Fighting for the Forty-Ninth Star

Fighting for the Forty-Ninth Star

C. W. Snedden and the Crusade for Alaska Statehood

Terrence Cole

University of Alaska Foundation
Fairbanks, Alaska

Distributed by University of Alaska Press
P.O. Box 756240
Fairbanks, AK 99775-6240

ISBN 978-1-883309-06-0

Library of Congress Cataloging-in-Publication Data

Cole, Terrence, 1953–
  Fighting for the forty-ninth star : C.W. Snedden and the crusade for Alaska
statehood / by Terrence Cole.
    p. cm.
  Includes bibliographical references and index.
  ISBN 978-1-883309-06-0 (cloth : alk. paper)
  1. Alaska—Politics and government—1867–1959. 2. Snedden, Charles Willis,
1913–1989. 3. Statehood (American politics) 4. Newspaper editors—Alaska—
Biography. 5. Fairbanks daily news-miner—History. 6. Alaska—Biography.
I. Title.
  F909.C69 2010
  979.8'02092—dc22
  [B]
                        2010021044

Cover and text design by Paula Elmes, ImageCraft Publications & Design

All photos and clippings courtesy of *Fairbanks Daily News-Miner* unless
otherwise credited.

This publication was printed on acid-free paper that meets the minimum
requirements for ANSI / NISO Z39.48–1992 (R2002) (Permanence of Paper
for Printed Library Materials).

second printing 2011

Contents

Foreword

by Charles L. "Chuck" Gray, publisher emeritus
of the *Fairbanks Daily News-Miner*

In 1949, I was a twenty-two-year-old printer (pressman) for the *Fairbanks Daily News-Miner*, a small newspaper that published five days a week with a circulation of thirty-five hundred. We had three Linotype machines; they were rundown and hadn't had professional care for many years. The paper was losing money and in late 1949, our owner, an aging Fairbanks industrialist named Austin E. "Cap" Lathrop, brought in a Linotype machinist from the Pacific Northwest to investigate what was wrong and offer recommendations on how to improve the operation.

My first memories of the Linotype expert, who in the spring of 1950 drove his panel truck-cum-machine shop up the Alaska Highway from Vancouver, Washington, were of his mechanical ingenuity and wood-working skill. I helped him build a work tabletop on a couple of old cabinets and was impressed when he put a beautiful finish on the table using shellac, an alcohol-based material made from, I believe, bug secretion. His name was Charles Willis (Bill) Snedden.

Snedden was smitten with Alaska and Fairbanks, and almost on impulse he offered to buy the rundown newspaper from Cap Lathrop. And that was how I would come to spend the next thirty-nine years of my life working for and with C. W. Snedden, one of the most remarkable men I have ever known.

Snedden suffered lifelong physical difficulties as a result of his World War II shipbuilding experiences. Consequently, when he came to Fairbanks he was semi-retired and learning to live with a bad heart and hearing difficulties. But that didn't stop him from transforming the *News-Miner* beyond recognition, with a massive investment in a new press in 1953, and another new press in 1965, when we became one of the first newspapers in the country to switch to "cold type" and offset printing. Working with Snedden's encouragement, the *News-Miner* led the industry in developing techniques for color printing on newsprint, and I was fortunate to play a part in that process.

Aside from Snedden's interest in producing a world-class newspaper, it was his treatment of his employees ("staffers," he liked to call us) that I remember. He demanded a certain amount of personal grooming for staffers meeting the public, and beards were a quick route to the "alumni club." But when one of us had a prolonged or terminal illness, it was half pay after other benefits were used up. When Congress enacted legislation in 1974 setting a statutory framework for Employee Stock Ownership Plans, Snedden was quick to investigate and adopt an ESOP for the newspaper. This allowed a certain percentage of before-tax profits to be used to buy company stock for employees. Consequently, when the newspaper was sold in 1992, employees shared $7 million from the proceeds of the sale. I also remember the time he called the company's travel agent and set up an all-expense-paid trip for two to Hawaii. The trip was for a local businessman and his wife who were both in poor health and were never supposed to know their benefactor. It is a small example of how Snedden lived his life.

To give an idea of what kind of a decisive man C. W. was, I particularly like to recall how the *News-Miner* came to own the *Cordova Times* in 1973. It also could be titled "How Compassion Overrules Common Sense"! Harold "Skip" Bonser, the eighty-one-year-old owner of the *Cordova Times*, was in failing health in the fall of 1973 when he contacted Snedden and offered to sell us his newspaper. Snedden was acquainted with Bonser due to Snedden's boating in Prince William Sound and was intrigued by the offer. So one morning I took off from Fairbanks to Cordova, four hundred miles south, in the *News-Miner*'s twin-engine plane, with two passengers, Snedden and *News-Miner* office manager Zelma Trafton. After lunch with Bonser, the three of us went to work.

Mrs. Trafton was assigned to visit city hall and collect tax-assessment records, population, and other information in order to determine the advertising potential of the town. Snedden and I looked over the company books and the printing equipment. The shop had nothing but outmoded hot metal machinery, and unfortunately Bonser still owed about $15,000 on it because of previous uncovered fire losses; Bonser's "friend" and insurance agent had pilfered the premiums!

By mid-afternoon the three of us rendezvoused on the sidewalk outside the Bonser building to compare notes. There was really not much worth buying, I thought. I estimated a cost for replacing the printing equipment, and did so with crossed fingers hoping for a negative decision, because I knew who would bear the brunt of a positive decision. Me! I would have to refit the shop.

But it took C. W. only moments to make up his mind.

"Let's go ahead and help Skip out," he said.

As best as I can remember, we paid off the Bonser loan and gave him an additional $35,000. He retired comfortably to Anchorage and died of prostate cancer two years later.

Fuller Cowell (who later went on to become publisher of the *Anchorage Daily News*) and his wife, Christmas Cowell, were selected from the Fairbanks operation to be the publishers at Cordova. We invested about $25,000 in new offset equipment and produced the first weekly edition with a full-color picture on the front page. Nothing like it had ever been seen in Cordova before! Eventually we put up a new building. The Cowells did a fine job and in 1975, as the oil pipeline was under construction, they saw the opportunity to establish a new newspaper in Valdez, the *Valdez Vanguard*. And it all started because C. W. wanted to help Skip out!

Causes! There was no end to the causes and campaigns Bill Snedden and the newspaper undertook. An early one was to replace the archaic electrical and phone system in Fairbanks with a system owned by the municipal government. And after the 1967 flood, the need for a community-owned hospital was obvious. Snedden co-chaired two successful fund drives to get the hospital built. The area needed a local refinery when oil flowed through our backyard. The newspaper promoted the financing that resulted in one. Snedden got on the board of Wien Airlines in an attempt to save this local pioneer airline, which was operating Boeing 737 aircraft, among others.

However, nothing topped Snedden's dive into the statehood effort from 1954 to1959 that is the focus of this book. It is a story that few outside his close circle of friends have ever known, and I am pleased to see it finally come to light. It is a chapter of Alaska history that richly deserves to be remembered by the state that he helped to bring to life.

The official unveiling of the forty-nine-star flag at the White House on January 3, 1959. From left to right: Ralph Rivers, Bob Atwood (holding out the flag), Fred Seaton, Ernest Gruening, Bob Bartlett, Mike Stepovich, and Waino Hendrickson. The four men in the center of the picture—Atwood, Seaton, Gruening, and Bartlett—were all newspapermen or ex-newspapermen who had played key roles in the statehood crusade. The key Alaska newspaperman missing that day was publisher C. W. "Bill" Snedden of the *Fairbanks Daily News-Miner*, America's farthest north daily newspaper. This book is the story of why Snedden belongs in the picture. University of Alaska Fairbanks Archives, Gruening papers, 1976-0021-00281.

Preface

A t noon on Saturday, January 3, 1959, in a small ceremony at the White House, President Dwight D. Eisenhower turned forty-eight states into forty-nine, when he signed the official proclamation of Alaska statehood. The admission of Alaska marked the end of the hardest road to statehood in the history of the United States. Alaska had been a U.S. territory for nearly fifty years, and an American possession for almost ninety-two years, when Eisenhower finally opened the door.

The prolonged wait for admission was due in part to the fact that Alaska was uniquely different from the forty-eight states that preceded it. Geographically, it was the first noncontiguous state. One statehood opponent claimed that once a distant territory like Alaska joined the Union, nothing could stop Italy from demanding to be admitted next! The forty-ninth state would have the most land (twice the size of Texas) and the smallest and youngest population; the longest coastline and the shortest road system; the highest prices (Fairbanks was 50 percent more costly than Seattle) and the fewest job openings; a vast potential for economic growth yet the narrowest existing economic base in America; a surplus of unmarried men and a shortage of unmarried women (there were one and a half men for every woman in Alaska). Alaska would become the only state not linked to America by train, and the only state whose capital could not be reached by road. Climatically, it would also have the coldest, wettest, and highest points in the Union, with the shortest days and the longest nights, and vice versa.

In the course of that presidential ceremony that changed the shape of the United States, President Eisenhower used a dozen pens to complete his signature. The first nine pens went to the dignitaries gathered round the president's desk who witnessed the historic ceremony. Seated on Eisenhower's right was Vice President Richard Nixon, with House

Speaker Sam Rayburn on the left. In the center immediately behind President Eisenhower's chair stood Secretary of the Interior Fred Seaton, the administration's key point man in the statehood contest. It was Seaton who was largely responsible for convincing a reluctant Eisenhower and others in the Republican Party to accept the idea that Alaska was ready to become a state. In the final Senate vote more Republicans than Democrats had voted in favor of admitting Alaska into the Union.

Immediately after the signing ceremony Bob Atwood, the publisher of the *Anchorage Daily Times*, the new state's largest newspaper, stood on a chair to proudly stretch out the new forty-nine-star flag for the camera. Standing in front immediately below the flag were Ernest Gruening and E. L. "Bob" Bartlett, the two men who had been elected as the first senators from the forty-ninth state, and Secretary Seaton. It was a most fitting portrait. While the four men differed greatly from each other in their political beliefs and personalities, all were veteran newspapermen who knew the power of the printed word. Each had played a major role in winning the fight for Alaska statehood.

Atwood had built the *Anchorage Times* into the largest and most influential newspaper in Alaska, and beginning in the mid-1940s his daily had been the most vocal proponent for statehood; Seaton was the publisher of the *Tribune* in Hastings, Nebraska, as well as a string of other small papers, and in addition to his formidable powers as secretary of the interior he used his family connections in the publishing industry to help spread the word about the merits of Alaska's campaign. Before Gruening had gone into government service as a New Dealer, he had a distinguished newspaper career and had once been the editor of the *Nation*, while Bartlett had begun his career as a reporter for the *Fairbanks Daily News-Miner*.

But there was another newspaperman not in the picture or at the ceremony, who by all rights should have been there, for he played an essential role behind the headlines in educating the U.S. Congress and the American public about the need for Alaska statehood. C. W. "Bill" Snedden was publisher of the *Fairbanks Daily News-Miner*, America's farthest north daily newspaper. Most Alaskans never knew the extent of Snedden's personal contribution in winning the fight for statehood, or the costs and sacrifices he had made for the cause. And fewer still understood the crucial role he played as publisher of a small-town newspaper that took up the twin tasks of opening the Arctic to oil and gas development and convincing the United States of America to add the forty-ninth star to the flag.

For this reason, Secretary Seaton had pledged one of the ceremonial pens to C. W. Snedden, who helped to prove the power of the pen and the power of the press to change the course of history. *Fighting for the Forty-Ninth Star* is the history that Snedden and the *Fairbanks Daily News-Miner* helped to write from 1950 to 1960, the decade that saw the birth of modern Alaska, marked above all by three developments he advocated: the coming of oil, the rise of the Alaska Republican Party, and statehood.

Acknowledgments

This book originally grew out of the work I was fortunate enough to do beginning in 2003 with the University of Alaska "Creating Alaska" project, under the inspired leadership of University of Alaska Vice President Karen Purdue, marking the fiftieth anniversary of the writing of the Alaska Constitution on the Fairbanks campus in 1955–1956. In the half-dozen years I have spent researching the life of C. W. Snedden and the statehood movement, I have accumulated many debts from friends and colleagues.

First of all, University of Alaska President Mark Hamilton was enthusiastic about the topic from the very start and was generous in providing encouragement and helping to secure financial support through the University of Alaska Foundation. Mrs. Helen Snedden was likewise supportive and did everything in her power to ensure the book be completed. So too did numerous *News-Miner* veterans, including Charles L. Gray, Fuller A. Cowell, Virginia Farmier, Marilyn Romano, Jack de Yonge, Debbie Carter, Dermot Cole, and Senator Ted Stevens, the former *News-Miner* attorney and Snedden's protégé and closest friend.

Among those friends and colleagues who kindly offered to read advance chapters and to make suggestions were Robert Meyerowitz, Michael Carey, Jerry McBeath, Mary Ehrlander, Larry Goldin, Michael Letzring, Marion Jones, Candy Waugaman, Henry Cole, Arthur D. Sellers, Vic Fischer, Claus-M. Naske, and William R. Hunt.

Michael Carey was gracious enough to share with me not only his unpublished paper on the friendship of Bill Snedden and Fred Seaton but also his insights into the early career of Ted Stevens as Fairbanks district attorney. My twin brother, Dermot, provided much information about the history of the *News-Miner* and early-day Fairbanks.

Many staff members at the university have been invariably helpful and supportive, particularly Chancellor Brian D. Rogers, Vice Chancellor

Jake Poole, and Emily Drygas at UAF Development; Kay Bullock, Tracie Cogdill, Cynthia Owen, and Breehan Yauney in the College of Liberal Arts Dean's Office; and Anne Aleshire, Wendy Frandsen, and Linda Levy in the Rasmuson Library.

The staff at the Alaska and Polar Regions Collection at the UAF Rasmuson Library was as always courteous and resourceful, especially Dirk Tordoff, Caroline Atuk-Derrick, Rose Speranza, and Peggy Asbury. Joe Hardenbrook was a great inspiration in the deft way he always ensured the ins and outs of the Creating Alaska project did not get too complex. My friend Lee Huskey at UAA always went out of his way to share his abundant supply of faith and optimism.

I have been most fortunate to have had wonderful teaching and research assistants who contributed ideas, energy, and enthusiasm, including Neva Hickman, Brittany Retherford, Cary Curlee, Leighton Quarles, Dave Drexler, Eleanor Wirts, Rudy Riedlsperger, and Artem Zhdanov. Director Joan Braddock of the University of Alaska Press, and editors Sue Mitchell and Elisabeth B. Dabney, were professional, friendly, and efficient as always, while Rachel Fudge did a great job of copyediting, and Paula Elmes worked her magic on the design and layout. Proofreader Theresa Kay did a thorough job for which I thank her.

Claus-M. Naske, the leading historian of the statehood cause, has generously shared material he uncovered in the National Archives and at the Eisenhower Library. For almost forty years, through good times and bad, he has been a mentor, colleague, and friend, and I have benefited once again from standing on his shoulders.

Finally, I would like to thank my three children, Henry, Desmond, and their new little sister Elizabeth, and my wife, Gay Salisbury. For far too long they have put up with the piles of books and thousands of photocopies and newspaper clippings spread out across the floor of the house. Thanks for tolerating my high tolerance for disorder one more time, because I would be lost in the chaos without you.

1

Ain't God Good to Fairbanks

In 1949 Austin E. "Cap" Lathrop was the richest resident in all of Alaska, but the eighty-three-year-old self-made tycoon was not a happy man. Among the many enterprises that Lathrop controlled the least profitable was probably the small daily newspaper in Alaska's second largest city, the *Fairbanks Daily News-Miner*. At a recent board meeting Lathrop had exploded when he looked at the *News-Miner*'s balance sheet, filling the air with expletives that could not appear in his family newspaper. Lathrop made it profanely clear to his attorney, "Judge" Ed Medley, that he wanted to know why the *News-Miner* was losing so much money and to rectify the situation as soon as possible. The man Medley hired for the job was a "newspaper doctor" from Washington State, thirty-six-year-old Charles Willis "Bill" Snedden.

Bill Snedden was born in Spokane in 1913 but raised by his grandparents in Vancouver, Washington, across the Columbia River from Portland, Oregon. He found his true calling while he was still a schoolboy, working part-time as a janitor in the print shop of the *Vancouver Columbian*. As he watched a typesetter working the Linotype machine, one of the most complicated contraptions ever invented, he had a realization that would set the course of his life.

"I saw a guy setting type," he said, "making more money than I was."[1] Snedden learned that a position on the Linotype was coming open because one of the typesetters was going to quit. Besides mechanical aptitude and skilled hands, another essential requirement for a Linotype man was knowing how to spell, and particularly knowing how to spell like a printer: upside down and backward. At thirteen he hired on as an apprentice printer at the *Portland Telegram*. To master the trade he lived with a

1

small dictionary in his pocket. "Morning, noon, and night, every time I had a spare minute, I went through that darn dictionary. You know that's one way to learn English, and it stuck with me." He had some college, at Washington State in Pullman and Oregon State in Corvallis, but his stubborn independence meant that formal education would never be his strong suit. "I think the teachers couldn't stand me," he once joked in an interview, "so they shipped me out."

Part of the problem was that he had to work his way through college in the depths of the Depression, and another was that he couldn't make up his mind about what he wanted to study. "I thought I was going to be an electrical engineer to start with," he said, "then I discovered what that was all about and didn't like it, so I switched to mechanical [engineering]. And I never got a degree in anything."

Snedden had a gift for tinkering with machines. By the time he was eighteen he was a journeyman Linotype operator, machinist, and electrician. He worked for some time selling, installing, and servicing Linotype machines for the Mergenthaler Linotype Company, and earned money on the side as a musician playing trumpet, trombone, and French horn in silent movie houses and dance halls. While playing at a Vancouver dance hall in 1933 he met his future wife, Helen; they were married the next year. While building their house he developed another profession: putting up spec houses as a contractor, eventually constructing and selling more than a dozen until Pearl Harbor.

The day after the Japanese attack Snedden tried to enlist in the navy, but since he had been born with a 50 percent hearing deficiency he was rejected out of hand. As Snedden put it, "I wanted to join the navy and those meatheads discovered I couldn't hear very well. So I got smarter and went down and joined the army and I bluffed my way through the first days." His military career did not last long. When he was sent to officer training in Fort Benning, Georgia, "the first guy I meet as I step off the train" was an old, previously retired soldier, "Major Painter." Snedden had sold him a house in Vancouver.

"He wondered what the hell I was doing there. I told him I'd come to win the war. 'Well,' he says 'yeah, but you can't hear.' And that was the end of that."

On his way home Snedden sat next to a man on the train who would become a superintendent at the Henry Kaiser Shipyard, then under construction in Vancouver, and found his war service. Snedden went to work at the Kaiser yard, rising to be an assistant superintendent responsible for about eight thousand machinists. The yard worked around the clock turning out ships during the war, including LSTs, Liberty ships, and pocket carriers almost six hundred feet long. "We shot one down the river every Tuesday morning for fifty-seven-some consecutive weeks."

The job was dangerous and stressful. Snedden and the other men slept on cots at the office and often did not go home for weeks at a time. "Three of us in the shipyard had about the same job and the other two guys dropped dead on the job—both of them," he later recalled. Snedden had his own health problems. As he would say, "My pump had gone bad. I was having heart trouble." It started one day when his crew discovered that a ship near completion had a "rough bearing" in a main turbo generator. "I crawled inside the casing and asked the crew to slowly turn the armature by hand while I felt the bearing journal for rough spots. Then someone by mistake closed the main switch." He was jolted by a charge of thousands of volts that melted all but the brim of his hard hat, and woke up later in a hospital. The shock had ruptured a valve in his heart, requiring open-heart surgery and almost a year of convalescence.

Following the war he branched out into other enterprises. He briefly ran a hardware stove in Vancouver before hitting on the idea of consulting for ailing newspapers. He knew the ins and outs of the Linotype business and he'd been a careful student of what would and would not work in pressrooms. Selling a paper the right Linotype machine meant he'd had to fully understand the operation. "I was exposed to the operating methods, operating problems, and problem-cures of many newspaper plants," he said. Thus he became a self-accredited "newspaper doctor."

"Anyone who was doing what I was in the Linotype field would have had to be a sleepwalker not to notice the efficiency differences among the various newspapers. So to become a 'newspaper doctor' was really very simple: merely remember the equipment, methods, personnel policies, etc. of the efficient operations you were exposed to, steal the good ideas, and use them on the sloppy operations."

He was never paid a fixed salary. Instead, he negotiated a percentage of the increase in profits over the previous three-year average. "The big wonder to me about this modus operandi," he said, "was that I never encountered—or even heard of—anyone else doing the same thing—or reasonably close to the same thing."

Snedden came to Medley's attention as the possible answer to the *News-Miner*'s problems due to his work with William H. Cowles Jr., the publisher of the *Spokane Spokesman-Review*. Medley called Snedden to set up a meeting in Seattle, but at first Snedden declined Medley's offer, because at the time the *News-Miner* had a circulation of only about three thousand. "I wasn't interested because it was too small. Even if you got an increase in all of the profits of an operation that size you wouldn't have much." In the end, however, there was one factor that outweighed all the others and convinced him to take the job, a reason that has brought many men to the Last Frontier: going to Fairbanks would be the perfect excuse to take the fishing trip of a lifetime.

The Lathrop Company agreed to pay his expenses, and Snedden flew Pan American to Fairbanks in December 1949 to make a preliminary investigation. After a short visit he agreed to return in the spring of 1950. He drove up the Alaska Highway in a panel truck rigged up as a traveling machine shop, equipped with a lathe, drill, welding tools, spare parts, and all the machinery needed for a newspaper repair man, as well as all his fishing gear. His eye was on the calendar, particularly the start of the fishing season. "I wanted to get the job done at the paper by the time the weather broke," he said, so he could spend several months relaxing with his son, Duane "Skip" Snedden, going after grayling and sheefish on the rivers of Interior Alaska, before driving back to Vancouver in the fall. It didn't work out that way. The three-month job he didn't want to take and the summerlong Alaska fishing trip that was his true motivation would turn out to be the start of a forty-year commitment to the farthest north daily newspaper in the United States.

Snedden's first impression of Fairbanks in the spring of 1950, however, was hardly enthusiastic. He got a room at the Nordale Hotel on Second Avenue, directly across the street from the offices of the *News-Miner*. A snap spring blizzard blanketed the city and at first he couldn't remember where he had parked his panel truck, now buried in the snow. It was a harbinger of the hard work to come. Fixing what was wrong at the *Fairbanks Daily News-Miner* was going to be a challenge. Its problems were deeply rooted in the management of the paper and the community it served.

In 1950 the *Fairbanks Daily News-Miner* was the oldest operating business in Fairbanks and the oldest daily newspaper in Alaska. Founded in 1903, it boasted the second-longest streak of continuous publication in the territory and was one of only three gold rush newspapers that still survived, along with the triweekly *Nome Nugget* and the weekly *Wrangell Sentinel*. Given the uncertain history of a typical gold rush town, and the even less likely chances of survival for a gold rush newspaper, the sheer endurance of the *News-Miner* was remarkable, particularly because the operation had nearly always been a money-losing proposition. The *News-Miner* owed its existence in no small part to the determination of two characters who dominated the history of the newspaper's first half-century: W. F. Thompson and "Cap" Lathrop. Two more dissimilar personalities could hardly be imagined, but as publishers they were both passionate boosters of anything that had to do with Fairbanks, even if neither ever succeeded in making the *News-Miner* turn a profit.

With his wicked pen, peculiar sense of humor, outrageous opinions, and unquenchable thirst for gambling, alcohol, and adventure, William Fentress "W. F." Thompson could have been created by Mark Twain. Thompson was never shy about expressing his editorial opinions in language that many of his critics—the crowd of "long-haired men and short-haired women"—thought unduly intemperate.[2] In person he was usually quiet and soft-spoken, unless, it was said, he had been too much in the company of "the great god Bacchus." After the onset of prohibition he once ran a banner headline across the entire front page of the *News-Miner* that read "Whiskey Is a Sure Preventative of the Influenza." A headline that he used repeatedly during those years was "The Evils of Prohibition." He claimed he owed his longevity to the fact that he "drank, smoke and chewed to excess" all his life.[3]

Even when sober, Thompson limped along the streets, as he had been crippled in a train accident as a young man. The tapping of his cane on the wooden sidewalk announced his arrival. Impeccably dressed and distinguished-looking, especially when his thick head of hair and neatly trimmed beard turned gray, he favored pinstriped shirts, high stiff collars, and a gray herringbone vest and suit coat; at work he doffed the coat and wore long black sleeve protectors to keep ink off his shirt. "He was slightly deaf," a coworker said, "and used this to ignore that which he considered not worth listening to."[4]

Popularly known behind his back as "Wrong Font" Thompson—"wf" was the common proofreaders' shorthand to indicate a mistaken typeface—W. F. usually called himself "The Old Man" or "Wandering Foot" for his proclivity to roam. Born in Michigan in 1863—the same year as Henry Ford—he joined the legion of western printers and newspapermen who traveled from camp to camp with portable presses and trays of type to spread the latest news, rumor, slander, or gossip. Not a great deal is known about Thompson's early life or education, but the discipline of school was not his style. He once claimed that as a young man he had been forcibly divorced from the Michigan Military Academy "for throwing a bottle at the Commandant's head (it was an empty bottle, and he had caught us taking the last drink from it)." Despite his lack of formal education, Thompson picked up a sizable vocabulary and a propensity to use it. "Writing with him was spontaneous," a friend said, "and coupled with a wanderlust, carried him through years of reckless adventure."[5]

"The only game we really know anything about," Thompson wrote of himself, "is the newspaper game, which consists in keeping the nearby public informed of that which they may be interested in (or pretend that they are), and if you are sincere in your work it is SOME job."[6] He said in 1920 that he had been printing and publishing for forty years in, among other places, Michigan, California, Arizona, Utah, Texas, Wyoming, Washington, British Columbia, Yukon Territory, and, finally, Alaska. In Washington alone he worked on papers in Davenport, Spokane, Tacoma, Des Moines, Steilacoom, Roslyn, Westport, and Sprague, sometimes running papers in two places at once. It was only when he came to Fairbanks in 1906 that he found his true home.[7] The boldface motto he adopted for the *News-Miner* may not have been grammatical, but whether he posed it as a question or an exclamation, it captured his feeling for the community: **"Ain't God Good to Fairbanks!"**

The origins of the *News-Miner* actually go back three years before Thompson arrived in Fairbanks. Another itinerant printer, George Hill, published the first issue of the *Fairbanks News* on September 19, 1903. Veteran Fairbanks printer Paul Solka Jr., who researched a detailed history of the *News-Miner*, thought that vol. 1, no. 1, was printed on a hand-powered, portable printing press. Solka believed it was probably printed on either a Washington Hand Press, a relatively compact press, as light as seven hundred pounds, invented in 1827 and a symbol of "country journalism" on which many small papers, including Vancouver's *Columbian*, first appeared, or an even lighter and more portable Army Press, so called because it "was designed in size and weight for transportation on a pack horse, and so constructed that it would be ready to print a few minutes after it was taken off the horse."[8] By 1904 the *News* had the distinction of being set on the first Linotype machine brought to Alaska, Mergenthaler Linotype No. 5801. (Like locomotive engines, all Linotypes were individually numbered, and they were often named by printers who became attached to them.) The following year Alaska's second Linotype was installed in the offices of the *Nome Gold Digger*.

When No. 5801 debuted in Fairbanks in 1904—the same year that the U.S. Government Printing Office in Washington, D.C., first adopted a typesetting machine—the Linotype was a remarkably modern piece of machinery for such an isolated mining camp. Alaska was the last of the current fifty states to get a Linotype machine, but the timing was still astonishing considering the remoteness of Fairbanks; the first Linotype in Washington State had appeared in Seattle just eleven years earlier, in 1893, and Fairbanks' Linotype was set up a mere six years after the first in Idaho (the *Idaho Statesman* in Boise, 1898), four years after the first in South Dakota (the *Deadwood Pioneer Times,* 1900), and three years after the first in Nevada (the *Reno Gazette,*1901).[9]

Even before it came to Fairbanks, Alaska's first Linotype had earned a reputation. No. 5801 had originally been sledded over the ice to Dawson City, Yukon, in 1901, new from the factory, at a total cost of about $9,000. It was an amazing feat, one that made that Linotype a legend in the newspaper business: the machine, which weighed nearly three tons, was hauled down the Yukon from Whitehorse to Dawson by horse-drawn sleigh in the middle of winter, a trip that took twenty-nine days, during which temperatures bottomed out at more than seventy degrees below zero. Though the horses and men were frostbitten, the machine made it to Dawson in perfect condition; "not a bolt was lost nor a rod bent." In fact, it operated so well in Dawson that it earned another distinction: No. 5801 was claimed by its owners to be the fastest Linotype in the world, running at about 110 rpm, or nearly twice the speed for which it was designed.

When the legendary electric machine arrived in Fairbanks in September 1904 via stern-wheeler from Dawson City, the *Fairbanks News* had no place to plug it in, as the city's electrical plant was not yet complete. Eager to get No. 5801 in operation, however, the pioneer printers rigged a system of belts and wooden pulleys and powered it by hand for several weeks. It worked splendidly—but, as the operator admitted, "we were certainly pleased when the power was at last turned on."[10]

In its inaugural issue, the *News* set guidelines under which it would serve the "the rich interior of this truly wonderful country" and made a promise—grammatical and typographical errors notwithstanding—to the people of Fairbanks: it had "enteted [*sic*] upon" its sacred mission of reporting the news "with a realizing sense of the grave responsibility which attaches to such a task. It will be the aim of this journal to keep the public informed upon all questions of general, local and national interest, as well as mining and kindred subjects. . . . By dealing with all questions which arise fairly, impartially and intelligently, we hope to acquire public confidence and esteem, and become a power for good in this community."[11]

⋯⋯✦⋯⋯

When W. F. Thompson arrived in Fairbanks three years later, "to engage in the dissemination of well-known truths," promoters of as many as five daily papers were in various stages of planning and preparation. Thompson briefly put out a sheet called the *Tanana Miner*, from which the *Miner* in *News-Miner* would eventually come, but he quickly went broke, claiming he lost about $40,000 of his and his investors' money in only nine months. Over the next three years, as the local newspaper wars continued, Thompson resurrected versions of the *Miner* in the creeks around town.

By 1909, many less optimistic souls believed Fairbanks, as a placer mining camp, was doomed. "There is a terrible spirit of depression here," one prominent Fairbanks businessman wrote in August 1909. "It is the sense that the camp is over and will decline fast. I hardly think it will go down so very quickly, but go down it surely will and perhaps just drop all at once. It seems everybody is trying to get away."[12] Thompson, who refused to believe that Fairbanks was dying, purchased the *Fairbanks News* in March 1909 and merged it with his *Miner*, giving the paper a new, hyphenated name: the *Fairbanks Daily News-Miner*.

Thompson's highly personal style was typical of nineteenth-century frontier journalism. Though he always used the editorial "we" and typically spoke of himself in the third person, he never pretended there were two sides to an argument. The *News-Miner* would only print the truth—as he saw it. Like his fellow editors, he consistently pleaded for businesses to advertise and residents to subscribe, all the while damning, slandering, and otherwise belittling his competitors; in Thompson-talk, the *Alaska Citizen* published across the Chena River was the "Garden Island Cesspool," and the *Fairbanks Daily Times* was the "Morning Peserator." Readers then expected editors to blast each other in print, like the New Mexico scribe who placed a curse on the rival who called him an unwashed liar, sneak, and thief: "May fortune flee from him, and evil cling to him all of his days; may death rob him of family; friends forsake him; disease waste his flesh; ghosts of women haunt his sleep, and in the end poor, miserable, loathed of men and despised by God, may the wretch sink into the grave and hell receive his soul."[13]

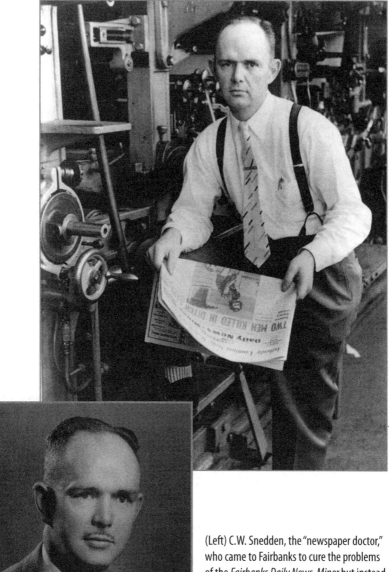

(Left) C.W. Snedden, the "newspaper doctor," who came to Fairbanks to cure the problems of the *Fairbanks Daily News-Miner* but instead ended up buying the newspaper himself. (Above) Snedden and "Alice," the new printing press he installed in 1953.

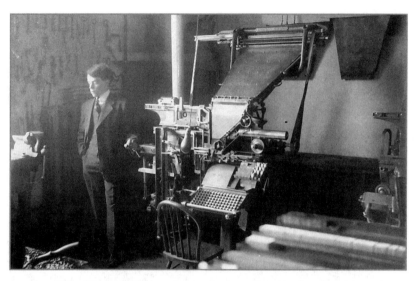

An early printer and Linotype machine in Dawson City during the gold rush, similar to the machine first brought to Fairbanks in 1904. Author's collection.

The *News-Miner* 1937 special edition announcing Austin E. "Cap" Lathrop's construction of the new facilities in the Lathrop Building.

MARVELOUS NEWSPAPER PRESS INSTALLED BY THE NEWS-MINER—prints one paper per second from a flowing white stream of newsprint and is the finest and latest equipment of the kind in the Northland.

The Cox-O-Type press, installed in 1937, printed one eight-page paper per second.

Chuck Gray, who decades later would become publisher of the *News-Miner*, and the Cox-O-Type used until the installation of "Alice" in 1953. Also in photo with Chuck is Lois Weber, "flygirl".

The *News-Miner*'s bank of Linotype machines in the 1940s. Editor Charlie Settlemier in back in hat. Paul Solka Jr., printer and newspaper historian, on near machine. Photo courtesy of Chuck Gray.

Under Cap Lathrop the *News-Miner* was the cornerstone of the anti-Gruening, anti-statehood "Axis Press."

===THE=== GOSS

ᏚᎧᏚᎧ

Patented 4-Deck
Straightline
Newspaper Printing
And Folding Machine

HIGHEST AWARD given to the Goss Printing Press Co. on their 4-Deck Straightline Press recently on exhibition at the Paris Exposition.

The only perfect machine that makes any number of pages — without the use of angle bars or turners. There are no complicated parts, everything is clear sailing from start to finish.

STRAIGHTLINE PRESSES are Prize-Winners and Money-Makers.

===== PATENTED AND MANUFACTURED =====
BY

THE GOSS PRINTING PRESS CO.

16th Street and Ashland Avenue, CHICAGO, ILL., U. S. A.

An early advertisement for a Goss Four Deck Straightline printing press, the same model as "Alice," the seventy-one-ton press from the *Sacramento Union* that Snedden purchased in 1953. The Straightline was capable of printing in four colors. It could roll off seven finished newspapers a second, a speed made possible due to its revolutionary design; one roll of paper per deck enabled the newsprint to flow in a straight line from the spool to the folding mechanism on the opposite end. Author's collection.

The *News-Miner* open house in the spring of 1954 marked the completion of the Chena Building and the unveiling of "Alice," illuminated in the picture window on First Avenue so that Fairbanks could watch the press in operation.

When the *News-Miner*'s last competitor, the *Daily Alaska Citizen,* went belly-up in 1920, Thompson claimed his newspaper might be given the sobriquet of the *Daily-News-Miner-Citizen,* explaining its pedigree this way: "Established in 1903 as *The Fairbanks News;* absorbed *The Tanana Miner* and became *The News-Miner;* took over the remains of *The Daily Alaska Citizen,* which had taken over the remains of *The Fairbanks Daily Times;* thus we accumulated a string of titles longer than your arm, which we have condensed into *News-Miner* and call it that; some others call it 'that damned sheet.'" Thompson said the full name of the newspaper should actually be the *Fairbanks News-Tanana Tribune-Tanana Miner-Chena Miner-Ridgetop Miner-Daily Alaska Citizen-Weekly Alaska Citizen-Fairbanks Daily News-Miner.*[14]

Following Thompson's death in 1926, Hjalmar Nordale did his best to modernize the paper, and made some notable improvements, but with limited funds and a badly outdated plant, there was not much he could do. The dawn of a new era came in November 1929, when Thompson's widow sold the newspaper to Captain Austin E. Lathrop.

Two years younger than Thompson, Lathrop had also been born in Michigan in the 1860s, and likewise received little in the way of formal education, leaving school in the ninth grade. Thompson's forte was writing, a skill that Lathrop never pretended to have, but the latter's prodigious energies and interests ran the gamut of modern commerce. His enterprises—draying, carpentry, sailing, construction, mining, trading, railroads, real estate, shipping, freighting, banking, movies, liquor, radio and newspapers—made him a veritable one-man chamber of commerce.

Lathrop started in business for himself when he was just fifteen, stump-grubbing with a team of horses for local sawmills in Michigan. He moved on to Ashland, Wisconsin, where he tried his hand at the hardware business, and then draying and contracting, which became his specialty. When downtown Seattle burned to the ground in 1889, he quickly headed west to Puget Sound, where a man with his talents would be in demand to tear down burned-out buildings and clear space for new structures. Dubbed the "Boy Contractor," by twenty-five he'd made a name for himself in the Pacific Northwest. The money he earned rebuilding Seattle, however, he lost in a railroad he built north of the city, when the financial markets collapsed in the Panic of 1893.

With nothing left to lose, he went north to start over. Seeing that the small gold strikes that had been reported along Alaska's Turnagain Arm were creating a demand for shipping, he scraped together the funds to purchase a 110-foot steam schooner, the *L.J. Perry*. He freighted along the Alaska coast for five years, particularly in Cook Inlet and Prince William Sound, becoming known forever after as "Cap" Lathrop. An old-timer once explained that in the early days of white settlement in Alaska, "Anyone who operated anything that could float was called Cap."[15] Still, Cap Lathrop was the only man among the Alaska seafaring and riverboat crowds known throughout the territory by the nickname itself. In his 1943 book *War Discovers Alaska*, correspondent Joe Driscoll tracked down Lathrop for a curbside interview in downtown Fairbanks. The title of the chapter was "Just Plain Cap." Driscoll claimed that most people in Alaska didn't ever know Lathrop's given names. "Today the old man is known as Cap Lathrop to hundreds who have never heard of Austin Eugene Lathrop. A. E. is a stranger to Lathrop himself, who speaks in the third person of Cap Lathrop and signs hotel registers with that monicker."[16]

As skipper of the *L.J. Perry*, Lathrop gained a distinct perspective on the resources of coastal Alaska. He tried his hand at prospecting for oil in the Cold Bay region before establishing a successful draying and transfer business, first in Cordova, when the Copper River and Northwestern Railway was under construction, and later in Anchorage, when the U.S. government began construction of the Alaska Railroad in 1915. In both Cordova and Anchorage he built large apartment buildings to the highest standards of construction, a mark of quality that became his trademark. In 1915 the Lathrop Building in Anchorage was claimed to be the "most commodious" structure in the city, with flooring that was "the best ever placed in an Alaska building." Lathrop was also one of the first builders in Alaska to use concrete, an unheard-of extravagance in a land where log cabins and tents were the norm. "Nothing," Lathrop was fond of saying, "is too good for Alaska."[17]

One industry that Lathrop pioneered in Alaska was the building of movie theaters, as he realized the new motion-picture industry offered boundless opportunities for entertainment-starved Alaskans. "The Empress Circuit," his chain of Alaska movie palaces, started with the first theaters he built, in Cordova in 1912 and Anchorage in 1916. Far riskier than showing movies was Lathrop's attempt to make them. Always willing to take calculated risks even if others thought them foolhardy, he saw more clearly than any of his contemporaries in Alaska the power of mass media, as would become clear later when he moved into newspapers and then radio stations. Lathrop calculated that Alaska-made motion pictures, besides their entertainment value, could be an invaluable tool in promoting the development of Alaska resources and educating the American public about the riches of the territory. Hiring a crew of professionals from the industry, he created his own movie studio in Anchorage in 1922, the Alaska Moving Picture Corporation. The only film he ever produced, however, a silent gold rush melodrama called *The Cheechakoes,* proved to be a financial and critical flop.[18]

While the film studio was a disappointment, another Lathrop enterprise started at about the same time would reap enormous rewards. Railroads ran on coal, and coal mines ran on railroads. Lathrop realized that with the pending completion of the Alaska Railroad in 1923, the rich coal fields on the northern edge of the Alaska Range, near Healy, were ripe for development. For decades geologists, government officials, and promoters had believed that the vast coal seams of Alaska held enormous potential, but the lack of transportation and high costs doomed every effort. The Alaska Railroad was about to change the equation. Huge high-grade lignite deposits in the Healy River coalfield—by one estimate up to nine billion tons—were easily accessible when the railroad completed a four-mile-long spur to the site of the mine. Lathrop led a group that became the Healy River Coal Corporation, which developed the largest coal mine in Alaska, producing about four hundred tons a day by the late 1930s. The coal from Healy River saved millions of trees; before Lathrop's mine went into operation, Fairbanks consumed an estimated fifteen thousand cords of wood a year for heat and light.[19]

The other ingredient that made the coal mine a success was gold. In the early 1920s mining engineers were laying the groundwork for the revitalization of the gold mining industry in Fairbanks. The Healy River Coal Corporation would play a crucial role. During and after World War I, high costs and exhaustion of the richest pockets of placer gold had sent total gold production spiraling downward year after year. By the 1920s, a new method of thawing frozen ground with cold water had greatly reduced the costs of gold recovery, making it feasible to bring in large-scale dredging equipment. Completion of the Davidson Ditch, a ninety-five-mile-long aqueduct that assured a plentiful water supply, allowed the Fairbanks Exploration (FE) Company to install a fleet of eight electrical dredges that could harvest gold in unprecedented quantities. The coal that ran the electric plant, which powered the dredges that dug the gold, came via the coal cars of the Alaska Railroad from Cap Lathrop's Healy River

Mine. The FE Company, the largest employer in Fairbanks, was by far the largest single user of Healy River coal.[20]

Lathrop's coal mine provided the foundation for the resurgence of the Fairbanks mining economy in the 1920s and 1930s, but his construction of the Empress Theater in Fairbanks in 1927 was the most visible symbol of his faith in the community's future. The theater was the first building in Fairbanks made of steel and concrete. At the theater's grand opening, on August 25, Lathrop told the hundreds crowded on Second Avenue, "awed by the subdued beauty of the magnificent new playhouse," that the building was his "gift to Alaska." For several years afterwards, Lathrop said that engineers from the U.S. Post Office "came to Fairbanks each summer and went over the walls of the theater looking for cracks and checks, and other signs that the winter freeze and spring thaws were about to bring the building tumbling down." Lathrop claimed that only after he had proved it would stand the test of time did government officials approve construction of a "modern steel and concrete federal building. Then other businessmen began to see that we could have something other than frame buildings."[21]

Two years after he built the Empress, Cap Lathrop purchased the *News-Miner* from the widow of W. F. Thompson. He made the deal only a few weeks after the 1929 stock market crash. To some extent, buying the paper was also an act of public service. "They asked me to help the woman out," Lathrop said, as other local businessmen were concerned that Mrs. Thompson would soon be broke, leaving Fairbanks without a newspaper of any kind. The new owner promised the paper would henceforth support the Republican Party (Lathrop was Republican National Committeeman) and "will be progressive in its dealing with the welfare of its territory, an expanse that may justly be claimed to exceed geographically that of any other daily newspaper on the American continent."[22]

Lathrop was not a newspaperman, and in the years he owned the *News-Miner*, his name did not appear on the masthead. Once he bought the paper, however, Cap's intentions were simple. "I just want to take my friends there," Lathrop said, "show them through, and tell them they've seen the best newspaper office and newspaper plant in Alaska."

To bring the *News-Miner* up to date required an enormous investment, which Cap never recouped in the more than twenty years that he owned it. When Lathrop had purchased the paper, he'd been disgusted with its "ramshackle building and aging machinery."[23] Most importantly the printing press, the *News-Miner*'s oldest piece of equipment, was Civil War vintage, a creaky, hand-fed, flatbed cylinder press that dated at least to the 1860s or 1870s, and broke down almost every week. Apprentice printer Paul Solka Jr., who started at the paper in 1922, remembered "the steel and iron of the complaining machinery had become crystallized and brittle with the vibration of passing years, and the mere tightening of a bolt that had worked loose often caused a casting to break as if it were glass." Several times in the 1920s it appeared that the old press was about to give up the ghost. "We don't blame the press for quitting," Thompson wrote after one critical breakdown. "It's too much to put upon any venerable press which has done more than its share of the world's work."[24] In about 1935 Lathrop brought in a one-revolution cylinder Babcock press to replace the old press, but this was simply a stop-gap measure as the "new" press was about the same vintage as the old, just in better condition.

Solka recalled that the composing room housed a motley collection of gold rush antiques, old enough to be in a museum. The large foundry type used for headlines and advertising normally had a usable life of about four years, but practically all of the *News-Miner*'s worn-out type was at least twenty years old. "Some slugs had been used for so long that they were rounded on the ends and edges, much as a much-washed pebble in a stream."[25]

The paper did boast two relatively new Linotype machines. One that Thompson purchased in 1922 was a Model 14, the second most popular Linotype ever made, offering a wide range of characters and fonts. Thompson claimed the Model 14 was so advanced it "will almost talk." Unfortunately, no instructions came with the machine, and the staff had to figure out how to put it together by themselves "out of almost a million pieces without blueprints or specifications of any kind." They made a few mistakes in the assembly, and as a result it never quite worked properly until a Mergenthaler factory representative came to Fairbanks about six years later and spent several days reassembling it correctly. (Solka remembered Thompson's "talking Linotype" fondly; he set his first line of type on the machine in 1924, and as it was still usable more than forty years later, he set his last line of type on the Model 14 when he retired in 1967. The old warhorse was scrapped for junk in the early 1970s, Solka wrote, "sent to the place that all hot metal typesetters have been consigned to by an ungrateful society dedicated to worship of the computer.")[26]

The major overhaul of the paper came in the late 1930s, when Lathrop erected a combination office and apartment building between First and

Second Avenues, at the time the most elaborate structure ever built in Fairbanks. The $500,000, four-story, concrete-and-steel "Lathrop Building," completed in 1937–1938, included the best apartments ever seen in Alaska at the time and a bowling alley in the basement. The centerpiece was the new home of the *News-Miner* on the first floor.

Crusty old Cap was always inordinately proud of that building. Eleven-year-old Skip Snedden never forgot meeting Lathrop for the first time in 1950. Skip was leaning against the outside of the Lathrop Building with his foot against the wall, patiently waiting for his dad, when Cap came walking down the street. The eighty-four-year-old tycoon did not mince words with anyone.

"Hey kid," he said, "get your goddamn foot off my building."

At the public unveiling of the new newspaper plant in the fall of 1937, a *News-Miner* writer, speaking from bitter experience, claimed the typical newspaper office was usually little better than a greasy garage adorned with "a helter-skelter arrangement of office desks and dusty, oil-soaked, ink-grimed machinery." Such had been the workplace of the newspaperman in Fairbanks since 1903, but no more.

Newspaper officials reportedly told Lathrop that the plans he had for the *News-Miner*'s expansion were more suitable for a newspaper in a city of two hundred thousand, not three thousand, but his philosophy was that building for the future required a commitment not justified by present conditions, and he had every faith that Fairbanks would continue to grow. Instead of the cramped quarters the paper had always known, the Lathrop Building provided a roomy business and editorial office "finished in mahogany and with every modern fixture and convenience." The compositors and printers, accustomed to the decrepit machinery of the Thompson years, found a room full of new devices, including a brand-new Mergenthaler "Blue Streak" Linotype machine, the first of its kind in Alaska, enabling one operator to set more type than five or six "type-stickers" doing the same task by hand. For job printing, the mechanical room had a Kelly automatic cylinder press, a Challenge paper drill, a Morrison "Perfection" stitcher, and a Diamond power paper cutter. At the heart of the plant was a brand-new press from the Goss Printing Press Company in Chicago, a Goss Cox-O-Type web press that was unlike any press ever seen in Fairbanks.

Before the *News-Miner* purchased its Cox-O-Type, the newspaper had been printed on one sheet and one side at a time. On the one-cylinder Babcock press, the pressman fed each sheet into the gripper. All the sheets had to be run through twice in order to print on the other side. On the new Cox-O-Type web press, paper was automatically fed into the press at high speed from a five-foot-wide, fifteen-hundred-pound roll that made a continuous web or stream of newsprint, and it required only one pass through the two cylinders on the fifteen-foot-long machine—in little more than one second—to print, cut, and fold an eight-page issue. The *News-Miner* could now print its run of about thirty-four hundred copies in only an hour, compared to the five or six it had taken before.[27]

The move from the sheet-fed Babcock to the web-fed Cox-O-Type brought the *News-Miner* out of the horse-and-buggy days, but the 1937 makeover was as far as Lathrop's modernization would ever go. A new rival entity took the luster off the *News-Miner* two years later, when Lathrop became convinced that the future belonged not to newsprint but to radio. In 1939, three floors above the "dream newspaper plant," he opened radio station KFAR, whose call letters stood for "Key For Alaska Riches."

KFAR radio went on the air at seven p.m. on October 1, 1939, when Lathrop took the microphone and said, "I hope you all derive as great a pleasure out of the programs on KFAR as we have experienced in building and planning the station. I feel very proud that I have been privileged to bring KFAR to my people."

The inspiration for the station had come from Miriam Dickey, Cap's longtime secretary and companion. Despite initial skepticism, Lathrop eventually became a full-scale radio enthusiast, promising to invest at least $100,000 or more in a one-thousand-watt station with RCA equipment that was to be "modern to the last word of engineering."[28]

In no time at all the station became irreplaceable, not least because when the Japanese bombed Pearl Harbor the engineers at KFAR were the first people in Alaska to know of the attack and called the U.S. Army to notify them that the war had begun. Commentators marveled repeatedly that with the arrival of KFAR isolated Alaskans now considered "their small portable radios as necessary as their guns, and watch their battery replacements as carefully as their stores of food."[29]

The beginning of KFAR was the beginning of the end for Lathrop's *News-Miner.* His ownership of both the newspaper and the radio station in such a small town posed new complications. Critics had often charged Lathrop with being a monopolist, and certainly he dominated the commercial life of the community as no one ever had before or since. In those days every street in Fairbanks was Lathrop Street. The coal from Cap's coal mine supplied the steam and electricity that ran the city; every time the lights went on in Fairbanks, every time the dredges scooped another bucket of gravel, it was due to Cap Lathrop. A man living in a home heated by the coal from Cap's mine, or in one of Cap's apartments, could apply for a loan at Cap's bank to pay for his children to attend Cap's university (Cap was vice president of the University of Alaska Regents). At the end of a hard day he could watch a movie in one of Cap's theaters, drink Cap's beer (Cap was the Olympia distributor), listen to Cap's radio station, or read Cap's newspaper.

With such dominance in a small market like Fairbanks, Lathrop's enterprises were naturally interconnected. As one man put it, the economic reality in Fairbanks was that "Cafe owners who do not buy Cap's beer need not apply for loans at Cap's banks."[30] But the dilemma for the *News-Miner* was that after 1939, Cap's newspaper could never compete with Cap's radio station. As Solka recalled, KFAR won the "hearts and ears" of Fairbanks and the bush, serving as an "indispensable link with the rest of the world." As a result, "Lathrop abandoned the *News-Miner* for this new and more flashy medium." In the hierarchy of the Lathrop Company, the radio station was clearly the favorite son for money, staff, equipment, and advertising dollars. There was a spirit of youth and enthusiasm in the radio station that was lacking at the newspaper. KFAR's staff—engineers and announcers such as Stan Bennett, Augie Hiebert, Bud Foster, and Al Bramstedt—was composed of twenty-year-olds with energy and optimism to match their pioneering industry.

As a famous sociological study in 1929 noted, the automobile, the motion picture, and the radio were the three great technological wonders reshaping American life. The three were not simply "a new way of doing an old thing" but "added new dimensions" to the lives of people across the country, bringing the world to people in their own homes, rich and poor alike. "With but little equipment one can call the life of the rest of the world from the air, and this equipment can be purchased piecemeal at the ten-cent store."[31] Bringing radio to Interior Alaska was one of Lathrop's proudest accomplishments.

In contrast to the forward-thinking spirit on the fourth floor of the Lathrop building, the tenor of the *News-Miner* offices was decidedly antiquarian. Even as staunch a defender of the printing trade as Paul Solka had to admit that the root of the problem was the backward-looking philosophy of his colleagues at the paper. "The *News-Miner* staff," he wrote, "sunk in the morass of gold-rush methods and ideology, was outclassed and outgunned. No wonder that Lathrop soon ignored almost completely his paper, preferring to bask in the reflected glory of KFAR."[32]

It was not hard to understand why more and more advertisers chose to spend their money on radio spots instead of newspaper ads, which only made the *News-Miner's* bottom line worse and worse. As the years passed, Lathrop grew ever more impatient with the continuing expense of operating the *News-Miner*. He came to regard the paper as a necessary evil if not a bottomless pit. One-time editor Art Bremer vividly recalled how reluctant Cap became in his later years to invest any additional funds in the *News-Miner*. A salesman once convinced Bremer of the merits of installing a more efficient, long-lasting type of fluorescent bulb that would provide vastly superior light for the men working on small type. In the short term the price tag for the conversion would run into thousands of dollars, but in the long run it would result in substantially lower electric bills. The salesman rigged up a sample in the composing room over one of the "stones" in the layout department. "The next time Cap was in I showed him the light, demonstrating how quickly the light came on when you pulled the switch, unlike the earlier fluorescent tubes," Bremer said. "I told him the price and how much it would save. Cap's only answer was an incredulous, 'You mean I got to spend *all that money?*'" Bremer quietly paid for the one light the salesman had installed and dropped the whole idea.[33]

Charles "Chuck" Gray, who started working for the *News-Miner* in March 1944 when he was a sophomore in high school, naturally was intimidated by Lathrop. Gray began working afternoons after school as a stereotyper "casting pigs and flat casts" used to create the plates that would be run on the press. He too recalls Lathrop's constant economy measures. "My earliest recollection of Lathrop is when he'd make a very infrequent trip through the place," he said, "and went around turning off lights. He told me right off the bat that if one took care of the pennies the dollars would take care of themselves."[34]

By the time Snedden arrived in Fairbanks in the spring of 1950, Lathrop had been turning the lights off at the *News-Miner* for so long that the paper was in sorry shape. As he had at the other ailing papers he'd diagnosed in his career, Snedden started with the machinery, the nuts and bolts of the newspaper plant, the composing room, the Linotype machines, the job shop, and the press, drawing up a list of what needed to be repaired, remodeled, or replaced. He then moved on to the bigger pattern of the workflow, diagramming a new layout of the back shop to coordinate activities between the departments.

In July 1950, Snedden handed Lathrop a twenty-page report detailing what needed to be done, including his recommendations about staffing, supplies, newsprint, technological innovations, and equipment.

Predictably, Lathrop did not want to hear what the newspaper doctor had to say. "Cap never got beyond the second page," Snedden recalled. "He told me, 'I don't need any dope from the Big City to tell me to spend another $100,000!'"

Snedden tried to convince Lathrop that the investment would pay handsome dividends; the *News-Miner* was fundamentally sound and in a ripe, expanding market. If the right steps were taken, he predicted, the rebuilt plant could be sold in a short time for at least 100 percent profit above any additional investment Lathrop would have to make.

Cap was not convinced. He said he'd be happy enough "to find some darn fool" who would pay fifty or seventy-five cents on the dollar for all of the money he'd wasted in the newspaper business in the last twenty years.

As Snedden recalled the conversation, Cap asked where he might find a buyer for the *News-Miner*.

"Right here," Snedden said.

The two men worked out a deal for Snedden to purchase the paper and shook hands on the spot. They left the details to be written up later; each man had a train to catch. Lathrop was on his way to inspect his Healy River Coal Mine. Snedden and his son Skip were going fishing near Mt. McKinley National Park. Together they rode south on the Alaska Railroad about a hundred miles out of Fairbanks. Lathrop disembarked at Healy. Snedden would never see him again.

The eighty-four-year-old Lathrop was killed at the Suntrana Mine on July 26, 1950. No one saw the accident that claimed his life. That morning he'd been supervising a crew repairing a washed-out bridge approach. After lunch he headed back alone, walking along the tracks; possibly he had a stroke, but apparently he slipped and fell beneath the wheels of a loaded coal car.[35]

Lathrop's passing, like W. F. Thompson's a quarter-century earlier, was the end of an era for Fairbanks. The man at the core of its commercial life since the 1920s was gone. Initially Snedden believed Cap's death was also the end of his plan to purchase the *News-Miner*. Nothing had been finalized in writing before the accident, and Snedden assumed the deal was off. However, at Lathrop's memorial service, fittingly broadcast across Alaska via KFAR, Judge Medley approached Snedden and asked if he was still interested in buying the paper. Lathrop's sudden demise had placed the Lathrop Corporation in a cash squeeze, and, according to Medley, Lathrop had called the morning before the accident and said, "That sucker you sent up here to look at the paper has agreed to buy it."

They quickly made all the necessary arrangements. The Lathrop Company was only too glad to sell the paper that had been such a financial drain for so many years and thereby also honor Cap Lathrop's last wish. Though all the details would not be worked out for months, less than a week after Cap Lathrop's death, on August 1, 1950, Snedden became the publisher of the *News-Miner*. He didn't plan to stay long. His intention was to rebuild the newspaper from the ground up, establish it as a profitable concern, and sell the entire plant within one or two years. But in fact Snedden's tenure at the *News-Miner* would last almost forty years, longer than W. F. Thompson's and Cap Lathrop's combined, and like his two predecessors, he would leave an indelible mark on the community he came to call home.

2

The Progress Edition

Cap Lathrop gave Fairbanks its first modern facilities, but it was Uncle Sam, Adolf Hitler, and Joseph Stalin who turned the old mining camp into a city. In the 1940s, the threat of totalitarianism and the demands of air power created a new economy and a new way of life in Interior Alaska. Almost overnight, the U.S. Army Air Corps supplanted gold mining as its main industry. Miners gave way to military men and construction workers on government payrolls, and digging for gold was replaced by digging ditches for roads and runways.

Construction of the Alaska Highway in 1942 provided an overland link to the Lower 48. The building of Ladd Field (later known as Fort Wainwright) and Mile 26 (which became Eielson Air Force Base) brought thousands of soldiers, airmen, and laborers to the Tanana Valley. Through the 1940s and early 1950s, Uncle Sam poured an estimated $100 million a year into the two air bases outside Fairbanks, far surpassing the value of all the gold dug out of the creeks in the previous fifty years. Between 1940 and 1950 the region's population quadrupled, and the little mining town on the edge of nowhere had become the northern outpost of America's defense perimeter, "the good right fist of Uncle Sam in Alaska."[1]

When Bill Snedden took over the *News-Miner* in August 1950, little more than a month after the start of the Korean War, both the town and its newspaper were struggling to cope with the enormous changes of the past decade and trying to adjust to life in the middle of a cold war zone. In 1950, the newspaper was as antiquated as the rest of the local infrastructure. Snedden's initial plan to remake the *News-Miner* into a healthy business was, in theory, not much different from salvage operations he'd performed on lagging newspapers in California and the Pacific Northwest. But as he came to appreciate what the community had to offer, it wasn't long before he gave up any thought of selling the *News-Miner*.

If Fairbanks were dug up and dropped in the Lower 48 it would be nothing more than the average county seat. But in Alaska, Fairbanks functioned as a major regional center along the lines of Seattle, Portland, or San Francisco. A 1954 survey by economist Richard Cooley, fittingly entitled *Fairbanks, Alaska: A Survey of Progress*, found that "the commercial and financial importance of the city far exceeds its size." It was the hub for a trading area of 227,000 square miles, equal in area to the entire states of Washington, Oregon, and the northern half of California. "No city in the United States, its territories, or insular possessions has so vast a tributary area," said another authority.[2] The chance to make the *News-Miner* into a vital force serving this huge hinterland—an area spectacularly rich in national resources—was too alluring to resist. By 1951, Snedden was determined to stay.

He purchased the old home of R. C. Wood, built in 1906 at the corner of First Avenue and Kellum Street that featured a large bay window and front porch with a lovely view across First Avenue to the Chena River. Dick Wood had been a prominent businessman in Fairbanks' early years, president of the First National Bank of Fairbanks. His showplace home and garden had been featured on picture postcards. Legend has it that when President Warren G. Harding made his historic visit to Fairbanks on July 15–16, 1923, to drive the golden spike on the Alaska Railroad, the Woods hosted him at the house. Wood was a friend and sometime business associate of W. F. Thompson, and during the presidential party's twenty hours in Fairbanks, the "Editor in Chief," as Thompson called him—Harding was a printer and publisher by trade—visited the *News-Miner* offices and hand-set a line of type that read "FAIRBANKS, ALASKA. W.G.H.," which Thompson said he would frame on the wall as a reminder that even a typesetter could grow up to become president.[3]

Snedden's preliminary report to Cap Lathrop had estimated that refurbishing the plant could cost up to $100,000. In fact Snedden would invest about four times that amount over the next several years. On the business side, the circulation department was in shambles. Despite the booming economy of Fairbanks in 1950, the *News-Miner* was mysteriously running in the red, averaging losses of about $2,000 a month, and so with every issue that rolled off the press the company went deeper in debt. Luckily, one of the key staff members Snedden inherited from Cap

Lathrop was Zelma Trafton, who would serve for decades as his book-keeper and business manager. Once he assigned Trafton to examine the books closely, she discovered an embezzler in the circulation department. The culprit was immediately fired, though no prosecutions were pursued because officials in the Lathrop Company feared it might reflect badly on their other interests.

In the Lathrop era no one had expected the newspaper to make money, and the *News-Miner*'s business practices had long been notoriously lax. As Chuck Gray recalled, "There was no visible effort to sell advertising," and those who did advertise were accustomed to paying about once a year. "Most advertisers figured that Cap didn't need the money anyway."

Officially wearing three hats in those early years as general manager, business manager, and advertising manager, Snedden revamped the entire business operation. Salesmen recruited to solicit classified and retail advertising were told to politely inform customers that space in the paper would now have to be paid for in a timely fashion. The publisher made house calls on local businesses to get acquainted, hearing their concerns and asking what the newspaper could do to help the community. But his philosophy was that reporters and editors had to make sure not to print stories that were simply free advertising. "Advertisers here (like everywhere else) periodically come up with 'great ideas' for publicity gimmicks which they feel sure we should publish as red hot news."[4]

As for the newspaper's editorial policy, Snedden was equally clear. The *News-Miner* would be "Independent Republican," in that order, with the proviso that "partisan politics is very definitely secondary to the best interests of Fairbanks, Alaska, and the United States," also in that order.

One of Snedden's earliest editorial innovations was the launching in November 1950 of the *News-Miner*'s annual "Progress Edition," patterned after the *Vancouver Evening Columbian*'s Progress Edition first launched in May 1928, which he remembered vividly from his youth. The *Columbian*'s seventy-six-page special edition had proudly claimed to be the largest edition in the newspaper's history, "or, for that matter, of any newspaper ever published in Southwestern Washington," and it recounted the "remarkable growth, prosperity and advance of civic ideals in Vancouver and Clark county."[5]

According to the *Columbian* (admittedly not dispassionate about the special edition) readers "literally gasped when the toiling carriers delivered their copies.... Surprise at the physical proportions of the issue was followed by wonder, amazement and pleasure as the citizenry settled itself in its favorite easy chairs and turned page after page to see the seemingly endless array of illustrations and articles touching upon virtually every phase of city and county activity." Once upon a time, the editor explained, Vancouver's slogan might have been "'It's good enough.' Today nothing is good enough for Vancouver and Clark county unless it is good enough for every community." The front-page banner headline read "CITY SHOWS BIG PROGRESS," and underneath it said "READERS URGED TO SEND EDITION TO THEIR FRIENDS."[6]

Like its Vancouver predecessor, the *News-Miner*'s Progress Edition was a promotional vehicle designed to tell the story of Fairbanks to the rest of the world. (The annual Fairbanks version, published until the 1970s, even included a mailing wrapper with printed postage rates to make it easier to send to friends outside Alaska.) "The *Daily News-Miner* is a robust 22 pages today," the first Progress Edition proudly explained in November 1950, "nearly three times its normal size. It goes forth containing two extra sections, 14 pages, devoted to Fairbanks . . . combining a look at the past with something of the shape of things to come."[7]

From that initial, modest fourteen-page supplement, the *Fairbanks Daily News-Miner*'s annual Progress Edition would grow year by year into the largest newspaper ever published in Alaska: 40 pages in 1951, 70 pages in 1952, 128 pages in 1953, and 144 pages in 1954, with the press run of the Progress Edition during those years nearly tripling from seventy-five hundred copies in 1951 to twenty-two thousand three years later. For a small newspaper like the *News-Miner,* the logistical and financial challenge of manufacturing this special edition was enormous: the 1954 issue totaled almost 3.2 million newspaper pages, of which about eight hundred thousand were printed in color.

The Progress Edition exemplified Snedden's view of the newspaper's role in fostering community growth.

> A city is not created by those who use it for financial gain, and take little or no interest in its welfare.... A great city does not exist in terms of concrete, or wood. It exists in the hearts of those who love it, and want to work for it.... This civic spirit is the foundation of our city. Big buildings, paved streets, and adequate utilities are essential to growth ... But only the hard work and devotion of

the average citizen and his family will make Fairbanks a great city.[8]

Beyond Snedden's boosterism, the pages of the Progress Edition reflected the city's remarkable transformation. "In the past, the name, 'Fairbanks' has been associated with board walks, muddy streets, ramshackle frame buildings and the brawling, sprawling activities of a typical boom town."[9] But rapidly the old wooden town of mud and dust was giving way to paved streets and concrete buildings. In 1953 reporter Maury Smith estimated that the total volume of concrete poured in Fairbanks the preceding year would make a pillar as high as Denali.[10] Elsewhere residents might be apt to take the combination of sand and gravel for granted, but not in a place like Fairbanks, where permanent investments had seldom before been made. Even in the 1952 Progress Edition, a headline read "Modern, Fireproof Concrete Buildings Newest Trend Here." The first concrete-block home belonged to businessman George Nehrbas in Slaterville. He experimented with many materials before constructing the first "cavity wall masonry house" in Fairbanks— two layers of blocks with dead air between for insulation—surrounded by a landscaped lawn "enclosed by a decorative concrete block fence." Nehrbas said he was convinced that Interior Alaskans "could live just as comfortably here as in the United States." According to the *News-Miner*, "The ultimate result was a home as modern as tomorrow with radiant heat one of the special features."[11]

The Progress Edition boasted that old-timers visiting Fairbanks would find it "hard to remember the yesteryears of 'log cabin town,'" and would instead be greeted by "many modern fireproof buildings of poured concrete and concrete block supplanting landmarks gutted by fire throughout the years." The overall impression of "the new type of construction is the air of permanence that is taking hold of Fairbanks. Instead of thinking in terms of 'making a pile to take home' elsewhere, Fairbanksans are planning their future right here."[12]

The one building that more than any other symbolized the changes taking place was the Northward Building. Though not the biggest erected in Fairbanks in those years (the tallest was the eleven-story Hill Building, later renamed the Polaris), the eight-story Northward Building—originally called McKinley Manor—opened in the spring of 1952 and took up an entire city block. "Newer than tomorrow," the Northward was Fairbanks' first large apartment building and its first shopping mall, complete with a restaurant, bar, coffee shop, barber, beauty salon, mail order store, dry cleaners, grocery, liquor store, drugstore, clothing store, lawyer's office, insurance agency, and bank. Residents in the 210 apartments—all of whom had access to "high heat incinerators" to vaporize bottles and cans—and protected by double-pane "twindows," designed not to frost over, could, it was claimed, go an entire winter without ever having to venture out into the cold. "Visitors strolling through the ultra modern new Northward Building . . . will have no idea they are in rugged Alaska's log cabin town of yester-year." Designed to be "nearly sound, earthquake and fire-proof," and built on a welded-steel frame covered entirely in aluminum, it was one of the largest structures of its kind in the world.

"From the air the new Northward building is this city's outstanding landmark," the *News-Miner* reported. "It looms up amidst the city like a . . . mountain," and pilots said that "the building glares in the sun" like a huge silver nugget. When novelist Edna Ferber, inspired by Ernest Gruening to write a book about the statehood cause, came to Fairbanks to research the project, she stayed at the Northward. In her novel, loosely inspired by Fairbanks, the "mountain of metal" became a symbolic structure called the Ice Palace, representing the many political, economic, and social changes taking place in Alaska in the 1950s.[13]

For the *News-Miner* itself progress was slow but gradual. To supplement the paper's existing battery of three Linotypes, Snedden added two new Comet models that could produce more lines per minute. The paper switched to a new typeface in May 1952, setting up all of its Linotype machines to run in seven-and-a-half-point Corona, claimed to be the "latest, most modern style of type. It has been designed to 'save reader's eyes' by making the paper more legible. . . . Corona type has been scientifically designed to make it easier to read and at the same time, make it possible for the newspaper to get a large amount of news in each edition."[14]

The major production bottleneck and design flaw in the newspaper plant remained the flatbed printing press. The Goss Cox-O-Type could only handle eight pages at a time, so in November 1952, Snedden announced plans for expansion, including buying a new press so large it would need an entirely new building.

Constructed in 1953, immediately east of the Lathrop Building, the Chena Building was a three-story structure fronting on both First and Second Avenues. Part of the wall in the Lathrop Building was knocked out to provide access. The long, narrow structure—50 by 143 feet—contained apartments and commercial offices on the top two floors, with a department store on the ground floor along Second Avenue. There was additional space for the *News-Miner* on the First Avenue side, where the pride of the newspaper, a new rotary press nicknamed "Alice," previously owned by the *Sacramento Union*, was ensconced in a two-story atrium, visible from the street behind a huge plateglass window.

Alice, named after the daughter of a former *Union* publisher (her name was inscribed on a bronze plate attached to the press), was about fifty years old, but in printing years that was hardly middle aged. Both printing presses and Linotypes were rugged pieces of industrial machinery with a life expectancy of many decades. To recondition the press, Snedden leased the Christy Gun Works in Sacramento. Before shipping the whole plant to Fairbanks, he spent months going over it piece by piece with a crew of machinists, oiling, repairing, and replacing all worn parts. "We took over the machine shop at night," Snedden said. "The reworked parts were sprayed with plastic for rust-proofing before crating and shipment."[15]

Alice was a Goss thirty-two-page straightline, four-deck rotary press, a vast improvement in both quality and speed; on a rotary press, unlike a flatbed, the curved plates on the printing cylinders enabled the stream of newsprint to flow faster through the press, and the four printing "decks," each fed by a separate spool of newsprint, offered vast capabilities for speedy four-color printing. When Alice was cranked up, the entire building shuddered. She was capable of turning out twenty-five thousand papers of thirty-two pages per hour; the old Cox-O-Type flatbed had to run eight hours to do what Alice could do in thirty minutes.

Editorially the biggest improvement was Snedden's new managing editor, John Joseph "Jack" Ryan. A colorful man of many monikers and Irish to the core, Ryan brightened the paper's pages as managing editor from 1951 to 1957. (Later in life "John J." added yet another title to his string when he officially changed his last name from Ryan to O'Ryan, claiming it was probably some dunderheaded, Anglo-Saxon bureaucrat who forced his ancestor to drop the "O" when he was dropped off the boat.) Born in Washington State in 1919, Ryan had come to Alaska in 1939 "on the trail of the lonesome dime" with high school friend Ed Braddock in a homemade twenty-seven-foot boat they christened the *Maggie Murphy* in honor of Ryan's mother. According to Ryan, his mother never thought it was quite the honor he did, and she always called the leaky craft "that thing." Hoping to become salmon trollers, Ryan and Braddock came north with neither money nor skill, and blamed their crazy adventure on the Scandinavian neighborhood in which two Irish Catholic boys were forced to grow up.

Remarkably, the boat made it all the way to Alaska, and Ryan spent two memorable summers trying unsuccessfully to get rich off the sea while attending the University of Washington journalism school in the winter. He finished college after a four-year hitch in the navy during World War II and returned to Alaska in 1948 to work for the *Ketchikan Daily News*, the *Anchorage Daily News*, and then the United Press bureau in Anchorage. In 1951, the same year that Norton published Ryan's first book, *The Maggie Murphy*, a whimsical account of his youthful sailing adventures in Alaska, Snedden hired him as *News-Miner* editor.[16]

Snedden thought Ryan was the fastest writer he ever knew, although the quick-witted Irishman had a well-deserved reputation for enjoying a drink now and again, or more precisely, again and again. It was an open secret that he kept a bottle in his desk drawer, and Ryan liked to tell how he could walk to his home on Tenth Avenue, eight blocks from the *News-Miner*, without ever getting cold, even when the temperature was sixty below. "First, I would dash from the *News-Miner* to the Cottage Bar, warm up a bit, then make a run to the Northward Bar. After this stop, I'd make a long dash to the Travelers Inn bar, and after a brief stop there, I'd arrive at my house, warm as toast."[17]

Both Ryan's sense of humor and his disorganizational skills were legendary. Jack de Yonge, a green reporter who worked under Ryan in the 1950s, remembered his old chain-smoking boss as "a hands-on editor. He always had his hands on your cigarettes."[18] On occasion Ryan could not remember where he parked his car, including once when he was double-parked in the middle of Second Avenue. Chuck Gray recalled the time when Ryan returned to the newsroom late one night after many hours of celebrating to find the reporters had ignored his repeated requests to clean up the office, so he took matters into his own hands. He "threw everything on every desk into the trash," causing quite a stir when the staff arrived the next morning to find all the desks empty and the garbage full.

In Snedden's view the *News-Miner* had a unique responsibility in its approach to the news. Unlike papers of similar size in the Lower 48, the *News-Miner* had to serve as both a local paper and big-city paper. "Because of our remote location practically none of our readers have access to a metropolitan daily newspaper upon which they can depend for national and international news. Consequently we must give our subscribers a reasonably comprehensive but concise (this presents a neat trick!) picture of national and international events, as well as thorough local coverage."

He believed the core of the paper had to be local news. School activities, city council meetings, church organizations, community clubs, youth groups, anniversaries, etc. could all provide a steady stream of raw material because "most readers are more interested in mundane local events than they are in happenings in some remote corner of the world." The plain fact was that except on the police blotter, people liked to see their names, their children's names, and their friends' names in the paper. "The more times we get names (when they are spelled right) into the paper, the more friends we have."

Snedden always believed some of the *News-Miner*'s most interesting contributors were in its stable of "bush correspondents," the freelancers ("stringers" in newspaper jargon) who periodically wrote about goings-on in their villages, from spots across hundreds of miles throughout Interior and northern Alaska such as Fort Yukon, Chicken, Tanana, Old Crow, Barrow, Bettles, and Kotzebue. Local correspondents were a staple for most small-town American newspapers, but the *News-Miner*'s cadre was unprecedented. "No other paper in the United States," Snedden believed, "could even come close to matching the human interest that is commonplace in the columns submitted by people out in the bush."[19] William Chapman White, a reporter for the *New York Herald Tribune*, wrote in 1952 that the *News-Miner*'s rural correspondents covered the usual—births, deaths, crimes, weddings, anniversaries, and pinochle tournaments—but in addition were just as likely to describe killing a whale, bagging a polar bear, or chasing a herd of reindeer. "Few local correspondents for American papers," White concluded, have "so much of the exotic at their doorsteps."[20]

During most of his six years at the *News-Miner*, Jack Ryan wore four of the main editorial hats as editor, managing editor, editorial page editor, and city editor. In that time advertising rates nearly doubled, circulation nearly tripled, and the paper's local news coverage was as good as or better than it had ever been before. Ryan quit the *News-Miner* in 1957 to set off on a new seagoing escapade he hoped to turn into a book; with Snedden as his co-signer, he purchased a new vessel and "for reasons of business and adventure," he set off to circumnavigate the globe.

He got as far as Florida but never managed to sail around the world or to write another book. Ryan returned to Alaska after statehood in 1959 and made a run for U.S. Congress, then bounced around on a series of newspaper and public relations jobs before winding up back in Seattle with the *Seattle Post-Intelligencer* from 1969 to 1986. When he died in 1995 at age seventy-seven of a heart attack, *P-I* columnist Jon Hahn described his old friend as "the poor man's Jack London who made every *Seattle P-I* reader richer for his on-the-road adventure stories." [21]

To this day the imprint of Jack Ryan still appears daily on page one of the *News-Miner* in the form of his alter ego, a little cartoon character named "Sourdough Jack." It was Snedden's idea to put a cartoon of a crusty old-timer on the front page with some witty comment about the news, but it was Jack Ryan's personality that brought Sourdough Jack to life. Staff writer Jim Leveque, who had a "flair for cartooning," was given the assignment to draw four images of Sourdough Jack—"smiling, frowning, acting aloof and being just plain thoughtful." Leveque claimed he got the assignment only because he was "the youngest person in the office and the only one who could be talked into doing it." Smiling Sourdough Jack made his first appearance on June 11, 1952. "Well, the city manager can pat himself on the back today, and claim he's finally got the dust problem under control," the old-timer said. "It's raining." [22]

Sourdough Jack caught on with the readers, inspiring theme dances, parade costumes, and even a book, *Sourdough Jack Sez*, published in 1954 with one hundred of Ryan's best gags. "There's 100 of my humorous sayings in this book," the Sourdough says on the cover. "Some people claim I'm a wit, but my wife says they're only half right." City affairs, potholes, booze, marriage, weather, loafing, and innate human gullibility were among the recurring themes of the old philosopher. Under Ryan's tenure "Sourdough Jack" might charitably be described as a lazy, unemployed, alcoholic, wisecracking, hen-pecked, crafty, cantankerous, stubborn old man who told the world exactly what he thought:

> This dust must be getting my wife down. She wuz complaining yesterday. Said she's sick and tired of seeing me come home with a snootfull.

> Cold weather is coming and its time fer me to relax. In summer, I go to a lot of trouble finding ways to avoid work. In winter, I stay in bed and quit being so plumb eager.

I'm gonna take a case of beer and go fishing Memorial day. I'll have something in common with each fish I catch. Both of us will be wet to the gills.

The construction boom is tapering off, and I ain't sorry to see it go. This is the first summer since 1942 that I been able to walk downtown without being afraid someone would offer me a job.

Wuz watching cars whiz down the highway yesterday. Decided Americans has gone speed wacky. Everybody is driving 80 miles an hour to get nowhere to do nothing and hurrying back so it won't take so long.

A guy from California called our city a far north slum yesterday. Afraid I can't argue with an expert. If he's from California, he knows a slum when he sees one.

When showing visitors around, I tell them Fairbanks is a modern city with paved streets, green lawns, parks and sidewalks. If they leave before the snow melts, they never know the difference.

Folks in the States is always hoping for a white Christmas, but we don't worry about that in Fairbanks. We always have a white Christmas, a white Thanksgiving, and a white Easter. One of these years, we'll probably have a white Fourth of July.

Sourdough Jack is the longest-running feature ever to appear in the *News-Miner*, spanning more than half a century and counting. In the *News-Miner*'s tribute to Ryan/O'Ryan when he died, columnist Dermot Cole concluded, "O'Ryan is survived by his former wife, his son, three daughters and Sourdough Jack."[23]

The other lasting legacy from Ryan's *News-Miner* tenure was a piece he did for Snedden in 1953, a story that was the most influential article he ever wrote, even though it was never published. Snedden had asked

Ryan for an investigative report on the pros and cons of Alaska statehood. The Ryan report did such a thorough sales job that the publisher would reverse the newspaper's long-established position, and give Snedden the cause of a lifetime.

3

Statehood Now!

When Bill Snedden took control of the *News-Miner* in 1950, he was so preoccupied with modernizing the newspaper plant that he gave little thought to the biggest issue overshadowing territorial affairs: whether or not Alaska should become a state. No newspaper in Alaska had opposed statehood more strenuously than the *News-Miner* under Cap Lathrop in the late 1940s. Snedden initially saw no need to change that position. But over the next several years numerous events would force Snedden to re-evaluate the entire question.

The quest for Alaska statehood in the 1950s was fueled by growing dissatisfaction with federal management of the territory. Complaints about the overarching federal bureaucracy and the lack of local control were especially pronounced in the aftermath of World War II, but the roots of the problem stretched back many decades. Alfred P. Swineford, the publisher of the *Ketchikan Mining Journal* who had served as the second governor of Alaska from 1885–1889, told a visiting group of congressmen in 1904 that Alaskans were Americans and deserved to be treated like Americans, not colonial subjects: "I would like to impress you with the fact that we want to be made American citizens, first and foremost; the right to govern and control our own domestic affairs; to work out our own destiny; to reap the just reward of our labors and sacrifices."[1] In 1915, a short-lived weekly newspaper called *The Forty Ninth Star* began publication in Valdez, saying, "The creed of *The Forty Ninth Star* is that all people should have an equal opportunity, and in order to get that opportunity they must govern themselves. To advocate and preach that doctrine from now, henceforth, until Alaska becomes the 49th star on the American flag, is the mission of this paper."[2] As a symbolic gesture, in March 1916, the forty-ninth anniversary of the Alaska Purchase, Alaska Delegate James Wickersham introduced the first Alaska statehood bill in Congress.

Alaskans in favor of statehood claimed all they wanted were the basic rights granted to citizens in the forty-eight states, including the right to vote for president, to elect congressmen and senators, and to control their lands and resources. As residents of a territory, they had none of these. Their cry for equal representation was based on one of the fundamental principles of the American system, even older than the Constitution itself. Since 1784, when Thomas Jefferson promulgated what became known as the Northwest Ordinance, the principle was established that new western territories, once they had reached a population of at least sixty thousand, thus demonstrating a minimum level of economic and political maturity, were entitled to apply for admission as new states, on equal footing with the others. This innovation was meant to ensure that the newly independent colonies would not themselves have colonies as the country expanded westward and the United States would not duplicate the tyranny of "taxation without representation" against which it had rebelled. "Where there is no crown," as H. G. Wells described the American commandment, "there cannot be crown colonies."[3] The creation of each new state affirmed this republican concept.

So deeply rooted was the anticolonial strain in American politics that when Senator Charles Sumner rose to defend the purchase of Russian America in 1867, he stated the "most important endowment" Congress could ever give to Alaska was to fully incorporate it under the republican form of government. "Here will be a source of wealth," he predicted, "more inexhaustible than any fisheries. Bestow such a government, and you will bestow what is better than all you can receive, whether quintals of fish, sands of gold, choicest fur, or most beautiful ivory."[4]

In the decades that followed, progress toward political equality and greater economic opportunity for Alaskans was torturous. The purchase had been Seward's brainchild, and with little political interest or reliable information about the new possession, the general public assumed the "American Siberia" was too cold, isolated, and remote to be of concern. For its first seventeen years under the Stars and Stripes, Alaska remained a political vacuum, ruled indifferently by military officers or treasury department officials assigned to the capital at Sitka. Except for a few minor measures, Congress took no action to extend the basic provisions of government to Alaska's citizens. In 1878, M. C. Berry, the customs collector, and the only federal official in Alaska, said that the "frozen truth" was that

Alaskans had no rights whatsoever. "A man may be murdered in Alaska," he said, "his will forged, and his estate scattered to the four corners of the earth, and there is no power in a court of chancery to redress it."

Congressional passage of Alaska's first Organic Act in 1884 led to the appointment of a figurehead governor and a district court judge, but this half measure—one writer called it a "phantom of a government"—provided no elective legislative branch, no effective executive branch, and nothing in the way of representative democracy.

The influx of thousands of gold seekers into Alaska in the 1890s and early 1900s forced Congress to enact a series of reforms. Most notably, in 1906 Alaskans were permitted to elect a nonvoting delegate to Congress, and in 1912, with the passage of the Second Organic Act, the right to elect a Territorial Legislature. The new legislature was only a tiny step toward genuine home rule, however, because the body had severely restricted legal authority, particularly when it came to dealing with lands and natural resources, the core of Alaska's potential wealth. A political scientist described the Alaska Territorial Legislature as "the most circumscribed legislative body functioning in any land which professes faith in democracy."[5] Just as nearly 100 percent of Alaska's land would remain federal property until the achievement of statehood in 1959, the major decisions affecting Alaska's future continued to be made by federal bureaucrats, Congress and the president, none of whom were responsible to or appointed or elected by the residents of Alaska. Political reality, as a writer for *Fortune* magazine explained in 1955, was a bureaucratic nightmare: "Cut a tree, build a house, harness a stream, shoot a bear or net a salmon on 99 percent of the land, and a bureaucrat will be on hand to say yea or nay." The "rule of red tape" that controlled the territory was seen by many residents as the dark side of the American democratic system. "The government of Alaska," a Juneau lawyer pronounced in 1936, "is the worst possible under the American flag."[6]

The iron law of bureaucratic inertia and the lack of a cohesive, practical alternative to nonresident, federal domination ruled Alaska until the 1940s. Ironically, it was the economic growth fueled by the massive increase in federal spending in Alaska during World War II, and creation of a new military/government-construction economy not based on natural resource extraction, that revolutionized the political and economic landscape and provided the critical mass for the drive to statehood. Another irony was that the man who carried the torch for the right of Alaska residents to enjoy "state's rights" was the last nonresident to be appointed governor of Alaska, a brilliant, brash, and outspoken New Deal bureaucrat

from New York, Dr. Ernest H. Gruening, who served as governor from
1939 to 1953.

— ··· —

An urbane, sophisticated intellectual with an MD from Harvard—though
he never practiced medicine—Gruening was a citizen of the world. Fluent
in four languages, he was a prolific writer and a fierce debater who made
his name as a muckraking journalist on some of the leading periodicals
in the country, including a stint as managing editor of *The Nation* in the
1920s. Although he held many responsible administrative positions in
his life, Gruening always remained a freethinking reporter at heart, more
comfortable as a critic than a decision maker, who thought of journalism
as "the most interesting and worthwhile" of all the professions."[7] After the
election of Franklin D. Roosevelt in 1932, he became one of the bright
young men of the New Deal. He rose to become head of the Division
of Territories and Island Possessions in the Interior Department, when
suddenly, in the fall of 1939, at age fifty-two, he was exiled from D.C.
to become Governor of Alaska, largely because he had repeatedly infuriated his boss, Interior Secretary Harold Ickes. Ickes was delighted that
Gruening had been banished to Juneau by President Roosevelt; though he
privately confessed he was "apprehensive of what may happen in Alaska"
when Gruening got there, Ickes trusted that he had seen the last of his
troublesome colleague and expected that Gruening would not last more
than a few months as governor.[8]

Confounding Ickes and all those who underestimated him, Gruening
would go on to have a long and fruitful second career in Alaska, starting
with more than thirteen years as governor, the second-longest term of any
territorial governor in the history of the United States, and then a decade
in the U.S. Senate following Alaska statehood. During his tenure in the
governor's mansion, Gruening earned more than his share of passionate
admirers and bitter critics. Supporters thought he articulated more clearly
than anyone before the ways that Alaska residents had been shortchanged
by the all-powerful fishing and mining industries, and the need for enacting a comprehensive new taxation policy. In public speeches, articles,
and books, Gruening blasted the endless cycle of territorial history that
President Theodore Roosevelt had bemoaned back in 1903 as he faulted
the absentee owners of Alaska enterprises, the men who came to Alaska
to "skin the country" and then leave, who opposed all efforts to pay the
taxes required if Alaska was ever to have any local government. Gruening

adherents praised his never-ending battle to raise taxes and retain a greater share in Alaska of the profits from natural resource development, and they were wholeheartedly behind his appeals for statehood as the only answer to ending nonresident rule in Alaska. "He has the tongue of the spell-binder," one pro-Gruening newspaper proclaimed in 1949, "the logic of Socrates and much of the charm of the late FDR. He has a way of making things seem important and getting others to see them that way."[9]

Even close Democratic allies of Gruening sometimes found the governor a difficult friend because he had all the subtlety of a jackhammer. "He broke up everything that was in his way," a colleague once said. "He bored through. He had the determination of sixteen men and a mind that was sharp and quick and ruthless."[10] Gruening's longtime protégé and confidant, the much loved E. L "Bob" Bartlett, explained early in his career how he tried to keep some distance between himself and Gruening. In 1943, before Bartlett ran for public office for the first time, he related, in a personal letter to Delegate Anthony J. "Tony" Dimond, the challenge of working with Ernest Gruening:

> I do not have to tell you that I have not followed Ernest Gruening slavishly.... His methods of doing almost everything have not been the methods which would be used by a person who had political "feel." He chooses to barge into a situation head on when a more cautious approach would serve him better ... [He] is too often inclined to forget that the reason we appointive officers are where we are [is] because some other men were elected.

Bartlett believed that those opposed to Gruening generally had no substantive comments to offer and merely attacked Gruening the person, not his ideas. Most repulsive to Bartlett was the obvious anti-Semitism that fueled some of the hatred of the governor. "They have assailed Gruening personally as a carpet bagger and as a Jew," Bartlett said, "and as a good many other things entirely unrelated to the problems at hand."[11]

Of all the Alaskans who took offense at Gruening in the 1940s, none felt the sting of the governor's presence more deeply than *News-Miner* publisher Cap Lathrop. Having earned his living in Alaska the hard way, and having gone broke more than once to prove it, Lathrop did not take kindly to being lumped by Gruening with absentee owners who earned enormous sums in the territory and shipped their profits to the Lower 48. Year after year the earnings from canneries, gold mines, banks, and mercantile stores ended up in Seattle, Chicago, or New York, leaving little behind in Fairbanks, Ketchikan, or Nome. Gruening thought an equitable tax system was the only way to ensure that an adequate slice of the profits from resource development remained in Alaska. "Too much going out, not enough staying here" was the slogan, Gruening said, that typified the principal illness of Alaska—but no private citizen had done more to reverse this trend than Cap Lathrop. Admittedly, Cap was the richest man in Alaska, and it was true that the territorial taxes he paid on his numerous enterprises were absurdly low: for example, there was a minimal license fee for banks ($250 a year) and motion picture theaters ($100), and even if the *News-Miner* and KFAR earned any profits—which they did not— neither would have been liable to taxation because newspapers and radio stations were not subject to the territorial tax code. Gruening dubbed Lathrop the "Commodore—Let the Public Be Damned—Vanderbilt of Alaska." Lathrop did pay a modest fee at his coal mine—a sum that Gruening called "infinitesimal"—but from Cap's point of view, the governor seemed to ignore that he had consistently poured his money back into Alaska, sparing no costs in buildings, machinery, equipment, and new enterprises.[12] As the years went by Lathrop made no secret of his opposition to statehood anytime in the near future, claiming that the territory could not afford the costs of running a full-fledged state bureaucracy.

When Gruening first encountered Lathrop in Fairbanks in 1940, the governor realized that the *News-Miner* was technically the best-equipped newspaper in the territory. (In contrast Gruening claimed Bob Atwood's *Anchorage Times* was "the poorest paper in the territory" in spite of having the "greatest opportunity.")[13] Though he could not approve of the *News-Miner*'s harsh anti–New Deal editorial policies, Gruening confessed that for the most part Cap always refused to use the newspaper as a political soapbox or as a vehicle to launch partisan crusades.[14] But he still thought the paper was too subservient to local business interests. Following an interview with a *News-Miner* staff member in August 1940, Gruening wrote in his private diary about a short conversation he had afterwards with the reporter.

> After I had given him my statement I asked him
> about journalism in Fairbanks and asked him what

"must nots," "keep-outs" and sacred cows there were. He looked [at] me somewhat in surprise and I recalled to him that I was a newspaperman. He then said, "Nothing whatever unfavorable to the FE [mining company] or any of its officials. The same for Northern Commercial, and practically nothing about labor." This is certainly a swell state of affairs since the first two mentioned companies practically control the economic life of Fairbanks and the entire surrounding country, plus the fact that they practically dominate the legislative delegation from the Fourth Division.[15]

The feud between Lathrop and Gruening erupted in the open after the governor presided over his first legislative session in the spring of 1941. When lawmakers soundly rejected a comprehensive tax reform policy proposed by Gruening, as well as a variety of educational and social measures, Gruening claimed the salmon lobby controlled the legislature, operating "on the principle that Alaska should spend as little as possible on its own needs" in order to keep taxes at a negligible rate. Frustrated by the "crude and shameless" performance of the lobbyists and legislators, he took drastic action. Gruening launched an unprecedented publicity barrage, taking his complaints about the legislature directly to the voters with a scathing "Message to the People of Alaska." He urged them to reject government of the lobby, by the lobby, for the lobby, which only represented "outside interests whose sole concern is to take out of Alaska as much as they can, as fast as they can, and leave as little as possible."[16]

Lathrop refused to run Gruening's message in the *News-Miner* or on KFAR. Infuriated by this "flagrant example of suppression" of the news, Gruening pushed forward a confidential complaint to the chairman of the Federal Communications Commission, blasting Lathrop for his joint ownership of the only two media outlets in Fairbanks and pushing for establishment of a government radio station to better serve the people of Alaska.[17]

By January 1948, having endured two terms of Gruening, Lathrop had had enough. Along with the rest of America he was convinced that Tom Dewey was certain to defeat hapless Harry Truman in the upcoming presidential election, so Lathrop spearheaded a campaign to deny Gruening another term. He also intended to use the *News-Miner* as a catalyst to revive Republican fortunes in the territory, now that sixteen years of

Democratic control of the White House (and therefore territorial patronage) by Roosevelt and Truman appeared to be ending. To that purpose Lathrop brought in a new managing editor of the *News-Miner*, William Strand, a veteran political and foreign correspondent from Colonel Robert "Bertie" McCormick's *Chicago Tribune*, the most bitterly anti-Roosevelt and anti-Truman metropolitan daily, which famously styled itself as "The World's Greatest Newspaper." As a correspondent for the *Tribune* Strand had written some critical articles about Gruening, and he was known as a "militant" Republican (years later he became head of public relations for the Republican National Committee). Pressman Paul Solka, who by this time had gone to work at *Jessen's Weekly* (and would himself come under fire from Strand for being a Democratic loyalist), thought Strand a Republican hatchet man who had come north to cut down Gruening.[18]

The first blow fell in March 1948 when the *News-Miner* broke with tradition and published a two-column front-page editorial, obviously written by Strand but signed by Lathrop, detailing all the reasons Gruening should go. In terms reminiscent of Thomas Jefferson's attacks on King George III, Strand claimed the governor "has tried to use the power and prestige of his office and the resources of the federal government to transfer to himself the initiative of the law-making powers of the citizens. It is the hallmark of all New Dealers." The editorial concluded that the U.S. Senate should reject Gruening's confirmation and wait until President Dewey could nominate a Republican in 1949. "The hope that the next President will be a Republican should be too bright at this point," Strand wrote, "to permit a GOP-controlled Senate to give serious consideration to this appointment of a Democrat to an important office such as the governorship of Alaska."[19]

News-Miner editorials and a barrage of letters complaining about Gruening had the desired effect: the U.S. Senate tabled the nomination, apparently leaving Gruening, for all practical purposes, a lame duck.[20] But when the November 1948 election did not turn out as expected Gruening got a new lease on his political life, and like Strand's old newspaper the *Chicago Tribune*, with its infamous "Dewey Defeats Truman" headline, the *News-Miner* botched the election. "Strand was so sure Dewey was going to win," former editor Art Bremer recalled, "that he prepared an election extra with a 'Dewey Wins' banner and all the stories slanted for a Republican victory. When Truman squeaked through, they got out the extra all right, but it was a mixed-up mess with everything but the top headline and lead story dealing with the victorious candidates headed by Governor Dewey of New York."[21]

Truman's victory and the Democratic sweep of the congressional elections in November 1948 was followed by Gruening's dramatic victory in January 1949, when the Alaska legislature finally approved an overhaul of the Alaska tax system and instituted a comprehensive income tax. In response Lathrop launched a last-ditch effort to block Gruening's confirmation. When the now Democratically controlled U.S. Senate agreed to hold hearings on the nomination, Lathrop brought a delegation of about half a dozen anti-Gruening witnesses to Washington, D.C., though to his chagrin they were outnumbered almost seven to one by Gruening supporters. From Lathrop's point of view the hearing ended disastrously; several of his witnesses proved to be less than credible, and one man admitted that his testimony had been written by Cap's secretary. When the hearing was over Gruening's nomination was approved unanimously and the full Senate went on to give him another four years in office.[22]

Still, the war of words between Gruening and Strand did not subside; if anything the conflict over the next year and a half between the governor and the *News-Miner* escalated, with each accusing the other of symbolizing all that was wrong with Alaska. At the Republican Lincoln Day Dinner in February 1950, Strand smeared the governor's wasteful and corrupt reign since 1939 as "a blot on the history of Alaska which not all the water of the Seven Seas can wash away," while Gruening blasted Strand one month later at the Democratic Jefferson-Jackson Day Dinner as a veteran of the ultraconservative school of "the *Chicago Tribune* whom Cap Lathrop had brought in . . . to . . . fight statehood, prevent the present governor from getting reappointed, and if re-appointed, prevent his confirmation."[23]

Gruening was still at the governor's desk and Strand was still in the editor's chair when Snedden took the helm of the *News-Miner* in the summer of 1950. During the early months of Snedden's tenure, the conflict between his editor and the governor reached its peak. In July Gruening had made the *News-Miner* a party to a $50,000 libel suit he had brought against the *Juneau Empire* for reprinting an *Empire* editorial that accused him of corruption in connection with federal funding for a civil aviation project. At that time the *Empire* was probably the only newspaper in Alaska that reviled Gruening as much as the *News-Miner*; publisher Helen Troy Monsen, daughter of John Troy, the man whom Gruening replaced as governor in 1939, went so far as to refuse to spell out Gruening's name in her paper. Whenever a story involved him, he was simply referred to as "the governor."[24] Along with the *Fairbanks News-Miner,* the *Juneau Empire* was one of four partners belonging to what Gruening derisively called the "Axis Press," the papers in the four largest cities—Anchorage, Fairbanks, Juneau, and Ketchikan—that opposed Gruening, taxes, and statehood; the others were the *Anchorage Daily News* and the *Ketchikan Fishing News.* Only two major newspapers favored statehood at that time: Bob Atwood's *Anchorage Times* and William Baker's *Ketchikan Alaska Chronicle.* Strand and his anti-statehood colleagues bristled at being compared in any way to Hitler, Mussolini, and Tojo. "There is no more an 'Axis Press' in Alaska," he said, "than there is a commissar governor who lives in a Kremlin in Juneau and meets from time to time with other officials whom he calls a Politboro [*sic*]."[25]

While three Alaska newspapers had reprinted the *Empire* editorial in question, Strand believed the governor had sued the *News-Miner* as an act of intimidation. "The hatred of the Gruening Administration for this newspaper is no secret to anyone," Strand said, claiming he was "proud of the governor's enmity" and that as a result of his "attack upon this newspaper and its editors" the *News-Miner* had been "elevated" into "the No. 1 force blocking his path toward absolute political control over the destiny of Alaska."[26] On the eve of the October election in 1950, Strand accused Gruening and his allies of making the *News-Miner* the central issue in the campaign. "The *News-Miner* did not make it so," he wrote. "It was made an issue by its political opponents and personal enemies, who have undertaken to run against this newspaper rather than on their records."[27] From the governor on down, he charged, the wheels of the Gruening machine "have been more thoroughly shaken and frightened by the *News-Miner* ... than by any other force or at any other time in their political careers." Strand denied the frequent charge that the *News-Miner,* because it opposed Gruening and his call for immediate statehood, was therefore somehow the "mouthpiece" of the canned salmon industry. "As far as this newspaper is concerned, it should be unnecessary to point out that it was published for nearly 20 years by Austin E. Lathrop, who was not for sale at any price and who accepted handouts from no one. No one ... told him what to think."[28]

At the height of the Gruening–*News-Miner* feud, news of the sale to Snedden had not yet been made public, and while the new owner would have been happy to retain the old *Tribune* man as editor, Strand had other plans, only agreeing to stay on until the arrival of Jack Ryan in February 1951. Afterwards Snedden remained friendly with Strand and the two men would stay in contact, because, in a strange twist of fate, after Eisenhower's election Strand was hired in 1953 to take Gruening's old job in the Interior Department as director of the Office of Territories and Island Possessions.[29]

Snedden shared Lathrop's and Strand's low opinion of Gruening. He bristled at the way Gruening repeatedly denounced the Seattle business community for not supporting statehood. "Unfortunately he attacked every businessman in Seattle who did not agree with his viewpoint," Snedden said, "and he attacked them for little or no reason at every opportunity. If no opportunity arose, Governor Gruening would create one."[30] Furthermore, in Snedden's mind the *News-Miner*'s stand against statehood had initially seemed eminently sensible, and quite popular in Interior Alaska. "At that time Fairbanks was undoubtedly the center of hard-core opposition to statehood in Alaska," Snedden said, "due in large part to Cap Lathrop's high personal prestige and the fact he kept his newspaper and radio stations continually pointing out the folly of any attempt to make Alaska a state."[31]

Proof of the strength of Fairbanks's opposition to statehood had come from a 1946 referendum, the only official advisory vote ever taken on the issue up to that time. Across Alaska the measure had passed by a 3–2 margin, with huge majorities in the affirmative in most of the dozen largest communities in Alaska. The highest percentages of urban "no" votes came from Nome (47 percent) and Fairbanks (44 percent), and as a consequence the overall tally from the 2nd and 4th Divisions went against statehood. In comparison only 22 percent of the voters in Ketchikan and 33 percent in Anchorage voted no on the nonbinding referendum.[32]

Lathrop and other statehood skeptics said they were not opposed to statehood someday, because to do so would have been akin to opposing motherhood. As KFAR and *News-Miner* reporter Georg "No E" Meyers phrased it, "Am I in favor of boys becoming men? Of course I favor statehood for Alaska."[33] While Gruening argued that Alaska's economic underdevelopment was proof of the need for immediate statehood, however, Lathrop claimed exactly the opposite, that Alaska's narrow economic base was evidence of the need to delay statehood and all its costs. Critics responded that Lathrop and the other "statehood not now" crowd were in fact arguing "statehood never" because they would never be willing to agree that the time and terms were suitable. [34]

Snedden's journey to supporting immediate Alaska statehood began when he was somewhat reluctantly elected to the Public Utilities Board for Fairbanks in October 1951.[35] While on the PUB, Snedden and the other board members discovered firsthand the financial cost of living in a territory, not a state, when the Fairbanks Municipal Utilities System sought $7 million in revenue bonds to finance a new power plant.

"I really thought the bonding houses were being facetious with us," Snedden said, "when they started quoting interest rates of around 6% at a time when many issues were going for less than 2%. . . . It was the first time that I saw graphically the . . . fantastically high costs we were being assessed because the entire territory was at the whim of a few congressmen and, particularly, the secretary of the interior—all located 4,000 miles away, and invariably all woefully uninformed about what conditions were up here."[36] Snedden said most of the bond houses "didn't even want to talk to us." They maintained that the inherent instability of the territorial economy and political structure, being totally dependent on distant federal decision makers, required an added premium if the bonds were to find a market.[37] "This was an experience that really opened my eyes," Snedden said, "to one of the aspects of being a 'second class American citizen.'"[38]

Another great factor in Snedden's education about the statehood cause was his growing friendship with Congressional Delegate Bob Bartlett. Like Gruening, Bartlett was a former newspaperman with equally strong convictions, but his background as a small-town reporter from Fairbanks, writing daily about neighbors and friends, required substantially more tact and discretion than the comparatively abstract and impersonal world of metropolitan muckraking in New York and Washington, D.C., in which Gruening had been schooled. People in small towns had long memories.

Shy and soft-spoken, Edward Lewis "Bob" Bartlett was a modest and unassuming son of Klondike pioneers, with a less-than-stellar résumé. A Fairbanks high school graduate and three-time college drop-out, he was a failed placer miner who chopped wood and went broke before deciding to become a newspaperman, learning his trade at the *News-Miner* under the tutelage of W. F. Thompson and Cap Lathrop. Despite Bartlett's meager academic credentials, the newspaper provided him with ample opportunity to polish a natural affinity for language, because for most of the nearly half-dozen years he worked at the paper in the 1920s and 1930s, he was the only reporter on the staff. When Cap Lathrop hired Bernie Stone, a hard-drinking tramp printer, as managing editor in 1930, the workload became even greater. One story goes that Bernie showed up at the *News-Miner* one morning with a thirst so powerful that he broke the glass on the front door in his hurry to find the bottle of "white mule" he had hidden in his office. When he could not find the bottle of bootleg whiskey, he accused Bartlett, who denied any knowledge of its whereabouts. Thereupon Stone noticed the broken glass in the door and demanded to know "who in the hell" had shattered the glass.[39]

Bernie Stone never let his typewriter do his talking for him. As Paul Solka delicately put it, "Bernie was adept with the spoken word to a far greater degree than the written phrase. As a consequence supplying copy for the paper fell almost entirely on Associate Editor E.L. Bartlett."[40] Bartlett rightly considered his title of associate editor of the *News-Miner* to be a dubious distinction, one that he had received only because Bernie had refused to give him a raise. As Bartlett liked to tell the story, it started after his childhood sweetheart, Vide Gaustad, finally agreed to marry him in the fall of 1930. His Depression-era salary as the *News-Miner* reporter did not go far. All the newlyweds could afford to eat that first winter were hamburgers and spaghetti. By the spring of 1931 Bartlett worked up the courage to tell Bernie that he needed a raise, if only to vary his diet. Bernie's response was that the *News-Miner* was struggling financially just like every other business in town, and could not spare an extra dollar, but instead he gave Bartlett a new title and put his name on the masthead as "associate editor."

"From that moment on," Bartlett wrote many years later, "the associate editor had an uneasy feeling that the ranks of journalism could not contain him much longer. His feelings in this regard were heightened by the derisive comments coming from fellow Fairbanksans . . . all of whom were aware of the fact that the editorial staff consisted of the editor and the associate editor."[41]

With or without his name on the masthead, Bartlett admitted that working for Cap Lathrop and barely getting by was not in his long-term plans. If he thought he had to remain a low-paid reporter at the *News-Miner* for the rest of his life, he told Vide, "I'd go out and shoot myself." He even considered looking around the Pacific Northwest for a small newspaper that could be bought with a low down payment and built into a paying proposition.[42] What dramatically changed Bartlett's life, however, was a series of articles he wrote for the *New York Times* in 1932–1933. As the Fairbanks stringer for the *Times*, Bartlett published a series on Alaska, the most important of which was an insightful profile in October of the delegate race between the incumbent Republican James Wickersham and

Democrat Tony Dimond, a former gold miner and well-respected attorney and territorial senator. While Wickersham at age seventy-five was the old warhorse of Alaska politics, first elected delegate in 1908, Dimond at age fifty-one was making a strong bid to become the first Democrat to capture the seat in a dozen years. Bartlett clearly admired Dimond's modesty and genuine personality, qualities that many others saw in Bartlett himself.

"He is almost entirely lacking in the political instinct," Bartlett wrote about Dimond.

> A Democrat of long standing, it may be said that never before has he sought office; the Territorial Senatorship was forced upon him. A prospector in his youth, an injury cut short his gold-seeking days and he turned to the study of law ... A reputation for honesty and sincerity of purpose, love of the Territory and his professional standing make him the most formidable candidate the Democratic party has placed in the field for many years.

Bartlett rightly predicted that Dimond would win the election.[43]

Tony Dimond had been a longtime friend of the Gaustad family in Valdez; Dimond and his wife had been witnesses at Vide and Bob's wedding in 1930. Following the 1932 election Vide had prodded her reluctant husband, who was so desperate to leave the *News-Miner* that he thought he could earn more money as a wood cutter on the Yukon, to apply instead for a job as the delegate-elect's secretary and administrative assistant. Impressed by Bartlett's knowledge of Alaska affairs, and his work for the *New York Times*, Dimond hired Bartlett to man his office in Washington, D.C.

Working a year and a half for Tony Dimond in the nation's capital in 1933–1934 was a turning point in Bartlett's career, his introduction into the world of government service and Democratic Party politics, though true to form Bartlett found life in Washington and the political world so little to his liking that he took the first chance he could to return to Alaska. In late 1934 he wrangled a job in Juneau as assistant director of the Federal Housing Administration, but he quickly realized he had no desire to spend his life watching the clock as a government bureaucrat. "There are nine of us all told," he wrote to Vide shortly after taking the FHA job, "and, honest to God, nothing to do but sit around on our fannies."[44]

The opportunity he wanted came when President Roosevelt appointed him in early 1939 to a four-year term as secretary of Alaska, the chief lieutenant to the governor of Alaska. During his four years in that post Bartlett became Ernest Gruening's closest ally. When Delegate Dimond announced in 1943 that after twelve years in office he would not seek reelection, Gruening wanted Bartlett to throw his hat in the ring. Vide Bartlett was adamantly opposed. She wanted Bob to remain in Alaska and keep his job as territorial secretary. Neither she nor Bob had particularly enjoyed living in Washington when he worked for Dimond. Bartlett was also reluctant as ever to push himself forward, believed he could not raise the money to finance a campaign, and doubted his ability to win an election. But Gruening was so eager to push Bartlett into the race (probably in part because he thought Bartlett would be more pliable than other possible candidates) that he tricked Dimond into prematurely endorsing Bartlett for the seat, virtually forcing Bartlett to put his name into contention.

Maneuvering Bartlett into running for office was one of Gruening's most astute political moves. Not only did Bartlett go on to win the 1944 election for delegate handily, but over the next quarter century the former *News-Miner* associate editor became the most respected and revered figure in Alaska politics. He won ten elections between 1944 and 1966 (seven as delegate and three as U.S. senator after statehood) during which time he averaged more than 70 percent of the vote; on two occasions he received about 80 percent of the vote, sweeping his opponents by a 4–1 margin. When Bartlett died in 1968, *Anchorage Times* publisher Bob Atwood said Bartlett's renown came in spite of the Alaska electorate's "individualism, divisiveness, sectionalism, arrogance, and clannishness." Somehow the ex-newspaperman from Fairbanks had done the impossible. "On ten different occasions," Atwood wrote, "the stubborn, unmanageable, belligerent and politically erratic populace of Alaska handed him the crown."[45]

Bartlett's political success was all the more astonishing because at first glance he hardly appeared to be a consummate politician. He was easy to underestimate. He did not have an air of breezy self-confidence and was never comfortable glad-handing a crowd. Even his closest supporters found it painful to hear him give public addresses; a colleague fondly called him "one of the world's worst speakers."[46] He likewise never won any prizes for sartorial elegance. Bartlett had the perpetually disheveled look of a man who had just come inside from working on his tractor. His youngest daughter, Susie, claimed he could put on a brand-new $200 suit, and in five minutes it would be as rumpled and worn as something he might have scavenged from a thrift shop.[47]

What he may have lacked in pressed pants or shined shoes, however, he more than compensated for in diligence, loyalty, and empathy, and as a result he was more popular than the causes he promoted. Even voters who didn't support statehood supported Bob Bartlett. As Alaska's longest-serving delegate in Congress, he earned a sterling reputation among his colleagues. Despite being a lowly delegate with no vote to horse-trade, he had a phenomenal record in getting legislation passed. From 1945 to 1952 he authored sixty-one bills that became law, more than any other member of Congress.[48] As Harry Truman once said of Lincoln, the secret of Bartlett's success was "a good head and a great brain and a kind heart."[49]

Like many other Alaskans, Snedden thought so highly of Bartlett that he came to think that there had to be more reasons in favor of statehood than he had previously believed, particularly after his experience trying to sell the revenue bonds for the Fairbanks power plant. In late 1953 Snedden decided that he needed an objective analysis of all the pros and cons.

"The day after Christmas I sent my editor, John J. Ryan, upstairs to a vacant apartment in our building," Snedden later said, "and told him I did not want to see him again before February—and at that time I expected two comprehensive briefs: one setting forth the merits of statehood, and one setting forth the merits of remaining a territory."[50]

Shortly afterwards Ryan came back to tell Snedden "to get someone else to write the 'con' side of the question." He could list the pros, but he couldn't honestly support the cons. After going over all the records and government hearings on the question, it appeared to him the rational arguments in favor of statehood were simply overwhelming and that there was no logical alternative.[51] "I sent him back to concentrate on the negative side," and though Ryan did as he was instructed, he again told Snedden none of the arguments against immediate statehood were legitimate.

Convinced by Ryan, as well as leaders such as Bartlett, Gruening, and Bob Atwood, Snedden decided to come out for immediate statehood in a full-length, two-column, front-page editorial written by Snedden and Jack Ryan on February 27, 1954, inspired in part by news that Sen. George Smathers from Florida had revived an old idea that the Territory of Alaska should be made a commonwealth instead of a state. "Our present status is literally an insult to American citizens," the *News-Miner* announced. "We cannot vote for President of the United States, and we cannot elect our own governor. . . . Here in Alaska, we live at the whims of federal agencies, and exist according to the will of congress. We are disfranchised, helpless American citizens living under a form of oppression almost as disheartening and tyrannical as that which brought about the Boston tea party, and the glorious American revolution of 1776." "Statehood Never" was no longer a viable alternative.

"The *News-Miner* has long advocated that we should try to build industry and develop the resources of Alaska before taking the long step to Statehood. But we are disheartened with this waiting, and waiting, while our destinies are twisted this way and that way by threats of filibusters, the whims of federal agencies and the uncomprehending attitude taken by many congressmen. . . .

"Alaskans should demand, STATEHOOD, NOW!"[52]

The *News-Miner*'s change of heart on the statehood question would cast a long shadow. Snedden said that initially many people in Fairbanks were "incredulous" at his decision.[53] "The *News-Miner* and myself were both about as popular around Fairbanks as a skunk in the parlor for some time."[54] It took years for old-guard admirers of Cap Lathrop to forgive Snedden. On his first visit to Washington State after the pro-statehood announcement, Ed Medley, the attorney for Cap Lathrop who had initially brought Snedden to Fairbanks in 1950, just shook his head in dismay.[55]

For Snedden personally, converting to statehood cost him a golden business opportunity. In the fall of 1953 Helen Troy Monsen, the publisher of the *Daily Alaska Empire* in Juneau, had inquired if Snedden would be interested in purchasing her newspaper. She had suffered some serious financial setbacks, including the protracted libel suit brought against her by Gruening, which she had lost. As a result she was on the verge of bankruptcy and needed to sell the newspaper almost immediately.

"I went down to Juneau and took a look at the operation," Snedden said. "It was a heck of a mess, to put it bluntly—worse than the *Fairbanks News-Miner* had been when I took it over."[56] After settling on the name of an independent newspaper appraiser, and giving her an initial down payment of $40,000 so she could continue to operate, they agreed that the closing date for the deal would be March 1, 1954. Two days before closing, however, was the day that Snedden had announced his support for statehood. When word reached Monsen of the *News-Miner*'s policy change, she was distraught. She could not bear the thought that her family's newspaper, which had battled the governor for so many years, and had essentially been driven into bankruptcy because of it, was nevertheless going to fall into the hands of the pro-statehood camp. Given Monsen's bitter feelings on the statehood question, Snedden regretfully decided that the only thing to do was to give up his option on the *Empire*, even though he was under no legal obligation to do so, and gave her one year to repay the $40,000 down payment interest-free.[57] The financial loss was only half of the equation. "Later I was tempted to regret this action," Snedden subsequently recalled, "as I believe the statehood battle would have gone much smoother if we had also been operating the *Empire*."[58]

In the years to come, the *News-Miner* and its publisher would play an increasingly important role in promoting the statehood cause, both publicly and privately in Alaska and Washington, D.C. No one appreciated the importance of Snedden's all-out commitment more fully than the *News-Miner*'s former reporter and associate editor, Delegate Bartlett.

"I shall be forever sensible and appreciative of what you in your personal capacity and through the *News-Miner* have done for the cause of statehood," Bartlett wrote Snedden in 1956.

> You are so close to the scene that perhaps you do not comprehend the significance that the change in the editorial policy of the *News-Miner* has meant. Before that time, it was not only statehood that was castigated and cast into the outer darkness; it was that almost every effort to advance the cause came in for constant and biting criticism. At Fairbanks, as at Juneau, the heavy hand of destructive rather than constructive newspaper policy in ever so many instances weighted the scales adversely. Now all that has changed in Fairbanks and you must, of course, be given the credit for that.[59]

As of 1954 the days when the *News-Miner* had anchored the Axis Press were long gone. But even as Statehood Now replaced Statehood Never, the newspaper was already fighting an equally bitter campaign on the local front: trying to stop the perpetual civil war that was life in the community of Fairbanks, Alaska.

"Progress" was the *News-Miner* mantra of the 1950s for the "Growing Metropolis" of Fairbanks.

Distributed nationally throughout the 1950s, the annual Progress Edition was the vehicle for convincing the rest of the United States of the bright future for Fairbanks and Alaska, even though Snedden admitted the special edition was "economic suicide" for a newspaper of the *News-Miner*'s size.

BIG PRODUCTION JOB—Preparing the 1957 Progress Edition for distribution was a task which commanded the energies of nearly 100 full-time and special employes of the News-Miner over a period of several months. Its 12 sections were printed two at a time and "stuffed" by hand. Shown working on this phase of production are Calvin Blevins and Hildegard Carr in first row and, left to right at rear, Otto Coon, Edith Foulen and Mrs. Lydia Burnett. *News-Miner Photo by Phil's Studio*

Hey Kids

ASK YOUR MOM AND DAD
TO GET YOU ONE OF THESE

BIG-NEW

GUIDED
MISSILE
BANKS

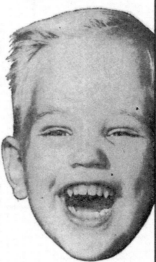

. . . ACTUALLY MAKES IT FUN TO SAVE! These large size, full 13 inches high; all metal Guided Missile Banks are offered as a special service by each office of the Alaska National Bank of Fairbanks. They are available to present Savings Account customers, as well as to new customers who open a savings account of $5.00 or more. The price is less than our cost — only $1.50 — with your savings pass book. Come In, Get Yours While They Last!

Open Your Savings Account Now

SAVINGS EARN **3%** TO $10,000

FOUR OFFICES

MEMBER FEDERAL DEPOSIT INSURANCE CORPORATION

To Serve All Your Banking Needs

of Fairbanks

- MAIN OFFICE—Northward Building 10 A.M.-3 P.M. Mon.-Fri.—10 A.M.-12 Noon Sat.

- AIRPORT ROAD BRANCH—Airport and Turner. 11 A.M.-6 P.M. Mon.-Fri.—11 A.M.-1 P.M. Sat.

EIELSON FACILITY — Baker Field House, E.A.F.B. 11 A.M. - 3 P.M. Mon. - Fri. — Closed Sat.

DELTA BRANCH — Delta Junction 11 A.M. - 3 P.M. Mon. - Fri. and 6-8 P.M. Fri. — Closed Sat.

Advertisements in the 1950s promoting the *News-Miner*'s circulation campaign.

FAIRBANKS CITY WATER

Safe, pure, clear water will be available this year to everyone within the city limits

Our Water Customers Say:

"No more grey and dingy looking laundry."

"No more yellow film on kitchen and bathroom fixtures."

"No more sticky, clinging scum in the bowl."

"No more chocking scale inside the piping."

To obtain city water at the favorable cost of connecting to the system under the present construction program, your application should be filed at once or by May 31, 1955 at the latest.

City of Fairbanks, Alaska
Municipal Utilities System
645 FIFTH AVENUE
TELEPHONE 2233

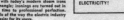
The Fairbanks Municipal Utilities System promised housewives that new electric appliances would "banish drudgery." Snedden's service on the MUS board, and the effort to sell its bonds, first alerted him to the financial burdens that came with territorial status.

Signs of the 1950s reflected in the advertising of the *News-Miner*, including its first ever television schedule when TV came to Fairbanks in 1955.

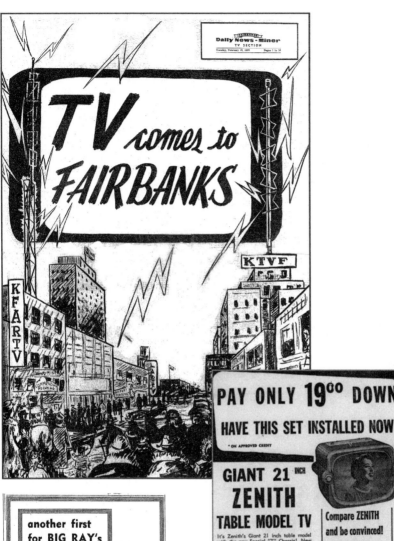

HOME WAS NEVER LIKE THIS—Five residents of Barrow who came to Fairbanks for Eskimo dancing on the Golden Days celebration program pay a visit to the News-Miner plant before flying home and are fascinated by a linotype machine operated by day foreman Irl Todd. The visitors are, left to right, Willie Sailak, Nita Ahnupkana, Bruce Nakapigah, Lena Ahnatook and Dorothy Tazruk.

A feature shot of parka-clad Barrow residents watching a Linotype operator at work.

The old prospector, "Sourdough Jack," named after editor Jack Ryan. Some of his choicest sayings were compiled for the book Sourdough Jack Sez.

Sitting beside garbage cans collecting dripping water after the deadly 1957 fire, the Linotype men went to work setting type in raincoats.

In 1957 *News-Miner* paperboy Joe Igelmund was proclaimed a hero; he smelled smoke when he was delivering the paper to Sig Wien's house on Lathrop Street and alerted the Noel Wien family next door in time to put out the fire.

News-Miner Photo by Phil's Studio

HE SMELLED SMOKE — Joe Igelmund, 12 - year - old News - Miner carrier is shown at the door of the Sig Wien home at 900 Lathrop St., delivering a paper just as he did Tues- day evening when he summoned the Noel Wien family next door because he smelled smoke in the house. A fire caused by a faulty deepfreeze motor was extinguished in the basement.

Rosy Portrait of City Drawn By Alaska Housing Officials

Gagnon Meets With Council, Planning and Park Commissions; Potter Takes Issue With Policy on Park Locations

A tentative portrait of a multi-million dollar annex to downtown Fairbanks, encompassing a hotel, high-storied apartment dwellings, and business houses, was painted last night for city officials by the Alaska Housing Authority.

Elmer Gagnon, urban redevelopment director of the AHA,

Counci
Commi
sion th
at leas
and W
areas
buildin
He a
depend
No o
the me
He r
of wha
No. 1 b
avenue:
nette
drawin;
buildin
Elks ha

All o
merely
final pl
the city
includi:
en.
The
ed, will
States
city wo
fund fo
been es
would
sale of
Gagn
going v
subject

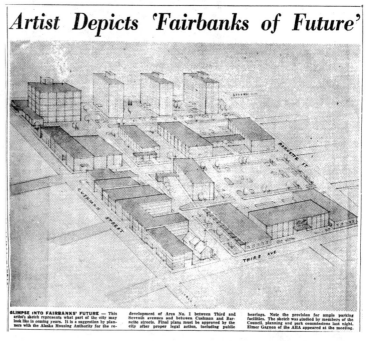

Artist Depicts 'Fairbanks of Future'

GLIMPSE INTO FAIRBANKS' FUTURE — This artist's sketch represents what part of the city may look like in coming years. It is a suggestion by planners with the Alaska Housing Authority for the redevelopment of Area No. I between Third and Seventh avenues and between Cushman and Barnette streets. Final plans must be approved by the city after proper legal action, including public hearings. Note the provision for ample parking facilities. The sketch was studied by members of the Council, planning and park commissions last night. Elmer Gagnon of the AHA appeared at the meeting.

The *News-Miner* took the lead in pushing to modernize Fairbanks. Although construction of a community-owned hotel and a slum clearance/urban renewal program west of Cushman Street (above) were marked by repeated frustrations, the completion of Wally Hickel's Travelers Inn in December 1955 (right) was a major landmark in Fairbanks history.

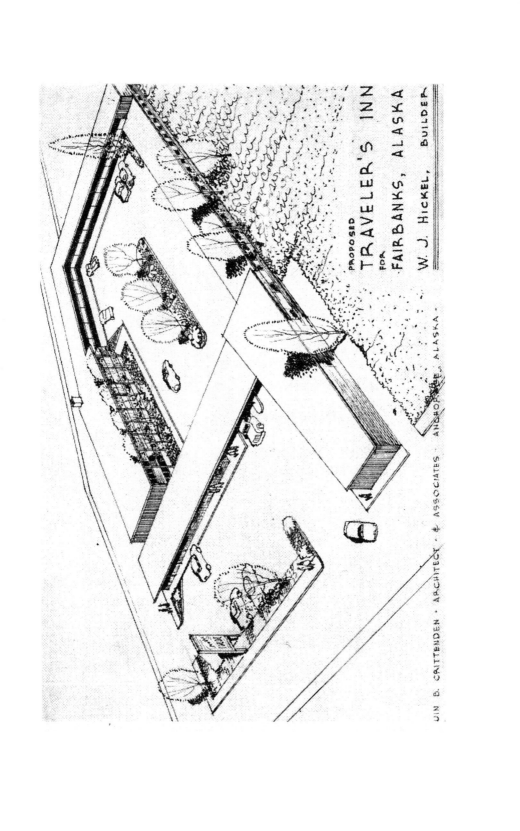

PROPOSED
TRAVELER'S INN
FOR
FAIRBANKS, ALASKA
W. J. HICKEL, BUILDER

JIN B. CRITTENDEN · ARCHITECT · & ASSOCIATES · ANCHORAGE, ALASKA ·

News-Miner attorney Ted Stevens's first law office in Fairbanks in 1953 was on the top floor of the new Polaris Building.

4

Breaking Stories and Making News

Bill Snedden believed the role of his *Fairbanks Daily News-Miner* was not merely to report the news but to articulate a vision for Fairbanks and Alaska and help make it come true. In that sense he was a classic small-town newspaper publisher, a booster and community builder who espoused what historian Daniel Boorstin called the "rhetoric of anticipation," an earnest faith "that the future could hold anything or everything."[1] Snedden's *News-Miner* not only chronicled what had already happened but also predicted many good things to come. Its annual Progress Edition may have been the most visible symbol of the *News-Miner*'s blueprint for the future, but every issue was a 1950s portrait of tomorrow.

Despite the constant danger of the Cold War and the threat of nuclear annihilation, the post–World War II era saw the expansion of U.S. power, prestige, and confidence as more Americans enjoyed greater prosperity and economic security than ever before. In contrast with the grim 1930s, the affluent '50s offered a time of unrivaled wealth and increased appetites. In an age of suburbs, shopping centers, tail fins, and interstate highways, never had so much been enjoyed by so many for so modest a cost. A child of the Great Depression, Snedden shared the 1950s faith in the inevitable march of progress and the conviction that a rising tide would lift anyone who could swim. His mission was to bring the benefits of twentieth-century commerce and industry to sparsely populated Alaska.

Fairbanks was a small oasis of 1950s civilization, a subarctic outpost with about thirty thousand people, fifteen thousand cars and trucks, two broadcast television stations, two radio stations, one twelve-lane bowling alley, eighty-four restaurants and bars, thirty-seven churches, forty-two gas stations, seven supermarkets, and fifteen drive-ins of various types (including a drive-in liquor store).[2] The *News-Miner* was one of Fairbanks's largest and most modern industries, boasting a year-round workforce of fifty-one people, a payroll of $400,000, and the so-called "fastest Gal in town" or "Alice," the four-deck Goss Rotary high-speed press that could have readily served a city of 150,000. Few other newspapers in the United States could match the *News-Miner*'s printing quality or extensive use of color. At a community open house in May 1954, more than a thousand people toured the *News-Miner*'s facilities to get their first close look at the marvelous machinery inside the new Chena Building. The "news factory" was the most high-tech manufacturing plant in Fairbanks, consuming two tons of newsprint a day and turning out more than a quarter-million newspapers a month.[3] Snedden had built the newspaper on high expectations. Fairbanks's current size did not warrant a press that could print and fold seven newspapers per second. "This plant is geared to the future of Fairbanks," he said. "A smaller and less expensive plant would have adequately served Fairbanks right now, but the *News-Miner* chose to prepare for the future because the publisher of this paper firmly believes that our city is on the brink of the greatest era of growth in its history."[4] Snedden predicted that within a decade the *News-Miner* would have to expand again. "I don't feel that our present plant will be adequate for much more than ten years. This city is located at the hub of America's arctic defenses and at the crossroads of over-the-pole air travel. . . . I believe that someday Fairbanks will be the largest city in Alaska."[5]

The source of Snedden's optimism was all around him. This speck of modern America, connected to the outside world by a single road to the south, was surrounded by hundreds of thousands of square miles where the human presence on the land was virtually invisible, an expanse of wilderness in every direction that seemed to offer infinite opportunity to remake the world, unlike the rest of the United States, where the frontier was closed and the maps filled in. Empty spaces invited big ideas to fill them.[6]

Two of the biggest ideas of that era, which the *News-Miner* wholeheartedly supported, were Project Chariot, a scheme to use atomic explosives to excavate a harbor on the northwestern coast of Alaska, and Rampart Dam, which would flood the Yukon Flats with an artificial inland ocean the size of Lake Erie.[7] Neither Chariot nor Rampart ever came close to fruition—both proved totally impractical if not illogical— but they symbolized the size and scope of the dreaming that had been behind the evolution of the United States from a small collection of struggling colonies on the Atlantic seaboard into the world's wealthiest nation, spanning the North American continent. Alaska boosters were the latest in a long line of promoters who believed there was room enough for atomic blasts and hydroelectric plants as well as superhighways, factories, pulp mills, tourist resorts, and gas and oil wells while still leaving millions of acres untouched.

Alaska was a paradise of promise, a garden of expectations, where the primal need to be useful and productive could be fulfilled in steel and concrete. It was the unfinished quality of life in Alaska that Snedden and others found most appealing. As a newcomer to Fairbanks wrote in 1953, the town felt and looked like "a movie set . . . where only a part of the props for the next act have been put up" and everything was "still a little unglued."[8]

Statehood would be the primary avenue to bring this transformation about, and Anchorage, where the statehood spirit was strongest, had grown much faster than Fairbanks since World War II and had come to be dominated by a young and enterprising business community. Fairbanks, on the other hand, too often seemed to be held back by a considerable part of its citizens who fiercely resisted any change, especially one that required cooperation. Cap Lathrop, who had businesses in both Anchorage and Fairbanks, thought the towns at the two ends of the Alaska Railroad had opposite personalities. Fairbanks was the anti-Anchorage and proud of it. In 1948 Lathrop said Anchorage "wasn't even Alaska anymore." The town was overflowing with new businesses and new people who "don't know anything about Alaska and don't give a damn." But Fairbanks was a different matter. "When I walk down the street in Fairbanks I meet old-timers I have known for years," Lathrop reflected. "Hell, Fairbanks is full of old-timers. That's the problem with Fairbanks."[9] Like Lathrop, Snedden would struggle mightily with the Fairbanks "can't do" philosophy. Pushing Fairbanks forward, he would more than once find himself at odds with powerful elements in the community.

— ❈ —

The biggest development in Fairbanks in the late 1950s, which the *News-Miner* advocated relentlessly, was the launch of Alaska's first slum clearance program, more politely known as urban renewal. If any town in Alaska needed radical plastic surgery, it was Fairbanks. In 1949 Hanson Baldwin, the *New York Times* reporter renowned for his expertise on military affairs, had said that some soldiers and airmen in Fairbanks lived in little more than "packing cases" that looked "like shacks from a 'hobo city'" and that these servicemen were "forced to live in what are probably the worst conditions under the American flag."[10] By one calculation, 50 percent of all the dwellings in the area were classified as "substandard" and casual visitors were likely to miss the charm of local construction completely.[11]

Ray Lentzsch, a visitor from Whittier, California, went down in Fairbanks history in 1957 when he published a piece in the *Whittier News* headlined "WILD FAIRBANKS A FILTHY TOWN," which the *News-Miner* republished in disbelief atop page one. According to Lentzsch, Fairbanks was a "flat, barren, dusty mud-hole" and he wondered why anyone would want to live amid such squalor. On the outskirts of town he'd passed a handful of crude homesteads gouged out by bulldozer; some had been abandoned while others were "in tumbledown condition with junk strewn around." He also noted a succession of "auto junk yards and huge heaps of smashed airplanes" from government surplus. "Drab-looking buildings" with gaudy names like "The Golden Slipper," "The Diamond Horseshoe," "The Mocambo," and "The Elysian Retreat" were hot spots populated with "disgruntled servicemen" and unemployed laborers passing the days and nights by "drinking themselves further and further into a hole." Lentzsch claimed he drove right through the center of town without realizing he had already passed it. According to Lentzsch the only bright spot in the three depressing days he spent in Fairbanks was the kindly policeman who refused to give him a ticket after he had been caught "doing 60 mph through a 25 mph zone on my way out of town." Lentzsch's theory was that the cop had taken pity on him. "He must have sympathized with the sad look on my face and realized why I was so anxious to escape Fairbanks, the most depressing town I have ever visited."[12]

In the weeks that followed Lentzsch's dismal portrait of life in Fairbanks, readers bombarded the *News-Miner* with letters. While most ridiculed his harsh opinions, some echoed the complaints. "There are nice things about [Fairbanks]," a newcomer named Willard Deal wrote, "but they are overshadowed by trash, junk, taxes, dirt, bugs, etc." Deal said he had been in Alaska for only a couple of months, but had no intention of staying in the choking dust hole called Fairbanks. "I have been here since June and have seen no mud. Dust, smoke, and bugs and mosquitoes by the millions, yes, but no mud." He pledged that as soon as he had enough money "for a plane ticket out of here, I should most certainly shake the dust out of my clothes and leave all of you to your dusty, smoky, god forsaken paradise."[13]

"I know what it's like," the wife of a serviceman wrote, "when you first arrive and see some of these old shacks [where] you have to pay over $100 a month rent. You feel like turning back and going home."[14] With decent housing, however, she thought she would be glad to live in Fairbanks, and it was with residents like her in mind that in the 1940s the city started planning a slum clearance program funded largely by the federal government. The original concept was to remove many of the small cabins and shacks on the "Line," the restricted red light district on Fourth Avenue between Cushman and Barnette Streets, though the urban renewal tract eventually expanded to include a thirteen-acre parcel west of Cushman between Third and Seventh Avenues. A survey by the Alaska Housing Authority reported that 115 of 132 structures were "substandard," with 83 judged to be "dilapidated," 78 classified as "overcrowded," 49 without baths, 47 without indoor flush toilets, and 26 without running water.[15] The wheels of bureaucracy grind slowly, however, and years of studies, lobbying, and lawsuits followed before the bulldozers finally started to move. Through most of it, Snedden remained convinced that urban renewal was key to the city's future, and the editorial page kept up a steady drumbeat of support. In a 1957 front-page editorial, the paper pleaded with local residents to help push it to completion: "THIS PROJECT IS UTTERLY VITAL TO FAIRBANKS! WE MUST COMPLETE IT; IF WE DO NOT, THIS CITY IS DOOMED TO SLOWLY DEGENERATE INTO NOTHING MORE THAN A FAR NORTH SLUM." At no cost to local taxpayers, the urban renewal program would make Fairbanks "A CITY THAT WE CAN BE PROUD OF, RATHER THAN ONE OF WHICH WE WILL BE ASHAMED."[16]

The slow progress made by government bureaucrats in carrying out the project was incomprehensible to Snedden. Even after the Safeway grocery chain—which became the first major tenant to build in the cleared tract—made its winning bid in August 1959, the *News-Miner* lamented that the pace of the program had "bogged down in red tape, apathy, indecision and inaction."[17]

Another key to the renewal of Fairbanks was the long and difficult campaign to build the Fairbanks Community Hotel. Of all the many projects that Snedden advocated in the pages of the *News-Miner* in the 1950s, perhaps none was more telling of the political and personal dynamics of the area than this ill-fated effort to build a locally owned hotel.

Visitors and businessmen who came to Fairbanks in the 1950s found the accommodations overpriced, run-down, and in short supply. The best place in town was the venerable Nordale Hotel, a creaking, gold rush vintage, three-story wooden firetrap on Second Avenue that featured thin walls, hard mattresses, and sawdust insulation. In the summer, the demand for beds was so steep that hotel keepers regularly farmed out new guests to private homes, hostels, and basements around town, or even double-booked rooms in the hotel, leading to surprise encounters for those not familiar with the practice. One visitor was shocked when the manager "put a strange lady in our room after midnight, not asking our permission before, just simply unlocking our door." In a 1953 survey an experienced traveler condemned Fairbanks for having the worst hotels in the country: "Poorest accommodations I have ever seen are in Fairbanks."[18]

In July 1952 a fire at the Pioneer Hotel killed five people and started the campaign to construct a modern fireproof hotel.[19] Fire was always the first fear of guests staying in wooden hotels. Evidence of the danger was an old territorial law, not repealed until 1957, that required every hotel room in Alaska to be equipped with a manila rope one-half inch thick, knotted every twelve inches, and long enough to reach the ground.[20] Fairbanks civic leaders realized it was essential for the city's future growth to offer lodging where a stray spark from a frayed wire or a drowsy smoker lying in bed would no longer be a death sentence. Snedden pledged the *News-Miner* would do all within its power to make the new tourist and commercial facility a reality. A new hotel would not be just another business; it would serve as the core of Fairbanks's commercial future. A modern hotel with accompanying restaurant, lounge, café, meeting rooms, and convention center would prove Fairbanks was more than just a military construction camp and herald the community's coming of age. "We cannot be a first class city," the *News-Miner* proclaimed, "without a first class hotel."[21]

The three-year struggle to build the hotel would become the largest community-wide campaign in local history, but it would painfully show irreconcilable divisions among rival business interests and the community malaise the *News-Miner* fought on so many divergent issues. The hotel saga would become a legendary example of Fairbanks's tendency to pull together in opposite directions.

At the start everyone realized that raising the estimated one to two million dollars needed for the hotel would be a hard sell. Given the seasonal cycle of the Alaska economy, hotels could hope for full bookings only about four or five months of the year, making it difficult to recoup the high construction costs. Furthermore, a military boomtown that might bust with the next federal appropriations cycle did not offer long-term stability.

To tackle the financial challenge, the Fairbanks Chamber of Commerce turned to one of America's fund-raising gurus, Myron D. Hockenbury, a hotel financial consultant from Pennsylvania. Over the previous four decades the Hockenbury firm, founded by his father, had raised more than $100 million and built more than 220 hotels found in small communities throughout Canada, Australia, and every state in the union. The "Hockenbury System," a grassroots fund-raising strategy that included contests, slogans, appeals, and gimmicks designed to whip up civic pride like a high school pep rally, was intended to convince residents that a modest purchase of local hotel stock was not only a civic duty but also a once-in-a-lifetime investment opportunity.

After investigating the Fairbanks market, Hockenbury told the *News-Miner* in the summer of 1953 that he had "never before studied a city" that so badly needed a new hotel.[22] In July and early August 1953, working with a representative of the Hockenbury Company, forty-five civic and business leaders formed the Fairbanks Community Hotel Executive Committee. Their task was to raise among themselves and their business associates an average of $10,000 each, or a total of $450,000, before starting the intensive second stage of the campaign, which would solicit donations from the general public. Snedden was one of about two dozen local businessmen who pledged $5,000 or more. The two largest contributors were the Bank of Fairbanks and the First National Bank of Fairbanks, which each promised $15,000.

By the first week of August a bitter fight had erupted over where to build the hotel, and the Hockenbury staff came close to deciding that the community was so fractious the funding drive would have to be canceled. While up to a dozen sites had been considered by Hockenbury, the dispute boiled down to two factions centered around the two banks that were the two largest contributors to the hotel fund and were located on the opposite sides of downtown Fairbanks: the Cushman Street crowd, centered around the First National Bank on the west side of the small downtown business district, and the Noble Street gang in the neighborhood of the Bank of Fairbanks (later called the Alaska National Bank of the North) to the east.

The Cushman and Noble Street factions acted as if they were hundreds of miles, not hundreds of feet, apart. *News-Miner* reporter Kay Kennedy covered the hotel campaign from the start. "That Fairbanks should find itself divided at Cushman street," she wrote, "seems unthinkable."[23]

The *News-Miner* offices were, fittingly, about halfway between Cushman and Noble, and Snedden tried to keep the community drive going despite the dispute. "We have taken no side in the issue of the hotel location, and we certainly do not intend to do so. Our goal is to see the hotel built.... We would greatly deplore the situation if a controversy over its location would split the community, and cause the fund raising campaign to fail." Snedden recommended the committee postpone any decision on the location until the pledge drive was finished. "After all the money has been raised, then there will be voting stockholders who can settle this issue fairly."[24]

The executive committee decided instead to hold an opinion poll by secret ballot among those who had pledged to buy hotel stock and bonds, and the results appeared to be decisive: 60 percent of the stockholders favored a site on Noble. The east side had won, but in a spirit of compromise, the board also selected Ed Stroecker, president of the First National Bank of Fairbanks on the west side, to be chairman of the hotel board. "The site is picked and we want everyone to get behind it," Stroecker said. "After all, the object is to get a new hotel for Fairbanks."[25]

With the divisive question of the site apparently settled, the hotel fund-raising campaign entered the next stage. An army of 130 volunteers constituted the general sales staff. Trained in the sales pitch by the Hockenbury staff and divided into teams to inspire friendly rivalry to raise the most money, the volunteers set out to knock on every door in Fairbanks. Progress reports and encouraging editorials appeared daily in the *News-Miner*. For as little as $10 a month for ten months, a resident could purchase the minimum $100 stake—consisting of $25 in stock and $75 in 5 percent bonds—that would pay a "double return": a financial return for the individual and a social return for Fairbanks. The *News-Miner* adopted the slogan "There Is No Such Thing As a Good City Without a Good Hotel. Let's Make Fairbanks a Good City." Outside the *News-Miner*'s new home in the Chena Building, then under construction, a large tally board was set up to track the investments, which averaged about $30,000 a day.[26] The new hotel was nothing less than "a test of citizenship." "Are You For or Against Fairbanks?" read one advertisement. "This question is directed squarely to every citizen. Are you on the side of the progressive citizens who have purchased securities in the New Hotel?"

At a victory dinner on Friday, September 4, 1953, the community celebrated the successful completion of the fund-raising campaign. The full-page banner headline in the *News-Miner* the next day read "OVER $800,000! HOTEL ASSURED." Engraved gold watches were given to the top salesman and team captains, while coveted "golden goat" awards were given to those who exhibited perseverance and dedication beyond the call of duty. The level of community support had been outstanding. One man alone had sold stock to ninety-one individuals. "It is difficult to find in Fairbanks today a person who had not bought a share of this project," the *News-Miner* said.

That glow quickly faded. When the hotel's board of directors was elected in November, it rejected the Noble Street site on the east side chosen by the interim board and voted to build the hotel on the west side, at Second and Turner. Those who had backed the east side location cried fraud, a blatant case of bait and switch, and once again the entire project was on the verge of collapse. "This deal sure stinks," claimed an angry subscriber named George H. Bush. "I bet you don't print this. I demanded my money back."[27]

Snedden urged both sides to compromise somehow for the good of the community. Again he promised the *News-Miner* would support any location, on the east side or the west side or halfway between, as long as the hotel was built somewhere. The newspaper's motto was "Let's Get It Built."[28] As weeks passed and neither faction made any steps toward a resolution, Snedden refused to give up.

> The *News-Miner* intends to press constantly for action on this hotel. We feel that the project is the most important movement that has been sponsored here in the history of this city. The future of every permanent resident depends to a large extent on this hotel. . . . We appeal to our local business leaders to put the interests of Fairbanks above their own interests.[29]

By early 1954 Snedden had devised a new strategy to break the deadlock by holding a secret ballot of stockholders. The *News-Miner* published a ballot of possible sites every day for a week in late January and early February 1954, asking stockholders to mark their preference and send it to the newspaper's bookkeeping office. Neither the Cushman Street nor the Noble Street factions were particularly pleased with Snedden's plan. The hotel's board reluctantly acquiesced, but only with the stipulation that the results would not be binding, while the board's critics claimed the newspaper's efforts were a diversion designed to prevent an official election. A group calling itself the Noble Street Progressives took out a full-page advertisement urging stockholders to boycott the *News-Miner*'s opinion poll and hold out for a binding vote by the stockholders. Their opposition puzzled Snedden, and he claimed the "progressives" were making an obviously bad situation worse:

> The News-Miner has recommended time and time again, that the issue of the hotel location be settled by the stockholders in a bona-fide vote. When such an election appeared impossible to achieve, we decided to poll the stockholders ourselves.... The "Noble Street Progressives" certainly can't accuse this paper of being unfriendly to them. We accepted their original site, and have fully agreed with them as to the necessity of holding a stockholders' election. But their obvious distrust of this election and their eagerness to inject new issues into an already "muddy situation" is not helping the hotel project, or the city, in our opinion. The News-Miner has only one objective in this poll and that is to expedite start of construction of the new hotel.[30]

The results of the *News-Miner* poll showed how sharply the hotel had split the community. While the site on the west side had won with 47 percent of the total votes, two possible sites on Noble Street had received about 46 percent of the voting shares combined.[31]

Once the newspaper votes had been counted, Snedden hoped the business community could settle their differences and "proceed to build this hotel with bricks, cement and wood—not hot air!"[32] But the quarreling continued, on and on. "We are somewhat hoarse from saying this, over and over again," the *News-Miner* pleaded in March 1954, "but LET'S BUILD THE HOTEL! Let those who are blocking progress for personal or business reasons take another look at the situation, and show a willingness to compromise, for the good of this community and every person in it. We can still build that hotel. Are we going to do it, or are we going to continue quarreling and PROVE that this city is too SMALL to build a BIG hotel?"[33]

After almost two years' worth of editorials, and thousands of words of encouragement, the *News-Miner* finally admitted in September 1954 that the hotel was "all but dead," killed by pig-headedness on both sides.

"It was a fine idea ... it spurred civic spirit to record heights during the fund raising campaign ... it was desperately needed, and it could have been ours."[34]

-- --⚬-- --

Only one ray of hope remained. Snedden urged the community to face the truth of how the hotel war had damaged Fairbanks's prospects and, before returning the stockholders' capital, see if there still might be another option. The answer turned out to be a blunt-speaking contractor from Anchorage: Wally Hickel, a former Golden Gloves welterweight boxing champion from Kansas, the son of a sharecropper, who proudly landed in Anchorage in 1940 with nothing but a handful of spare change in his pocket. It was the most famous thirty-seven cents in Alaska history, the seed capital for what would become Hickel's fortune from building houses, shopping centers, apartment buildings, and hotels.

Hickel's first tourist facility was the Anchorage Travelers Inn, Alaska's first modern motel, opened in 1953. As Hickel told the story, he believed so strongly that Anchorage needed such a facility that even after local banks turned the project "down cold," he went forward. Like Teddy Roosevelt, who proudly boasted that he took the Panama Canal Zone while Congress debated, Hickel built the motel while the bankers procrastinated. He claimed he actually finished the Travelers before he had a construction loan. The motel was an instant success, and Hickel enjoyed proving naysayers wrong. "I never tried to do anything someone else had already done," Hickel wrote years later in his autobiography. "I always looked for problems that had not been answered, needs that had not been met."[35] By that standard the Fairbanks community hotel fiasco was tailor-made for Hickel. "People were beginning to call me a plunger," he wrote, "a gambler eventually bound to roll snake eyes."[36]

Hickel figured if Fairbanks contributors who had previously pledged for the community hotel would pledge to grant him a $225,000 loan at 5 percent interest, that would be all the leverage he would need to raise the additional half a million or more that the hotel he envisioned would cost. "I'm not up here to try and sell anything, or to try to talk anybody into anything," Hickel said in Fairbanks in November 1954. "If my offer isn't satisfactory, then I'll invest elsewhere. I'm making a straight business proposition, in which the people of Fairbanks act as 'little bankers,' putting up the necessary share of local participation capital to make it possible for me to finance the balance."[37]

Snedden threw the *News-Miner* completely behind the Hickel plan.

> From the very start, this newspaper has given full
> support to the Community hotel project ... The
> publisher of the News-Miner has invested a fair
> sized chunk of money in the hotel corporation,
> and virtually every member of the staff has pur-
> chased stock in the proposed structure. We have
> devoted countless editorials to the task of boost-
> ing the hotel, and we have also devoted a tremen-
> dous amount of news space to this project ... The
> News-Miner may seem slightly biased on this
> hotel subject. Frankly, we are biased. We harbor
> a deep conviction, that Fairbanks must have this
> hotel facility.[38]

Many stockholders of the Community Hotel transferred their shares
to Hickel's new endeavor, prodded by a cut-out coupon that ran on the
front page of the *News-Miner* and read in part:

YES! . . . I WANT TO PARTICIPATE IN
FAIRBANKS **NEW HOTEL!**

Please pay the amount forthcoming to me on my stock
and bond refund to Walter J. Hickel's Fairbanks Travelers
Inn, Inc. in exchange for second Mortgage 5% bonds.[39]

The drive to raise money for the Travelers Inn took on aspects of
a revival meeting. In addition to the *News-Miner*'s "Hotel Goal" meter that tracked the campaign's daily progress toward $225,000, KFAR
Radio staged a marathon fund-raiser on the air in January 1955 that
netted more than $14,000 in bond purchases. Challenge grants on the
radio broadcast included a $200 bond purchase to hear Mayor Douglas
Preston's rendition of "My Wild Irish Rose." But the highlight came
when three local men, including Snedden, volunteered to have barber
Rod Wolff cut off their mustaches while announcer Al Bramstedt described the action snip by snip. Snedden let his mustache go in exchange
for a pledge of $500 in bonds.[40] Snedden's donated mustache, along with

those of Don McCune and George Nehrbas, were framed and hung on the wall of the Chamber of Commerce until the completion of the Travelers Inn, over the inscription "Never have so few given so much for so many."[41] The funniest stunt in the hotel bond drive was Lonnie Hall's promise to ride a cow into the Northward Building and to milk her in the Northward Bar. Hall rode and milked Clarabelle as promised, to the delight of the bar's patrons, receiving in exchange another $1,300 in funding for the hotel.[42]

Wally Hickel's Travelers Inn in Fairbanks, twice the size of the Travelers Inn in Anchorage, was constructed in only seven months and two days. It opened for business on December 17, 1955. More than two thousand people came out to see the new hotel at its grand opening. "I told you I would do it," Hickel reminded the crowd, "and what I had in my heart and had in my mind when I said I would do it—this is it."[43] Mayor Preston said the Travelers Inn was "far beyond our wildest dreams." Local merchant and city councilman Byron Gillam praised both Hickel and Snedden for making the new hotel a reality. Fairbanks had to survive a "two years struggle within itself." It would have never happened, he thought, without Snedden's support. As a reporter on the scene noted, "Gillam praised the *News-Miner* for keeping the idea of a new hotel drive alive through the columns of the paper."[44]

For Snedden, the opening of the Travelers was a landmark in Fairbanks history, one he greeted with a special twelve-page section of the *News-Miner*. Never had one business and one building meant so much to Fairbanks. As the *News-Miner* said, the term *motel* was "a poor word for the luxurious, modernistic structure" that Hickel had built, because the Travelers Inn offered the finest accommodations available anywhere in Alaska.[45]

~ ~ ~

Snedden thought the completion of the Travelers Inn was evidence of what the community could do—with a little help from Anchorage—when it got together. Too often causes in Fairbanks that required a co-ordinated group effort for support, such as schools, libraries, hospitals, youth and cultural programs, medical care, etc., remained grossly deficient for a population that had more than doubled in five years and was soon to double in size again. The *News-Miner* reminded residents what it took to be a good neighbor, not just by preaching—which came natural enough to anyone with an editorial page.

The newspaper's major charity drive of the year was at Christmas. For decades the annual *News-Miner* Christmas Fund raised thousands of dollars for needy families, fire victims, and orphans. The *News-Miner* bore all the administrative costs, and working with the Christmas Clearing House, a local group that handled the distribution of food packages and toys every December, it helped brighten the dark days for many children and helped some families simply survive the winter. In 1954 one disbursement went for "purchase of insulation, food and fuel for family with three children whose inadequate home was so cold the baby had frozen its hands indoors."[46] Every dollar was spent directly on those who needed it, and every penny was accounted for: of the $3,277 raised by the newspaper in 1957, for example, the balance remaining at the end of the season was eighty-four cents.[47]

The *News-Miner* raised the money through "Santa's Christmas Calls," a daily column that "called out" members of the community by name in the weeks before Christmas, urging them in a lighthearted way, with a bad pun or two, to make a small donation. Sometimes the subjects of these friendly extortion notes were simply picked at random out of the phone book, but "Santa"—in these examples, editor Jack Ryan—usually selected his targets with care.

> **Al Seeliger** is president of the Chamber of Commerce. No doubt he'll boost Santa's Christmas fund. Al, would you advertise your generosity? Just drop a small donation in Santa's pot. (It's not a chamber pot, either Al.)

> **Judge Vernon Forbes** is the new man on the bench in our District court. We know he's a man who will want to help little Kids. Judge, would you make a motion towards your pocketbook? Santa would like to have you hand down a small donation to the Christmas fund.

> T'was the night before Christmas.
> And all through the houseovich.
> Christmas joy was insured
> By **Johnny Butrovich.**

(Santa is sending the bill for that free advertising to the Alaska Insurance Agency.)

Santa is eyeing **Dr. Arthur S. Brown**, the optometrist. We are going to test his generosity. How about a fitting donation, Doctor? If you fail to respond, you'll make a spectacle of yourself.

Tom Roberts, manager of the Commercial Printing company, is the generous type. Santa is pressing him for a contribution. Will Tom keep the Christmas drive rolling?

Gene Immel is the friendly proprietor of Gene's Auto Service—the Studebaker-Packard agency. We'd like Gene to put Santa's Christmas fund in high gear. Five dollars would be a nice transmission Gene.

Bob and Grace Hoitt are the genial proprietors of the Music Shop. We'd like them to [be] instrumental in providing a happy Christmas for an unfortunate kid. They'll send Santa the right note. Do you dig me, folks?[48]

The *News-Miner* Christmas Fund was part of the inspiration for what became the Fairbanks United Way, the first of its kind in Alaska. Previously, every charitable organization in town, including the Boy Scouts, Girl Scouts, USO, YMCA, Alaska Crippled Children, Salvation Army, and the Red Cross, had run its own fund-raising, hitting up the same businesses and individuals again and again and generating donor fatigue. "Fund drives for worthwhile purposes go on and on in Fairbanks," the *News-Miner* stated in August 1954. "But, sometimes we wonder if all this money being donated to charity is wisely divided and profitably used." Snedden believed the solution was a "Federated Drive" that would unite all of the volunteer groups under one umbrella that would hold one big fund-raiser a year and have a central organization to ensure an equitable and honest distribution of donations.[49] "Fairbanks has gone as far as it

can," an editorial argued, "on our haphazard methods of collecting funds
for the needy and for worthwhile organizations."[50] Naturally, some of the
local volunteer groups were initially reluctant to give up their traditional
fund-raisers. But Snedden was a member of the board of directors of the
Chamber of Commerce, and working behind the scenes with Chamber
manager Don Dickey, the new organization became a reality in 1955, as
ten agencies pooled together in the united Federated Fund Drive—later
known as the United Way.[51]

The creation of the Fairbanks United Way in 1955 revolutionized charitable giving in Fairbanks. It was a high-water mark of cooperation that
stood in contrast to the affairs of the city government. Even those who
loved the community had to admit that a large percentage of the population belonged to the "Whatever It Is—I'm Against It Party." Institutional
flaws caused by the hypergrowth since 1940 made the divisions worse.
"The fact that this city has problems," the local Planning and Zoning
Commission concluded in 1952, "some of which are not conducive to . . .
healthy urban life, is not unusual." Due to the sheer speed of the city's
expansion, no city planning had ever been done. "The defense effort here
is making a spectacular impact," the commission stated, "which defies
analysis" and exacerbated "the 'normal' abnormal" pattern of Fairbanks's
economy; consequently, many civic problems were simply too overwhelming to even begin to tackle.

For instance, the Fairbanks city hall was so small, the *News-Miner*
reported, that whenever "the council meets in its undersize chambers,
spectators and interested taxpayers are practically choked with smoke in
the tiny room, before the meeting is half over." Snedden urged the city
to undertake some long-range planning and come up with a proposal to
build a new municipal building that could serve as a symbol of the city's
progress. "We believe local citizens would take pride in such a building,
and that this structure would do much to improve the efficiency and 'es-
prit de corps' of the city's employees."[52]

Even worse than the city hall was the Fairbanks city library. When
the George C. Thomas Memorial Library had been built at the corner
of First and Cowles in 1909, funded by a donation from a Philadelphia
philanthropist who wanted the lonely miners in Alaska to have a peaceful
place where they could read and smoke at the same time, it was the most
commodious library and reading room ever constructed in Alaska, but

half a century later the gold rush relic was long overdue for remodeling or replacement (although it would go on to serve as the local public library for another two decades). The *News-Miner* said in 1957 that the old "prehistoric quarters" housing the library needed to be replaced, and the volunteer members of the library board must start planning and raising money instead of continually reducing services to the community as the building fell apart. "The disquieting fact about the Library's dilemma," the *News-Miner* concluded, "is that nobody seems to be taking any real interest in the situation." This was in painful contrast with Anchorage, where former mayor Zach Loussac had provided the funds to build a state-of-the-art public library, while "Fairbanks is watching its library sink . . . If it is neglected for a few more years, a stick of dynamite may be the only answer."[53]

Snedden was also mystified by the city's inept response to civil defense. Everyone in Fairbanks in the 1950s recognized that the community could be a likely target of Soviet bombers or missiles, and construction of the Distant Early Warning (DEW) Line had brought home the reality of the nuclear threat.[54]

As the aviation editor for the *Los Angeles Times* reported in 1955, the pilots stationed at Ladd AFB were standing by around the clock in a ready room equipped with "a firemen's pole for quick scramble slide to the ground floor" in order to be airborne in less than five minutes in the event of a Soviet strike.[55]

On June 15, 1955, Fairbanks, Anchorage, and Juneau were slated to be part of a nationwide civil defense drill called "Operation Alert 1955," a mock H-bomb attack on key American cities liable to be attacked in case of nuclear war. The initial plans imagined that "an atomic bomb would be presumed to drop on the center of Fairbanks," and the key to survival, a local official said, was evacuating the city in no more than two hours, the amount of lead time experts thought might come before an attack. "Current thinking in CD preparedness," the *News-Miner* explained, "lies toward evacuation, rather than to seek underground shelter, as a defense against nuclear weapons."[56]

In Alaska on H-Day there was an "orderly evacuation of residents in Anchorage and Juneau," though an official claimed at one point there were four thousand cars on one of the six routes leading out of Anchorage, and the territorial offices were not evacuated in Juneau because "the test started at 6:30 a.m. before government employees reported for work." In Fairbanks the *News-Miner* reported that all military dependents were safely evacuated in a slow and measured fashion from both Ladd and Eielson Air Force Bases, beginning at 6:30 a.m. For about forty-five minutes a "steady stream" of 650 cars, moving along at about five miles an hour, left Eielson by the south gate and then drove four miles up the Richardson Highway to the north gate. The wives and children living at Ladd had a much longer stint as atomic refugees in the mandatory drill. About five hundred cars left Ladd AFB and were required to drive fifteen miles to the turnaround at North Pole and back, spending about two and a half hours on the road.[57]

The roads of Fairbanks itself, however, were already so torn up due to military and civilian construction projects that civil defense officials decided the city could not survive even an imaginary H-bomb attack and called off the local exercise. "This is a terrifically bad season for a dispersal test in Fairbanks," the civil defense director explained. "With $100,000,000 in defense contracts, this city would suffer real hardship if the test went off as planned. I realize that an attacker would pay no attention to whether we have a building season in Fairbanks or not," but he feared the "bad will" a botched exercise would garner.[58]

It took the city of Fairbanks another two years to craft a mass evacuation plan to deal with an atomic attack, a plan that would have funneled residents to three "safety havens," relatively safe spots from fallout at Ester, Chatanika, and Airport Road.[59] Concerned that the information was not being disseminated widely enough, in April 1957 the *News-Miner* printed a map of the officially approved evacuation routes for Fairbanks and a list of "defense necessities" to be kept at the ready at all times, including outdoor clothing, five days of emergency food and water, a first aid kit, extra batteries, a shovel, a pistol or rifle, and at least a half tank of gasoline.[60]

The confused state of civil defense in Fairbanks mirrored the community's general disorganization. The lack of consensus on how best to handle costly civic problems meant that the task of running the city was often next to impossible. Year after year public officials and city employees were targeted for abuse, accused by one group or another of fraud, incompetence, or dereliction of duty. The Fairbanks brand of arctic hysteria swept the community like an annual witch hunt despite the best efforts of Snedden and the *News-Miner* to keep the peace. Between 1950 and 1958,

Fairbanks went through eight city managers as well as a long parade of police and fire chiefs. "Fighting city managers seems to be a highly regarded sport in Fairbanks," the *News-Miner* explained, "even if the battle is over subjects which . . . did not warrant the fuss that followed. Anyway, in this town city managers suffer from their occupational disease—arrows in the back—most of the time."[61] "So far as we are concerned," the paper said on another occasion, "Fairbanks would be much better off if we could keep our ship of municipal government on an even keel, and avoid the storms that periodically rock it wildly."[62] When Superintendent of Schools Mariette Pilgrim came under fire one year, a member of the school board proudly justified his position by stating he was "in favor of a male superintendent. Men are easier to talk to and will listen to both sides of any argument more readily."[63]

The *News-Miner* generally tried to remain above the fray in the perpetual civil war of Fairbanks politics. The paper opined that all who volunteered for public service should be accorded respect. "About all the average councilman gets out of life in Fairbanks," the *News-Miner* stated, "is grief."[64] On other occasions the *News-Miner* sympathized with the council as it tried to juggle "five hot potatoes" at once. "Every time they throw one up in the air, another one comes down."[65] This did not prevent the paper from occasionally having a little fun at the expense of the city and its most obvious failing: the rutted, potholed patches of mud laughingly called streets. "They aren't really streets in the strict sense of the term," read one editorial nugget of wisdom. "They are wagon trails" so cut with ditches and excavations that it was usually impossible to ever get from here to there.[66] To illustrate the depths of the problem, readers saw a glorious front-page picture in April 1957 of a woman supposedly drowning in a giant lake in the center of a Fairbanks street, though luckily a man outfitted in full scuba gear was on his way to rescue her. As the caption explained, the "fair damsel" was fortunate, as it was only because she was "standing on a city road grader at the time the photo was shot" that her head was above water.[67]

But try as they might to remain upbeat about city affairs, Snedden and other responsible citizens found that recurrent infighting poisoned the atmosphere for everyone. "Our city government seems to be descending," the *News-Miner* complained in 1957, "into a world of petty bickering, controversy, strife, low blows, [and] trickery."[68] Shortly thereafter, a typical front-page editorial headlined "Silly Controversy," which could have appeared on any number of occasions over the years, claimed: "A person who is not deeply involved in the current city name calling contest must wonder if Fairbanks has lost its collective sanity. A handful of citizens, who are so bitterly involved in this controversy they appear to be unable to think of anything else, have disrupted city functions, and have filled the air with vile adjectives and words of hate."

Fairbanks was dealing with "a hundred and one problems, projects and plans," including "dusty, pitted streets, a dire housing shortage; a vast city construction program," but instead of tackling these serious issues residents were on a witch hunt "investigating each other, digging up 'dirt' against this person and that person, calling names and placing monkey wrenches in the wheels of our city government." "We have been carrying on like children," the editorial concluded. "Now, PLEASE, let us settle this matter like men.... FAIRBANKS IS MAKING A FOOL OF 'ITSELF' IN THIS CIVIC CONTROVERSY. LET'S GET IT OVER WITH RIGHT NOW!"[69]

When the local school board in August 1957 refused to sign a pupil transportation contract with the territory as required by a new territorial law, it left hundreds of local children without school transportation at the start of the school year. On this as on many other occasions, Fairbanks was alone in its stubborn refusal to put disagreements aside in favor of the greater good. "Everywhere else in the territory," the *News-Miner* sadly explained, "pupils will ride to school in buses . . . This school district alone out of dozens in Alaska is still making difficulties over the school bus issue." Both the legislature and the courts had spelled out the steps to pay for student bus service "and every school district in Alaska has taken it without quibbling—every school district, that is, except one."

The *News-Miner* found itself at the center of another acrimonious controversy in 1957 over Snedden's failed effort to have the Territory of Alaska take over the wholesale distribution of alcohol as a means to help stop bootlegging in rural areas and raise millions of dollars in tax revenue. By noon the following day the wholesale liquor dealers had withdrawn thousands of dollars in advertising orders from the *News-Miner*. Snedden refused to heed the boycott. "If the liquor wholesalers in Alaska wish to 'browbeat' us financially for speaking up, that is their business. We would rather have that revenue, but if we have to sell our principles to enjoy it, they can keep the money. The policy of this newspaper will continue to be dedicated to the public interest, as we see this interest. No advertiser, however large, is going to dictate our editorial policy. Period."[70]

Alcohol continued to be the source of many of the community's most serious problems. Every day the *News-Miner* editor was besieged with people asking to keep their names out of the newspaper for one reason or another, though the usual culprit was drunk driving. At a time when many people considered it a rite of passage or a symbol of machismo, the *News-Miner* continually reminded all that a drunk behind the wheel was a potential murderer on the loose. Shortly before Christmas 1954 reporter Chuck Hoyt volunteered to test the territorial police department's new "Harger Drunkometer," the first breath analyzer in Fairbanks. Before purchasing the new Drunkometer—which had initially been developed by Indiana University professor R. N. Harger in 1938—drunk driving in Fairbanks had always been a matter of a patrolman's opinion; with this machine, officers could for the first time determine a suspect's blood alcohol content. The point of Hoyt's test was to demonstrate to the public the reliability of the new machine; after about two and a half hours and seven shots of one-hundred-proof whiskey, Hoyt's blood alcohol reading was .193 percent. "A police officer or your wife may listen to alibis," Hoyt concluded, "but that machine won't." His warning to all those who thought they could trick the machine was blunt: "The Drunkometer . . . can't be fooled."[71]

Snedden's policy was that names of criminals were never withheld from publication. "An editor who must push aside the request of a weeping mother requires a heart of stone," Jack Ryan wrote. "Yet, it is absolutely necessary that a fair newspaper print all the news, without giving certain people 'breaks' that are not given to others. Most important, having one's name in the paper is a part of the penalty that must be paid for lawbreaking."[72] Critics who believed that the paper would protect the rich and powerful refused to hear otherwise. When a woman called the *News-Miner* in 1957 to ask that a name be withheld from the police blotter, she "got the answer that everybody gets—the *News-Miner* doesn't leave out the name of anybody who is arrested." Furious, she responded that "she was going to watch our paper to see whether we published the name of a 'real bigshot' who got into trouble over the weekend. She wouldn't tell us who." The editor responded: "We don't recognize any genuine biggies among the names of drunks, drunk drivers, etc. who went through the police mill here in the past few days. But if we left him out, lady, it was because his name wasn't in the police records, because the *News-Miner* believes the only way to run an honest newspaper is to treat everybody alike."[73]

Some city officials—accustomed to being able to control what did and did not appear in the newspaper—would discuss some matter or another in an open public meeting, and retroactively announce "that's off the record" whenever they didn't want something to be printed in the next issue. While sympathetic to the mayor and council, and conceding that generally their "lot is to sow hard work, and reap a harvest of headaches," the paper refused to go along. Snedden's stance was that truly confidential information should be discussed in a rare executive session, but that in order to have a transparent, democratic system, the public's need to know should not be compromised. "The *News-Miner* reporters will not observe any further requests to keep information which they hear at council meetings out of the newspaper," it stated. "While we agree the council has a problem in this matter, we can't agree to solve it by preventing a reporter from writing what he or she hears at a public council meeting."[74]

The recurring city battles were reflected in other policy changes in the newspaper. Most visibly, the *News-Miner* began to devote significant column inches to letters to the editor. Letters had always been a staple of American journalism, but it was only in the 1950s that the *News-Miner* made them a prominent feature in order to reflect more divergent points of view. Naturally there was always a correlation between the heat of the issue and the volume of letters, and while the letters seldom shed much light, they were often entertaining or inflammatory. "Anyone blind in one eye and can't see out of the other has noticed any number of blunders in the way things are done in the city of Fairbanks," read one typical missive.[75] For several years an inmate confined to a mental hospital in California regularly wrote the paper, having "obtained our address because of his very confused interest in Alaska. His letters consist of thick envelopes filled with drawings of fantastic projects which he is recommending that Alaska build."[76]

Many letters targeted the *News-Miner* itself for failings real and imagined. In 1954 a fan of Sen. Joseph McCarthy was bewildered by the publisher's decision that the paper would no longer run any stories about the Communist-hunting senator from Wisconsin on page one.

> Sometimes when I pick up your newspaper I say to myself, "These fellows who run this paper are as good as the *New York News* at home." But other times you act like a bunch of little kids. What I'm referring to is your ban on McCarthy off the front

page. What's the matter with you anyhow [*sic*].
Don't you realize that when a person is worthy
of the front page, whether he be good or bad he
should be there. So put McCarthy back where he
belongs, on page one.

The editor's terse response was that "Tail-gunner Joe's" headline-
hunting days were over in Fairbanks. "We put him where he belongs every
day. Page two, or three."[77]

Though letters were often ungrammatical, illogical, and ill-tempered,
Snedden refused to restrict their publication. Some readers complained
that the editor should "show greater care in the selection of letters which
are published," but this was antithetical to the *News-Miner*'s stated policy
of offering a free and uninhibited public forum. "The truth is that the
editor doesn't attempt to select what letters are sent to the printer ... As
long as a letter is not libelous, not profane or indecent, and is on a subject of general interest, it will be published. The editor will not interpose
himself as a censor between the readers who write and the readers who
only read."[78]

The *News-Miner* never made any secret of its political sympathies.
In a territory that the Democratic Party had dominated for two decades,
it was a Republican newspaper that invariably backed GOP policies and
candidates—with the notable exception of Delegate Bob Bartlett.

Snedden's campaign to craft a better future for Fairbanks coincided with the national revival of the Republican Party in Dwight D.
Eisenhower's first term. The GOP's renaissance would play a key role in
reforming law and order in Fairbanks, especially when Snedden teamed
up with a fiery young Harvard attorney from California named Theodore
Fulton Stevens, who would become his lifelong friend, confidant, and
protégé, beginning with their joint crusade fighting crime in Fairbanks
in 1953.

5

The New "Ike Age" in Alaska

Dwight D. Eisenhower's landslide in the November 1952 presidential election meant that for the first time in a generation the GOP would have all three levers of legislative and executive power in its grasp: the House of Representatives, the Senate, and the White House. Not since the 1920s had the Republicans been in control on both ends of Pennsylvania Avenue. The Republican revival would bring new policies and personalities to the fore across the country, but nowhere would the resurrection of the GOP have greater impact than Alaska.

The District of Columbia may be only one ten-thousandth the size of Alaska, but it was the source for the ten thousand and one rules that controlled all aspects of life in the northern territory. Unlike the forty-eight sovereign states, which enjoyed some measure of independence and local control, the Territory of Alaska was a federal foster child. Congress could veto any act of the territorial legislature, and the president had nearly absolute power to appoint whomever he chose to the federal agencies that oversaw the territory. No matter how well intentioned they may have been, those who decided what was best for Alaskans never had to answer to Alaskans. Territorial status may have been a government for the people, but it was not by the people of Alaska.

Without an intervening layer of state government, Alaskans in territorial days were instantly affected whenever a new tenant arrived in the White House or a shift in power took place on Capitol Hill. The coming of the new "Ike Age" for Alaska, as one newspaper derisively called it, would see a radical transformation from the New Deal/Fair Deal

Democratic days of Roosevelt and Truman and allow Republicans to try
their hand at the helm of territorial affairs for the first time since before
the Great Depression.[1]

The resurgence of the Republicans in Washington was paralleled in
Juneau. In the 1952 territorial elections, swept along with the enthusiasm for Eisenhower, the Alaska Republican party took control of both
the territorial house and senate for the first time since 1931. For most
of the 1930s and 1940s, Republicans were almost as scarce in Alaska as
in Alabama or Arkansas; Democrats dominated the "Frozen North" the
same way they ruled the "Solid South." Over a span of five territorial elections between 1932 and 1942, Democrats won 112 seats in the Alaska
Legislature compared to only eight seats for Republicans; in the legislative sessions of 1935, 1937, 1939, and 1943, either the house or senate
went 100 percent Democratic.[2] Though the Alaska GOP would put up a
more respectable showing in the Truman-era elections between 1946 and
1950, until the arrival of Eisenhower it still bore the earmark of a permanently disgruntled minority.

Alaska's GOP had been in opposition for so long, with no patronage jobs to offer loyal supporters, and therefore no serious responsibility
for governing in the past quarter century, that by the early 1950s it had
warped into an organization that stood against everything and for nothing. In particular, the Republican Party in Alaska was perceived as the
party against statehood, as with a few notable exceptions the effort to join
the union was seen as a Democratic initiative. A critic who wisecracked
that Alaska's GOP had been so fractious, ineffective, and cranky for so
long that it was little more than "an angry old man in each town" was not
so far from the truth.[3]

As a dedicated Republican, Snedden naturally believed the new political alignment in Washington and Juneau offered a fresh opportunity
to unify the Alaska GOP and shape it into a political counterweight to
Alaska's Democratic machine. While military and government spending
had sustained the Alaska economy since 1940, and any dip in federal appropriations threatened economic catastrophe, the Republicans promoted
lower taxes and limited government as a way of fostering natural resource
development, believing a resource economy was likely to be more stable
and long-lasting than relying for survival on federal handouts. It was expected that the military buildup and construction program might run
dry within three years, so the need for a replacement for federal dollars
loomed on the horizon.[4] Snedden thought the classic Republican virtues
of hard work, individual initiative, and free-market competition would

prove to be popular—generally, people who came to a place like Alaska were not eager to have someone tell them what to do—and provide the postmilitary private enterprise economy needed for the future.

——◆◆◆——

Snedden's hope of building a permanent Republican majority in Alaska took a giant step forward in the spring of 1953, when he began to vigorously promote the career of Theodore Fulton Stevens, a bright and energetic young attorney representing the *News-Miner*. What started as a simple business relationship gradually evolved as Stevens became Snedden's protégé and one of his dearest friends and most trusted confidants. Ultimately, Stevens would also become the most influential politician ever to hold office in Alaska, the longest-serving U.S. Senator in the history of the Republican Party, and the largest presence Alaska has ever known in Washington. The meeting of Snedden and Stevens was a turning point in the lives of both men—and in the history of modern Alaska. In the spring of 2000, about half a century after Snedden and Stevens first became acquainted in Fairbanks, a committee designated Ted Stevens the "Alaskan of the Century."[5]

Few senators or congressmen in U.S. history have meant more to one state than Stevens did to Alaska. From Prince William Sound to Kotzebue Sound, his legacy is everywhere. He helped to author every landmark piece of Alaska legislation since the 1950s, including the statehood act, the authorization of the Trans-Alaska Pipeline, the Magnuson-Stevens two-hundred-mile limit, the Alaska Native Claims Settlement Act, and the Alaska National Interest Lands Conservation Act. While critics have charged him as one of the worst pork-barrel spenders in American political history, Stevens and his legions of supporters have countered that he was only out to garner Alaska's fair share. His passion to protect and advance Alaska, combined with a formidable work ethic, a ferocious disposition directed against those who raised his ire, and an expert knowledge of political stagecraft made him one of the all-time maestros of the legislative process.

Ted Stevens was the third of four children, born to George and Gertrude Stevens in Indianapolis on November 18, 1923.[6] Like Snedden's, his early childhood was difficult. His parents divorced when he was about six; George, an accountant who lost his position during the Depression, suffered from severe eye problems and eventually went blind. After the divorce Teddy was first sent to live with his grandparents in Indianapolis.

From a young age, he did all he could to help support the strapped family, which included not only his disabled father but also a mentally retarded cousin. One of his first jobs was hawking newspapers in the early 1930s. "I remember selling lots of newspapers on the day of the Lindbergh kidnapping," Stevens told reporter David Whitney of the *Anchorage Daily News*.

His life changed dramatically in 1938, at age fifteen, when he moved to Southern California to live with his aunt and uncle. He relished the warm beaches and sunny days. Though he always received excellent grades, Ted and several close friends at Redondo Union High School spent all the time they could spare—and then some—swimming and surfing the California coastline. A self-described "beach bum," he cruised the coast in a 1931 gold Pontiac convertible and rode the waves on a $40 wooden surfboard that "cost almost as much as my car."

As it did for many Americans, Pearl Harbor changed Stevens's life forever. He had long dreamed of learning to fly. His aunt and uncle's house was only about five miles from the Los Angeles Airport, and as a teenager with no money "many times our entertainment was to go watch the planes come and go." On his first attempt to enlist he failed the eye exam, which Stevens maintained was because he had "strained his eyes" in an engineering course. After a daily regimen of "eye exercises" he tried again, this time with the U.S. Army Air Corps, where the recruiters now thought Stevens could see clearly enough to fly for Uncle Sam. On March 15, 1943, nineteen-year-old Private Ted Stevens reported for duty. Within a year he was flying C-46 and C-47 cargo planes throughout the China Theater in support of the Flying Tigers. "We transported everything," one of Stevens's fellow pilots recalled, "from bombs to Chinese troops to gasoline." In recognition of his wartime service, Stevens received the Air Medal, the Distinguished Flying Cross, and other honors.

One month after he was discharged as a first lieutenant in March 1946, Stevens enrolled as a second-semester freshman at UCLA and joined the swarm of ex-GIs on the fast track through college. He earned a BA in political science with a minor in economics in only seventeen months. Professors were invariably sympathetic and flexible with the returning servicemen, eager to give credit for military training, and "anxious to help us get on to somewhere else." For Stevens, who was most inspired at UCLA by James Allan Clifford Grant's course in constitutional law, somewhere else became Harvard Law School.

After three years at Harvard—including one summer as an intern at the U.S. Attorney's Office in Los Angeles—Stevens earned his law degree and was quickly admitted to the bar in both California and Washington, D.C.[7] Evidence of his scholarly work at Harvard came in an essay he published in the *Harvard Law Review* in 1950, "Erie R.R. v. Tompkins and the Uniform General Maritime Law."[8] For a man who would devote most of his career to demanding that Alaska receive equitable treatment from the federal government, on a level playing field with all the other states, it was appropriate that Stevens's essay—which the U.S. Supreme Court cited as recently as 1986—focused on the difficulties of the uniform application of the law. In twenty-five densely packed pages he explored the implications for maritime law of the famed "Erie Doctrine," a strong philosophical and legal affirmation of states' rights. Once called the "'Pole Star' of contemporary legal scholarship," the Erie Doctrine came out of a 1938 decision by Justice Brandeis, which held that a federal court hearing a case involving more than one state "must apply the law of the U.S. state in which it is sitting."[9] As Stevens explained, the justification for the Erie case "rests solely upon the principle that state courts should have the power to determine the scope and effectiveness of rights created by the states in the exercise of their Constitutional powers."[10]

Fresh out of Harvard, Stevens went to D.C., where he worked for more than two years with Northcutt Ely, a prominent Republican attorney and legal expert on natural resources and water rights who had been executive assistant to the secretary of the interior in the Hoover administration. In early 1952 Stevens married Ann Cherrington, a graduate of Reed College working at the State Department on a project involving the United Nations. She was following in the footsteps of her father, Dr. Ben Mark Cherrington, the esteemed chancellor of the University of Denver, who years earlier had been the first head of the State Department's Division of Cultural Relations and among the many authors credited with helping to draft the charter of the United Nations.[11]

Though Stevens's parents and in-laws were Democrats, he favored the GOP and energetically volunteered on the Eisenhower campaign in 1952, assisting with the Republican Speakers Bureau in Washington, D.C.[12] After Ike's election he had hoped to receive a legal position in the Interior Department. However, the new president instituted a hiring freeze, and as a result the next job that Stevens landed was four thousand miles away, in a small legal office on the top floor of the Polaris Building in downtown Fairbanks.

Stevens had first become interested in Alaska affairs while working for Ely on a legal case representing the Usibelli Coal Mine, which after the death of Cap Lathrop was the major coal supplier for Fairbanks and the military bases. Fairbanks attorney Charles Clasby, of the firm of Collins and Clasby and a director of Usibelli Mines, had been left shorthanded when a young associate in his Fairbanks office shot himself in the head with a .38 revolver only one day after receiving his license to practice law.[13] It was this twist of fate, and a $600 advance from Clasby, that led Ann and Ted Stevens to head north to Alaska. They took the backseat out of their 1946 Buick, crammed it full of all their personal belongings (what didn't make it inside was strapped on the roof of the car), and drove up the Alaska Highway to Fairbanks in April 1953. The young couple had plenty of confidence but no money. As Stevens has said, Wally Hickel may have come to Alaska with the equivalent of one quarter, two pennies, and a dime, but Stevens had him beat: "[Hickel] likes to say that he came to Alaska with 37 cents in his pocket. I came $600 in debt."[14]

On April 16, 1953, a small article on page thirty of *Jessen's Weekly* in Fairbanks announced Stevens's arrival via the Alaska Highway: "New Attorney at Collins, Clasby." The article explained that the new Harvard-trained attorney from D.C. had become interested in Alaska while working on the Usibelli account. Like a harbinger of things to come, the final sentence stated: "He also worked with details of legislation pertaining to Alaska for the Congress."[15]

The law office of Collins and Clasby was mostly Charles Clasby. The senior partner, eighty-year-old E. B. Collins, one of the grand old men of the Alaska legal profession, had been the first Speaker of the House at the first session of the Alaska Territorial Legislature in 1913, and had practiced law in Alaska since 1915. But Collins had semi-retired in 1948, and the growing firm, which included four stenographers, two attorneys, one bookkeeper, and one secretary, needed all the legal brainpower they could find. Less than three months before Stevens drove into Fairbanks, Clasby had opened a new suite of offices in the penthouse on the eleventh floor of the Polaris Building, giving the firm the "most modern law offices" in Fairbanks. The nicest feature of the new space at the top of the tallest building in Interior Alaska, besides the large picture windows that offered "a breathtaking view of downtown Fairbanks" and the modern furniture, including "leatherette chairs," was the concrete construction. "Mostly," Clasby said, "we are happy to be in a building where we don't have to worry about fire."[16]

The *News-Miner* was one of Collins and Clasby's clients, and Stevens was introduced to Snedden not long after arriving in town. The two men hit it off almost immediately. At the time Stevens was twenty-nine and Snedden was thirty-nine. Stevens called Snedden "Father" and Snedden called his young protégé "Son." Though one was a Harvard lawyer and the other a Hard Knocks graduate, they had much in common. Both had been raised by relatives other than their parents; forced to take responsibility for themselves at an early age, they had little tolerance or sympathy for those too indifferent to do the same. Stubborn, combative, and accustomed to sitting at the head of the table, they preferred to give rather than receive when it came to orders. They thought of themselves as realists who appreciated the rightful power of government to help build a better society, but they were generally fearful that the government could do much ill in the name of good. Intensely private men, not given to public displays of affection or grandstanding, they both saw the world with a stern moral clarity and certitude.

Above all Snedden and Stevens prized loyalty and trust. One liberal congressman who later battled with Stevens repeatedly over the years appreciated the same directness in the man that Snedden prized: Stevens would never "slap you on the back and lie like hell," said Rep. David Obey of Wisconsin. He was not the type who would "lie and hope you didn't notice where they put the third comma in the second sentence that obscures what they really meant to do."[17]

Stevens, who once famously described himself in a congressional hearing as "a mean, miserable S.O.B.," rightfully earned a reputation for his explosive temper. "Though he's not a big fellow," Sen. William Proxmire (D-Wisconsin) once said, "he has a loud and distinctive voice." According to a profile by the *Congressional Quarterly*, the booming voice from Alaska was heard in the world's most prestigious debating society almost immediately after he took office in January 1969, when the green freshman fearlessly took on two powerhouse Democrats from New England with nearly thirty years of senatorial seniority between them, Ed Muskie of Maine and John Pastore of Rhode Island, who were opposing President Nixon's nomination of Alaska Governor Wally Hickel to be secretary of the interior. From that day forward, the *CQ* report noted, "colleagues have known that debate with Stevens can quickly degenerate into a shouting match."[18]

"We all joke about his temperament," said Sen. Tom Daschle (D-South Dakota). "We sometimes say it is hard to understand how a guy from so cold a state could be so hot under the collar."[19] Though Snedden had a risible temperament himself, it was he who first tried to school Stevens in ways of using his temper more effectively. Like his young friend, Snedden had a wide streak of tenacity and stubborn independence; they both could be pugnacious and intractable. On more than one occasion "Father" and "Son" made the sparks fly at the dinner table at the Sneddens' house in Fairbanks. Stevens recalls it was Helen Snedden who had to act as the referee. "You guys are arguing too much," she would say. "Ted, you go home." One memorable night, the Stevens and Snedden clans were enjoying a peaceful stay at Williamsburg, Virginia, when the discussion between the two men grew so heated, to the horror of both Ann Stevens and Helen Snedden, that a neighbor called the police. "The only problem Ted had was that he had a temper," Helen Snedden recalled. "My husband helped and guided him along the way. He kind of steadied him, like you would do with your children. My husband taught him the art of diplomacy."[20]

After less than five months at Collins and Clasby, Stevens resigned effective August 31, 1953, when he was appointed acting U.S. Attorney for Fairbanks by District Judge Harry E. Pratt.[21] Clasby, a former U.S. Attorney himself in Nome and Anchorage from 1939 to 1945, was disappointed in Stevens for taking the government post. He claimed Stevens had enough talent that he would earn far more money if he continued in private practice. Snedden, however, thought the federal prosecutor's job was not only a good career move for Stevens but also a way of improving the dismal record of law enforcement in Fairbanks.

In 1953 Fairbanks's record for intra-city feuding reached an all-time low with a total meltdown of the police department. Personnel squabbles, management blunders, and professional incompetence ripped the department to shreds that year, leading to the firing of two police chiefs within less than ten months and a nearly complete turnover among officers on the force. Dissatisfaction with Police Chief Ray Skelton first erupted publicly in February 1953. Five of thirteen officers, including the police captain, quit or were fired within a span of three days; two more would resign about a week later (and Skelton would fire two new replacements about two months later).[22] According to the chief the terminations were due to differing opinions about law enforcement practices, in addition to "flagrant insubordination and lack of discipline within the police force."[23] Snedden believed the disintegration of the police department had robbed the public of the protection it deserved. "We do not quibble with the chief's right to hire or fire police officers," the News-Miner stated. "But we certainly wish he would fire people one or two at a time."[24] The city council received a petition signed by 194 residents asking them to fire Chief Skelton, while an ad supposedly from the "S.S.S."—"Skelton's Skeleton Supporters"— took out an eye-catching half-page, boldface advertisement in the *News-Miner*, an alleged all-points bulletin calling all "THIEVES, THUGS, BURGLARS AND MURDERERS" to launch a crime spree.[25]

One man called the ad "disgraceful" and demanded that whoever placed it should apologize.[26] The president of the local Junior Chamber of Commerce said the "open invitation to promote crime" was deplorable and "goes to an unnecessary extreme in ridiculing our law enforcement agency."[27]

For his part Snedden thought it "pure hogwash" that the satirical ad would incite a crime wave. While the advertisement may have been less than subtle, the paper's editorial policy was that the *News-Miner* was a soapbox for anyone who cared to express an opinion. "We are charged with a great responsibility to the public in connection with freedom of speech, and we will always lean over backward to see that this free expression is not arbitrarily cut off. Even if you think the *News-Miner* is a lousy, no good newspaper, you have a right to say so in the *News-Miner*."[28]

In response to the turmoil in the police ranks, city manager Donald Eynick declared that henceforth "the Police Department is on probation in the eyes of the council and citizens" and must "prove that the council's faith in them is justified."[29] Unfortunately, the worst was yet to come. In April 1953 the community was stunned when in the space of less than a week, two men—Merle "Bearpaw" Nugent and Verner Peterson—died while in the custody of the Fairbanks City Police. Both had been jailed for drunkenness. Suffering from severe cases of alcohol withdrawal, they had received no medical attention.

Peterson had been arrested on a Friday and suffered delirium tremens and violent convulsions in his jail cell for the next three days until he collapsed and died Tuesday morning. Other prisoners said that "Peterson was out of his mind most of the time."[30] While confined in the dungeonlike jail in the basement of city hall, he tore the plumbing fixtures out of the cell and had to be moved so his screams would create less of a disturbance. The autopsy of his badly bruised body revealed he also suffered from acute starvation, kidney and liver failure, as well as excess fluid in the brain, lungs, and stomach. (Peterson was offered only one meal in five days. City prisoners were normally fed coffee and bread twice a day, except for Mondays, Wednesdays, and Fridays, when they received a single hot meal instead of the second serving of coffee and bread.) A hastily convened coroner's inquest ruled that the police department was to blame. "We find," the jury concluded, "confusion and lack of understanding among police officers responsible for his death."[31]

Snedden was as horrified as anyone about what was going on in the police department and in the city jail, which the *News-Miner* took to calling "the black hole of Fairbanks."[32] The paper asked why Peterson was allowed "to suffer in his cell, while screaming, delirious" for three days, and the police did nothing to ease his pain. "To die of the DT's, if that is what he had, must be a horrible experience. That human being had certain God given rights, wretch that he may have been. To let him scream in agony for three days is not a humane treatment."[33]

⋯ ━◆━ ⋯

The 1953 turmoil in the city police department coincided with a crisis in federal staffing at the offices of the U.S. Marshal and the district attorney caused by the disarray in the territorial Republican Party from top to bottom. For a generation the Alaska GOP had been a squabbling, token opposition party, and old habits died hard. Due to a shortage of competent applicants and fierce disagreements among Republicans over who should be given which job, most territorial political offices remained in Democratic hands for up to a year after Eisenhower's election. It was enough to make a Republican strategist privately inform the White House that the infighting and incompetence augured a swift and complete Democratic return to power in Juneau by the next election.[34]

Most notably, the inability of the Republicans to unite on a suitable candidate as the new governor of Alaska caused an embarrassing situation that enabled Democrat Ernest Gruening to remain in power until April 1953. The two main Republicans vying to replace Gruening were a pair of rival Anchorage businessmen: hotel man Wally Hickel, the builder of the Travelers Inn, and Elmer Rasmuson, the president of the National Bank of Alaska. Other party officials backed pilot Bob Reeve, who had unsuccessfully run against Bob Bartlett in the 1952 delegate race.

Unable to agree on a candidate, the Eisenhower administration concluded that Governor Gruening would have to stay in office through the 1953 legislative session. Incomprehensibly to Snedden, bickering Republicans had kept an unrepentant New Dealer like Gruening in office rather than select a fellow Republican from a rival faction.[35] "We feel that the party has only itself to blame," the *News-Miner* said.[36] Though Snedden would have preferred that a businessman like Hickel or Rasmuson occupy the governor's mansion, he urged all Republicans to back the compromise candidate, Alaska regional forester B. Frank Heintzleman, a nonpolitical, lifelong civil servant from Juneau, who finally landed the job, though only after protracted weeks of maneuvering and mudslinging.[37] "In the last election," the *News-Miner* lamented, "the Republicans made much fuss over the 'mess in Juneau.' We agree that there is a mess in Juneau, but we see an elephant wallowing in that mess now—not a donkey."[38]

Heintzleman, who was admittedly more comfortable cutting down trees than stumping for votes, had no public record to stand on; while he may have been the least objectionable man to become governor, he remained highly unpopular with many Republicans, especially the pro-statehood segment of the party from Anchorage, which feared he was the candidate of the salmon industry. Snedden repeatedly came to Heintzleman's defense, claiming that without unity, the party be unable to achieve any of its goals. "The success or failure of the [Heintzleman] administration depends to a large extent on the Republicans in Alaska, and the support they give . . . It is up to the Republicans in the territory . . . to heal wounds and differences created during the 13 barren years when the [Gruening] Democrats exercised complete control of the Alaska capitol."[39]

Heintzleman's top aide, veteran newspaperman Bob DeArmond, who tried to steer patronage jobs to worthy applicants, found the chorus of complaints unrelenting. By August 1953, after only four months in the governor's office, DeArmond said he'd concluded "that of the 128,864 people reported by the last census to be living in Alaska, 128,863 of them are dissatisfied. We haven't yet heard from the one remaining."[40] DeArmond explained that trying to replace Democratic political appointees with Republicans was not simple. Many Democratic office holders had simply refused to tender their resignations. Most of the decisions on political jobs were actually made in Washington, and the D.C. bureaucracy was moving at its normal crawl. But there was no denying that the GOP pool of qualified job seekers was neither wide nor deep. "There are a number of applicants for marshal and judges," DeArmond wrote on August 24, 1953, "but only a few who can pass the FBI check." For most jobs the governor had only heard from "ne'er-do-wells and a few November Fifth Republicans who were in the previous administration," and as far as DeArmond knew, there was "not a single applicant" for the vacant district attorney positions in either Juneau or Fairbanks.[41]

In Fairbanks Truman's appointee, U.S. District Attorney Robert J. McNealy, had submitted his resignation after the election of President Eisenhower, as did U.S. Marshal Frank X. Chapados.[42] McNealy wanted to leave office and go into private practice in Fairbanks by February 1, 1953, but the Department of Justice refused to accept his resignation because the Republicans did not yet have a successor in line.[43] As a result the post remained in limbo for almost nine months. By the time of McNealy's last official court appearance as DA on August 14, 1953, his replacement had still not been identified, but the *News-Miner* had a favorite candidate in mind. "Speculation in the legal circles of Fairbanks," the *News-Miner* reported later that day, "favor Theodore F. Stevens of Collins and Clasby's law office as the likely successor to McNealy."[44]

Stevens may have been a young and inexperienced newcomer to Alaska with no trial experience, but Snedden thought his decisive attitude and tough personality would make him an ideal choice as the new prosecutor. As DA he could supplement the community's meager police force, and it would also help groom Stevens as one of the new breed of young Republicans Snedden hoped would come to the fore of Alaska affairs.

On the last day of August 1953, Judge Harry E. Pratt appointed Stevens as acting U.S. District Attorney for the Fourth Judicial Division headquartered in Fairbanks. At the time, Stevens had been in Alaska for little more than four months, and he had yet to take the Alaska Bar Exam. (As a courtesy he had been admitted to the Alaska Bar provisionally in May 1953, until he found time to take the test.) At age twenty-nine he was the youngest DA in the history of Fairbanks.

The fiery young prosecutor and the publisher embarked on a crusade to shake up the local law enforcement scene. The partnership Snedden and Stevens forged in Fairbanks from 1953 to 1956 set the pattern for later battles they would fight side by side in D.C., especially the struggle for Alaska statehood, and it created a bond between the two men that never wavered. More than thirty years later, when Snedden was enduring a long and painful bout with throat cancer, and wondering out loud "how much mileage" he had left, he fondly recalled in a letter to Stevens their early days together as among the happiest of his life. "Been a long time," he wrote Stevens, "since the energetic D.A. and a one-horse publisher got together to correct the woes of the world."[45]

As acting DA beginning in September 1953, Stevens would be relentless in tackling gambling, prostitution, and drug dealing in Fairbanks, hoping to prove to the Justice Department that he deserved a permanent appointment as prosecutor, which required presidential approval.

Snedden's top priority was to ensure that Stevens received the permanent post as DA, and the *News-Miner* applauded every step he took in his war on vice, including the way he handled a particularly brutal crime that landed the novice prosecutor and the *News-Miner* in the center of what remains to this day the most notorious and baffling murder in the history of Fairbanks.

6

The Rise of Ted Stevens

Law enforcement has never been an elementary proposition in Alaska. This was especially true in early territorial days. Isolation, the harsh climate, and a shortage of lawmen, lawyers, jails, and judges, combined with the greed of the gold rush mentality, spelled constant trouble. "There are in this country," a nineteenth-century Alaskan Treasury Department official complained, "as God-abandoned, God-forsaken, desperate, and rascally a set of wretches as can be found on earth. Their whole life is made up of fraud, deceit, lying and thieving, and selling liquor to the Indians."[1]

By the time Bill Snedden and Ted Stevens joined forces in Fairbanks in 1953, legal professionals might have been forgiven for believing Alaskans' morality had not appreciably improved. "Partly because of Federal apathy towards Alaska's needs," the *News-Miner* wrote shortly after Stevens took office, "law enforcement . . . has been woefully weak for years and continues to be one of the chief problems of this territory."[2] The basic troubles still stemmed from the unholy trinity of illegal alcohol, gambling, and prostitution.[3]

A Danish journalist who visited Fairbanks in 1948 said the Fourth Avenue "Line" might appear to an outsider to be an anachronism, but "up there its significance is obvious and therefore understandable, in a pioneer country with the men outnumbering the women, it simply must exist."[4] In that same vein a man in 1957 bemoaned the "do gooder, blue noses" who wanted Fairbanks to be something that it could never be. "This is now and will be for years to come a land of and for men. The laws of nature say man must have a woman. . . . You know and I know he's going to find it."[5]

Military officials at Ladd Air Force Base did not share this laissez-faire attitude toward the Line. In the 1940s, they threatened to place Fairbanks off-limits unless the community took action. Sporadic reform campaigns were launched beginning in 1948, but by early 1952 conditions were worse than ever, according to undercover investigators from the American Social Hygiene Association, a nonprofit public health advocacy organization formed in the early twentieth century to fight prostitution—euphemistically known as the "social evil"—and venereal disease.[6] At the request of the Defense Department, ASHA conducted a confidential survey in January 1952 that

> showed that the old prostitution district within
> a stone's throw of the United States government
> building in Fairbanks was again inhabited by pros-
> titutes. Along one street [Fourth Avenue] practi-
> cally in the center of the city fifteen houses of
> prostitution were observed to operate on almost
> a twenty-four hour basis. Prostitutes were seen in
> the windows of their crib-like quarters soliciting
> all potential customers who chanced to pass by. . . .
> On paydays these resorts were very busy. A steady
> stream of customers were observed entering and
> leaving practically all the houses. Some customers
> had to wait for the prostitutes of their choice.[7]

Snedden thought the ASHA report required immediate action. "The city fathers should not try to 'hush up' the situation," the News-Miner warned.[8] In the weeks that followed local law enforcement, including city police, federal agents, and MPs, undertook what the News-Miner dubbed "Operation Versus-Vice," an all-out surveillance campaign to shut down the Line and end prostitution in the entire Fairbanks area.[9] Within two months city manager Evan Peterson reported to the council that the united front of law enforcement had shut down most of the cribs for the time being, but he warned the suppression effort would have to continue permanently, lest the red lights and all the associated evils rise once more. "Prostitution is not something that walks alone," he told the council. "It is followed, hand in hand, by drug addiction, burglary, beatings, rollings, drunkenness and others forms of vice and crime."[10]

When Ted Stevens took office as acting district attorney on September 1, 1953, he had no intention of letting any criminals go free. During his nearly three years as DA, Stevens would become the most proactive and animated prosecutor in Alaska history, with Snedden backing him every step of the way. The DA's office on the third floor of the Fairbanks Federal Building at Second and Cushman Street became the nerve center of an investigative task force headed by Stevens that not only tried to punish the guilty but also worked to keep serious crimes from occurring in the first place.

Over the decades legends have grown about Stevens's crime-fighting career in Fairbanks, most notably his penchant to go with the U.S. Marshals on raids fully armed. Those who disliked the DA said his reputation as a gunslinger was a sign of his rashness. In 1958 a rival charged that while Stevens was in office he made "nightly forays into the South Fairbanks area with a .45 Colt strapped to his hip, with which gun he would sometimes threaten those whom he had discovered in some minor infraction of the law. This excited derision amongst the denizens of South Fairbanks. In the bars and nightclubs, they sang ribald songs about Stevens' unprofessional conduct."[11]

Though the young DA did carry a gun, and did participate in major arrests, the myths surrounding his career have grown more flamboyant as the years have passed. For instance, in 1994 Anchorage reporter David Whitney interviewed former Alaska Supreme Court Justice Jay Rabinowitz about the legendary "gun totin' D.A." Though Rabinowitz had not been in Alaska at the time—he only arrived in Fairbanks in 1957, one year after Stevens left office—he had heard how "U.S. marshals went in with Tommy guns and Ted led the charge, smoking a stogie and with six guns on his hips." Stevens believed the basis for this story was a prostitution, narcotics, and illegal alcohol raid in which he recalled wearing a holster with a gun. "It wasn't two guns. I never had two guns. . . . Someone saw us coming back in or going out of the federal building that day and said, 'Jesus Christ, there's the damn district attorney carrying a gun.'"[12]

When Stevens became DA he found a backlog of about one hundred pending cases. The *News-Miner* agreed this was intolerable and during Stevens's second week in office urged community support to streamline local law enforcement and ensure that justice would no longer "become lost in the Federal building." Speedy trials had not been the norm in Fairbanks for years. "Men who have been arrested for serious offenses, including narcotics charges, are released on bail, and then they go free for months simply because the D.A.'s office is unable to get to the case in a reasonable length of time. Meanwhile, witnesses leave town, memories become dim, and the offender's chances to 'beat the rap' become better each day." As a result, the *News-Miner* concluded, "a criminal in Fairbanks has excellent chances to evade the penalty for his crimes."[13]

To clear up the accumulated cases meant long hours with short staffing. Snedden thought Stevens did more work in his first two months than his predecessors had done in the previous two years.[14] Before Stevens took office, the *News-Miner* said, "the wheels of justice . . . creaked on dry axles here in Fairbanks." Under the new DA, justice was no longer delayed or denied. "We have seen two offenders, one a narcotic peddler and the other a safe cracker, arrested and sentenced with breathtaking speed. The safecracker started his sentence in McNeil's Island penitentiary the same day he was arrested. Two others caught in the safe cracking offense were indicted by the grand jury the same day they were captured."[15]

Stevens's colleagues in the U.S. Marshal's office were also impressed by his dedication. "Many times we find him still in his office after midnight," Marshal Al Dorsch wrote. "Whenever there is a call for night duty he is available and anxious to participate, thus having been on hand when several arrests have been made."[16] The young DA's court tally for the last quarter of 1953 was remarkable. In fifty days in court he dispatched about fifty criminal cases, resulting in thirty-five pleas of guilty, thirteen convictions (bank robbery, accessory to bank robbery, interfering with the FBI, sodomy, selling liquor without a license, and assault with a deadly weapon), three acquittals, and three dismissals. Dorsch thought Stevens's performance was the best of any district attorney in the history of Fairbanks.[17]

Stevens supporters such as Dorsch and Snedden believed it was the DA's effectiveness that prompted a revolt by the local bar association in the fall of 1953, when fourteen of the sixteen lawyers in Fairbanks secretly tried to block his candidacy for the permanent presidential appointment as Fairbanks District Attorney. At a closed meeting of the Tanana Valley Bar Association, in late October 1953, the members petitioned the U.S. Department of Justice to deny Stevens the permanent position, claiming he was too young, immature, and inexperienced to handle the job.[18] Even Stevens's former boss, Charles J. Clasby, signed the petition, as did Mayor Ralph Rivers, Fairbanks city attorney William V. Boggess, and former district attorneys Robert J. McNealy and Everett W. Hepp. His fellow attorneys thought the acting DA had proven to be arrogant, dogmatic, and thin-skinned. The formal resolution stated Stevens "has failed to exercise mature judgment and reasonable discretion" and was not "qualified to perform the duties of United States Attorney."[19]

The opposition to Stevens was both professional and personal. His style struck many of the older attorneys as arrogant, and those accustomed to business as usual didn't appreciate his hard line on crime. Furthermore, of the sixteen practicing lawyers in Fairbanks, only three were Republicans; while two of the Republican lawyers—Mike Stepovich and Julian Hurley—had signed the anti-Stevens petition, the acting DA's only public supporter among the bar was the third Republican, Maurice Johnson. "I think Stevens is doing a good job," he told the *News-Miner*.[20]

Mayor Rivers, the U.S. Attorney in Fairbanks from 1933 to 1944 under President Franklin D. Roosevelt, privately wrote Delegate Bob Bartlett about the bar association's dislike of Stevens. "Theodore Stevens, under a temporary appointment, is a man of integrity," Rivers said, "but has antagonized nearly all of the lawyers because of officious attitude, lack of humor and mature judgment. He also seems to be imbued with the presumption that everybody is guilty" and too hastily prosecutes on "flimsy complaints." Rivers accused the young DA of trying to "run the steamroller over everybody when practical or compromise solutions are at hand for flimsy cases."[21] He wondered if Bartlett might be willing or able to block Stevens's advancement. "I realize this is a Republican show," Rivers wrote, "but the lawyers wanted me to tell you their point of view."[22] Bartlett responded that since he was now in the Democratic minority he would not be involved in the decision. "I doubt whether I could help or hurt him much in the Department of Justice these days. My advice is not being solicited!" Moreover, Bartlett said, not everyone agreed that Stevens was unsuited for the job. "I'm obliged for your comments concerning Ted Stevens," he wrote Rivers, however the delegate had received another report "diametrically opposed" to that of the Fairbanks attorneys, one that "saluted Ted as an able U.S. Attorney who ought to be appointed to the position."[23]

Marshal Dorsch believed the accusations against Stevens were politically motivated. He wrote to his old friend Bill Strand, the former *News-Miner* editor and now a high-ranking official in the Interior Department, urging Strand to come to Stevens's aid. "I . . . want to sing the praises of our young Court Appointed D.A.," Dorsch said. "I feel that he has in his short term of office set an example as a prosecutor that has been far above any predecessor's accomplishments during my 21 years of residence in the community." At the opening of one trial, Dorsch said, he overheard a defense attorney tell his colleague they would have no trouble in dealing with the rookie DA, saying "we'll knock his ears down." But as Stevens quickly piled up confessions and convictions, "the Democrats apparently decided that he was going to be a factor to reckon with" and turned on him. "So we have a young man, with a clean cut Republican background, whose worst fault . . . is that he is doing an outstanding job of prosecuting the criminal element. . . . We need this man. I am fully convinced that if we can keep him we are going to break up this crime situation which has harassed the community for some time now. Stevens is capable, honest, sincere, fearless, a hard worker and weighs his judgment carefully."[24]

Outraged by the bar association's attack on Stevens, Snedden complained to Governor Heintzleman that the "worthy gentlemen" of the Fairbanks bar were only proving themselves to be lazy, incompetent, and hypocritical. "It is my sincere opinion that this young chap Stevens is about as good a man as it would be possible to find for the district attorney's job. I am well aware that he does not have much . . . experience; however, he appears to be very intelligent, conscientious and hard-working." According to Snedden the Fairbanks attorneys were motivated by professional spite and jealousy, because Ted Stevens was disrupting the old-boy, Democratically ruled legal fraternity that had for so long mismanaged the law in Fairbanks.

> It appears to me that the reason the attorneys do not like Stevens is the fact they are going to have to get in and work to represent their various clients, as Stevens is going to do his best to see they are prosecuted and law enforcement is carried out in the manner in which it should be. There has been [sic] far too many cases in the past here in Fairbanks, where offenders went scott-free because the district attorney's office did not bear down on prosecution. The result has created a situation where law enforcement is at a regrettable low ebb—and the welfare of the general public is suffering considerably. . . .
>
> The law enforcement situation here has been about as close to intolerable as I believe any place could possibly be. We are doing our best with the newspaper to make people aware of the fact, and help to see that the situation is corrected.[25]

In a letter to Attorney General Herbert Brownell Jr., Snedden claimed that "the only reason local attorneys are opposed to Mr. Stevens is the fact that *he is doing too good a job in dispatching the duties of the position.*"[26]

Others who advocated harsher treatment of lawbreakers shared Snedden's notion that defense attorneys habitually and unfairly impeded criminal prosecution in the territory. During the Truman administration, Juneau District Court Judge George Folta had complained in 1952 that U.S. Attorneys and their deputies in Alaska were so poorly paid that they were usually the least-experienced lawyers in the courtroom, novice law school graduates "pitted against veterans who do their utmost, under our archaic system of criminal procedure, to perpetuate the sporting theory of justice in the trial of criminal cases." Folta said he repeatedly watched crafty defense counsel "make a farce of each trial, to run it off on a tangent; to try one collateral issue after another, in fact to try every thing and everybody except the merits and the defendant." Lacking courtroom savvy, the government lawyers seldom knew how to respond. "All too often," Folta wrote, "the prosecutor is unaware of what is taking place." This tepid prosecution meant that criminals and their advocates often had an easy day in court, an advantage that defense counsel were naturally loath to give up.[27]

When rumors about the bar association's action against Stevens appeared in the *News-Miner*, supporters of the district attorney rushed to his defense, angered at what they thought was a partisan smear campaign, since none of the lawyers would publicly comment or even admit that they had in fact taken a stand against Stevens. "It seems more than revealing," wrote Rev. G. T. Charlton of St. Matthew's Episcopal Church, "that the *News-Miner*'s reporter could not find a single member of the local Bar Association who was willing to admit that he had voted against the permanent appointment of Mr. Stevens as U.S. Attorney. . . . This would seem to indicate that these gentlemen are aware that their action is not popular with the public, and they are not willing to take responsibility for it."[28]

On behalf of the Fairbanks Ministerial Association, Charlton wrote a private letter to the U.S. Attorney General, elaborating the fine job the ministers felt Stevens was doing to eliminate crime. Previous prosecutors, Charlton said, had been ineffective and incompetent. "Many charges were summarily dismissed, many simply shelved and never brought to trial." In the short time Stevens had been in office, Charlton continued, the prosecutor had reversed this pattern. In only a few months Stevens had put on more trials and earned more "convictions than we are accustomed to seeing in the period of a year." He claimed that the general public was behind Stevens, but not the coalition of bar owners, politicians, and gamblers:

> ... this diligent work by the U.S. Attorney has offended the local (and very powerful) liquor interests and gambling interests. These men are influential in the City Council and in civic affairs generally, although they represent only a small minority of the citizens of the area. They have frankly requested that certain illegal practices be permitted and have offered thinly veiled bribes to the U.S. Attorney. Finding him incorruptible, they have persuaded the local Bar Association to withdraw their support of Mr. Stevens for his permanent appointment. This was not hard to do because the other lawyers were finding it difficult to defend their clients against Mr. Stevens' prosecutions.[29]

Snedden answered the secret attacks on Stevens with a series of supportive editorials, urging the Republican party to unite behind the district attorney and asking why attorneys should have more say than the general public in determining who becomes prosecutor, especially since attorneys and district attorneys were natural and inevitable adversaries. "Attorneys are paid to defend," the *News-Miner* said, "and the district attorney is paid to prosecute. The D.A. represents the people of Alaska, and the attorney represents his client. It is scarcely wise to allow the defenders to have a hand in the choosing of a prosecutor."[30]

A recurring theme among supporters was that the bar association did not represent either the people of Fairbanks or their best interests. "I do not know the man personally," one admirer of Stevens wrote the Justice Department, "my opinion is based solely on the stands he has taken on issues as acting district attorney the past months. He strikes me as being forthright and honest in the face of powerful opposition and corruption in local governmental affairs. Many of us [citizens of Fairbanks] hope that the bar association will not prove so powerful as to deprive us of the good government which we so sorely need."[31] The corruption was so bad, and the contempt for Stevens so deeply rooted, said one citizen who had served nine months on a federal jury, that jurors routinely received threatening, anonymous phone calls at home, trying to intimidate potential jurors and personally attacking the district attorney. [32]

Admittedly, Stevens's experience at Harvard Law and in D.C. had not prepared him for the world he encountered at the Cushman Street courthouse, especially in the person of Fairbanks's most flamboyant defense attorney, Warren A. Taylor. Among the lawyers who signed the petition against Stevens, none would battle him more bitterly than Taylor, an old frontier barrister who had never seen the inside of law school but had been practicing in the territory since 1927, and was the senior Democratic legislator from Fairbanks. Hot-tempered and combative, Taylor was the most experienced defense attorney in Fairbanks in the 1950s, known for his theatrical style and novel arguments in defense of long-shot, high-profile clients. For example Taylor represented a thirty-two-year-old unemployed law student from New England named Henry Mason; he appealed Mason's DWI conviction on the grounds that the "Drunkometer" recently adopted by the police to test blood alcohol was too sophisticated an instrument to be deployed correctly by the poorly trained local officers. According to Taylor the police had mistakenly assumed his client was drunk after "a few beers" only because of his "Boston accent" and the "three-syllable words" he was fond of using (an argument which the jury did not find convincing).[33]

Taylor's tactics in the courtroom repeatedly pushed Stevens to the boiling point. A sensational "white slavery" prostitution trial in 1954, Stevens's biggest trial during his tenure as DA, featured dozens of exhibits, and a "multitude of witnesses" for the prosecution who were brought to Fairbanks at great expense from Colorado, D.C., Texas, British Columbia, and Anchorage. Taylor called Stevens himself to the stand as the last witness for the defense. This unusual step was intended to embarrass his young adversary and to undermine the government's case by intimating that the DA was guilty of prosecutorial misconduct. With Stevens in the witness chair, Taylor asked him if "he knew he was lying" when he had badgered one of the alleged prostitutes, initially the government's only witness, who had subsequently recanted her confession to the FBI. Stevens fired back at Taylor's "obnoxious" behavior until the judge called for order and "told them to confine the proceedings to matters relative to the case before the court."[34]

Snedden thought Taylor's actions in Juneau as the leader of the local Democrats were as irritating as any stunt he pulled in the courtroom.
Taylor charged the *News-Miner* repeatedly distorted his positions. "I have
been misquoted and misconstrued so many times during the present session of the legislature," Taylor wrote the editor in 1955, "that I am beginning to believe it is intentional."[35]

But Taylor's stock with Snedden and Stevens reached its all-time
low when he took the floor of the territorial house in February 1955 and
launched a blistering personal attack on two of Alaska's district court
judges, George Folta and J. L. McCarrey. At issue was a bill before the
legislature that would have changed Alaska's code of criminal procedure by the substitution of a single word. Rep. Stanley McCutcheon, a
Democratic lawyer from Anchorage, called it the "may-must" bill. "The
bill was my idea," he said. "I wrote it, put several of the lawyers' names on
it and introduced it." He initially considered it a "do-gooder," he said, one
of a succession of innocuous bills introduced that session, including one
adopting the ptarmigan as Alaska's official bird, another making "Alaska's
Flag" the official anthem of Alaska, and a third adopting the official design of the Alaska flag.[36] Unlike those measures, however, the "may-must"
bill caused an uproar.

⸺ ⸱⸺⸱⸺ ⸱⸱

Since 1899, the law in Alaska, based on a provision in the old Oregon
Code, had technically stated that criminal defendants "must" present a defense at the opening of trial proceedings. According to McCutcheon, such
a requirement "compels the defendant to testify against himself" and was
therefore a clear violation of the Fifth Amendment. For decades this provision remained a dead letter. "No judge, within my knowledge or within the
knowledge of the elder members of the Bar, had ever required the defendant to state his defense notwithstanding this provision of the statute. . . .
Frankly, most of us did not even know the existence of this statute." That
changed when former prosecutor George Folta ascended to the bench in
1947 and began to require all defense attorneys in his courtroom to adhere
to the provision by stating their defense at the start of proceedings.

According to McCutcheon, Judge Folta did not have the impartial
attitude the job required. He said Folta had "a prosecutor's viewpoint in
the trial of a criminal case," so much so that defense attorneys groused
that whenever Folta was presiding, there were "two prosecutors in the
court room and no judge."

Working with Warren Taylor, who chaired the House Judiciary Committee, McCutcheon proposed to revise the statute by changing "must" to "may," to ensure that the entire burden of proof lay on the prosecution. Judges Folta and McCarrey, however, lobbied against the change, with McCarrey warning the revision could mean a 75 percent drop in convictions. "What the defendant can do if the amendment goes through," McCarrey wrote to legislators, "is wait until the government has put on its entire case and then fabricate a defense which the district attorney could not rebut."[37] During the floor debate in Juneau, Taylor said Folta was the only judge he'd ever heard of who enforced the mandatory defense rule. Folta responded, saying Taylor was paid to protect criminals, while as a Judge he was "interested in protecting society."[38] The next day Taylor took the floor and delivered a forty-five-minute attack on Folta and McCarrey, blasting the judges' interference in the legislative process, calling McCarrey "stupid" and labeling Folta a confessed atheist and a "hanging judge." The letter McCarrey wrote to legislators was, he said, "the most asinine statement I ever heard from a judge in Alaska or in the states."[39]

Taylor's speech made headlines across the territory. The next day the *News-Miner*'s front page read:

LEGISLATOR ATTACKS U.S. JUDGES
Warren Taylor Delivers Tirade on floor of House in Juneau

According to the Associated Press, seasoned politicians called Taylor's speech "one of the bitterest personal attacks ever delivered on the floor of Alaska's legislature," while other Democrats insisted Taylor's views were his own and not those of his party. Fellow Democratic legislator and attorney Seaborn J. Buckalew, of Anchorage, a former district attorney, rose to apologize. "It shocks my conscience," he responded quietly, "that judges should be torn apart on the floor of the legislature."[40] The *News-Miner* condemned Taylor for his "reckless and destructive" slander. "Smearing our judges in a name calling speech in the legislature serves only to weaken respect for courts, law and order."[41]

Ted Stevens responded to Taylor's speech by initiating disbarment proceedings against him. Taylor's comments, he said, had demonstrated "that he is an unfit person to enjoy the privileges of the legal profession." Stevens alleged that Taylor had violated the ethics of the American Bar Association when he publicly "attacked, maligned, abused, attempted to discredit, ridiculed and denounced" the judges.[42] He asked for the FBI to determine if it was true, as rumored, that Taylor had once been convicted of a crime, or had been implicated in a prostitution ring in Kodiak during World War II.[43] Stevens maintained that Taylor had violated a fundamental precept of the American justice system. "It is the duty of the lawyer to maintain towards the courts a respectful attitude," Stevens wrote. "Judges, not being wholly free to defend themselves, are peculiarly entitled to receive the support of the bar against unjust criticism and clamor."[44]

Stevens's disbarment proceedings against Taylor brought a unanimous protest from the Alaska House of Representatives, even though the body refused to pass judgment "on the propriety or impropriety" of Taylor's remarks. McCutcheon, the original author of the "may-must" bill, admitted that Taylor "was out of line" and had gone "far overboard in his criticisms," but defended Taylor's right to blow his cool. "It was regrettable that . . . the young and inexperienced District Attorney in Fairbanks saw fit to file a disbarment action against Warren," McCutcheon wrote former Governor Gruening. "In the first place, Warren was clearly within his legislative immunity when he was arguing in the defense of a measure then pending before the Legislature. . . . Both judges were out of line in using their official judicial position to influence the Legislative branch of government."[45]

Democrats particularly were furious with Stevens. "Have just read of the debauchery instigated by a petty politician with a viewpoint to disbar one of Alaska's ablest attorneys," Bob Blodgett wrote to the *News-Miner*. "Such is so typical of the Republican regime in all channels of our government today . . . I am thankful to my God that our forefathers did not endow our nation with a Republican totalitarianism. Bully for Warren A. Taylor."[46]

Though Stevens's attempt to disbar Taylor failed, the case had a major impact on the Alaska legal profession: it helped ensure the enactment of the 1955 integrated bar bill, which, among its other provisions, removed the policing and disciplining of lawyers from the office of the U.S. Attorney to the newly established Alaska Bar Association, which was created by the legislation. Judge Folta told Stevens that the integrated bar bill, which he opposed, would have been repudiated by the governor if not for the fracas with Taylor. Governor Heintzleman actually "had his veto message prepared against the integrated bar bill when the announcement came of the filing of the disbarment action against Taylor,"

Folta wrote Stevens, adding that that news, which Taylor released, forced Heintzleman to let the bill become law. "It seems that in this particular fight we don't get a single break."[47]

Taylor never forgave Stevens. When he heard a rumor in 1958 that Stevens was being considered for appointment as a federal judge for Fairbanks, he couldn't contain his disgust. "Due to [Stevens's] extreme bullheadedness," Taylor wrote Bob Bartlett, "his animosity toward all who oppose or disagree with him and his total lack of knowledge of law, it is the consensus that Stevens' appointment would be catastrophic for this division. He is petty, spiteful, overbearing, intolerant and insulting; and in fact possesses all the attributes a judge should not have."[48]

The last word on Taylor's legal standards may have come from the U.S. Ninth Circuit Court of Appeals. In *William Bergen v. United States of America* Stevens defended the government against a passenger who claimed he had been injured in a derailment caused by the negligence of the Alaska Railroad. Reading the brief Taylor submitted on behalf of Bergen, the appellate judges were astounded by Taylor's unprofessional style. Taylor's brief, they said, "hardly conforms to any of the requirements of this court except that it is correctly entitled, is written in the English language, appears on paper and is signed by counsel." If Taylor continued to ignore the Federal Rules of Civil Procedure, they warned, "it is inescapable that some clients will pay dearly for his indifference."[49]

Taylor and the other thirteen attorneys from the Fairbanks bar association who tried to block Stevens's appointment as U.S. Attorney in 1953 did not give up easily, even after President Eisenhower officially appointed Stevens to a full term on March 30, 1954.[50] Opposition to Stevens's approach to law and order only increased as he expanded the functions and fully utilized the powers of his office. At the same time, Snedden stepped up his editorial support for the young district attorney's new way of doing business. Stevens spearheaded formation of a comprehensive interagency crime investigation unit called the Crime Squad. Staffed by representatives from the city police, territorial police, and marshal's office, it dealt with major felony cases as well as prostitution, illegal alcohol, and gambling. Its dual purpose was to hunt criminals down and keep "a continuous eye on offenders" in order to keep the next resident from being "robbed, slugged or shot." Stevens liked to say that "big crimes grew out of small vice," and the Crime Squad was the tool to dig out vice by the roots.[51] The fruit of its labor, according to the DA, was a steep drop in venereal disease and prostitution: "With fewer 'girls' liquor sales declined sharply in certain establishments and some bar owners raised a fuss with the agencies. They complained that the squad was too efficient."[52] Stevens and Snedden were sure it was this efficiency—and the resultant discomfort of some prominent Democrats and their friends—that inspired a political backlash intended to kill the Crime Squad.

Like the fight with the Tanana Valley Bar Association, the dispute over the Crime Squad stemmed from personality clashes and partisanship, but also from a fundamental difference in attitudes about crime and the necessity of punishment, between those who wanted Fairbanks "open" and those who preferred it "closed." In frontier parlance, the police and prosecutors in an "open" camp preferred to look the other way when they came upon minor illegal activities, while officials in a "closed" town shut down every card game, crib, and unlicensed saloon they could find.

Stevens stood by the "closed" position much more firmly than his immediate predecessor in the DA's office, Robert McNealy, who had said he preferred a "gambling balance" that took a relatively tolerant view of most games of chance, a position that he thought represented the "majority of liberal, free thinking citizens that gamble a bit or leave it alone, that take a drink or leave it alone." When he had been in office McNealy said he and the U.S. Marshal were not intolerant radicals out to insist on the letter of the law; they would enforce only the laws supported by "the MAJORITY of the citizens of the Fourth Division. Our federal appointment does not make us crusaders."[53]

When Stevens took over as DA he denied he was planning a "concerted drive to stamp out gambling in the Fairbanks area," but warned that as a federal prosecutor he had no authority to enforce only popular laws; gambling was expressly prohibited by the terms of the Alaska Organic Act, and when evidence of it surfaced he was bound to shut it down, from pinball machines to crap tables and card rooms. The threat made some gambling establishments think twice. A *News-Miner* reporter found signs on a row of machines in one bar that read "due to action of D.A. this machine cannot be played."[54] Meanwhile, a reporter on undercover assignment one night with $40 of the *News-Miner*'s money played "scores and scores of pinball games, lost most of his money, then reported back." He found that practically every place in Fairbanks with a pinball machine was illegally paying winners.[55]

Though he understood why Stevens could not condone illegal activity, Snedden thought a more practical and realistic solution, given the history and makeup of Fairbanks, was to tax the small-stakes gambling that was taking place all over town. While the city clearly had no authority to legalize an illegal activity, a gambling license for pinball machines and punchboards would draw a clear line between small-scale gambling the community could tolerate and the large-scale vice it could not. "Some people are going to say that the *News-Miner* favors a wide open town, with unrestricted gambling. They will say the *News-Miner* is suggesting legal pinball machines and punchboards as an entering wedge that will eventually open this area to wide open gambling. We are doing no such thing. . . . We are only recognizing a situation that exists, and suggesting a step we believe is sensible."[56] Mayor Rivers agreed with Snedden. "What's wrong," the mayor asked, "with over the counter instead of under the table payoffs"? From city hall's point of view, the "penny ante stuff" of pinballs and punchboards did not rise to the level of real gambling since the payouts were so small. "As long as we have it anyway, we might as well bring it out in the open and make some money off of it." [57]

The stakes in the gambling war were raised irrevocably when a city council member supporting the proposed gambling tax wrote an ill-considered letter to U.S. Attorney General Herbert Brownell Jr. asking him to forbid Stevens from interfering with Fairbanks's favorite pastime. Snedden printed Councilman Ted Mainella's eye-opening letter to the attorney general and the response he received from the Justice Department.

"Here in the Territory of Alaska," Mainella wrote the chief law officer of the United States, "petty gambling is a traditional form of recreation and has always been recognized as such. . . . However, it is apparent now to everyone here that the newly-appointed acting District Attorney Mr. Ted Stevens, who is a 'Cheechako' or newcomer to Alaska, has undertaken, on his own initiative, to interfere with this recreation." Mainella's chief complaint was that in an attempt to block the taxing ordinance, Stevens had threatened "to strictly enforce the laws on gambling within the city of Fairbanks thereby inferring that the ordinance considered by the council was somewhat illegal."

Assistant Attorney General Warren Olney III drew the task of responding to Mainella's treatise on gambling, federal law, and the "somewhat illegal" doctrine. He found the councilman's mastery of the finer points of precedent less than stellar. "Your objection is apparently based on the grounds that illegal gambling has gone unscathed for so long that it should enjoy exemption from attack. . . . Neither custom nor use can render legal that which the law determines an illegality. We can only regret that disregard of the law in the past has created a present atmosphere in which complete law enforcement is regarded as 'interference.'" According to Olney, Stevens had no choice but to enforce the laws as written: "We cannot, of course, speak for the Fairbanks City Council but the assignment of the United States Attorney is the complete and impartial administration of all statutes, regulations, and ordinances falling within the jurisdiction of this office. We would consider any lesser performance a dereliction of official duties."[58]

Despite the fact that the U.S. Attorney General's office had made it clear that DA Stevens had the duty to shut down gambling "irrespective of any taxing ordinance that may be passed by the city council of Fairbanks," proponents of the gambling tax persisted.[59] Mainella claimed Stevens was bluffing and wouldn't dare "interfere" with the gambling tax. "The district attorney," he charged, "is just playing hero."[60]

In late December 1953 a bitterly divided city council debated Mainella's gambling ordinance for two weeks. The *News-Miner* opposed the final measure because it included card games, and Snedden thought it would be unenforceable. "It is not that we feel card games with a low limit on stakes would be harmful here. . . . We don't think there is any way the city could enforce the limit. How could policemen watch a hundred different card games going on in this city each night, and ascertain that a $5 limit was not being broken?"[61]

The majority of the city leaders, however, disagreed with Snedden and the Department of Justice, and by a 4–2 vote the council authorized the city of Fairbanks to tax illegal pinball machines, punchboards, pinochle tables, pangini tables, and $5 limit poker tables.[62] The victory for the gambling proponents was short lived. Mayor Rivers, as Sourdough Jack phrased it, pulled an ace out of his sleeve to beat four of a kind. "As it became apparent that the gambling tax has passed," the *News-Miner* reported the following day, " . . . a silence fell over the crowded council chambers." At that moment Rivers stunned the council and the audience by announcing he would veto the ordinance. Five votes were needed to override. Rivers had killed the tax. As far as he knew, the city clerk said, no Fairbanks mayor had ever vetoed a council ordinance before.[63]

Rivers, who had at one time supported the gambling tax, said he'd come to believe its "detrimental effects would far outweigh the anticipated license revenue."[64] The ordinance would put card room operators in jeopardy, the mayor indicated, because "the District Attorney and Marshal would be forced to 'lower the boom' in line with enforcing the basic law against gambling." Additionally, the tax would also threaten "raffles and other petty gaming devices for charitable and community purposes, which

I consider sufficient to satisfy the proclivity of the average person to take a chance, along with card playing by people in their own homes."[65]

‐‐ ‐‐

The defeat of the gambling tax signaled that, under Stevens, the community would be more "closed" than ever before, but the debate about how vigorous the district attorney should be wasn't over. Opposition to Stevens's authority came to be centered on the actions of the Crime Squad, and his opponents were heartened in late 1954 when Territorial Police Superintendent A. P. Brandt announced his officers would no longer belong to the DA's special investigative unit. Brandt said his men were spending too much time on crimes inside the city limits of Fairbanks, including prostitution and gambling, and since territorial law mandated his primary duty was to provide police protection to unincorporated areas, henceforth he would restrict his agency's regular operations "to the rural areas and the highways." Further, Brandt said, Stevens's Crime Squad was an un-American intrusion on personal freedom and local authority. "The pattern for the establishment of an all-embracing State Police organization is a European one, patterned after the Gendarmerie Systems of Germany and Spain. . . . The policy of local control of law enforcement organizations is an elementary principal [*sic*] of American Democracy, and an important buttress against the development of the totalitarian state."[66]

Snedden took strong exception to Brandt's interpretation and the superintendent's nearly impenetrable bureaucratic language. He printed Brandt's full letter to Stevens on the editorial page "although we were certain that nobody could fully grasp a meaning from that welter of statements. All Mr. Brandt did was make use of about 2,000 words to give a simple answer . . . 'NO.'"[67] Since 90 percent of the people of Alaska lived within incorporated cities, Snedden maintained it made no sense for the force to protect only the remaining 10 percent, leaving the vast majority of Alaskans to fend for themselves.[68] "Some of our most prominent residents habitually keep revolvers handy because they have little confidence in law enforcement and public protection as it now exists."[69] The residents were not getting their money's worth from their taxes if all the territorial police did was to give speeding tickets. "If somebody is murdered in town," the *News-Miner* remarked, "the murderer had better watch his speed if he makes his getaway on the Richardson highway."[70] In Snedden's mind the Crime Squad under Stevens "was the finest form of law enforcement this city has seen in a long time" and the public demanded it continue. "We've seen our share of murders and vicious armed robberies in this town," the *News-Miner* said. "We would feel much more secure if we had a cooperating squad keeping its fingers on the pulse of the underworld . . . and . . . the activities of some of our ruthless characters."[71] The *News-Miner* challenged the superintendent directly:

> We would like to remind Mr. Brandt that here in Fairbanks, some of the foulest crimes in the history of our territory have been committed. . . . Rarely, we repeat, RARELY, is an offender brought to justice for a murder or an armed robbery in this city. Yet, our law enforcement agencies are 'too busy' to get together and sponsor an organization devoted to crime prevention and detection. . . . WE ARE WIDE OPEN FOR ANOTHER UNSOLVED MURDER. YOU WHO ARE SITTING AT HOME READING THIS EDITORIAL COULD BE MURDERED TONIGHT, AND THE ODDS ARE THAT THE MAN WHO KILLED YOU WOULD NEVER BE ARRESTED.[72]

To help buttress Brandt's policy change, two Fairbanks lawyers serving in the Territorial House of Representatives tried to change the law to force the dissolution of the Crime Squad. Rep. Hubert Gilbert (D-Fairbanks) introduced bills that would have prohibited both territorial police and U.S. Marshals from operating inside the boundaries of first-class cities such as Fairbanks unless specifically requested to do so by local police or the governor. Gilbert was the Fairbanks city magistrate, and a former assistant U.S. Attorney before Stevens's arrival. It was no secret that the bills were inspired by the jurisdictional, personal, and ideological difficulties he had with Stevens and the Crime Squad. If passed they would have severely restricted the DA's authority. Joining Gilbert in support of the measures was Rep. McNealy (D-Fairbanks), Stevens's immediate predecessor as DA, who claimed, according to a press account from Juneau, that due to the demands of Stevens's crime unit, "the territorial police had been spending most of their time in Fairbanks while complaints were coming from outlying areas that they had no protection. McNealy added . . . that they spent too much time hanging around bars in the city."[73]

Snedden thought Gilbert's bills were an open door to increased corruption, and the *News-Miner* condemned them repeatedly. "Alaska's cities are bursting their seams due to sudden growth, often poorly financed and frequently beset by serious problems and controversies. They need help, all the help they can get, in carrying out law enforcement duties. If cities are stripped of aid from the Territorial Police and the marshal's office ... law enforcement is certain to be weakened greatly within larger cities under terms of Mr. Gilbert's bill."[74] The bills, in Snedden's opinion, would "set up perfect conditions for vice, graft, and corruption in Alaska cities" and place the people "at the mercy of whatever element wins control of the police force" without any institutional checks or balances.[75]

The anti–Crime Squad bills failed to pass and, thanks to an upwelling of public support in Fairbanks, the city, territory and federal officials created a new crime-solving task force, for which the *News-Miner* took some credit:

> We feel that this has come about partly because
> of our editorials and partly because of the inter-
> est in the situation shown by a citizens' committee
> here, and partly because of the laudable attitude of
> our legislators. . . . Therefore the News-Miner will
> cease 'harping' on this subject. . . . But we promise
> this: The next time we become convinced that the
> public is not getting a fair measure of return from
> money expended for law enforcement here, we will
> 'howl' again. . . . [76]

If any single case encapsulated the reasons why Stevens and Snedden thought the Crime Squad was necessary, it was the brutal murder of businessman Cecil Wells in October 1953, a crime that would shadow his entire career as district attorney. Wells was the owner of Wells Alaska Motors, the local GM dealer, and one of Alaska's most prominent businessmen. A member of the Elks Lodge, the Lions Club, and the Presbyterian Church, he had been in the automobile business in Alaska for almost thirty years.[77] In Fairbanks, as a hard-boiled account of his murder in a pulp magazine later put it, the name Cecil Wells "carried more weight than a Japanese wrestler."[78] He had just stepped down as president of the Fairbanks Chamber of Commerce and had recently been elected president of the All Alaska Chamber of Commerce, which required him to travel widely across the territory and the Lower 48 on behalf of Alaskan concerns. An accomplished private pilot, he flew a new Cessna aircraft to Fairbanks in April 1953 that he had picked up at the factory in Kansas. "He also took out time to go to Washington," the *News-Miner* said, "where he worked on tax incentive legislation, communications, land withdrawals and other matters affecting Alaska."[79] Wells had ambitions that went far beyond Alaska. He and five other Fairbanks entrepreneurs, led by contractor Lloyd Martin, announced plans in September 1953 to build the tallest apartment building in Hawaii, a twelve-story structure towering over the beach in Waikiki. "We mean business," Martin told the *Honolulu Advertiser.* "We're not just arousing the public over a dream."[80]

Wells's personal life was complicated. He was fifty-one and had four ex-wives; his last wife, Diane Wells, was thirty-one and had two ex-husbands. If Cecil had not been slain, it looked as though Diane would have shortly become ex-wife number five. Between them they had eight marriages, at least eight children, and six divorces—and by March 1954, one murder and one suicide.[81]

Shortly after seven a.m. on Saturday, October 17, 1953, Diane Wells—invariably described in the *News-Miner* and elsewhere as "a pretty blond"—was found by her neighbors crawling and screaming hysterically in the hallway on the eighth floor of the Northward Building, outside her apartment door, badly beaten and bleeding from the head. Inside their double suite Cecil was lying dead under the sheets with a huge bullet wound in the head. The double banner across the top of the *News-Miner* later that day told the story:

CECIL WELLS MURDERED IN BEDROOM; WIFE, DIANA, FOUND BADLY BEATEN

The Wells murder and assault had taken place on the top floor of the finest residential building in downtown Fairbanks. If Cecil Wells could be murdered in his bed and his wife savagely beaten about the face without neighbors raising an alarm, no one could be considered safe anywhere in town. What made this slaying all the more terrifying was the bungled response by Chief E. V. Danforth and the Fairbanks Police Department. The police failed to get any fingerprints at the scene of the crime, saying there "were only a few smears," and the bloodstains in the apartment revealed nothing. "Tests of blood taken from Mrs. Wells, the rug, mattress, shoe and wall of the bedroom proved negative," a lab technician explained, "owing to the inadequate equipment at the Fairbanks Clinic where the tests were done." The police also misplaced crucial evidence—the pajamas Diane was wearing the night of the attack somehow disappeared that morning and were never found again—and clearly misinterpreted the crime scene.[82] For hours after Cecil's body was discovered the Fairbanks police were reporting that he'd been bludgeoned to death, his skull smashed "by blows inflicted by some sort of instrument," but when Dr. Paul Haggland examined the corpse Saturday afternoon, he quickly found a .38-caliber bullet hole above the left ear and an exit wound on the opposite side of the skull. "When Dr. Haggland made this discovery during the examination," the *News-Miner* reported, "he said the bullet or the ejected cartridge should be in the bed. He then shook the bedclothes and the ejected cartridge dropped out. The slug was found in the pillow . . . under Wells' head."[83]

Worst of all, in Stevens's opinion, Chief Danforth, who had come under fire repeatedly for missteps since taking office in the spring, was refusing to cooperate with the district attorney's office, the U.S. Marshal, or the territorial police, shutting them out of the case completely. Danforth denied that, however, saying he was only trying to keep the investigation proceeding in an orderly fashion. Snedden blasted the local police in a page-one editorial that same afternoon, headlined "Crime Out of Control."

> In the shocking killing today, the usual friction between law enforcement agencies was quick to show itself. The city police took over the investigation of the crime, excluding marshals and even the district attorney's office. No report of the murder had been made to the D.A. up until noon today.
>
> The majority of our law enforcement officers in this region are only bystanders today, and the city police carry out complete investigation of the crime.
>
> We hope fervently that the police can solve this shocking murder. But we can't see why they should try to do it alone. . . .
>
> The city police, territorial police and the marshal's office should be working together as one unit, doing their utmost to stamp out lawlessness in this area.
>
> As things stand now, we have three agencies working against each other in many cases, and the

criminal is the big winner. WE NEED COORDI-
NATION AMONG OUR LAW ENFORCMENT
AGENCIES, AND WE NEED IT NOW![84]

On Monday morning Stevens said he would force Chief Danforth to allow full participation of federal and territorial officers in the Wells investigation, but it took a five-and-a-half-hour marathon meeting in the DA's office to make the chief acquiesce.[85] Stevens's rationale was simple. Unlike a state with a state court system having jurisdiction over most criminal cases, Alaska's district courts were all federal courts, and therefore all felonies in Alaska were automatically under federal jurisdiction. Snedden applauded the move by Stevens to get involved in the investigation.

"Both the territorial police and the marshal's office were 'shouldered out' of the investigation into Cecil Wells' death," the *News-Miner* stated. "Today, the D.A. took action to force the participation of both offices in the current investigation. This is certainly a wise move. When we have a dozen or more qualified men standing on the sidelines as a shocking murder is being probed, the situation doesn't make sense."[86]

The conflict between Danforth and Stevens over the handling of the Wells case came to a boil a few weeks later, when the federal grand jury that Stevens had impaneled concluded that the chief was "not qualified" and should either resign or be fired.[87] Danforth accused the DA of misusing the grand jury for a personal vendetta against him. "In the first place, it is not up to the grand jury to tell the city council how to run city government," Danforth stated. "Mr. Ted Stevens, the district attorney, has had a hostile attitude toward me ever since the murder of Cecil Wells. . . . Clearly, the D.A. has used the grand jury by presenting his differences with me to act for his own selfish interests."[88]

The *News-Miner* welcomed the grand jury's recommendations and urged the city to heed its advice, most notably to get rid of the chief of police and to support Stevens. "We stand behind the 19 members of the grand jury," the *News-Miner* pledged, and asked every honest citizen to stand "BEHIND EVERY HONEST PUBLIC OFFICIAL WHO FIGHTS THE ROTTEN CRIME SITUATION THAT NOW EXISTS IN THE FOURTH DIVISION."[89] Mayor Rivers condemned the *News-Miner* for its "loose statements about rottenness, lawlessness and intolerable conditions," denied that the city was experiencing a crime wave, and charged that the grand jury's attack on Danforth, egged on by the district attorney, was "a blow beneath the belt."[90]

To the satisfaction of Snedden and Stevens, Danforth resigned as Fairbanks chief of police on November 30, 1953.[91] By that time Stevens believed the Wells case had been solved. Eighteen days after Cecil's murder, Stevens convinced the grand jury to indict the widow, Diane, on a first-degree murder charge, along with Johnny Warren, a part-time grocery clerk and jazz drummer in Fairbanks. Warren, the leader of the Johnny Warren Band, had allegedly been having an affair with Diane since early September, and Stevens believed they had conspired to kill her husband. The DA thought he could present a reputable case with the contradictory statements Diane had made and a twenty-three-page statement Warren had given Oakland police, in which he confessed to sleeping with Diane even though he denied any connection to the murder. Warren also admitted he had owned a .38-caliber pistol, which he claimed to have sold the day before the crime, and that he had been at the Northward Building on the night of the shooting and had hurriedly left town at five o'clock the next morning—all coincidences, he claimed.[92]

What made the Wells and Warren indictments a front-page scandal was that Warren was part African-American. The salacious details of the affair between a blonde bombshell and a "colored" jazz drummer accused of premeditated murder made headlines around the country. The blonde-and-the-deadly-drummer story even hit the pages of *Newsweek* and *Life* magazines, not to mention *Official Detective* and *Front Page Detective*. The sensational treatment in *Life*—which called it "The Case of the Beat-Up Blonde"—could have been lifted from an installment of Perry Mason. It featured a picture of Diane's badly bruised face and a series of photos from the *News-Miner*, including a staged reenactment of the crime with Diane playing herself and *News-Miner* editor Jack Ryan playing the part of one of the masked intruders she said had assaulted her.[93]

One of the *News-Miner* photographs that appeared in both *Life* and *Newsweek*, as well as countless newspapers around the country, was a shot by staff photographer Jim Douthit of a banquet at the Fairbanks Country Club, which included all three principals in the Wells-Warren-Wells murder–love affair triangle: in the foreground to the left are Cecil and Diane Wells, talking and eating at the banquet table, while in the background on the far right Johnny Warren is beating the drums. "This picture was carried on the wirephoto circuits to virtually every newspaper in the United States," the *News-Miner* explained about a year after the murder. "It has appeared on national newsstands about once a month since the sensational shooting took place."[94] On the day of the indictments of Wells and

Warren, the *News-Miner* dug the country club photo out of the archives and gave it large play on top of the front page, with the ill-starred trio identified by arrows. The caption read in part "Diane Wells is gazing into the eyes of her husband and smiling, as he smiles back."[95]

The next day Dr. Harvey Anderson wrote an angry letter complaining about the "ludicrous caption" and the paper's inability to resist sensationalizing the story. Anderson complained the entire coverage of the Wells case had been a clear-cut example of "lead poisoning" by the newspaper staff. The editors of the *News-Miner* felt it necessary to respond:

> Reader Anderson is entitled to his own opinion of News-Miner coverage of the Wells case. One thing we would like to point out however is that the News-Miner has been very careful to present facts in this case accurately, and we have NOT been handing out "jazzed up news." We have made mistakes in quoting witnesses on occasions, and we have reported some evidence incorrectly, but we have, in every case where we discovered our mistake, gone over the point again and corrected ourselves in print.
>
> We have not handled this case in a sensational manner, and if reader Anderson doesn't believe this, he should check on what newspapers in the States are printing.[96]

One interested reader who agreed that the *News-Miner* was handling the Wells story straightforwardly compared to other publications was Diane Wells. She said she'd been "snowed under" by long-distance calls from reporters with papers such as the *New York Herald American*, the *San Francisco Examiner*, and the *London Daily Mail* and she appreciated the responsible way the *News-Miner* was handling the case. "In view of all the false rumors, speculation and even some facts that are circulating," Wells wrote, "I believe the News-Miner has shown admirable restraint in its reporting. In each case where I have been the newspaper's source of information, I have been quoted practically word for word."[97]

Stevens wanted to try Diane Wells and Johnny Warren together because, he said, it was "a plain and simple case of murder, and nothing else." The attorneys representing Wells, Charles Clasby—Stevens's former employer—and Walter Sczudlo, asked for separate trials for the defendants, in separate cities, claiming that if her case was not severed from Warren's, racial prejudice would make it impossible to receive justice. Sczudlo told the court that ever since the murder the "young and attractive" widow "has been the object of a morbid and sensational journalistic effort to implicate her romantically with the co-defendant, Johnny Warren, who is a part Negro, part time musician." The "lurid" implications by both the local and national press had shifted the question from who shot Cecil Wells to who was sleeping with Diane Wells. Because of this tabloid treatment from every newspaper, including the *News-Miner*, "the death of Cecil Wells has reached a secondary role" compared with Diane's love affairs, raising an "implication of social misconduct on the part of Mrs. Wells far overshadowing the charge of murder." Sczudlo argued that "racial prejudice and bias . . . would be generated in the court if the two were present at the same time," and that furthermore "the alleged relationship between the two would be more in the minds of the jurors than the murder itself."[98] For example, the *Newsweek* story about the case the previous week was called "Drummer and Blonde."[99] As further proof, Sczudlo said, the judge only had to look around: "there were many more people in attendance in the court room listening to the hearing than there were at Cecil Wells' funeral." Additionally, he submitted clippings about the case into evidence, including an editorial, photos, and articles that had appeared in the *News-Miner*—one headlined "Diane Wells, Johnny Warren Nabbed"—and the "more lurid stories from the states and other cities in the territory." It was this coverage, Sczudlo claimed, that had "kept the murder alive."[100]

Stevens rebutted all the charges, denying that the newspapers had created a prejudicial atmosphere. According to the *News-Miner* reporter at the courthouse, "District Attorney Stevens defended the local papers in their coverage of the case, saying it was good reporting and nothing else that has kept the case alive," and that "the only racial prejudice he was aware of rested in the defense counsel's mind."[101]

The first-degree murder trial for Diane Wells and Johnny Warren was scheduled to start on April 5, 1954, but they never had their day in court.[102] On March 9, 1954, in a hotel room in Hollywood, California, Diane Wells swallowed thirty sleeping pills. A cryptic suicide note read: "For one thing, I am guilty too for ever seeing Warren. If Warren is guilty. . . . One thing is for sure, Cecil is dead and I must be the cause of it, one way or another."[103]

Though the charges against Johnny Warren stayed open for another six years, the suicide of Diane Wells essentially ended any hope of bringing him to trial. Stevens privately told a sergeant with the Los Angeles Police Department in 1955 that without Diane he didn't have enough to convict Warren unless additional evidence could be found. "Because of the nature of the testimony we had," Stevens said, "most of it being Diane's statement and proof that we had that the alibis she had were not true, we sort of know that we will lose Warren if we go to trial, yet they are afraid if they press us to go to trial we are liable to win, so we are both sitting on the side of the fence looking at each other."[104] In a bitter courtroom battle with Warren Taylor in 1955, Stevens did win a perjury charge against William Colombany, a ballroom-dancing instructor who was one of Diane's confidants. But whoever shot Cecil Wells was never brought to justice.[105]

Stevens never had another case with the notoriety of the Wells murder. He resigned as Fairbanks district attorney in June 1956, and initially he hoped to be transferred to Juneau. When that fell through he left the Justice Department and accepted a post in Washington, D.C., as a legislative counsel for the U.S. Department of the Interior. Upon the announcement of Stevens's resignation, Snedden praised his young friend's hard work, character, and discipline, which he believed Stevens had demonstrated every day on the job in resisting the "heavy hand of pressure groups who would 'open the city' to gambling or vice." Despite a tiny staff and huge workload, Stevens had "enforced the law, prosecuted violators with vigor, and resisted all pressure put on him to 'overlook' illegal activities."[106]

The junior attorney who had come north with no trial experience was returning to Washington as a veteran prosecutor with the battle scars to prove it. His temper might not have noticeably improved, but Stevens left Fairbanks with a far deeper appreciation for the limitations and opportunities of life in territorial Alaska, an invaluable education for the role he would play as Snedden's chief contact in the Eisenhower administration during the crucial years of the statehood fight from 1956 to 1958.

Fairbanks U.S. attorney, 1953–1956, Theodore Fulton Stevens.

C. W. Snedden (right) and his protégé, former News-Miner attorney Ted Stevens.

TANANA VALLEY BAR ASSOCIATION
FAIRBANKS, ALASKA

November 19, 1953

Honorable Herbert Brownell, Jr.
Attorney General of the United States
Washington, D. C.

Dear Sir:

    We, the undersigned, members of the Tanana Valley
Bar Association of the Fourth Division, Territory of Alaska,
are opposed to the appointment of Theodore F. Stevens as United
States Attorney for the Fourth Division, Territory of Alaska.
Mr. Stevens has served as United States Attorney under a
temporary appointment, as endorsed by the Tanana Valley Bar
Association, for approximately three months and has failed to
exercise mature judgment and reasonable discretion in the
exercise of the duties incident to that office. We believe
that he does not have the experience or is qualified to perform
the duties of United States Attorney.

    There are sixteen lawyers admitted to the bar, and
practicing law in the Fourth Division of Alaska. If a qualified
man can be found, a large majority of us would be pleased to
recommend his appointment.

                                     Respectfully submitted,

After Stevens's first three months as acting DA, fourteen of the sixteen attorneys practicing in Fairbanks protested that he should not be given the permanent presidential appointment and sent this formal complaint to U.S. Attorney General Brownell. Snedden believed the lawyers were angry primarily because the rookie prosecutor was doing too good a job and making the defense attorneys work too hard to defend their clients. Author's collection.

A front page photo of Ted Stevens (center) and his assistant George Yeager (right), being sworn in by long-time court clerk, John B. "Dixie" Hall, as United States attorneys in Fairbanks on April 15, 1954. At the request of the *News-Miner* this was the first occasion photographs were ever allowed inside the Fairbanks courthouse.

The *News-Miner*, Stevens's faithful ally during his three-year reign as district attorney, cheered his permanent appointment despite the strong objections of local attorneys.

Personalized ...
PRINTING is the specialty of the Daily News-Miner Commercial Printing Department ... Quality printing designed to fit YOUR need at reasonable cost.

FAIRBANKS
Daily News - Miner
America's Farthest North Daily Newspaper   Member of The Associated Press

WEATHER
Partly cloudy tonight, increasing Thursday with light snow. The low tonight -10, high Thursday 1; not last night -5, high yesterday 4. The temperature at noon today -1. Sunrise Thursday 6:41 a.m., sunset 5:55 p.m.

VOLUME XXX   10c Per Copy   FAIRBANKS, ALASKA, WEDNESDAY, MARCH 5, 1953   Eight Pages   No. 95

Ladd Commander Blasts Fairbanks Vice Conditions

Politicians Set Their Sights On Primaries

New Hampshire Voters Undecided As Election Nears

By The ASSOCIATED PRESS

'52 Winter Carnival Queen To Be Selected Tonight

By PHOEBE CLARK

Weeks Field Injunction Is Denied Here

City Learns Of Unpaid Utility Bills

Local Insurance Man Wins Honor

Milk Truck Foils Prison Break Plan At Walla Walla

WALLA WALLA, Wash., March 5

Internated Scot Inally Lands Job

LONDON, March 5

Gen. Smith Demands Cleanup; Seeks Aid of Local Chamber

Ladd Chief Says Military Authorities Will Take Strong Measures to Protect Servicemen From Vice If Fairbanks Officials Don't Act

By JIM DOUTHIT

Here's Job List Today

FEMALE HELP

MALE HELP

Alaska, Japan Being Guarded By New Radar-guided Jets

American Planes Bag Five MIG's

SEOUL, Korea, March 5

Lou Larson Wins Cribbage Tourney

Treasury Official Is Questioned

WASHINGTON, March 5

Portland Visitor Addresses C. of C.

PROPOSED SPORTS ARENA

Prostitution, gambling, and a flood of alcohol were at the core of Fairbanks's perennial vice problems. Stevens's attempts to "close" the city generated ferocious opposition. Stevens gained notoriety by carrying a gun and accompanying police on high-profile arrests that landed on the front page, such as that of bar owner "Curly" Urban for murder (right), photographed as he was being cuffed and led off to jail.

Nightclub Operator Arraigned On 1st Degree Murder Charge

By CHUCK HOYT

Leon Devere Urban, also known as Curly, was arrested at 7 o'clock Saturday night at the Alibi club on a charge of first degree murder.

Urban, 45, was charged with beating Myrtle Patricia Cathey on or about January 22, ultimately causing her death January 31 in St. Joseph's hospital.

ANNOUNCING THE OPENING
of the
DRIVE-IN LIQUOR STORE
AT THE CORNER OF 13th and GILLAM

**Opening Special
SEAGRAMS "7"**

$**4**^{29} Fifth

Now . . . you can drive in and fill your liquor needs from a fine selection of "name" brand liquors . . . all at popular prices. There's plenty of parking space . . . fast service at the new DRIVE-IN LIQUOR STORE . . . come out today, avoid the rush and confusion.

OPENING SPECIAL

GILBEY'S GIN

$**3**^{59} Fifth

Lots of Parking • Competitive Prices

at the new, convenient

DRIVE-IN LIQUOR STORE

Fairbanks had a plentiful supply of liquor stores and bars (left and below), which inspired *News-Miner* reporter Chuck Hoyt (right) to put the Drunkometer to the test, in order to prove that police were serious in the battle against drunk driving. Dissatisfaction with the local police department in 1953 prompted a controversial ad in the *News-Miner* (lower right), urging "Thieves, Thugs, Burglars and Murderers" to start a crime spree.

NEW and BEAUTIFUL

*Fairbanks' Most
Beautiful Cocktail
Lounge has a*
"New Look"

TODAY . . . .

WE WANT TO INVITE ALL OF OUR FRIENDS AND CUSTOMERS DOWN TODAY TO INSPECT OUR ULTRA PLUSH NEW DECOR

**OPEN AT:
4:00 P.M.**

MECCA BAR

549 2nd   Dial 5500

Chuck's
NEVADA BAR

The beautiful showplace
of Alaska's Golden Past

REMOVING THE BULLET FROM THE HEART OF SOAPY SMITH — SKAGWAY — 1898.

Only one of our famous early day photographs hanging today on our walls.

SEE
SNAKE HIPS
from
Dawson, Y.T.

SEE
LIVENGOOD
Alaska's last stampede town—1915

SEE THE FABULOUS Collection of Pictures and Antiques of Early Alaska

SEE
**FAIRBANKS
BURNING**
1906

Meet Your
Friends
Here For
A Cool Drink

SEE
The Stampede
Through
**CHILKOOT
PASS**

605 FIRST AVENUE

Reporter Tests Drunkometer

Machine Bares Condition Of Accused Drivers Here

(Editor's Note: The Territorial police have obtained a Harger Drunkometer for use in determining the guilt or innocence of drivers accused of operating a vehicle while under the influence. Charles R. Hoyt, News-Miner staff reporter, volunteered to take a test under supervision of the police. His story, printed below, shows that the new drunkometer is accurate and will prove, to the decimal point, the amount of alcohol a driver has consumed. Local motorists should keep this mind during the coming holiday season.)

By Charles R. Hoyt

What one won't do for the sake of science.

When approached by Lt. Wm. Trafton of the territorial police to test their new Harger Drunkometer and carry a picture story about the test in the News-Miner, my editor, Sourdough Jack Ryan declared the paper very willing to go along with the tests and would even furnish a guinia pig, in the shape of myself, of course.

I thusly volunteered to demonstrate to wayward drivers the futility of driving after leaving one's favorite pub, because I learned at an early age that gasoline and strong spirits do not mix. (I used to drive the garbage truck).

Test Arranged

The test was arranged and scheduled for 3 p.m. last Monday. With typical efficiency, Ryan, photographer Jim Douthit and myself arrived at the territorial police headquarters, an hour late, but raring to go. Ryan and Douthit, I mean. I was the one to sample the 100 proof bottle of Country' Fair whiskey in copious quantities and go down in the annals of the territorial police as a martyr, but by no means immune to future arrests. In fact I am now quite vulnerable, as my capacity is known.

The Harger Drunkometer is a small deceptive looking machine, that looks innocent, but take it from one who learned from sanity to insensibility, an alcoholic driver is a cinch for a $250 rap. because that machine just can't be fooled.

Patrolmen Present

Present at the test were Territorial Patrolman Burton Finley, who was to give the test; Lt. Snyder of the Air Force who was to act as official observer, and Lt. Trafton, who purchased the whiskey used by myself who is hereafter referred to as the "subject".

In the terminology of the Territorial police, the subject, had his first two ounces of 100 proof whiskey, chased by water at 3:48 p.m. The Subject was given a card sorting test, which he completed in 40 seconds with no mistakes. A reaction time test on a gadget of Lt. Snyder's that simulates a car gas pedal and brake pedal situation was given, with the elapsed time the Subject was able to take his foot from the gas pedal and apply the brakes to an emergency being .413 hundreds of a second. A color blindness test

victims stay away from this test as the floor is slanted.)

Another Harger test was given one and a half hours after the first drink with the result determining that .157% of alcohol was in the blood system. This was approximately eight ounces of whiskey in the subjects blood, and brands the subject as definitely under the influence.

After the seventh and final drink, the Subject sorted the cards in 50 seconds with no mistakes, but his reaction time was down and an attempt to walk the straight line with head back, eyes closed and hands at side was again a miserable failure.

Again Tested

Twenty-five minutes later, Subject was again given the reaction test, with the result slightly better than the previous test, and he sorted the cards in 50 seconds with no mistakes.

A third drunkometer test was given two hours from the time of the first drink. The results found .165% of alcohol in the blood.

At two hours and 37 minutes from the first drink, the Subject was again given the test, with the finding being that he had .193% of alcohol in the blood. About 11 ounces of whiskey in the blood. According to the test, the Subject has about reached the maximum point of intoxication.

Balloon Used

At this point, the Subject wishes to make clear that the amount of alcohol in the blood of a person is determined by blowing up a balloon, generously furnished by the Territorial police for just this purpose. The drunkometer measures accurately the amount of alcohol which is being given off by the Subject's lungs. This is a perfect indication of how much alcohol there is in the Subject's blood.

The innocent balloon, a child's toy in normal life, is capable of

DRUNKOMETER TEST BEGINS—Here is Charles R. Hoyt, News-Miner staff reporter, pictured as he commenced the Drunkometer test under the supervision of Territorial police. Hoyt volunteered for the test, in an effort to prove the accuracy of the meter. He proved that as more and more whisky was consumed out of the bottle, the Drunkometer showed a larger percentage of alcohol in his blood with an amazing degree of accuracy. The Drunkometer, shown in foreground, can't be fooled.

THIS IS THE DRUNKOMETER—Here is the Harger Drunkometer, a new gadget that proves beyond doubt whether the person being tested is drunk or sober. Territorial police have put the meter in use in an effort to bring drunken drivers to justice. A police officer's finger points to the indicator which shows the percentage of alcohol in the subject's blood.

SPECIAL SECTION
Honoring 50th Anniversary of Powered Flight . . . Second section of today's issue, page 9.

⎯⎯⎯ FAIRBANKS ⎯⎯⎯
Daily News - Miner
"America's Farthest North Daily Newspaper" · · · Member of The Associated Press

WEATHER
Generally clear and cold tonight, becoming partly cloudy on Sunday. Low tonight, 12. High Sunday, 35. High yesterday, 45. Low last night, 15. Noon temperature 30.

VOLUME XXXI   10¢ Per Copy   FAIRBANKS, ALASKA, SATURDAY, OCTOBER 17, 1953   Fourteen Pages   No. 244

CECIL WELLS MURDERED IN BEDROOM; WIFE, DIANA, FOUND BADLY BEATEN

Pioneers of Aviation Are Honored Here

News-Miner Prints Special Section To Mark Occasion

35 Killed as Heavy Blast Rocks Carrier

Seek Cause of Explosion on Fighting Ship

BOSTON, Oct. 17, (P)—An explosion and flash fire turned the lee-deck compartments of the aircraft carrier Leyte into a smoke-choking inferno yesterday.

JOHNSON APARTMENTS FIRE—

PROMINENT BUSINESSMAN DEAD—Cecil Wells, owner of Wells Alaska Motors and president of the Alaska Chamber of Commerce.

Wife Crawls for Assistance; Police Seeking Death Clues

Cecil Wells, prominent Fairbanks businessman and president of the All-Alaska Chamber of Commerce, was found bludgeoned to death in the bedroom of his eighth floor apartment in the Northward building shortly after seven o'clock this morning. The murder was discovered when his pretty wife, Diana, bleeding and beaten, crawled to the door of a neighboring apartment and aroused the tenants.

Police who arrived on the scene found that Wells' skull had been injured by blows inflicted by some sort of an instrument. He apparently was killed in his sleep. His skull was apparently cracked, and there were small holes in it apparently inflicted by a protrusion on the death instrument. There was no evidence that he had been shot.

At 7:15 a.m. this morning, Mrs. Wells beat on the door of apartment 812, just across the hall from the suite of rooms occupied by the Wells. The occupant, Mrs. Alley Drywood opened the door and found Mrs. Wells in the hall floor, badly beaten, with blood dried on her face. Mrs. Wells screamed to Mrs. Drywood to call a doctor. She was hysterical and incoherent.

Police and ambulance drivers arrived on the scene. Mrs. Wells, still hysterical, blurted out this story.

WERE IN BED

She said she and her husband were in bed when she heard an intruder in the bedroom. The intruder made her husband get up. She leaped from the bed and ran to the front room where she shot a second intruder who beat her severely. She said she didn't remember anything after that.

Police found a wallet belonging to Cecil Wells on the hall floor of the building, a few feet from the front door of the Wells apartment. The wallet was empty.

BAD CONDITION

Wells appeared to be in good bad condition fire department ambulance drivers Marv Ramos and John Madson decided to rush a doctor immediately, before attempting to take Wells to the hospital. Doctor Donald McLean of the Fairbanks clinic answered the call and immediately went to the scene. He gave emergency treatment to Mrs. Wells, and the woman was then taken to the hospital. She was told that her husband was dead but she didn't seem to comprehend this fact. She kept pleading, in the drives to "take him to the hospital, take him to the hospital." She told them that her husband was hurt worse than she.

NO ROBBERY MOTIVE

In spite of the fact an empty wallet was found near the body, Chief of Police E. V. Danforth, who is personally conducting the investigation of the crime, said that robbery apparently was not the motive. There were many valuables in the apartment that were not touched, he said.

Police found crushed flower pots, dirt and broken flowers on the floor of the apartment. This was the only indication that a struggle had taken place. There was considerable blood in the apartment, both on the death bed where Wells' body was found and on the floor. There was a trickle of dried blood on the floor, apparently made by Mrs. Wells, which extended from the point where smashed flower pots were found to the door of the apartment.

FOUND ON BACK

Wells was found lying on his back, in a relaxed position, with the covers over him. There was every indication that he had been killed in his sleep.

Businesses were found on the davenport. The couple had been packing to leave for Anchorage today to attend CAB hearings scheduled next week. According to friends, Mr. and Mrs. Wells had attended the late show last night, and later went to their apartment. Then, they had guests, and drinks had been served. It was not known what time the guests departed.

Police said today that they had not yet identified the murder instrument. However, Chief of Police Dan-

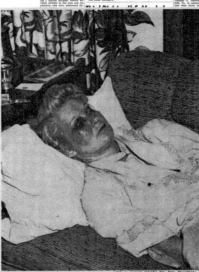

(News-Miner Photo by Jim Douthit)

THREE DAYS AFTER—Mrs. Diana Wells, widow of slain businessman Cecil Wells, is pictured above as she recovered from the effects of a beating administered to her during the crime. The picture was taken last night, three days after the blows were showered on her face. Both eyes are still black, her mouth is swollen, her face is puffed and colored yellow and blue and she has lacerations about the scalp as well as her face.

Mrs. Wells Describes Terror Of Sudden Attack in Apartment

By JOHN J. RYAN

Speaking tearfully, through swollen lips, Mrs. Diana Wells last night described how two brutal intruders killed her husband and beat her beyond recognition.

Three days after the crime, Mrs. Wells' eyes are still shiny black, her jaw is puffed, her nose is lumped out of shape, her lips are swollen and thick, and there are lacerations scattered on her face and⊕

The murder of Cecil Wells and the brutal beating of his wife, Diana, was prosecutor Stevens's first and highest-profile case. The unsolved crime would shadow his entire tenure in the U.S. Attorney's office.

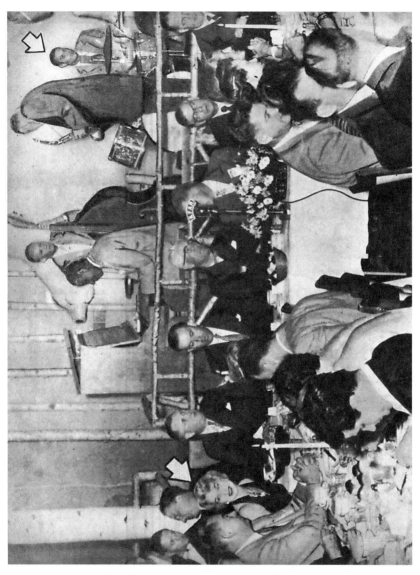

By chance at a banquet at the Fairbanks Country Club, *News-Miner* photographer Jim Douthit happened to photograph all three individuals in the Wells/Warren love affair-murder-suicide triangle. Two months after the murder, the newspaper ran the photo again, this time with arrows pointing out the principals. "The arrow at right points to Johnny Warren, colored drummer at the club," the caption stated, while the arrow on the left shows "Diana Wells...gazing into the eyes of her husband and smiling, as he smiles back." Seated at the head table immediately behind and left of Mrs. Wells is former *News-Miner* editor Bill Strand; to the right of the KFAR microphone is Delegate Bob Bartlett.

The bungling of the Wells case by local officials pitted DA Stevens against the chief of police. The grand jury and the *News-Miner* sided with the DA. With the suicide of Diane Wells in the spring of 1954, the case against Johnny Warren collapsed.

7

States' Rights and Civil Rights

Delegate Bob Bartlett was "immensely heartened" when he learned on March 5, 1954, that the *News-Miner* had joined the statehood camp. "I have moved over on the bench to give you plenty of room," he wrote Jack Ryan, and asked the editor to airmail two copies of the paper's first editorial supporting statehood to his office in Washington.[1] A week later Bartlett felt comfortable enough to begin addressing Snedden on a first-name basis. "Everyone else refers to you as Bill Snedden so I trust you will permit me to abandon the formality which has heretofore marked my salutations to you in correspondence."[2] In return Snedden dropped "Mr. Bartlett" as well, marking the start of a friendship and collaboration across party lines that would last until Bartlett's sudden death almost fifteen years later.

"Anyone who has read the *News-Miner* regularly is aware that we are admirers of the policies of the Republican party," Snedden wrote in October 1954 when he first endorsed Bartlett for reelection. "But," he added, "the *News-Miner* is an Independent newspaper," and though Bartlett may have been the titular head of the Democratic Party in Alaska, Snedden thought the delegate's "long and valiant battle to win full citizenship for all Alaskans" meant he deserved the support of all Alaskans, regardless of political affiliation.[3]

As a new convert not disillusioned by the repeated defeats of the past, and not yet fully cognizant of the scope of the entrenched opposition in Washington, D.C., Snedden hoped optimistically that the statehood battle might be won within a matter of months. "The *News-Miner* will do what it can towards advancing the cause of Statehood in the very sincere hope that something can be accomplished during the present session of Congress."⁴ But Delegate Bartlett warned Snedden that the chances of passing a statehood bill in 1954 were not favorable. "I cannot make any prediction on the possible outcome of the statehood effort" anytime soon, but he said if he "were a bookmaker" he would take odds against it.⁵

Bartlett had good reason for pessimism. By 1954 the statehood cause for Alaska and Hawaii had bogged down in a Byzantine political stalemate on Capitol Hill that showed no sign of ending. Alaska statehood bills had been introduced in every session of Congress since 1943, only to be repeatedly defeated by congressional inertia, inaction, and political intrigue. These measures did not wither from a lack of public sympathy or support. In the United States in the 1950s the prospect of admitting Alaska and Hawaii into the Union was about as popular as peace and prosperity. Year after year opinion polls registered less than 10 percent of Americans opposed to Alaska statehood, but this abstract affection had never been translated into concrete political action. "Just about everyone in the country seems to be for statehood," Bartlett once said, "except this group in the Congress."⁶ George Gallup said the congressional stalemate over admitting Alaska and Hawaii was a classic case of the "lag between public opinion and legislative action."⁷

Snedden and many other residents not intimately familiar with the ways of Washington, D.C., assumed congressional inaction was largely due to the widespread myths about Alaska as a frozen wasteland. Based on the misinformed comments he had read about Alaska in the *Congressional Record* Snedden figured the best service the *News-Miner* could offer in the statehood fight would be to provide continuing education about the territory for senators and congressmen, as a way of rebutting the opposition's continual repetition of half-truths and wholehearted lies about the territory. For instance, Sen. George A. Smathers (D-Florida) had picked up the bizarre notion that the reason there was no road to Alaska's capital city of Juneau—which is built on rock every bit as solid as any part of the North American continent—was that the entire community had been constructed on some sort of floating iceberg. "Because Juneau sits on an ice formation which continues to move back and forth with the change of the seasons," Smathers authoritatively told one of his Florida constituents, "it is impossible to build roads as we presently know them, to Juneau."

Anchorage Times publisher Bob Atwood, who never particularly cared for Juneau himself, thought this was "just about as crazy a statement as anyone could make" and proof of the senator's "enormous stupidity." It left him wondering "where Juneau has moved to today?"[8]

Snedden thought the "appalling ignorance and misconceptions prevailing among the learned gentlemen in our nation's capital" about Alaska was proof of the "tremendous educational job" needed to paint "a true picture of what the facts and conditions are up here."[9] It led him to suggest that the *News-Miner* underwrite publication of a booklet that would summarize the essential facts about the territory, particularly "stressing what Alaska as a State has to offer the United States," and mail it with a cover letter to every member of Congress. "I would appreciate your opinion," he wrote Bartlett, "as to whether this project could possibly be of any practical effect."[10]

While such a booklet could be a valuable reference, Bartlett urged Snedden to save the money. Given the volume of mail that congressmen received on a typical day, he thought at best no more than 5 percent would ever read it. But as a former reporter used to working on a short string, Bartlett cautiously offered another plan. "I do have an alternative suggestion which may not be worth a hoot. Could you print a special section in the *News-Miner* incorporating the same text you would use in the pamphlet and surround it with some advertising to help pay its way?"[11]

Following Bartlett's suggestion, Snedden and Ryan prepared a six-page "Statehood Edition" published on Friday, April 9, 1954, including more than a half-dozen editorials and features summarizing all the reasons why Alaska deserved the rights and responsibilities of full statehood immediately. The 1954 statehood special was the first in what would be a four-year flood of words flowing from the editorial pages of the *News-Miner* trumpeting the facts of Alaska as it was, and the promise of what it could be.

The supplement at first glance was indistinguishable from a regular issue of the newspaper, but closer reading revealed differently. The weather forecast on the top of page one should have been a hint: "the business climate in Alaska will improve with statehood. As things stand now, expansion is bogged down, and enterprise is snowed under by high taxes and excessive cost of living. Naturally, Alaskans have no control over this weather."

A disclaimer made clear that this issue had only a single purpose: "We hope it is thoroughly understood that this special edition is not NEWS reported as such. This paper is made up entirely of editorial opinions of

the *Fairbanks Daily News-Miner.*"The lead editorial stated the only thing
remarkable about the six-page supplement was that the sixty men and
women who worked at the *News-Miner* and produced it, all of whom
were natural-born U.S. citizens, were denied the full rights of American
citizenship. "You who live in the United States and read this newspaper
are fortunate. You have the precious rights of an American citizen. We,
who have published this paper, do not have these rights." Unable to vote
for president and lacking a "voting voice" in Congress, the "members of
this newspaper staff are in a boat with some 180,000 other Alaskans. All
of us are disfranchised, helpless Americans."

Snedden's April 1954 statehood special tackled questions such as
"Why Statehood?," "Is Alaska Ready?," "Can Alaska Afford It?," and "Is
Alaska American?" These would be the same arguments supporters and
opponents would debate endlessly over the next four years, as none of the
substantial questions would ever change. The issue's underlying theme,
the argument that lay at the core of Snedden's belief in the need for
statehood, was that fundamentally Alaska was no different from any of
the forty-eight states, and that Alaskans were no different from other
Americans, except that territorial residents were denied the basic democratic rights of their fellow citizens.[12]

The page-one aerial view of downtown Fairbanks might as well have
been captioned "Anywhere, USA." The description said Fairbanks could
easily be mistaken for "a thousand different cities in the United States"
with a "modern business district including two structures that rank as
'skyscrapers.' A glance at this picture proves that Fairbanks is an American
city in every sense of the word 'city.'" Other pictures on the inside showed
a group of well-fed dignitaries at a typical Chamber of Commerce dinner,
a classroom at Point Barrow proving "that children learn the three 'R's'
in the most remote parts of Alaska the same as they do in public schools
of our large American cities," and one of the true signs of modern urban
America, a U.S. Postal Service van with thirteen local postal workers "who
launched door-to-door mail delivery service in Fairbanks."[13]

Snedden's goal was to counteract the charges that because the population was too small, the distances too far, and the climate too cold, the
territory could never afford self-government. But the facts were not always enough. When conservative Nevada Democrat Sen. George "Molly"
Malone said Alaska did not deserve statehood because it was noncontiguous and lacked population, Bob Bartlett said a skeptical reporter was
shocked to hear that argument from a senator representing the most
sparsely populated state in the United States, a desert wasteland whose

economic livelihood rested on atomic testing, divorce, and gambling (and had been home to only some twenty thousand people when it became a state in 1864). Momentarily stunned, according to Bartlett, the newsman "reeled back and then pressed forward to renew the assault by asking, 'But how can a man from Nevada say that?' Molly leaned forward confidentially, put his hand to his mouth and whispered, 'But we're in.'" [14]

As Malone's dirty little secret revealed, the most serious roadblocks to Alaska statehood had nothing to do with its distant location, fragile economy, or small population. The reality was that the fate of both Alaska and its sister territory Hawaii were intertwined in partisan and sectional disputes unrelated to conditions in the territories. The heart of the "Alaska Question" was not primarily if Alaska was ready for the United States, but was the United States, and particularly the U.S. Congress, ready for Alaska? This was because Alaska's campaign to join the Union ran head-on into the underlying power structure of the Union itself. The admission of either Alaska or Hawaii threatened to disrupt the prevailing balance of power on Capitol Hill between Democrats and Republicans, and northern Democrats and Dixiecrats, and to weaken the entrenched political strength in Congress of the Old South, where the battles over states' rights and civil rights were seen as a bitter continuation of the "War of Yankee Aggression" by other means.

＊＊＊＊＊

Officially, the Democratic Party had been in favor of immediate statehood for both territories ever since President Truman's endorsement in the 1946 State of the Union message, but the truth was far more complex. As the campaign promises played out the majority of Democrats favored admitting Democratic Alaska first, while Republicans thought Republican Hawaii should receive preferential treatment, and as a result both territories were repeatedly blocked. Decision makers on Capitol Hill admitted to the *New York Times* in 1953 that partisan politics "calls the tune on whether Hawaii or Alaska should get priority for admission as the forty-ninth state of the United States." Congressional leaders "make no secret of the fact that party politics is the primary reason why Democrats place Alaska first, and Republicans place Hawaii first in considering the statehood question."[15]

If one party or the other had been in a dominant position, perhaps the statehood question might have been resolved relatively quickly; however, at no time in American history had the Senate been so evenly divided for so long. Throughout the 1950s neither party ever had a secure upper hand. From the convening of the 82nd Congress in 1951, to the adjournment of the 85th Congress in 1959, no more than one or two seats separated Democrats and Republicans. "Political control of the Senate," one editorial writer noted, "has often hung on a heartbeat since 1950."[16] This was literally true in the 83rd Congress from 1953 to 1955, Eisenhower's first two years in office, when due to the deaths of nine sitting senators and one resignation, and the subsequent interim appointments and elections, the Senate had twenty-four changes in the balance of power, with Republicans in control for eleven different stretches, Democrats seven times, and the two parties tied on another six occasions.[17]

Ostensibly power may have been almost evenly divided between Republicans and Democrats, but in truth the Southern Democrats from the old Confederacy and the border states comprised a unified bloc of their own, a de facto third party of Dixiecrats—most often allied with Sen. Robert Taft's (R-Ohio) conservative wing of the Republican Party—that pushed a radically different agenda. With a few notable exceptions, the self-styled "Constitutional Democrats," wanted neither Alaska nor Hawaii to be admitted.

Since the early years of the Republic, suspicions about westward expansion had always lingered in the South. Creation of new states invariably spurred nervous calculations regarding future control of the U.S. Senate, with the future of slavery, the South's "Peculiar Institution," at the heart of the debate. Resigned that the North with its swelling population would dominate the House of Representatives, the Senate became increasingly the citadel of the South, the fortress where the rights of minority white slave owners could be protected from the majority of Americans who opposed slavery. To preserve the fragile ties that bound the Union, free states and slave states usually entered in pairs, such as Indiana and Mississippi (1816–1817), Illinois and Alabama (1818–1819), and the famed Missouri Compromise of 1820 (which among other provisions admitted Maine and Missouri). But the westward march of statehood threatened the survival of slavery, as Southerners knew the West lacked the climatic and economic conditions required for slaveholding, and therefore they cast a cold eye on potential new western states that might naturally restrict the expansion of human bondage, leading eventually to a filibuster-proof majority in Congress that would promote abolition.

As the tribulations of Alaska and Hawaii would demonstrate, Southern suspicions about new states lingered long after Appomattox. In the 1950s Southerners feared the addition of four new senators from outside the South, whether Republicans or Democrats, would permit a coalition of northern Democrats and liberal and moderate Republicans to gain a two-thirds supermajority and enable it to invoke cloture to cut off debate. This would have stripped the South of its doomsday weapon, the filibuster, the right of unlimited debate through which a minority of Southerners could talk any legislation or proposed legislation, motion, rule change, or confirmation to death, by refusing to give up the floor, and thereby stopping all business in the Senate until the majority accepted defeat. For decades the filibuster had been the South's last line of defense, preventing federal anti-lynching laws and stopping federal guarantees for civil rights, voting rights, and fair labor practices that "Constitutional Democrats" deemed an unwarranted imposition on the rights of the states. Stopping Alaska and Hawaii from entering the Union therefore became a southern priority. And the southern bloc was perfectly aligned to keep them out, not only because the near-equal division of the two parties gave the Dixiecrats the swing vote, but also because the Dixiecrats were the gatekeepers of Congress.

Thanks to the one-party rule of Democrats in the South, which gave many southern politicians virtual lifetime tenure, as well as the seniority system, the filibuster, and southern mastery of parliamentary procedure, the South garnered a disproportionate share of legislative power. This was particularly true in the Senate. As one writer claimed in the 1950s, the U.S. Senate was the Confederacy's "unending revenge" for Gettysburg and "the only place in the country where the south did not lose the war."[18] Up to the 1950s Southern politicians had been so extraordinarily effective at halting civil rights legislation designed to protect the rights of African-Americans that the last time the U.S. Senate had passed a civil rights bill, Ulysses S. Grant was president and Union troopers were still on patrol in Dixie.

Focused on the need to stop Alaska and Hawaii, in order to stop cloture and civil rights legislation, the southern obstructionists were ready to use any parliamentary weapons in their bag of tricks to keep the two territories at bay. "All last week the southerners whanged away at Hawaii," Bartlett wrote in late March 1954. "Some of their arguments against statehood for that territory not only border on the ridiculous, but stray clear across the border."[19] Southerners proved repeatedly more willing to fight against Alaska and Hawaii than supporters were willing to fight for them. The unfortunate truth, Bartlett said in 1953, was that the majority of Americans "who are for statehood in a generally affirmative way do not regard it as a burning issue."[20] And even though the Dixiecrats were a minority, the finest legislative generals were on their side, starting with Richard Russell of Georgia, the mastermind behind the opposition to admission of any new states.[21] "Like the heroes of the Confederacy whom he admired," the *New York Times* wrote when Russell died in 1971, "Senator Russell fought for an old South that is dying because it was founded on racial injustice. But like those Confederate captains, he held his ground tenaciously, maneuvered his outnumbered forces with consummate skill, and earned the respect of his keenest foes."[22] The Southern advantage strategically was that all they needed to do to win was to fight a holding action, because delay was a formidable legislative weapon. Once, when a friend chided Russell that filibustering against civil rights was just postponing the inevitable, he admitted that with a little luck he might be able to stop the legislation for only another ten years, but with a lot of luck he might prevail for the next two hundred.[23]

When statehooders such as Ernest Gruening realized the implacable nature of the southern opposition, inspired solely by the cloture-filibuster issue, he found it "extremely depressing." For all practical purposes it left fully one-fifth of the Senate in an "unthinkable position" far beyond the reach of rational politics. "The southerners are obsessed with this issue," Gruening said, "to the point of allowing it to dominate their entire course of conduct."[24]

The man who understood better than anyone else the implacable and desperate nature of the southern opposition to statehood was a fellow son of the South, George H. Lehleitner, an eccentric New Orleans businessman who became the most unlikely champion of Alaska's cause and one of Snedden's closest allies and collaborators. Despite an impoverished childhood—his formal schooling stopped after elementary school because he had to go to work to help support his family—Lehleitner, born in 1906, was a congenital optimist, a cheerful and enthusiastic soul blessed with the natural gift of salesmanship and the ingrained conviction that "no" today might be "yes" tomorrow. "Nobody," his wife once said, "could resist George." Bob Bartlett claimed he could swear "freely and without the possibility of successful contradiction from anyone" that George H. Lehleitner was "one of the mightiest salesman who ever undertook a selling assignment."[25] In the 1930s Lehleitner founded a successful wholesale company that bore his name dealing electric refrigerators and other consumer appliances, but the day after Pearl Harbor he put aside his commercial interests for the duration and enlisted in the U.S. Navy. Subsequently Lehleitner received command of the U.S.S. *Rotanin*, a Crater-class navy cargo ship that sailed throughout the South Pacific in 1944 and 1945.[26]

While on tour in the South Pacific, Captain Lehleitner found a book in the ship's library by a former *New York Times* reporter that changed his outlook on life forever, Clarence K. Streit's *Union Now*. Streit had spent most of the 1930s covering the travails of the League of Nations in Europe. "The world as seen from Geneva," Streit had written in 1931, "appears an Alice in Wonderland world, devoted to the propositions that all nations are created superior, the part is greater than the whole and the day is longer than the year."[27] Horrified at the revival of militarism, the rise of Nazism and fascism, and the inability of the League to do anything constructive about the growing threat to peace, Streit devised a radical plan for the reorganization of the globe, an "Inter-democracy Federal Union" of the world's fifteen leading democratic countries based essentially on the U.S. Constitution, to serve as the nucleus of an eventual one-world government uniting all the peoples on earth. According to Streit, the U.S. Constitution "is already universal in its scope" and perfectly set up to accommodate new partners in freedom. "It allows for the admission to its Union of any state on earth. It never even mentions territory or language. It mentions race and color only to provide that freedom shall never on that account be denied to any man."[28] Streit envisioned that once the democracies were united in "The Union of the Free," its inevitable success would naturally lead other countries to flock to the banner of universal peace and freedom, in the same way that the original thirteen states had absorbed an additional thirty-five states by the 1930s.[29] Taking his lead from Jefferson, Streit wrote a "Declaration of Inter-Dependence and Union" that began: "When in the course of human events it becomes necessary for one free people to unite with other free peoples, and form a common government embodying the fact that they do depend on each other for their freedom, a decent respect to the opinions of mankind requires that they should declare the causes which impel them to the Union. We hold these truths to be self-evident. . . ."

The proposed "Declaration of Inter-Dependence" promised further that a new Constitution for the Union would "provide that non-members shall be admitted to full membership as states are admitted to the U.S.A.—on a basis of equality with the founders. . . . until The Union shall gradually become the government of all mankind and armament be reduced to a world police force."[30]

When Lehleitner came upon Streit's book in the waning months of World War II, he became for the rest of his life a "devout disciple" of Streit and the Federal Union movement. He was most impressed by Streit's "prediction that other and greater conflicts would follow unless the older democracies amalgamated into a Federal Union whose overwhelming strength" would halt "future would-be Hitlers and Napoleons" before they started. "The brilliance of your idea, Clarence," he wrote Streit in a ninetieth birthday wish in 1986, "and its enormous significance for free men everywhere, struck me with great impact and continued to occupy my mind."[31]

Not long after coming upon Streit's book in 1945, Lehleitner landed in the territory of Hawaii for the first time, offloading hundreds of Japanese prisoners of war. "This was my first contact with Hawaii, and I was shocked to see this progressive and loyal community, American to the core, operating under a wholly un-American system of government, whereby its Governor was a presidential political appointee, and its 400,000 inhabitants were without voting representation in our national Congress."[32] He was outraged and distressed at the hypocrisy of "supposedly fighting a war to maintain our own freedom and to restore it to others from whom it had been stripped—and we Americans were depriving almost a half million of our fellow citizens of many prime essentials that were the proper entitlement of free men!"

After Lehleitner returned to civilian life in New Orleans in the spring of 1946, making the world safe for a unified democracy became the goal of his life. "Because I share, with Clarence Streit," he wrote Sen. Russell B. Long in 1955, "his conviction that neither armament, nor armies, nor treaties, nor dollars, can provide us with enduring security from Communism, I also hold his view that our own salvation—and that of other free men—lies in complete political and economic amalgamation with those who share our fundamental traditions and political beliefs."[33] As his contribution to "The Union of the Free" Lehleitner adopted the cause of Hawaiian statehood, convinced that bringing Hawaii into the American Union would be an essential first step toward bringing the United States into the World Union, since "a nation which was not yet ready to extend the equality of statehood to a segment of its own people, because of their ancestry, and, because they were 2,400 miles removed from the nearest state, had a long road to travel before it would accept the idea of federalizing with other peoples even further away."[34]

For about seven years Lehleitner focused his statehood crusade exclusively on Hawaii, since the common wisdom was that Hawaii was more economically developed than Alaska and thus a more likely candidate for quicker statehood. It was also believed that as soon as Hawaii was admitted, Alaska would follow quickly on its heels. But in truth the two states were caught in the same ideological and partisan trap that by the mid-1950s threatened to derail statehood for both territories permanently.

Lehleitner found some senators and representatives opposed to admitting new states because it would diminish their own relative power; this was especially true in the House of Representatives. Previously, the House typically added new seats to accommodate new states, as was done for the last time in 1912 with New Mexico and Arizona. Fearing that if it grew any larger the House would become too unwieldy to conduct business, members agreed in 1929 to cap membership permanently at 435, so any potential new seats for Alaska and Hawaii would have to come at the expense of the existing states. No representatives were eager to vote themselves out of office. As one congressman confessed to Lehleitner the fixed number of seats "makes each member feel that an affirmative vote might eliminate his or her district at some future date of reapportionment."[35]

Lehleitner understood why his fellow Southerners opposed the admission of new states, even if he detested their general attitude. According to his calculations in 1956, anti-statehood Southerners held "11 of the 16 key committee chairmanships in the House, and 7 out of 12 in the Senate. Moreover, the Majority Leader of the Senate [Lyndon Johnson] and the Speaker of the House [Sam Rayburn], and the Chairman of the all-important Rules Committee of that body [Howard Smith], are ALL Southerners. . . . and outspoken opponents of statehood!" And these powerful men did not stand alone. "Even were those presently holding committee chairmanships and other key positions to pass from the political scene, the picture would not be altered materially, as the Congressional Directory reveals that opposed Southerners also occupy 16 of the No. 2 spots on the basic Congressional committees!"[36] Lehleitner said the situation became even worse when Sen. James Eastland of Mississippi became chairman of the Judiciary Committee, leaving eight out of the Senate's twelve standing committees under the control of statehood opponents. "The anti-statehood tide is still running strongly against us!" Lehleitner wrote in 1956. "The current fight on segregation, and the bitterness and schism it will engender certainly won't help."[37]

If the civil rights struggles in the 1950s and 1960s were the final campaigns of the Civil War, the two territories were the last hostages of the Lost Cause. Protecting the states' rights of the South meant denying Alaska and Hawaii the rights of statehood. As Lehleitner warned his northern allies in 1957, "when one of these Southerners tells you that he is very much concerned about 'States' Rights' what he really means is that he is very much concerned about the issue of segregation." Lehleitner said he mentioned this "simply to guard against the possibility" that someone might "take those fellows seriously when they profess a deep concern about 'States' Rights.' I can only repeat that their REAL concern is primarily about the segregation implications."[38]

From his vantage point as vote-less delegate in Congress, Bartlett knew better than anyone that much of what happened on Capitol Hill was not what it appeared to be. He also understood the real motivation of the Southerners, their solemn oratory aside. "The fact is that the southern boys when they hit out at either Hawaii or Alaska are skirting and avoiding the two issues which are of fundamental concern to them—racism . . . and . . . Civil Rights."[39]

A journalist quoted in the *News-Miner*, who saw the Dixiecrats kill statehood in one session "dead as a dodo" without ever having to vote against statehood itself, was both appalled and impressed by the skill of the Southern Democrats. "Merits or demerits of the statehood issues did not enter into the picture, but adroit parliamentary maneuvering did. The Dixiecrats are adept parliamentarians. Many of them never have been to Alaska, know little about the territory and apparently care less." The only thing "they did care about was preservation of the present two or three vote margin by which they now can prevent the senate from . . . halting filibusters on . . . civil rights."[40]

As if the problems of civil rights and partisanship on Capitol Hill were not enough, however, an added liability for Alaska was the opposition of the Eisenhower administration. Unlike Truman, who gave Alaska his full-fledged support, Eisenhower said financial and strategic questions convinced him that Alaska was not ready for its own star. In his inaugural State of the Union address in 1953, Eisenhower urged Congress to take immediate action to admit Hawaii, but pointedly made no mention at all of Alaska. "To my mind," as Eisenhower told a news conference some weeks later, "not yet has the Alaskan case been completely proved. It is more of a dependency than it is a separate and self-supporting region."[41]

Symbolic of the Eisenhower administration's resistance to statehood had been the selection of veteran forester B. Frank Heintzleman to replace Ernest Gruening as governor of Alaska in the spring of 1953.

Heintzleman, age sixty-four, was the "anti-Gruening," an amiable bachelor and aging federal bureaucrat with more than three decades' experience in Alaska, and a solid reputation as a career civil servant who would stay out of the headlines, do what he was told by his bosses in the Department of the Interior, and play by the rules. Heintzleman had no political enemies, vendettas, or ambitions, and no passion for the statehood cause. His candidacy was backed by those who believed, as he did, that the statehood issue was "a little premature."[42]

The sum total of replacing Truman with Eisenhower, Gruening with Heintzleman, and a Democratic Congress with a Republican House and Senate changed the political calculus in the statehood battle considerably. Even Snedden came to believe that Eisenhower's policies toward Alaska during his first term were both shortsighted and inexcusable. "Alaskans have reason to doubt," the *News-Miner* lamented in April 1954, "that the present administration has a warm spot anywhere in its heart for the North."[43]

⁕

The *News-Miner*'s message that Alaskans were denied the most basic rights of self-government that all Americans held most dear echoed the outraged appeals to simple justice that fueled the civil rights campaign in the 1950s and 1960s. While no one could seriously claim that the constitutionally restricted rights of territorial residents or the other indignities of life in a territory approached the vicious brutality and terror suffered by black Americans—no Alaskans were ever lynched for trying to vote—the long-denied wish for equal treatment under the law was the impetus behind both the civil rights' struggle in the segregated South as well as Alaska's fight for full civil rights as a state of the Union. Ernest Gruening—who never suffered from a loss of words or an excess of modesty—struck the civil rights theme most memorably when he imagined what Lincoln would say if the Great Emancipator could comment on Alaska's crusade for liberty in 1954, eighty-seven years after the U.S. Purchase of Alaska.

> Four score and seven years ago our fathers bought
> on this continent a new territory and admitted
> its inhabitants to the enjoyment of all the rights,
> advantages, and immunities of the citizens of the
> United States. Now we are engaged in a great civil

struggle testing whether that territory, or any territory, so deceived and so frustrated can longer
endure without them. We are met to dedicate
ourselves to this struggle. The administration may
little note nor long remember what we say here.
But we can never forget . . . It is for us the living
in Alaska to dedicate ourselves to the cause for
which such measured words of devotion have been
uttered; that we here highly resolve that those
pledges shall not have been made in vain; that
this Territory under God shall have a true birth of
freedom and that government of its people by its
people and for its people shall come to our piece
of earth.[44]

The noble sentiments of Lincoln (updated by Gruening) underscored
the irony of the repeated rejection of Alaska statehood in the 1950s by
congressional leaders and the Eisenhower administration. The vast majority of the U.S. population thought America's government should live
up to its professed national ideals and give Alaskans the representative democracy they desired, but this was not translated into Congress.
Veteran congressmen were likely to be bombastic defenders of the Pledge
of Allegiance, the flag, and the Fourth of July, but whenever high ideals
came into conflict with self-interest, even the most self-evident of truths
could be conveniently denied and disregarded.

With the Congress fractured four ways—liberal and moderates for
both Alaska and Hawaii, Democrats generally for Alaska, Republicans
generally for Hawaii, and Dixiecrats (and most conservative Taft
Republicans) for neither Alaska nor Hawaii—and the Eisenhower administration openly hostile, the stage was set for perpetual stalemate of
the statehood cause. Alaska's struggle to become the forty-ninth state
would be the political equivalent of pulling the sword out of the stone.
More than ever this seemed to be the case by 1955, when instead of coming closer to the long-cherished goal, partisan politics seemed to be pushing statehood ever further away.

For Lehleitner the darkest hour in the statehood battle came on May
10, 1955, when the U.S. House of Representatives, by a majority of forty-
eight votes, rejected a combined Alaska-Hawaii Statehood Bill by returning it to committee. (Joining the two territories together in a single bill
was always the preferred poison pill of opponents as it invariably united

opponents of either territory and the opponents of both.) "The day of that reversal," Lehleitner recalled, "will always be remembered by me as the absolute low point in the statehood struggle."[45]

Distressed at the failure of the campaign for Hawaii, Lehleitner concluded by 1955 that perhaps Alaska could lead Hawaii into the Union instead of the other way around. In that year Alaska's leaders, stung by the repeated rejections from Congress, had decided to take matters into their own hands; rather than continue to wait for the politicians in D.C. to act, they intended to hold a constitutional convention and draft a blueprint for the proposed State of Alaska to prove once and for all that the far north was ready, willing, and responsible enough to take its place in the Union. But what if the new constitution was not enough? Without adoption of a bold new strategy Lehleitner feared that the ever-increasing delays and disappointments of past defeats could halt any serious consideration of statehood for years to come, if not forever.

With this in mind Lehleitner decided he had to go to Alaska. The charming salesman from the Deep South came north with a unique plan to shake-up the statehood movement and send a message to Congress.

8

"We Are Right and Congress Is Wrong"

In spite of the prodigious effort put into producing it, a daily newspaper has a shorter shelf life than a vase of cut flowers. As soon as an edition hits the street, the staff must prepare to do it all over again. Over the years Bill Snedden would publish hundreds of millions of words in this cycle of daily obsolescence, which is what made his work for the Alaska Constitution such a notable exception.

The *News-Miner* was a midwife at the birth of Alaska's constitution in Fairbanks in 1955–1956, when delegates trying to somehow break through the congressional stalemate blocking statehood gathered to create the foundation for the State of Alaska. Snedden's plant not only cast in hot type the original parchment copies of the constitution individually signed by the delegates, but it also printed the first copy of the constitution distributed to the people of Alaska. However, most importantly the *News-Miner* played a key part in ensuring that the Alaska Constitution was acceptable to and accepted by the people of Alaska.

The convention's importance, the *News-Miner* predicted in September 1955, "cannot be overestimated.... It doesn't matter that Congress has turned a deaf ear to Alaska's Statehood appeals. We are right, and Congress is wrong."[1]

Some statehood leaders initially opposed the convention. In 1953 *Anchorage Times* publisher Bob Atwood, the chairman of the Alaska Statehood Committee, feared a state constitution "would give foes of statehood a 'target to shoot at' and they would point to its shortcomings as evidence Alaskans can't even make their own laws."[2] In June 1954 Atwood was still dismissing it as a crackpot scheme that would sidetrack the statehood movement. "The suggestion that the constitution should be drawn before Congress acts, is fundamentally unsound," he wrote. "It is like suggesting that a man should build a house before the blueprints are drawn."[3] In light of repeated defeats in Congress, however, the belief that a constitution needed to be drafted grew, culminating in the 1955 session of the Territorial Legislature that approved $300,000 for a seventy-five-day convention to be held in Fairbanks on the campus of the University of Alaska from November 1955 to February 1956.

The News-Miner welcomed the convention and the decision to hold it in Fairbanks, and it charged that critics who claimed the territory was wasting hundreds of thousands of dollars "because the Federal government would pay for it if and when Congress ever grants Alaska statehood" were statehood opponents singing a different verse to the same old tune. The Wrangell Sentinel even called the Fairbanks gathering an "outlaw convention" because it had not been authorized by the federal government. "In our opinion, these charges have no validity whatsoever," the News-Miner responded. "If Alaskans want Statehood, and we believe the vast majority of them do, they should be more than willing to pay the costs of a Constitutional Convention."[4]

The hope was that the university campus would provide a nonpartisan, academic setting free of the typical legislative intrigue in Juneau. Laws from the legislature were subject to change by the next session but the articles from the convention would be permanent, or at least not easily amended or discarded. Building a strong foundation for a future state demanded a higher standard of excellence. As the University of Alaska student newspaper the Polar Star boasted, the campus was the logical site for the convention because the "impartial academic air of the University would relieve all external pressures on the delegates."[5] Former governor Ernest Gruening, the guest speaker at the convention's opening, echoed the feeling of many Alaskans when he said, "There are a number of inspired actions that accompanied the creation of this Convention . . . Perhaps the most was selecting the University of Alaska as a site for holding it. A University is really the keeper of the soul of a modern society and . . . this Convention . . . has that inspirational quality, and it will succeed."[6]

Realizing that the *News-Miner* would be the newspaper of record for the drafting of the constitution, Snedden went to great lengths to prepare for the most intensive reporting job the paper had ever attempted. To give the delegates' deliberations the daily attention they deserved and to be able to disseminate the news stories as widely and rapidly as possible required a major upgrade of the *News-Miner*'s communications and transmitting capabilities. "We had a dickens of a time trying to figure out how we could get adequate coverage of the convention," Snedden recalled. Telephoning from downtown Fairbanks to the university campus was problematic. "There were only a few lines, and all lines had at least six parties on them, some of them 10 or 12." Snedden installed a few regular phones and a teletype machine in the new Student Union Building where the delegates would meet (later renamed Constitution Hall) and linked the teletype to the outside world by a phone line that the *News-Miner* staff rolled across the frozen ground. "One of our reporters discovered an old cable, surplus from an abandoned military site, which we appropriated, and for the next three miles our connecting wire was a cable which was simply strung through the brush and the snow." This system enabled the *News-Miner* reporters at the convention to file their stories on the Associated Press circuit to Seattle. During the convention the *News-Miner* flow of copy on the line out of Constitution Hall was so heavy, Snedden said, that "we had trouble with the AP office in Seattle because we were . . . monopolizing too much of the wire!"[7]

Filing stories directly to Seattle was an innovation. It was only after September 1, 1954, that AP members in Alaska had a dedicated news-wire, a two-way circuit twenty-eight hundred miles long connecting them with Seattle. Before then, the teletype at the *News-Miner* was a one-way receiver that took in only about nine thousand words a day (at the rate of one word a second) on the regular lines of the Alaska Communications System, running for no more than two and a half hours every morning, including thirty minutes of sports at five a.m., one hour of general news at seven a.m., thirty additional minutes at ten a.m., and thirty final minutes at twelve-thirty p.m., right before press time. For the rest of the day the teletype was quiet. With the installation of the dedicated circuit in 1954, the Seattle AP bureau started sending stories to Alaska AP members throughout the day and most of the night. "When the *News-Miner* staff gets to work in the morning, we find news all over the place," Jack Ryan wrote. "There'll be 20 feet of paper streaming from the teletype with news from every corner of the globe."[8]

When the convention opened it appeared for a time there might not be much news coming out of their deliberations. On day three the rules committee suggested that all committee meetings be closed. The proposed rule read: "The deliberations of the Standing Committees shall not be open to the public except upon invitation of the Committee." This was the opposite of what had been suggested by the convention consultants. As delegate Burke Riley, the chairman of the rules committee, tried to explain, "The word 'not' was inserted and that was qualified with the addition of the words 'except upon invitation of the Committee.'"[9]

Delegate John Hellenthal, an attorney from Anchorage, immediately objected, worried that this would change the tone of everything the convention tried to do. "I think we would put ourselves open to the well-deserved criticism that we are meeting in secret session, which has an ugly connotation." He urged the committee to simply use executive sessions if sensitive personal matters had to be discussed. "Now if the occasion develops that crackpots or someone (I don't think there are many crackpots in Alaska) start plaguing us, then we can take a prophylactic rule such as the one recommended here, but in the absence of that demonstration I think that this rule has no place before our body. I have been through this before with city councils where they elected to meet 'secretly' is the word the newspapers always use, and I tell you that it does not work, and I see no need for it." Anchorage delegate Victor Fischer agreed; the public had the right to know what the delegates were doing, because the "Convention is being held in behalf of all of the people of Alaska. We hope that sometime or another many Alaskans will have an opportunity to come to College and listen in on some of these sessions. . . . I think it is our responsibility to the public to give them an opportunity to watch this Convention at work."

Most of the vocal delegates, however, seemed to back the rules committee's proposal for closed meetings. A typical sentiment came from attorney and former Fairbanks mayor Ralph Rivers, who said, "We don't want to have them open to the public while we try to develop a consensus of our thinking . . . We think the committees can do better work if the public is there on invitation."[10] Warren A. Taylor, the flamboyant Fairbanks attorney, agreed with Rivers. "I have been chairman of a great many committees. I think it would not be for the best interest of the committees doing efficient work to allow the public to indiscriminately come into these little committee rooms, take up your time, distract your thoughts from matters of great importance."[11] Although he was a newspaperman and editor of the *Juneau Independent*, delegate George Sundborg also supported keeping the public and press out of meetings except by invitation. "I feel we do have to have the freedom which we would have in committee only if we can speak without having a lot of people sitting around breathing down our necks. . . . I just don't think that business can be conducted efficiently if the public is walking in and out wandering around through these committee rooms all the time we are trying to do serious business." According to Sundborg, neither the Alaska Legislature nor the U.S. Congress generally allowed open committee meetings. "Hearings are but committee meetings, I've been excluded from them many times, in Congress." Above all he pointed to the example of the original Constitutional Convention in Philadelphia in 1787, which operated entirely in secret, prohibiting its members from "even reporting outside of the halls of the Constitutional Convention . . . what had gone on, therein and they came out with a pretty good result."[12]

After a brief recess the delegates agreed to a compromise wording. While it sounded more welcoming than the rules committee's proposal, it was functionally identical, closing all meetings but leaving it to the discretion of each committee to decide if and when to admit the public: "The deliberations of the Standing Committees shall be open to the public at such times as may be designated by the respective committees."[13]

Snedden thought closing the committees was an outrage. He didn't want his reporters, "who have been strained to the utmost to keep up with the convention doings," wasting their time getting clearance to attend meetings that should be open to the public in the first place. The *News-Miner* blasted the convention's decision:

> We hope the delegates realize that the news con-
> cerning this convention which is appearing in the
> newspapers printed in their home towns isn't being
> distributed throughout the Territory "by accident."
> There's a lot of hard work connected with . . . keep-
> ing the folks around the Territory who are paying
> the bill for the convention informed as to what is
> going on. This constitution is the property of the
> people of Alaska and we feel they have a right to
> know how it is being drafted. . . .
>   Since most of the work of the convention in
> the future will be accomplished at the committee

meetings, the new rule, in effect, clamps what amounts to press censorship on the . . . proceedings. Frankly, WE PROTEST.

The *News-Miner*'s position was that it had been "charged with 'covering' this event for virtually all of the newspapers and radio stations in Alaska." It wondered "how we will be able to accomplish our task in the face of the obstacles this new rule imposes. We are very disappointed with the attitude of the delegates on this matter. In our opinion, they have opened a great exercise in Democracy with a very undemocratic act."[14] Even giving the appearance of excluding the people from the making of their constitution would violate the principles the delegates were supposed to uphold. Former Governor Gruening had told the delegates that the most important word in Alaska's constitution would be the second shortest word in the English language: *by*. This was so, he said, because it was the one word that had been absent in the eighty-eight years since the 1867 purchase, the "little preposition 'by.' Many things have done for us; even more things have been done to us, but very little have we been permitted to do by us."[15] Snedden's view was that a constitution "by" the people could not be created without free access by the press.

Snedden's protest against the "open by invitation only" policy had the desired effect. Stung by the criticism, the delegates revised the rule once again, though the final version was an exercise in legalistic legerdemain, stating that all *hearings* would be public, and that all *meetings* could be opened given public notice—a distinction not lost on the *News-Miner*, which pointed out that it "skirts the issue of public meetings and apparently leaves it open to interpretation."

Proof that the attorneys on the rules committee had left themselves a loophole came when Warren Taylor tried to add the words "except when in executive session" to the promise that all convention hearings would be public. As Ralph Rivers then had to explain with some embarrassment to his fellow delegates, hearings were by definition always open to the public anyway, but meetings were an altogether different matter. "That last sentence in Rule 19 says 'All committee hearings shall be public.' You don't have hearings in executive sessions. This does not say 'all committee meetings' [shall be public] but 'all committee hearings' shall be public. With that thought, Mr. Taylor, I think the matter should be left the way it is." And the modified rule was left standing, explicitly stating that public hearings could not be closed to the public, but at the same time clearly implying that committee meetings could be.

Still, no matter what the rules said, a shift had occurred, and the "invitation only" policy had been discredited. As one reporter noted at the end of the wrangling over the wording of the rules, the "interpretation given by Burke Riley, chairman of the Rules Committee, was that the meetings would be considered to be open."[16] In a history he authored about the convention, Vic Fischer, the Anchorage delegate who opposed the closed-meeting rule from the start, said after the debate no more was ever said about excluding the public from their deliberations, and "there is no record or recollection of any committee formally calling a closed meeting."[17] A week or so after the closed meeting brouhaha, the *News-Miner* stated that everyone seemed to be happy with the resolution. "The delegates quietly agreed to let the press sit in on any session it chooses. . . . The committee sessions have the sound and high quality of university seminars on the graduate level. The tenor of the meetings is serious and questioning."[18]

Early on, convention president Bill Egan had commented on this spirit to the *News-Miner*. "It's wonderful and maybe a miracle to see how these fifty-five people have left politics out of this convention."[19] The university campus helped inspire a collegial and academic atmosphere, unlike the smoke-filled barrooms in the capital. "In a Juneau restaurant during legislature time people of different sides of the fence wouldn't sit within half a mile of each other, but here they are at the same table and talking too."[20]

Snedden had decided from the beginning that the *News-Miner* would assign a reporter full-time to the proceedings, thinking that the more people knew about the way the constitution was being drafted the better the final product would be and the more likely voters would be to embrace it. The coverage in the *News-Miner* was the only daily contemporaneous account of the proceedings, and Snedden believed the newspaper's vigilance helped lend an air of openness to the proceedings that ensured the public there had been no back-room dealing.

On rare occasions other reporters would be in evidence at the convention, including a writer from the *New York Times* who arrived in the final days, but *News-Miner* staffer Florence Douthit was the only reporter on the story for seventy-five days, and her husband, Jim Douthit, was the *News-Miner* photographer who took all the official photographs of the delegates at work. The convention itself issued no substantive press releases, so the Douthits' stories and pictures were a crucial record of what was taking place in Constitution Hall. Florence was such a constant presence at the meetings that the delegates came to think of her as another member of the convention.[21] On the last day of the proceedings they gave her a standing ovation for her faithful and fair coverage. George Sundborg, chair of the Style and Drafting Committee, made a formal presentation to the reporter, who was seven months pregnant at the time. "Mrs. Douthit, on behalf of the delegates to the Convention, we are very happy to present this to you. . . . It is a baby cup . . . to be inscribed with the following message . . . 'Bestowed by grateful delegates upon an unborn child named Douthit who abided quietly throughout the Alaska Constitutional Convention and never offered an amendment.'"[22]

The delegates also recognized the job the *News-Miner* had done to keep the public abreast of the proceedings. Delegate John Hellenthal, who had battled for the meetings to be open, put forward a resolution that stated "the *Fairbanks Daily News-Miner* and its president and publisher, C.W. Snedden, and its staff . . . be commended for their honest, scholarly, objective, and courteous reporting of matters dealing with the progress of the Convention."[23]

Though Snedden spent most of his energy promoting public access to the convention, behind the scenes he played a critical role in quietly laying the groundwork for the most innovative measure put before the delegates, George Lehleitner's quixotic scheme to garner national attention for the statehood cause (and thereby further his larger goal of creating the United States of the World). It was a bold step Lehleitner had been peddling unsuccessfully in Hawaii for years, but he had concluded in 1955 that perhaps Alaska, on the occasion of its constitutional convention, might be the territory to take the plunge. Lehleitner's plan was that the territory, instead of waiting to be asked into the Union, should act as if it already were a state and elect a slate of senators and a congressman to send to Washington, D.C., who would demand to be seated as the duly elected representatives of the people of the State of Alaska. He called it the "Tennessee Plan," because the sixteenth state in 1796 had been the first to force the issue by electing a shadow slate of senators and congressmen, and in the nineteenth century other territories subsequently followed Tennessee's lead, including Michigan (1837), Iowa (1846), California (1850), Oregon (1859), and Kansas (1861).[24]

Not everyone thought that a tactic last used before the start of the Civil War had any relevance in the real world of 1955. When they first learned of Lehleitner's scheme, two of the most prominent statehood leaders—Bob Bartlett and Bob Atwood—thought it was a screwball stunt, likely to be offensive to the more traditional-minded senators and congressmen it was supposed to persuade. They could hardly imagine why real senators from the forty-eight real states, who were so protective of the perks and prerogatives of the Senate, would welcome ersatz "senators" from a "state" that was still a figment of the imagination.

But while Atwood rolled his eyes at Lehleitner's plan—even though later he was drafted as the Republican nominee for one of the Senate seats after the people of Alaska approved it—Snedden saw the attraction of this bold stroke almost immediately. He believed that the ingenious plan of the salesman from New Orleans, in conjunction with the convention itself, might be the dramatic gesture that was needed, a powerful one-two punch that could break the political and partisan stalemate on Capitol Hill.

Snedden also saw the Lehleitner charm. He realized that even when the little Louisiana man with a bow tie disagreed strongly with statehood opponents, he somehow managed to be gracious and hospitable, a Southern gentleman who tried not to give or take offense in the heat of battle, and refused to hold a grudge. Naturally at ease when talking to his fellow Southern Democrats, who controlled Congress, Lehleitner was so effective that he actually convinced some of them to back statehood, most notably Louisiana Sen. Russell Long, who, despite remaining an avowed segregationist, came to be a strong supporter first of Hawaii and then of Alaska under Lehleitner's spell. Long's conversion came at a political cost. When he defected from the Dixiecrats on Hawaii, national columnist Drew Pearson reported that other Southern "Democratic senators are treating Russell Long . . . as if he had political B.O."[25]

In fact, the concept behind Lehleitner's Tennessee Plan was not so different from an idea that Snedden had endorsed a year earlier. "It strikes us," the *News-Miner* had stated in October 1954, "that Alaska could do much more to promote the Statehood cause." Besides calling a constitutional convention, the *News-Miner* had recommended at that time that Alaska "set up a complete State government composed of non-paid, unofficial public office holders, such as a governor of the State of Alaska, a lieutenant governor, and other similar officials" to "show the nation that we mean business in our quest for the full rights of American citizenship. . . . Even if we are facing opposition in Washington, we should carry out our end of the task as completely as possible."[26]

When Lehleitner came to Fairbanks for the first time in September 1955, before the convention began, to pitch the Tennessee Plan to Snedden, the *News-Miner* publisher thought the Louisiana man was one of the most remarkable individuals he had ever met, and like virtually everyone else who came in contact with him, he was completely in awe of the devotion and selflessness shown by this public-minded entrepreneur, navy veteran, and philanthropist and his hurricane-like enthusiasm for his favorite subject: Alaska-Hawaii statehood.

The two self-made businessmen shared a single mind when it came to the sacrifices of time and money they were ready to make for statehood. Lehleitner figured he spent about $100,000 of his own money on the fight, and while Snedden never tallied how much he was out of pocket—when a reporter from *Time* asked in 1958, his retort was "Too damn much—just ask my creditors"—he probably volunteered as much or more than Lehleitner.[27] Snedden battled so strenuously for Lehleitner's Alaska-Tennessee Plan that Bartlett paid him the highest compliment in a note to an Anchorage colleague in 1956: "Bill Snedden is sparkplugging the whole business; for my money he is developing into another George Lehleitner, praise be."[28]

Lehleitner called Snedden the "tower of strength" who made the Tennessee Plan a reality, especially considering Atwood's resistance. Snedden's work behind the scenes, he said, combined with what he did with the *News-Miner*, was the "most important single contribution to the acquisition of statehood of anybody from Alaska," including the heroic efforts of Bartlett and Atwood.[29] The pages of the *News-Miner*, Lehleitner said, were the best evidence of the good things that were happening in Alaska and why the territory deserved statehood. "While Bill Sneddens are hard to come by, in Alaska or anywhere else in this world for that matter," he told one skeptical congressman, there were enough energetic Alaskans with Snedden's sensibility that the territory would be able to carry its fiscal and political responsibilities as a full-fledged member of the United States. Lehleitner thought the Fairbanks publisher and his *News-Miner* were Exhibit No. 1 in the case for Congress giving the forty-ninth star to Alaska.[30]

Even though Bartlett always remained skeptical of the Tennessee Plan idea, he agreed with Snedden that Lehleitner's obvious disinterestedness helped the Louisiana salesman articulate the truths at the core of the statehood fight better than anyone else. "For how, indeed, can we hope to influence Asians and Africans, Europeans and Latin-Americans, to follow US—rather than communism or some other 'ism'—if we show such little faith in our own philosophy of government," Lehleitner once wrote. When Bartlett read those "moving and eloquent" words that Lehleitner had sent to House Speaker Sam Rayburn, he claimed it touched even his old heart "which believes all good words about statehood but beats faster only when such as yours are spread upon the record."[31]

The idealism and passion Lehleitner brought to the cause of the territories far from his home on the Gulf of Mexico, without any desire for personal or professional gain, was inspirational and refreshing. It could also be exhausting for those who didn't know what they were getting into when they started to communicate with him. Lehleitner was a Louisiana windstorm of words, a slow-moving but inexhaustible talker with a drawl and a perpetual smile who could go on for hours about the practical, philosophical, or political aspects of the statehood quest.

Given the solemn way Alaskans undertook writing their constitution in 1955, Lehleitner's framing of the moral implications of the denial of statehood had particular resonance. As with the admission of every new state in the past, the genius of the American system was that the addition of Alaska and Hawaii would reinforce the vows and truths to which the country had been dedicated in 1776. "We MUST recapture the faith of our Washingtons, Jeffersons, and Lincolns," Lehleitner wrote, "each of whom fervently believed that material progress is the *fruit* of freedom, rather than the reverse being true."[32] Lehleitner argued that if Alaska and Hawaii were denied, the whole country and the cause of world peace would be diminished, because communist sympathizers could rightfully conclude that Americans did not practice what they preached. "And, because I so believe, I work for statehood," he said.[33]

While Lehleitner privately briefed seventeen of the fifty-five delegates on his visit to Alaska in the fall of 1955, he preferred to remain out of the public eye until after he had a chance to make a formal public presentation in a plenary session in January 1956, and for that reason Snedden agreed to keep Lehleitner's scheme out of the newspaper. The two men feared many Alaskans would instinctively look askance at any proposal—especially one as radical as the Tennessee Plan—from an outsider. They worked to build support behind the scenes first, particularly with the members of the convention's committee on ordinances since the plan would be submitted as a supplemental ordinance, not an integral part of the constitution itself.

The strategy to keep the Tennessee Plan under the radar failed when Bob Atwood broke the story on the front page of the *Anchorage Times* in early December 1955, labeling it a "bombshell" buried on page five of the

Ordinance Committee's special report. The tone of the *Times* story had dark implications. It explained that Fairbanks attorney Robert McNealy, Ordinance Committee chairman, had admitted that Lehleitner had "brought the matter before the committee unofficially." The committee had unanimously endorsed the idea, but McNealy was forced to go on record promising that all "points in opposition to the plan ... will also be submitted to the convention and the people of Alaska."[34] Atwood had been chairman of the Alaska Statehood Committee since 1949, and he clearly took Lehleitner's contention that "statehood advocates have been too passive in their support" as a criticism. An earlier story in the *Times*—headlined "Louisianan Says Alaska Statehood Farther Away"—quoted Lehleitner saying that "Alaska statehood supporters have 'done ourselves a disservice by believing our own propaganda' that statehood is inevitable" especially in light of bitter resistance from Southern Democrats. "The only real fire injected into the statehood fight has been put into it by the opponents. They don't just object—they're militant in their opposition."[35]

Atwood resisted Lehleitner's more strident approach. In an editorial on the Tennessee Plan he was pointedly noncommittal and urged what he called "cautious consideration" before the convention took any steps. "If the Tennessee Plan is understood thoroughly it may be that Alaskans would want it despite the pitfalls," Atwood wrote. "At present we, like many others, are finding it a difficult decision, too. We are like the boy who is on the high dive platform for the first time. ... Should we climb down by the ladder, or should we overcome our fears and dive in?"[36]

As Snedden and Lehleitner had anticipated, the breaking of the Tennessee Plan story in Anchorage launched a volley of criticism and ridicule. The executive board of the Anchorage Republican Women's Club denounced the proposal as wasteful, insulting, and downright foolish, about as sensible in 1955 as endorsing whale-bone corsets, horse-drawn carriages, or powdered wigs. "This plan was adopted by other states one hundred or more years ago," the club wrote, "at a time where there was no radio, TV, airmail, long distance telephone, railroads, planes, or automobiles—at a time when Washington, D.C. could be reached from California only by covered wagon or around the Horn. We hardly think Alaska wishes to be classed in the same state of economic development as California was at the time it was admitted to the Union in 1850."[37]

Snedden told Lehleitner that Atwood's hasty publicity about the Tennessee Plan and his skeptical editorial "distressed me very much." As a result Snedden was forced to come out in mid-December with his own editorial in response to the controversy Atwood's stories had precipitated.

"Actually, delegates to the convention have discussed this matter only 'backstage,'" Snedden explained, "and it has not yet come up for debate or official discussion." Snedden made the *News-Miner's* position clear.

> Frankly, if this proposal comes before the convention, we intend to back it 100 per cent. Alaska has nothing to lose in this matter of obtaining Statehood, in our opinion. We are no closer to Statehood than we were 55 years ago. Surely, such a dynamic move as sending elected representatives to Washington to demand our rights as American citizens would focus national attention on our plight, and possibly persuade Congress to grant us Statehood.

At the very least it would "put Congress 'on the spot,' and force congressmen to make a clear cut stand for or against the American tradition of Democracy."[38]

Despite his endorsement of the Tennessee Plan, however, Snedden promised the *News-Miner* would not launch a publicity crusade, believing that a hard sell could destroy the spirit of the convention. "As much as we favor this plan, we do not intend to open a campaign of editorial 'pressure' to force delegates to take up the issue. In our opinion, the convention is not an ordinary political body, and should not be subjected to the ordinary brand of Alaskan political maneuvering. . . . Yes, we favor the Tennessee Plan, and when it comes up for discussion at the convention, we will support it."[39]

Snedden may have been certain that the Tennessee Plan was the correct way to proceed, but unfortunately the one person whose support would be most crucial to its success, Bob Bartlett, was still not convinced. Snedden recognized from the start that the Tennessee Plan would rise or fall depending on Bartlett's attitude, and he lobbied him relentlessly. "I have spent several hours discussing the 'Tennessee Plan' with Bob Bartlett," Snedden confided to Lehleitner three weeks after the start of the convention, "and I am sorry to say that Bob is still not completely sold on it."[40]

Bartlett knew the conditions in D.C. better than anyone in Alaska, and though he said he admired the boldness of the plan, he feared the powers in Congress might take strong offense to it, making his job as delegate infinitely more complicated. In mid-December he explained his doubts to convention president Bill Egan. "It is a matter of real regret to me that I am apparently one of the few not yet completely persuaded as to its efficacy," he said. While Lehleitner's idea might have made sense in the 1850s, he worried it was a hundred years out of date. "I sense a difference in attitudes, speaking historically, between the present and the time when the plan was so successfully used."[41]

Bartlett's doubts were similar to those expressed by Robert Estabrook, editorial page editor of the *Washington Post and Times Herald*, who had told Lehleitner, "The principal reservation I have is that it has been nearly 100 years since the procedure was tried. The real problem that statehood advocates are faced with is that the United States generally, and Congress in particular, has experienced hardening of the political arteries."[42]

Still, Bartlett said he had to agree with Lehleitner that unless "some new, bold and yet unknown revolutionary device is employed, statehood may be in the position of unanimated suspense for a long time to come. I have been so wrong so frequently in the past on this subject that it perhaps ill becomes me now to drag my feet in respect to any decent proposal. . . . Notwithstanding, I just am not an enthusiastic supporter."[43]

After weeks of intense private lobbying by Snedden, Lehleitner, and others, on January 20, 1956, just three days before Lehleitner was scheduled to appear before the convention, Bartlett finally agreed to publicly endorse the Tennessee Plan, in part out of sheer desperation. The delegate's political assessment was grim. Given the negative attitude of the Eisenhower administration and the Southern stranglehold on Congress, the prospects for statehood were "bleak" unless some new strategies were tried.

"The Tennessee Plan . . . could jar the nation and the Congress from lethargy," Bartlett wrote, and "provide the fulcrum needed to jar statehood from dead center, or to use another metaphor . . . remove the key log creating the jam." He hoped any resentment toward an officially unofficial congressional team from Alaska "would be far . . . outweighed by the benefits" and that this "daring and . . . imaginative" gesture could give the statehood quest a new lease on life in the American consciousness.[44]

Spurred by Bartlett's declaration of support—even if belated and reluctant—the delegates were primed to welcome Lehleitner with open hearts and minds. During the course of the convention Lehleitner was one of several dignitaries—including Bartlett, Atwood, and Gruening—invited to address the delegates but no one was greeted with more warmth and enthusiasm. On the evening of January 23, 1956, Lehleitner was symbolically escorted into the convention hall by Wally Hickel and Alex Miller, the respective Republican and Democratic national committeemen for Alaska, showing the bipartisan support Snedden believed was essential if the plan was to have a chance. "It is not often," Egan told the delegates and a packed gallery, that

> we Alaskans have an opportunity to extend our gratitude to one who has so unselfishly dedicated a considerable portion of his life's endeavors towards fulfillment of a principle and purpose solely for us. Such, however, is our good fortune this evening for with us on this rostrum is a young man who over the past few years has expended a considerable part of his time and personal fortune in an unyielding determination to secure a rightful place in the brotherhood of states for Alaska and Hawaii.[45]

Lehleitner's rousing call to action, "The Tennessee Plan: Admission of the Bold," included a review of the half-dozen territories the Tennessee Plan had helped to become states and a blunt description of the current congressional deadlock caused by partisanship and Southern zealotry. Without the Tennessee Plan he thought statehood was doomed. The challenge was there for the delegates to accept or reject. It was time for Alaskans to take the initiative. The Tennessee Plan was the right tactic "for an aggressive attack. No people in history ever accomplished anything worth-while without making a commensurate effort. No nation has ever won a war by remaining on the defensive. *Deeds* win wars . . . and achieve ideals!"[46] When he finished his remarks the delegates and spectators erupted in a rousing standing ovation. The delegates were so touched by his dedication, sacrifices, and "complete selflessness" that they unanimously voted to make Lehleitner the honorary fifty-sixth delegate of the Alaska Constitutional Convention and the "ambassador of good will from this convention to the people of the United States and to the members of congress."[47]

The day after Lehleitner's appearance, Snedden's editorial argued that adoption of the Tennessee Plan would reap a whirlwind of favorable publicity in the nation's press and "bring forcibly to the attention of the American people the fact that Alaska exists under virtually the same oppressive system of government that caused our forefathers to revolt in 1776." By claiming their rights as American citizens to elect and send a delegation to Washington that would demand to be seated, Snedden thought, Alaskans could once and for all drop the "'hat in hand' approach to statehood" that had failed miserably and force the intractable elements in Congress "to make a stand, before the eyes of the world, on whether or not America, the leader of the Free Nations, is going to tolerate colonialism in her own back yard."[48]

Snedden's enthusiasm for the Tennessee Plan—or the Alaska-Tennessee Plan—was shared by most of the delegates. The most spirited defense came from Marvin "Muktuk" Marston, the loquacious Anchorage businessman and real estate developer, who thought of Lehleitner as a modern-day knight errant, a "'Sir Galahad' who came here from the South and presented this great program. . . . I think it's a terrific story, and I think that it is now or never for statehood and . . . the Tennessee Plan is the only course; if we turn that down, then we have wasted our time here."[49] Though realizing that the Tennessee Plan was a risk, the delegates were emboldened to push ahead. "Sometimes we need to take a step into the unknown," said delegate Yule Kilcher from Homer. "There is never a guarantee to anything. The only course is to walk on." Delegate Frank Barr said that Alaska, like a turtle, "won't get anywhere without sticking its neck out."[50] By a vote of 47–5 (with three absent) the delegates approved appending to the Alaska Constitution the Alaska-Tennessee Plan Ordinance, which—if ratified by the voters—would provide for the election of two provisional U.S. senators and one U.S. congressman. (The five nay votes stemmed from the convention's reluctant decision that due to time constraints and costs, the Tennessee Plan candidates would have to be nominated by party conventions instead of primary election.)[51]

The Tennessee Plan had struck a nerve. Unlike the body of the constitution itself, the Tennessee Plan Ordinance was a direct challenge to the U.S. Congress and the American people, and some delegates, inspired by the audacious spirit of Lehleitner's vision, wanted to make the challenge even more explicit. Three days before the convention was set to adjourn, the Committee on Ordinances proposed a section that essentially gave Congress a deadline for granting statehood to Alaska: January 4, 1959. If statehood was not achieved by that date, the proposal stated, the Territorial Legislature would be entitled to hold elections and to make the

Alaska State Constitution the law of the land in Alaska, an act of brazen defiance bordering in the minds of some delegates on outright secession or rebellion.

Those in favor of the statehood deadline argued it was simply a way to strengthen the Tennessee Plan, claiming that merely sending a delegation to Washington was a half-hearted measure unless there were explicit consequences if they failed to be seated in Congress, and that Alaskans should be prepared to go the distance and elect their entire state government regardless of any further delays by Congress and the president. As Seaborn J. Buckalew, an Anchorage lawyer born in Texas, phrased it, the delegates had approved "a watered-down version of the Tennessee Plan.... I will give those hillbillies credit, they went all the way; and I am a little disappointed that we have elected to modify the plan."[52]

The debate over the statehood deadline and the effort to put more teeth in the Tennessee Plan prompted the most incendiary arguments in the entire seventy-five days of the Constitutional Convention, with delegates citing Patrick Henry and 1776. Steve McCutcheon of Anchorage said, "If the Congress of the United States does not see fit to extend us statehood in view of the fact that we send back our duly elected officials to the United States Congress, then we just have to take some other act which is more forceful."[53] Thomas Harris of Valdez urged restraint. "I have often wondered in studying history," Harris said, "how revolutions get started. I think this would be a good way to start one.... We are talking about mutiny."[54] Jack Coghill of Nenana, who proved to be a faithful reader of "Sourdough Jack," cited the *News-Miner* icon for what might happen if the statehood deadline were approved: "if we passed this section ... we would be doing just exactly what Sourdough Jack said the other day. He said the next meeting of the constitutional convention delegates will be when the Department of the Interior lines us up to shoot us for treason."[55] Finally John Hellenthal, a Juneau lawyer, dismissed the deadline talk as complete nonsense. "I don't think we should threaten or hold a pistol or a club over Congress," he said. "I don't think we should make damn fools out of ourselves. Now the South once threatened to secede from the Union and we fought the bloody war of the States. I can't see that anything can be gained by adopting this wild course of conduct, nothing whatsoever."[56] Ultimately caution triumphed over confrontation, even though fully one-third of the delegates voted in favor of the deadline they believed would have been part of a "full Tennessee Plan."

As the convention neared its conclusion the pressmen and back shop crew at the *News-Miner* who would print the new state constitution worked overtime as they took a steady stream of proofs and corrections regarding style, grammar, and punctuation.[57] By the time the convention adjourned *sine die* on February 6, 1956, the final document that rolled off the presses at the *News-Miner* was probably better than anyone could have expected at the start of the proceedings.

Snedden concluded—like many others—that it was Egan's performance as president that was crucial in fostering the spirit of harmony and goodwill that prevailed. Given the usual track record of the Alaska Territorial Legislature, and the normal bitter partisanship that dominated every session and election cycle, the nonpartisanship of the delegates had been unexpected. While the university setting helped to set a cordial tone, Snedden insisted Egan's deft but kindly and fair-minded chairmanship deserved most of the credit. Egan proved to know when to use or not use the gavel, giving every delegate the feeling that his or her point of view had been heard, even those on the short side of a vote. "Bill was on his toes every moment," Snedden wrote Bartlett a week after the convention adjourned, "and consistently kept discussion on the floor confined to the issues at hand, which as you can well imagine was no small task at times."[58] The convention had far exceeded Snedden's expectations in both its performance and its product, and "could not have been carried on in a more efficient manner, or by more able and conscientious delegates."[59]

Egan and Bartlett thought Snedden also deserved a goodly amount of credit for keeping the convention going forward on a positive track due to the *News-Miner*'s reporting and editorials. Bartlett thought the *News-Miner*'s help was doubly remarkable because Snedden had shown so much strength of character by reversing his views on statehood only two years before. "Bill Snedden is quite a fellow," Bartlett wrote Egan. "When he first came to Fairbanks and took over the *News-Miner* he was adamantly opposed to statehood. Memory dredges up many meetings between us, he on one side regarding statehood and I on the other. Yet he is a man of basically sound instincts and when he has convinced himself as to the justice of a cause he doesn't mind, as so many people do, switching positions." Bartlett thought having the *News-Miner* as the convention's paper of record was an incalculable benefit best appreciated by considering a different scenario. He asked Egan to imagine what would have been the case if instead of meeting in Fairbanks, where the delegates enjoyed the steadfast support of the *News-Miner*, they had met in Juneau, home of the most rabid anti-statehood newspaper in Alaska. "Just think of the atmosphere you would have been living in," Bartlett wrote Egan, "had you met in a community where the *Daily Alaska Empire* is just that except on Sundays! It would have been poisonous and it might have been ruinous."[60]

When the Alaska Constitutional Convention was all over, Bill Snedden thought the convention itself and the legal framework it produced were testaments to what Alaskans could do. The convention "has served a dual purpose," the *News-Miner* concluded. "It has produced an outstanding document, and it has given Alaska a new sense of unity. We have found that citizens from every corner of the vast territory can sublimate their own sectional and personal interests to achieve progress for all the people of Alaska." The constitution, the *News-Miner* boasted, would be Alaska's "Declaration of Independence" from territorial bondage.[61]

Besides setting Alaska's "Declaration of Independence" in type and printing the original one hundred copies reserved for the delegates, dignitaries, libraries, and schools, the *News-Miner* printing plant also produced 61,500 copies—the largest press run in its history to date—of a special Alaska Constitution insert, distributed by arrangement with the Alaska Statehood Committee, to all the major newspapers in Alaska as well as key newspapers in the Lower 48, that gave the public its first look at Alaska's proposed framework as well as a comprehensive account of the document's crafting. At Snedden's suggestion the *News-Miner* also produced two thousand nine-by-twelve-inch envelopes to mail copies of the constitution insert—with a transmittal letter from Bill Egan—to top federal officials, high school and university libraries across the country, and every congressman and senator in the United States.[62]

Like most Alaskans, Bob Bartlett got his first look at the final Alaska Constitution from the *News-Miner* insert, which he thought the best special section the *News-Miner* had ever published and "one of the very best special editions I have ever read anywhere." He saved one of the first two Snedden had sent as a personal keepsake and warned that anyone who tried to borrow it "is going to have to fight to get it from me."[63] "The coverage job you are doing is magnificent," Bartlett wrote, "and I am as sure as sure can be will result in dividends when the April 24 votes are counted."[64]

There were a few vocal critics of the constitution, mostly in southeast Alaska. The most virulent of all was a disgruntled Juneau Democrat, Peter Wood, who said the delegates had been a motley assortment of "gut-less wonders" and "hack politicians," and these "much-vaunted, holy framers" had produced a document that "set the stage for graft, corruption, dissipation of resources and chaos." According to Wood the constitution was "worse than nothing" and would ensure the "biggest patronage grab in history" by the "Gruening-Bartlett clique," dictating that as a state Alaska "would become another Missouri under Boss Pendergast, another Louisiana under Boss Huey Long, another New Jersey under Boss Hague." As much as Wood despised the constitution, however, he thought the "silly" Alaska-Tennessee Plan was even worse—an "asinine" idea. "A two-week junket to Washington, D.C. by three elected 'congressmen' might be all right," he said. "They would get the expected publicity and come home, as usual, but why put these three unofficial derelicts on the taxpayers' neck for six years, or four, or two?"[65]

Wood also attacked the constitution supplement written by the *News-Miner* staff as "a carefully written professional job" of subtle propaganda "designed to lull the voters into complacency in appraising this document." Snedden refuted Wood's charges immediately. Though the Statehood Committee had purchased 50,500 copies of the insert to distribute, no one outside the offices of the *News-Miner* had any editorial control whatsoever about what went into it. "Prior to publication, no delegate to the constitution or member of the Alaska Statehood Committee had the slightest idea of what this special section would be, other than an understanding that it would contain the full text of the constitution. Our special constitution section was a part of a regular edition of the *News-Miner*. . . . We as a newspaper reported the convention and the constitution exactly the way we saw it." While the publisher admitted that he and his newspaper often expressed strong convictions—including the belief that every Alaskan should enthusiastically back the constitution and the Alaska-Tennessee Plan that Wood despised so bitterly—the opinions of the *News-Miner* "are not and never have been for sale."[66]

In a letter to the editor one bitter critic of the *News-Miner*'s editorials in support of statehood and the constitution blasted the "princely sum of $300,000" wasted on the constitutional convention. "Needless to say, serious minded tax-paying citizens can but wonder how it came about that they have been called upon to finance such 'august deliberations.'" He also questioned the motives and the money behind George Lehleitner, asking "how it came about that a citizen from Louisiana was invited to address the deliberative body on the merits of the 'Tennessee Plan.' Would it be pertinent to inquire who financed his junket?" Snedden issued a blunt reply: "Mr. Lehleitner paid for it entirely—and we will vouch for that with an affidavit if necessary."[67] It had always been a matter of principle for Lehleitner not to accept any funds while battling for Alaska and Hawaii statehood, so when convention president Egan had apologized that he could not volunteer to pay his travel costs, Lehleitner had set him straight. "I would not have accepted reimbursement for the same had it been tended by the convention, as during my eight years of effort on behalf of statehood I have always scrupulously avoided the acceptance of any reimbursement for any expenses incurred. . . . lest anyone misconstrue the payment of expense monies as a form of compensation for my effort."[68]

As the date of the ratification election on April 24 approached, Lehleitner grew increasingly concerned about the fate of the Alaska-Tennessee Plan. Snedden expected that the constitution would be ratified by a substantial margin, perhaps even in southeastern Alaska, the hotbed of anti-statehood feeling, but the Tennessee Plan—which the *Ketchikan Daily News* dubbed an "expensive white elephant"—was a more doubtful proposition.[69] The *Anchorage News* blasted the Tennessee Plan as a "gimmick" and a silly game that "could prove very embarrassing not to say expensive" as it would require taxpayers to subsidize "a useless delegation of remittance men" to send to Washington, D.C.[70]

While the constitution could be seen as an abstract affirmation of the ultimate shape of the future state, requiring only support for "eventual statehood," the Alaska-Tennessee Plan was a de facto referendum on the question of immediate statehood, and Lehleitner worried that not everyone was aware of the damage that would be done by either a narrow victory or an outright rejection. He warned Snedden that if the Tennessee Plan were "defeated, it would be my guess that every opponent of statehood in the Congress would point to its defeat as conclusive evidence that Alaskans do not wish statehood at this particular time! And it would seem to me a plausible argument." A negative vote "would be just short of tragic" and might delay statehood for twenty years or longer.[71] He thought passage of the Tennessee Plan would be as vital as approval of the constitution, because without the Tennessee Plan to breathe life into the statehood cause, the constitution, even if approved by the voters, would sit on the shelf and be forgotten. "I cannot help but believe that if the Tennessee

Plan Ordinance is NOT approved, there will be precious little benefit to be derived from ratification of the Constitution itself."[72]

The *News-Miner* found itself the lone newspaper in Alaska strongly supporting both the constitution and the Tennessee Plan. "The *Anchorage News*—and to a lesser degree the *Ketchikan News*," Snedden wrote Bartlett three days before the election, "have been blasting both the Constitution and the Tennessee Plan, with emphasis of course on the latter. The only paper doing much fighting for both of these is the *News-Miner*."[73]

When the votes were tallied on April 24 the good work of the delegates was ratified by a landslide. By a margin of more than 2–1 territorial residents approved the constitution of the future State of Alaska, and by a smaller margin (about 3–2) they also endorsed the Alaska-Tennessee Plan. Snedden thought the vote proved that Alaska owed an enormous debt to the members of the Constitutional Convention, "who not only drew up an outstanding document but who devoted considerable time and effort to the task of correcting misunderstandings of the constitution, and defending it from attacks of those who willfully interpreted it wrongly."[74]

Of all the major cities in Alaska, Fairbanks gave the constitution the biggest majority by far, with 80 percent of the votes going for ratification; Anchorage cast 73 percent, Juneau 60 percent, and Ketchikan only 47 percent. Bartlett thought the strength of the vote in Fairbanks and in small communities throughout the Interior—the Athabaskan village of Nulato cast all of its sixty-two votes for the constitution—demonstrated the influence of the *News-Miner*'s extensive coverage and Snedden's editorial support.[75]

The big question after the ratification vote was who would run for the slots in the Alaska-Tennessee Plan seats. Lehleitner and Snedden had long since decided that the keystone of the delegation must be Bob Bartlett. Snedden thought that with the voters' approval of the Alaska Constitution and the Alaska-Tennessee Plan, it was vital for Bartlett to take the next step and throw his hat in the ring, as he would be a shoo-in to become Alaska's first "Senator-elect."

Bartlett told Lehleitner there were few people in Alaska whose counsel he valued more than Snedden's. "Like you, I rely very substantially upon his judgment," Bartlett said. "[T]hat he is one of the moving and most powerful forces for statehood today is to state the obvious."[76]

Thus Bartlett would not find it easy to say no to the Tennessee Plan that Lehleitner and Snedden believed in so strongly, especially because in their minds the plan was predicated on Bartlett's participation.

Lehleitner tried his powers of persuasion first. In a note to Egan, Bartlett described how Lehleitner started pressuring him to run in March 1956. "George wrestled with me for perhaps three hours," Bartlett wrote. "He is a very convincing man. He feels it is essential for me to offer my services as a United States Senator. He believes my occupying that position and holding that title, however unofficial, would be highly advantageous to the cause of statehood. He cites reasons extending almost from here to there."[77]

Even before the constitutional ratification election, Bartlett had privately tried to break the news to Lehleitner and Snedden that he did not intend to run on the Tennessee Plan, believing that the job of being a congressional delegate was incompatible with the duties of a Tennessee Plan senator or representative. The delegate felt he already had so many responsibilities to the people of Alaska that holding both positions would be a dereliction of duty. "If I were two guys in one," Bartlett told one associate, "there is nothing I would like to do more than to be Delegate and try to advance the cause of statehood simultaneously as a TPer. But I am not."[78] He also was worried that taking a Tennessee Plan seat would open him to charges of seeking statehood for personal gain. "It could be said and would be said that my interest in statehood was personally in self-aggrandizement rather than the cause itself." On the other hand if he stood aside and let others take the seats, "I think everyone would be bound to be impressed by the fact that I was seeking to the very best of my ability to put into effect a plan which would do me out of a job. Then I should think people would be more than ever inclined to say that Bartlett was selfless and without any doubt whatsoever sincere in every way in his advocacy of statehood, and with no thought of himself at all."[79]

Despite Bartlett's continued resistance, it was obvious that neither Snedden nor Lehleitner believed that he ultimately would be able to turn down a Tennessee Plan seat, which would guarantee him an eventual seat in the U.S. Senate. The realization that Bartlett was genuinely going to say no came only a few days before the April 24 election.

"This was such a lovely day," Snedden wrote Bartlett on April 21, 1956,

> until I opened envelopes from Lehleitner marked
> "strictly personal." The roof slowly caved in as I

read copies of George's April 11 letters to you and
your April 13 reply.

. . . Bob, I have never for a moment given serious consideration to the possibility that you might
not accept the candidacy of one of the posts of the
Tennessee Plan. . . . It was so obvious to me—and
I assumed it would be to you—that E.L. Bartlett
constituted the brightest of the three stars around
which the chances of the Tennessee Plan would
revolve.[80]

Bartlett was crucial to Snedden's and Lehleitner's hope of placing
the Tennessee Plan "above politics" and ensuring a bipartisan effort that
would appeal to both Democrats and Republicans in Congress; they were
convinced that a split delegation with one senator from each party would
be the best signal to wary Republican members of the U.S. Senate that admitting Alaska might not automatically ensure two additional Democrats,
as was generally expected. With the opposition of Southern Democrats,
the territory had no chance of becoming a state without bipartisan support. A unity ticket would be the logical approach.

Lehleitner was typically exuberant in his support of a bipartisan TP
delegation; it would make "rare political good sense," he thought, because Alaska "could then count upon attracting support from BOTH
sides of the aisle. Unquestionably, we will need liberal support from both
Republicans and Democrats if we are to succeed."[81]

Snedden's thinking was that since the Tennessee Plan was itself a
departure from normal politics, why not go a step further and abandon
the notion of partisan advantage to make a sacrifice for the greater good
of all Alaskans? Though Snedden never hid his Republican allegiance,
he argued that politics must be adjourned to enact the Tennessee Plan,
just as the Constitutional Convention delegates had done during their
seventy-five-day marathon in Fairbanks, because "as far as achieving
statehood is concerned—we in Alaska are Alaskans first, and Democrats
or Republicans second." Party regulars from both camps would be skeptical, but to keep the bipartisan spirit of the Constitutional Convention
alive, he suggested a dream ticket behind which he thought all Alaskans
could unify: Delegate Bob Bartlett and University of Alaska President
Ernest Patty (a Republican) for the two Senate seats, and Constitutional
Convention President Bill Egan (a Democrat) in the House.[82]

Without Bartlett, Snedden predicted the Tennessee Plan's chance of success would be reduced by at least 50 percent.[83] "Where—Oh WHERE, in Alaska are we going to find the men who can do the job?" He only hoped a miracle would happen, "such as Bob Bartlett changing his mind—or even more unlikely, a trio of capable, outstanding candidates for the Tennessee Plan suddenly emerging from one of our melting snow banks."[84] Barring a change of heart on Bartlett's part, Snedden thought all he had done with Lehleitner might have been a waste of time. "It appears to me . . . that Alaska is at the crossroads—and one of our strongest leaders, E.L. Bartlett, appears to be heading for a wrong turn at that crossroads. Guess about all I can do is pray that he will change his mind before he actually gets started!"[85]

Bartlett's refusal to run was a serious obstacle to the coalition scheme. So too, as Snedden had expected, was the intransigence of the Republican Party. On the eve of the GOP convention Snedden challenged the Republicans, in a *News-Miner* editorial, to work with the Democrats to create a fusion slate for the Tennessee Plan offices. "Could our two political parties set a precedent for America that would show the unity and pride in our Territory" as "Alaskans carry out their battle for the full rights of American citizenship?" He urged the two parties to work together in an "enlightened manner" to fill the three seats, with the Republicans giving way to the Democrats, or vice versa, when "the other party has a man of obviously better qualifications . . . It would be an unprecedented act of cooperation between rival parties that would demonstrate . . . that Alaskans place the welfare of the Territory far above politics."[86]

The Republicans thought nominating a Democrat was heresy. According to a reporter at the 1956 convention, Snedden's proposal "was shouted down and the convention adjourned only minutes after delegate Lawrence A. Moore of Anchorage told the gathering 'we have nominated three of the finest men in the country—I see no need for compromise.'"[87]

Though stung by the Republican rejection, Snedden still refused to give up. At his prodding, in the hope of keeping some pressure on the Democrats, the GOP Tennessee Plan Senate nominees, *Anchorage Times* publisher Bob Atwood and Fairbanks insurance agent John Butrovich, agreed that either would be willing, as Butrovich put it, "to step aside and support a coalition candidate if a compromise platform can be

effected—and if the Republican party thinks another man is better fit-
ted . . . for the position." Of course the only "better man" anyone could
envision was Bartlett, and everyone knew he had no intention of partici-
pating. The GOP also remained coy about which nominee would run for
which Senate seat, hoping to forestall any Democratic advantage.[88]

The Democrats likewise rejected a coalition by nominating three
party stalwarts: Gruening and Egan for the Senate and Ralph Rivers for
House.

Bartlett and Egan thought that, at least subconsciously, Snedden's
real goal in promoting a fusion ticket headed by Bartlett was to stop the
election of Ernest Gruening to one of the Senate seats.[89] Snedden didn't
try to hide his fear of Gruening becoming a senator. "I am certain," he told
Egan, "that if Gruening is one of our elected Senators that the effect is
going to be bad—very bad—for Alaska."[90]

Gruening had never disguised his willingness to throw his entire
wardrobe into the Tennessee ring. Only two days after the approval
of the Tennessee Plan, he was acting as if he were already leading the
Tennessee Three, telling Mildred Hermann, the secretary of the Alaska
Statehood Committee, that he planned to blanket America with copies
of the "Let Us End American Colonialism" speech he had given at the
Constitutional Convention: "When I get through the country will know
about Alaska's colonialism! Every political scientist, every editor, every
radio commentator, and a great variety of clergymen, lecturers, writers,
and opinion formers generally, are getting the speech with a personal letter. And all Congressmen."[91]

Putting the members of Congress at the tail end of the list of those he
hoped to convince may have been an oversight, but the tone of Gruening's
approach still revealed the showboating style that appalled Bartlett
and Snedden. Bartlett would publicly support Gruening for one of the
Tennessee Plan Senate seats while privately admitting that one of the
reasons he did not want to run was Gruening's domineering personality.
"I am 52 years old now, not 35 as I was when Ernest and I started our association. I could not and would not abide the utter control he would seek
to exercise in every matter involving execution of the TP. This would be
especially the case because while I admire him . . . so greatly in so many
ways I think he is as politically naïve today as when he started out. Which
is to say plenty. I want none of it."[92]

Even though Bartlett readily told Democratic colleagues he could not accept the "coalition agreement so ardently desired by Bill Snedden," he agreed with the publisher that the candidates for three seats should be "divorced from the ordinary run of politics," and "should not be considered candidates in the ordinary definition of the term." "I feel very strongly that for many and persuasive reasons the Tennessee Planners should not be coupled with the rest of us of the common herd."[94]

However, keeping politics out of the Tennessee Plan proved impossible. Both Republicans and Democrats were so convinced they could capture all the seats for themselves that any notion of compromise with the other party was out of the question. There was also the matter of future strategy and political control. One Democratic official wrote a blunt assessment to the chairman of the Democratic Central Committee. "Bob Atwood is a nice guy, so is Johnny Butrovich, but they are in the opposition camp and running on a Republican ticket, and if either of them should win it would be a real victory for them and it might give them just what they need to begin to rebuild a strong Party, and we can't let that happen."[95]

In the end, to Snedden's dismay, the Democrats swept all three of the Tennessee Plan seats in the October general election, choosing Ernest Gruening and Bill Egan for the Senate and Fairbanks attorney Ralph Rivers for the House. The straight Democratic Alaska-Tennessee ticket was a fatal flaw as Snedden and Lehleitner saw it, because "one couldn't expect much enthusiastic support from most Congressional Republicans" if all they could see when they looked at Alaska was two more senators on the Democratic side of the aisle. Lehleitner thought this "defect" was corrected somewhat when subsequent Alaska statehood bills required new elections to be held upon admission, which would give Republicans another chance at the seats.[96] But for now the voters had spoken, and the Gruening-Egan-Rivers team, working in conjunction with Bob Bartlett and the Alaska Statehood Committee, would carry the fight to Capitol Hill in early 1957, where the odds against Alaska were still daunting. Said Lehleitner: "We have one hell of a big public relations job ahead of us!"[97]

The Tennessee Plan would never live up to Snedden's expectations as a weapon in the statehood fight. Though he remained on the surface a strong defender of it, he knew that for all practical purposes the solidly Democratic delegation would be unable to make any headway with the Republicans in Congress or with the executive branch. Given Eisenhower's dismal track record on Alaska matters during his first term, it was not clear that anyone, let alone three uninvited Democrats, would be able to change the administration's course.

9

"Giveaway McKay" and
"The Garbage Man"

Like many Democrats in the 1950s, Bob Bartlett could never comprehend Dwight D. Eisenhower's philosophy or his appeal—any more than most contemporary Republicans had been able to understand Truman or FDR. Ike had been the Supreme Allied Commander in Europe and had spearheaded the Normandy Invasion, yet it was hardly unusual for opponents to denigrate his administrative talents and intellect. "My views on the general are not at all objective," Bartlett told Paul Solka in 1954. "I have never been persuaded as to his abilities and nothing he has done since he moved to 1600 Pennsylvania Avenue has detracted from an earlier firm belief that although he has been a favored child of fortune he does not rank in the company of such military men as Marshall and Bradley."[1]

Most contemporary journalists had a similar disdain for the president's skills. Eisenhower became famous at press conferences and public appearances for his circular syntax and wayward sentences, which often left audiences and reporters wondering what the president was thinking—or if he was thinking at all. However, as confidants knew at the time, and historians would learn years later once his presidential papers were open for inspection, the public image of Ike as America's detached but genial and grandfatherly golfer-in-chief was far wide of the mark. He was anything but the slow-witted, indecisive, and uninvolved leader that his critics charged. Maneuvering behind the scenes, he manipulated the perception of his administration to further his political agenda. Eisenhower's style was a continuation of his military habits by other means; he was a president who operated on a need-to-know basis, a master of misdirection, always keeping his opponents guessing as to where he stood and where he might be going. Ike knew the power of information as well as any chief executive in history, and realized the less he said the more options he preserved. During his "hidden hand" presidency, as it would come to be called, Ike never showed half his cards. He maintained in his memoirs that his reputation for being inarticulate and out of touch was perfect cover when he needed to avoid a sensitive issue or disguise his actual strategy. As he told his press secretary, James Hagerty, shortly before the start of a critical press conference in 1955, "Don't worry Jim, if that question comes up, I'll just confuse them."[2]

Ike's handling of Alaska was a textbook case of the strengths and weaknesses of his style of management, as he confused everyone about where he stood on statehood and why. From the public record it was obvious he preferred to pretend as if he had never heard of the Territory of Alaska. Ike neglected even to mention Alaska and its statehood aspirations in his first two State of the Union messages, in 1953 and 1954, all the while urging immediate action on the admission of Hawaii. When he begrudgingly referred to Alaska in 1955, he could hardly have been more evasive about Alaska and more explicit about Hawaii: "As the complex problems of Alaska are resolved," he told Congress, "that Territory should expect to achieve statehood. In the meantime, there is no justification for deferring the admission to statehood of Hawaii."[3] Though he repeatedly said there were both financial and national security reasons why he doubted Alaska's suitability and readiness for statehood, he refused to elaborate, and what little he did say was seldom completely logical or comprehensible. Since the president intentionally never made a definitive public case, statehood supporters found it impossible to counter his objections. No one could debate the position of the Commander-in-Chief if they couldn't find it.

Most confounding was that Ike distanced himself so effectively from the political problems of Alaska's admission that the public perception during his first three years in office was that the agency calling the shots on Alaska was not the Oval Office, or the Pentagon, but the Department of the Interior, headed by Douglas McKay, whose record of political bungling was so egregious that the White House reportedly had one staffer permanently on the McKay desk, a full-time assignment responding to letters attacking Secretary McKay.[4] It was McKay's misfortune to become the administration's Alaska scapegoat, a role for which he was suited all too well.

McKay was a longtime Chevrolet and Cadillac dealer from Oregon. Snedden, who was somewhat familiar with him, initially had high hopes for what McKay could do for Alaska, especially since Snedden's close confidant, former *News-Miner* editor Bill Strand, was given one of the top posts under McKay. Those expectations hit the rocks soon enough. McKay's troubled three-year tenure at the Department of the Interior, from 1953 to 1956, would prove Ike's biggest political liability in his first term. Though he was also a former Oregon legislator, mayor, and governor, McKay readily admitted he was temperamentally more of a salesman than a politician, administrator, or bureaucrat. "At heart," he told a friend, "I am still a Chevrolet dealer."[5] His bitter home state rival, Wayne Morse, U.S. Senator from Oregon, dismissed McKay as nothing but a "small-town garage owner."[6] The interior secretary who referred to himself as "the old car peddler" floundered repeatedly in high-profile controversies. His attempt to manage the Alaska statehood question was one.

Republican insiders acknowledged that when it had come to doling out patronage jobs in the first Eisenhower administration, most of the conservative Taft Republicans had been relegated to the Department of the Interior, and that while McKay was a kindly man, he was never strong enough to establish firm control over his agency.[7] A former associate said that the Taft contingent in the Interior Department—including one bureau chief who "was back about 1880 in his thinking"—dominated the department's policies so thoroughly that McKay ended up looking like "a dinosaur of all dinosaurs."[8] The Eisenhower policy of creating "partnerships" with private entities to develop the public domain led conservationists and Democrats to tar the secretary with the ignominious nickname of "Giveaway McKay." In 1954 Bernard DeVoto, a prominent author and historian of the West, claimed that in the space of McKay's first eighteen months on the job, he and his lieutenants had not only gutted the professional staff of the Interior Department but had also reversed seventy years of American conservation policy that strove to protect the nation's natural resources, substituting instead a policy of "reckless destruction for the profit of special corporate interests." According to DeVoto, under McKay the Eisenhower administration had a perfect record in wanton waste. "Every move in regard to conservation that the Administration has made has been against the public interest."[9]

McKay's policy shifts and blindness to the art of public relations made him a prime target for those who disliked the administration. As longtime journalist Elmer Davis crudely put it after attending McKay's first introduction to the press, "this man does not know the lower outlet of his alimentary system from a hole in the ground."[10] But McKay boasted he was unfazed by such harassment. "I've sold automobiles for 32 years, and I was once a second lieutenant in the Army, so I've been cussed by experts. It doesn't bother me a bit."[11]

McKay's inability to deal with the press was made painfully obvious when he came to Alaska in the summer of 1954. His ineptness would help derail both statehood and the most promising economic prospect on the horizon: the development of oil and gas on the Arctic Coast of Alaska. Through all the turmoil, Snedden, mostly out of loyalty to Strand, was one of the last editors to give up on McKay.

As McKay was about to make his first visit to Fairbanks, in July 1954, a *News-Miner* editorial urged everyone to be on their best behavior during the dignitary's visit. "Any local resident who is contemplating shooting his neighbor next week," Jack Ryan wrote, "should postpone the deed at least seven days."[12] Snedden believed McKay's trip "will be a golden opportunity for public spirited citizens. We should impress the secretary with the fact that this area has a great future, if only the Federal government will give us a fair chance."[13]

When he was governor of Oregon, McKay had unequivocally recommended Alaska for statehood, but since becoming interior secretary he had become another apparent master of equivocation and indecision; as far as Alaska was concerned, he might as well have been "Secretary Delay" of the "Department of Indecision." Testifying before Congress in April 1953 McKay parroted what had long been the Republican dogma, that Alaska should become a state only under the right circumstances, "when it is ready." Asked if he thought Alaska was ready, he replied that he was not prepared to say one way or the other. "I've never been there. There's a difference of opinion on that. A great many persons think they [Alaskans] are not. I can't say."[14]

When McKay came to Fairbanks he addressed a banquet crowd at the Fairbanks Golf and Country Club, stoutly defending the Eisenhower administration's first year and a half in office. He urged Alaskans clamoring for statehood to be patient. After all, the Republicans had been in power for less than twenty months, but there had been "20 years of Democratic rule when there was no statehood for Alaska."

Eager to take what good news he could find in the secretary's remarks, Snedden thought that the request to give Ike and the Interior Department the benefit of the doubt was reasonable enough. "We at this newspaper have been impatient," Snedden admitted, "for we see much that needs to be done here in the Far North. After listening to Secretary McKay, we are comforted, for he showed clearly he is dedicated to do everything within his power to right the economic and social wrongs in Alaska."[15]

Even if immediate statehood was beyond McKay's power, there was one "economic wrong" entirely under the purview of the secretary of interior that McKay could have righted instantly had he chosen to do so. Snedden pleaded with the secretary to revoke Public Land Order 82, a World War II measure that prohibited all private development north of the Brooks Range, in the Alaska Arctic, because of its oil and gas potential.

--- ⚜ ---

Since the early 1920s, the federal government had reserved the most promising petroleum land in the north for national defense purposes, starting with the creation in 1923 of Naval Petroleum Reserve No. 4 (Pet 4), an expanse of twenty-three million acres. Twenty years later, in the midst of the oil shortage during the Second World War, the Interior Department closed off an additional twenty-five million acres, encompassing the entire North Slope, an area about the size of Nebraska. Acting Interior Secretary Abe Fortas, under orders from Secretary Harold Ickes, signed Public Land Order No. 82 on January 22, 1943, withdrawing all potential oil lands in Alaska. PLO 82 included within its boundaries all of the roughly 48.8 million acres north of the Arctic Divide between the crest of the Brooks Range and the Arctic Ocean, including Pet 4, "for use in connection with the prosecution of the war."[16] It was perhaps appropriate that PLO 82 never specified the war the Interior Department had in mind, because the closure lasted for the duration of not only the Second World War but also the Korean Conflict and the Cold War through the 1950s.[17]

In the first decade after the enactment of PLO 82, the U.S. Navy's Office of Naval Petroleum and Oil Shale Reserves spent close to $50 million searching for oil north of the Brooks Range. No other potential oil field in the world posed more brutal logistical, climatic, and technical challenges. During nine fields seasons the navy and its contractors drilled forty-four core tests and thirty-six test wells (of which ten were at least a mile deep). Most of the drilling was inside Pet 4, but geologic and seismic surveys were performed across the entire arctic region. About 180 miles south of Barrow the navy discovered a medium-size oil field at Umiat, in the northern foothills of the Brooks Range, with estimates of up to one hundred million barrels of recoverable oil, as well as a nearby gas field of "major size" across the Colville River (and just outside the border of Pet 4) at Gubik, possibly containing up to three hundred billion cubic feet of natural gas.[18] According to the testimony of John Reed of the U.S. Geological Survey's Navy Oil Unit, the fifty-mile-long Gubik anticline was enormous. "So far as is known," Reed told Congress, "there is no oil in that structure. It is all gas, the quantity is very large. We can't even measure it."[19]

The U.S. government's exploration for arctic oil from 1944 to 1953 came at an opportune time. There had been sporadic interest in Alaska oil development since the gold rush days, but no one had ever found any significant deposits because, as historian Bob King said, "they were look-ing for oil in all the wrong places."[20] During the first half of the twen-tieth century, the only commercial oil production in Alaska came from the tiny field at Katalla east of Cordova, where a small refinery oper-ated until it burned down in 1933. During its two decades of operation, Katalla produced only 154,000 barrels (by comparison, that would later be about three hours' worth of production from Alaska's Prudhoe Bay at its height).[21]

A private oil and gas industry hardly existed in Alaska before the 1950s. In 1949 only one oil and gas lease was under contract in the terri-tory, covering a scant 2,560 acres, and it didn't produce a drop of oil. But the rush was about to begin. Within five years there would be more than one thousand leases (1.8 million acres) under government contract, with eight major oil companies hunting underground—Richfield, Humble, Phillips, Shell, Union, Texas, Ohio, and Standard of California— and within another five years more than fifteen thousand oil and gas leases would cover 32.1 million acres, an area about one-fifth the size of Texas.[22]

The Alaska oil rush dates from 1953–1954. Not only were the first private wells since the 1930s bored into Cook Inlet and the Alaska Peninsula, but after several years of debate over the cost-effectiveness of its program, the navy finally decided to shut down exploration activities on the North Slope, raising the possibility of private development.[23] A naval review board had concluded in 1952 that while the work in Pet 4 was valuable for developing arctic technical expertise and exploring for additional resources, not enough oil had been found to justify its retention as a strategic reserve. No matter what further discoveries might be made in the future, Pet 4 was so isolated and inaccessible the navy board argued it was the "least desirable of all existing reserves for use in emergencies." It was "of questionable value, due to the difficulty and extreme vulnerability of any practical means of transportation" and "should be transferred to another Government agency for administration at such time as feasible," most likely the Department of the Interior.[24]

Once the navy announced it was ending its operations in the National Petroleum Reserve, the Alaska Development Board asked federal authorities, in March 1953, to return to the public domain all of the nearly fifty million acres under Pet 4 and PLO 82, in order to let private industry try its hand on the North Slope.[25] With the major oil companies scrambling for acreage across southern Alaska, Snedden realized that Fairbanks was ideally located to profit from private exploration north of the Brooks Range, the largest geologically favorable oil and gas province in the United States—but only if the Interior Department lifted PLO 82. As early as 1954—before Alaska had a single oil well in production—he believed that hydrocarbons on the North Slope were the key to Alaska's future, and that Fairbanks had the most to benefit from the development of oil and gas in the Arctic. "It is obvious that Fairbanks lies close to great oil wealth," he wrote in September 1954. He agreed with geologists who thought the territory's oil reserves would "someday . . . be Alaska's biggest sources of income."[26]

For this awareness of the latent importance of arctic oil and Gubik gas to Fairbanks and Alaska, a realization that helped convince him of the feasibility of statehood, Snedden credited his friend James W. Dalton, son of the famed gold rush trailblazer Jack Dalton and a 1937 mining engineering graduate of the University of Alaska. (He was also the husband of Kathleen "Mike" Dalton, who would toil as a *News-Miner* reporter for many years.) Jim Dalton was a quiet, retiring man who earned a reputation as a logistical and technical genius in arctic construction and technology. As the last general superintendent of Arctic Contractors, the civilian firm charged with exploratory work for the navy in Pet 4 from 1946 to 1953, he was well placed to appreciate the underground wealth in the arctic oil reserves.[27] When the navy decided to mothball Pet 4, Dalton was certain that the gas field at Gubik was ripe for commercial exploitation, and he convinced Snedden to push for repeal of PLO 82 and to promote construction of a 465-mile-long natural gas pipeline from Gubik to Fairbanks.

Little more than a month before coming out for statehood, Snedden announced the newspaper's campaign for North Slope natural gas. "The News-Miner is dedicating itself to an all-out battle to open the great gas reserves of Arctic Alaska," Snedden wrote in a front-page editorial on January 12, 1954.[28] Relying on information from Dalton, Snedden said the methane gas was "high quality" (97 percent pure) with low moisture. While most natural gas lines in the Lower 48 were buried, this one could be laid directly atop the frozen ground so as not to disturb the permafrost. "Dry natural gas will flow in coldest of weather," eliminating the need for insulation "since the gas cannot freeze."[29] There were estimates that twenty million cubic feet of Gubik gas per day could be piped to Fairbanks, cutting energy costs in the community anywhere from 30 to 60 percent and supplying local needs for the next thirty years. Snedden believed that "no natural resource in Alaska . . . could do more for Fairbanks and the Interior" than the Umiat-Gubik gas fields. He was determined to help make the gas line a reality. The essential first step was to have the gas fields released from the government withdrawals "that hold these lands captive."[30] "IF THE FEDERAL GOVERNMENT IS TRULY INTERESTED IN EXPANDING THE ECONOMY OF THE FAR NORTH," he concluded in capital letters, "THIS LAND WILL BE RELEASED."[31]

In 1954 Dalton published what became Snedden's bible for the Gubik gas line and the PLO 82 repeal movement, an eighty-two-page report for the Alaska Development Board titled "Possibility of Commercial Development of Gubik Gas Field and Use of Natural Gas as a Source of Heat and Power in the Railbelt Area of Alaska." "The purpose of this report," Dalton stated in the introduction, "is to promote the commercial development of Alaska's natural gas resources."[32] Before publication of Dalton's Gubik report, Snedden said, most of the pertinent information about Gubik and PLO 82 existed only in "James Dalton's head or his files."[33] Dalton's report was not light reading; crammed with tables of statistical data and financial calculations, it provided a wealth of geologic, economic, and technical information about the development of the gas field and construction requirements for a gas line from the North Slope to Fairbanks.

With Gubik gas, Dalton predicted, the economy of Interior Alaska and the entire railbelt to Anchorage could become a subarctic industrial powerhouse. "Cheap fuel in the form of natural gas may make practical the establishment of smelting plants for production of antimony, tungsten, copper, molybdenum, and gold and silver." Fertilizers and chemicals could also be manufactured. Just as coal fired Pittsburgh's iron and steel plants, so too, Dalton believed, Gubik gas could make Fairbanks a hub for producing cement and ceramics.[34]

Dalton also argued that making Gubik gas accessible to Fairbanks served a national security need in keeping with the original intent behind Pet 4 and PLO 82, since the biggest immediate beneficiary of opening the Gubik gas fields would be the U.S. military. Every year Ladd and Eielson Air Force bases consumed about twice as much energy for electricity and heat as the entire civilian sector.[35] Substituting natural gas for some of the fourteen million gallons of fuel oil that the air force had to ship north every year by tanker and train would both save money and reduce energy consumption, thereby slowing the "depletion of oil reserves within the continental limits of the United States."[36]

Years later, when the largest oil field ever found in North America was eventually struck on the coast of the Arctic Ocean at Prudhoe Bay, on land once closed to development by PLO 82, Snedden occasionally told readers that no one should forget Jim Dalton, a man who hated to see his name in the newspaper. Snedden thought Dalton more than anyone else was the catalyst for private development of the arctic oil plains by "quietly and methodically" pushing for repeal of PLO 82 to develop Gubik, an effort that ultimately opened up the Prudhoe Bay oil field for exploration and development. In the 1960s and 1970s Snedden repeatedly tried to honor Dalton for his groundwork on the North Slope, but the quiet man from Fairbanks would have none of it. Only with his death in May 1977, not long before the first oil started to flow south to Valdez in the Trans-Alaska Pipeline, could Snedden give Dalton his due. Now James Dalton, he wrote, "can no longer protest being recognized. . . . All Americans, particularly Alaskans, owe a great debt of gratitude to James W. Dalton. . . . Unknown to all but a small handful of Alaskans was the fact that . . . Jim Dalton was largely responsible for making possible today's Prudhoe Bay petroleum development." Dalton refused to take out any oil leases in the millions of acres in the former PLO 82 withdrawal—a policy that Snedden also followed—so as not to be accused of even an appearance of a conflict of interest. "If I made offers to lease [ground area within PLO 82]," he told Snedden, "people might think that all I had in mind in writing the reports was to make a pile of money for myself. We can't have that. All I want to do is to help Alaska develop so that we Alaskans can stand on our own feet."[37]

In 1968, six years before a year-round, overland link between Fairbanks and the Arctic Ocean existed, Snedden first proposed that the path to Prudhoe Bay should someday be called the "Dalton Trail." This came to fruition in 1981, when the Alaska Legislature officially named the North Slope Haul Road from Livengood to Deadhorse the "James W. Dalton Highway."[38]

In 1954 the trail that Snedden and Dalton wanted to build was to Gubik, and the roadblock was PLO 82. Snedden had thought McKay would probably announce the repeal of PLO 82 during his short visit to Fairbanks, but instead of taking action, McKay kept promising he would take action soon.

"I am well aware of the great desire of the people of Fairbanks for the opening of the Gubik gas area," McKay told local civic leaders, adding that he was working as quickly as possible to clear away the red tape, and suggested it would only be a matter of days or weeks. "When the papers reach my desk they will be signed promptly."[39] But that was before Washington, D.C., columnist Drew Pearson got hold of the story.

Few journalists in American history were as eagerly read and thoroughly despised as Pearson. For almost forty years, tens of millions of readers in about six hundred newspapers—almost twice as many as the next most widely syndicated editorial column—followed Drew Pearson's daily feature "Washington Merry-go-round," a combination of hard news, gossip, scandal, scoops, exposés, and insider politics about Congress, the White House, and the executive branch. In a 1944 poll of Washington correspondents, Pearson's colleagues in the national press corps voted him the most influential opinion maker in D.C., the "Washington Correspondent who exerts through his writings the greatest influence on the nation." He received twice as many votes as his closet competitor, Walter Lippmann, and more votes than all the remaining twenty-one columnists on the list combined.[40] But in the same poll his colleagues also judged him to be one of the least accurate men in the business, less than average when it came to "reliability, fairness, and ability to analyze the news."[41] Styling himself a courageous crusader against corruption and hypocrisy, Pearson operated on the principle that occasional lapses in facts were outweighed by the value of bold charges that might be true. One unsympathetic biographer claimed that Pearson "probably made more enemies, published more loose or unfounded charges, called more names, published more guesses and inventions, pursued more vendettas ... than any other man in journal-istic history."[42] Pearson said he had been denounced by three presidents (Roosevelt, Truman, and Eisenhower) and fifty-four senators and con-gressmen. Sen. Joe McCarthy of Wisconsin accused Pearson of being a "perverted," "greedy," "degenerate" Communist tool intent on destroying America, and cited forty-four people who, he said, agreed that Pearson was a liar.[43]

Far more eloquent than McCarthy was Tennessee Sen. Kenneth McKellar, who in the course of a single memorable speech in April 1944 about the "lying human skunk" named Drew Pearson, took up more than three pages in the *Congressional Record*, stretching the limits of the English language to describe his contempt for the "ignorant ass" and "low-lived, double-crossing, dishonest, corrupt scoundrel, who claims to be a col-umnist." McKellar indignantly denied Pearson's charges that he was a Tennessee hillbilly with the worst temper on Capitol Hill; according to Pearson an enraged McKellar in a heated debate once pulled a knife and charged a colleague on the Senate floor, as if he were a Hatfield dispatch-ing a McCoy. In his rebuttal, McKellar described himself as a normally temperate man with a genial disposition; he stoutly denied that he was a hillbilly or had ever drawn a blade in anger in the Senate chambers. He called the knife story a "willful, deliberate, malicious, dishonest, intensely cowardly, low, degrading, filthy lie" that was "the most false, most dam-nable, most outrageous, the most colossal lie I have ever read about myself or anyone else." In the course of his increasingly heated remarks—after which the seventy-five-year-old senator was so worked up that he fainted and needed attention from a doctor—McKellar also called Pearson an "ignorant, blundering, lying ass," "an infamous, dirty, low-down, mean, lying scoundrel," "a natural born-liar ... a congenital liar, a liar by profes-sion, a liar for a living ... a liar in the daytime and a liar in the nighttime," and an "ignorant liar, a pusillanimous liar, a peewee liar, and ... a paid liar."[44]

Cultivating enemies and creating controversies was one secret of Pearson's success. A writer for *Time* once speculated that Pearson's popu-larity was due to the drama of his high-wire attacks, always on the edge of libel, or beyond.[45] It is generally thought that Pearson was accused of libel more than any single journalist in history, though the columnist never kept precise count of how many times he was sued, allegedly be-cause this would have been too convenient a weapon for his adversaries to use against him. One assiduous journalism professor, who conclud-ed that the name Drew Pearson was "synonymous with libel actions,"

authored a book about the libel history of Pearson's column and tallied at
least 108 suits brought against him or his column asking for about $100
million in total damages.[46] Every year from 1939 until his death in 1969,
Pearson was in court somewhere fending off lawsuits. Fortunately for
Pearson, who for obvious reasons could not carry libel insurance, he lost
only one case in his career, a $40,000 judgment in 1953 for impugning
the reputation of a former assistant attorney general. As his 107–1 record
demonstrated, despite the incendiary language and frequent false statements of the "Washington-Merry-go-round," libel was never an easy
thing to prove.[47]

Ironically, when the tables were turned, the lesson about the limits
of libel law known so well by Pearson the defendant was not familiar to
Pearson the plaintiff. Against the advice of his wife and his own counsel,
Pearson filed at least fifteen suits against those he claimed had libeled
him, seeking tens of millions of dollars in damages. He never won a single
suit, but his most important defeat concerned the *News-Miner*—and it
increased the rights of journalists like Pearson to say what they wanted
about public figures like Pearson.

Pearson v. Fairbanks Publishing Co. Inc. and C.W. Snedden was a celebrated 1958 lawsuit for $176,000, prompted by two *News-Miner* edi-
torials that labeled Pearson the "garbage man of the Fourth Estate" and
explained to readers, "Not wishing to distribute garbage with our newspaper, we have dropped Pearson."[48] Of course Pearson had been called much
worse than a "garbage man" by more prominent people and publications.
Time once said he had been called "more kinds of liar . . . than any man
alive," and some were printable.[49] FDR said Pearson was a "chronic liar."
President Truman had famously called him an "S.O.B.," and Pearson relished that appellation so much that he adopted it as his moniker. He enjoyed telling the story of how he once received a letter in the mail that had
no name, street, city, or country on the envelope; it was addressed simply
to "The S.O.B." The title of his 1950s serialized memoir was "Confessions
of an S.O.B." and he bragged that he wanted the inscription on his tomb-
stone to read "Here Lies an S.O.B."[50]

The Snedden-Pearson feud that culminated in the long-running "garbage man" case—which played out its final act in 1966 when Justice John
Dimond of the Alaska Supreme Court ruled that Pearson's "writings frequently did not conform with facts and were therefore worthless," so that

calling him a "garbage man" was not a "reckless disregard" of the truth—
actually began a dozen years earlier when Pearson almost single-handedly
thwarted Snedden's campaign to repeal PLO 82 and in the process halted
any realistic chances for the development of oil and gas on the Arctic
Coast of Alaska for years to come.[51] In the summer of 1954 Pearson believed the Eisenhower administration was in the pocket of the oil industry. ("During his eight years in the White House," Pearson later charged,
"Eisenhower did more for the nation's private oil and gas interests than
any other President."[52]) The columnist had suspected McKay's ulterior
motives from the first day he met him. "Called on the new Secretary of
Interior, Douglas McKay," Pearson wrote in his diary on March 9, 1953,
"a nice guy but a political phony if I ever knew one. He has no conception whatsoever about the basic fundamentals of protecting the public
and would give away the entire national domain if he thought he could
get away with it." In his mind McKay came off like a cheap used-car
salesman with a guilty conscience. "He employs the tactic of talking fast
and lengthily, a strategy frequently used by smart politicians who want to
avoid embarrassing questions."[53]

When Pearson learned of the campaign in 1954 to repeal PLO 82, he
portrayed it as nothing short of another Teapot Dome, the notorious oil-
leasing fraud in the 1920s that had sent Interior Secretary Albert B. Fall
to prison for bribery. In back-to-back columns distributed nationwide on
September 30 and October 1, 1954, Pearson accused "Generous Doug"
McKay of being "hell-bent" on a "dynamite-laden" proposal, a "hush-hush"
scheme to "turn over the vast oil reserves of Alaska to private exploitation
despite the objections of Naval officers and career men in his own Interior
Department." In his typical shotgun style—a *Time* writer said a Pearson
paragraph usually read like it was scribbled on the back of an envelope
"in a lurching taxicab"—Pearson headlined the story "ALASKAN OIL-
RESERVE TAKES ON SHADES OF TEAPOT DOME." He labeled the
PLO 82 repeal campaign, and the effort to interest private firms in Umiat
oil and Gubik gas, "the biggest Bonanza the oil industry has been handed
for some time." He accused McKay of secretly planning to "give" $50 mil-
lion worth of geophysical research—the amount the navy had spent on
Pet 4 exploration—to his friends in the oil industry, insinuating it was an
underhanded deal brokered by oil company executives now working in the
Eisenhower administration.[54]

Snedden thought Pearson's columns on the arctic oil and gas fields
were "a big shovelful of 'political bulloney,'" full of "vicious mistruths"
as ridiculous as any anticapitalist propaganda emanating from Moscow.

"These particular columns ... distributed all over America," the *News-Miner* complained, "consist of half truths skillfully manipulated to create an impression that is completely false." The Navy had no use for natural gas whatsoever, and Gubik was outside of the Pet 4 boundary and under sole jurisdiction of the Secretary of the Interior. The *News-Miner* had been publicly campaigning throughout 1954 to get traction on releasing the oil lands and building the Gubik gas line. Those pushing the idea were hardly the mythical cabal of shadowy "MILLIONAIRE OILMEN" concocted by Pearson, but rather small-time Fairbanks entrepreneurs who hoped the untapped reserves of natural gas could heat their homes and businesses.[55] "The 'plot' to 'grab' Arctic oil lands which Mr. Pearson reported is a complete figment of his own imagination."[56]

To Snedden's dismay, however, the damage had been done. Millions of readers saw Pearson's columns about the arctic "Teapot Dome," and Secretary McKay, fearful of yet another "give-away" charge, reversed his tracks immediately, abandoning any serious effort to repeal PLO 82. McKay had been so scared by Pearson's attack that he refused to use his authority to restore PLO 82 to the public domain, and instead passed the buck to Congress, which had no responsibility for the matter. "Douglas McKay has all the courage of a rabbit," claimed George Sundborg of the *Juneau Independent* and the former head of the Alaska Development Board. "Doubletalk Doug" had promised to remove the federal freeze on the arctic oil and gas lands, but now was claiming that he had been misunderstood. McKay was even quoted as saying that the idea of practical oil development in the Arctic was preposterous anyway. "The ground is so frozen," McKay supposedly said, "I can't see why the oil companies would want them [*sic*]."[57]

McKay's about-face on PLO 82 after Pearson's tirade was discouraging, but Snedden refused to give up his campaign to open Gubik. Continuing to work behind the scenes with Strand and McKay, he even tried one last time after McKay had announced in the spring of 1956 that he would resign and return home to Oregon to run against Senator Wayne Morse. When Snedden happened to find himself at the same hotel as McKay in Portland in March 1956, he seized the opportunity. "McKay checked in at the hotel while I was still standing at the registration desk and I had a very good opportunity to discuss [PLO 82] ... with him the following day."[58] However, McKay never did anything about PLO 82 except talk about it, and though Snedden considered the secretary's inaction a huge missed opportunity, few Alaskans outside of Fairbanks shared his indignation.

In the 1950s the oil and gas resources on the Arctic Coast were generally considered to be neither rich enough nor accessible enough for practical development, so the projected economic benefits were judged not worth the inevitable political heat—as demonstrated by the success of Pearson's attack. When word had first surfaced in early 1954 that the opening of the arctic reserves might be included in the 1954 statehood bill, Bob Bartlett had feared that any "provision abolishing Naval Petroleum Reserve No. 4" tacked onto statehood legislation would be "loaded with dynamite." The delegate noted, however, that if Secretary McKay genuinely wanted to lift the portion of PLO 82 that covered Gubik, he could do so with a stroke of the pen. He wondered why McKay would dither about tying PLO 82 to any legislation unless the real motive was to sabotage the statehood bill.[59] Bob Atwood sensed the same danger. "Don't Mix Oil and Statehood," he warned in an editorial. According to Atwood, the effort to settle the "Arctic oil question" with a rider in the statehood bill would be "one of the worst things that could happen for Alaska" and would further complicate the political calculus of entering the Union. "The reserve on the Arctic rim of Alaska," Atwood wrote, "has no bearing on statehood."[60]

A new formula for releasing PLO 82 would have to be found, but that would have to wait for the appointment of a new secretary of the interior, Fred Seaton, and a stroke of political genius by Seaton and Snedden that would not only open the door to oil and gas exploration on the Arctic Coast but would create the largest conservation unit in American history, the nearly nine-million-acre Arctic Wildlife Range. Meanwhile, it was true, as Atwood said, that the oil and gas reserves on the "Arctic rim" would play no role in statehood for Alaska, even though those resources would ultimately answer the fundamental statehood problem: How could the State of Alaska support itself? Time would prove that the riches on the Arctic Slope in PLO 82, as Snedden and Dalton believed, would be the financial bedrock of Alaska's future—but if it had been left up to McKay, Alaska would have had neither oil nor statehood.

10

"Start Acting Like Ladies and Gentlemen"

Douglas McKay's missteps regarding Alaska's political future originated in the spring of 1954, at what seemed like an opportune moment for the Republican Party. Until that time the consensus in Washington was that for partisan reasons Republicans would continue to favor Hawaii and block Alaska. The *News-Miner* reported with no comment about a satirical skit at the 1953 Gridiron Club dinner in Washington, D.C., contrasting the GOP's support for Republican Hawaii with its cold shoulder for Democratic Alaska. To the tune of "Sweet Leilani," an "Alaskan Eskimo" sang a mournful dirge as "a Republican chorus" danced the hula:

> Sweet Hawaii, G.O.P. flower,
> Leaders smile on statehood just for you.
> They say you'll give them extra power,
> While I have votes so few.
>
> Poor Alaska, we are forsaken.
> We have no Wai-ki-ki like you
> No hula girls to charm the Senate,
> You are their dream come true.[1]

In January 1954, Nebraska Sen. Hugh Butler, the heavyweight Republican chairman of the Senate Committee on Interior and Insular

Affairs, and the most forceful anti-statehood Republican in the Senate, shocked his friends and enemies by switching his position and coming out in full support of admitting Alaska.[2] Butler was a Taft Republican to the core, and the most influential GOP policy maker on Western affairs in the Senate, who could have become secretary of the interior if Taft had won the presidency. As an unapologetic isolationist—Eisenhower was too much of a New Dealing internationalist for his taste—Butler opposed foreign aid, Social Security, and free trade, and had once been aligned with the Nebraska Protective Association, an affiliate of the Ku Klux Klan.[3] Besides these sterling conservative credentials, the Nebraska Senator had for years been the GOP bulwark against admitting Alaska to the Union, making him the bête noire of the Alaska statehood movement. His off-hand comment before he had gone to Alaska in 1953 that he wanted to hear from the "little people" in Alaska, to see if they supported statehood as much as the Democratic party bigwigs and political aspirants who typically testified at Senate hearings, had inspired the formation of a grass-roots group known as "The Little Man for Statehood Club." When Butler held hearings in Alaska he was besieged by members of the "The Little Man Club"—both men and women—who wore buttons and signed petitions that said "I'm a Little Man for Statehood."[4]

Butler's endorsement of statehood in January 1954—at about the same time that Snedden had decided to shift the *News-Miner's* position—was a turning point. Publicly, Butler claimed he'd changed his mind because he believed Alaska could finally support itself; privately, he admitted there were other considerations. "It may surprise you to know that this time I'm for statehood for Alaska," he confided to a former colleague in the Republican caucus in January 1954. "I'm coming out stronger than horse-radish for it because I'm not going to let the Democrats take the ball away from us."[5] Writing to one of his closest advisors, he admitted that politics dictated the change of tactics:

> I am still no more enthusiastic than you are for the
> [Alaska statehood] legislation, but the battle at the
> moment is between the two parties as to who gets
> the credit for the statehood bills. . . . You don't have
> to argue with me that a fellow really ought to be
> a statesman instead of a politician in a matter like
> this, but the big majority in both parties are politi-
> cians this time and not statesmen.[6]

Confident that Alaska statehood had become a winning national issue for Republicans, Butler told Eisenhower and Republican Senate Majority Leader William Knowland that it would be "very helpful, politically, with respect to the country as a whole" for the GOP to "clearly and unequivocally" support statehood for both Alaska and Hawaii. "I am convinced that the majority of Americans do favor statehood for both Territories."[7]

Senator Butler hoped that Interior Secretary McKay and his staff could get Eisenhower aboard a Republican statehood bandwagon, but most of all he wanted the president to take "a clear stand, one way or the other," as he believed the White House's refusal to clarify its position was hurting GOP prospects.[8] McKay and Undersecretary Orme Lewis met with the president and a few top aides in the White House on the morning of March 2, 1954, to try to garner Eisenhower's support for Alaska statehood. The meeting did not go well. McKay was poorly prepared; he lacked any understanding of why Eisenhower was doubtful about admitting Alaska, and furthermore Ike seemed to know more about Alaska than his secretary of the interior. McKay timidly turned the presentation over to Lewis. As Lewis recalled more than twenty years later, they were seated in a small semicircle around the president's desk, and for a few seconds when it was his turn to speak, he was panic-stricken. "Ike switched his chair around," Lewis said, " . . . and looked at me and said, 'Mr. Lewis, this better be goddamned good.'"[9]

It wasn't good enough. After listening politely for about twenty minutes, the former five-star general replied that partisan political advantage aside, he was not about to do as McKay and Lewis were asking because in his mind Alaska was both too vulnerable and too strategically important to be a state. Just the day before the White House meeting, Ike had said that he was glad for any action that would keep the Alaska statehood bill "on the shelf," telling press secretary James Hagerty—who recorded the president's comment in his diary—that he "couldn't think of a better place for it. Can't understand Alaska statehood. It's an outpost."[10]

To Eisenhower, Alaska was the front line of the Cold War, where the Pentagon needed the freedom to move troops into place at a moment's notice without interference from state or local officials, especially in the remote regions closest to the Soviet Union. Since entering West Point in 1911 he had devoted more than forty years to anticipating and countering threats to the security of the United States, and his concerns about Alaska defenses were hardly new.

In 1947, as army chief of staff, General Eisenhower made a two-week inspection tour through Alaska. Upon his return he reported that the military facilities in Alaska needed to be strengthened and expanded immediately, warning ominously that Japan's capture during World War II of the Philippines (where he had served under General MacArthur from 1935 to 1939) was "an example of what can happen when such outposts were not properly defended."[11] Stalin reportedly had deployed a huge army of several hundred thousand on the Chukotka Peninsula in the late 1940s "to ensure that Soviet forces could attack the United States" and "to land in Alaska in the event of war."[12] Over the western horizon, Stalin's industrialized Siberia, with millions of people, hundreds of thousands of troops, and a string of slave labor camps, was a fearful prospect. The situation in Alaska only deteriorated further, in Eisenhower's view, with the Soviet deployment of its first atomic bomb in 1949 and the continued improvement of Russian long-range bombers. In the spring of 1950, by which time Eisenhower had resigned from the army to become president of Columbia University, the retired general made national headlines when he warned of the Soviet threat to Alaska, saying that strengthening Alaska's army garrisons was the nation's first strategic necessity. He urged the Truman administration and the Pentagon to triple the troop strength in Alaska to protect the triad of strategic air bases outside of Anchorage and Fairbanks—Elmendorf, Ladd, and Eielson—that were the foundation of America's northern defense perimeter.[13] "I don't cry wolf," Ike told the Senate Appropriations Committee.[14]

At the time of Eisenhower's 1950 warning about Alaska's precarious defenses, the widely respected *New York Times* military editor, Hanson Baldwin, reported that the Pentagon realized Alaska was "vulnerable both to air bombardment and to airborne assault." One frightening scenario was the landing of even a single company of Soviet troops "at Nome, or in the Outer Aleutians, or in the Kenai Peninsula." Such an incident would be a propaganda coup, forcing the United States to drive them out at enormous cost, just as occurred after the Japanese occupation of Kiska and Attu Islands in the Aleutians in 1942–1943. Another danger was an airborne assault on the Anchorage and Fairbanks airbases that would also give the Soviets a disproportionate advantage. "Seizure of these fields," Baldwin wrote, "would bring a good part of Alaska under enemy domination and would force the United States to allocate a material part of its strength to checkmate the enemy." Yet a third nightmarish possibility was a Soviet fire bombing attack or atomic raid on Anchorage and Fairbanks that would not only wipe out Alaska's two largest cities but also neutralize the air bases and "leave our troops scrabbling around in the snow, struggling not against the enemy, but for shelter and survival."[15]

By 1954 President Eisenhower was no less concerned about Alaska's strategic situation. At the meeting with McKay and Lewis, perturbed that his Interior Department had missed the signal importance of Alaska to U.S. Armed Forces, the Commander-in-Chief spread a map of Alaska across his desk as if he were giving a lecture to junior officers at the U.S. Army War College and explained the implications for hemispheric defense. Almost as an afterthought, he took a pencil and drew a circle around western and northern Alaska and told Lewis, "Now if we had control of this area we'd have no problem. Otherwise we're sunk."[16]

The president had drawn a line in the tundra. Henceforth he never wavered in his determination that national security concerns somehow needed to be addressed before Alaska was ready for statehood, and if a new state were to be born, the boundary lines would have to be redrawn in order to meet his objections. Yet the president's specific objections as well as the location of the line and the rationale for it were impossible to pin down. (At one point Bartlett would complain that "so many map makers are busy in so many ways that every whipstitch brings a new proposal as to where the boundary line should run. It all adds up to a bunch of nonsense in any case."[17]) The shifting line was symptomatic of the administration's entire approach. A definitive explanation of the president's reasoning was never articulated, mystifying both Democrats and Republicans on the Hill and even the members of his own executive agencies. Democratic critics accused Eisenhower of political partisanship while Republicans such as Butler, who thought the refusal to endorse Alaska hurt the GOP's prospects nationally, believed the president was not partisan enough.[18]

There were good reasons for Taft men to doubt the president's GOP credentials. Democrats had tried to draft General Eisenhower for the presidential nomination in 1948 and 1952, and before Ike defeated "Mr. Republican," Ohio Sen. Robert Taft, for the GOP nomination in 1952, even Sherman Adams, the head of New Hampshire's "Eisenhower for President Committee" (and eventually Ike's White House Chief of Staff) did not know if Eisenhower belonged to the Republican Party.[19]

Clouding the picture even further was the embarrassing revelation that back in 1950 at a speech in Denver, private citizen Eisenhower had spoken in favor of immediate statehood for both Alaska and Hawaii. When that became known, President Eisenhower fudged the question at a press conference with typical Eisenhowerese: "I was not responsible at that moment for the national security of the United States. I didn't bear the responsibility I do now. . . . I don't mean to say that I have changed my mind. I still think that any territory of the United States has got a right to strive to achieve the standards normally accepted for statehood, but we have got a very, very difficult, tough problem up there."[20]

When pushed by a reporter at a press conference in July 1954, he admitted in a classic bit of circumlocution that as a territory Alaska would not necessarily be "easier to defend," but it would be "easier to use, because . . . it is under the absolute control of the central government."[21]

— ·—·—· —

No one in Alaska had to be told that a territory was "easier to use" by the federal government. Resentment against such ease of use was the whole purpose of seeking statehood. But if a territory was not "easier to defend" than a state, what exactly were the president's objections to statehood? Even the members of Ike's own administration could not answer that. As head of the Interior Department, McKay should have been the administration's lead voice on Alaska affairs, yet he and his staff never formulated a clear direction on Alaska for internal use, let alone for the public. McKay and several of his top officials actually admitted to the press that they didn't know the administration's views on statehood. Bartlett never ceased to be astonished that McKay "consistently insists that he is stating a personal opinion and not representing the President. For the love of goodness, if the Secretary of the federal department chiefly concerned with the Territory cannot speak for the administration in a proposition involving the Territory then who can?"[22]

Despite Ike's impeccable military credentials, few people outside the administration believed his argument that Alaska had to remain a territory for purposes of national defense. "If there was ever a phony reason for not recognizing statehood in Alaska," said Oregon Senator Wayne Morse, "that is one."[23] Bartlett suspected that rumors about national security were "being instigated by statehood opponents" because "the most powerful curse which could be laid on statehood would be to assert that its granting would be in derogation of our military position in Alaska."[24] As Bartlett predicted, statehood opponents such as Sen. A. W. Robertson of Virginia tried to get all the mileage they could out of the security scare. In a unique twist, Robertson confidentially argued that Alaska was impossible to defend from the Soviets under any circumstances, but fortunately, since it was only a territory, it would not have to be held to the "bitter end [as if it had been] a State of the Union." According to Robertson, there was a "conspiracy of silence in the press" about what was at stake, but the Pentagon knew full well that

>Russia could land in Alaska two or three hundred thousand men any time she sees fit. In that contingency, the only practical thing to do would be to evacuate the people of Alaska, because we would have no power in the world to meet such a land force ... As an experienced soldier, Eisenhower, of course, knows the impossibility of defending Alaska under such circumstances, and that is primarily the reason why he has announced that he is against statehood for Alaska.[25]

When Robertson shared his views with the White House, the president's deputy assistant, retired general Wilton B. "Jerry" Persons, commended the Virginia Senator's reasoning. "The arguments you make," Persons wrote, "are certainly very persuasive."[26]

Others were not as easily persuaded. Almost all Alaska residents seemed to share Snedden's belief that the administration's supposed national security reasoning was insincere.[27] "If the Russians attack Seattle tomorrow," Bartlett asked, "will a bill be put through the Congress immediately revoking statehood for Washington[?]"[28] The fundamental philosophical question was the continued legitimacy of civilian control of the armed forces, and the delegate wondered if for some supposed reason "the military branch cannot operate properly under America's normal system of government should we abolish that system and substitute another?"[29]

Snedden was as baffled as anyone during Eisenhower's first term by the president's opposition to Alaska statehood. "Why the administration is against Statehood remains a mystery," a *News-Miner* editorial complained in May 1954. Despite the vague references by Eisenhower to defense matters, top officials at the Pentagon continually denied there were any military reasons to keep Alaska from joining the union, and the chief of the air force had gone on record supporting statehood, so the *News-Miner* had to conclude that the national security excuse was "most curious, to say the least. If there are defense considerations that are blocking Statehood, our top air force and army officials don't know about them."[30]

Faced with the impossible task of reconciling Ike's opposition to statehood with Butler and the GOP's newfound enthusiasm, the White

House and the Department of the Interior crafted a solution that pleased almost no one: partitioning Alaska along the Eisenhower Line—misleadingly known as the McKay Line—with the more heavily populated and economically developed southern and eastern sections, including the southeastern Panhandle and the Anchorage–Fairbanks railbelt and roadbelt, becoming a state and the more lightly populated western and northern regions remaining a territory. In essence it placed the administration in the position of being for and against statehood at the same time. The notion was that Alaskans would be more satisfied with half a loaf than no bread at all. It was a serious miscalculation. Eisenhower's team quickly learned that most Alaskans were prepared to starve rather than take the crumbs offered by the Interior Department.

Governor Frank Heintzleman was the fall guy left with the unenviable task in April 1954 of announcing and taking dubious credit for the administration's half-Alaska strategy, and he was met with a near universal chorus of condemnation and spontaneous revolt across the territory from both Republicans and Democrats. Snedden thought partition made no economic sense whatsoever because it would deprive Alaskans of the vital resources that they would need to support statehood, such as the potential oil and gas deposits in northern Alaska. "We would prefer that Alaska remain united," Snedden said. But he was at least willing to give the administration the benefit of the doubt. If partition was just a temporary tactical change and not a strategy shift, "then possibly Alaska would be better off to accept Statehood a parcel at a time, rather than all at once. The important thing is to win Statehood, by some means or other."[31]

Few others shared Snedden's view that half a state was better as a start than no state at all. "I . . . will never find it satisfactory to split Alaska," Barrie White of Operation Statehood wrote, "particularly in such an arbitrary manner. . . . On this issue, it's *all or none* with me—and everyone else I know up here who's been around the Territory long enough to call himself a permanent Alaskan."[32] Delegate Bartlett's office was inundated with angry telegrams and letters. "The storm of protest is terrific," he said. "I have never seen the equal of it."[33] The outcry was so explosive that reading some of the "vigorous" language in one telegram, Bartlett said he felt "as if I had a lighted firecracker in my pants pocket about to go off."[34] Both Republicans and Democrats united against the "ridiculous," "absurd," "nefarious," "simple-minded," "preposterous," "drastic," "rotten," "disgraceful," "infamous," "outrageous," "shocking," "lame," "misguided," "inexcusable," "bomb-shell," "stab-in-the-back," "below-the-belt" suggestion that Alaska needed to be torn apart in order to be acceptable.[35]

One distressed resident said partitioning Alaska was nothing short of a "national sacrilege."[36] There were calls for the governor's retirement, resignation, or impeachment. "Put it in big type on the front page," a Skagway man telegraphed the *Juneau Independent*. "Heintzleman must go."[37]

As unpopular as it may have been with 99 percent of the public, McKay continued to support the ill-advised partition plan or some variant of it for the rest of his time in office, insisting that Alaska would have to be cut in half along one line or another if it expected to join the Union. In February 1955 he dismissed all of northern and western Alaska as "barren wildernesses" that "could be nothing but a burden on an infant state." And he continued to pass the buck with a vague recommendation that "congress should examine with care the strategic importance of these areas to the nation's defense, in the light of world conditions."[38] Oregon Democratic Sen. Richard Neuberger blasted McKay's partition plan as making Alaska "a kind of twilight-zone" that would be "half military reservation and half state . . . sort of a centaur, half man and half horse, but actually no adequate version of either."[39] Adlai Stevenson quipped that McKay's partition proposal was like offering to lighten a man's burden by cutting off his head.[40]

Most Alaskans instinctively hated the idea of splitting the territory. Bill Egan spoke for many when he said he'd sooner see statehood's chances killed for now rather "than take any compromise along the lines of the Heintzleman proposal. The darn fool."[41] But others were less sure. Snedden, Bartlett, and others believed that the administration's proposal, backed by key members of Congress, was the only practical alternative on the horizon. Butler, now the Republican champion of statehood, told Atwood partition was the "only opportunity" for admitting Alaska and that it was an idea all Alaskans would have to get behind eventually, even if begrudgingly as Snedden did. "Personally, I'd like to have given you every inch of the Territory," Butler wrote, "but I am convinced we're not going to get it through in that form."[42] In a confidential memo Bartlett recorded the gloomy outlook: "Alaskans had better begin giving serious consideration to some plan for partitioning Alaska along the general although not the specific lines proposed by Governor Heintzleman." The delegate tried to be stoic. "We must view this dispassionately and objectively in clear realization that we are not calling the shots now." Those who were calling the shots seemed determined to carve up the territory. "They are not asking advice from Bob Atwood on this subject of divisions. They are not asking advice from me. So far as I know they are not asking advice from anyone in Alaska."[43]

The administration may not have been listening to anyone in Alaska, but that only made the complaints louder. Hundreds of telegrams poured into the White House urging the president to clarify his position and to reject the Interior Department partition proposal. On behalf of the *News-Miner*, editor Jack Ryan cabled Eisenhower to ask him where he stood: "As one of Alaska's oldest and most influential newspapers which supported you for President while you were still in uniform we would feel honored if you would explain to us your stand on Alaska statehood." Ryan queried, "Why should we be required to come into the Union stripped of all our really promising resources?" and then asked what was the real story behind the national security claims: "[I]f America can defend 48 states, can't she defend one or two more? If America can defend Korea and Indochina effectively, can't she defend her own citizens[?]"[44]

But no definitive answer was forthcoming from the president. Even Bartlett had to admit that he had never been so confused about what was happening inside the administration and why. "You hear rumors and rumors of rumors," he privately explained. "You can't pin it down."[45]

Out of this confusion came one final, dramatic effort to get straight answers about Eisenhower's beliefs, setting up a historic confrontation between the president and the people of Alaska. In May 1954 more than fifty Alaskans volunteered at their own expense for a bipartisan "Statehood pilgrimage" to D.C. on an Alaska Airlines DC-4 to lobby Congress and the administration. Operation Statehood, the citizens' group based in Anchorage that had evolved out of the "The Little Man for Statehood" movement, organized the trip. Snedden did all he could to encourage Fairbanks residents to make the journey. "The flight to Washington," he wrote, "will impress congressmen that Alaskans mean business."[46]

Snedden sent editor Jack Ryan and his wife as the *News-Miner*'s representatives on the statehood flight. Perhaps Sourdough Jack summarized the adventure best: "Found out one thing in Washington. Congressmen is people that Alaskans can depend on. No matter what, the answer is always 'No.'"[47]

The old sourdough could have been quoting Nebraska Republican A. L. "Doc" Miller, the influential chairman of the House Interior Committee. Representative Miller told the delegation flat-out that if Alaskans wouldn't settle for partition "you will probably get nothing." According to Miller, statehood was doomed unless the entire area north of the Yukon and west of Galena could be reserved as a permanent military reservation "with no chance for future annexation by the new state."[48] House Speaker Joe Martin (R-Massachusetts) was just as blunt. He said in his mind Alaska was "physically, financially, and economically" not ready to join the Union.[49] According to Bartlett, Martin told someone privately that he was against statehood "because the country is too cold and no one wants to live there."[50]

The highlight of the trip came on May 13, 1954, when a group of fifteen representatives from the Alaska contingent met for a quarter of an hour with Eisenhower in the White House. The president had been warned that Governor Heintzleman had come under intense fire for recommending the partitioning of Alaska, leading Assistant Secretary of Interior Lewis to suggest in a briefing memo that it "would be most helpful to Governor Heintzleman and the Republican Party if the President made a few complimentary remarks to the delegation concerning the Governor's activities."[51]

No one in the room ever forgot the confrontation that sunny Thursday morning at the epicenter of American political power. It came after weeks of tension since the partition plan had first surfaced and frustration heightened by the belief that Ike had been kept in the dark by the Interior Department. The future of Alaska hung in the balance as Operation Statehood President Barrie White, along with thirteen men and one woman from the north, accompanied by Governor Heintzleman and Delegate Bartlett, filed into the Oval Office. To show a unified front the bipartisan group was evenly divided between Republicans and Democrats from across the territory, including both the Republican and Democratic National Committeemen from Alaska, Wally Hickel and Ray Plummer; a senior Republican and Democrat from the Territorial Senate, John Butrovich and Bill Egan; the Democratic Mayor of Fairbanks, Ralph Rivers, and the Republican Mayor of Cordova, Dr. Will Chase; an Eskimo from Dillingham, Miles Brandon, and a housewife from Anchorage, Helen Fischer.

The meeting started informally, with Ike half leaning against the front of his desk as the Alaskans assembled in a semicircle before him. Butrovich, the senior Republican in the Territorial Senate, had been chosen as their spokesman. Bartlett watched with pride as the forty-four-year-old Butrovich, whom he had known since they were both children in Fairbanks, stood up to "Mr. Big," "looked him right in the eye and let loose. . . . John didn't back an inch, figuratively or literally."[52] For about four or five uncomfortable minutes the Alaskans listened as Butrovich

lectured Eisenhower, watching the president's face grow noticeably red-
der as Butrovich explained why they had come all the way to Washington
and the elementary principles of American democracy that were at stake.
"We have heard many reasons why we should not be granted statehood,"
Butrovich told the president, but none, he said, had any merit. "We feel,
Mr. President, that the issue of statehood is not a local issue nor is it a domestic issue. It is, in our opinion, an international issue. The government
of the United States of America has extended its influence throughout the
entire world. We have, as a people, and you, Sir, as an individual, brought
hope . . . to oppressed people everywhere." Therefore it was impossible to
understand why Ike would not lift the telephone and make the call that
would get the statehood bill pried out of the congressional committee
where it was hopelessly stuck.

"Sir, we think that you are a great American, but . . ."

Butrovich's memory of the meeting years later was that he inadvertently paused a moment too long after the word "but," giving the redden-
ing Eisenhower the chance to caustically interject something to the effect
that he was "glad that at least you think I am a loyal American."

As Eisenhower started to steam, Butrovich pushed on: "but . . . we are
shocked to come here and find a bill which affects the lives of more than
150,000 Americans bottled up in a House committee when a nod from
you could bring it out."[53]

By the time Butrovich had finished, Eisenhower's face was "almost
fiery red" and according to Bartlett his crimson complexion made him
look like he was "fixing for a stroke of apoplexy."[54]

"John was eloquent," Bartlett said. "John was firm, John was a spokesmen of whom we could be proud. He fixed the leader of the free world
right smack in the eye . . . speaking firmly and yet respectfully. . . . The
Eisenhower temper was almost visibly contained. But John kept on boring in."[55] According to Butrovich, on his way out of the Oval Office that
morning Chief of Staff Adams shook his hand and said, "I think you've
just made your first and last trip to the White House."[56]

"An outspoken Alaskan told President Eisenhower exactly how
residents of the territory feel about Statehood," Jack Ryan wrote in the
News-Miner the next day. It was a "Straight-from-Shoulder Talk" the
sub-headline read, but there was no sign that Butrovich's earnest eloquence had "softened the chief executive's opposition."

"All persons present," Ryan explained, "agreed that the President appeared to redden" during the course of the Butrovich sermon, and the
gloomy banner headline summarized the encounter:

IKE UNMOVED BY STATEHOOD PLEA

"He did not say he was against Alaska statehood," Ryan wrote of the president's response, "but neither did he say he was for it. He left the Alaskans with the definite impression that he was in sympathy with their request for the rights of citizenship, but he was not in favor of granting Alaska Statehood now."[57]

Even if the blunt message from Butrovich had done nothing but irritate the president, Alaskans were proud that someone from the territory had finally looked Ike in the eye and explained what it felt like to be denied the full rights of American citizenship. The red-faced general-turned-president clearly was not used to being called on the carpet in the Oval Office, and organizer Barrie White felt it necessary to offer a modest apology. "If our plea was couched in strong terms," White explained in a short note, "we are sure you realized it was merely a measure of our intense sincerity."[58] White assured Eisenhower that all Alaskans were "very conscious of the tremendous burden you carry" as the leader of the Free World and had meant no disrespect. Four days after the Alaskans' meeting with Eisenhower in the White House, the Supreme Court under Chief Justice Earl Warren issued its historic unanimous ruling in *Brown v. Board of Education* outlawing segregation in public schools. White thought the timing was perfect for the administration to follow that landmark case and give Alaskans the political equality they deserved. "Coupled with the recent decision on segregation by the Supreme Court," White wrote, "I cannot conceive of any stronger record of progress by this administration in the field of human rights."[59]

The consensus among the Alaskans was that former *News-Miner* editor William Strand, director of the Office of Territories, was the chief anti-statehood force at the Interior Department, still promoting the same policies he had espoused for years in Fairbanks under Cap Lathrop. They mistakenly believed that it was Strand, not Eisenhower, who was the real stumbling block in the administration.

The bitterness against Strand exploded shortly before the Alaska delegation departed Washington. At a farewell cocktail party at Strand's home, the host took GOP Committeeman Hickel—the one-time Kansas amateur welterweight champ—to a back room to discuss some confidential party matters, where polite conversation quickly evolved into a shouting match. At the time it was hardly unique for GOP gatherings in Alaska to erupt into rhetorical violence. Hickel had come to power backed by the pro-statehood "Young Turks" of the GOP in Anchorage, who had staged a successful revolt against the party's longtime power broker, "Boss" Al White of Juneau, and the philosophical, regional, and generational divisions between the factions were still raw. Perhaps the "P" in Alaska's GOP should have stood for "Partition" as Democratic presidential hopeful Adlai Stevenson joked when he came to the territory in 1954.[60] Before Hickel's ascent, Alaska's Grand Old Party was neither grand nor effective, but it most certainly was old, with Strand, the apparent architect of partition, solidly on the side of the old guard.

The main issue between Strand and Hickel was choosing a replacement for retiring Judge Harry Pratt in the Fourth Division in Fairbanks. Hickel wanted the post to go to Mike Stepovich, a young Fairbanks attorney, but Strand insisted he was in charge of patronage jobs for Alaska and that he had a candidate from the Lower 48 slated for the job. (Eventually the judgeship would be given to Vernon D. Forbes of North Dakota, with a Democratic newspaper slamming the selection as "the worst example in recent times of a carpetbag appointment in complete disregard of the wishes of Alaskans."[61]) According to Hickel, Strand boasted that he was in charge of setting policy for Alaska and that he "didn't give a damn about any or all Alaskans." He said Strand even accused the young Alaska Republicans generally and Hickel personally of being traitors for not supporting Heintzleman and the administration's partition plan. An account in the *Anchorage Times* claimed that when "Hickel asked how anyone could expect to sell Alaskans a scheme that has no purpose and no advantage," the director shot back: "You don't sell it to them—you tell them. You stuff it down their throats."[62] The Strand-Hickel "bout," according to Atwood, the Anchorage publisher, "smoked out" the foes of statehood, and was proof that the former *News-Miner* man had "virtually proclaimed himself 'dictator' of Alaska," leading Atwood's *Anchorage Times* to issue a page-one banner declaration:

STRAND BRANDED 'DICTATOR'

Atwood contended that the revelation of this petty tyrant's machinations was the missing piece of the puzzle, the key that revealed the partition plan as "a nefarious scheme to complicate the legislative process and divert congressional action up a blind alley that would lead to nothing." He thought Strand was the rotten core of the administration's statehood opposition thwarting the will of the people. "There is no joy in discovering that a high official is basing his actions on personal hate and vindictiveness."[63]

Snedden took strong exception to Atwood and others who chose to scapegoat his friend and former editor, and to the Alaska Republican party's subsequent passage of a resolution that flayed Strand for his support of partition and his "dictator-like attitude in party affairs in which he ignored the wishes of Alaskans."[64] Snedden's response to Atwood was an editorial recapping "Strand vs. Hickel," in which the *News-Miner* argued that a few "heated words" at a cocktail party amounted to little more than a rattling teapot. "We believe that tempers flared . . . and some things may have been said that should not have been uttered. But we doubt if this exchange of words . . . constitutes anything very significant."[65]

From Strand's perspective, Atwood's attack was another example of the arrogance and immaturity of many statehood proponents. Like his mentor Senator Butler, Strand pledged that he had been converted to the statehood cause, but as a midlevel bureaucrat in the executive branch he could not be a vocal advocate and continue working for Eisenhower. Since Strand said he was nothing but a "small spud" in the Interior Department, it would have been unthinkable of him to break ranks. The former five-star in the White House was not accustomed to hearing subordinates speaking publicly out of turn. "You know how long I'd be in this job," he said, "if I came out for statehood—one week."[66] Strand admitted long afterwards that McKay's Interior Department was caught in a politically untenable position: pushing partition due to unspecified military concerns—concerns that actually came directly from Eisenhower—as a prerequisite for statehood, but, because they could not be more explicit, continually "forced to endure a lot of noise and abuse from the far north."[67]

Failure to recognize that Strand's policies were an effect of Eisenhower's opposition to statehood—not the cause—revealed how far out of touch the leaders of Alaska's statehood movement were with the inner workings of the administration, but the members of the Interior Department were equally blind to political conditions in the territory. This was never more apparent than when Strand accompanied McKay to Alaska on the secretary's ill-fated 1954 summer tour of the territory. The day before the relatively warm reception they would receive from Snedden and others in Fairbanks, the trip soured when McKay, still smarting from the "dictator" flap with Atwood and what he perceived as the rude behavior of the Alaska delegation in D.C. six weeks earlier, uttered a few poorly chosen words that would be long remembered. At a gathering with Operation Statehood in the Anchorage Westward Hotel, McKay started angrily lecturing Alaskans that they were not going to get statehood anytime soon principally because they would not accept partition, and then launched into a tirade, accusing them of belligerence, incivility, and a lack of gratitude, and that he was "sick and tired of getting kicked around by Alaskans."

"There isn't one thing done by this administration that you approve," McKay said. "You've given Bill Strand the devil and Strand was probably one of the hardest workers for statehood." Charges in the press about the Interior Department had been "just a bunch of horsefeathers." He said it was time for all Alaskans to come politely with "hat in hand" instead of making demands and to "get back down to earth and start acting like ladies and gentlemen."[68]

McKay's outburst hit a new low for poor taste and bad politics. A cabinet member scolding prominent Alaskans as if they had been a naughty group of teenagers caught smoking behind the barn was a front-page blunder. Even the sympathetic *News-Miner* headlined the secretary's "tongue lashing" as the gaffe that it was:

McKAY FLAILS STATEHOOD GROUP
Tells Anchorage Audience to Act Like Ladies, Gentlemen[69]

Bob Atwood said the secretary's "verbal thrashing" came out of nowhere like "the roar of a jet plane" above a Sunday picnic, because no one had expected a visiting dignitary to act like such a bully and a boor.[70] An irate Alaskan said McKay had the swagger of a "jail master or a tyrant" and his diatribe could have been written by a "Goering, Goebbels, or Malenkov."[71]

In an open letter to McKay the members of Operation Statehood said Alaskans were not about to "approach public officials with our 'hats in hand' which is a polite way of saying on our hands and knees." "Little children sometimes go 'hat in hand' in seeking something they know they shouldn't have. Oppressed peoples drop to their knees before tyrants and despots in begging for bread, or their lives," but Operation Statehood promised McKay that Alaskans would never "go 'hat in hand' before any servant of the people in stating what we believe to be our rights as American citizens."[72]

After hearing of the "shocking exhibition" in Anchorage of McKay's "dictatorial, arbitrary, tyrannical attitude," Oregon Sen. Wayne Morse went to the floor of the U.S. Senate and called his fellow Oregonian a "mental peanut" and a "stage character tyrant" who had been "autointoxicated by his own stupidity." "Well, who does he think he is? A young Hitler? Have we got to the point where free American citizens, even though they are second class citizens in Alaska, and not given the right to vote . . . have to take that kind of abuse from a Secretary of the Interior?"[73] Morse reminded McKay that by the terms of his oath of office he owed his ultimate loyalty only to the American people, and therefore it was a dereliction of duty to repeatedly claim he personally favored statehood but officially could not speak in support because he was only Eisenhower's "hired hand." Such an excuse might have been legitimate for a low-level functionary, but not the top appointee in the U.S. government responsible for the welfare of Alaska. "What the Secretary of Interior ought to recognize is that in his position he has the duty to advise the President; and if he is for statehood, he ought to be willing to stand for statehood himself, irrespective of what the President's views are."[74]

Snedden seldom found himself agreeing with Morse in style or substance, but he ultimately had to admit that Douglass McKay had neither the influence nor the ability to promote the two most important federal initiatives for Alaska's economic and political future. Elimination of PLO 82 and the creation of all Alaska as the forty-ninth state were linked like the proverbial chicken and egg, but McKay's inaction ensured that neither would come first. The *News-Miner* boiled down McKay's apparent philosophy to a simple catch-22 proposition: "Alaska is not yet ready for Statehood, and furthermore, we are seeing to it that the Territory is never ready."[75]

The only hope for Alaska was for "Giveaway" McKay to go back home to Oregon as soon as possible, and when Eisenhower replaced McKay in 1956 with a Nebraska newspaperman named Fred A. Seaton, everything was about to change.

11

The Seaton Revolution

The first chance that Alaskans ever had to vote for president of the United States was April 24, 1956, the same election in which the voters approved the Alaska Constitution and the Alaska-Tennessee Plan. Though the results of the presidential popularity poll did not count, they added up to prove that Alaskans liked Ike almost as much as the rest of America did. In the nonbinding presidential preference primary on the April 24 ballot, President Dwight D. Eisenhower outpolled both Adlai Stevenson—the Democratic standard-bearer in 1952 and the eventual nominee again in 1956—and Sen. Estes Kefauver, Stevenson's chief rival for the Democratic nomination.[1]

The support for Ike cheered Snedden almost as much as it dismayed Alaska Democrats. "I simply am unable to understand the size of the Eisenhower vote," Bartlett wrote Bill Egan two days later. "If people had gone out against the constitution and the Tennessee Plan and voted for Eisenhower at the same time it would have made sense. Yet here they are plugging for him while endorsing the two propositions. Is it that they don't know Eisenhower is against statehood?"[2]

Anchorage Democratic leader Wendell Kay was just as hard-pressed to account for the personal popularity of Ike in Alaska and wondered how any Alaska Republicans would be able to balance "their love for Eisenhower" and their support for statehood. How could they ride on Eisenhower's coattails "when the coattails are going the wrong way?"[3]

It was true that up to 1956 President Eisenhower was the single most important opponent of Alaska's statehood bid. Bartlett said there was so much political fog surrounding statehood that the only thing he was really sure of, beside the solid core of southern opposition, was the importance of Eisenhower: "If Eisenhower would only come out for statehood and twist the arms of the House leadership," he wrote in March 1954, "statehood would be ours this year."[4]

Despite all the other obstacles, it was impossible for anyone to seriously imagine Alaska joining the Union unless Eisenhower changed his views. Without the president's endorsement, the speech making about Alaska on Capitol Hill was all for naught.

But the tea leaves for Alaska were about to change. One month after Alaskans voted for Eisenhower, the man who would eventually convince Eisenhower to vote for Alaska was tapped to become secretary of the interior. Fred A. Seaton, a forty-six-year-old White House Assistant and veteran Nebraska newspaperman, who had briefly served in the U.S. Senate in 1951–1952, would engineer the transformation of the Eisenhower administration from an intractable adversary into an unabashed advocate of statehood. No one else in Ike's cabinet could have wrought such a remarkable turnaround, and the fact that Alaska would become a state in 1959 is a permanent testament to Fred Seaton's personal influence, principled convictions, and political skills.

Among the president's most trusted confidants—Seaton nearly became Ike's chief of staff in 1958—the self-effacing cabinet secretary, who called himself a "liberal-conservative," was one of the core group of Eisenhower supporters from the 1952 campaign. Respected by members of both parties, Seaton was well known on Capitol Hill as a practical man with an open mind and an engaging sense of humor. Cool under fire and calm in a crisis, he proved repeatedly he was the problem solver in Ike's administration, the man who knew how to get things done.[5] When he died in 1974, his obituary in the *New York Times* fondly recalled that Seaton's "aggressive temperament" was combined with such a thoroughly "disarming manner" that no one in Washington "was wiser in the ways of not giving unnecessary offense."[6]

--- ---

Seaton was a reserved and shy man, but gifted with innate political acumen and charm honed during a lifetime around politicians and the press.[7] He was born in 1909 in Washington, D.C., when his father, Fay N. Seaton, was serving as executive secretary for Republican Kansas Sen. Joseph L. Bristow (the senator who would nominate Abilene native Dwight D. Eisenhower for West Point in 1910). The Seaton family moved in 1915 to Manhattan, Kansas, where Fay Seaton bought his first newspaper, the *Manhattan Mercury*. By the time he died thirty-seven years later, in 1952, the formidable media holdings of Fay Seaton and his two sons, Fred and younger brother Richard, spanned five states—Kansas, Colorado, Nebraska, Wyoming, and South Dakota—and included seven daily newspapers, three radio stations, two weekly newspapers, and one semimonthly magazine, *Western Farm Life*, which reached 160,000 families in ten states.[8]

Working for the family company in the midst of the Great Depression in 1937, Fred Seaton and his wife, Gladys, departed Kansas for the small farming and college town of Hastings, Nebraska, "The Queen City of the Plains," to take charge of the Seatons' newest acquisition, the financially troubled *Hastings Tribune*. The young publisher quickly put the *Tribune* solidly in the black. While the community of Hastings had a population of only fifteen thousand, Seaton attracted daily subscribers across a wide swath of the farming belt, and within three years "The Voice of Nebraska's Great Southwest" had a phenomenal circulation of ten thousand. Seaton was claimed to have been the first publisher in Nebraska to use wire photos and the first to utilize three wire services.[9] The *Tribune* became nationally renowned for its editorial and production quality. In 1940 the National Editorial Association honored the *Hastings Tribune* as the finest small-town daily newspaper in the United States. At the annual meeting of the NEA in New York that year, the *Tribune* received four first-place awards, for typography, newspaper production, job printing, and "general excellence." In addition it earned a second-place award for best special edition and a third-place honor for its editorial page.[10] The *New York Times* praised "our Nebraska contemporary" for its "make-up, its news, its variety of reading matter, its pictures," and the community that supported such a fine publication. "Hastings is a college town," the *Times* noted, "and *The Tribune* one of its most distinguished professors."[11]

Though Seaton would always remain a newspaperman at heart—one of his favorite quips was "The ink won't come off"—he also had the political bug from an early age, earning a well-deserved reputation as a maverick liberal Republican. As a youth back in Kansas he had been an organizer of young Republicans for Hoover in 1928, and personal secretary for Governor Alf Landon during his presidential bid in 1936. In Nebraska he served two terms in the legislature, ran the successful Nebraska primary campaign of Harold Stassen in 1948, and served a one-year stint in the U.S. Senate in 1951–1952 when the incumbent died in office (and Seaton declined to seek election in his own right), before coming out as one of the first to endorse Eisenhower in early 1952.[12]

THE INVENTION OF COLOR PRINTING

With the installation of "Alice" in 1953, the *News-Miner* began to invent and perfect many of the techniques of color printing on newsprint that would became standard in the industry in the following decades. Snedden and his chief lieutenant, Chuck Gray, took particular pride in these technological breakthroughs that enabled the *News-Miner* to lead the industry in the quality of four-color reproduction, at a time when most newspapers were nothing but black ink on off-white paper. "In a world of color," a trade journal complained in 1958, "most newspapers persist with drab black and white." In comparison the *News-Miner* was a veritable rainbow. By the late 1950s the *News-Miner* was one of only a few dozen newspapers in the world regularly printing full-color news photographs that were sharp and rich. Most of the images in the following section feature sample pages of the *News-Miner's* color work. Some of the originals have faded with age, and by modern standards of color printing it may seem difficult to appreciate just how striking these originals would have been a half-century and more ago. Few newspapers in the country were half as colorful as the farthest north daily in the United States.

The front page of the special statehood edition published June 30, 1958, featured from left to right Fred Seaton, Mike Stepovich, and Bob Bartlett admiring a flag with seven rows of seven stars, underneath a portrait of President Eisenhower.

For the annual Christmas edition Snedden often commissioned retired printer Paul Solka Jr. to do a painting of early-day Alaska, such as this cheerful scene of a newsboy in front of the old *News-Miner* offices in the 1920s on Third and Cushman Street, decorated with W. F. Thompson's slogan: "Ain't God Good to Fairbanks!"

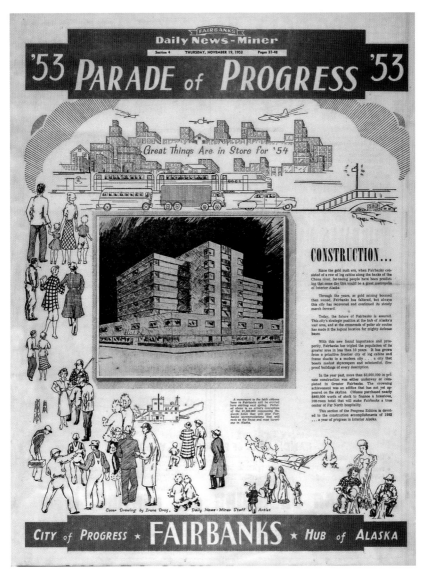

The construction section of the 1953 "Parade of Progress" edition was adorned with clip art of a Fairbanks with skyscrapers that never would be. Featured in the center is an artist's conception of the proposed community-financed hotel that also never materialized, due to friction between those who wanted it built on the west side of Cushman Street and those who wanted it on the east side.

A page out of the tenth annual Progress Edition in 1959, featuring an inset picture of the new Bunnell Building on the University of Alaska Fairbanks campus.

CITY
NEWS
IN BRIEF

What's Your
PLEASURE...
Whatever you want, Classified helps
you find it. If you're things to sell,
rent or buy—use Want Ads. Dial
5662 NOW.

FAIRBANKS
Daily News - Miner

LATE
HOME
EDITION

"America's Farthest North Daily Newspaper" · · · Member of The Associated Press

VOL. XXXVI   15c Per Copy   FAIRBANKS, ALASKA, THURSDAY, JUNE 5, 1958   Twenty Pages   No. 133

IKE URGES ACTION ON STATEHOOD

Wisconsin Tornado Kills 29

Many Buildings Pulverized By Sweeping Cyclone

MENOMONIE, Wis., June 5.

Knowland To Support Alaska Even If Alone

Statehood Discussed at Republican Conference; Pennsylvanian Declares Statehood Needed To Draw Capital

WASHINGTON, June 5.

Death Claims Legislator Ken Johnson

ANCHORAGE, June 5.

Flames Threaten Homestead

Plumbers Vote To Strike

Decision Here On Teamsters

Teenager Joins McKinley Climbing Expedition

SEATTLE, June 5.

T33 Plane Explosion Kills Two

ANCHORAGE, June 5.

Correspondent Tells Saga Of Statehood Bill Strategy

By A. ROBERT SMITH
WASHINGTON, June 5.

WEATHER

DIANA IN THE SPRINGTIME—Blonde Gloa Robertson aims at a target

LATE
BASEBALL
RESULTS

National League

Sourdough Jack
Sez:

A Portrayal of Outdoor Living in Alaska

Special Section Today, Pages 11-20

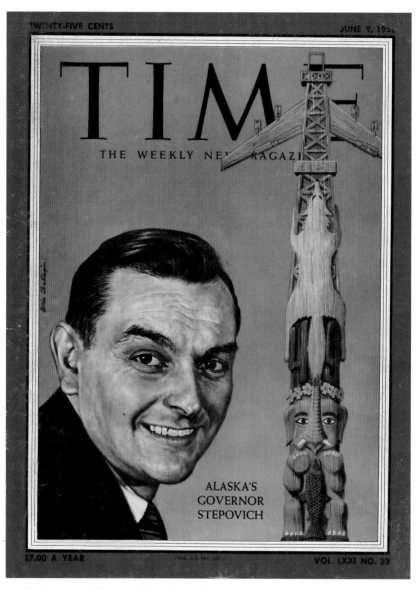

TIME

THE WEEKLY NEWS MAGAZINE

ALASKA'S
GOVERNOR
STEPOVICH

Snedden's greatest publicity coup during the statehood campaign was landing Governor Mike Stepovich (with the GOP totem pole/oil derrick/bomber in the background) on the cover of *Time* on June 9, 1958, three weeks before the final vote in the Senate. The Stepovich story was the most widely read article about the statehood crusade.

Daily News - Miner
PROGRESS EDITION, Wednesday, Nov. 20, 1957—Section 3, Pages 25 to 36

ALASKA'S FIRST FAMILY symbolizes the vibrant, dynamic Alaska of today. Gov. Mike Stepovich, born in Fairbanks, is pictured with his wife, Matilda and seven children in the Governor's Mansion in Juneau. The youngest son, Theodore, rests in his father's arms. The other children, left to right, are Antonia, Marla, Dominic, Mike, Jr., Peter and Christopher.

ALASKA .. its Status Today

The pattern of recent and present growth in Alaska is that of expansion within the limits permitted by territorialism. There is an important difference from the status which applied in the western states on the eve of their own statehood, however. It is that Alaska enjoys instantaneous communication and rapid transportation with the rest of the nation. The territory has bustling cities, fine schools, a great university, a good road and air network. Alaska is a frontier, but a modern and appealing one.

*is reflected in its youth,
its aggressive leadership,
its determination to
become the
Forty - Ninth State of the Union*

Snedden took every possible occasion to keep Governor Stepovich and his entire family in the public eye, such as this portrait of Mike, Matilda, and the first seven of their thirteen children, under the kindly gaze of President Eisenhower in the 1957 Progress Edition.

The front page of the *News-Miner* after the Senate vote to admit Alaska on June 30, 1958. Snedden arranged to have about 1,600 copies of this joyous edition flown overnight to Washington, D.C., on a U.S. Air Force B-47 Stratojet to prove "how close the newest state was to Washington in this day of jet transportation." While the headline that day of the *Anchorage Times*—WE'RE IN!—better captured the spirit of the occasion, the *News-Miner's* was factually more accurate because Alaska would not officially enter the Union until six months later, when Ike signed the presidential proclamation on January 3, 1959.

From the start he was one of the key members of Eisenhower's inner circle and proved his value to Ike as a public relations wizard during the biggest crisis of the presidential campaign, when he helped orchestrate one of the biggest publicity coups and turning points in modern political history: Richard Nixon's 1952 "Checkers Speech." When word of running mate Nixon's "secret expense fund" from wealthy Californians was disclosed in September 1952, money which Nixon said he needed "to support my fight against communism and corruption in government," the scandal threatened to derail the entire campaign. According to a *New York Times* report, "It was Mr. Seaton . . . who almost alone kept his head when the story broke. . . . It was he who planned the strategy that eventually put Mr. Nixon on the air to explain the contributions—an address which turned the affair into an asset for the Eisenhower-Nixon candidacy."[13] Following the election *Time* magazine speculated Seaton could become postmaster general, and Ike's younger brother, Milton Eisenhower, suggested that the Nebraska newsman be appointed commissioner of the Federal Communications Commission.[14] Instead, however, Seaton chose to return home to attend to personal matters and the family business until September 1953, when Ike pulled him out of his short-lived political retirement to help restore public confidence at the Department of Defense, where his assignment was to salvage "what prestige he could for the military during the 1954 Army-McCarthy hearings." Later he joined the White House staff as chief deputy to Chief of Staff Sherman Adams as an all-around political and public relations fireman, handling all kinds of testy issues, including the often incendiary task of patronage, so well that the RNC chairman called Seaton a "damn smart politician."[15] Thus it was hardly a surprise that in the spring of 1956 Eisenhower once again tapped Seaton to handle a strife-torn agency when he asked him to take over the Department of the Interior, where the public perception of scandalous mismanagement of the nation's natural resources under Doug McKay had become an embarrassing political liability in advance of the 1956 reelection campaign.[16]

When Seaton's nomination came up for consideration by the full Senate, it took less than ten minutes for his former colleagues on the Hill to unanimously confirm his appointment. Even Sen. Wayne Morse, the most bitter conservationist critic of the Eisenhower administration, admitted Seaton was an excellent choice, proof enough in the words of the *Washington Post*, that Seaton was "sensitive, progressive and broad-gauged," a man "admirably equipped to give the Department the sort of nondoctrinaire direction it needs."[17] As a "liberal-conservative" Seaton said he endorsed the Eisenhower definition that a true liberal was a person who could be "liberal toward other people and their troubles and who seeks out remedies for them, and at the same time is conservative with other people's money."[18] Further evidence that he was no conservative ideologue came from none other than the John Birch Society: the head of the far-right-wing group reported with disgust that during Seaton's brief tenure in the U.S. Senate the "so called Republican" from Nebraska had earned the highest marks of any GOP senator from the Americans for Democratic Action.[19]

Seaton's first task as secretary of the interior would be to ensure that the Interior Department ceased to be a major concern in the 1956 campaign and to deprive the Democrats of a potential campaign issue, a task for which he was admirably suited. For good reason Fred Seaton was called "the perfect antidote" to Douglas McKay in substance, style, and personality. McKay had been likely at any moment to stick his foot down his throat, while Seaton was congenial, self-assured, and relaxed, able to defuse difficult situations with a light touch of self-deprecating humor. Where McKay had made a habit of falling into political traps by foolish off-the-cuff remarks that made headlines and "unnecessary political controversy," as one of his top aides later admitted, Seaton was always mindful of what he wanted the lead story to be. While McKay was perfectly willing to grant newspaper interviews and had a friendly attitude toward individual reporters, he refused to hold press conferences; after almost three years in office, he had given only one formal press conference, the least of any member in the entire cabinet.[20] Seaton, on the other hand, a master at the art of public relations, was unrivaled as a press conference virtuoso in Washington, D.C.

Throughout the West, where the purple mountains and the open ranges were generally owned by Uncle Sam, the interior secretary was typically the local landlord and therefore the unfriendly face of the federal government; Seaton's approach was to overcome any natural suspicion by acting like a concerned neighbor instead of a distant bureaucrat. After attending one Seaton press conference in late 1957, veteran Washington columnist George Dixon said the secretary's down-home Nebraska style was as "local-yokel as an old-fashioned barn-raising." Other cabinet secretaries might deal with world peace, outer space, and the national debt, but he said Seaton was more likely to be quizzed about "what he thinks about a new culvert at Hound's Gap." Dixon was surprised at how comfortable Seaton was in dealing with the press and witnessed the "refreshing" style of the "smiling and debonair Interior chieftain" tame the most callous members of the press corps. "Not one reporter crowded Seaton," Dixon wrote in awe, "and some of the nastiest crowders in the business were present. One irritationist whom I have seen enrage Ike, infuriate Dulles and make Benson want to go back to the farm just nodded cheerfully" when Seaton answered his pointed question with a gentle brush-off: "The matter hasn't yet come to my attention. Sorry."[21]

But matters of style and public relations were hardly the only differences between McKay and Seaton. Among the many changes that Seaton would institute at the Department of the Interior, none would be more far reaching than his policies toward Alaska, particularly his rejection of partition and his support for statehood, conservation, and arctic oil and gas development.[22]

Seaton had been an unabashed advocate of immediate statehood for all of Alaska for years. During his brief spell in the U.S. Senate in 1952, his first and only substantial speech had been a declaration of unqualified support for statehood. Now as interior secretary, he made no secret that he had not changed his mind, but neither had Eisenhower, and if the president could not be persuaded, Seaton said he would have to follow the dictates of his conscience. As he explained in regards to another controversial issue, "When the President of the United States has taken a position, if I cannot convince him of some other course, I feel it is incumbent upon me either to follow out his policy or to resign."[23]

What practical effect Seaton might have on administration policy was an open question. During the brief and cordial confirmation hearings by the Senate Interior Committee—during which some of his old colleagues still called him "Senator Seaton"—the nominee testified that he would "be glad to do everything I can . . . so that Alaska can become a state." His pledge was to "try to persuade President Eisenhower to favor immediate admission of Alaska as a state," with the proviso that "certain areas" would have to be "set aside for national defense purposes as a condition for admission."[24] In other words, the poison pill of partition was still the quid pro quo. But Seaton's deft ability to defuse difficult questions was on full display. "If those withdrawal terms can be worked out," he told the Senate committee, " . . . I certainly would do everything I could to convince the President that we should have . . . statehood for Alaska immediately. I do not think that would be much of a job."

"You mean withdrawing the land," asked Sen. Henry "Scoop" Jackson (D-Washington), "or convincing the President?"

As the room erupted in laughter, Seaton nimbly answered, "I will let you speak as to that, Senator."[25]

A. Robert Smith, the *News-Miner's* Washington political correspondent, concluded that while "most observers expect Seaton to be more aggressive than was his predecessor Douglas McKay in trying to win White House support for his ideas," the new interior secretary was nevertheless "expected to find himself acceding to the chief executive's wishes on this question."[26]

Upon Seaton's appointment Anchorage city planner and Constitutional Convention delegate Vic Fischer told Delegate Bartlett that he had considered writing a letter to Seaton "expressing appreciation of his statehood position," and the fact that Fred Seaton wasn't Douglas McKay. Fischer wondered that perhaps "if enough people" wrote polite letters to Seaton, the new interior chief "might even get the impression that we are 'ladies and gentlemen.'"[27] Bartlett told Fischer that Seaton "is a decent, honorable guy" but could not predict how effective he would be in reversing the administration's course. "Whether or not he will be able to convince Eisenhower is something we will learn by and by but at least . . . Seaton will have his heart in it in contrast with you know whom."[28]

Except for the president himself, the secretary of the interior, the "Czar of Alaska," was the single most influential official in the U.S. government as far as the territory was concerned. Fred Seaton would take an intense personal and political interest in Alaska, spending more time there than any previous interior secretary in history. And when it came to Alaska affairs, Secretary Seaton, the Nebraska newspaperman from Hastings, would listen to no one more carefully than C. W. Snedden.

Secretary Seaton and Snedden collaborated so closely together on Alaska matters from 1956 to 1960 that many mistakenly assumed they were old friends going back decades together in the newspaper business. For his part Snedden never recalled exactly when he had first met Fred Seaton. In later years he assumed it might have been in the 1930s or 1940s when he had been traveling throughout the western states as a Linotype expert or newspaper consultant, or perhaps at some other gathering of newspapermen. But it is clear from their surviving correspondence that it was only following a meeting in Seaton's office in Washington, D.C., in December 1956 that the two men really began to get to know each other personally.[29] Their partnership was a natural fit. Sharing a common background as small-town entrepreneurs, printers and publishers, Western boosters who prided themselves on the ability to see the world as it was, but armed with the editorial weapons to promote possibilities that could be, they both came to agree that the unique opportunities of Alaska and the peculiar political limbo in which it was frozen demanded aggressive action by the Eisenhower administration.

Naturally having the ear of the man who had the ear of President Eisenhower paid big dividends, but as Snedden realized, what made the new interior secretary so invaluable for the statehood cause and the Alaska Republican Party was that before the Seaton revolution at the Interior Department, statehood supporters had no practical access to the levers of power in the administration.[30] Since Alaska statehood had always been predominately a Democratic cause, Eisenhower's 1952 election had left the traditional champions of statehood in the Washington wilderness. After two decades in control of the White House, the national Democratic establishment found it hard to think of Eisenhower and his men as anything but usurpers. Ike's appointment of three top cabinet officers, each with ties to General Motors, had prompted Adlai Stevenson's famous quip that the New Dealers and Fair Dealers had been rousted out by the "car dealers" (one of whom was Douglas McKay).[31] What was good for General Motors may or may not have been good for the country, but as the new interior secretary in 1956, Fred Seaton brought the conviction to the top level of the Eisenhower administration for the first time that what was best for Alaska, and Alaska's Republican Party, was best for America, and what was best for America was Alaska's immediate admission as the forty-ninth state.

Seaton took the oath of office as the thirty-sixth secretary of the interior on June 8, 1956, the same day that President Eisenhower formally accepted Ted Stevens's resignation as U.S. Attorney. The following day Stevens officially started duty as special assistant to the solicitor of the Department of the Interior, and was shortly thereafter reassigned to become the legislative counsel for the entire agency, responsible for coordinating the department's position and language on all pending legislation, including the Alaska statehood bill.[32]

The chain of events that took the Fairbanks DA back to Washington, D.C., and a key post under Seaton in the Interior Department—the agency that he had first hoped to work for back in 1953 before going to Alaska—began with an episode in 1954 during Douglas McKay's unfortunate "act like ladies and gentlemen" tour. At the time of Secretary McKay's arrival in Fairbanks, District Attorney Stevens learned from McKay's staff about the Interior Department's legal dispute with E. W. Lauesen of McKinley Park Services, Inc., the concessionaire at Mt. McKinley National Park Hotel, a drafty wooden barracks near the park entrance on the Alaska Railroad that had been a marginal operation for years. Lauesen had been operating the hotel for more than a year, but since no official contract with him had ever been approved by the secretary's office, it was the government's position that he should be evicted from the premises. McKay's staff asked for Stevens's assistance to negotiate a timely resolution of the lingering dispute.

On his own volition Stevens flew down immediately to the park on July 29, returned again on August 4–5, and filed an interim report on August 6 with the Civil Division of the Justice Department directed to Assistant Attorney General Warren E. Burger (who fifteen years later during Stevens's first year in the U.S. Senate would be confirmed as chief justice of the U.S. Supreme Court). Stevens's forceful approach produced results. Within less than a month the long-running soap opera with the park concessionaire had been resolved, and an experienced park service contractor had taken over the hotel. Impressed by Stevens's rapid resolution of the matter, Assistant Secretary Fred Aandahl commended him in September 1954 on behalf of McKay for the "most cooperative and effective manner in which you assisted in terminating the unauthorized use by McKinley Park Services, Inc. of Government property. . . . A situation which could have been highly detrimental to the Government's operation of the Park was averted, largely through your efforts."[33]

Having earned his stripes with his resolution of the hotel concession, Stevens also assisted the Interior Department the following year when he testified before a congressional committee about the mental health bill then under consideration by the House, wading into what became a torrid political and bureaucratic struggle. Though he played a minor role, it would be the first of many national debates in which Stevens would become involved, even if in a small way, dealing with the clash between the reality of life in Alaska and the perceptions of those in the Lower 48.

In Alaska Territory the care of the mentally ill was a direct responsibility of Congress entrusted to the Department of Interior, and since 1904 the agency had contracted with a private "Nervous Sanitarium" in Portland, Oregon, known as Morningside, to care for mentally and emotionally troubled Alaskans. Black humor in Alaska about the natural progression of life from youth to old age was "Inside-Outside-Morningside," meaning those who left Alaska to go "Outside"—anyplace but Alaska— would sooner or later end up in the Morningside mental hospital.[34] By the early 1950s the Interior Department was fully cognizant that the federal commitment process in Alaska, which had not changed since 1905, and the warehousing of mental patients in the aging Morningside Sanitarium was nothing short of a crime, but the entrenched system in place for half a century, protected by politicians, bureaucratic rust, and inertia, proved extraordinarily difficult to reform.[35]

For seven years the Interior Department had "vigorously supported" efforts to find an alternative to Morningside and to modify the outdated federal laws under which the territory was forced to operate, most particularly the archaic commitment procedures, but all efforts had been blocked in Congress.[36] Despite every setback Bob Bartlett—one of whose uncles had been briefly committed to Morningside decades before—continued to champion the enactment of long-overdue reforms. As Congress wrestled with how to improve the deplorable situation, New York Congressman Leo "Obie" O'Brien's territorial subcommittee of the House Interior and Insular Affairs Committee—the gatekeeper subcommittee that handled up to 90 percent of all legislation having to do with Alaska—decided to hold hearings in the territory in the fall of 1955 to "investigate any matter within its jurisdiction," including mental health.[37]

The 1955 Alaska tour of O'Brien's territorial subcommittee was a marathon. According to Chairman O'Brien's estimate, the hardest-working subcommittee in politics crammed about ten months' worth of hearings by Washington standards into only three weeks, traveling thousands of miles and hearing from more than two hundred witnesses in twenty locations across the length and breadth of the territory.[38] O'Brien's congressional trek across Alaska was the most ambitious and wide-ranging investigation ever held in the territory, and the end result was more than fifteen hundred printed pages of testimony, on topics so broad and disparate that the title for the encyclopedic-sized compilation of proceedings was simply

Alaska, 1955. The committee hearings would have a profound impact on the mental health issue, statehood, and Congressman O'Brien himself, a liberal Democrat with a sparkling sense of humor from upstate New York.

On his final day in Alaska, O'Brien announced his conversion at the Juneau public hearing. "I think your greatest problem in Washington lies in the fact that many Members of Congress are indifferent to your problems. . . . I was one of the indifferent ones. . . . But that indifference has been dissipated in the last two weeks." Admitting that he had learned more about Alaska in the previous fourteen days than "I did in 4 years in a remote committee room in Washington peering at maps," he pledged that he and his fellow representatives would go back home as changed men and women, determined to help solve the problems in Alaska that only Congress could address. "I am very sure that you will be better off, the Government of the United States will be better off, and we will be better off individually and collectively for having spent this time in the Territory." True to his word, O'Brien would become a passionate defender of the rights of Alaskans, adopt the territory as his special responsibility, and would become what he called the "quarterback" for the Alaska Statehood Bill in the House of Representatives.[39]

Of all the testimony O'Brien heard on his 1955 tour of Alaska, no story impressed him more deeply than the tale he heard from Ted Stevens about the unjust federal treatment of mental patients. Stevens appeared before the O'Brien subcommittee in Fairbanks on September 15, 1955, marking the first time he ever officially testified in a congressional hearing. He was invited at the special request of committee member Bob Bartlett, who thought Stevens's firsthand experience as a court official with involuntary commitment procedures would be persuasive, but it took some bureaucratic maneuvering to get him to the witness table. The Department of Justice had not taken an official stance on the Alaska mental health legislation, and the agency was not about to have the northernmost U.S. Attorney in the land start setting policy for it. When Stevens's initial request to his superiors for permission to talk to the committee had gone unanswered, Bartlett sent a special telegram six days before the hearing to Deputy Attorney General William P. Rogers in Washington asking for action: "Will greatly appreciate your granting United States Attorney Theodore Stevens permission to appear as witness before House Interior Subcommittee which will convene in Fairbanks September 15, so he may present testimony in connection with Alaska Mental Health Bill and pertinent matters. I believe his opinions would be helpful in determining final draft of language."[40] After some bureaucratic dithering the Justice

Department agreed three days later to let Stevens appear, on the condition, as the memo written for the files stated, "that if he had to give an opinion to be sure he made it clear that it was his personal opinion and did not reflect the views of the Department. He said he . . . would follow my instructions."[41]

Never lacking for a strong opinion—or hesitating to express it—the fiery DA made it clear to the House subcommittee that in his personal view the inhumane federal policies toward mental patients in Alaska were a stain on the conscience of anyone involved in the entire process. Some on the committee had opposed the changes to the commitment procedures that the Interior Department had suggested, but Stevens begged them to reconsider. Under the existing federal rules mentally ill men, women, and children in Alaska were treated not as patients but as criminals, because a jury trial was the only tool for involuntary commitment. It was not uncommon for individuals to be charged, arrested, jailed, and committed to Morningside fifteen hundred miles away without ever having seen a psychiatrist or medical practitioner of any kind.

Too many times the DA had participated in this miscarriage of justice, an antiquated remnant from the dark ages of mental illness. Generally the commitment paperwork began with the filing of a written complaint with the local U.S. Commissioner or judge asserting that an individual "was an insane person at large." The law required that the alleged insane person be arrested and confined by the U.S. Marshal in federal jail with all the other prisoners, until a six-member jury could be impaneled to decide whether he or she was "guilty" of insanity. The "guilty" vote had to be unanimous.

When the Interior Department had asked a prominent group of medical experts to evaluate Alaska's mental health policies back in 1949, the psychiatrists and clinicians were appalled to find that such a barbarous and unscientific procedure as the insanity jury, completely divorced from medical science and "utterly out of line with present concepts and methods of psychiatric treatment," was still the official practice of the U.S. government in Alaska. The panel published a stinging indictment in the *American Journal of Psychiatry* in 1950 that decried treating sick people like prisoners, confining them in the overcrowded, unsanitary jails in the territory—especially the federal jail in Anchorage, a "fabulous obscenity" unsuitable for any human occupation.[42] In the six years since that investigation, nothing had changed, and Stevens thought one did not need an MD to see that insanity trials were a barbaric way to treat sick people.

From his perspective as a prosecutor, asking uninformed citizens off the street to make a clinical diagnosis was a medical and legal travesty.

A jury might as well have been asked to diagnose brain cancer, diabetes, or scarlet fever. The most heartrending cases involved children. In one notorious instance, which Bob Bartlett found most repulsive, a seventeen-day-old infant accused of insanity was jailed, tried, convicted, and sentenced to Morningside.[43] Likewise a twenty-month-old toddler—whose mother had charged that the baby was insane—had been committed to Morningside, joining seventeen other children younger than eight years of age at the sanitarium in 1955.

"The insanity jury system is archaic," Stevens said. "It places in the hands of laymen the right to determine . . . a person's mental capacity."[44] During the twenty-four months since Stevens had taken office as U.S. Attorney, there had been sixty-seven insanity hearings in Fairbanks—about one every two weeks—and it was the worst part of his job. "There is no way you can put a foot in the stomach of a prosecuting attorney quicker than making him participate in an insanity hearing. . . . I really have a very great respect for juries, but not with insanity."

Chairman O'Brien then asked Stevens if a six-member jury with no medical training might be "just as likely to send a sane person to an insane asylum as they would be to free a person who was insane?"

"That is true," Stevens said. "I have witnessed a person I would consider normal—maybe my judgment is not too good—but a person I have considered normal gets on the stand. They get a little nervous. I am a little nervous right now although I am before juries constantly. Yet a man who is really insane, I have watched them and they are very lucid."[45]

Usually such little time was given to the insanity proceedings—as little as fifteen or twenty minutes—that it would have been impossible for even a trained professional to make an informed judgment so quickly. On one occasion Stevens had been warned in advance to encourage a suspected mental patient to talk as long as he wanted, because only then would the true extent of his psychosis be revealed. The man started out speaking calmly and coherently; they let him talk for nearly two hours, when suddenly his demeanor became unhinged. "The gentleman took off his shoe," Stevens recalled, "and began reading a poem about the Statue of Liberty and gave us a political speech."

The story of the shoeless man obsessed with the Statue of Liberty sparked Chairman O'Brien's legendary sense of humor. "You would not say that a delivery of a political speech was a symptom of insanity, would you?"

Amid a chorus of laughter Stevens responded, "Please do not tell the Department."[46]

That moment of levity aside, Stevens's dismal message about the barbaric state of Alaska's legal procedures for the mentally ill was painful for all to hear. "There is no one, apparently, in the entire chain of command," O'Brien summarized, "including yourself, members of the jury, Department of the Interior, Department of Health, and Education and Welfare, and the Department of Justice who likes what is going on."[47]

Snedden wholeheartedly backed the effort to reform the "vicious system of handling the insane that is a blot on the Federal government's record in Alaska." No clearer example existed of how little power territorial residents had over their own destiny than the inability to change the rules about insanity. "This system, imposed on Alaska by the Federal government, [has] been condemned by every medical authority who has studied it. Yet, Alaska was helpless because the Territory has no voting representative in Congress to lead a battle to change this vicious practice of jailing the mentally ill."[48]

While true enough that Alaska had no votes to trade, the territory did have Bob Bartlett. Theoretically, Alaska as a territory was represented by all ninety-six Senators and 435 Congressmen, but it was Bartlett, the conscience of the U.S. Congress, with his earnest powers of polite persuasion and impeccable reputation, quietly cajoling colleagues to do for Alaska what the territory could not do for itself, who made sure Alaska's voice was heard. Bartlett's remarkable ability to deal with his colleagues on Capitol Hill even though he had no favors to give in return, a skill that would prove its value most notably during the final push for statehood, was fully evident during the mental health debate, when he enlisted Rep. Edith Green of Portland to sponsor the bill in order to help neutralize opposition from Oregon. Even though the reforms would mean the end of the federal contract with Morningside, and probably cost her some prominent local supporters, motivated by Bartlett she agreed to work against the parochial interests of her own district in favor of a greater good, helping the sick of Alaska. This noble gesture on the part of Representative Green did not go unnoticed. A *News-Miner* editorial described it as a selfless act that epitomized a true servant of the people. "We say, that greater courage has no congressman or congresswoman who would risk the loss of support in his or her own State to help residents of a Territory who can offer no votes in an election."[49]

Outside the state of Oregon, voting for the Alaska Mental Health Bill at first seemed to require little or no courage on the part of anyone in Congress. In the wake of the 1955 congressional hearings in Alaska, the measure passed the House on a voice vote with minimal opposition on January 18, 1956. Snedden thought the worst was over. Since there were "no avowed enemies" of the legislation in the Senate, and the Interior Department and President Eisenhower were solidly behind it, he expected that the new mental health procedures would quickly become the law of the land, meaning "mentally ill persons in Alaska will no longer be arrested, jailed, tried by jury, and escorted to Morningside Hospital. . . . They will be examined by competent specialists, and treated in an Alaskan institution where they will be within reach of relatives and friends." The House vote was a rare victory of "considerable magnitude," the *News-Miner* wrote, demonstrating "that when the people of Alaska become aroused, and unite in support of good legislation, they can score gains in Congress."[50]

Within weeks that optimism was shattered by a strange twist of events which would prove yet once again that as far as Alaska was concerned, what the residents of a territory may or may not have wanted was inconsequential compared to what Congress heard from voters back home. The Alaska Mental Health Act passed by the House, HR 6376, became the centerpiece of a bizarre conspiracy theory, which one bemused observer in William F. Buckley's *National Review* said caused the biggest outbreak of mass hysteria and "panic since Orson Welles landed his Martian invaders" with *The War of the Worlds* in 1938.[51] The Alaska commitment procedures Stevens had addressed in his testimony were the focal point of an acrimonious national debate, so far-fetched and delusional it could have been hatched inside the walls of Morningside itself, that revealed how ill informed the rest of the country remained about the reality of life in the northern territory, and how vulnerable Alaska would continue to be as the target of popular delusions in American politics.

Not long before the mental health bill had passed the House, a little-known right-wing group claimed the new law would authorize construction of a massive federal concentration camp to house thousands of American political prisoners. "We could not help remembering that Siberia is very near Alaska," one alarmist with a good memory warned, "and . . . we were wondering if it could be an American Siberia." It was a case of putting two and two together and coming up with two million: Alaska is close to Siberia and cold like Siberia, so therefore Alaska is a prison camp like Siberia.

A California conspiracy theorist published a widely quoted article titled "Siberia, U.S.A." that became the catchphrase of the movement. It alleged that the Alaska mental health bill was a covert attempt "to establish a concentration camp for political prisoners" that would "place every resident of the United States at the mercy of the whims and fancies of any person with whom they might have a disagreement, causing a charge of 'mental illness' to be placed against them, with immediate deportation to 'SIBERIA, U.S.A.!'"[52] Because the proposed legislation modified commitment procedures in part by changing the rules for insanity jury trials—though not eliminating them, as Stevens had recommended—the extremists charged it "takes away all of the rights of the American citizen to ask for a jury trial and protect him from being railroaded to an asylum."[53]

O'Brien said somehow the opponents of the mental health bill had convinced themselves that the U.S. government was about to string "a barbed wire fence around a million acres in Alaska, into which we would pour anyone in your district or mine, at whom we might point a finger."[54] Because the big lie took less effort to comprehend than the little complex truths of real life, for too many gullible and uninformed Americans who knew little about Alaska—except it was close to Siberia—and even less about modern mental health practices, the prison camp story was easily digestible. Common sense is not always the active ingredient in politics, and since Alaska was so strange and foreign to most Americans anyway, the "frozen north" found itself to be fertile ground for the preposterous. As a sparsely populated, politically impotent region, the territory of Alaska served handily as a blank canvas where nightmares and dreams of those who lived elsewhere could be projected, and no more powerful specter existed in America in the 1950s than the fears of mind control, indoctrination, and global communism.

Both Snedden and Stevens were distressed and indignant about the distortions spread in the "underhanded" and outrageous "Siberia, U.S.A." anonymous editorial that had started to appear in newspapers around the country in early 1956. The *News-Miner* reprinted the Siberia charges simply because it would otherwise have been so unbelievable to anyone in Alaska that such charges could be taken seriously. "Obviously, it came from some source," the *News-Miner* concluded, "that is hostile to Alaskans, to their ambitions for Statehood and their desires to create a modern system for committing and treating the mentally ill."[55]

The combination of paranoia and misinformation about Alaska destroyed any chance of Senate passage of HR 6376. When it finally appeared as if all prospects of mental health reform had been stymied yet again, the great conservative Arizona icon in the Senate, Barry Goldwater, found the solution to appease the radical right. On Goldwater's prodding the Senate stripped from the bill all the specifics about the commitment procedures that helped spur the right-wing backlash, and to the relief of all who truly cared about the tortured souls plagued with mental disease, the pared-down bill sailed to passage. Instead of spelling out how the mentally ill in Alaska would be treated, the final law simply gave the territorial legislature the "authority comparable in scope to that of the States and other Territories" to deal with mental illness and a one-million-acre land grant to pay for it.[56] This adroit editing sidestepped the concentration camp specter without changing the main thrust of the bill: to stop the brutal treatment of mental patients in Alaska, and to allow new, more humane commitment procedures to be instituted.

By the time the Alaska Mental Health Enabling Act, which put the district attorney and the Interior Department out of the insanity business, became law in 1956, Stevens had joined the staff of the Interior Department. His move back to the capital in 1956 was as much a surprise to himself as anyone else. Originally Stevens had intended to remain with the Justice Department as a U.S. Attorney in Alaska, but he had wanted to move to Juneau. After being recruited to apply for a vacant position in Juneau, he had submitted his name for consideration for the transfer in early 1956 but was surprised to get a telegram from Assistant Attorney General William Rogers on March 1, 1956: "Prior commitments make transfer to Juneau impossible." Stevens was disappointed, surprised, and puzzled. "In many ways I am sorry about this," Stevens wrote. "I did not decide overnight to try for the Juneau spot."

He had run his transfer request by all the officials of the Alaska GOP, from local party members on up to and including national committeeman Wally Hickel and Governor Frank Heintzleman and had never received any hint that the request would be summarily rejected. He explained to a friend that he had purposely not contacted anyone else on his behalf because "I was informed that *no* appointments would be made in Alaska without clearance from the local organization. That is the route I chose, and, apparently, it has not benefited me to do so." He speculated that someone in the Alaska GOP might have sabotaged his candidacy, and that instead of relying on local support alone, he should have asked for help from the two Republican senators from his home state of California,

Bill Knowland and Thomas Kuchel, especially since it had been a recommendation letter from Senator Knowland that had helped him to win confirmation by Eisenhower as DA in Fairbanks back in 1954.[57] "Perhaps I should have called upon the Senators from California for support, and I may still try to do so." While mulling over future possibilities, including an offer from a law firm in Southern California, he had decided that remaining in Fairbanks was not an option under any conditions.

"It has been a pleasure to work with the [Justice] Department," he wrote William Rogers after receiving the telegram with the bad news. "I am indeed sorry that I feel compelled to sever my connection with it. Naturally, because I sought clearance from the local Republican organization, my desire for the transfer is well known. I would not feel justified in remaining with the Department under the circumstances."[58]

As Stevens had feared, the story of his transfer request begat a rumor around Fairbanks that he was being forced out of office. Snedden came to his aid by running a short news item: "U.S. District Attorney Theodore Stevens replied to rumors that he was 'resigning under pressure' with an emphatic denial today. Stevens told reporters in Fairbanks he has an offer from a firm in California and may go to work there this year."

"'There is no pressure from the Department of Justice or anyone else,' Stevens said heatedly. 'No one has asked me to resign.'" According to the *News-Miner* account, the young DA had "held the position of U.S. Attorney for nearly three years, acting with probably more vigor than any predecessor in the Fairbanks office."[59] In fact Stevens's quitting was the last thing that the Department of Justice really wanted, because at the time more than forty felony cases were awaiting trial in Fairbanks and the DA said unless the department kept the staffing at full force "this place will be in an uproar."[60]

Since assuming the DA job in Fairbanks in 1953, Stevens's ties to Washington had hardly languished, in part because he had attended the annual U.S. Attorneys' conference in the capital each October, the one chance that enabled attorneys in the field to have personal contact with the administration. Living in Alaska made attendance at these meetings no small task. In 1955, for instance, Stevens and his family had taken a thirty-four-day combination business and vacation trip, which included picking up a new car in Seattle and driving across the country and back again, with stops in New York City; Cambridge (for his five-year class reunion at Harvard); Washington (for the U.S. Attorney conference); Denver (to visit Ann's parents); Manhattan Beach, California (to see Ted's relatives); and San Francisco (to argue a case before the Ninth Circuit) before Ted drove back up the Alaska Highway to Fairbanks, while Ann flew home with the children.[61]

Of all Stevens's contacts in the capital, the most important was Elmer F. "Ben" Bennett, a Stanford Law graduate from Colorado six years his senior and an expert on resource and antitrust law, who would help bring Stevens into the Interior Department.[62] Bennett had been the top aide to Sen. Eugene Milliken (R-Colorado) from 1951 to 1953, when Stevens had been working on a Colorado matter with Northcutt Ely. (Bennett would subsequently join Ely in the 1960s as a partner in the law firm of Ely, Duncan & Bennett.) In 1953 McKay had picked Bennett to be the legislative counsel for the Department of Interior in the Office of the Solicitor, where his performance over the next three years impressed both Congress and the White House.

Even in a city with thousands of bureaucrats, the bureaus in the mammoth five-acre fortress of the Department of the Interior, seven stories high with six wings and more than three miles of corridors, had gained a notorious reputation for inefficiency and indifference to congressional inquiries on pending legislation. "It was a scandalous situation from the point of view of the committees on the Hill," Bennett recalled two decades later. From his two years with Senator Milliken's staff, he knew firsthand that too often Interior staffers were not likely to return phone calls or answer memos, and since normally "a congressional committee will not schedule a hearing or take any action on a bill" until a response is received, "it served bureaucratic purposes very often just to let a request from the Hill for departmental views just rot on the vine by never getting an answer up there."[63]

As legislative counsel Bennett reorganized the flow of work with specific duties and deadlines for all bureau chiefs on legislative inquiries and instituted a new system that funneled correspondence with Congress through his office. Previously the legislative liaison "had been largely a paper-shuffling office," but now it assumed "the entire responsibility for coordinating the department's position on legislation."[64] In this expanded role Bennett had frequent dealings with all of the senior White House staff, including presidential assistants Fred Seaton and Jerry Persons, a retired general who was Eisenhower's longtime army confidant and close friend.

Impressed by Bennett's performance, Persons set the wheels in motion in early 1956 to have Bennett transferred to the White House staff, and so at the same time that Stevens was looking for a way out of Fairbanks, the Interior Department was in the search for a new legislative counsel. Bennett called Stevens, urging him to come to the Interior Department, as did Acting Solicitor J. Reuel Armstrong.[65] On Bennett's recommendation, McKay agreed to hire Stevens, the only wrinkle being that McKay was resigning—in reality forced out by Eisenhower—and to be replaced by Fred Seaton. Thus at the time that Stevens had agreed to come to the Interior Department the agency was in a state of flux, caught in limbo between McKay's departure and Seaton's arrival.

Stevens started his new job at the Interior Department on June 9, 1956, only one day after Seaton had taken the oath of office. For the first few weeks his title was special assistant to the solicitor, but by mid-July he was reassigned officially as a legislative attorney and assumed Bennett's old post of legislative counsel.[66] Gradually brought along and encouraged by Bennett—at Seaton's request Bennett had stayed on at Interior to become the secretary's top aide—Stevens slowly became part of the inner circle. Mentored by Bennett and Seaton, during the next four and a half years Stevens would climb up through the ranks of the Department of the Interior, taking a series of increasingly demanding positions, culminating with his appointment in 1960 as Interior Department Solicitor, the chief law officer of the entire agency.[67]

"The Department of Everything Else," as Interior's grab bag collection of bureaus has been called, offered Stevens a wide range of opportunities as a young lawyer to expand his professional expertise, not to mention working closely with the secretary of the interior, Congress, and the White House. Stevens soon began attending private strategy meetings at the White House every Saturday morning chaired by one of Ike's top assistants, Bryce Harlow, designed to coordinate the administration's legislative priorities; Stevens's job was to ensure that Seaton's priorities from the Interior Department were given proper recognition in the president's overall agenda.[68] Though Stevens had many duties, during his years on Seaton's staff questions regarding Alaska were never far from the front burner, as the ubiquitous role of Interior in running the Territory of Alaska, and the ongoing push for statehood that would be orchestrated by Seaton and Stevens out of the offices of the Interior Department, lent extra importance to Stevens as the department's acknowledged Alaska expert, signified by the famous hand-lettered sign on his office door that read "Alaska Headquarters."

Though Snedden was delighted with Stevens's new job at the Interior Department, he grew increasing distressed in the summer and fall of 1956 when Seaton, the Eisenhower administration, and the Republican Party continued to appear "indifferent" to the needs of Alaskans. In the run-up to the October 1956 elections for the Alaska-Tennessee Plan seats, Bill Strand—who had been transferred to the post of information director at the Interior Department—told Snedden that even with Seaton at the helm there would be no official change in the Eisenhower administration's stated policies, dimming the faint prospect, Snedden feared, of electing even a single Republican to one of the three ATP seats. Further bad news came from the top leadership of the national GOP, when RNC chairman Leonard Hall reportedly concluded that the Republican cause in the Alaska election for October 1956 was "an irretrievably 'lost cause.'" Hall therefore said he did not want to push Ike to shift his Alaska policy because "it would be injudiciously risking the President's personal prestige were this move to fail to exert any influence on the election's outcome."[69]

It was only after the Republicans had been shut out in the Alaska-Tennessee Plan election that Snedden became determined to get through to Seaton and encourage a new strategy for the administration. Sending back three Democrats in the ATP delegation made it imperative, he believed, to find some way of turning around the Interior Department's Alaska policy. "I am very much interested in Alaska statehood, and advancing the cause of the Republican party in the process," Snedden explained to Seaton in November 1956. "Perhaps I am presumptuous, but I believe I have a formula which will accomplish both, and am willing to devote the time and expense for a Washington trip to present my ideas to you if you are interested." Snedden was quick to admit, "I am no politician, but . . . I know the newspaper business and by necessity know how public opinion is formulated. We can have a Republican 'State of Alaska' if given a minimum of assistance from Washington!"[70]

Snedden's persistence paid off. After three or four letters had arrived from Fairbanks, an aide in Seaton's office attached a note to the most recent correspondence: "If Secy. Seaton goes to Alaska, he better be sure to see this man."[71] Snedden also called Elmer Bennett directly, who penned a note to the secretary: "Mr. C. W. Snedden of the *Fairbanks News-Miner* called me late yesterday afternoon from Fairbanks. . . . He is known as a dedicated Republican and feels confident that the Republicans can take over the territorial government in two years if the Administration move promptly to take the ball away from the congressional Democrats on the handling of Alaskan problems."[72]

Furthermore, working behind the scenes with Strand and Stevens, Snedden was already helping to craft an administration statehood bill that would put the executive branch in front of the issue. "Strictly confidentially between you and I," Snedden wrote George Lehleitner in early December, "it appears I am making headway with the Administration on the Statehood matter. There now appears a possibility that the Administration will strongly back a statehood bill, and push it off with a bang shortly after Congress convenes." Ted Stevens had quietly sent him a copy of a proposed statehood bill for his comments and suggestions. It had been written in longhand because the legal staff wanted to keep it secret, avoiding the possibility of a leak from the stenographers' pool. This caused other problems since the lawyers could not write legibly. Snedden said "attempting to decipher the long hand correspondence" was frustrating beyond belief. "They are both extremely poor writers and honestly I can't interpret some of their scribbling."[73]

Penmanship aside, Snedden's principal concern was that the bill must not include any reference whatsoever to partition, because President Eisenhower still seemed intent on carving up the territory as the prerequisite for statehood. For some reason Eisenhower still insisted on saying the people of Alaska were "confined almost exclusively to the southeastern corner," and the *News-Miner*'s bitter rejoinder was that these words "reflect shocking ignorance concerning Alaska on the part of the President," so it was obvious that the lobbying job ahead would be daunting.[74]

When Snedden finally managed to have a face-to-face strategy conference with Seaton at Interior Department headquarters in Washington, D.C., on December 18, 1956, the two newspaper publishers hit it off famously. Snedden came away from the meeting more optimistic than ever. He was further encouraged after Seaton made a ten-day trip to Alaska in late January 1957, including spending a day and a half with Snedden at Fairbanks, where the two men had in-depth conferences on politics, Alaska, and newspapers. "I had several long discussions with the secretary while he was here totaling approximately 5 hours," Snedden briefed Lehleitner. "Incidentally, apparently I was the only person he talked to any length of time in Fairbanks—as least the only person he talked to alone."[75]

From Snedden's perspective the only thing that might have made the secretary's Alaska visit more fruitful would have been if Ted Stevens had accompanied him to the territory. Stevens's absence was not due to any lack of effort on Snedden's part, as before Seaton had left Washington he had urged Elmer Bennett: "I believe I mentioned to you that my belief that Ted Stevens would be of great value on the trip if he can be freed for that length of time. From my acquaintance with Ted I know that he has a good level head on his shoulders, is well acquainted throughout the Territory, and should prove of considerable value as to proper local contacts."[76]

Snedden's great overriding concern, which he expressed repeatedly to Seaton, was the fear that the administration still seemed convinced that partitioning the territory was the only possible method of overcoming Eisenhower's resistance. Snedden urged Seaton to consider other options. "In subsequent conversations with Elmer Bennett in your Department, and Gerald Morgan at the White House it became apparent that the word 'partition' is a very pertinent point in the proposed Alaskan Statehood Bill. I hope very much that administrative objections can be achieved in another manner, and that particular word does not have to be included in the bill, as I consider it 'political dynamite' throughout the Territory."[77] He repeated the message to Bennett. "I certainly hope that the Administration and the Interior Department conclude that the word 'partition' is a nasty word throughout Alaska, and it is not included in the new Alaska statehood bill. If the objective desired by the Administration can be gained by some other methods—or at least the word partition replaced with a synonym—Republican popularity in the Territory will be greatly enhanced."[78]

Though the danger of even talking about partition might have been beyond obvious to Snedden, rumors floated around the capital in January and February 1957 that the Eisenhower team would not relent. Even Seaton had warned a group on his visit to Fairbanks in January that Alaskans would have to back the administration, even if the bill was not "entirely palatable." "I'm not saying you're going to have partition," he had told a group of civic and business leaders at the University of Alaska, but "you may get something approximating it."[79]

On the eve of the long-awaited congressional hearings in March 1957, Gruening feared he knew what the Interior Department's pound of flesh would be. "We are waiting eagerly—perhaps a bit anxiously—to know what Fred Seaton . . . will spring as the price of the administration's support for statehood. He has broadly hinted that it will be partition and we have already made clear our objections. However he has warned us that if we fight the administration's proposals, whatever they may be, we will lose its support and thereby the statehood bill!"[80] What Gruening did not know was that two days earlier at an interdepartmental conference in the White House office of presidential assistant Jerry Persons, Interior

Counsel Ted Stevens sketched out a strategy to meet Ike's national security objections that avoided partition.

According to Stevens's presentation at the White House, there were at least half a dozen incontrovertible reasons why partition was the wrong answer to the defense question, reasons that he and Snedden had been mulling over the past three years. Politically and economically, he argued, partition was a bankrupt proposition. Creation of a formal "militarized zone" encompassing northern and western Alaska and lying outside the boundaries of the new state would not only be prohibitively expensive, it would also disenfranchise about twenty-four thousand people and needlessly damage the reputation of the United States internationally and hurt the Republican Party politically. There were "vast mineral resources" in the northern and western reaches of the territory "necessary for the full development of the more populated areas of Alaska," and at the top of that resource list was Snedden's top priority: Gubik. "The Gubic [*sic*] gas field," Stevens wrote in his memo for the White House conference, " . . . is a known gas structure . . . estimated to contain 300 billion cubic feet of gas. . . . The opening of this field may well provide the incentive for extensive oil and gas exploration in this area."[81]

Stevens emphasized that the connotation of the word *partition* itself would strike a sour tone around the world, and the "international repercussions which may be expected" would strike at the credibility of the United States. "'Partition' has been used . . . to describe actions in Korea, Viet-Nam and Germany," Stevens wrote, and it would be foolhardy to treat Alaska like one of those Cold War flash points. "We have been informally advised by the State Department that the creation of a dependent, voteless area, by the United States, resulting from partition of Alaska, would meet with disapproval internationally, and that such action would probably have to be defended in the United Nations."[82]

Partisan logic also played a part. For the Alaska GOP the stakes were high because "the Democrats in Alaska have gambled on use of the Tennessee Plan to gain admission as a State." The Democratic Party's refusal to make the Tennessee Plan a bipartisan lobbying tool had put them in a winner-take-all position on partition. If statehood were achieved, the Democrats could take the credit; if statehood were blocked, the Republicans would get the blame. Partition would play into the hands of the ersatz Tennessee Plan congressional delegation by giving them a ready-made excuse for failure, and since partition was political poison in Alaska, it "would provide an almost foolproof certainty that the

Democrats would win senatorial and congressional seats in Alaska for many years to come."[83]

Most important of all Stevens had concluded that the president and the Defense Department could reserve areas for "exclusive federal control" that would meet the president's standards without partitioning the territory in any way. "We have been advised informally that the Departments of State, Defense, and Justice are in accord." For some years one plan on the table had been the establishment of large "military reservations" to the north and west of the Eisenhower-McKay Line as a possible solution to the strategy question, but this had never been endorsed because it seemed to require that the Pentagon and the White House would have to tip their hand in advance to the Soviets, enabling them to see just what areas were most strategic.[84] The key to Stevens's proposal was that it would retain the element of surprise and "give the President the right to establish areas of exclusive Federal control after Alaska becomes a State. . . . This is the fundamental difference between the McKay amendments and our plan of action." According to Stevens, being able to disguise future intentions would mean the Pentagon "will not have to telegraph our defense plans by stating now what areas it needs in the future for security reasons."[85]

Reserving the right to make future withdrawals as a type of strategic insurance policy would not only keep all of the president's options open beyond the Eisenhower-McKay Line—modified to become the "Porcupine-Yukon-Kuskokwim" or "PYK (pronounced 'Pick') Line"—but it would also allow the future state of Alaska to have the same external boundaries as the territory of Alaska. North and west of the Porcupine, Yukon, and Kuskokwim Rivers, however, in an area ten thousand square miles larger than Texas, the new state's internal boundaries could be modified at will, at the sole discretion of the Commander-in-Chief.

On the morning of Monday, March 11, 1957, six days after Stevens made his presentation at the White House, the Eisenhower administration finally made public its new statehood position, adopting the reasoning, strategy, and even the language of Stevens's proposal about the PYK national defense withdrawals. In remarks by Secretary Seaton—delivered by Undersecretary Harold Chilson because Seaton was confined to Walter Reed Hospital recovering from back surgery—the Interior Department had banished the word *partition* from its vocabulary. From the first sentence of Seaton's statement, the Eisenhower administration's new no-partition PYK policy suggested by Snedden and Stevens was at the forefront of its strategy: "Before we proceed . . . let me make this clear: The administration's position is that all of the Territory of Alaska should become the State of Alaska. However, because of the unique position of Alaska, we ask the Congress and the people of Alaska to grant to the President, the Commander in Chief of all our Armed Forces, special powers with respect to defense in this area."[86]

A good portion of Seaton's statement was lifted directly from the memo Stevens had written for the White House a few days earlier, citing the "vast mineral resources" in the remote regions "which are necessary for the full development of the population centers already established," and noting in particular the Gubik gas field in PLO 82 and the proposal to build a $45 million gas line to Fairbanks.[87]

Seaton's statement on the morning of Monday, March 11, implied the two magic words all Alaskans were waiting to hear, and supplied the crux of the *News-Miner* headline that afternoon:

NO 'PARTITION'

The promise of no partition brought a mixture of relief and exhilaration to both Democrats and Republicans. Bob Bartlett's instant response was that it "sounds all to the good." He stressed that the "big thing to remember is—this is not partition."[88]

In Juneau AP reporter Bill Tobin hurried to gather reactions from the members of the Territorial House and Senate. "I've never been so happy in my life," said Democratic National Committeewoman and Rep. Helen Fischer of Anchorage. She had been one of the fifteen Alaskans in the Oval Office the day Butrovich had lectured Ike about the denial of democracy, and Fischer thought that Seaton's remarks showed such a complete reversal on the part of the administration that "statehood for Alaska is virtually assured this session of Congress." Another jubilant Democrat, Stevens's old nemesis Warren Taylor, called Seaton's remarks "the brightest light we have ever discerned on the horizon of statehood." Acting Governor Waino Hendrickson said, "It allays any fears of partition. This was what I personally had hoped for."

As the news from Washington broke in Juneau, Senator Earl Cooper (D-Anchorage) rose to read an account of Seaton's testimony on the floor of the Territorial Senate. Cooper called it "very heartening news. I feel the fears . . . that the administration bill might include partition have been eliminated." Likewise Senate President Vic Rivers, the brother of Tennessee Plan Rep. Ralph Rivers, called the news "very encouraging. It brings Alaskans one step nearer to their goal of statehood on an acceptable basis—that of statehood without partition." On the House side the twenty-one members of the Democratic majority relished the breaking news and the caucus reported to be "elated." Finally, no one could be happier than Democratic Rep. Jim Von Der Heydt of Nome, who cheered that his region would not be excluded from the future state. "Those of us from northwestern Alaska are tremendously pleased by the statement by Secretary Seaton in that Alaska statehood does not include the concept of partition."[89]

Snedden, who could not admit that he had played a part in shaping the legislation, praised the proposal "as a wonderful surprise to Alaskans. It contains no 'partitioning' clause whatsoever." In his words it was an "extremely good bill" with "virtually no 'unpalatable' provisions" that "should please every Alaskan" and "greatly hasten the dawn of a new era in Alaska." And he gave all due credit to the man at the top of the Interior Department. "We feel that this bill reflects, to a large degree, the friendly, open-minded attitude which has been taken toward Alaska by Secretary of the Interior Fred A. Seaton."[90]

Stevens's proposal for "national defense withdrawals" beyond the PYK line would become the substance of Section 10 of the Alaska Statehood Act, the critical compromise that enabled the president to have all the benefits of partitioning Alaska without doing so. Because no Section 10 withdrawals were ever made by Eisenhower or any other president, critics and historians have in hindsight tended to disregard or misunderstand the significance of the PYK line. But that is the blindness of looking backwards, only possible once the fear of partition had been forgotten, because PYK was always more important for what it didn't do: it didn't exclude any part of Alaska from statehood by partition. In his 1967 recounting of the statehood saga Gruening said the PYK was simply a "face-saving formula for the administration" that was "meaningless and of no significance" because it gave the president powers that he already had.[91] As Stevens had admitted at the White House conference, and Seaton would testify, presidential authority to exercise unilateral federal jurisdiction in an emergency was extensive, and more than half of all the states by either statute or constitutional provision had similar guarantees. But a loaded gun need not be fired to have an impact, and the mere existence of Section 10 as a "strategic insurance policy" was just enough to let Eisenhower reluctantly acquiesce to Seaton's wishes about Alaska. If nothing else, the PYK proposal—which is still the law of the land—is a permanent reminder of the Cold War tensions that shaped the state of Alaska, and the silent depths of Eisenhower's staunch resistance to the territory becoming a state.

The PYK enabled Seaton, thanks to the help of Stevens and Snedden, to win the statehood battle with Eisenhower. Now the war would enter a new phase in Congress, where the outcome remained very much in doubt.

12

"Second-Class Citizens" and the "Lunatic Fringe"

By the spring of 1957 hearings about statehood for Alaska had become a familiar routine on Capitol Hill that testified to the congressional habit of talking much and doing little. "I have worn out at least two pairs of pants listening to statehood hearings," Rep. Leo O'Brien said. "My mind is thoroughly made up on this subject. I am enthusiastically for statehood for both Alaska and Hawaii."[1]

The old arguments about Alaska had been hashed over so many times that all the players knew the full script by heart. The territory was either a sparsely populated, isolated wilderness, with no economic prospects, or it was a treasure trove of resources, with unlimited potential and a population that had been denied the basic rights of American citizenship for too long. Like a singer with only one song, Bob Bartlett said he feared boring his colleagues with the details of the statehood story yet again because all of them had heard his performance "so many times that if I were to omit a single comma" they would know it was missing. It pained him to recall the number of statehood hearings they had endured in the previous ten years: 1947 in Alaska and Washington by the House; 1949 in Washington by the House; 1950 in Washington by the Senate; 1953 in Alaska by the House and in Washington by the Senate; 1954 in Washington by the Senate; 1955 in Washington by the House and the Senate. Cumulatively Bartlett counted 3,323 pages of printed statehood hearings, totaling about two million words.

"Every argument that could be devised by man against statehood has been offered to this committee in the past," Bartlett told the Senate

Interior Committee, "and every such argument has been refuted."[2] Bob Atwood thought the typical anti-statehood clichés registering on the far end of the sanity scale—such as the fear mongering during the mental health debate in 1956—were paranoid fantasies on about the same level as "the world is flat, the flying machine is not here to stay and the law of gravity ought to be repealed." Because the most common myths about Alaska were repeatedly used as excuses to justify congressional inaction, these delusions proved resistant to reason and virtually immune from logical scrutiny, no matter how often they were denied or rebutted.[3]

Perhaps Sourdough Jack had the best answer of all. During the 1957 celebration of Golden Days, the annual summer festival and parade honoring the history of Fairbanks, the *News-Miner* published a four-page extra edition on full-sized newsprint with the old-timer's head on the cover and the headline "All the Valid Arguments Against Alaska Statehood." Inside, all three pages were blank.

Snedden sent about fifty copies to key senators and congressmen "as valuable reference material," and the first reply came back from Tennessee Sen. Estes Kefauver. "I have heard opponents to Alaska Statehood argue on the floor of both bodies," Kefauver wrote, "and I think on pages 2, 3, and 4 you have covered the arguments in full."[4]

Regardless of the torrent of wasted words and empty rhetoric spilled into the Potomac, several surprises were in store when the final round of statehood hearings came to order on Monday, March 11, 1957, at ten a.m., with Congressman Leo O'Brien of the House Subcommittee on Territorial and Insular Affairs presiding. It was immediately evident that these proceedings would be quite different from any that had gone before.

For one thing, the people of Alaska had now adopted an official state constitution, which greatly simplified the task before Congress. Previous statehood bills had been "enabling acts," which included lengthy procedural steps required to enable the territory to become a state—most important, the drafting and approval of a suitable constitution—but henceforth all statehood legislation would simply be straightforward "admission acts."[5] Furthermore, thanks to the Alaska-Tennessee Plan, Alaska now had a trio of elected—but officially unrecognized—representatives in Washington, D.C., lobbying for statehood: "Senator" Gruening, "Senator" Egan, and "Representative" Rivers. In theory, four heads working the halls of Congress should have been better than one, and publicly Bob Bartlett had made an elaborate showing of welcoming and working with the ATP men, but in reality he was merely trying to put the best face on a bad situation. Privately, both Bartlett and Snedden concluded that the three "would-be" legislators would not be much help.

Though he never admitted so publicly, Snedden felt Lehleitner's Tennessee Plan, which the Fairbanks publisher had done so much to bring about, had gone wrong from the very beginning. As soon as the three Democrats had been elected in October 1956 they seemed unable to work as a unit. This became all too apparent when Gruening refused to accompany Egan and Rivers on a nearly seven-thousand-mile-long automobile trip in the middle of winter from the steps of Constitution Hall on the university campus in Fairbanks to the steps of the Capitol in Washington, D.C. At its heart the ATP was a public relations stunt, and Snedden had envisioned the cross-country caravan ride—with the three men and their wives driving together in three specially marked new white cars—one Mercury, one Pontiac, and one Chrysler—as sixty-six hundred miles and at least fifteen states of free advertising, including a celebrated stop in Nashville to honor the home of the original Tennessee Plan. Snedden pleaded with Gruening to join Egan and Rivers on the road to D.C. "I fully realize that the caravan trip will be in no sense a 'joyride' and that three weeks of traveling might prove an undue hardship," but he thought it vital for all three ATP men to join the trek. "It is essential that Alaskans stay . . . united in this statehood drive," Snedden wrote, but he could not convince Gruening to even come to Fairbanks to wish the other two men farewell, let alone get behind the wheel himself.[6]

Gruening's absence was the first of many disappointments to come. As Rivers and Egan prepared to leave Fairbanks on the morning of Monday, December 10, carrying forty-nine flags with forty-nine stars— one each for the existing forty-eight and the expectant number forty-nine —the temperature was almost forty-nine degrees below zero, and Rivers's Pontiac refused to start. After hours in the garage, and installation of a new battery and a new head-bolt heater, two-thirds of the Tennessee Plan started off through the ice fog, only to have Egan's Mercury freeze up later that day and require the assistance of a tow truck some two hundred miles south of Fairbanks, by which time the mercury in the thermometer stood at fifty-five below.[7]

Egan admitted he was not comfortable behind the wheel, but the cold temperatures up north would be a mild nuisance compared to the crazy drivers he would encounter down south. Never having had to navigate through traffic before, he found driving in the United States to be "a lot different than driving the old delivery car around good old Valdez." By the following summer he could look back on the trip with a bit of humor, shocked that he had made it from Fairbanks to the East Coast without getting a ticket or putting a dent in the Mercury.

> From the time we started going into Tacoma, Everett and Seattle on a rainy night in December I was really having one hell of a time trying to figure out what I would do at the next turn or intersection in the road or street. Ha! Neva hung on without too much complaint all the way across the country. Had I been her, and if I knew then what I know now, I'd have jumped out as soon as we hit the State of Washington border.[8]

During their wintertime whirlwind three-week tour of the United States—in the course of which Gruening flew in to meet them at Portland and Nashville—the ATP men and their wives generated a smattering of local headlines and mild curiosity, but no national coverage in magazines, radio, or television. Upon their arrival in Washington, D.C., the news blackout and the cold shoulder continued. As Bartlett later said, neither the country nor the Congress were excited by the arrival in the capital of the free world of three anomalous characters chosen to unofficially represent the people of Alaska; Gruening, Egan, and Rivers were not about to rival the Cold War, civil rights, or the hydrogen bomb for newspaper coverage and TV time. Bartlett privately admitted that the publicity campaign of the ATP was nothing other than a "massive failure."[9] Meanwhile, the executive branch looked upon the Tennessee Planners with outright disdain. "We must concede," the News-Miner admitted in a January 1957 editorial, "that the fact that all three Alaskans are Democrats does not help their cause with the Administration."[10] For more than four months Eisenhower even refused to see the three Democrats, only relenting finally for a twenty-minute courtesy call at the White House in the first week of May 1957.[11]

Even with members of their own party, neither Egan nor Rivers proved to be particularly effective salesmen. Egan was a shy, retiring sort, not used to introducing himself to strangers, and Rivers made so few contacts that after a considerable time in Washington he could not introduce Snedden to a single Democratic member of the crucial House Rules

Committee, and could probably recognize fewer than a dozen members of the entire House of Representatives.[12] While Gruening was his usual irrepressible self, buttonholing anyone and everyone, many—including both Bartlett and Egan—felt he was too aggressive. Egan was soon handicapped by a broken eardrum, but he heard so much of Gruening with his good ear that he shortly refused to have anything more to do with him.

The Tennessee Planners had been elected with the full expectation that they—like previous Tennessee Plan delegations in the nineteenth century—would automatically ascend to the House or Senate upon the achievement of statehood. Gruening's ATP letterhead—designed by Paul Solka in the *News-Miner* back shop—said in bold typescript across the top:

UNITED STATES SENATOR
From the 49th State of Alaska

Realizing too late that claiming to be a U.S. senator from a state that did not yet exist might strike observers in Washington—particularly Republicans—as arrogant and presumptuous, Gruening and the others modified the letterhead by hand-printing the word "ELECT" after the title, but this only seemed to accentuate the problem. "Senator-elect" Gruening sent a letter to Eisenhower asking in vain for a meeting as soon as possible; in the president's files a scribbled memo to White House counsel Jerry Morgan was attached to Gruening's request: "Jerry, Note Gruening's use of *Senate letterhead* (!) The Gruening [i.e. Tennessee] Plan will leave Bartlett out—and is he mad?"[13]

Republican resentment that acceptance of the Tennessee Plan guaranteed two Democratic senators—the situation that Snedden had hoped to avoid with the coalition ticket—plus the widespread notion that it also unfairly forestalled any chance for Delegate Bob Bartlett to try for an eventual seat in the Senate, spurred a bipartisan congressional consensus that the statehood bill required new elections for both the Senate and the House, in essence nullifying the elections of the Tennessee Planners. Thus marginalized by Congress, shunned by the administration, and ignored by the media, the Alaska-Tennessee strategy that Snedden and Lehleitner had launched with such great hopes would have gone out with a whimper, except for the bulldog determination, eloquence, and intellectual firepower of Gruening. Though ill suited for the tedious and delicate process of lobbying for votes in Congress, and habitually more inclined to lecture than to listen, the "Phantom Senator," as he took to calling himself, never flinched from the spotlight of the bully pulpit he craved. While the Tennessee Plan itself may have failed in its original design as a publicity stunt for winning friends in Congress—Bartlett believed the ATP did not result in a single additional vote for statehood—it provided Gruening all he needed: a platform to articulate to the American public the fundamental questions of the statehood quest, in a manner only he could do.[14]

In sharp contrast to the confrontational and sensational style of Gruening was the more subtle approach of Interior Secretary Fred Seaton. In a battle of words and wits no one could equal the erudition of Gruening, but to win a fight in Congress required other skills once the speeches were over. Secretary Seaton would make the congressional hearings in the spring of 1957 a watershed in statehood history. The PYK proposal crafted by Ted Stevens under Seaton's leadership had bridged the gap between what Eisenhower demanded and territorial residents would accept; this piece of legislative magic had given Seaton the freedom to unleash the Interior Department as the most potent weapon of the pro-statehood forces. By rejecting partition and backing statehood for the entire territory, Seaton swept away the years of indecision and confusion about where the administration stood and why, making statehood for Alaska appear to be a genuine possibility for 1957. Thanks to Seaton, for the first time since Truman had left the White House four years earlier a parade of top officials from both the Defense Department and the Interior Department—including Legislative Counsel Ted Stevens—came before Congress to press for Alaska to become the forty-ninth state.

Ironically, at these hearings, where Seaton's role was of such crucial importance, he was the man who wasn't there. Throughout the eighteen days of testimony from March 11 to 29, he remained confined at Walter Reed Medical Center with a slipped disc and a severe case of sciatica, so the campaign to convince Congress was left to Under Secretary Chilson, assisted by Stevens, while behind the scenes in his hospital room Seaton continued to orchestrate the statehood strategy in his bathrobe.[15]

Seaton's approach was simple. With the Republican administration fully committed, the secretary pressured Congress to stop talking and take action. He challenged the sharply divided House and Senate to stop the maneuvering that had barred the doors to the two territories for so many years, pressing lawmakers to forget their personal interests and prejudices in favor of full equality for all American citizens, no matter where they lived. He urged that a bipartisan coalition come together to do what should have been done long ago.

"As for myself," Seaton said,

> I haven't the slightest concern as to whom or which political party gets the credit for Hawaiian or Alaskan statehood. Simple justice demands that each be admitted to the Union. Republicans or Democrats, the people of these Territories are Americans, and I know of nothing in the Constitution of the United States which gives preference to one political party or the other or, more importantly, sets up political party affiliation as a test of fitness for statehood.[16]

While Seaton's unequivocal support for Alaska's admission was plain enough, the legal impact of the Interior Department's PYK amendment was more nebulous. As drafted by Stevens, Section 10 reserved to the president the right to withdraw any amount of land, at any time, north and west of the red line along the three rivers for national defense purposes, with "exclusive jurisdiction" reserved to the United States, but what precisely this might mean for this region larger than Texas was uncertain.

One House committee member predicted that the executive branch would probably withdraw the entire 276,000 square miles and should do so promptly; another thought any defense withdrawals would be equivalent to "a modified form of martial law and military government" under a continual state of emergency. Under Secretary Chilson stressed, however, that the administration preferred to think of Section 10 as a military "insurance policy," a permanent provision enabling the president to take whatever actions he deemed necessary, without interference, or the need to declare a state of emergency or martial law.[17] And yet despite this blanket guarantee of executive authority, Chilson affirmed that the Interior Department's intent was for existing state laws to remain in effect inside any "exclusive jurisdiction" withdrawals, as long as they did not violate defense needs, and perhaps continued to be administered by state or local officials, if the executive branch were so willing.

The PYK goals may have appeared to be mutually exclusive, if not a complete contradiction—total flexibility for the Commander-in-Chief on the one hand, with maximum local control on the other—but the proposal seemed to promise both sides just enough of the reassurance they needed, as long as the point was not pushed too hard. For instance, Delegate Bartlett asked what might happen if the area around a small unincorporated Native village such as Point Hope on the Arctic Coast were withdrawn. Chilson, who had never been to Alaska, and frankly had no idea where Point Hope was located, asked Stevens to help fill in the blanks. Stevens explained how the PYK withdrawal might impact state laws in the village regarding alcohol. As Stevens told Delegate Bartlett:

> The amendment provides that the laws of the State applicable in that area become Federal laws as of the time of the withdrawal. Those [state] laws will still govern . . . the liquor situation in that area at the time. The enforcement problem is the final problem, and the section provides that the laws shall be administered by the President's designated representative and . . . in most instances it could be assumed that that would be the person who was administering them already.[18]

Bartlett complained of the "element of uncertainty" inherent in the measure, because the amendment explicitly reserved all decisions about the extent of local control to the discretion of federal officials. But the delegate admitted that the verbal testimony of Chilson, Stevens, and others was reassuring, as what they told the committee indicated that "state authority would be maintained to a much greater extent than might be inferred in the language" of the amendment, and that the Eisenhower administration had no intention of using the PYK as a ruse to keep half of Alaska under quasi-territorial control. To get that promise explicitly on the record, Bartlett responded to Stevens and Chilson—as politicians are often wont to do—with a statement posed as a question: "In other words, there is no intention here to put the people at Point Hope, or those similarly situated anywhere within that area north and west of the line, under tight Federal control?"

"That is not our intention," Chilson replied. "Our intention, Delegate Bartlett, is to preserve, so far as at all possible, the right of self-government in the people up there, even though a withdrawal is made."[19]

In the Senate hearings Stevens explained that the unique feature of the Section 10 proposal was the exclusive right to guarantee future withdrawals even after statehood. Stevens told the senators that he had lived in Alaska for more than three years, and that he was confident the PYK amendment would be "acceptable to the Alaskans. They know, the people of Alaska know, that area of north and west Alaska is strategic. They are willing to accept the administration's proposal."[20] Buoyed by the reassuring testimony of Chilson and Stevens, Bartlett wholeheartedly endorsed the creation of the military withdrawal zone. "I think I speak for all Alaskans," Bartlett told the Senate committee, "in saying that this principle is perfectly acceptable to us. . . . I have not had a single objection to it from any source within the Territory."[21]

Alaskans found the PYK to be a welcome alternative to partition, but if anyone imagined that the new initiative and the strong backing from Seaton and the Eisenhower administration would make the statehood bill sail through Congress, that notion was shattered on the second day of the House hearings, when Snedden appeared at the witness table.

Snedden's arrival in Washington, D.C., as one of the first witnesses in support of the administration's proposal—he testified before any of the three members of the Tennessee Plan delegation—was a sign of just how close he and Seaton had become in the short time since their first conference in Washington in late 1956 and Seaton's trip to Alaska in early 1957. The natural rapport and compatibility between the two small-town publishers blossomed into a close personal friendship, giving Snedden a direct pipeline to the "Czar of Alaska," as interior secretaries were called. Never before in all of Alaska history had any secretary of the interior established such a tight bond with a resident of the territory, and this quickly forged alliance would begin to pay dividends immediately.

Snedden offered to come to Washington to appear as a witness for the administration in the March 1957 hearings, and for both partisan and ideological reasons, Seaton thought having Snedden as a leadoff witness was an excellent strategy. A Republican businessman and newspaper owner would naturally carry more weight with the conservative faction that was the biggest stumbling block to statehood.

Snedden's presentation before the House subcommittee started cordially enough as Chairman Leo O'Brien gave him a warm welcome, from one ink-stained newspaperman to another. O'Brien fondly recalled the subcommittee's hearings in Fairbanks two years previously.

"In a great many subjects that come before the committee," O'Brien announced to his colleagues, "your chairman cannot pose as an expert, but I do have some slight knowledge of the newspaper business and I want to say to the next witness that one of the things that impressed me most in Alaska during the time I was there was the alert, progressive press which exists in the Territory of Alaska. High on that list is your own newspaper, sir."[22]

In his prepared statement, Snedden tried to articulate the familiar reasons why he and many others believed that "statehood for Alaska is absolutely essential to the welfare of the Territory and our Nation."

"I base my conviction on one essential fact—that the Territorial form of government is un-American, undemocratic, stifling to free enterprise, and damaging to the morale of the people."

He then described the innumerable "headaches and heartaches connected with being in business in Alaska," including higher freight rates, interest rates, and capital requirements. "I have the rare privilege," he said, "of printing my newspaper on the most expensive newsprint" in probably the entire world, costing more than $200 a ton. He thought the federal government should do something to utilize Alaska's forestry products, but he argued that the worst example of the neglect of its "untapped resources" was the Gubik gas field, still locked up by PLO 82, the "temporary" withdrawal made in 1943.

> Thousands and thousands of hours have been spent by Alaskans toward what should be the comparatively simple matter of making this area available. The majority of those working on this . . . including myself, have no immediate personal interest in the actual development, and no immediate personal gain. We simply cannot see any logical reason for this great resource to lay idle year after year when development shows definite feasibility, and will contribute so much in reduced costs to Alaskan and to all taxpayers of our great country as well as "paving the road" for many other types of development. . . .

Snedden claimed that with development of Gubik gas, the military in Alaska could conservatively see their fuel bills cut $1.4 million a year, "and even in this day of inflation that seems like a lot of money to me."[23]

Alaska's relative economic poverty in the midst of such fantastic natural riches was, he maintained, due entirely to federal neglect. "We contend that, beyond a shadow of a doubt, the fault lies right at the feet of the United States." Alaskans were "second-class" citizens who wanted only "the rights and privileges of first-class American citizenship" typically taken for granted by residents of the forty-eight states.

> I believe that some of you are "spoiled." ... [L]ike the child of a fortunate family, you have forgotten what it is like to be in want. ... You cannot know how you miss the rights of American citizenship until you have done without them day in and day out, through the years. ... These may seem like small things to you who have them, but I am convinced after my years of residence in Alaska that they are the greatest handicaps of all.[24]

Over the decades Alaskans had made the practice of decrying the ills of federal neglect a solemn ritual, and for more than fifty years the cry of second-class treatment—such as Snedden had described—had been standard fare in editorials and stump speeches. On Capitol Hill, however, the language of Alaska politics was obviously a foreign dialect, because the ranking Republican on the committee, Rep. A. L. "Doc" Miller of Nebraska, one of the most powerful statehood foes in Congress, thought Snedden's remarks were both offensive and misguided.

"If I were a businessman ... and read your statement," Miller shot back, "Alaska would be the last place I would want to go. Because I think you made the best argument against statehood for Alaska that I have heard." What bothered him most of all was the charge of second-class citizenship. "I do not know why you refer to 'second-class citizens.' It makes me a little hot under the collar. You are not more second class than Hawaii or the Indians of this country or anybody else. And I rather resent that statement. I rather resent the statement that you read into the record as to your 'colonial form of Government.' I think it is wrong."

Congressman Miller charged that becoming a state would not solve any of the underlying economic problems that Snedden had addressed, and wondered "how in the world would statehood change the cost of newsprint" or anything else in Alaska?

> You still have a high cost of production and high cost of transportation. You used to have two steamship lines going to Alaska. You do not have

any now. . . . You used to have a thriving gold mine
industry in Alaska. You do not have that now. . . .
Millions of dollars have been spent in Alaska trying to find gas and oil, but they have not found it,
at least in quantities that could be used. So I do
not know how statehood would change all that.
You discourage me about statehood. If I took your
statement as to the cost of vegetables and everything, I would think you are not mature enough.
You cannot support yourselves.[25]

Miller said that folks in parts of Nebraska had to pay a high rate on
bonds "and we do not consider ourselves second-class citizens. . . . But apparently Alaska does. This is the part I do not like about your statement.
I think it is ill-advised and gives the committee the wrong impression
and the country the wrong impression as to what might happen if you
had statehood in Alaska." For Miller the bottom line was a simple one:
"[I]nstead of making statements about the cost and how you are second-
class citizens, I hope you will get down to the economics of it to see if you
are able to exist as a state. That is what I would be interested in."[26]

When Doc Miller had finished scolding Snedden, Democratic
Congressman James Haley of Florida followed in a similar vein. "I regret
that a statement of this kind should be in the record. . . . I have heard a
great deal since I have been in Congress about 'second-class American citizens.' I do not consider the people of Alaska second-class American citizens. Neither do I consider the people of Hawaii second-class American
citizens. You are following traditionally the pattern of all the Territories
that came into this great Nation."[27]

At that point Leo O'Brien rose to Snedden's defense in as diplomatic
a tone as possible, praising Alaskans as "first-class people" who were nevertheless "second-class citizens."

One of the things that I like best about serving
in Congress is that men can disagree very violently and still remain friends. The gentleman from
Florida and the gentleman from Nebraska have
said that they regretted the insertion of the witness' statement in the record. I cannot share their
views. I appreciate the statement, and I agree with
it, because while I regard the residents of Alaska

as first-class people, I think we cannot deny, unless we want to deny our Constitution itself, that
they are at the moment second-class citizens. . . .
Because anyone who is subject to taxation without
representation is a second-class citizen.[28]

The flap over Snedden's charge of "second class citizenship" was the
lead for reporters covering the hearing and made headlines the next day
in both the *New York Times* ("Alaskans Status Stirs Inquiry Tiff") and
the *Washington Post* ("Statehood Hearing Witness Rebuked On Calling
Alaskans '2nd Class Citizens'").[29] And when "Senator-elect" Gruening
appeared to testify, he too joined in the fray. Gruening told the committee his initial intention had been simply to "declare my deep conviction
that Alaska was ready for statehood" and then offer to answer questions,
believing it hardly necessary to repeat yet again the same old statehood
arguments heard year after year. But he said he changed his mind when
Snedden's rather innocuous comments about second-class status "had
aroused the ire" of certain committee members. "As I share his view, and
I believe that view is shared by the majority of Alaskans . . . I desire to
go into the matter at some length" to detail the ninety years of neglect of
Alaska by the power brokers in Washington, D.C., and to prove the fact of
second-class citizenship. "Now, I have no desire needlessly to raise issues
which are perhaps controversial and may be needlessly irritating to certain
members of the committee. . . . However, discussion, debate and dissent
have been called the three 'D's' of democracy, and I feel that buttressing
the facts . . . about the colonialism which the United States has practiced
in Alaska" will explain why statehood is needed and how it will work.[30]

In his treatise on ninety years of neglect Gruening said "the list-
ing of discriminations" against Alaska "could go on almost indefinitely."
While some costs in Alaska were naturally high, others were artificially
inflated by government action or inaction. As a result "it cost about twice
as much to live in Alaska as in the United States," meaning the citizens
of the territory labored every day under a double burden made worse by
federal action.

Probably the most intolerable of these acts was the Merchant
Marine Act of 1920—commonly known as the Jones Act after its sponsor, Washington Senator Wesley L. Jones—a federal law originally designed to protect the U.S. maritime and shipbuilding industry. Among
other things the law required all shipping between U.S. ports to be
done in American-built-and-owned bottoms. This restriction placed a

disproportionate financial burden on the territory as it relied almost exclusively on its maritime lifeline. "Alaska is handicapped by the highest transportation costs in the world," Gruening said, "and by far the highest anywhere under the flag. . . . The people of Alaska pay the price. That is what Bill Snedden . . . was seeking to convey to you when he related that he was paying the highest cost of newsprint of any publisher under the Stars and Stripes." Gruening called Snedden "a typical American who has gone up to the last frontier to make his way and is burdened by the results of manmade discrimination imposed, through Federal legislation," to favor a specific industry in the United States. "That is colonialism."[31]

As another example Gruening cited a case where the Congress had cut funding for road construction in Alaska's national forests by two-thirds, shifting $7 million to national forests in the Western states. "I ask you," he challenged the committee, "is the action of the Congress, in effecting a unique discrimination against voteless Alaska in favor of the States with voting representatives, an example of colonialism or is it not? And if it is not colonialism, what is it? And if the victims of this $7 million discrimination are not second-class citizens, what are they?"[32]

At the conclusion of his testimony Gruening held up a copy of his 1954 history of the territory published by Random House with the deliberately provocative and premature title *The State of Alaska*. (If Gruening could adopt the title of U.S. senator prematurely, he saw no harm in anticipating the birth of the new state five years before it happened.) "At the risk of seeming to advertise the product . . . I will be very happy to present a copy of this book to every member of the committee who has not got one. It is called *The State of Alaska*, and it goes very definitely into all of these discriminations and cites chapter and verse in which all the documentation can be found."[33]

Some of the extreme sensitivity about the phrase "second-class citizenship" was the suspicion that the charges of the "un-American" treatment of Alaska by the federal government sounded suspiciously like communist propaganda, particularly since Alaska was on the doorstep of Siberia. Suspicion of communist infiltration in Hawaii was common enough, but Chairman O'Brien wanted to make it clear in the record that any Alaskan accusations of "un-Americanism" on the part of the federal government were inspired only by the Red, White, and Blue. To that end O'Brien introduced FBI statistics that indicated there were 22,575 communists in his home state of New York, compared to only ten card-carrying Reds in all of Alaska, equaling about one lonely communist for every sixty thousand square miles. Per capita, New York had a communist ratio of one for every seven hundred people, compared to one to sixteen thousand in Alaska. Only three states among the forty-eight tallied fewer communists than the territory: Kansas with six; Wyoming with four; and Mississippi with one.[34]

Obviously, Alaska was hardly a bastion of Soviet sympathizers—except in comparison with Mississippi—but to those not familiar with the local sense of political sarcasm the rhetoric on occasion sounded a secessionist beat. Faced with the indifference of federal bureaucrats, Alaskans often joked that if the territory were an independent country the United States would probably treat it with more respect. As a symbolic gesture, back in 1951 seven members of the territorial legislature had proposed a memorial asking the United Nations to help establish the "Republic of Alaska" as a poke in the eye to Uncle Sam. Snedden once suggested to Lehleitner that if the Tennessee Planners were not warmly received in Washington, D.C., perhaps they would generate more headlines if they were to try Ottawa instead. Bob Bartlett relished a 1957 letter to the editor of the *News-Miner*, which suggested that Alaska should declare war on the United States, and follow this up immediately by a declaration of unconditional surrender, with a simultaneous request for foreign aid.[35] Inspired that this was a surefire way to ensure unlimited U.S. investment in Alaska, Bartlett made this tongue-in-cheek plan the theme of a rousing dinner speech for statehood in Washington in early 1957. As he explained to Snedden, "I told the audience that . . . I was no longer for statehood; stating this reversal had come about by reason of a letter which had recently been published in your paper. There must have been a couple of hundred people there and they all seemed to enjoy it."[36]

Apparently some members of Congress did not have such a sharp sense of humor. Recalling Bartlett's speech, Gruening made a similar quip to the members of the House subcommittee, and like the flap over Snedden's comment about second-class citizenship, the response showed the inability of some members of Congress to comprehend the nature of Alaskan discontent, or to tell the difference between a throwaway line and a threat. The outraged congressman this time was Utah Republican William A. Dawson, who thought Gruening was flying the flag of treason.

> Mr. Dawson: Governor, I am rather disturbed at your statement on page 25 to the effect

that: '*Some Alaskans have at times mused how much better off we would have been if for just a few years in the last decade we had hoisted a foreign flag.*'

You do not seriously believe that, do you, Governor? . . . Do you really believe you would have been better off under a foreign flag?

MR. GRUENING: Will you read the next sentence?

MR. DAWSON: Yes, I have read it, but I assume you put that statement out for some purpose. You go on later and apologize for it, but you still leave the statement there. . . .

MR. GRUENING: I didn't apologize for it. I said no one thought that except in jest.

MR. DAWSON: It is a serious statement.

MR. GRUENING: When we . . . noticed that these foreign countries could get almost anything they asked, we would say rather humorously—or perhaps wistfully—"If we hoisted a foreign flag we could get all this stuff."

Of course nobody took it seriously, nobody meant it seriously. And I made that clear. And if it wasn't clear, I'll make it clear now. We prefer even our second-class citizenship in America to citizenship in any other country in the world. . . .

MR. DAWSON: We in the States make the same statement . . . we give aid to foreign countries, why should we not give aid to our States? . . . And none of us think for one minute that we would rather be under a foreign flag.[37]

If ever more proof had been needed that Alaskans did not enjoy the full equality and respect accorded to other U.S. citizens, it was the tone and the tenor of congressmen such as Dawson and Miller, the imperial "what gives you the right" attitude toward Snedden, Gruening, or anyone else from Alaska who dared criticize Congress for not living up to the ideals of the U.S. Constitution. Like any beleaguered or disenfranchised minority before or since asking for equal treatment under the law, the Alaskans were met with puzzled stares, if not uncomprehending hostility, from power brokers who could not imagine the value of equality to those denied it.

At this juncture the debate took yet another unexpected turn when Doc Miller decided to take it upon himself to poll the people of Alaska through the pages of the *News-Miner* and other newspapers and radio stations in the territory, to ask if Alaskans really had a genuine desire to join the Union at all. Initially, Snedden took the Nebraska congressman's opinion poll as a harmless diversion, since the overwhelming approval by voters of the Tennessee Plan six months earlier—a de facto vote on immediate statehood—and the enthusiastic support for the constitution itself, seemed ample proof of majority sentiment, not to mention a decade of official votes, such as the 1946 referendum in favor of statehood, as well as legislative memorials urging immediate statehood passed by every Territorial Legislature in the past ten years—with those in 1953, 1955, and 1957 approved unanimously in both the House and Senate.[38]

Despite these repeated demonstrations of popular support, however, for several years a shadowy organization known as the Alaska Referendum Committee had unsuccessfully pushed for another vote, claiming the issue of "immediate statehood" had never been put to the test. This was the spur for Miller's straw poll. What Miller apparently didn't realize, however, was that the entire membership roll of the Alaska Referendum Committee, comprised only a single person, an off-beat Fairbanks character named Alice Stuart, who—as the old adage goes—always had both feet planted firmly in the air.

It might be a stretch to call Alice Stuart a marginal character on the Alaska political scene; she was far off the edge of the right-hand margin in the realm of cranks and crackpots with a story to tell that every newspaper publisher knows all too well. But nevertheless the one-woman band behind the Alaska Referendum Committee would leave a lasting mark on the history of the territory. A perpetually unsuccessful candidate for political office in Fairbanks, and a die-hard opponent of statehood, Stuart had lived in Alaska since 1940 and had been engaged in a variety of odd jobs, including office work and selling advertising. Starting in about 1953 she became the self-employed publisher of "The Alaska Calendar for Engagements," an inexpensive, plastic, spiral-bound desk diary, illustrated with black-and-white "photographs of the beauties of scenic Alaska" that she sold out of her suitcase for about three years.[39] In 1953, when the Republicans came to power in the Territorial Legislature, Stuart was a typist in the Senate offices, and apparently it was there she first hatched the plan of holding a referendum that she believed would demonstrate Alaskans preferred to remain a territory. She claimed the hysteria for Alaska statehood was the plot of a tiny cabal of self-serving, fast-talking office seekers, led by Bob Bartlett and Ernest Gruening, and backed by the *Anchorage Times* and the *Daily News-Miner*. In her mind it was only the politicians, "pressure groups," and the powers-that-be that wanted statehood, not the people. Bartlett's rejoinder was that "Alice Stuart constitutes in her own small frame the most persevering and at the same time misguided pressure group in the entire vast Territory of Alaska."[40] When the unsuspecting *Topeka Capital* in Kansas ran an editorial on "Dissension in Alaska" about the demands of the Alaska Referendum Committee, Snedden tried to explain to the managing editor the nature of this grassroots movement, which stemmed from a solitary root. "We have questioned Alice several times as to the identity of the Referendum Committee. However, she can 'never remember' exactly what it consists of."[41]

Her line of reasoning appeared to be that she was one of the people, she opposed statehood, and thus the people were opposed to statehood. "All I am," she said, "is a woman in Alaska, which is a man's country. I am not even married, do not even have a husband backing me up."[42] According to Stuart the statehood question was so contentious in Alaska that it was one of the forbidden topics for polite dinner conversation, to which Bill Egan answered: "It is my humble observation that the pros and cons of statehood for Alaska have been the subject of more discussion at dinner tables, in polite and impolite society, in public forums and in the press of Alaska than has any other subject during the past 12 years."[43]

Wrapped in the rhetoric of the American Revolution, Stuart claimed a new referendum was not another delaying tactic, but simply common sense. "Proponents talk about taxation without representation, how about statehood without representation—without the known will of the residents? . . . In the cause of Justice and to insure Alaskan internal tranquility . . . an up-to-date referendum is needed."[44]

In May 1954, a few days after John Butrovich and the Operation Statehood delegation had met with President Eisenhower at the White House, Stuart had made *News-Miner* headlines when she went to 1600 Pennsylvania Avenue herself, trying to deliver a petition with 1,420 signatures asking for her statehood referendum. Eisenhower's staff was a bit perplexed by this odd woman from Fairbanks. In a memo to White House Counsel Bernard M. Shanley, Assistant Counsel J. William Barba explained his peculiar encounter with the head of the "Alaska Referendum Committee."

"Miss Alice Stuart from Fairbanks, Alaska presented a petition on behalf of the Alaska Referendum Committee today. . . . Ms. Stuart advised that the above Committee is a name adopted by her and that she is really the Committee." He reported that Stuart was "very disappointed that she was not permitted to present her views to the President. She felt she was being discriminated against by reason of the fact that he saw a group from Alaska last week." In all truth the White House at the time was certainly receptive to Stuart's message of delaying statehood, if not to Stuart herself. Across the bottom of the memo Shanley scribbled: "She doesn't have to worry."[45]

Back in Fairbanks many were shocked by the news of Stuart's lobbying campaign, because apparently many of the individuals who had signed her petition, including the *News-Miner* staff, did so because they had believed she was lobbying *for* statehood and not trying to delay it. "Many people who signed that petition favor immediate Statehood," the *News-Miner* explained, "and Miss Stuart knows that. She is using our signatures to defeat a bill which we favor." While the *News-Miner* blasted Stuart for misrepresentation, she did have a defender. Sparing no adjectives in the thesaurus, Jack Little wrote that the *News-Miner's* "scurrilous attack" against Stuart was an example of the paper's "contemptible, cheap, mean, miserable brand of yellow journalism," a "disgusting, repulsive, extremely offensive, malicious and unwarranted attack upon a lady," by a "mishappen [*sic*], mistaken, mislead, mismanaged, misprinted and mistuned organ."[46]

By the spring of 1957 the Alaska Territorial Legislature had refused Stuart's request for a referendum in three successive legislative sessions, and the seemingly inescapable electoral evidence of the will of the people demonstrated by the support for the ATP and the constitution might have dissuaded anyone with less dedication or more common sense, but she refused to give up her quest. On a visit to the East Coast in early 1957 she had read of the upcoming statehood hearings, and she delayed her return to Fairbanks in order to testify.

Arriving at the witness table for the House hearings with an armful of clippings and papers, including an excerpt from John F. Kennedy's recent book *Profiles in Courage*, she told the committee, "Do not be frightened of all of that. That is just reference material."[47]

Though she had prepared and submitted a written statement in advance, as all witnesses were required to do, she only got as far as the first sentence of her testimony before she started reading random quotes and statistics from her stack of references. "I do not know if any of you are from Philadelphia," she said, "but I have something I cut out of a *Philadelphia Inquirer*, and it says right in the headlines. . . ." After listening for several minutes the committee staff attorney interrupted her to point out that only about "one tenth of one percent" of her comments were from her prepared statement, and he inquired if she intended to return to it: "I will be back to the statement," she said, "as soon as I read three paragraphs in the Acting Governor's message to the 23rd Legislature," at which point Chairman O'Brien gently suggested that Miss Stuart get back on track, "because frankly, I, for one, get lost."[48]

Stuart blasted the "tyrannical" Alaska legislature, which had not only repeatedly refused to support her proposed referendum but also appropriated money to support the Alaska Statehood Committee and to call the constitutional convention. She thought it was all much too confusing and claimed she and other Alaskans deserved a simple vote on "the bull's eye question" they had been denied: "'Are you in favor or against immediate statehood for Alaska'—which means we are ready to eat beans to support it, that we are ready to accept the responsibility as well as the honor."

In response O'Brien said Alaskans had already enjoyed multiple "opportunities to fire bull's eyes" against statehood if they had wished, including the 1946 referendum, the election of the constitutional convention delegates, and the election of the Tennessee Planners. He bantered with Stuart until finally they had this exchange:

"Mr. O'Brien, I think you can fool all the people some of the time and some of the people part of the time, but I do not think you can fool all of them all of the time. I do not mean you."

"Thank you," O'Brien said.

"I mean the proponents," Stuart continued. "I think if it were put to a vote, they would find out they had ceased fooling the people in Alaska, and that is why they are afraid to let it come to ballot."[49]

When the hearings opened in the Senate ten days later, Stuart was back on the witness stand, but the senators were less tolerant of her stream-of-consciousness testimony that their colleagues on the other side of the Capitol had been. If there was so much opposition to statehood, members of the Senate committee asked, why was it that on March 11— the same day that Representative O'Brien had opened the hearings before the House subcommittee—the Alaska Territorial Legislature had passed a unanimous resolution asking Congress to grant statehood to Alaska within nineteen days, by March 30, 1957, the ninetieth anniversary of the purchase of Alaska, so that henceforth "liberation day" from Russian colonial bondage could also be known as "Statehood Day." When Stuart nevertheless insisted that if a ballot were "held today I think it would very likely go against immediate statehood," Sen. Henry M. "Scoop" Jackson of Washington was incredulous: "In other words, you feel that the people in a vote would override the unanimous vote of the Territorial legislature, House and Senate, in which they ask that there not only be immediate statehood, but that it be completed by the end of this week, March 30. I guess that is as immediate as anything can be."[50]

Sen. Clinton P. Anderson of New Mexico made the same point: "Not one person in the legislature of Alaska in House or Senate subscribed to your point of view. Would you not think this committee, having decent regard for the wishes of the representatives of the people of Alaska, ought to grant what the legislature asked and not what you asked?"

Stuart gave the same answer she always used: "I think they have forgotten 'government shall be with the consent of the governed.'" Senator Anderson shot back, "No, they have not," and tried to explain that Alice Stuart did not have veto power over everyone in Alaska. "Consent of the governed does not mean that everyone has to consent but only the majority has to consent. . . . Here you have it unanimously. How many more can you get? This is everybody in the legislature."[51]

Clearly, most congressmen and senators who heard Stuart's testimony thought her referendum crusade was the obsession of a misguided eccentric, but not Doc Miller. To Snedden's astonishment, the Nebraska doctor not only took Alice Stuart's complaint seriously, but he also decided to do something about it. He announced he would poll the people of Alaska himself through the territory's news outlets. On March 20 the congressman wired the *News-Miner* as well as four other newspapers and ten radio stations, asking them to help conduct an anonymous poll of the public asking the Alice Stuart question: "Do you favor immediate statehood for Alaska?" Representative O'Brien blasted Miller's request, saying it was nothing but a "dilatory tactic" that "wouldn't be worth the paper it's printed on." Alaska's four elected officials in Washington, Delegate Bartlett and the three Tennessee Planners, likewise thought this a flimsy excuse to stuff the ballot box with straw votes and suborn the will of the registered electorate. What would stop a single person—such as Alice Stuart herself—from sending in tens, hundreds, or even thousands of responses? A simpler recipe for political manipulation could hardly be concocted.

In a joint statement Bartlett, Gruening, Egan, and Rivers said that this alleged opinion survey inspired by Alice Stuart would have no validity as an indicator of the territory's willingness for statehood, especially since "Alaskans have repeatedly and emphatically demonstrated their desire for statehood now" in a series of officially monitored elections. "Whatever the merits of a further referendum might be, and it seems they are nebulous, we can see no good purpose to be served by such a poll."[52] Bob Atwood thought Miller's "weird poll" was intended only to delay and defeat statehood. "The folly of the congressman's poll has been cited by his colleagues in Washington," Atwood said. "It is obvious to Alaskans. . . . He is more interested in confusing the issues and dividing Alaskans than he is in discovering new truths."[53]

Snedden thought Miller's "so-called poll" was an insult to the democratic process, and further evidence—if it were needed—of the second-class status of Alaska citizens; otherwise the House member from the fourth congressional district of Nebraska would not dare to so lightly dismiss the sworn testimony of Alaska's duly elected delegation, its legislature, and the tens of thousands of formal votes Alaska residents had already cast directly or indirectly for statehood in the previous years. Snedden enjoyed the suggestion of *Juneau Empire* editor George Sundborg, who said the logical response would be to ask the people of Omaha "to send us unsigned letters on how they like being just across the creek from Iowa."[54]

But regardless of his personal views, Snedden felt forced to comply with Miller's request. He ran the poll question on page one, though the wording he chose clearly indicated it was under duress:

POLL

In response to a request from representative Miller of Nebraska, the News-Miner *prints the following poll form:*

I am

FOR_____

AGAINST_____

Immediate Statehood for Alaska

Signed_____

Fill out this form, if you wish, and mail to the News-Miner. *We will forward all ballots to Representative Miller.* [55]

In the days that followed the launching of Miller's off-hand opinion survey, the congressman claimed the anti-statehood replies flooded his mailbox, running at least 2–1 against statehood. Miller professed to be "amazed" at the number of "thoughtful letters, good sound letters" written by those who opposed statehood, while in contrast, "many of those in favor are merely cards, probably an inspired postcard program put on to stimulate people to send in postcards."[56] When Snedden realized the impact Miller's strategy might have, he warned *News-Miner* readers they could no longer ignore what had initially seemed like such a foolish exercise.

"It seems that the only people who are bothering to vote are those who are bitter on the subject . . . We are printing the poll form again. We appeal to everybody to vote. . . . Whether you consider this ridiculous or not, please fill out a ballot and mail it to the *News-Miner*. We have to take this poll seriously, it seems, to prevent a small group in Washington from harming the Statehood movement seriously."[57]

When Miller ultimately released the results of his straw poll, the final tabulation—not surprising to Snedden and others—was against "immediate statehood" by almost three to one, with 1,340 opposed and only 503 in favor.[58] A skeptical senator later wrote Alice Stuart that in "Congressman Miller's so-called poll" there was "no requirement for voting nor limitations on the number of times any person, whether qualified or not could vote," and therefore technically there was "no reason that you yourself" could not have personally cast all of the thirteen-hundred-plus votes against statehood, in the same way that Delegate Bartlett might have voted in favor of statehood at least five hundred times!

According to Snedden, on the days that the paper ran the form for the "post card poll" the *News-Miner's* newsstand sales jumped dramatically, and the only possible conclusion was that an "aroused minority" appeared to have voted early and often, making arguments, the *News-Miner* said, that were "untrue, unreasoned, or beside the point," expressing the frustration of "the crack-pot fringe that always welcomes a chance to jibber their views—on any subject."[59]

Generally the "crack-pot" contingent blamed newspapers like the *News-Miner* and the *Anchorage Times* for inventing the need for statehood and thwarting the will of "Me the People." As one participant in Miller's survey said: "The promoters who have control of the press in Alaska are too far advanced toward this fraud against the genuine Alaskan to allow a representative vote."[60] But there was one Alaska newspaper publisher in 1957 lashing out daily against statehood as a diabolical scam and raising the stakes in the war of words against the *News-Miner* to an unprecedented level—William Prescott Allen, or WPA, the spectacularly flamboyant and always unpredictable owner of the *Juneau Empire*.

Ironically, it was Snedden himself and his conversion to the statehood cause that was responsible for bringing WPA to Alaska in the first place. When Snedden's proposal to buy the *Juneau Empire* had been canceled in 1954 because Helen Monsen would not sell to an editor favoring statehood, the financially ailing newspaper went back on the market. In June 1955, for an estimated $235,000—rumored to be about $70,000 above what Snedden had been willing to pay—Monsen sold the *Empire* to Allen, owner and publisher of the *Laredo Times* in Laredo, Texas, and the *Montrose Daily Press* in Montrose, Colorado.

When Bob Bartlett first learned of the sale of the *Empire*, he was gleeful that the worst newspaper in Alaska would finally have a new publisher, though given Monsen's snub to Snedden the previous year, he had no expectations of any improvement in its editorial policies. "It is to be assumed," he wrote, "that the new owner is of the proper political faith; otherwise it is doubtful if Helen would have sold." Bartlett was a silent backer of the liberal weekly the *Juneau Independent*, edited by George Sundborg, and the delegate wondered if this would "be an appropriate time to make the big switch over to a daily? If the new owner paid anything such as the price Helen is rumored to have wanted then he bought himself a bad deal, indeed."[61] The gossip in Juneau was that Allen was not much of a newspaperman anyway and probably made his money in oil wells. According to Sundborg's old colleague Jack McFarland, "[W]e won't have anything to fear from Mr. Allen if the *Empire* is cast in the image of the Montrose paper, which . . . is the lousiest newspaper published anywhere."[62]

On his first trip to Alaska after buying the *Empire* in 1955, WPA's "Texas personality" made an indelible impression on all those he encountered, including George's wife, Mary Sundborg, and the Mother Superior in charge of the Juneau Catholic hospital. As George Sundborg detailed for Bartlett, Allen gave them both the full Texas treatment.

> Mary relates that [Allen] visited the hospital and asked to see the Sister Superior. When Mary went to summon her, he was half way in the super sacrosanct nuns' quarters on her heels before she shooed

him back out. The old sister is deaf. Allen pumped
her hand and said "My name is Allen. I guess
you've heard of me. I've just bought a newspaper."
Went on to say he lives across the street from a
Catholic institution of some kind and the sisters
there would never forgive him if he were to return
without visiting the sisters at the hospital. After he
left Sister Superior remarked to Mary that she had
just talked to a crazy man. That he told her he had
just bought a newspaper (she thought he meant
one copy at 10 cents).[63]

Not everyone who encountered Allen assumed he was a mental patient, but the Texas publisher did seem to have too large a personality
for a single human being. A 1942 profile in *Time* headlined "Conquest
of Mexico"—Allen was a descendant of William Hickling Prescott,
the famed nineteenth-century American historian who wrote the classic works *The Conquest of Mexico* and *The Conquest of Peru*—described
WPA as a "hotheaded, crusading editorialist" who was truthfully more
"a Western Hemisphere propagandist than a newspaperman." Since the
1920s he and his Laredo newspaper—Laredo prided itself as the "Gateway
to Mexico"—served as an unofficial conduit between the Mexican and
American governments. Many of his subscriptions were sold south of the
border, and the *Laredo Times* was probably the first English-language daily in the United States to include a Spanish supplement. For his service in
the advancement of better relations across the Rio Grande, Mexico City
bestowed two of its highest honors on WPA: the "Order of the Aztec
Eagle" and "Military Order of Merit."[64]

WPA's greatest moment in the national spotlight, however, came in
1956. Distressed at claims about rampant crime in the streets of Laredo,
he launched a statewide campaign blasting Texas as the "most corrupt
state in the nation." Apparently, his strategy was that the best way to defend the reputation of Laredo was to attack Fort Worth four hundred
miles away. After WPA published a series of front-page editorials in the
Laredo Times accusing unnamed dirty officials in Dallas and Fort Worth
of running a gambling syndicate of fifteen hundred illegal pinball machines and taking kickbacks from vice operators, charges that the Fort
Worth DA called "the ramblings of an uninformed person" and the police
chief dismissed as "absurd," Allen was hauled before a Fort Worth grand
jury. When the "distinguished looking" sixty-year-old publisher refused

to reveal the confidential sources of his information, he was found in contempt of court, fined $100, and jailed, exchanging his "matching silk tie and pocket handkerchief" for striped coveralls.[65] Though released the next day when he admitted that all of his information had in fact come from an "anonymous letter," WPA's arrest and one-night stand in the Fort Worth jail generated national headlines and only spurred him onwards. The publisher, who once drove to Austin with a truckload of brooms, asking ministers from around the state to join him in a ceremonial sweeping of the state capitol steps, took to driving around Texas in a loudspeaker-equipped car blasting corrupt city and state officials, for which he was briefly arrested and jailed again in Beaumont, Texas.[66]

As he paid his fine in Beaumont and moved on to Port Arthur, where he had also been charged with disturbing the peace with his loudspeaker, WPA vowed to continue his anti-corruption crusade across Texas and pledged to launch yet another populist campaign, "a nation wide drive against federal income taxes," beginning his fight against the IRS with his recently acquired newspaper in Juneau, Alaska. WPA hoped to turn Alaska into the biggest tax loophole in the country, urging President Eisenhower to declare the territory exempt from all federal taxation for twenty years.[67]

Alaskans hardly needed a man from Texas to tell them they should not have to pay taxes; for years statehood skeptics had been pushing the idea of a "tax moratorium" to spur Alaska development, claiming a tax-free zone along the lines of the Commonwealth of Puerto Rico was a viable alternative to statehood. Details of what Bob Atwood called the "mystical panacea" of commonwealth status for Alaska were never spelled out by anyone, possibly because turning Alaska into Puerto Rico was a constitutional as well as a geographical impossibility. Nevertheless, nothing would deter WPA and others from imagining a commonwealth paradise of tax-free windfalls beyond the grasp of the Internal Revenue Service.

Commonwealth was an intentionally vague and pleasant-sounding word resonating back to seventeenth-century England and colonial America. The principle behind the Puerto Rican–style "commonwealth" of the twentieth century—which bears no resemblance whatsoever to the Commonwealths of Massachusetts, Pennsylvania, Virginia, or Kentucky, where the term was synonymous with *state*—required a tortured constitutional reading as logically and ethically dubious as the "three-fifths compromise" or the Dred Scott decision. Following the Spanish-American War Washington needed to justify why America's newly acquired colonial islands—the Philippines, Puerto Rico, and Guam—were intrinsically different from older territories such as Oklahoma, Arizona, or New Mexico—and could never become candidates for statehood.

America had been founded on the creed that colonies were intrinsically evil, and since 1787 all U.S. territories had simply been states waiting to be born, but fear and uncertainty about what these new "insular possessions" might portend for the future demanded a new interpretation of the Constitution. In a series of landmark legal decisions in the early 1900s known as the "Insular Cases," the Supreme Court ruled there were two fundamentally different Americas after 1898 that were separate and unequal: "incorporated" and "unincorporated" territories. These "incorporated" or traditional territories were a permanent part of the United States slated for eventual statehood, subject to all the rights, privileges, and protections of the U.S. Constitution, while the new islands taken from Spain were "unincorporated territories" or "insular areas" that were not a *part* of the United States but merely temporary *possessions* belonging to the United States and not automatically granted citizenship or full constitutional rights. In essence these decisions enabled the U.S. government to acquire colonial possessions without breaking the fundamental law of the land, because the justices had ruled that the Constitution did not "follow the flag," except when it flew over an incorporated part of the country.

According to the court Congress had already incorporated both Hawaii and Alaska, and that step could never be undone. Alaska's incorporation dated back to the 1867 purchase from Russia, as the Treaty of Cession approved by the Senate and signed by the president had promised: "The inhabitants of the ceded territory . . . shall be admitted to all the rights, advantages, and immunities of the United States." Therefore, while the U.S. could grant independence or otherwise treat the Philippines or Puerto Rico without regards to constitutional safeguards, or grant them preferential tax treatment for example, as a result of the 1867 treaty it could no more give away Alaska than it could give away Montana.[68]

In the 1930s, as a first step on the road to Filipino independence, Congress had created a special new legal status for the Philippines called a commonwealth. Not until 1952 did Puerto Rico receive that designation, though calling it a commonwealth did not "change Puerto Rico's fundamental political, social and economic relationship to the United States," as it had already acquired a local legislature, an elective governor, and one nonvoting "resident commissioner" in the U.S. House of

Representatives.[69] Puerto Ricans—like Filipinos before them—had never paid federal income taxes, but the exemption had nothing to do with its recent designation as a self-governing commonwealth. The tax exemption was due to its status since 1898 as an unincorporated possession of the United States.

As the debate heated up about Alaska and Hawaii statehood in the 1950s, the path of Puerto Rico seemed to offer an easy alternative to hardcore Southern Democrats and conservative Republicans opposed to admitting either territory. Four senators joined to take the lead in championing the commonwealth cause for Alaska and Hawaii: A. S. "Mike" Monroney of Oklahoma, J. William Fulbright of Arkansas, George Smathers of Florida, and Price Daniel of Texas. Arguing that forty-nine states would be one too many, Monroney wrote an article in *Collier's* magazine entitled "Let's Keep It 48." Granting statehood to Alaska and Hawaii, he said, would radically alter "the shape and the very nature of the United States," and he recalled the ominous warning of Nicholas Murray Butler, the noted American educator, presidential advisor, and 1931 Nobel Peace Prize winner: "Under no circumstances should Alaska, Hawaii or Puerto Rico, or any other outlying island or territory be admitted as a state in our federal union. To do so, in my judgment, would mark the beginning of the end of the United States as we have known it." According to Senator Monroney, opening the statehood door to Hawaii or Alaska would be a ready invitation to not only Puerto Rico but also the other insular possessions, including the Virgin Islands, the Marshalls, the Carolines, and the Marianas. And with the specter of World War III more places would demand to get in. "Anything might happen in an atomic-hydrogen-bomb war," Monroney wrote. "Already Australia and New Zealand ... have looked to us for security, and we have treaties of mutual defense with them. Will they someday wish to enter our Union as states? How many states would Australia be made into? In the Caribbean are many British, French, Dutch and independent islands, ranging in size up to Cuba. ... [T]hey, too, might want statehood." A proliferation of new states would shift the balance of power in the U.S. Senate to "foreigners" far from America's traditional shores.

Though some politicians proposed other constitutional roadblocks to dissuade new statehood applicants, such as denying full representation in the Senate, or only admitting new states by a vote of three-fourths of the existing states, commonwealth status seemed to be the only probable option. Unlike new states, commonwealths without congressional representation would not threaten the national balance of power, and in exchange for no representation, Monroney believed there should be no federal taxation. It sounded fair to the man from Oklahoma. "Aside from the lack of full representation in the national Congress, it would be almost impossible to find material differences between commonwealth and state status."[70]

Senator Monroney may not have been able to tell the difference between a commonwealth and a state, but most Americans knew otherwise. The Scripps-Howard newspaper chain called the "no representation—no taxation" deal a bribe that was constitutionally "dubious" and morally "indefensible."[71] Most authorities seemed to believe that the "uniformity clause" of the constitution would prohibit giving Alaska any tax breaks, because as an incorporated territory "all federal tax laws apply uniformly to Alaska, just as to any other part of the United States." Furthermore even if it were constitutional, Monroney's proposed tax exemption, the bait on the commonwealth hook, was a political leap of faith; what would it profit a senator or congressman to raise taxes on his own constituents in order to give tax exemptions to others? As then–Interior Secretary Douglas McKay said, passing legislation to abolish federal taxes in Alaska was about as likely as passing a bill to "replace the stars and stripes on the American flag with the hammer and sickle."[72]

The senators desperate to keep Alaska out preferred to ignore the legal distinction between incorporated and unincorporated territories, even though it was as fundamental as that between citizenship and slavery. An Alaska Commonwealth would have been a breach of the Constitution and the bond of the perpetual Union, because no legal means existed to force a part of the United States to remain forever voiceless and voteless. Whatever label it might be given, a commonwealth denied congressional representation was nothing but a colony, and permanent colonial status with second-class citizenship was impossible under the American system. The editor of the *Alaska Weekly* thought trying to steal the rights and responsibilities of U.S. citizenship out from under the people of Alaska in this cowardly fashion verged on senatorial treason:

> There is nothing better than to be an American.
> There could be nothing worse than to be an ex-
> American, paying no taxes to America, sending no
> representative to the Congress, denied any voice

in the affairs of America. We say to those who dream—fantastic as the dream may be—of taking Alaska out of America ... Your nightmare is not for us. Go, go to Russia, go to the land where a constitution is nothing but a scrap of paper....

... Alaskans are Americans and Alaska is America. They are one and the same, now and forever, and the only good thing that can be said of the ridiculous Commonwealth suggestion is that its very utterance proves that freedom of speech is still one of the rights of any American, no matter how lacking in common sense.[73]

Try as he might Bob Bartlett said that he never fully understood the half-baked proposal that Monroney and others meant by commonwealth; but the delegate was certain that to commonwealth advocates in Alaska it meant one thing and one thing only: "the possibility of being able to become exempt from the payment of Federal taxes."[74] The prospect of finding a legal way to never file a 1040 form again kept the tax-free commonwealth dream alive among those in Alaska opposed to statehood, and WPA was its most passionate champion.

Allen not only refused to believe that exempting the territory from federal taxation was impossible, he also became convinced that anyone who doubted this approach was a dupe or a criminal. In his mind high taxes and corruption were two sides of the same coin, and he charged that statehood supporters who dismissed the tax moratorium or commonwealth were no better than the crooked officials he was battling in the Lone Star State. About one month after WPA had gone to jail in Texas in 1956 for the second time, he was the featured speaker at the annual meeting of the Alaska Press Club in Anchorage. Despite his scant Alaska résumé—this was his first visit to any part of the territory outside the Panhandle—and never having lived in Alaska himself, the Texas publisher scolded pro-statehood editors in Alaska such as Snedden and Atwood for conniving with "crooked and corrupt politicians who rob the treasury and merely reside in Alaska so they can selfishly eat out of the public trough." He claimed that the *News-Miner* and the *Anchorage Times* had to be honest and accept the necessity for a ten or twenty-year tax moratorium before even considering statehood. "When all the press of Alaska begins to tell the public the truth about this subject," he said, "and the milking of the taxpayers is stopped, this dream for Statehood will come true."[75]

Nationally, the tax-free Alaska commonwealth option withered after Congress rejected the Monroney bill in 1955, but on the last day of O'Brien's subcommittee hearings in March 1957, Seattle Congressman Thomas Pelly revived it once again, claiming the tax advantages of the Puerto Rico–type arrangement would allow Alaska to develop far more rapidly than would be possible under the fiscal burden of immediate statehood. When pushed on the constitutionality of an incorporated territory becoming a commonwealth, Pelly said he was not qualified to render an opinion as "the only law I know came from a correspondence school course." But he said that was a question only nine justices could answer since "like man, the Congress of the United States proposes; and, like woman, the Supreme Court of the United States, disposes."[76]

Despite the caveat that abolishing federal taxes in Alaska was no more likely than doing away with death, Pelly's argument that the Supreme Court might ultimately find commonwealth for Alaska acceptable after all, combined with the confusion caused by the Alice Stuart–Doc Miller referendum fiasco, gave fuel to WPA's tax revolt fire. No matter how long the odds or remote the possibility, rational arguments could not dampen the fervor of true believers intent on living in a tax-free paradise. One of the other anti-statehood editors in southeast Alaska pointed out that "none of the present states paid income taxes while Territories." The *News-Miner* had to add the necessary footnote: "Of course they did not. The last state was admitted in 1912. The income tax amendment was not added to the Constitution until 1913."[77]

Thanks to such selective, circular thinking, the commonwealth talk continued to bubble. Bartlett thought that every editorial from Allen, "no matter what the real theme of the editorial was supposed to have been," eventually "wound up on the subject of tax moratoriums."[78] By early April 1957 *News-Miner* editor Jack Ryan warned that commonwealth was "rapidly becoming a 'trump card' of the Statehood opposition in Alaska. It is winning adherents, and I fear that this movement is going to outrun Statehood supporters if we don't watch it." No matter how many times the *News-Miner* explained that commonwealth was a legal and political impossibility, the enticing prospect of escaping from federal taxation had an irresistible appeal that made it next to impossible to counteract. Ryan recommended that Bartlett and the Tennessee Planners tackle the issue head-on.

> I suggest that if the Statehood bill appears abso-
> lutely doomed in this session of Congress our Ten-
> nessee plan delegation write up a Commonwealth
> bill and drop it in the hands of Congress. Make
> this bill good—put into it all the provisions for
> the 10-year federal income tax moratorium that
> supporters of this measure are wildly promising.
> Of course such a bill won't pass, but by doing this,
> the fraud of the Commonwealth movement can
> be unmasked.[79]

Neither Snedden nor Bartlett agreed with that approach, though
Bartlett shared Ryan's view that commonwealth was still a threat. "I
thought we had laid the ghost of commonwealth forever," Bartlett said.
"But here we go again." He thought introducing a commonwealth bill
destined to fail would only give even more ammunition to the hopelessly
unrealistic commonwealth crowd. "I should be willing to take an oath
signed in my own blood that attainment of commonwealth with tax exemption . . . and all the rest of it would be infinitely more difficult than
statehood. Statehood has been on a long and perilous road. We know all
about that. But the statehood road would be a veritable boulevard as compared with that for commonwealth."[80]

To combat what Snedden called the "Commonwealth Fraud" the
News-Miner started running a series of editorials laying out the facts
of the case with lessons in constitutional history, describing the Insular
Cases, the differences between incorporated and unincorporated territories, the fact that *commonwealth* and *tax exempt* were not synonymous,
and the unique tax status of Puerto Rico that could not be applicable
to Alaska. "We people in Alaska have no more chance of getting such
freedom from taxation than have the people of New York, Oregon or
California. The supreme court has ruled that Alaska is part of the United
States, and hence it is unconstitutional to give Alaskans any tax freedom
that is not given to ALL THE CITIZENS OF THE UNION."[81]

Snedden said only someone with a "feeble grasp" of political reality,
like W. P. Allen, believed that Congress would waive income taxes for the
territory, even if it were constitutionally possible, and he never ceased to
be astounded at the Juneau publisher's "mis-statements, misinterpreta-
tions and manipulations of his versions of 'the facts.'"[82]

"In my opinion it is a darned shame," Snedden wrote Bartlett on
April 18, 1957, "that when Mr. Allen moved to Alaska from Texas he

forgot to bring all his possessions with him . . . particularly his brain."[83] That same day Snedden ran a front-page editorial headlined "Lunatic Fringe" blasting the man he started to refer to as "Alamo Allen" for his "dim Texas view of Alaska's Statehood aspirations." Snedden wrote that Alamo "has been referring, darkly, to a 'minority lunatic fringe' in Alaska" opposing his war on taxes. "We agree with him that there may be a 'lunatic fringe' in Alaska, but we think it is rather cruel of him to refer to his admirers in that manner." The editorial included a lengthy letter from the three Tennessee Planners that debunked WPA's commonwealth and taxation arguments one by one. Snedden told Bartlett his goal was to tie a "knot in Mr. William Prescott Allen's tail. As you can see from the enclosed front page editorial, the result is about as subtle as a sledge hammer."[84]

Snedden's "Lunatic Fringe" editorial spurred an immediate response from WPA. Even by the standards of Alamo Allen it was bizarre: a rambling telegram two legal-sized pages long targeting Ernest Gruening and the other Tennessee Planners as the prime examples of thieving politicians. To prove his sincerity and to demonstrate the waste of tax dollars spent on the Tennessee Plan, WPA offered to put his money where his front page was with an outrageous sporting proposition.

"I wager the assets of the *Daily Alaska Empire*," he cabled Snedden, "against the assets of the *Fairbanks News-Miner* that there will be no law granting statehood to Alaska during this session of congress. . . . Let me suggest that if you have any doubt you may lose your wager you have those favoring the Tennessee Plan underwrite your loss."

According to Allen the purpose of the bet was to help force the media in Alaska to be honest about the true costs of the statehood campaign and the Alaska-Tennessee delegation, which WPA charged had already bilked Alaskans out of approximately $600,000. WPA claimed professional office seekers such as Gruening had helped make Alaskans the most overtaxed people under the American flag. "None of this robbery of the taxpayer could go on if the newspapers, the radio stations, and television stations of Alaska were honest enough to stand up and tell the people the real truth. The real truth is that the enemies of statehood are the politicians who keep piling heavy taxes on the great and fine Alaska people."[85] Despite what he wrote in the *Empire*, WPA professed to have the highest respect for Snedden. "Personally I think a great deal of you Mr. Snedden and think you are an asset to Alaska. Therefore any of your published statements concerning me or my publication are considered as friendly and constructive, and for the eventual benefit of Alaska. In no way am I taking offense or will I take offense to any statement made in the *News-Miner*."[86]

In addition to wagering his newspaper against Snedden's, WPA also offered to debate Gruening, "the most able politician ever to come to this great territory," within the next two weeks in Fairbanks—under the stipulation that "this debate shall be properly advertised on the front page of your newspaper each day for at least a week prior to the debate, and a nominal charge shall be made, the proceeds to go to the Alaska Press Association."[87]

Snedden was delighted with WPA's long telegram, pleased that the "Lunatic Fringe" editorial and the letter from the ATP delegation "got under his skin a little." Convinced that the more Allen opened his mouth the more people would see what a fool he was, and consequently be able to see through the commonwealth "smokescreen," Snedden was anxious to make the debate a reality, offering to pay Gruening's round-trip air fare from Washington to Fairbanks out of his own pocket. "It is of course absolutely certain," he wrote Gruening, "that you would murder Allen in any debate."[88]

The following day Snedden ran the telegram from the "Alaska-Texas Publisher" in full, starting on page one. He also responded to the "Texas-Size Bet Against Statehood" with a counterproposal, an Alaskan-sized wager against commonwealth: "Perhaps we Alaskans—or at least this Alaskan—find the Texas way of doing things a little difficult to grasp. Perhaps I think too much of my Alaskan newspaper (particularly since I have no other newspapers in Texas or elsewhere) to consider its worth as lightly as you evidently evaluate the *Juneau Empire*."

Snedden figured his investment in the *News-Miner* was worth about twenty times what Allen had in the *Juneau Empire*, and that "anyone foolish enough to wager $20.00 against $1.00 would be just as foolish as, for instance, saying that Alaska can ever be relieved of Federal taxes." But he had a counterproposal for his Juneau rival. The *News-Miner* would wager $100,000 that "Commonwealth status, with an accompanying 20-year moratorium on Federal taxes" would not be granted to Alaska anytime in the next ten years. "If such a moratorium becomes effective you win the bet," Snedden promised, with the money to come from the savings on federal taxes the *News-Miner* would no longer have to pay to Uncle Sam over the next ten years! "If it is not granted by May 1, 1967, you lose and you owe the *News-Miner* $100,000."

Snedden also upped the ante on statehood. "Since it is apparent you feel that granting statehood will be equivalent to sounding the economic death knell for all business in Alaska, including newspapers," Snedden promised to purchase the *Juneau Empire* upon the granting of statehood, with the price to be determined by impartial appraisal. "This will 'get you off the hook' you seem to feel is inherent in Statehood economic conditions, and will enable you to make a move to that great Utopia of Puerto Rico."[89]

In the end WPA refused any wager or debate at all, claiming that when Gruening could not make it within the deadline that Allen had imposed, Gruening had backed out. To try to set the record straight and set up an another time for a possible debate Snedden called Allen long distance on the morning of Friday, April 26. In a transcription of the forty-minute conversation—Snedden would tape and transcribe important phone calls on his Dictaphone in order to keep a record—Allen announced he had written his debate speech and had "mailed it to the *Washington Daily News* as a paid advertisement." As Allen told Snedden on the phone, "Well, I don't see any point in talking about something that I have already printed and is being run as an ad in Washington."[90]

After Snedden got off the phone with Allen, he immediately wired Bartlett with the latest of WPA's antics, explaining that Allen might take part in a debate in Washington after all: "I urge you wire him immediately offering either Ernest or Bartlett or both take him on. Perhaps I am sadistic but that's something I want to see. With Texas size best wishes, Bill Snedden."[91]

Bartlett was stunned by Allen's "debate speech." It was so wrong about everything it might have made more sense if it were read upside down and backwards. "It is a lulu," Bartlett wrote Snedden. "It is fantastic. It bewilders one. It leaves one dizzy."[92]

Gruening meanwhile told Snedden on the phone that "he saw absolutely no sense in debating 'that lunatic' in Washington," but Snedden warned they could not afford to ignore Alamo. Not only did WPA claim to be friends with the two most important Texans in Washington, D.C., Senate Majority Leader Lyndon Johnson and Speaker of the House Sam Rayburn, but no matter how unbelievable Allen's tax-free fantasies in the *Empire* might be, the daily repetition of such nonsense was having an effect.

"I emphasized to Ernest," Snedden wrote,

> and I wish to reiterate ... to you Bob, that we should not sell Allen short. While I consider him an eccentric screwball, to overlook the obvious fact that he [is] creating quite an impact in the Territory which is adverse to statehood is the height

of foolishness. . . . Someone should definitely show
Allen up for the oddball that he is, in my opinion.
Whether this can be done, and just how it can be
done, is beyond me at the moment.[93]

Bartlett agreed that WPA's misstatements needed to be addressed.
"Certainly I cannot dispute your contention that we must pay heed to
WPA. It is true that his assertions are so wild as to be almost fantastic;
nonetheless, repeated almost daily in the EMPIRE they are bound to
make an impression on part of his reading public."[94]

As Snedden had feared, the impact of Alamo Allen would be long-
lasting; the radioactive half-truths he spread would prove impossible to
eradicate. More than any other single person, it was Allen who sowed the
seeds and propagated the greatest myth of the Alaska statehood struggle,
a big lie still repeated today, that a tax-free commonwealth had been a
viable option for the territory, the road not taken that statehood proponents had deliberately ignored and hidden from the people of Alaska.
Even Jay Hammond, the fourth man to become governor after statehood,
who had opposed statehood in the 1950s claiming Alaskans had been
"statehoodwinked," believed decades later that commonwealth had been
a genuine alternative. As Hammond wrote in his 1994 autobiography,
"Some of us believed commonwealth status, such as Puerto Rico's, might
avoid imposition of federal income taxes and yet achieve a greater degree
of self-government. But little reasoned debate was allowed. Anyone daring even to question statehood was branded either a 'pinko,' a paranoid."[95]
In fact, as Bartlett told WPA in many different ways, a commonwealth
with no federal taxes really was nothing but a figment of the imagination,
"divorced from reality, a fantasy . . . a dream which cannot in a practical
world be expected to come true."[96] "In claiming that Alaskans could ever
achieve complete freedom from income taxes for any number of years," as
Snedden repeatedly said, "statehood foes were perpetuating a fraud as big
as Texas."[97]

Ironically, Alamo Allen would have the final say when it came to
public testimony about statehood for Alaska. Out of the millions of
words from countless witnesses who appeared before Congress in the
previous half century urging more self-government for the territory, the
last words on the last page of the last Senate report in the 1957 hearings
came from a lengthy telegram Allen sent to the U.S. Senate about his
commonwealth crusade and blasting Snedden once again for the second-
class citizen remark.

THE CRY OF SECOND-CLASS CITIZENSHIP AN UN-
TRUTH. NOBODY IN ALASKA EVER BEEN SECOND-
CLASS CITIZENS. THIS MERELY POLITICAL
PROPAGANDA OF BAD POLITICIANS.[98]

While the myth of the lost commonwealth may have been a WPA legacy, Alice Stuart also left her mark on the historical record. In response to her referendum obsession and Doc Miller's "straw poll," Ted Stevens and Snedden came up with a plan they hoped would neutralize the referendum red herring forever, by including a requirement for a referendum in the statehood bill itself. Legally there was no need whatsoever for a statehood bill to be put to a vote of the people; states were admitted by Congress, not by popular vote. However, Stevens explained to Bartlett that building a referendum into the bill as a prerequisite for statehood "would be a good way to pull the rug out from under [opponents] such as Alice Stuart."[99] Bartlett was inclined to agree. At the very worst it could do no harm because once the bill was finally passed by Congress "all will be over except the rejoicing." After meeting with Stevens, Bartlett explained the strategy to Bob Atwood:

> Ted Stevens, legislative officer for the Interior De-
> partment, came up the other day with a proposal
> that we take the steam out of people like Alice
> Stuart by inserting a provision in the bill for a
> referendum vote on the proposition of immediate
> statehood. It seemed sensible enough to me then
> because (1) it would not require a special election,
> (2) it would be ratified by an overwhelming vote
> and (3) ought to swing even the diehards.[100]

As finally drafted, the statehood bill did require the referendum that Stuart had wanted, and the results of the election, held in August 1958, answered the question definitively: by a 5–1 margin they wanted statehood, immediately.

Paradoxically, the same faction in Congress that professed, like Alice Stuart, to believe so strongly in the virtue of popular sovereignty and the will of the people, that claimed Alaskans had to prove they were ready for statehood by yet another vote, would do everything in its power in 1957–1958 to thwart the vote on Capitol Hill from ever taking place at all. As the final phase of the struggle to force Congress to vote began in the summer of 1957, Snedden would be reminded more than ever that some of the most powerful men in the United States were no more rational when it came to the topic of Alaska statehood than Alice Stuart or Alamo Allen.

13

Mixing Oil and Politics

As the last statehood hearings ground to a close in Washington, D.C., in 1957, and the opponents of admission were preparing new roadblocks, the political economy of the territory was already in the midst of a fundamental transformation, thanks to the rise of the Republican Party and the discovery of oil. The emergence of the Alaska GOP as a voice for statehood and the 1957 oil strike on the Kenai Peninsula portended things to come, depicted symbolically on the June 9, 1958, cover of *Time*. The issue featured a large portrait of a smiling young man named Mike Stepovich, whom Seaton had appointed Governor of Alaska the previous year. (Ever after the inside family joke was that this was the only time that Mike Stepovich was ever on *Time*.) In the background was a rendering of a rocket-like Alaska totem pole/oil derrick numbered "49" adorned with a figure of a blue GOP elephant at the base. At the top the oil platform was equipped with a set of wings and four jet engines, about to blast off into space.[1]

The man behind the *Time* cover story was Snedden. Not only had he engineered this journalistic coup, but he was also responsible for helping make Mike Stepovich the new face of the Alaska GOP, and the preeminent spokesman in the party for statehood, though not without controversy.

Alaska's new governor, installed in the summer of 1957, was a hometown boy. At thirty-eight, Mike Stepovich of Fairbanks was the youngest territorial governor in the history of Alaska and the first and only one to be born in Alaska. Fred Seaton had settled on Stepovich in early May after a long and embarrassing hunt to find a replacement to B. Frank Heintzleman, who had retired in January 1957 shortly after his sixty-eighth birthday. The failure to fill the post for the next four months left Alaska's territorial government in the hands of Secretary of Alaska Waino E. Hendrickson throughout the entire 1957 legislative session. To Snedden, the difficulty in finding a replacement for Heintzleman was further evidence of the disarray of the Alaska Republican Party and its "juvenile" tendencies. Faced with twenty or thirty potential candidates passionately backed by one faction or another, the selection process bogged down in a nasty feud. However, Snedden thought the resolution of the governor issue and Seaton's influence would encourage the local GOP boys to "put on their long pants and start to grow up, and get down to business." He made only one promise to Seaton: "the *News-Miner* is going to do the best job it can in building regard for the Republican party and the Administration."[2]

Snedden said that early in the process he was offered the governor's post by Seaton but turned it down, feeling he had neither the qualifications nor the temperament for the job.[3] Thereafter four leading candidates emerged, Wally Hickel of Anchorage and three men from Fairbanks: Territorial Senator John Butrovich, University of Alaska President Ernest Patty, and businessman Les Nerland. Snedden's favorite was Nerland, followed by President Patty. When none of these could either be persuaded or cleared for the job, Butrovich suggested the name of his legislative protégé in the Territorial Senate, Mike Stepovich.

Initially Snedden tried to have Seaton reconsider, hoping he could find someone with a better track record on statehood. "To the best of my knowledge," Snedden wrote Seaton, "Mike has never taken a positive stand on the merits of Alaska statehood, and naturally I would prefer to see the Governor's chair occupied by a person ... wholeheartedly advocating statehood."[4] Though he liked Stepovich personally, he believed the young and easy-going Fairbanks attorney lacked the gravitas for the job. A reluctant lawyer, who famously lost his papers on the way to try his first case, Stepovich was more comfortable on the golf course or the baseball field than in the courtroom. As a star first baseman in college who had hoped to turn pro, he had gone to law school only after his mother insisted he needed a "real job." He also had a full family life. Stepovich would gladly explain to anyone that he and his wife, Matilda, had a "Step by Step" plan to have an even dozen little Stepoviches—a goal they actually surpassed, not stopping until the arrival of number thirteen.

Despite Snedden's reservations, as soon as Seaton gave Stepovich the nod in May 1957, the publisher promised to provide all the support he would need as the party's and Seaton's nominee. Behind the scenes Snedden was the young governor's principal advisor, speechwriter, and mentor over the course of the following year, tutoring and promoting Stepovich each step of the way. With the assistance of Snedden and the *News-Miner* Stepovich quickly became Alaska's most visible and popular Republican in the statehood cause, and the only GOP official in the territory who could be a potential rival to Delegate Bartlett or the Alaska-Tennessee delegation. In fact, Snedden would become such an obvious pillar of strength for Stepovich and work so closely with his administration—the *News-Miner* always had a friendly word for Governor Mike—that the Democrats would assume erroneously that he had been the publisher's first choice for the governor's mansion all along.

Stepovich plainly had to grow into the role for which he was being groomed, and at first others had been as skeptical about Stepovich's political acumen as Snedden, considering him little more than a "featherweight." First impressions aside, however, Stepovich's importance to the GOP and the statehood cause as a youthful and vibrant model of Alaska's future was evident immediately. When Ted Stevens learned that Seaton planned to send his right-hand man, Elmer Bennett, to Stepovich's inauguration, the message was clear: the secretary was signaling that he "intends to give Mike's administration broader responsibilities in the government of Alaska than ever before.... In Washington no one represents Seaton more effectively than does Bennett."[5]

It was not long until Snedden came to believe that Seaton's selection of Stepovich was a stroke of genius; the charming, charismatic, athletic young governor with the irrepressible smile and the ever-growing Kennedy-like brood of children—the "seven little iches" soon to be joined by the eighth "ich" in Juneau—was the fresh new face of the Last Frontier. "We Like Mike," the Alaska version of the Eisenhower campaign slogan of 1952, was a slogan on many lips and inspired a "lady poet" in Anchorage to put Mike and Ike together:

> Now Ike and Mike live much alike
> In houses palace-like they say.
> There's Ike in Washington, D.C.
> And Mike in Juneau, still T.A. [Territory of Alaska]

"Please, Ike," says Mike, "look northward now
The whole of Alaska asks of you.
She's been a territory long enough;
She wants to be a big state too."

And Ike to Mike has said like this:
"She'll make a state both rich and fine."
So she is hoping striving still,
To hear them say, "You're forty-nine."[6]

Snedden did all he could to keep Stepovich in the news and stress his statehood fervor. For instance, one "special" news item from Washington, an unsigned item probably written by either Snedden or Stevens, described how Secretary Seaton and his staff also liked Mike. The article, headlined "Mike Makes Favorable Impression," said the "vigor of the youthful 38-year-old governor has drawn quite a contrast in the minds of Washington officials" with his senior citizen predecessor.

> Stepovich has also got off to a good start with his boss in Washington by the good press he has received in his first seven weeks in office. From all appearances, the new governor is well liked wherever he goes. More important in political considerations is the observation by Seaton and his associates that Stepovich has not emerged as a controversial figure. He and his outspoken statements in behalf of statehood have evoked praise from men of both parties.[7]

Boosting Stepovich in the *News-Miner* was a simple proposition, but drumming up press attention outside Alaska required far more lobbying and legwork. Thanks to Snedden's indefatigable campaign, Stepovich garnered all the national publicity that the publisher had once thought the Alaska-Tennessee delegation would deserve. A few weeks after Stepovich's inauguration Snedden wired Ted Stevens for help in setting up a color photo session for the new governor and Secretary Seaton: "Please advise soonest whether . . . you can obtain services top notch photographer who understands color. Considering full page color photo Seaton [and] Stepovich . . . with 49 star flag in background for possible use when . . . statehood bill passes. Possibility *Life* using same shots."[8]

As the *Wall Street Journal* commented on the Alaska political scene in April 1958, beside backing statehood "the most popular move the G.O.P. has made here was the President's appointment last May of Mike Stepovich," and even if he wasn't a "great orator nor a particularly original political thinker," he had a common touch that many found endearing. "It's a foregone conclusion here," the *Journal* explained, that in the event of statehood "Mike is too popular not to run for something," perhaps governor or senator.[9]

A political reporter for the *Washington Post* thought Stepovich an essential political counterweight to Alaska's four Democrats in Washington—Bartlett and the three Tennessee Planners—and was therefore of incalculable benefit on the GOP side of Congress. Republicans, who had previously pushed so hard for Hawaii ahead of Alaska, seemed to be softening their stand, he wrote, and were willing to adopt the "Alaska First" strategy of the Democrats. "One reason for the improved GOP interest in Alaska is said to be Mike Stepovich.... In Stepovich, Republicans think they see GOP gold in those cold Democratic hills."[10] To assure fearful Republicans that Alaska as a state would not be an automatic win for Democrats every two or four years, on Snedden's suggestion Stepovich came out with a prediction meriting a front-page *News-Miner* headline: "Stepovich Predicts GOP Seat." The governor announced that in spite of the past strength of the Democratic Party, the rejuvenated Alaska GOP, of which Stepovich was the symbol, had a chance with statehood to possibly capture two of the three seats in the congressional delegation, while "at least one Republican senator is a sure thing."[11]

Though time would prove him to be a terrible prognosticator—Stepovich also predicted that Alaska as a state would have at least two million residents within ten years—out on the stump for statehood, the self-effacing, mild-mannered Stepovich, provided with speeches usually written by Snedden, radiated an unpretentious warmth, humor, and charm that enabled him to connect with total strangers.[12] He appeared on Edward R. Murrow's influential news program *See It Now* and also did a lighthearted stint on the game show *What's My Line?* But the greatest journalistic coup of all was when Snedden convinced editors in New York to make Stepovich only the second Alaskan ever to grace the cover of *Time*—Ernest Gruening had been the first in 1947—and profiled his accomplishments in a glowing tribute.*

---

* The third Alaskan to make the cover of *Time* was Governor Sarah Palin, in 2009.

The lyrical portrait of Stepovich in *Time*, based largely on information supplied by Snedden, was the single most widely read story on the statehood quest ever published. "For more than anything else," *Time* explained, "statehood is a matter of heart, a spirit singing," and in this version Stepovich was the headliner of the chorus and the lead soloist. "Time Magazine Tells Nation About Stepovich and Alaska" reported the *News-Miner*. The weekly news magazine depicted the challenges facing "Stepovich's Alaska" and how he handled himself like a latter-day Lincoln.

> Mike Stepovich typifies the pioneer's sense of destiny better than any Alaskan governor before him. A Republican appointed by a Republican administration, Stepovich handles himself like a man of the people, and the people—65 percent Democrats, 35 percent Republicans—like him that way. What they like best is his open-faced friendliness, his native talent for conveying to doubters "outside" what Alaska is about. . . . Unschooled in the well-oiled sophistication expected of governors, he is content to make his points with an earnest warmth that radiates when he waits his turn in a bowling alley or a barbershop—or a territorial committee meeting. And beneath all of this is the tough mettle that was born in him and strengthened on the cold, hard anvil of Alaskan living.[13]

Democrats were less than pleased at the attention that Snedden generated for Stepovich, but Bartlett tried to take it philosophically, seeing that the Stepovich stories were "very obviously . . . directed toward the political campaign which will follow in the event of statehood. . . . I am tickled right down my funny bone all through the rest of my skeletal structure at the terrific credit which is being heaped on Mike Stepovich. The national publicity which he is receiving as the chief proponent of statehood is as amusing as it is startling. For my part, I think some of it is justified." He said while certain Democrats were opposed to giving Stepovich any credit for his support for statehood since it was so "contrary to his previous feeling on this subject and the change came about so recently that one is entitled to laugh a bit if not audibly," the delegate believed the important thing is that he is now on "our side" and much good could come from having a visible Republican advocate who "is working hard and has quite obviously a sincere devotion to statehood."[14]

———

The same month that Seaton hired Alaska's new governor, Snedden found a new editor for the *News-Miner*, former constitutional delegate George Sundborg, one of whose first tasks would be to help Snedden draft Stepovich's inaugural address.[15] Oddly enough, Snedden's new editor came to Fairbanks, indirectly at least, thanks to his Juneau nemesis William Prescott Allen. At the end of April 1957 Sundborg's weekly *Juneau Independent* was about to go bankrupt. The liberal, pro-statehood paper had a sizable circulation, but due to a lack of advertising revenue it had never been financially stable since its founding five years earlier. When Bartlett—who two years previously loaned Sundborg $6,000 to keep the paper afloat—learned of the newspaper's imminent demise, he was more concerned about Sundborg's future than the outstanding debt. He said he and other friends "devotedly wish that in . . . your hour of need we could offer you something tangible rather than the only thing we can give, our sincerest sympathy." He tried to give Sundborg a pep talk, but a realistic one. "Things are grim," Bartlett wrote Sundborg on May 1.

> They will be grim for a long while. I know that as well as you do. You will have to wind things up. You will have to try to sell out. You will have to seek a job and the horror of it is where shall you seek and what. That won't be easy. It will be extremely difficult. But you can and will surmount everything so long as you do not lose faith in yourself. This you must not do. The George Sundborg of May 1, 1957, is even a better man than the George Sundborg who went into the *Independent*.[16]

Bartlett hoped that Sundborg's savior might be Bill Snedden. Perhaps the Fairbanks publisher could be convinced to take an interest in the *Independent*, if nothing else as a counterweight to Alamo Allen's daily anti-statehood propaganda. Snedden agreed enthusiastically. "I have a transaction in progress to purchase the weekly newspaper in Juneau," Snedden wrote privately eight days later, "with the principal objective to acquire the circulation list (which is about the same size as the *Daily*

Alaska Empire). I will suspend the weekly if the transaction works out, and honor the unexpired prepaid subscriptions with the *News-Miner*— which should perhaps change the thinking of a few individuals in southeast Alaska."[17] However, before the deal could be consummated, Snedden said a better solution surfaced when other parties "appeared on the scene who were interested in purchasing the operation and keeping the paper going," while Snedden hired Sundborg to succeed Jack Ryan as editor of the *News-Miner*, only the second change of editors in the seven years he had owned the paper.

George Sundborg was an odd choice for at least two reasons: not only was he a liberal New Deal Democrat, but he was also an intimate protégé and longtime associate of Ernest Gruening. Though Snedden would eventually come to regret hiring Sundborg and conclude it had been the biggest mistake of his professional life—just as Sundborg would later regret taking the post at the *News-Miner*—initially the common ground they found in fighting for statehood would make their political and personal differences less pronounced.

As it was Snedden already had his own difficulties with the Alaska Republican Party. Local GOP leaders were still angry that the *News-Miner* had called for a unity ticket in the Tennessee Plan campaign, and had endorsed Bartlett outright for reelection since 1954. John Butrovich told Sundborg, who in turn told Bartlett, "the Republicans here will never forgive Snedden for coming out for you for Delegate." While Snedden had loyally backed the GOP national ticket with financial support in 1956, and had given money to both John Butrovich and Bob Atwood in their failed campaigns for the Tennessee Plan Senate seats against Gruening and Egan, he had pointedly refused to support the GOP's "territorial or divisional fund campaigns."[18]

Hiring a Democrat to be his editor made Fairbanks Republicans even more suspicious, a situation from which Snedden took some wry satisfaction, since he had such a low opinion of the local party hierarchy. Not long after Sundborg had arrived in Fairbanks, but before Stepovich departed for Juneau, Fairbanks Republicans got together to confer with the new governor, and it turned into a gripe session about the *News-Miner*. "Well, the Republicans had a meeting last week," Sundborg told Bartlett, "and really raked Snedden and me over the coals, I was told by Snedden, who got it from John Butrovich, who was present. Snedden seems to be amused about this. The meeting was held to get in the last licks with Mike. Butrovich said the GOPs who are narrowest between the horns were holding forth about my being made editor and they were muttering imprecations, when Mike took the floor and really 'flang' his arms around"—Stepovich had a tendency to whirl like a windmill while speaking—"and told them off."[19]

Bartlett repeatedly warned Sundborg always to remember that even if Snedden sometimes thought the local GOP was nothing more than a mutual admiration society of incompetents and complainers, the *News-Miner* was still a GOP newspaper owned by a till-death-do-us-part Republican publisher, and as editor he owed his loyalty first of all to Snedden, though that would hardly stop Bartlett from occasionally wishing it were otherwise. In August 1957 Bartlett was particularly incensed by a front-page *News-Miner* editorial that gave sole credit to Eisenhower, Seaton, and Stepovich for a Democratic piece of legislation that granted three air carriers certificates to fly to Alaska; he wrote an angry and "highly confidential" letter to Sundborg spelling out the truth as he saw it. "This letter is written to register a complaint; goodness knows I realize that the *News-Miner* has a right to be a Republican newspaper. Nevertheless, I cannot refrain from writing you on a personal basis to report that it was a darned good thing the bathroom was close at hand when I read the front page editorial in the *News-Miner* for August 26." While he thought Seaton's influence at the White House might have been important in avoiding a presidential veto, the delegate claimed Stepovich had done almost nothing to promote the legislation. "There are some of us here who worked on that bill for, at a guess, 40 or 50 or 60 or more hours in the aggregate.... And it was a Democratic Congress which passed the bill. And it was a Republican President who scared the boys almost to death because they feared he would veto it."

He was not writing with any purpose except to vent his anger and make himself feel a bit better. "All of this is from one Democrat to another," he closed. "It is not from a Democrat to the Democratic editor of a Republican paper who does and always should (or at least I so believe) faithfully carry the paper's policies."[20]

When Sundborg received Bartlett's letter he tried to explain what had happened. "I can understand your reaction to our editorial," Sundborg wrote at four o'clock in the morning after an all-nighter at the office. "The facts are that Bill Snedden sent me a telegram from Juneau saying, as I recall, run an editorial on the front page commending Seaton, Stepovich and Eisenhower.... Believe me, I had the thoughts you had. I think you can appreciate that with the boss not here I could do nothing but what he specifically directed." Sundborg said he had tried to "give Bartlett credit a few times (where richly due)" but he could not overreach because as a

Democrat and an outsider he felt he was "still suspect around here and I do not want to destroy what effectiveness I may have when and where it really counts." He signed off his letter, "With regards from one Democrat to another."[21]

Bartlett was frantic that Sundborg had misunderstood him and followed with another confidential note to citizen Sundborg, not editor Sundborg. "My goodness, man, I hope I made it plenty clear in venting my spleen in writing you ... that there was no intention of implying that George Sundborg in his individual capacity was giving Ike and Fred and Mike exclusive credit.... The letter to you was partly in frustration, partly in admiration at a cleverness in Republican operations heretofore lacking. They ain't pitching liken they were. Unfortunately."

Fearing that Sundborg might put his *News-Miner* job in jeopardy by displays of Democratic partisanship, the delegate said he always appreciated "your crediting me with this and that. Happy as I am to see my name in print for whatever reason (almost) ... this has worried me a bit. You must not stick your neck out. I am *completely* understanding of your position, which assuredly must not be imperiled for political reasons." [22] Because of Sundborg's long affiliation with the Democratic Party, he was a natural conduit for relaying gossip and inside information to Bartlett and Gruening. For instance, Sundborg relayed to Bartlett Snedden's plan for a color photo of Stepovich and the forty-nine-star flag and explained how Delegate Bartlett had been deleted from the picture. "I don't remember whether I wrote to you about the flag," Sundborg wrote on July 11, 1957:

> Bill Snedden got the idea one day that while Mike Stepovich was in Washington it would be a good idea to get a color picture of him with Seaton and a 49-star flag, all of which would be used when we get statehood.... I told him you ought to be in the picture. He communicated this to Washington, I know, because yesterday I saw an answer from Bill Strand. It said Seaton had decided yes, that Bartlett should be in the picture, but Strand explained that it took so long to buck this question up to the Secretary and get an answer that the photographer arrived on the scene and there wasn't time to summon Bartlett. It seems, however, that the picture which was shot was unsatisfactory, being only a 35 mm. slide, which won't do for our

engraver, so all is to be done over some time when
again Mike is in Washington. Bill Snedden says all
is clear now to have you in the picture next time.
We will see.[23]

Sundborg might have concealed his low opinion of Stepovich to
Snedden, but he made no effort to hide it in his correspondence with
Bartlett. For example, Sundborg described the process of drafting
Stepovich's inaugural address.

About Mike's speech, he worked it over again or
had someone do it before he went down to Juneau.
Came back to show us. What he had done was
keep practically everything I had written and then
put back in practically everything I had thrown
away from his earlier draft. Result was curious,
but widely acclaimed. I was amused tonight when
Alex [Miller, Alaska Democratic Committeeman]
said to me he didn't think Mike was smart enough
to say some of the things he did, especially patting
you and the TP boys on the back. As this was a
pure invention by G. Sundborg, I was amused. I
was interested too to note that everything that Bill
Tobin picked out of the talk to quote in his AP
story was my language.[24]

Later in the summer Sundborg described the speech Stepovich gave
at the dedication of a memorial to pioneer bush pilot Carl Ben Eielson at
Eielson Air Force Base. He was less than charitable.

Mike needs somebody to write his speeches. He
gave one at the Ben Eielson monument thing last
Saturday which was absolutely the worst thing I
ever heard, and I have heard a few.... Mike appeared about 15th on a program of 16 speakers,
and he dwelt not only on good ol Carl Ben at
some length, but he went into the total subject of
Alaska, its resources, problems, production, people,
climate, history, etc., until I was afraid we would all
faint there in the warm sunshine.

According to Sundborg both Snedden and John Butrovich were up-set with the speech. "For God's sake, Mike," he claimed Butrovich said, "next time make it a sprint, not a marathon."[25]

By September 1957 the rumor mill around the *News-Miner* was that Governor Mike Stepovich, because of his youth and charisma, would make a formidable candidate against any Democrat. Sundborg wrote Bartlett:

> Lately I have heard a lot of talk about who might come out on top if Stepovich and Bartlett should run for the same office and, surprisingly, all who have speculated to me have concluded that Mike would triumph. I think that is complete fantasy, but it goes to show you that the boy is indeed pop-ular for the nonce.... My guess—you would lick the pants off him. Mike is riding high. Because he hasn't done anything. That can't go on forever, as we know. All of his mistakes are ahead of him, while you have been around for a long, long time doing superlatively well, and everyone knows it.

He also told Bartlett about a conversation Snedden had with Seaton. "I should tell you that [Snedden] had a telephone call not long since from Seaton offering him the job now held by Hatfield Chilson [assistant sec-retary of the interior]."[26]

"You amaze me in relating Seaton's offer to Bill," Bartlett replied. "I felt they were close, but had no idea it was on this basis. What I can't figure out, among other things, is how and when and where this closeness developed."[27]

Bartlett's surprise at Snedden's backdoor channel to Seaton revealed an elemental truth about the information gap and lack of trust between the two parties: even though Democrats and Republicans were both fighting for statehood, as a result of the partisan divide behind the scenes maneuvers were routinely hidden from the other party. While Snedden did not know about Sundborg's secret correspondence with Bartlett, for example, Bartlett did not know that Snedden had recommended—to no avail—that Seaton offer Bartlett a high position in the administration so he could be "'kicked upstairs' to remove him from the Alaska po-litical picture in the event we achieve statehood." As Snedden explained to Seaton:

Bartlett is not particularly interested in running for Governor, and would rather remain in Washington as a U.S. Senator. However, I am reasonably certain that Bartlett would not file against either of the two Tennessee Plan Senators in another election. This may be a "far-fetched" possibility, but if he could be given some type of appointment which would satisfy him sufficiently to leave Alaska politics for at least one election, I believe it would be a wonderful thing for the Republicans, and would give us a good chance at another key post.[28]

Controlling the executive branch equipped Seaton and the GOP with avenues of power invisible to the Democrats. Since the Interior Department had such multifarious duties and responsibilities, every state and every congressional district in every state could benefit from the favors that could be bestowed by the secretary of the interior, giving Seaton a powerful lever to move reluctant legislators off the fence. According to Snedden, Seaton "used every resource he had at hand in his position as a cabinet officer and a member of the Administration in power—and those resources were very substantial. Through him we had trading stock ranging all the way from federal judgeships to new facilities in parks and national monuments to an additional star route on some rural post office—encompassing many, many things in between."[29] Reminiscing years later, Snedden reminded Stevens that so much of what they had been able to do under the guidance of Seaton had never become public knowledge. Even a fellow Republican such as *Anchorage Times* publisher Bob Atwood, who lacked the personal rapport with Seaton that Snedden enjoyed, was usually as much in the dark as any of the Democrats. "Uncle Fred, yourself and I got a lot done," Snedden said, "and watched the Alaska-Tennessee planners and old friend Bob Atwood scramble to take the credit. At times fairly often—they did not know what or how something had happened. But that didn't slow down their modest efforts to be on hand to take a bow when the bouquets were handed out."[30]

Perhaps the most sensitive Seaton-Snedden-Stevens strategy about which outsiders never knew was the campaign to revoke or modify Public Land

Order 82 in order to proceed with the development of the Gubik gas field. If ever there were a political minefield on the Alaska tundra, it was how and when to remove PLO 82. Revoking this public land order demanded extreme caution in order to prevent a reoccurrence of the $50 million "Giveaway McKay" scandal that Drew Pearson had blown up in the face of Secretary McKay three years earlier and eventually helped to drive him from office. McKay had left the GOP particularly vulnerable to charges of handing out the nation's natural resources to contractor cronies for next to nothing, and Seaton's Interior Department had to be particularly vigilant in the manner in which it opened the public domain to private development. If the lifting of PLO 82 were handled incorrectly, it would not only derail the effort to develop the arctic reserves of oil and gas but it would most assuredly put the entire statehood campaign at risk.

Conservationist groups in 1957 had only a fraction of the clout on Capitol Hill that the environmentalists would garner in the 1960s and 1970s; however, as the charges against "Giveaway McKay" had proved, the protection of America's natural resources was a potent campaign issue and an ever-increasing concern to the American public. As one columnist claimed on the eve of the 1960 presidential election, both Republicans and Democrats had been hoping to find a "giveaway" charge to use against the other ever since McKay had been sent back to Oregon.[31]

The danger was that Alaska statehood might come to be seen as the greatest "giveaway" of the decade. Since about 1953 the general consensus had been that in order to support itself financially the state of Alaska would need a vastly larger federal land grant than any previous new state in American history, in the neighborhood of about a hundred million acres of choice land, an area larger than the entire state of California. All previous Western land grant states had received designated one-square-mile sections of land in a checkerboard pattern, but to ensure Alaska did not end up owning thousands of square miles on random glaciers and mountaintops, it would be permitted to select the lands it wanted in larger parcels as necessary. In 1957 Doc Miller—who had long championed making the land grant as large as possible—temporarily succeeded in raising Alaska's proposed share of the public domain to 182 million acres, thereby adding an area almost the size of Montana on top of the California-sized grant. The wary Alaska delegation unanimously opposed Miller's largesse and were fine when it was dropped back down, believing 103 million acres was more than enough. There was a lingering suspicion that perhaps Doc was simply trying to insert a "poison pill" in the bill, or as Ted Stevens put it, "to love us to death." Leo O'Brien told Miller that too much land for the new state would be too much of a good thing. "I know that milk is very good for kittens," O'Brien said. "I also know that you can drown a kitten in milk." Most certainly the fear was that too large a land grant would bring the wrath of conservationists and prompt the cry of "giveaway." "There are a great many people, especially in the East," Gruening warned, "who would oppose the Federal Government getting rid of a much larger portion of the public domain in Alaska. I think that [182 million acre] provision, which I doubt whether Alaskans would want, might jeopardize the bill."[32]

The possibility that Alaska statehood might be seen as a "giveaway" edged one step closer to reality when a nightmare scenario emerged in the 1957 congressional hearings. Bob Bartlett called it the "unholy alliance . . . completely beyond my comprehension" of salmon canners and conservationists, both of whom argued—though for diametrically opposite reasons—that Alaska was too "politically immature and irresponsible" to manage its own wildlife resources. Essentially the salmon industry feared the State of Alaska would be too restrictive on commercial fishing, while conservationists feared the state would be too lenient. Two of the most influential conservation groups in the country, the Wildlife Management Institute and the National Wildlife Federation, claimed that a future State of Alaska would let commercial fishing interests destroy the great salmon resources of the North Pacific. A third organization, the Izaak Walton League, was all set to join in the opposition to statehood, except that Executive Secretary Burton Atwood was the brother of Bob Atwood, and he helped to block any action on an anti-statehood resolution. Bartlett could not smile at the irony of seeing that "conservation groups made common company with the canned salmon industry."[33]

"Now we have the salmon industry," Bartlett warned, "which has openly fought statehood for years having unexpected allies in the conservationists who not only defend but insist on continuing federal control of the salmon fishery despite the shockingly bad record of the federal government in its failure to conserve that resource."[34] The delegate had fought for years to transfer control of the fisheries of Alaska to the territorial government, and so he was particularly distressed when the House Interior Committee amended the bill—at the behest of the salmon canning industry—so that federal control of fisheries could continue for up to five years or more after statehood. Bartlett said he "almost collapsed" at the news.[35]

Outside a union of the KKK and the ACLU, an odder political alliance could hardly be envisioned, but as different as the constituencies and reasoning of the canners and conservationists may have been, the fact that these rivals had come together to reach the same conclusion—stop statehood—was ominous. While the salmon lobbyists were a known and expected quantity, businessmen and corporations naturally protecting their profits and self-interest, the conservationist community was of an entirely different type and character, posing a potential threat the statehood movement had never encountered before. As Snedden believed statehood had three unimpeachable allies: motherhood, freedom, and apple pie. At the conclusion of every debate, the moral issue of the right of self-government was statehood's trump card. But equally sacred as a noble ideal was the conservation of natural resources, and under the right circumstances this might have evolved into the one political issue that could have neutralized statehood's motherhood edge on the national scene.

In the closing weeks of the statehood fight, "giveaway" would be the epithet of choice for those Southerners desperate to stop the admission of Alaska, decrying statehood as a vast land grab from the public domain. The chairman of the all-powerful House Rules Committee, Virginia Democrat "Judge" Howard W. Smith, the "unlegislator" known more for his ability to block legislation instead of passing it, who would keep Alaska statehood bottled up in his committee for almost an entire year, hit on the conservation theme as his last gambit. Though his genuine concern was obviously to block civil rights legislation and to stop the erosion of Southern power that would come from the admission of Alaska, Judge Smith belatedly realized that the easiest route to the moral high ground was conservation, blasting the statehood bill as "the greatest giveaway of potential natural resources in the history of our country" and probably the "greatest giveaway in the history of the world." Though normally a hard-line defender of states' rights, he was willing in this case to argue that federal control of Alaska's land was a sacred duty, and he decried the statehood bill for its wholesale theft of natural resources that "belong to all of the people of the United States."[36] Picking up the same theme Missouri Democratic Rep. Clarence Cannon, chairman of the House Appropriations Committee, labeled the Alaska statehood measure "an iniquitous bill which would give away more resources than have ever been given away in our history."[37]

Pennsylvania Congressman John P. Saylor, a statehood supporter and one of the most dedicated conservationists in Congress—he would be the driving force behind the passage of the 1968 Wild and Scenic Rivers

Act—responded that Judge Smith's attempt to "smear the cause of state-hood with a giveaway label" was nothing "but a red herring out of the creel of an avowed opponent of statehood." Smith refused to back down. "There are so many compelling reasons why statehood should not be granted to the frozen areas of Alaska that it is difficult for me to know where to start," he claimed. "I have said that this was the greatest giveaway of natural resources in the history of this country—and it is."[38] When Doc Miller asked Judge Smith exactly how small the land grant should be so as not to constitute a "giveaway"—one hundred million acres? fifty million acres?—the judge inadvertently confessed that the extent of the acreage didn't really matter to him at all. "I am opposed to statehood for Alaska, whether it involves giving them one acre or one million acres or two million acres." Nothing in the entire bill "from the enacting clause to the concluding paragraph ... would be acceptable to me."[39]

Bartlett took umbrage at the "giveaway" charge. "In the earlier days of the statehood movement," he explained to one suspicious congressman, "we were licked more than once because it was contended that the bill before the Congress offered Alaska so little by way of its own resources that the state would not be financially solvent." It was in response to this criticism that the generous land and mineral provisions of the statehood bill had evolved, and while Judge Smith now claimed it would be uncon-scionable for the new state to receive mineral rights, Bartlett said that Alaska was bound to be a better steward of its own resources than absen-tee owners or distant federal bureaucrats. Claim owners on federal lands could acquire fee simple title, enabling private citizens and corporations to "come into possession of all the minerals to be theirs forever and a day. But a very careful safeguard has been written into the statehood bill. The state will never be able to dispose of the minerals outright. It must lease them. And the people of Alaska are alert to the need for careful survey and scrutiny." On top of these legal protections, the federal government was keeping more than its fair share, with about one hundred million acres "in reservation for one department or other of the federal govern-ment. Much of this, as you can well imagine, is the best land available."[40]

The black humor of the "giveaway" charge was not lost on Snedden, since this was the exact opposite of what the traditional anti-statehood claim had always been, that Alaska wasn't worth giving away even if some-one could have been forced to take it. For example, New York Republican Rep. John Pillion reduced it to numbers. He claimed "approximately" 90 percent of Alaska was "wholly worthless and wastelands that have no immediate prospect for development or improvement or exploitation."

Pillion did not explain how he arrived at this sad figure, but even for a man from Buffalo it was hard to imagine a more hopeless-sounding piece of property on earth. California Republican Craig Hosmer claimed Alaska was so poor it might have to emulate Nevada and "resort to gambling and easy divorce laws to support statehood," and he warned that world conditions prove that areas in chronic economic distress "are breeding grounds for trouble."[41] In the face of such claims Snedden enjoyed Atwood's summary of the way statehood opponents seemed to have both sides of the debate covered. Statehood would either be the "giveaway" of a treasure chest of riches or the curse of a "bleak, desolate, uninhabitable and worthless place that never could support statehood, anyway."[42]

Snedden's rejoinder was that statehood would not be a "giveaway" but a "give-back," returning resources to the care of the local people who admittedly had the most to lose as well as to gain. If true conservation was a "never-ceasing struggle against waste and spoil and neglect," as Seaton said, for ninety-one years the "federal deepfreeze" may have been preserving Alaska, but only at the waste of its human potential. "The land which Uncle Sam will turn over to the state will not be wasted by a bunch of robber barons," the *News-Miner* promised, but put to work by people who know that the "best conservation is not that which locks resources away but which results in wise use."[43]

A combination of factors helped prevent the cause of conservation from sounding the death knell for Alaska statehood. One was timing. Within the following decade environmentalism became a political movement with formidable clout, and Howard Smith's arguments about giving resources to the state of Alaska that rightfully "belonged to the American people"—in spite of the transparency of his pro-segregation motives— would have resonated loudly across the Capitol. But in 1958 the notion of a wilderness ethic had not yet breached the mainstream, and *Silent Spring*, the Wilderness Act, the Santa Barbara oil spill, Earth Day, and Greenpeace were all still in the future. Wildlife advocates, hunting and fishing organizations, and conservation groups in the 1950s had influence, but nothing like the power that environmentalists would wield in years to come. Still, timing and the political tide were not all. The immediate reason why conservation was the dog that didn't bark in the Alaska statehood fight in 1957–1958 was the political skill of Fred Seaton with canny advice and assistance from C. W. Snedden.

Seeing the threat of a conservationist backlash against statehood on the horizon, in early 1957 Seaton thought the repeal of PLO 82 was probably too dangerous to contemplate. On a visit to Seaton's hospital room in the spring of 1957, Snedden said the grim news he heard from the secretary was to "forget any ideas I may have about getting all of PLO 82 released."[44] By mid-June, however, Snedden had further thoughts as he hinted in a letter to Ted Stevens. "Ted, I told Seaton I was afraid to take any chances on adversely affecting our statehood bills with possible repercussions on announcing release of PLO 82. Wish I hadn't said so now, as am becoming convinced it can be handled so it won't hurt."[45]

The opportunity Snedden saw was the possibility of making a trade-off that would mollify the conservationist community enough so that Seaton could go ahead and lift PLO 82 without causing the predictable uproar. For several years the cherished dream of the Wilderness Society and other conservation organizations had been the establishment of an arctic wilderness area in the extreme northeast corner of Alaska, seeing it as "an ideal chance to preserve an undisturbed natural area large enough to be biologically self-sufficient."[46] Snedden's idea was that if the conservationists could get their reserve dedicated, it would take the heat off simultaneously abolishing PLO 82. In a confidential letter to Seaton dated July 9, 1957, Snedden explained his proposal would enable the Gubik gas fields to be released from PLO 82 without any "repercussions" that would have an adverse effect on statehood, and "of course want to see the administration and Governor Stepovich get the maximum 'political mileage' out of the publicity on the announcement." As Snedden wrote Seaton:

> Have been doing some discreet checking with Wild Life and Conservation groups, both in Alaska and on the west coast. Appears at present that if you can see the way clear to release all of PLO 82, rather than only the area adjacent to the Gubik structure, and shortly thereafter give your official stamp of approval to the permanent refuge presently being sought by the Wilderness Society group (in the northeast corner of Alaska), we may very well have a vociferous and important group offering strong rebuttals to any possible criticism arising over the revoking of the PLO 82 withdrawal.[47]

Seaton's scribbled note on the margin next to Snedden's suggestion was "check into this." Meanwhile Ross Leffler, Seaton's assistant secretary of the interior for fish and wildlife, was on a fact-finding tour of Alaska. The day after Seaton received Snedden's letter, Leffler officially announced in Fairbanks that the Interior Department was going to sponsor creation of an "Arctic wildlife area" in northeastern Alaska. Pointedly, this giant conservation unit would not be a "wilderness" but a "wildlife area," where fishing and hunting, in addition to mining and mineral leasing, would still be permitted. "This proposal would be a substitute for a wilderness area which has previously been suggested for the same region," Seaton explained four weeks later to Snedden. "I understand the general proposal is strongly supported by the organizations interested in the matter."[48]

With continued prodding from Snedden, by the fall of 1957 Seaton had determined to go ahead along the lines that Snedden had suggested; he would announce that he would be modifying PLO 82 in conjunction with a request that Congress establish an arctic wildlife sanctuary encompassing millions of acres. As a personal favor, Snedden asked Seaton to wait to make the official announcement until Wednesday, November 20, in order to coincide with the publication of the 1957 Progress Edition of the *News-Miner*. "From our standpoint I can't think of a better day for a banner story and front page picture on Public Land Order 82. Circulation will be in excess of 50,000, with about 30,000 being distributed to strategic points throughout the states." He hoped the secretary's staff might be able to arrange a photo shoot featuring Stepovich looking on while Seaton was signing the order, while another section of the special edition would lead off with a color photo six columns wide of Governor Mike, Matilda, and the seven Stepovich children.[49]

Seaton agreed to do everything he could to comply with Snedden's request, timing the announcement for a November 20 press conference in Washington so the *News-Miner* could break the story in the Progress Edition released later that day in Fairbanks, and even providing the photo, shot in advance, of Stepovich looking over Seaton's shoulder to run on the front page. While conservationists were most enthused by the subhead on the lead story, "Part of PLO 82 Area Set Aside for Wildlife Refuge," the bold headline across the top of the page, which Snedden called "the best banner this sheet has ever carried," capsulated the true significance of the historic occasion as far as he was concerned: "SEATON OPENS ARCTIC GAS, OIL." The story behind the banner headline, as Stevens later explained to Snedden, was the quid pro quo for the wildlife reserve. "Bill—we can thank the people who wanted the wildlife range for the

PLO 82 action. Once [Seaton was] convinced . . . that the two should and could go together and that the wildlife range was close to the conservationists heart, everything went better."[50]

At the time Snedden was certain about the historic significance of the PLO 82 announcement he had broken in the *News-Miner* that afternoon. "We have a feeling that this day, November 20, 1957, will long be remembered in the annals of Alaska development. Today's action by Secretary of the Interior Fred A. Seaton opening up the untold natural riches lying to the north of us should launch a new era of progress for the territory."[51]

The role of the *News-Miner* in battling for the creation of the Arctic Wildlife Range as a means of promoting the development of arctic oil has been little understood or appreciated. In retrospect the November 20 headlines marked only the first step toward the lifting of PLO 82 and the beginning of Seaton's fierce three-year struggle to create the Arctic Wildlife Range. What was truly remarkable, however, was that the joining of these initiatives on November 20 had exactly the effect that Snedden had hoped. In the midst of the furor that raged from November 1957 to December 1960 over establishment of the wildlife range, the lifting of PLO 82 evaporated as a political issue, ignored by the press and the public, and forgotten by those who had been so irate at Douglas McKay for proposing a similar move three years before.

Many Alaskans, particularly Democrats, were incensed at the arctic wildlife proposal. Residents who could not understand why the normally pro-development *News-Miner* had endorsed the creation of the arctic reserve beat up the newspaper on almost a daily basis. A typical protest came from Fabian Carey of Fairbanks: "After watching the bureaucrats grab off all the choice slices of Alaska for the past lo so many years, I fail to see how you can condone this phony land grab on ANY basis." Another biting letter, which the *News-Miner* refused to run only because it was unsigned, "called the editor a 'liar' and 'silly.' It labeled as 'childish thinking' our reference to Alaska as a place 'which is still in its youth and where human beings are going to be trying to live in harmony with their environment many centuries into the future.'"

The *News-Miner* campaigned tirelessly for the nine-million-acre reserve, as Snedden believed it was a small price to pay for opening an area to oil and gas development more than twice its size. "It is certain," he wrote in one editorial, "if Alaskans will stop rocking the boat, that the 20,000,000 acres adjoining [the proposed reserve] . . . will be opened to development. Raising a furor at this time can result only in holding up

final release of this valuable PLO 82 area which contains so much promise." Furthermore, protestors risked the danger "that Alaska might again
incur the powerful opposition of conservation organizations in the States
who maintain that Alaskans have no stability when confronted by small
pressure groups. This opposition could defeat not only the release of PLO
82 but also larger goals like statehood."[52]

While Bartlett said accepting the wildlife range in exchange for lifting PLO 82 was giving in to political "blackmail," Snedden wrote that
opponents reminded him of a greedy little boy "who has just been given
a pie much larger than he can eat but who cries anyway when someone
tries to cut a small sliver out of it." Besides, Seaton's crafty compromise
seemed a perfect solution that would let the chubby boy not have to surrender a single bite of pie anyway. While the range would be a wildlife
sanctuary, it was by no means to be classified as a wilderness. Most experts
thought the region had few prospects for either mineral or oil and gas
development, but in the unlikely event such resources were discovered, the
proposal specifically allowed subsurface development "in accordance with
regulations which will protect and preserve the wildlife and the primitive
character of the land."[53]

Ironically, by the closing days of the Eisenhower administration, when
Alaska had finally achieved statehood, the Arctic Wildlife Range was still
being stymied in Congress, now blocked by the power of Alaska Senator
Bob Bartlett. As a result, on December 6, 1960, Seaton was forced to
create the Arctic Wildlife Range by executive order, issuing PLO 2214
establishing the 8.9-million-acre Arctic Wildlife Range, which was immediately followed by PLO 2215 revoking PLO 82. In thanking Seaton
for the "priceless gift" of the Arctic Wildlife Range executive order,
Wilderness Society director Olaus Murie said he could hardly find the
words to express his joy: "In establishing this area . . . you have truly done
a great good for untold generations to come."[54] Swept up in the emotion
of the creation of the wildlife range, Murie overlooked the simultaneous
lifting of PLO 82 that would open the Arctic to oil and gas development.

Snedden's November 1957 forecast of the future was both naively
optimistic and shrewdly prophetic. While Gubik gas never panned out as
the resource bonanza that Snedden and others had predicted, the creation
of the Arctic Wildlife Range had permitted the opening of twenty million acres immediately to the west, where more than twenty billion barrels
of oil under Prudhoe Bay lay waiting to be discovered.

While in the long run the most important headline in 1957 may have been the opening of northern Alaska to oil and gas development, at the time the biggest petroleum news in the territory was from the Kenai Peninsula, where Richfield announced on July 23 that it had hit oil in a wildcat well two miles deep on the Swanson River, the first commercially viable discovery in the territory. According to an Interior Department official, the Swanson River discovery sparked "a tremendous amount of enthusiasm bordering on mass hysteria" in Anchorage. Initial reports of nine hundred barrels a days were on the high end—the actual production turned out to be more like five hundred a day—but considering that the previous 165 wells sunk in the territory had all been dry holes, "the mere fact that this well has been found has been the biggest thing that has ... happened to Alaska since the 'Gold Rush' days." A Colorado editor said the "Kenai oil fever" was going to make the territory rich indeed. "If the Kenai Peninsula is as wet with oil as it appears, Alaska has it made like Texas."[55]

The possible ramifications of adding oil to the statehood equation could be enormous. Scripps-Howard staff writer Albert Colegrove, who visited Alaska in 1958, said wherever he went in the territory that spring the "A-B-Cs" of conversation were statehood, oil, and aviation. Since the lack of economic development was the standard rationalization against granting statehood—one congressman complained that Alaska's basic problem was that it was "long on politics and short on economics"— Swanson River could negate that argument, and some observers speculated it might also help with "some members of Congress from the oil producing states, especially Texas and Oklahoma, who have a great respect for the economic value of oil." According to *News-Miner* Washington correspondent A. Robert Smith, "Oil companies traditionally have preferred to do business with states rather than the federal government," though one oil man he talked to believed "the oil industry would probably not get involved in the statehood fight, one way or the other."[56] In the spring of 1958, with information supplied by Snedden, the *Denver Post* summarized the potential impact of the Gubik gas fields and the Kenai oil fields, and predicted "this vast oil and gas potential with its wide economic side effects might prove the deciding factor ... at long last" in the statehood battle. "The Alaskan oil gamble could well pay off in the biggest prize of all—statehood."[57]

In the final hours of the Senate statehood debate on June 30, 1958, one senator thought the Kenai oil discovery was an ace in a hole in the ground, the trump card that would finally put to rest the notion that Alaska could not afford to run its own affairs. "Now, happily, with the discovery of oil in Alaska," said Clinton P. Anderson of New Mexico, "it is quite probable that the new State will receive substantial revenues from its oil lands. Therefore, we can expect that Alaska will be a worthy State, adequately financed, and will take her place in our great Union of States on a basis of full equality in every respect." This estimate proved to be right on the mark. As Bill Egan, the state's first governor, admitted to Bartlett in 1961, "If oil had not been struck on the Kenai in 1957, our financial outlook would simply be impossible."[58]

But just as with the Arctic Wildlife Range, the Kenai oil strike presented some serious political complications, largely because the discovery well was inside the Kenai National Moose Range, once again alarming national conservationist organizations, which believed the federal leases should have never been sold in the first place.

"The oil rush stirred up powerful conservationist lobbies in far-off Washington," a *Time* correspondent noted. "To stop the drilling they lined up for battle against the oilmen."[59] Traditionally, government policy was to stimulate development by making oil and gas leases readily available to anyone with a pencil, a map, and twenty-five cents; in unproven geological formations noncompetitive leases could be had for an annual fee as low as a quarter an acre.[60] As one expert on the history of oil and gas leasing wrote in 1963, "statutory authority makes virtually all lands of the United States available for oil and gas development."[61] On public lands the secretary of the interior had great latitude in setting regulations, and during the McKay regime conservationists were in an uproar, as his policies greatly accelerated the granting of oil leases in national wildlife refuges, which had previously been largely off-limits. McKay's administration had approved almost two-thirds of all the oil and gas leases granted on refuge land since 1920, including the leases filed in 1954–1955 in the Kenai National Moose Range upon which Richfield would strike oil. A writer in 1956 said the granting of the oil leases in the Kenai Moose Range was a "flagrant" example of a "giveaway" of "publicly owned natural resources for the benefit of private interests." This was part of the "invasion of national wildlife refuges" by oilmen, the *New York Times* lamented, that would have "disastrous results for wildlife conservation."[62]

Following the oil srike on the Kenai, the nascent Alaska oil industry ground to an almost immediate halt. Richfield needed additional acreage on the moose sanctuary in order to develop the oil field, but due to an existing Interior Department freeze on approving new leases in all wildlife refuges until Seaton could finalize new leasing guidelines, the company capped the well and waited. Meanwhile, the backlog at the land office swelled to unmanageable proportions, as speculators in Anchorage flooded the Kenai and southcentral Alaska with almost five thousand new lease applications, covering about twelve million acres.[63] In the fall of 1957 an "informed official" in the Interior Department said conservationists were "practically ecstatic" when Seaton announced he was going to "restrict further oil and gas development on wildlife refuges" throughout the Lower 48. The big exception was Alaska, where under certain restrictions the secretary planned to continue to "allow oil companies, such as Richfield, to sink more wells to tap Alaska's underground wealth."[64]

Snedden was relieved that once again his friend Fred Seaton had come through with a sound policy proposal. Even the oilmen generally believed "that they got a good deal in Alaska," and thus it was all the more troubling to both Snedden and Bartlett that Tennessee Plan Senator Ernest Gruening took the lead in blasting the Interior Department for not throwing the entire Kenai National Moose Range wide open to oil development. According to Gruening, the proposed Interior regulations were "too restrictive" and bureaucratic, and as a longtime civil servant he said he knew the color of red tape. In his mind Interior's proposal "reads like a prospectus for an obstacle race." "Having served for 18 years in the federal government I can recognize in the language the plasm of protracted procrastination." Gruening suggested that the two-million-acre moose range could easily be cut in half, if not eliminated entirely, to accommodate the growing population in the Anchorage area. And while on the subject he suggested the government should also abolish the Chugach National Forest.[65]

Gruening contended that the real purpose of the moose range was not for the moose anyway, but for people. "I don't believe we should conserve moose for the sake of future moose," Gruening was fond of saying. "We preserve them so that future generations of human beings can see moose, and photograph moose, and hunt moose." Gruening called it inherently unfair for the government to allow a homesteader only 160 acres, while every single moose on the range had on average about five hundred acres on which to roam.[66] The former governor told a Kenai man that he could not

> imagine a greater bonanza for Alaska ... than the discovery of oil. It will mean the wildest kind of development—roads, housing, employment and a

chance to get our fuel cheaply. We should all get
vigorously behind it. The idea that it will damage
any existing values is nonsense. Modern oil exploration and drilling is performed on an entirely different basis than it was in the early days, when you
saw oil rigs next to each other almost like sardines
in a box, and oil seepage on the ground, etc. Those
conditions do not exist anymore.[67]

In his enthusiasm over the Kenai strike Gruening was oblivious to
the impact the oil discovery might have on conservationists; they would
hardly welcome the "wildest kind of development" even if it had not been
on a federal wildlife reserve. Furthermore, the outlandish suggestion to
reduce or completely eliminate the Kenai National Moose Range—by one
of Alaska's three elected statehood lobbyists—was hardly reassuring to
wildlife groups already inclined to believe that Alaskans were too careless
and irresponsible to be trusted with resources from the public domain. Any
effort to scale back the moose range, Bob Smith wrote in a dispatch from
Washington, "would likely set off a howl of protest from organized conservation groups.... Some of these groups are critical of any regulations
which would even allow oil development on the moose range." One such
organization was the National Wildlife Institute, already on record opposing statehood. Vice President C. R. Gutermuth claimed the "frenzied"
elected officials in Alaska bent on destroying the moose range provided
additional proof that the territory was not ready for self-government.[68]

According to "Judge" Winton Arnold, the leading lobbyist for the
salmon packers, Gruening's oil lobbying was inspired primarily by his
search for campaign contributions. Bartlett learned from Arnold—who
wanted "the oil industry to be created in Alaska in a hurry to take the
tax heat from the salmon industry"—that Gruening's oil lobbying was
inspired primarily by his search for campaign contributions. Arnold informed Bartlett that Gruening was trying to secure funding from the oil
industry to finance his anticipated campaign for the U.S. Senate once
statehood was achieved, and had seen top officials at both Richfield and
Shell before his public testimony on leasing regulations.

Another political complication was a simmering controversy about the
legality of the oil leases. A bitter rivalry in the Anchorage community

between locals who had been clever enough to grab noncompetitive leases on the Kenai and those who hadn't led to a nasty fight among the most powerful men in Alaska that threatened to burst into the open and cause irreparable harm to statehood. In one corner stood two of the staunchest supporters of statehood: Elmer Rasmuson, president of the National Bank of Alaska, and his brother-in-law Bob Atwood, publisher of the *Anchorage Times*. In the other corner was Rasmuson's biggest competitor, Dan Cuddy, president of the First National Bank of Anchorage, as well as developer and Republican committeeman Wally Hickel, and Norman Brown, publisher of the anti-statehood *Anchorage News*. While Rasmuson and Atwood had participated in a leasing pool that owned a share of the Richfield strike, the Cuddy-Hickel faction had thought the oil leasing speculation had been a fool's game and had not joined in. According to Bartlett's inside source, Wilbur Wester, an associate of Rasmuson and Atwood, the "ire" of the First National Bank crowd had "reached the explosive stage when Standard Oil of California, after entering into a partnership agreement with Richfield, et al, made a very sizeable deposit in the National Bank of Alaska."

Bartlett wrote a lengthy confidential memo to himself summarizing what Wester told him. Apparently Wally Hickel was furious with Seaton because he had been "passed over for the Governorship," and as a result, according to Wester, Hickel was complaining bitterly about the noncompetitive leases and Seaton's hand in their approval, claiming the ground should be reopened on a competitive basis. As part of the campaign to invalidate the leases, the *Anchorage News*, financed in part by the Cuddy family, had prepared a "purported news article" that would be a bombshell aimed at Seaton. "The headlines for it even had been prepared," Bartlett wrote. "Those headlines and the body of the story were to accuse Atwood and Seaton by name of perpetrating another Tea Pot Dome scandal" in the Kenai Moose Range where the Richfield leases had been improperly authorized by the Interior Department. "At any rate," Bartlett wrote in his memo, for some reason "it was decided not to print this article."[69]

One of the more trivial complications that arose from Gruening's attack on Seaton's Kenai policies was the impact on what Snedden called "Operation Cake." This was Snedden's plan—assisted by the Fairbanks Chamber of Commerce—to airmail Seaton a cake from Fairbanks to Washington, D.C., in the cargo hold of a Boeing 377 Stratocruiser for the secretary's forty-eighth birthday on December 11, 1957. But this was no ordinary cake: the size of a dining room table, about five feet long and three and a half feet wide, weighing 165 pounds, and covered with fifty-five pounds of icing, it was thought to be the largest cake "ever flown on an airplane." Baked by Fairbanks chef Peggy Goldizen with fifty-five pounds of flour, eighteen pounds of shortening, twelve dozen eggs, twelve quarts of milk, and one pound of salt, the cake was decorated with icing portraying a map of Alaska and the inscription "As Secretary of the Interior You Take the Cake . . . Happy Birthday Fred Seaton from your friends in Fairbanks and all Alaska. We hope we're '49' NEXT Year Ourselves."[70]

Originally, as Bartlett noted, Snedden wanted him to present it to Seaton on December 11 "in company with the Planners." However, on December 9, the day before Gruening would be publicly testifying against Seaton, Bartlett went down to the Department of the Interior where Seaton's assistants "George Abbott and Ted Stevens suggested to me it would be preferable if I made [the] presentation without being accompanied by Ralph and Bill and Ernest. I wormed out of them what it was all about, or at least part of a story." Abbott and Stevens "said they thought it might be misconstrued if Ernest were to be received by Seaton" in light of Gruening's intemperate remarks about the moose range and they feared "conservationists would regard this as a pat on the back for E.G. and the position he was assuming. Actually, I thought I detected that this was only part of the story and that deeper and more important reasons underlay their request. . . . Anyway, I went alone to present the cake."[71]

Unlike Bob Atwood, Snedden had refused to take part in any oil or gas leasing, fearing the appearance of a conflict of interest would compromise his independence as a publisher. When Snedden got wind of serious allegations against Seaton and Atwood regarding the Kenai oil leases in late December, he immediately relayed the information to Stevens. In turn Stevens—whom Seaton and Snedden had nicknamed "Crisis Stevens" for his knack of finding problems—informed Secretary Seaton in a handwritten note two days before Christmas, 1957. "Bill Snedden called me Saturday evening. He said that he thought you should know that the Anchorage reaction to the Kenai leasing problem was getting intense and that a new issue was involved. Apparently someone discovered that the Richfield lease was [allegedly] issued while a stop order on all leasing on wildlife areas was in effect." Snedden had a few suggestions on how the problem could be handled, which Stevens relayed to Seaton:

> You may wish to have someone in the Department state that the reason no new leases have been issued on Kenai is that the whole problem of oil and gas development on such wildlife areas is being studied by the Department. This would calm the Alaska people down, Bill said. He also said that he realized that there wasn't much that could be said right now, but that a statement that the problem was being studied was called for because the people up there assume nothing is being done at all.[72]

When Bartlett personally met with Seaton some weeks later, he wrote another confidential memo confirming that Seaton was obviously "very concerned" about the attempt to "name him and Bob Atwood in a Teapot Dome sort of conspiracy in connection with the Kenai oil leases." Bartlett said Seaton "talked on and on" about the Kenai controversy. "It is obvious that it bothers him. I was happy to learn that he is not provoked at Bob Atwood for having taken the editorial position regarding Kenai oil and at the same time having lease applications there. He is aware of a belief, as I was long before talking with him, that Wally [Hickel] will do anything to try to drag Seaton down because Seaton did not appoint him Governor."[73]

Snedden's contribution to quelling the Kenai controversy was to try to hush Ernest Gruening in an editorial headlined "Oil vs. Moose . . . Pipe Down, Ernest." The *News-Miner* scolded Gruening for his "hysterical" rhetoric and "unnecessary vehemence" and begged him to consider the impact of his inflammatory comments on conservationists, especially since Seaton's proposal that would allow a continuation or even expansion of oil leasing inside the moose range was highly favorable to oil interests in Alaska.

Seaton had said that oil and moose could "live together harmoniously in multiple use of the land, under workable regulations," and Snedden could not comprehend why Gruening was so insistent that the moose must go.

> What the people denouncing and belittling the moose lose sight of, we fear, is that if they succeed

in blocking the plan of the Interior Department . . . they will be closing the Kenai National
Moose Range, and very likely all other wildlife
lands in Alaska, to oil and gas leasing. They lose
sight of the fact that the conservationist group is
large and extremely potent politically throughout
the United States. If this group should be stirred
up to work against us, the development of Alaska
will be hamstrung. So might a good many other
desirable things, including statehood.

After Gruening publicly criticized Seaton for supposedly valuing
the moose of Alaska more than its people, Bartlett told Snedden that
Gruening was breaking his promise that he and the other Tennessee planners "would work for statehood and statehood only . . . because an expression on any other subject might hurt statehood." Beyond that Gruening
was usurping his duties as delegate. "So long as I occupy this job I am the
only elected official empowered by the people of Alaska to speak on any
and all subjects. When the people don't want me to do that any more they
can get rid of me at the ballot box."[74]

In "Pipe Down, Ernest," Snedden echoed Bartlett's views that nothing good could come from Gruening's misadventure in the Kenai Moose
Range. By charging "like a bull moose in the Kenai controversy," the
News-Miner said, Gruening was doing serious damage to the statehood
cause. "We suggest he make a quiet about-face and charge back out of
the woods to work in those greener pastures where he has been so much
more effective."[75]

In the end Fred Seaton hit on one of his typically ingenious legal
and political compromises as a solution to the Kenai oil leasing debacle:
the Kenai Moose Range would be both open and closed. The Interior
Department opened the northern half of the range—which included
Swanson River—and closed the southern half. Since oil never comes out
of the ground without a stack of lawsuits, a court fight over the validity of the Richfield leases eventually landed in the U.S. Supreme Court.
In 1965 the high court unanimously upheld the original Richfield leases of Rasmuson-Atwood et al., vindicating the actions of the Interior
Department.[76]

In the final tally oil had little to do directly with the approval of Alaska statehood. Certainly the events of 1957 did not hinder Alaska's cause, and were at the very least modestly helpful. But while the leading players had black gold and natural gas on their minds, Seaton's skillful handling of the Kenai Moose Range crisis, and the release of PLO 82 with hardly a trace of controversy thanks to the Snedden strategy of linkage with the Arctic Wildlife Refuge, helped ensure that Alaska would not be kept out of the union on the grounds that it was a "giveaway" of resources that belonged to the American people.

But claims that the Kenai oil strike actually lubricated the wheels of statehood are another matter entirely. The question has arisen only because of a straightforward issue of chronology, which is not identical to cause and effect. It was on July 25, 1957, only two days after the revelation of the Kenai oil strike, that Alaska statehood earned the endorsement of its most crucial ally next to Fred Seaton: the Speaker of the House of Representatives, Sam Rayburn of Texas. There is no evidence that it was the oil find on the Kenai that spurred Rayburn's conversion; the dates on the calendar are probably nothing more than a mere coincidence, as by Texas or Oklahoma standards Swanson River was simply not that important. A multimillionaire independent oilman in the Senate, Oklahoman Bob Kerr of Kerr-McGee—his campaign slogan had been "I'm just like you, only I struck oil"—did vote for statehood in 1958, after being seen as the one vote responsible for defeating statehood in the Senate in 1952.[77] Gruening would suggest in later years that Kerr changed his vote due to pressure from the chairman of the board of Phillips Petroleum, but that is unlikely.

A Fairbanks attorney originally from the Sooner state told Bartlett in February 1958 that the story he had heard in the Oklahoma oil patch was that in spite of the Kenai, Senator Kerr and his firm had no interest in petroleum prospects in Alaska.

> His oil company, Kerr McGee, did the drilling in the Yakutat area for Phillips, as you may remember. Evidently, it was a little expensive and not too successful, and Kerr McGee seems to be a little sick of Alaska. I do not know if this will influence Senator Kerr's thinking regarding Alaska statehood, but I don't believe it will help it. People, generally, did not seem to be too interested in Oklahoma regarding Alaska statehood.[78]

Like Kerr, Rayburn also had other things on his mind besides oil in Alaska, and odds are the Speaker probably could not have found the Kenai Peninsula on a map. Rayburn was much more concerned in July 1957 with the civil rights bill that his protégé and fellow Texan, Senate Majority Leader Lyndon Baines Johnson, was trying to push through a bitterly divided Senate. Rayburn's true motivation in coming round to support Alaska statehood apparently had nothing to do with Alaska at all, and was instead just a very small part of an ambitious scheme to help LBJ become the next president of the United States.

President Eisenhower famously fumed when more than a dozen Alaskans, pictured on the front page, went to the Oval Office in May 1954 to plead for statehood. According to Delegate Bob Bartlett (far right), Ike's face turned fire engine red as spokesman John Butrovich gave his straight-from-the-shoulder talk.

The *News-Miner* float in the 1956 winter carnival portrayed Uncle Sam as the dastardly villain denying his paternity of Alaska.

Anchorage Daily Times

READ BY ALASKANS EVERYWHERE

THIRTEENTH YEAR · PHONE 26301 · ANCHORAGE, ALASKA, MONDAY, MAY 10, 1954 · 12 PAGES · PRICE 10 CENTS

FORECAST

Fair tonight and Tuesday; Low tonight, 61; high Tuesday, 84.

ALASKANS TOLD TO TAKE PARTITION OR 'NOTHING'

A 3 LA

Lee Bettinger Labels Plan Stall Tactic

Saylor To Introduce Bill To Force State Measure On Floor

WASHINGTON (P) — Chairman Miller (R-Neb.) of the House Interior committee today told statehood-seeking Alaskans if they won't settle for partitioning of Alaska "you probably will get nothing."

He made his statement at a meeting with more than 50 Alaskans who arrived here early today to do what they can to spur Alaska statehood.

ALASKA SPLIT?—The shaded area in this map of Alaska shows the part which Gov. B. Frank Heintzleman has proposed for immediate statehood as a compromise in the congressional dispute over the Alaska-Hawaii statehood issue. This would leave about half of Alaska (indicated by white portions in map) in territorial status. Heintzleman advanced the suggestion in Washington, D.C., Saturday.

The 1954 Interior Department plan to partition Alaska (above) and a more generous modification by congressional Republicans (above right) generated ferocious opposition throughout the territory. The compromise solution under Interior Secretary Fred Seaton in 1957, with the details crafted by attorney Ted Stevens, was the "PYK Line" (right), the dotted line on this 1958 map that appeared in the *News-Miner*; land north and west of the Porcupine, Yukon, or Kuskokwim rivers could be withdrawn for military purposes by the president at any time.

NEW PARTITION PLAN

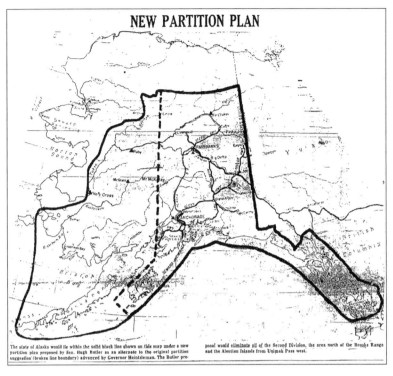

The state of Alaska would lie within the solid black line shown on this map under a new partition plan proposed by Sen. Hugh Butler as an alternate to the original partition suggestion (broken line boundary) advanced by Governor Heintsleman. The Butler proposal would eliminate all of the Second Division, the area north of the Brooks Range and the Aleutian Islands from Unimak Pass west.

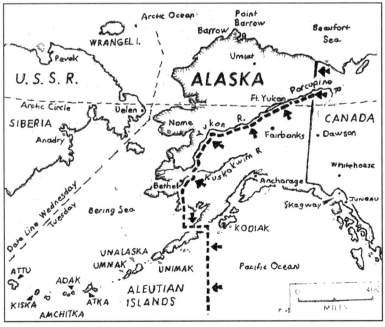

ALMANAC
Tuesday, June 8, 1954
Daylight Today 19 Hrs. 06 Min.
Sunrise 2:39 a.m.   Sunset 9:33 p.m.
Temperature Yesterday
Maximum....65   Minimum....49

Anchorage Daily Times
READ BY ALASKANS EVERYWHERE

FORECAST
Increasing cloudiness tonight; cloudy
and cooler Wednesday. Low tonight,
50; high Wednesday, 60.

THIRTY-NINTH YEAR   PHONE 56201   ANCHORAGE, ALASKA, TUESDAY, JUNE 8, 1954   12 PAGES   PRICE 10 CENTS

STRAND BRANDED 'DICTATOR'

McCarthy Aide Considers U. S. In Loyal Hands

WASHINGTON (P) — Roy M. Cohn testified today he never heard Secretary of the Army Stevens say anything to indicate "the Red Communists any better than I do."

And Cohn agreed—in response to a suggestion from Army counsel Joseph N. Welch—that the "government is really in the hands of patriotic individuals" and is "not really in the hands of traitors."

He testimony came at a session of the McCarthy-Army hearings where the production and mood seemed to be a shade calmer than it had been...

Tells McCarthy To Consult Psychiatrist

WASHINGTON (P) — Sen. McCarthy today is "better go to a psychiatrist."

Symington issued that that advice as he and McCarthy bandied...

Alaska's Dictator

THE DICTATORIAL ATTITUDE of the director of the division of territories in Washington was revealed in a story published in the Anchorage Times.

This revelation was shocking.

It disclosed that an appointed bureaucrat in Washington holds himself higher and of greater power than the United States Senate.

It showed that the man thinks he is the absolute ruler of Alaska and that if statehood is coming it must be on his terms.

It showed than an appointed bureaucrat looks down on one of Alaska's elected officials and demands that the bureau's policies be supported and defended.

The entire episode was un-Democratic and un-American. It was a worse demonstration than anything ever staged by the late Secretary of the Interior Ickes who was noteworthy for his efforts to ride rough-shod over the hopes and aspirations of Alaskans.

This situation is one that cannot be overlooked or ignored because it is grotesque and unpleasant. Alaskans are going to have to face it because the director of the division of territories is a key man in the present federal administration at Washington.

IN EVALUATING the shocking dis-

the living room after other Alaskans had departed. Col. M. R. Marston heard some of the conversation as he walked through the living room and overheard a few of the remarks.

This newspaper made careful investigations before printing the story and determined that the sensational and shocking account was true in every detail except one. The one error was the statement that the rumpus in the upstairs bedroom was so noisy it was heard downstairs. We could find nobody who could verify that statement, although it is entirely possible that somebody did hear it downstairs. This point is of such minor importance its accuracy would not add or detract from the verity of the rest of the story.

THE STRAND ATTITUDE was revealed in Washington after the Alaskans had spent a week trying to find why statehood legislation was being blocked and why a partition scheme had been proposed.

The Alaskans had been frustrated all week. They proved that important misinformation had been given them. They found that there was an iron curtain of knowledge which they were not allowed to penetrate. The true origin and purpose of the opposition and the partition scheme was never given to them. Numerous officials brushed them off with vague and unsatisfac-

STATEHOOD FOR HAWAII ONLY APPEARS UNLIKELY

Bill Without Alaska Must Top Big Hurdles In Senate-House Parley, New Senate Vote

By A. ROBERT SMITH
Times Washington Correspondent

WASHINGTON — The administration's plan for sidetracking Alaskan statehood in an effort to secure Hawaii from the present congressional stalemate on the issue is considered a long shot at best by veteran Capitol Hill observers.

With only eight weeks to go before the House and Senate adjourn for the year, administration leaders led by the Department of Interior have mapped out a prospective plan of action on Capitol Hill which they hope will work as follows:

1. Within the next week or so [illegible] A. L. (Doc) Miller of the House interior com-

[illegible] Of the seven situations on that roll-call vote, four were Democrats who announced they favored Alaska and three were Republicans who announced Republican opposition.

Hence the administration's intention to bring Hawaii to a vote while keeping Alaska out must initiate some provision for changing some votes in the Senate, where sentiment is divided 48 to 48 against them, judging by the March 11 tally. That's why observers believe the plan is a long shot at best.

McKay Alaska rary Set

WASHINGTON P — The Interior announced today that McKay will arrive [illegible] on July 17 to start his inspection tour of...

Paper Reports Heated Talk With Hickel

Interior Man Boasts Congress Won't Pass Alaska Statehood Bill

A conference in Washington in which William Strand, director of the division of territories, allegedly proclaimed himself "dictator" of Alaska, was revealed in Alaska this week.

The conference was with Walter Hickel, newly elected Republican Committeeman. It took place during a crowded party at the Strand residence when the Operation Statehood delegation was in the capital city pressing for statehood last month.

First publication of the story came in the Juneau Independent which failed to quote its source. Hickel said he did not release the story, but he admitted that it had few errors as it was published.

As related by the Juneau paper, Strand and Hickel went into conference in an upstairs room of Strand's home while other Alaskans remained downstairs for the social gathering.

Hickel sought Strand's aid in obtaining an Alaskan for appointment on an Alaska...

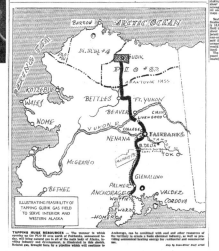

Through a special arrangement between Seaton and Snedden, set up by Ted Stevens, the Interior Department announced the proposed opening of the Arctic to gas and oil exploration and the simultaneous creation of the Arctic Wildlife Refuge on page one of the *News-Miner*'s 1957 Progress Edition. Also prearranged was the photo of Governor Mike Stepovich looking over Seaton's shoulder.

Index
Classified ..22-27
Comics 42, 43
Editorial 14
Games 55
Night Clubs ..34
Pictures ..22, 23
Radio, TV 39, 40
Society 56
Sports 56-51
Theatres ..57-59
Women's ..20-23

 **The Washington Daily News**

27th Year—No. 134   DC, 7-7777   Entered as Second Class Matter at D. C. Post Office

CITY EDITION   **TUESDAY, APRIL 1, 1958**

 Weather
Mostly sunny,
warmer. High,
56; low, 38. Fair
tonight. Sunset
weather t o m or
row.
Today at:
8 a. m. 41

5¢

This Little Man ————————————————————→

Stalls a Vote by These 11 Men...

And Defeats the Will of This Entire Body...

The "This Little Man" front page was inspired by Snedden, targeting the yearlong delay of statehood by House Rules Committee Chairman Howard W. Smith. Photo courtesy of Helen Snedden.

Rep. Howard W. Smith (D., Va.) has been reported as saying that Alaska can become a state "only over my dead body." As chairman of the House Rules Committee, Mr. Smith has been stalling to prevent a vote in his committee to bring the Alaska bill to the House Floor—altho the merits of statehood have been studied and decided favorably by the House Committee on Interior and Insular Affairs. A majority of the members of Mr. Smith's rules committee favor statehood and will so vote if given a chance. A majority of the House favor statehood; so do a majority of the Senate. In public opinion polls, the American people favor statehood by a ratio of 8 to 1. But Rep. Smith stalls ...

An Awakening Giant

(An Editorial)

CONGRESS frantically hunts a plan to spend billions and coax back the boom. But it can't find the time for a ready-made plan which historically always has been a stimulant to prosperity, and which wouldn't cost the taxpayers anything.

This is the bill to grant statehood to Alaska.

Here is a vast, rich land, ripe for development. For 91 years it has been a territory, kept in pocket by the Federal Government, its resources virtually untapped, migration from the states effectually discouraged.

Lumber, power, oil, gas, mining and other industries can exist in Alaska now only by sufferance of the Federal bureaucracy, which controls 99 per cent of the land. Federal domination, as congressional committees repeatedly have pointed out, has shackled the growth of the territory.

"In all ways," said the Senate Interior Committee last year, "Alaska is a dynamic and spectacular land. No area of the world offers a more promising challenge to the man of vision. This making giant is the America, there have been 35 additions to the Union. And each time a new state has been admitted, the national economy has surged ahead.

"Statehood has never been a failure," the House Interior Committee said.

In Alaska, the United States has, potentially, a lasting spur to the economy comparable to the opening of the West. And the nation is well supplied with men of vision eager to meet this promising challenge,

---

The core of the opposition to Alaska statehood always came from southerners, who feared Alaska would tip the balance of power against segregation. For this reason, keeping Alaska out of the Union was in essence another way of keeping black children out of white schools.

What's Your
PLEASURE ...
Whatever you want, Classified helps you find it. If you've things to sell, rent or buy—use Want Ads. Dial RE3 7077.

FAIRBANKS

Daily News-Miner

"America's Farthest North Daily Newspaper" — Member of The Associated Press

VOL. XXXVI   15c Per Copy   FAIRBANKS, ALASKA, TUESDAY, JUNE 17, 1958   Ten Pages   No. 143

LATE HOME EDITION

SOUTH OPENS FIRE ON STATEHOOD

U.S. Flies In Arms To Beirut

Rebels Fire
On Quarters
Of Christians

BEIRUT, Lebanon, June 17.

—ALASKA STATEHOOD—
Senate Consideration in Capable Hands:
(An Editorial)

WASHINGTON, D.C., June 17, 1958.

Dixie Solon Contends Bill Unconstitutional

'Grave Legal Questions' Raised by Military Reservation Provision of Alaska Measure, Argues Thurmond

WASHINGTON, June 17.

Two New Ordinances Approved

Cohen's Wife Gets Divorce

LOS ANGELES, June 17.

City Sets Hearing on Annexation

BLM Fire Fighters Use Borate Slurry Bombers

Mississippi Calls Alaska Bill 'Mistake'

WASHINGTON, June 17.

French Troops Will Withdraw

TUNIS, June 17.

Despite Rumors, Slankard Still City Manager

WEATHER   *Two Killed*

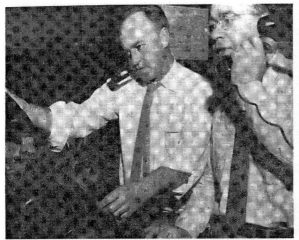

News-Miner Gets First News of Vote

First word to reach Alaska of the U. S. Senate's historic vote extending statehood to the territory came to the newsroom of the Fairbanks Daily News-Miner.

By prearrangement, t h e newspaper's Washington correspondent, A. Robert Smith, placed a long distance call to George Sundborg, News-Miner editor, when the roll call began in the Senate chamber. This was to insure an open wire for the 3,500-mile distance.

The call was made from the press room adjoining the press gallary. Smith and Sundborg exchanged pleasantries until the vote was completed, when Smith said:

"Here it is. You're in. The vote was 64 to 20."

The vote was completed just at 8 p.m. (2 p.m. Fairbanks time.)

Word of the decision was

SOUND THE SIRENS, RING THE BELLS —A message touching off Fairbanks' celebration of the passage of the Alaska statehood bill is telephoned to civil defense officials from the News-Miner newsroom by George Sundborg, editor, right, as Perry Torbergson, city editor, takes the news off the Associated Press teletype.

News-Miner editor George Sundborg (right) and city editor Perry Torbergson, as Snedden relayed the news to them of the passage of the statehood bill by the U.S. Senate on June 30, 1958.

With Senate passage of the statehood bill, the Fairbanks Shake and Steak announced its "Move Over Texas" statehood specials dedicated to Lyndon Johnson and Sam Rayburn. Photo courtesy of *Fairbanks Daily News-Miner*.

C. W. Snedden and "Flight Hostess" Marita Sherer on the half ton of "statehood day" newspapers the *News-Miner* publisher had arranged to have shipped overnight to Washington, D.C., by the U.S. Air Force on June 30–July 1, 1958, a stunt to demonstrate to Congress how close Alaska was in the jet age to the nation's capital. Photo courtesy of Helen Snedden.

President Lyndon Johnson (right) listening to Sen. Ernest Gruening (center) and Sen. Bob Bartlett (left). More than anyone else, Bartlett always believed that the two men most responsible for Alaska statehood were LBJ and his mentor, Speaker Sam Rayburn.

Wally Hickel (right) became Alaska's first Republican governor in 1966, and in turn he appointed Snedden's friend and protégé, Ted Stevens (left), Alaska's first Republican senator in 1968. Stevens would go on to become the longest-serving GOP senator in American history.

Fred Seaton (seated) at his office in Washington takes a call from Alaska Governor Mike Stepovich in Juneau, marking inauguration of the new "White Alice" phone system completed in Alaska by the U.S. military in 1958. Listening in from right to left: Ted Stevens and Anthony Lausi of the Interior Department and C.W. Snedden.

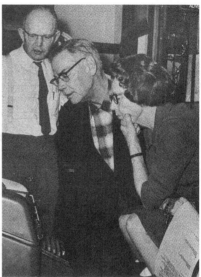

(Above left) Snedden during the 1967 Fairbanks flood. (Above right) checking election returns on the *News-Miner* teletype with Bob and Vide Bartlett. (Bottom) looking back, Snedden believed that the fight to make Alaska a state was the most rewarding experience of his career. He succumbed to cancer in August 1989 at age seventy-seven.

14

"The Lord and Lyndon"

Bob Bartlett never forgot the time or the place: it was shortly after noon on July 25, 1957, outside the restaurant of the U.S. House of Representatives. Looking back he came to believe, as he told Snedden and others, that hot Thursday afternoon in the corridor of the U.S. Capitol was the moment everything changed for Alaska, the first in a series of unanticipated and inexplicable twists and turns he could never fully unravel. The delegate had just finished eating lunch with Bill and Neva Egan when the three Alaskans met Speaker Sam Rayburn in the hallway. Bob introduced Neva and Bill, and the Speaker pointedly told the Tennessee Plan senator, "I hope you *are* a Senator someday!" Rayburn then asked Bartlett to "come over as quickly as possible" to his office to discuss "the wisdom of calling the statehood bill up at this time." As best as Bartlett could remember, the Speaker's exact words were "Bob, I doubt the wisdom of going ahead now." The delegate later wrote, "He did not go into details. He didn't need to."[1]

Initially this appeared to be a terrible development. "Not now" and "wait till next year" had always been the most effective arguments against statehood, and in a deliberative body with a running clock delay was typically the preferred weapon of choice to kill unwanted legislation. The best way to stop a bill was simply to slow it down, and it was hard to take delay as anything but a defeat, particularly when the word came directly from the Speaker of the House himself. Rayburn's message was further confirmation of what Bartlett knew only too well: that the rules of Congress were not written to make it easy to challenge the status quo. The system was intentionally designed to keep the past upon its throne by providing many ways to kill new proposals, even those supported by the majority. Parliamentary hurdles and procedural barriers were hidden all along the winding road through Congress, offering a multitude of opportunities, British historian and diplomat James Bryce had written in *The American Commonwealth* in 1888, "by which a minority can make itself disagreeable." In one way or another, Bryce said, "nineteen-twentieths of the bills introduced meet their death, a death which the majority doubtless deserve."[2] Pushing any piece of legislation through Congress, supporters needed to prevail in every skirmish, every step of the way, while opponents could easily lose every battle except one and nevertheless still win the war.

— ◦◦◦ —

On May 23, 1957, Leo O'Brien's House Subcommittee on Interior and Insular Affairs had approved the Alaska statehood bill by a 17–5 margin. "The victory yesterday morning in the territories subcommittee was a glorious one," Bartlett wrote Snedden. Behind the overall 3–1 margin of victory was even more good news: the vote showed strong bipartisan support, with nine Democrats and eight Republicans in favor. Of the five nay votes, only one was a Republican, New York Rep. John R. Pillion, not necessarily one of the most sensible men in Congress. An obsessive anticommunist of Hungarian ancestry, he would gain notoriety as the author of the 1961 "Pillion Resolution," which would have formally declared war against ninety-eight different communist parties around the world. Pillion believed the Warren Commission was a communist-inspired cover-up of the Kennedy assassination, and he was so fixated by the communist threat that according to Drew Pearson he once went to the South Pole "looking for live Communists." The *News-Miner* designated this "strange New Yorker" as the "most ardent anti-statehood congressman of them all." He was convinced that letting in Alaska or Hawaii would be tantamount to inviting "Soviet agents to take seats in the United States Senate." Pillion also proposed amending the constitution so that future states would no longer automatically have the right to two senators. In his mind statehood had nothing to do with democracy or freedom but was an attempt by the international communist conspiracy to infiltrate the U.S. Senate.[3]

The four other nay votes were equally fanatical that control of the Senate was the fundamental issue, but stopping civil rights legislation, not communism, was their primary goal. "Each Democratic vote against us was cast by a member from south of the Mason-Dixon line," Bartlett wrote, and he gave the roll call to Snedden: "Rogers of Texas, Haley of Florida, Shuford of North Carolina, and Rutherford of Texas."[4]

The committee vote was unmistakable evidence that Southern Democrats were as formidable an obstacle as ever, and not about to be swayed by economic statistics or moral appeals about the right of Alaskans for equality and full citizenship. Bill Egan wrote Snedden that "segregation feeling is so strong among the southerners that it would be foolish to hope that we can expect many more votes from that area than the votes of those few who have been dedicated to our cause in the past."[5] The immediate roadblock was the House Rules Committee chaired by Democratic Rep. "Judge" Howard Smith of the Eighth District of Virginia. The Rules Committee controlled almost all legislation getting to the floor and was in essence a third house of Congress, with Judge Smith's power nearly rivaling that of Speaker Sam Rayburn and Senate Majority Leader Lyndon Johnson. Dedicated to the Southern cause, and violently opposed to civil rights legislation, Smith was intent on keeping the statehood bill locked up in his committee at all costs. No Southerner was blunter in his rejection of Alaska, or any other possible new states, than Judge Smith. His stock response to the notion of adding any new states, in any combination, at any time, could have been summed up in only three words: *I am opposed*. As the Judge so memorably put it on the floor of Congress in 1955:

> I am opposed to statehood for Alaska. I am opposed to statehood for Hawaii, I am opposed to both of them together, I am opposed to them separately. . . . I am opposed to Puerto Rico, I am opposed to the Virgin Islands, I am opposed to all of them. I want to keep the United States of America on the American continent. I hope I have made my position clear.[6]

Impatient with the wiles of Congress, Snedden kept hoping to conceive a grand gesture to leap though the remaining legislative hurdles. "If we only had a 'big gun' ready to bring into action right now," he wrote Bartlett on May 27, "perhaps it would do the trick and get the bill out of the rules committee and onto the floor of the House." He wondered if one way of dramatizing Alaska's plight might be "a real strong series of editorials advocating" that Alaska threaten to secede from the Union and join up with Canada, or appeal to the United Nations and declare outright independence. "Of course I do not seriously believe that Alaskans would ever vote favorably on such a proposition. However, the fact that we were so thoroughly disillusioned with the way Uncle Sam is treating us that we are even considering the idea should bring quite a bit of publicity. Naturally, the hoped-for results would be for Uncle to reach out and grab us by the coat-tail and pull us into his happy family of states." Snedden told Lehleitner this gimmick would "create enough furore that Uncle Sam would take us in in a hurry—if for no other reason than to hush us up." Snedden admitted to Bartlett that perhaps he was "smoking the wrong kind of tobacco" but flirting with Canada or declaring independence was the best he could think of. "I know you have been through this battle several times before . . . and doubtless have felt several times in the past that success was in sight. While I do not have the benefits of that background, somehow I have the definite feeling right now that success is almost within our grasp—and if we are halfway smart we can dream up something which will enable us to close our fingers on that elusive golden apple of statehood."[7]

As the weeks passed Snedden grew increasingly concerned that the moment of victory was almost at hand, but only if the pro-statehood forces were ready to close the deal as soon as possible. He felt time was running out. "The more I cogitate on the matter," he wrote Bartlett in late June, "the more I am convinced that we should do everything possible to push the bill in the Senate also. It seems to me that if it is not pushed through the Senate before recess there are so darned many things that may happen [between] now and next January. I believe it will be extremely difficult to generate as much interest in Alaskan Statehood next winter as we have across the country today." His biggest fear was that Eisenhower might decide he needed Fred Seaton's help in another agency, perhaps at the Department of Agriculture, where the embattled Ezra Taft Benson had inherited McKay's mantle as the biggest political liability in the cabinet. Though he had no "inside information" about an impending transfer of Seaton, he surmised "there is a good possibility the President may decide to shift him to another post" sometime before January 1958. A new secretary of the interior would never work "for us as efficiently and sincerely as Seaton is today," and so while "the wonderful team fighting for us" in the Department of the Interior was still intact, an "all-out drive" had to be made.[8]

Bartlett's strategy was to proceed with high hopes and extreme caution. When the bill was passed out of the full House Interior and Insular Affairs Committee chaired by California Democrat Clair Engle, it was slated next to go to the Rules Committee chaired by Howard Smith of

Virginia. Unless Smith's Rules Committee granted the bill a "rule" or resolution authorizing it to be taken up by the full House, it would be DOA;
nevertheless, Bartlett refused to confront Rayburn directly about forcing
Smith to issue a rule, rightly fearing what the answer might be if he put
the Speaker on the spot. Rayburn had long been so notoriously anti-
Alaska statehood that back in February 1954 Bartlett had warned Bob
Atwood that in the event the Republicans were able to bring in Hawaii
that year, and the Democrats regained control of Congress in the midterm
elections, "only death would keep Sam Rayburn from becoming Speaker
of the House and Lyndon Johnson from becoming Majority Leader in
the Senate," and they "might figure that admitting Alaska would only be
to double the mistake." Bartlett said he could "see no possibility whatsoever of persuading Rayburn that he should be an advocate instead of an
opponent of statehood."[9]

Through June and early July 1957 there were no signs that Rayburn's
hostile attitude had changed whatsoever. Therefore Bartlett made sure
that he would not get "no" for an answer from Rayburn about pushing the
statehood bill onto the floor in 1957, by not posing the question at all. "I
very deliberately have refrained from having a heart to heart talk with the
Speaker on this subject. Even yesterday I didn't seek to do so," Bartlett
wrote Snedden on June 4. The previous day the delegate had a brief meeting with Rayburn, during which he had merely elicited a promise from
the Speaker that "expeditious consideration would be given Alaska statehood" and that the bill would not be frozen in the Rules Committee. "It is
my intention to hold my fire until Clair Engle is ready to seek a rule. Then
I shall have my talk."[10]

When the delegate from Alaska finally had his "heart to heart" with the
Speaker of the House on July 25, 1957, it was hardly what Bartlett had
expected. After running into Rayburn outside the House restaurant,
Bartlett and Leo O'Brien sat down apprehensively in "Mr. Sam's" office
to hear the details. The Texas Democrat began by admitting what they
already knew: he had first come to Congress in 1913, only one year after
the forty-six states had become forty-eight with the addition of Arizona
and New Mexico, and for decades had been an intractable foe of Alaska's
statehood cause. As Speaker of the House since 1940, except when the
GOP was in the majority in 1947 and 1953, he had maneuvered to stop
both Alaska and Hawaii on numerous occasions. But now it was 1957

and Rayburn said that while he still opposed Hawaii, he had changed his mind about Alaska, and promised he would hereafter do his best to make it the forty-ninth state. The only caveat was that his judgment and "44 years experience dictated that this was the wrong time to press for action" in either the House or the Senate. Nearing the end of a congressional session was always a time of high tension, "when most everyone is mad at most everyone else." This had been a particularly intense summer in the blistering heat of Washington; "tempers were frayed in the House because of so much controversial legislation" and "the Speaker said he thought Alaska statehood would be harmed and not helped if it were to come on the floor at this season when almost everyone was short-tempered and everyone wanted to get away." He wanted to put the statehood bill on the shelf until January 1958.

Before they had gone into Rayburn's office O'Brien had told Bartlett that he "would not fight postponing action now provided he were able to secure from the Speaker a promise for action not later than January; otherwise, he was disposed to say very bluntly that he would do everything in his power to by-pass the Rules Committee. But Leo didn't even have to bring the proposition up since the Speaker did so voluntarily. So that is the way it is."[11]

Being forced to follow Rayburn's lead on good faith alone was hardly an unusual position for a delegate with no trading stock of any sort. As Bartlett once described a typical busy day at his office, "I have been wheeling today. It would be an exaggeration to add 'dealing' because my understanding . . . is that you have to have some power before you can 'deal.' That is something I am without!"[12]

The *News-Miner* tried to adopt that same philosophical attitude in an editorial on "The Statehood Delay." "If there is one thing Alaska has learned in 90 years of being a stepchild of the United States of America, it is patience. We were asked yesterday to be patient yet a while longer. . . . The turndown illustrates . . . the inferior position of a territory at the nation's table. We take what is handed to us, and if we don't like it, that's just too bad." The only hope was that Rayburn would be true to his word and speedily bring the bill up for consideration in January. Otherwise his promise would be "another case of someone being for us in the abstract but against us when it comes to . . . action. We will find out when the second session of the 85th Congress opens next January."[13]

Before Rayburn had shut the statehood drive down on July 25, Snedden had been confident that a successful vote in the House of Representatives was imminent. Only two weeks earlier a *News-Miner* status report on

"How Statehood Stands" explained an "overwhelming victory" was "anticipated by all who have been watching progress of the measure through the 85th Congress."[14] And only three days before Rayburn called a halt, Bill Egan said his "crystal ball" showed the statehood picture in the House was "extremely promising at the moment," predicting full House approval with 265 votes in favor, "give or take 10 either way."[15]

Still in a state of shock the day after meeting with the Speaker, Bartlett composed his thoughts in a confidential memo to share with Snedden and other correspondents entitled "MEMORANDUM WHICH WILL NOT BEAR A TITLE." His despair at the delay had not yet worn off. "Since we have been confidently looking forward to a very early hearing before the Rules Committee, subsequent granting of a rule and consideration by the House, this decision was bound to be disappointing. But it has been made and although we shall never know for sure it may be that the Speaker's judgment in this was better than those who wanted to proceed."[16]

Knowing how frustrated Alaskans would be at the news, Bartlett had asked Rayburn to immediately brief the Tennessee Planners so that they could bear the brunt of the criticism he knew was sure to land on all their heads. The only saving grace was that "for the first time I should not be going home with the heat on me to explain why no action was taken on statehood; rather, the burden this time would be on the Tennessee Planners."[17]

Bartlett did not want to have to defend Rayburn's decision, because he knew to Alaskans specifically and Republicans generally it would be indefensible. No matter how sound Rayburn's political and tactical reasoning may have been, he had made up his mind without consulting anyone from Alaska. Furthermore, Rayburn had not consulted with anyone in the Republican Party or the Eisenhower administration. To help make the decision appear more palatable, the *News-Miner* portrayed the Tennessee Planners and Bartlett as having "accepted Speaker Sam Rayburn's advice" about waiting till 1958, though in reality they were not accepting a suggestion as much as following an order.[18] There was no way to disguise the fact that Rayburn had not talked with anyone on the other side of the aisle and the lack of consultation spoke much louder than all the hollow boasting of bipartisanship. Bartlett warned the Speaker that "the Republicans here and in Alaska will make much of the fact that a Democratic Congress failed to put the statehood bill through either house," and Rayburn promised that he would get together with Majority Leader Rep. John W. McCormack of Massachusetts and "issue a strong statement . . . so the world will know that this is not a move on his part to kill the bill but rather one to promote its chances for enactment."[19]

In any event Rayburn's message of justification was neither clear nor forceful, and the political fallout struck immediately. Seaton wired Snedden pinning the failure to move the bill forward squarely on the tail of the Democratic donkey, and the message landed in a front page *News-Miner* editorial recapping the "11th (or whatever number it is) running" of the statehood sweepstakes: "The determination by the Congressional leadership to take no action on Alaska statehood legislation during this session of Congress," Seaton wrote, "is a matter of keen disappointment to me, as I know it is to all friends of statehood for Alaska." Seaton called it a "regrettable delay" and a "new disappointment." The *News-Miner's* view was that Delegate Bartlett and the Tennessee Planners had done their best, but Rayburn's refusal to consult with the GOP was proof of the partisan way it was being handled. And Snedden lamented once again that the Tennessee Planners were all Democrats. "This newspaper thinks the quest would have been more fruitful if at least one of the good men we sent to Washington to represent us had been a Republican." Snedden concluded the record would show that while "the Republican Administration did everything within its power to obtain favorable action," it had been the Democratic leadership of the House that made the call to defer action until 1958.[20]

According to Bartlett the "cleverly done" Republican response to the Rayburn announcement, which included a few words from Governor Stepovich—probably written by Sundborg or Snedden—was sent out as an Associated Press dispatch "to build up the impression that the Republicans have done everything except commit hari-kari to bring about statehood and have been thwarted by the ornery Democrats." When Bartlett showed Seaton's statement and the *News-Miner* story to Rayburn, the Speaker was furious. "The sons o' bitches," he said. Rayburn dictated a short response to Bartlett, who took it down in pencil and gave it immediately to the "newspaper boys":

> As I explained to Delegate Bartlett last week, and later the same day to Senators-elect Egan and Gruening and Representative-elect Rivers, I am for the bill, and I am for the admission of Alaska as a state into the Union. The only reason for setting the bill over until January was because of the lateness of the session and the confusion that always obtains at a time like this. The people of Alaska

can be assured again that they will have their day in court. This is not a partisan issue and I do not intend to treat it as such.[21]

In the long run Rayburn's unexpected and unequivocal endorsement of Alaska statehood was invaluable. In the language of Capitol Hill, where code words and innuendo were so often finely tuned weapons of imprecision, enabling agile politicians to stand and sit on both sides of the fence at the same time, the blunt promise Seaton had forced out of Rayburn would resonate long and loud in the months to come, quoted repeatedly to make sure the Speaker would not forget: "I am for the bill, and I am for the admission of Alaska as a state into the Union."

No single vote for Alaska statehood would ever mean more than that of Sam Rayburn. "SPEAKER BACKS STATEHOOD BILL" read the *News-Miner* banner, and underneath Leo O'Brien claimed that Rayburn's endorsement alone would add "at least 20 votes" when the bill reached the House floor. As a consequence the New Yorker was ready to lay 3–1 odds "the Alaska bill will pass the House next winter."[22] The question was whether this delay would turn out to be a temporary tactical retreat or a crippling strategic blunder; it all depended on whether Rayburn could be trusted. He had given no reason for his sudden conversion to the cause that he had opposed for so many years, and it was natural to suspect his motives. Perhaps his promise of a January hearing was a legislative trap, but given the reality of the congressional power structure, there was no choice but to trust him.

Lehleitner knew the Southern politicians who controlled the levers of power as well as anyone, and he was suspicious. Disappointed at the shelving of the House bill, he was particularly fearful, as he explained to Bartlett and Snedden, about Rayburn's true intentions.

> IF Sam Rayburn really IS now to be numbered among our friends . . . and IF he really has pledged that the bill will be brought up next January, there is much to be said for postponing action until that time. . . . Does it not seem to you . . . that the real answer as to whether or not postponement represents a further advance—or a defeat—is to be found in the integrity of Sam Rayburn's promise that action would be forthcoming next January?[23]

Within one week after walking out of the Speaker's office, Bartlett had become more confident that Rayburn's promise was a stunning victory. "At the outset we were mightily discouraged," Bartlett admitted to Lehleitner. "At the conclusion not so." However, the proof would have to wait until 1958. In the event that "things should go to pot early in the next session," he agreed with Snedden and Lehleitner that "we must search around for some more forcible means of entry," but he warned the range of options was limited. "Just what those means might be goodness only knows. I don't. But I have thought and thought and thought about it." He was certainly not ready to endorse their idea of pretending to secede or asking for United Nations intervention, because "even at the point of extremity we must restrain ourselves from going too far." Meanwhile, for the time being Bartlett urged everyone to once again swallow an extra dose of patience and put their faith in the Speaker, because "until such time as there is an absolute demonstration to the contrary, I am bound to believe Sam Rayburn to be a man of honor and a man of his word."[24]

The "controversial legislation" that forced Speaker Rayburn to take the statehood bill off the table was the great civil rights fight of the summer of 1957, which would see the torturous passage of the first Civil Rights Act since Reconstruction. This momentous challenge was for Rayburn both a matter of honor and practical politics. He and his protégé in the Senate, Majority Leader Lyndon Johnson, who was gearing up to run for president in 1960, were dealing with the burning issue that could no longer be denied, the giant elephant in the Democratic caucus that was tearing apart both the country and the Democratic Party. Nothing in American history was as divisive and deadly as the question of race relations, and as the nation began to wrestle seriously in the 1950s and 1960s for the first time with the legacy of slavery and Jim Crow, not since the Civil War had the country seemed to be so close to the brink of violent rebellion. The traumatic struggle for equal rights touched all aspects of American life, as somehow an entirely new means had to be invented to guarantee the right to vote, to attend a good school, to eat at a clean lunch counter, or to sit in the front of the bus, regardless of skin color or the sanctity of "state's rights." Because it was clear that the only method of ending segregation was an expansion of federal power, potentially every bill in Congress had broad civil rights implications.

One year earlier the 1956 "Southern Manifesto" signed by 101 Southern senators and congressmen—ninety-nine Democrats and two Republicans, comprising almost the entire Southern contingent in Congress outside of Texas—declared the Supreme Court's 1954 *Brown* decision to be an exercise of "naked" federal power overriding "established law," creating an "explosive and dangerous condition . . . inflamed by outside meddlers." The manifesto put the rest of the country on notice that the South was preparing a campaign of massive resistance on all fronts and would not go down in Congress without a fight, even if it meant the destruction of the Democratic Party.[25] Seen through the prism of Southern resistance to civil rights, the statehood bills for both Alaska and Hawaii posed a double threat: the bills were civil rights measures that would guarantee equal political rights to the citizens of the territories, but more importantly, the addition of four new senators from outside the South would dilute the power of the minority Southern Democrats to block all other civil rights legislation. Behind all the "congressional dilly-dallying" about statehood, the *Detroit News* commented in 1957, was "nothing more than the fear of a bloc of southern senators that the new states would elect senators who would be anti-segregationist supporters of civil rights."[26] For this reason keeping Alaska out of the Union was for most Southerners no less a priority than defying the order of the U.S. Supreme Court to desegregate Southern schools. In effect, keeping Alaska out of the Union was another method of keeping black children out of white schools.

Despite a preponderance of contemporary evidence, the fundamental connection between the statehood drives for Alaska and Hawaii and the civil rights movement was intentionally ignored by almost everyone. Only much later would Daniel Inouye, Hawaii's first congressman and longtime senator, be free to admit that the Hawaii Statehood Act was "a pure and simple civil rights bill."[27] The same can be said of the Alaska measure; however, even modern historians have been fooled by the 1950s rhetoric that intentionally disguised the big picture.[28] The most perceptive analysis remains that of Hawaiian scholar Roger Bell. In his 1984 book, *Last Among Equals: Hawaiian Statehood and American Politics*, Bell demonstrated conclusively that the "anti-civil rights faction" of the Democratic Party was the perpetual stumbling block over which both territories had to pass, and it was particularly "the relationship of Hawaii and Alaska statehood to other civil rights legislation in Congress which was decisive." According to Bell, "Failure to appreciate the relationship between statehood and the Southern position on civil rights has obscured from most observers . . . the real obstacles to admission."[29]

In the 1950s statehood had of necessity to be isolated from the radio-active issue of civil rights, because in the political climate of the time total separation offered the only viable option. Even one drop of civil rights sentiment appeared as if it would be fatal to the statehood cause. When the civil rights debate began to boil in early June, Gruening raised the alarm about what might happen if statehood and civil rights were to collide in the Senate, and he warned Bartlett about the danger of statehood being linked even superficially with the civil rights movement.

"Ernest said that it was hard to comprehend the emotion aroused in southerners by the Civil Rights issues," Bartlett wrote in a memo to himself, "and if the two bills were to be associated even in respect to timing, it might be disastrous," so Gruening proposed that the Senate Committee on Interior and Insular Affairs intentionally stall its version of the statehood bill until 1958. Bartlett was appalled. "I thought it would be simply devastating politically at home . . . if it became known that any one of the Tennessee Planners or I became known as author of a move to slow statehood for whatever reason."[30] Within a few weeks, however, Bartlett was equally alarmed by the escalating war of words. "The southerners are in good voice and staying power," he quipped to Sundborg. "It is altogether likely that they will be inclined to discuss the situation at some length." By that time Bartlett privately had come to accept Gruening's thought that the civil rights question was so explosive that it would be beneficial if statehood did not surface in the Senate until the second session, at which time the raw emotions might have begun to dissipate.[31]

No one was more sensitive to the association of statehood and civil rights than the Louisiana-born-and-bred George Lehleitner. He too had the same premonition that Alaska could fall victim in the Southern mind to guilt by association with the civil rights crusaders unless they were extraordinarily careful. At the end of September 1957, while the 101st Airborne Division was at that moment protecting nine black children at Central High School in Little Rock, Arkansas, under orders from President Eisenhower, Lehleitner alerted Snedden that the message must somehow get to the president, his speechwriters, and the rest of the administration—perhaps through Seaton—that Ike and his staff should never utter the names "Alaska" or "Hawaii" in the same sentence with the term "civil rights." Lehleitner believed Harry Truman had made a "grievous error" in 1948, from which the statehood movements for the two territories had never fully recovered, when he included the Alaska and

Hawaii statehood bills as part of his comprehensive civil rights package, a set of measures that alienated the Southern Democrats and helped spur Strom Thurmond to break away that year with the "Dixiecrats."

> The net result was that those members of the Congress who were most sensitive to the impact of a civil rights program, received from the President's message confirmation of their suspicions that statehood for the Territories would represent two steps in the direction of the passage by the Congress of onerous civil rights legislation. In other words, Bill, I hope very much indeed that the President will take deliberate pains to disassociate statehood for the two Territories . . . with the 'civil rights' program in any way, shape or form.

Lehleitner was reluctant to see the obvious commonalities between Alaskans and African-Americans both fighting for the right for full representation, if for no other reason than the disastrous political consequences that might arise if the two causes were grouped together:

> Although, in a sense, statehood for the two Territories would be an extension of 'civil rights' to the people of Alaska and Hawaii, I am confident you share my opinion that there is no relationship between the enfranchisement of ALL Alaskans and Hawaiians and the granting of this and other rights of citizenship to the negro citizens of our Nation. And, because the two are completely disassociated subjects, I do hope special pains will be taken by the President to see that these separate issues are not linked together by any manner of association. Were that to happen, I'm afraid the end result would be catastrophic.[32]

This dire forecast of catastrophe was completely out of character for Lehleitner—normally he and Snedden shared the affliction of incurable, entrepreneurial optimism—but the acrimony and bitterness that had been on display in the closing months of the first session of the 85th Congress was ample explanation.

Even the Washington weather was historically miserable in the summer of 1957, as the city suffered through the worst drought since 1872, and tempers flared in Congress as it struggled to pass the first civil rights bill since 1875. This titanic clash between the South and the rest of the nation seemed to herald a seismic political realignment with major implications for the statehood fight, as well as everything else in American society. On June 18 a liberal-moderate, Republican-dominated coalition in the House—90 percent of the Republicans voted in favor of the bill—passed the Eisenhower administration's civil rights bill in spite of the near-unanimous opposition of Southern Democrats. The more than 2–1 margin of victory in the House—286 to 126—seemed to suggest the emergence of a new political geography that portended well for the chances of statehood. As the *News-Miner*'s Washington correspondent, Bob Smith, reported in late June: "A new political alignment in Congress, emerging out of the throes of the hot civil rights fight, may raise the question of statehood for Alaska and Hawaii to the status of a major issue before very long." According to Smith's analysis, the "new alignment consists of a majority of Republicans and most northern Democrats who have teamed up to put the civil rights bill through the House, and over bitter objections from the South, to place it on the Senate calendar. Shattered in these moves was the working coalition of conservative Republicans and southern Democrats that has held the whiphand in Congress," the same "old conservative coalition that proved to be highest barrier to statehood for Alaska and Hawaii. The bitterest foes of statehood are among the conservatives of both parties who want no change in the status quo. So long as that conservative coalition operated, statehood bills had little chance of being enacted."[33]

In fact, Southern power was cracked, not shattered. The contest in the Senate would prove to be every bit as ferocious as had been expected. At the time Senator Johnson was gearing up for a serious run at the White House, hoping to become the first president from the Deep South since before the Civil War, and passage of a civil rights bill was essential for him to have any chance of victory. To broaden his appeal LBJ was branding a new image for himself as a moderate Westerner instead of a segregationist Southerner. Though both Rayburn and Johnson were true-blue Texans and Southerners—Rayburn was the son of a Confederate solider and Johnson the grandson—they were also the national leaders of the Democratic Party, the two men responsible for holding the fractious Democratic coalition together. As a result they constantly had to balance the conflicting demands of the northern and southern, liberal and conservative wings of the party, tacking back and forth across the Mason-Dixon

Line to keep the two warring factions from an irreversible split. Rayburn famously eschewed any simple description of his political philosophy, claiming to be neither a conservative nor a liberal. "I always say without prefix, without suffix and without apology that I am a Democrat."[34] Johnson, on the other hand, was all things to all people. The only way to describe Lyndon, said Texas Governor John Connally, was to use "*every* adjective in the dictionary." His ten-gallon personality encompassed the entire political spectrum, so that depending on the day, the issue, and the audience, he could sound as liberal, conservative, or moderate as the occasion demanded—and sound as if he meant it to the core of his soul.[35]

Taking a moderate enough stance on most issues to at least mollify northern liberals—neither Rayburn nor Johnson had signed the 1956 "Southern Manifesto"—they were still solidly conservative enough in the eyes of the South to maintain impeccable credentials as Southern statesmen. William S. White, chief congressional correspondent for the *New York Times,* said they were the "indispensable" Democrats to both sides of the party divide, the two men who tied the room together.[36] Without Rayburn and Johnson, the Democratic Party as a national force might have ceased to exist.

LBJ's presidential hopes were naturally dependent on keeping the party united. Johnson's mentor in the Senate, Richard B. Russell of Georgia, the unrivaled leader of the Southern bloc and the most effective defender of segregation—and a key opponent of admitting Alaska or Hawaii—acknowledged that "we can never make him [Johnson] President unless the Senate first disposes of civil rights," and so together he and LBJ designed a strategy to give the North a taste of what it wanted, a Civil Rights Act, and give the South as much as it could tolerate, an ineffectual Civil Rights Act of "form without substance." Instead of the standard Southern strategy of open defiance, blazing straight ahead across open ground with a filibuster, the new, more sophisticated tactic of Johnson and Russell was to agree to an armistice, and with the threat of the filibuster always waiting in the wings, to sit down and acquiesce long enough in order to be able to modify the bill behind closed doors to their liking, and then ram it through. The end goal was to try to appease the North without pushing the South to the brink of revolution.[37]

Johnson and Russell realized that as much as the diehard Southern senators—LBJ called them the Confederates—would detest the passage of any civil rights legislation, it would be far worse if the Senate failed to pass it. Failure would not only doom LBJ's presidential bid, but relying on the filibuster in this case would be a senatorial Pickett's Charge, inviting a tactical and strategic defeat that could likely enable liberals and other Southern opponents to muster the necessary votes to change Senate rules limiting debate and strip them of the filibuster. Thus the South was faced with the prospect that if it dared to use the biggest weapon in its political arsenal it might lose the ability to ever stage a successful filibuster again. It was for this reason that when Strom Thurmond broke with Russell and the Southern strategy and decided to wage a one-man filibuster against the civil rights legislation by himself on August 28–29, 1957—setting the still-unbroken record for a single Senate "speech" of twenty-four hours and eighteen minutes—Russell blasted Thurmond's stunt as "a form of treason against the south" because under the circumstances there was "nothing to gain and everything to lose."

"There was not a man among us who was not willing to speak against this iniquitous bill until he dropped in his tracks," Russell said in defense of his strategy, after Atlanta Congressman James C. Davis accused the Southern senators of "surrendering" by refusing to stage a filibuster. "We would have done so, but for the conviction . . . that a filibuster was certain to make a bad bill infinitely worse." Instead, Russell said he had chosen to extract the fangs of the hated civil rights act in order to "keep the withering hand of the Federal Government out of our schools and social order," and he proclaimed it "the sweetest victory of my 25 years as a Senator from the State of Georgia."[38]

Compared with later civil rights legislation, the 1957 Civil Rights Act was pitifully weak and largely ineffectual, but as toothless as the 1957 act proved to be, its passage would be an unexpected landmark in American history. It was the passage of the Civil Rights Act in 1957, as one columnist predicted that year, which made Senator Johnson of Texas "the first Southern Democratic leader since the Civil War to be a serious candidate for the presidential nomination." Though LBJ failed to win the Democratic nomination in 1960, he agreed to be the vice presidential nominee in order to broaden the appeal of the ticket in the South. With Kennedy's assassination in November 1963, Johnson was unexpectedly catapulted into the Oval Office and would ultimately push through a fundamental and largely peaceful revolution in civil rights as president in 1964 and 1965.[39]

Drew Pearson had written in 1957 that it was "the unanimous opinion of Senate observers that passage of the . . . civil rights bill without a filibuster can be attributed solely to Sen. Lyndon Johnson of Texas. They also agree that his backstage maneuvering was sheer genius and that he should go down as the greatest political general of all time."[40] Historians have since tried to understand more fully the process by which LBJ was able to pull off this legislative marvel; Robert Caro, the author of the definitive biography of Johnson's congressional career, *Master of the Senate*, devoted almost half of the nearly twelve hundred pages in his book to an exploration of how LBJ conducted the civil rights campaign in Congress that summer. This was the exercise of power politics at its highest level, a tireless campaigner running his ninety-five Senate colleagues into the ground, buttonholing, dealing, trading, yielding, intimidating, listening, asking, demanding, cajoling, pleading, threatening, stalling, pulling, pushing, and counting, always counting. One of Bartlett's correspondents praised Johnson's work that summer, saying the passage of the 1957 Civil Rights Act was a work of political alchemy that was nothing less than "reconciling the irreconcilable," a phrase that Bartlett admired as a fellow politician, believing this was the highest a man in his line of work could aim. Johnson's 1957 Civil Rights Act was an invention of creativity, ingenuity, and hard work far above the normal range of human ability, the *Mona Lisa* of politics. As one senator said, "No one except the Lord and Lyndon is sure exactly how he accomplished it."[41]

What the Lord may have had to do with the passage of Alaska statehood a year later may likewise be beyond human understanding, but if the Civil Rights Act was the legislature miracle of 1957, the Alaska Statehood Act was that of 1958, and both Rayburn and Johnson played a big role. Given the improbable manner in which the statehood bill slipped through Congress in May and June 1958, some professed to believe that they saw the hand of a higher power in the making of the state of Alaska. On May 27, 1958, the eve of the final House vote, Ted Stevens admitted that the opponents of admission appeared to have prevailed as the masters of parliamentary tactics yet once again, and that nothing was left except to hope that God might still be on the side of statehood after all. Stevens called Snedden that night in Fairbanks to give him the bad news, and the transcript of their phone conversation read as follows:

> STEVENS: They pulled a sneaker on us. It was a sneaky trick.
> SNEDDEN: What do you think about tomorrow boy?

STEVENS: Well—it's a hard guess. It is an up-
hill road now. We [are] fighting to save ourselves
now instead of to get the bill through. . . .
SNEDDEN: Can you think of anything else we
can do?
STEVENS: Yes, go down the street to St.
Mathews [Episcopal Church in Fairbanks] and
borrow the church for the night.
SNEDDEN: Church? And do what?
STEVENS: Use it for the night. It's time to pray,
my friend. There is nothing else we can do now.[42]

Rep. Leo O'Brien, the official "author" and manager of the legislation on the House floor that made Alaska a state, called the House approval of HR 7999 a flat-out "miracle." On the long night of despair before the vote, he too had thought all was lost, and confessed that the way the "yeas" magically materialized in the last vote was beyond his comprehension, unlike anything he would ever witness again. Similarly, George Lehleitner believed so many obstacles suddenly and inexplicably disappeared in the final days that the only possible explanation lay in the realm of the super-natural; Lehleitner claimed to see the hand of God himself in the ways and means of how Congress dealt with statehood in 1958.

"I told both Bob Bartlett and Bill Snedden," Lehleitner later wrote Stevens, "and will unhesitatingly repeat this conviction to you—that each passing day makes me more humbly aware that the bill could not have been enacted without the Lord's intercession on our behalf; there were so many obstacles the melting of which could not be attributed to any other factor but Divine intercession."[43]

Aside from the imponderable question of supernatural forces, the tortured path of Alaska statehood through Congress remains mysterious enough, as every legislator or lobbyist had a different story to tell and in the chaos of the battle no single person was ever in a position to take in the full picture. Even Alaska's top official at the nucleus of the statehood campaign, Delegate Bartlett—who admitted to being a terrible prognos-ticator with a badly bent divining rod—grew increasingly frustrated by how many wrong predictions, rumors, "and rumors of rumors" he heard daily from otherwise reputable sources. "I become so irritated by the spec-ulative guesses on statehood," he griped to Snedden, "that if time ever af-fords I have in mind to undertake a vast and worthy research project . . . in an effort to discover the percentage of time they hit the ball. My estimate

without any research is that their percentage . . . would be lower than Yogi
Berra's recent batting [average]. I think that was .208."[44]

The confusion was everywhere. In March 1958 Lehleitner said that
after talking with twenty top officials in Washington, including six key
House members, five senators or their staffs, the three members of the
Tennessee Plan, three "well-informed newsmen," two members of the
Interior Department (one of whom was Ted Stevens), and Delegate
Bartlett, he observed that "the most striking characteristic . . . was that
NONE of my twenty contacts was precisely sure what WAS taking place;
even less were they certain of what WOULD happen. And, least of all
was their unanimity on what SHOULD be done next!"[45]

The inscrutable trinity at the heart of the matter included the secretary
of the interior, the Speaker of the House, and the Senate Majority Leader.
Fred Seaton, Sam Rayburn, and Lyndon Johnson, respectively, turned
around the White House, the House of Representatives, and the Senate
on the Alaska question. Lacking any one of these men, Alaska might never have joined the Union at all. It was hardly a secret that Seaton was the
heavyweight champion fighting for Alaska on the Eisenhower team and
had thrown the entire Interior Department into the fight, despite the fact,
as his Alaska point man Ted Stevens later admitted, that Seaton and his
crew "were violating the law as it was—we were lobbying from the executive branch."[46] But while Secretary Seaton's modus operandi was obvious
to everyone, the thinking of the top two Democrats in Washington, D.C.,
was an entirely different story. In truth "Mr. Speaker" and "The Leader"
could not afford clarity lest they irrevocably offend one end or the other of
the Democratic spectrum. Certainly, neither had Seaton's enthusiasm for
admitting Alaska; at most they were reluctant supporters only because the
alternative was worse. Just as with the civil rights compromise the previous year when they had gone to such great lengths to avoid a filibuster, the
two Texans seemed to agree that stopping statehood was a strategy they
could no longer afford to wage at all costs, particularly if Johnson was to
prove to a national audience that he was worthy of the White House.

When Rayburn and Johnson shifted from negative to neutral on the
statehood question, the Texans opened the door for Alaska. But the explanation for this change of heart was never clearly articulated or explained
to anyone, not even the head of the Alaska Democratic Party. Bartlett
admitted that he never knew exactly why his two colleagues from Texas
decided to let statehood proceed. "For whatever reasons," Bartlett remi-
nisced in 1963, "Sam Rayburn and Lyndon Johnson came to the conclusion in 1958" to no longer stand "in the way of statehood. . . . Rayburn's

opposition faded, and I do not pretend, in all honesty, to know the reasons." Bartlett was only certain that if "either of them in 1958 turned thumbs down, statehood would never have come to Alaska." At another point, he said statehood would never have happened "if Johnson and Rayburn had not changed the signal from red to green before either House in 1958. I have seen these fellows operate for a long while. If they had chosen to turn thumbs down instead of thumbs up no pressures which we could have brought to bear would have sufficed to gain consideration of that bill."

Knowing the reality of how Congress worked, Bartlett thought Alaskans—particularly Ernest Gruening—tended to underestimate how crucial the House Speaker and the Senate Leader were in making statehood a reality. "The plain fact of the matter is that after all of us Alaskans have finished congratulating one another . . . statehood came only because . . . Rayburn and Johnson stood aside."[47]

In retrospect, the reason Rayburn and Johnson as the national leaders of the Democratic Party gave the green light to Alaska must be interpreted in the context of the exploding passions over civil rights, the North–South split in the Democratic Party, and LBJ's presidential ambitions. It appears inescapable that the two Texas Democrats concluded that allowing the admission of Democratic Alaska—even if it further eroded the power of the South to hold back civil rights legislation—would be a relatively small price to pay in order to help keep northern liberals comparatively content; while the South would remain adamantly opposed to bringing Alaska in, aware Republican Hawaii would not be far behind, the main goal was to prevent a permanent rupture in the Democratic Party and keep Johnson's hopes alive for the 1960 primaries, the same logic that had prevailed in the civil rights fight of 1957.

Forcing the Southern Old Guard inch by inch to accept the necessity to compromise on statehood, just as he did with civil rights, Senator Johnson made it possible for Alaska to become one of the United States. The difference, however, was that while Johnson knew he needed the Civil Rights Act, the Alaska Statehood Act was not a priority from his perspective. "Rayburn and Johnson stood aside," as Bartlett said, a far cry from actively steering the bill past the road blocks in the House and Senate, and that was why Snedden would play such a crucial role in the final months of the battle.

15

"A Snowball in Hell"

The second session of the 85th Congress opened on January 7, 1958. Sam Rayburn's pledge the previous July had been that Alaska statehood would be at the top of the House agenda. "We won't have anything to do then," Rayburn had promised, "everyone will be happy." But thirteen days after Christmas, the Speaker of the House had nothing to celebrate; he now told the press he expected a "very heavy session and considerable controversy," leaving a veteran reporter to observe that in spite of the cheerful "hectic moments of handshaking and backslapping" that accompanied the start of every legislative gathering, "it was obvious that . . . the Eighty-fifth Congress had come back to Capitol Hill in a serious and disputatious mood." All Rayburn was willing to say on January 7 regarding the Alaska statehood bill was that it would be brought up for consideration "some time during the session, but I can't say when."[1]

As events would unfold that winter and into spring, the delays continued and the frustration mounted. The months on the calendar turned from January to February, then to March, April, and May; the cherry blossoms bloomed, withered, and died, all the while with the statehood bill still trapped in the tomb of the Rules Committee, and even Bartlett would begin to doubt Sam Rayburn's vaunted reputation for straightshooting and fair dealing.[2]

The day before the opening of Congress, Snedden had written Bartlett explaining he was on his way to Oregon for medical treatment, and he would anxiously be awaiting the good news they anticipated the following day from Speaker Rayburn. "If you get the Statehood Bill through

Congress by January 16," Snedden gladly wrote Bartlett, "let me know in Portland and I will come back to Washington" directly.[3]

When Rayburn failed on January 7 "to say that he was going to have the bill brought up tomorrow, or at worst the day after," Bartlett reported that he and Leo O'Brien would meet with the Speaker as soon as possible to plot a strategy. Within a week they had the meeting with Rayburn, and the news Bartlett had to share with Snedden was not good.

"He told us positively the bill will not come before the House of Representatives this month." Far worse, the Speaker could not even guarantee that the House bill would reach the floor before the Senate took action on its version of the legislation. Bartlett tried to reassure Snedden, as much as himself, that Rayburn had not done what he appeared to be doing: "I do not yet believe and cannot believe and will not believe that once having given his word (which he did without any pressures being exerted at all) that Speaker Rayburn will let us down. I am bound to assume that so far as he is concerned it is a matter of timing in light of considerations which he must give to the entire legislative program."[4]

Bartlett was always "guardedly pessimistic" about anything having to do with Congress. Years of experience had taught him never to take a vote for granted. But within two weeks even his natural caution and skepticism suddenly vanished, as it appeared Rayburn and Johnson might come through for Alaska after all. On January 28 Bartlett breathlessly dictated a jubilant but highly confidential note to Snedden. He had just come from a meeting with a "Senator of the Democratic persuasion who ranks way, way up there," and the scoop was that the statehood bill would be passed by the Senate, without a filibuster, inside of three weeks. The top four tidbits of news were:

1. The Alaska statehood bill would come to the floor of the Senate within the next 10 days.
2. The Alaska statehood bill would be passed in anywhere from three days to one week after debate started.
3. There would be no filibuster from Southern senators, although to protect the record they might in individual cases feel compelled to talk at length.
4. Arrangements had just about been perfected (outside the Southern camp) to prevent any move from northern Democratic liberals or friendly Republicans who would seek to tack Hawaii on to Alaska.

The good news did not end there. Reportedly, the Republican minority leader in the Senate, William F. Knowland of California, had signed on to the strategy of making sure Hawaii would not be tied in the Senate to Alaska, which had always in the past been a fatal attachment. Furthermore, it was the Majority Leader himself who was the mastermind behind the entire plan. "Lyndon Johnson is not only agreeable and amenable to the strategy; he devised it and is carrying it out now." Bartlett closed with the cheery thought that all Snedden would have to do next was pack his grip and be ready to travel on a moment's notice in order to be on hand for the Senate vote. He pledged to make sure someone would "flash the word to you as soon as we know it."[5]

Snedden said that the news of the Johnson plan was "the most welcome message I have ever received," especially because the delegate, "seasoned . . . by years of fighting this battle," was invariably "more conservative and less optimistic than Snedden" and that "makes me feel . . . there is indeed firm ground to be jubilant." Giddy with delight, Snedden wired Bartlett back immediately about waiting for the "flash" of the news of the Senate vote:

RE YOUR JANAURY 28TH LETTER
HURRY. IN FACT DOUBLE HURRY.

C.W. SNEDDEN

Bartlett's response was equally cheerful, despite his usual sense of foreboding:

HURRYING TO POINT OF OCCASIONAL TRIPPING.
DANGER ALWAYS IS SOMEONE WILL MOVE CLOCK
BACK IN DARKNESS OR GOAL POST BACK
IN OPEN DAYLIGHT.

E.L. BARTLETT[6]

Perhaps a warning sign that all was not well should have been apparent on January 27, when Bartlett had met with Secretary of the Interior Seaton at the Interior Department. They were supposed to talk about oil regulations for the Kenai Peninsula, but oil was not at the top of Seaton's agenda for Bartlett that Monday afternoon, and "the conversation was opened by the Secretary with these very words, 'Did you read Drew Pearson's column yesterday?'"

In his Sunday column Pearson had included a brief note headed "The 49th State" which had obviously come from Gruening. Back in 1952, according to Pearson, "Alaska's hard working governor Ernest Gruening" had converted then-Senator Fred Seaton of Nebraska to support Alaska statehood. Pearson then ostensibly praised Seaton for being "one man in Washington who doesn't deviate from his convictions," even though the real point of the column was to take a swipe at Eisenhower: "The other day, Ernest Gruening, now ex-Governor of Alaska but elected by the Alaskan people as their 'senator' to Washington, dropped in to see Seaton again . . . 'How do you feel about Alaska now?' asked Gruening. 'I feel just the same way,' replied the Secretary of the Interior. 'How about your boss?' Gruening asked."

According to Gruening, according to Pearson, Seaton's answer was vague and noncommittal: "Seaton did not definitely commit the President, but indicated that the administration would probably be for Alaskan statehood."

Pearson then went on to throw a few more jabs. He predicted Hawaii would not be added to the Alaska bill in the upcoming session of Congress for two reasons: the growing strength of the Democrats in the islands had dimmed the "enthusiasm" for Hawaiian "statehood on the part of the present Republican administration" and the obsession of Southern Democrats with the "race question" in Hawaii had not dimmed. Pearson closed with a barbed wisecrack: "The first Senator from Hawaii under statehood would probably be of Chinese ancestry."[7]

Pearson's article implied that Seaton's inability to "commit" the president to Gruening "the other day" was recent news, when in fact Gruening had not called on Seaton in almost a year, and in the meantime the administration had officially and repeatedly committed itself to both Alaska and Hawaii. Additionally, Pearson's garbled revelation about the plan to dump Hawaii was sure to rile Republicans, and the Chinese senator slur would do the same to Southern Democrats. "Seaton is a mild-mannered man," Bartlett wrote, "and he displayed no temper at all, but left no doubt . . . that he was distressed by what Pearson had written and thought it might well be very hurtful to statehood." The secretary's griping about Gruening went on: "'Can't anyone keep Gruening quiet?' asked Seaton, fully aware that EG had been the source of the Pearson story. 'Can't anyone in Alaska tell him to be quiet now?' He seemed to demand an answer. I gave it. 'No.' 'Is he becoming senile?' Seaton wanted to know. This I denied."

"This thing is getting horribly mixed up!" Bartlett concluded, though he didn't know at the time that much worse was yet to come.[8] A week after Pearson floated the story that the Republicans were abandoning Hawaii, a reporter asked President Eisenhower at a White House news conference if he planned "to push for statehood legislation for Alaska and Hawaii" in the current session of Congress.

"Well, I'll say this," Ike responded. "It has been in every message I have put in since 1953.... Now, what I personally would like to see them—the two bills coming on simultaneously—that is what I'd like to see them."[9]

Ike's grammar may have been typically convoluted, but his main point was clear enough: he wanted Congress to deal with the two territories "simultaneously." When the Associated Press moved the story on February 5, it set off alarms, since the most effective weapon against Alaska had long been Hawaii, and vice versa. Within minutes Snedden immediately telegrammed Seaton and phoned Stevens asking for an explanation because acting "simultaneously"

> GENERALLY REGARDED DEATH KNELL ALASKA STATEHOOD AND CERTAIN CAUSE TREMENDOUS ADVERSE REPERCUSSIONS ALASKA. IMMEDIATE CLARIFICATION EXTREMELY IMPORTANT.

The day before the news conference Republican congressional leaders had met with the president and his staff, and complained to Ike about LBJ's plan to leave out Hawaii. Unfortunately, Seaton was ill and unable to attend, so there was no one to make a strong stand against the danger of adding Hawaii into the statehood mix: "Ben and Chilly [Elmer Bennett and H. O. Chilson] said that the Leadership meeting didn't go too well," Stevens reported to Seaton. "Ben thinks it may be necessary for you to speak to the President about the virtues of separate bills."[10]

On February 6 Senate Minority Leader Knowland launched the GOP response to LBJ's Alaska plan. Knowland announced that "the Administration considered it inadvisable for Congress to take up Alaska statehood legislation without considering Hawaii statehood also." Knowland informed Senator Johnson that the Republicans wanted assurances from the Democrats that the "Hawaii bill should be called up for Senate consideration immediately following the Alaska bill," and if such a deal was not forthcoming the Republicans in the Senate would be forced to make a move to combine the two bills into one.[11]

Snedden was incredulous at Knowland's announcement because it seemed to him to be a deathblow to statehood's chances. According to George Sundborg, who relayed the story to Bartlett, on February 6 Snedden tried "frantically to reach Seaton all that day after our stories came in on Knowland's announcement. He could not talk to Seaton or even find anybody in the Interior Department who had heard about the Knowland statement. Finally Stevens called him. I sat in Bill's office as Stevens talked with him for more than half an hour."

The phone call between Stevens and Snedden was a heated affair.

> STEVENS: Hello, Bill.
> SNEDDEN: Yes, Ted?
> STEVENS: How are you?
> SNEDDEN: Getting madder by the minute.
> STEVENS: Well, Bill I just can't understand this. Mike [Stepovich] just called me and he was all upset about this and I heard that you had called Lorne [Seaton's assistant]. You know why Knowland has done this, don't you?
> SNEDDEN: Know what he is doing?
> STEVENS: Yes.
> SNEDDEN: Yes, he is scuttling Alaska statehood for Christ's sake.
> STEVENS: The hell he is, Bill. . . .
> SNEDDEN: Well, Jesus you ought to see our AP and UP press dispatches, Ted.

Stevens's argument was that Knowland and the Republicans were merely asking for fair play for Hawaii to ensure it would be brought up immediately after Alaska. Such a promise from LBJ would in turn guarantee the bills would remain separate, removing any pressure from Republicans to join with the Southern Democrats to combine the bills and kill them both. If Johnson would not assent, the failure would be on his shoulders and the Democratic majority, not on the Republicans, but Stevens was confident Johnson and the Democrats would not take that risk.

"We can't afford," Stevens said, "to say we are going to forget about Hawaii"—the Drew Pearson allegation—simply because the islands had narrowly elected a Democratic delegate "by an eighth of an inch" for the first time in twenty years. Hawaiian statehood was a popular cause in the Golden State, where Knowland was running a lackluster—and ultimately unsuccessful—campaign for governor of California, and he could not be seen as abandoning Hawaii. The Republican rationale, according to Stevens, was that the only way Knowland "can demand that the Republicans stay away from the motion" likely to come from Southern Democrats to combine the two bills will be the promise for immediate action on Hawaii, which will "put the monkey right on Johnson's back."

"Knowland has taken the only course of assuring that we [are] satisfying both sections of our party. And to me it's ABC. It's the best move we could possibly have had—if this thing gets joined now it's Johnson that did it, because he would not assure fair play. And, it's just that simple."

"Well, maybe it's ABC to you," Snedden replied, "but those first three letters of the alphabet to me are Greek or something, Ted—guess I'm just dumber than hell, but I can't see how we are going to gain anything from our public relations standpoint."

Toward the end of the phone call Snedden had begun to warm ever so slightly to Stevens's argument, but he was still highly skeptical of what might turn out to be a case of reckless brinkmanship.

STEVENS: You should realize how much of a victory this really is. . . .

SNEDDEN: Well, you know from my viewpoint, Ted—I guess I [may be] dumber than hell, but . . . we got two ships fighting a battle and [our ship sinks]. . . . Well, there may be cause to bounce around in your lifeboat shouting with glee, but that's the way it looks to me at the moment.

STEVENS: All Johnson can do is come back and say, "Oh, I'll assure you that as soon as we consider Alaska we will take up Hawaii and the thing will be in." It's just that simple.

SNEDDEN: OK, if he will say it now.

STEVENS: Well, what else can he say?

SNEDDEN: Well I think maybe you got it there. It's beginning to make a little daylight as far as I am concerned, Ted. The only thing is whether we can sell it to the people or not. . . .

STEVENS: Well, when the thing comes through and it works then you can crow about what Knowland's done. . . .

SNEDDEN: Oh sure, we can crow about it all to beat hell then, if it works . . . but if it doesn't work, Ted, then, Jesus Christ, then we're dead.

STEVENS: Well, then if it doesn't work then you gotta' blame Johnson for not agreeing to fair play and that's all.[12]

Secretly Sundborg sent Bartlett a transcription of the Dictaphone recording of Snedden's phone call with Ted Stevens. "I would deserve to be skinned alive for sending this to you for any other purpose than to try to get the statehood battle back on the track, which is Bill's real purpose too. There is probably nothing in it you haven't heard elsewhere, but I thought you would be interested, and also reassured, to notice Bill Snedden's reaction to the big news from Washington."

Sundborg warned Bartlett not to divulge the fact that he had sent him the phone transcript and other materials.

Now Bob you know how embarrassing it would be to me if Bill Snedden learned I had sent you some of this stuff ... so I know you will handle it with your usual adroit sophistication. I really have no right to be spilling a lot of stuff from this office, and would not do so except for the good purpose of keeping you informed. Bill is a peach and mustn't be betrayed. But I am afraid that may be just what is happening to him, and not by any Democrats.

The *News-Miner* editor suggested Snedden had been stabbed in the back by his own party. Sundborg's conspiracy theory—a popular Democratic one—was that the GOP stalwarts such as "Knowland, Nixon, Eisenhower, Sherman Adams and the unseen hands which have so much to do with what eventually happens in Washington" had realized that LBJ had worked out a compromise whereby the "southern Democrats were willing to let Alaska come in." Thanks to Johnson, the GOP leaders had inadvertently found themselves "practically across the threshold of helping to shove two more Democrats into the Senate.... They couldn't come out publicly to stop statehood for us, or slow it down, so they did this."

"I feel sorrier for [Snedden] than anyone," Sundborg wrote Bartlett. "He has been the real statehood boy in the Republican camp and what they are now doing to him is murder. I suspect that when he gets back there they will find out it is murder.... Bill Snedden is our most powerful weapon to straighten the Republicans out, if that can be done and if it is not too late."[13]

Bartlett honestly admitted that he did not understand what was behind the Knowland statement. "Statehood seemed within our grasp before this administration announcement was made. Now the future seems uncertain."[14] He interpreted Knowland's move from a vastly different point of view than Stevens. "Bill, I tell you in all frankness," the delegate wrote Snedden, "that everyone with whom I have talked except Ted Stevens believes that this [Knowland announcement] is a move to hurt statehood, not help it." At the very least, Bartlett complained, the failure to brief the Democrats beforehand was unpardonable—though perhaps Bartlett did not recall Rayburn's failure to do likewise. "Even if it was a sound reason . . . behind the Republican strategy which I am totally unable to fathom would it not have been well, Bill, for them to talk with us first and to brief us in an effort to explain their position? I think so. I think the comments we made were rather mild and altogether charitable in view of the devastating impact of the Knowland announcement."[15]

Helen Fischer, Democratic National Committeewoman for Alaska, informed Bartlett that the Knowland announcement had seemed to extinguish any trace of hope. "Everyone's down in the mouth about Statehood. You can see the difference all about. Everyone had been busy making plans for the victory. Now the 'let down' is more noticeable than ever before." Bartlett wrote back that he wished he could send "cheering news to boost your low spirits on account of recent developments concerning statehood. But, alas, no glad tidings can be conveyed from here." Confidentially, Bartlett told the Alaska Statehood Committee in early March that statehood no longer had a "Chinaman's chance" in the session, and publicly he had said that unless one House of Congress passed the statehood bill by May 1, "I'm afraid we're done for."[16]

The delegate thought if Knowland was serious, his "proposal . . . is a mortal blow because it seems elementary that Johnson will have to convince his southern colleagues that Hawaii is not in the picture at all now if they are to go along with Alaska." But Bartlett would admit privately that the national Democratic Party would be equally to blame if Republican pressure on Hawaii did "prove to be mortal," because "sometimes I have the feeling that some of our Democrats need only such an excuse as that provided by Knowland to escape taking decisive and affirmative action."

Since the Democrats were in control of Congress, naturally Alaska—presumed to be a safe Democratic stronghold—had moved ahead of presumably Republican Hawaii for consideration; that was part of the bargaining chip that Johnson had used on the Southern delegation. A de facto strategy of "Alaska Only and Don't Dare Mention Hawaii" had been the operating assumption on the House side for the past year. "Certainly there has been no secret about Leo O'Brien's intention to keep Hawaii bottled up in his subcommittee [until Alaska was approved]. And so far as I know, no Hawaiians have raised real objections to this. The discerning Hawaiians are aware of the fact that statehood for them cannot be long delayed if Alaska makes the grade."[17]

Meanwhile, President Eisenhower would have rather forgotten about Alaska instead of Hawaii, and privately told his top advisors he would find it difficult to accept statehood for Alaska without Hawaii. At a meeting with GOP legislative leaders on March 4, Eisenhower hinted that a veto of the Alaska bill was not out of the question, if a deal on Hawaii could not be reached. Notes of the meeting compiled by a staff secretary stated that in regards to "Hawaiian-Alaskan Statehood,"

> [t]he President said he would be extremely con-
> cerned over what he should do if the Congress ap-
> proved statehood for Alaska and not for the other;
> it would be nothing but a political maneuver to
> take one and let the other die. He felt certain Ha-
> waii had a claim to priority on the basis of eco-
> nomic development. He said he just didn't know
> if he would be able to concur in taking the poorer
> claim [for Alaska]; certainly he would need lots of
> advice.

In response to Ike's concerns, Seaton advised that if LBJ failed to deliver on Hawaii it would spark a "nation-wide protest"; however, he also warned the president that if "Republicans insist on tying together the two measures, then they would also have to suffer the blame for the defeat which was inevitable." Trying to be both realistic and pragmatic, Vice President Richard Nixon suggested that Hawaii would certainly follow in the wake of Alaska and it didn't matter which came first: "admission of these two new states was bound to occur eventually, just as the St. Lawrence Seaway was bound to come. He [Nixon] felt should the Congress vote to admit Alaska, the President would have no choice but to sign the bill. The President commented that he was still reserving judgment."[18]

For Democrats the core of the problem was that a Hawaiian promise of any sort was a deal breaker for the Southerners on Alaska. O'Brien said Hawaii was the ultimate red flag. "Once you inject Hawaii in the debate," he said, "then you get the response, 'Won't we one day be asked to admit Puerto Rico, the Virgin Islands, then Jupiter and Saturn and Mars?'"[19] According to Bartlett, LBJ's compromise had explicitly ruled out the threat of combining the two territories, the very threat that Knowland's proposal would supposedly prevent. The "southern group had become reasonably reconciled to Alaska statehood," Bartlett wrote. "They were not for it; they never would be for it. But they were ready to hold their noses and let it go through, or so we were informed. This was with the understanding that the Hawaii bill would not be called up." Knowland's request for a Hawaiian guarantee for 1958 had kicked out the props under LBJ's compromise proposal, and as a result Bartlett had heard that Georgia Sen. Dick Russell, the powerful leader of the Southern delegation, was "on the war path. Russell is reported to have told Lyndon Johnson that unless definite guarantees are provided that Hawaii will not be taken up this year it may be necessary for the southerners to talk 'four or five weeks' on the Alaska bill. This is equivalent to serving announcement of a filibuster."[20]

Bartlett met with Lyndon Johnson the morning after Knowland's bombshell. He learned immediately that the Majority Leader would not expend any more political capital on the Alaska cause. "After all," as Johnson freely admitted, "the hard core of my support is from the South," and he portrayed himself as beleaguered by Senator Russell and the other Southerners who had no wish to compromise further. Since Knowland had played his Hawaii card, Bartlett wrote, "Dick Russell has apparently been giving Johnson fits on this issue." For the previous six months Bartlett had been hoping that LBJ would publicly endorse Alaska statehood as Rayburn had done, but the Knowland move seemed to exhaust any trace of enthusiasm he might have had in that direction. He seemed to be using Knowland as an excuse to wash his hands of statehood.

LBJ told Bartlett an improbable and completely implausible tall tale about why Sam Rayburn had endorsed Alaska statehood anyway. Known for his obsessive quest to hold all the reins of power, the Majority Leader—sounding like an earnest and uneducated poor boy just in from the hill country who knew nothing about the devious ways of Washington, instead of the most powerful man in the United States Senate—claimed he had first heard the story of Rayburn's Alaska decision only the night before.

"Sam is older, he has more prestige, he was able to come out for state-hood where I can't right now," Johnson slowly drawled, as if every word were true. He said he had even asked Mr. Sam "how it was that he did come out for it."

"'Well,' Rayburn told Johnson, 'they just kept after me so long I finally gave in.'"

Following his meeting with Johnson, Bartlett had nothing but bad news to record in a most glum confidential memo. LBJ had no interest in brokering a new deal and seemed willing to let statehood on Knowland's terms die. The Majority Leader did not even want Bartlett to reveal their meeting to the press.

"I started out by asking him if it would be all right for me to comment on this meeting with him with the hope that I could include in my press release some announcement from him. He said it would be better not to do so." Johnson's only recommendation for Bartlett's press release was not helpful. "He advised me to blast the Republicans."

> I asked him if he were for Alaska statehood. He said he had voted against it before. I knew that. He said he didn't know. A lot of mail is flowing in from Alaska against statehood, according to Johnson.... He said he might even find it neces-sary to vote against the bill.... Near the end of the conversation I turned to him and and asked ... "Lyndon, do you think Alaska will have statehood this year?" His answer was: "No."[21]

Johnson confirmed that one particular source of the mail "flowing in from Alaska" was coming by way of Laredo, Texas, from the prolific pen of a man both Johnson and the Alaskans knew all too well: William Prescott Allen.

Alamo Allen made no secret of the fact that he was using all his Texas connections to stop Alaska statehood and to keep his dream of common-wealth and a ten-year tax moratorium on the table. To spread the word Allen paid for a rambling anti-statehood editorial advertisement in the *Washington Daily News*, charging among other things that communists controlled the Alaska and Hawaii statehood cliques and the two territories "would undoubtedly run a race in case of war to see which area would voluntarily join the Communist block first," and since Alaska was "next door to Russia" it would likely win. The Georgia guru of the Southern delegation and Senate mentor of LBJ, Richard Russell, professed to be so impressed by Allen's wise editorial that he placed it in the *Congressional Record*, claiming it dealt with the impracticalities of statehood in a "more realistic fashion than almost any other material I have ever seen on the subject." That anyone, especially a senator as distinguished and powerful as Richard Russell, could take Allen seriously was beyond Snedden's comprehension. In a series of three editorials the *News-Miner* responded that Alaskans would need "little convincing that William Prescott Allen . . . is whackier than the March Hare" and his charge that "Alaska is crawling with leftists . . . awaiting the signal to run up the red flag" was "pure moon madness," but unfortunately those in Washington like Senator Russell were too easily deceived. "One of the nicest things we can think to say about Mr. Allen's editorials," the *News-Miner* concluded, "is that they do not appear very often."[22]

As infuriated as Snedden and Bartlett were at Allen's charges, however, Bill Egan was the man who really told him off. It happened at a meeting in Bartlett's office that Allen had requested with the delegate and the Tennessee Planners.

"I . . . suggested that Mr. Snedden should be added to the group," Bartlett recounted. "Mr. Allen agreed. We met. Mr. Allen informed Messrs. Snedden, Egan, Rivers, Gruening and Bartlett that statehood was lost, that we had been 'double-crossed.'" According to Allen, "Statehood doesn't have a chance of a snowball in Hell," and he was about to launch into a discussion of why they should adopt his commonwealth crusade when the normally mild-mannered and soft-spoken Bill Egan stood up and shouted that Alaskans did not "need anyone from Texas" to accuse them of treason or "to tell them what was best for Alaska." At that point Allen shouted back, "You are a bunch of phonies," and stormed out of the room, slamming the door behind him.[23]

While Allen's claims of communism were clearly a figment of his imagination, he was hardly alone in believing that the statehood supporters had been deceived by Rayburn and abandoned by Johnson. Early one Sunday morning that spring as Bartlett was entering the House Office Building he encountered Louisiana Democratic Congressman Otto Passman, a statehood supporter thanks to his close friendship with George Lehleitner. Passman warned Bartlett that Rayburn was double dealing.

"Otto asked me about statehood," Bartlett wrote Lehleitner. "He thinks we have been done in. He thinks Mr. Speaker is basically still against us. He thinks Mr. Speaker will, indeed, let the bill go through the House but at such a late date and after having made suitable arrangements in the Senate that he knows there is no prospect at all of its passing this year." Bartlett speculated that perhaps Passman's notorious opposition to foreign aid had warped his thinking about Rayburn, and since "the leadership is probably bearing down on him . . . it may color his thinking about statehood."[24]

The truth was, however, that Bartlett did not know what was going to happen. The only thing of which he was really sure was that both political parties were responsible for the "intolerable delay." In late March Bartlett recapped what had taken place so far in the session for his friend Barrie White in Anchorage, a Republican and former delegate to the Constitutional Convention. There were few answers, but many questions.

"Where are we? Where are we going? The answers, long sought, continue to be hidden as they have for many a year past."

"I cannot tell you why the bill was not scheduled in either the House or the Senate or both in January or February. So far as I can discover, there was no good reason. . . . Perhaps that is one of the reasons why it was not brought up—because the circumstances would have been too advantageous for us. Who knows?"

He could not say for sure what might have happened if Knowland had not issued his demand for Hawaii to follow immediately behind Alaska.

> Neither do I know whether the administration had an honest intention of trying to achieve statehood for both territories this year, or whether it thought Alaska's chances would be aided by this maneuver, or whether it desired to kill both. Neither do I know whether there was substance to the story that Alaska would be scheduled with Hawaii out of the way. I can't say of my own knowledge that the Democratic leaders did not receive the Knowland announcement with inward joy in that it gave them an excuse to do nothing. So, so far as the political and partisan considerations are concerned, both parties can be damned or praised with equal fervor.

As always it was the ticking of the congressional clock counting down toward adjournment that posed the ultimate threat. Legislation at the end of the session seldom had an easy path, which was why Rayburn's failure to follow through on his promise seemed so sinister. "We had every right to expect ... that statehood could come up early in the session. Those pledges remain unredeemed and here we are once more with time running out. . . ."

"This has all been gloomy," Bartlett closed. "It is necessarily so because the events have been gloomy." But though most signs of hope had vanished, a few glowing embers still remained. Just as Bartlett had finished his recitation of the dismal events of the previous three months, he was reminded, "I have just read a letter written by Mr. C.W. Snedden ... in which he stated a personal conclusion that the prospects are bright. . . . Perhaps because of long experience, I shall not go so far as Mr. Snedden but I shall say that we still have a good fighting chance and no opportunity to explore and exploit that chance will be neglected."[25]

It was in these dark days that Snedden and his comrades in the Fourth Estate would bring the full power of the press to bear on Congress.

16

The Power of the Press

In the dark months of 1958, Snedden's stubborn streak of optimism and unflagging perseverance helped ensure that no avenue for promotion of the statehood cause would be left unexplored. Buoyed by the confidence that Seaton was on their side, he was relentless. Even though it was obvious to everyone else—particularly Bartlett—that the congressional odds remained daunting, if not insuperable, Snedden kept insisting to anyone who would listen that, in spite of the rules of logic and Congress, they would ultimately and inevitably prevail, and soon. At least in Snedden's mind it seemed to him that every new day statehood prospects were "better right now than they ever have been in the past."[1]

Occasionally Bartlett's spirits would soar, and when they did he used Snedden as the gold standard of positive thinking. During one brief moment of cheer, the delegate wrote Lehleitner, "I am wildly optimistic. More optimistic than Bill Snedden could possibly be even . . . at white heat."[2] But the difference between Snedden and Bartlett was that Bartlett's zeal never sustained the temperature of Snedden's.

"Bill Snedden called me last night from New York," Sundborg wrote Bartlett in early April. "Said not to worry, statehood will be a fact by the end of this session." Bartlett thought Snedden was naive. "The telephone call [from Snedden] notwithstanding, I insist upon worrying about statehood. Worse, I believe there is some reason to worry about it!"[3]

Meanwhile, at the same time that Bartlett saw doom, Snedden's letters and editorials continued to pound away at the notion that the skies were brighter and the sun was still shining on statehood as never before.

"In my opinion," the *News-Miner* quoted Fred Seaton, "the possibility of passage of this statehood legislation is better today than it ever has been before." Snedden even coined a slogan that caught on with no one but him: "Alaska is going to be a state in '58!"[4]

Snedden's confidence stemmed from his unshakable faith in the power of perseverance and positive thinking, not to mention the innate obstinacy that had made him temperamentally so well-suited for working with a contraption as complicated as the Linotype machine. His intractable belief in the innate righteousness of their fight for democracy made him an irresistible force. "Our cause is just," he wrote in one front-page editorial, and despite the "bigoted opposition" from congressmen such as Rules Committee chairman Howard Smith "in this great democracy of the United States of America right will prevail. Let us not be discouraged."[5] He did not, could not, would not believe that the United States government would knowingly continue to deny the people of Alaska their full rights and privileges as U.S. citizens, and he literally refused to listen to anyone who would tell him otherwise. "I shall say that [Snedden] more than the rest of us is admirably suited in these missionary endeavors," Bartlett said. "That is because if he doesn't like what the other fellow is saying he can and I am sure does turn off his earphone."[6]

No individual spent more time and money on the statehood crusade in its final two years than Snedden, even to the detriment of his health; he collapsed at one point due to a flare-up of his old heart ailment suffered during the war, but despite repeated warnings from the doctor, he refused to slow down. Nothing would get in the way of what had become his life's passion. "You start off with something as a hobby," Snedden told a *Time* reporter. "Pretty soon it's an avocation. And then it's an obsession."[7] Lehleitner, no slouch at knocking on doors himself, judged Snedden to be "in a class by himself among the statehood supporters." "I don't believe I exaggerate one iota when I say that no one—myself included—invested as heavily of his time and his money in the cause of statehood as did Bill Snedden!"[8]

Snedden's sacrifices in these months were all the more remarkable because on Saturday night, November 23, 1957, the city of Fairbanks had been devastated by a deadly fire that almost destroyed the plant of the *News-Miner*. The fire had started in a pile of trash on the second floor of the Lathrop Building, quickly engulfing the third floor in flames.

Miraculously, only one person died in the fire. To the horror of the community, Druska Carr Schaible, a popular University of Alaska professor and wife of local physician Dr. Arthur J. Schaible, was killed from smoke inhalation as the Fairbanks Fire Department watched helplessly; the department's longest ladder was too short to rescue her as she stood screaming from her third-story window.

Only later was the blaze discovered to have been arson. The culprit, a fourteen-year-old *News-Miner* paperboy, had been the first to report the fire to authorities; he confessed he was "just goofing off with matches."[9]

Even in the midst of the flames, city editor Chuck Hoyt was on the teletype to the Associated Press in Seattle. "Our building is on fire here. A lot of apartments are on fire upstairs.... We will be off the air for awhile." Editor George Sundborg, who had crawled out of his third-floor apartment when it filled with smoke, quickly took over for Hoyt in the newsroom and continued until the teletype went dead. "Cause or location of main fire not yet known. They are pouring water in here and the place is filling with smoke."[10]

The *News-Miner* suffered extensive flooding damage; water destroyed most of its supply of newsprint and disabled its phone system, electrical system, and the four Linotype machines. Starting Sunday morning the staff and the community—and a visiting Linotype machinist—pitched in to help the *News-Miner* dry out and retool. Even though the Linotype operators and their machines had to be shielded from the "rain" that continued to drip upon their heads for the next several days, amazingly enough the paper was able to get to press on time Monday afternoon.

"I want our readers to know," Snedden wrote, "that it was the combined efforts of some wonderful people who made possible the publication of the *News-Miner* today—full size and on deadline. Of course the nucleus of 'operation submarine' [was] the finest group I have ever seen assembled on one newspaper staff, who just 'forgot' to go home and stayed at the plant swimming around to get the job done."[11]

It would take many months to completely repair the Lathrop Building—estimated to cost $500,000—and for the insurance adjusters to pay the newspaper's claim for its damages—estimated at $100,000. "Have just about concluded the matter with the insurance adjusters," Snedden wrote Bartlett in late April, "and it appears that I am still the owner of the newspaper, even if by but a small margin. Seriously, we came out all right in the adjustment, assuming they get around to make out some checks inside the next month or so."[12] The staff heard only too clearly when the reconstruction of the building began in May 1958, so the *News-Miner* began running this page one announcement:

> PLEASE BE PATIENT if you are unable to con-
> tact the News-Miner or Commercial Printing Co.
> business offices by telephone before 5 p.m. during
> the day.
>
> PHONES CANNOT BE HEARD in our offices
> during a good share of the day due to jackham-
> mers tearing out concrete floors and ceilings as the
> Lathrop building is reconstructed following the
> recent fire. Our telephone operators (those who
> have not already lost their minds, that is) are doing
> the best they can under the circumstances ... If
> you don't reach us the first time (or can't be heard
> after you do reach us), please leave your number
> so we can call you back when the jackhammer op-
> erator pauses momentarily, or—PLEASE CALL
> BACK AGAIN.[13]

Even while grappling with the aftermath of the Lathrop Building fire, Snedden found statehood consumed most of his attention. Between mid-February and early July 1958 Snedden was typically camped out in Washington, sometimes for weeks at a time, living out of his suitcase in a small room in the Hotel Washington—a cubbyhole he said was just large enough that he could "change his mind in it"—about four blocks from Stevens's office at the Department of the Interior. During the daytime he was such a fixture in the halls of the government bureaucracy that Stevens said Snedden became "an unofficial employee" of the agency. Many nights he caught a cab out to Stevens's home in Alexandria, where the two men would plot their statehood strategy, working around the glass table in the kitchen until long after dinner and on into the early hours of the morning, drafting editorials, letters, speeches, and position papers to be planted with newspaper columnists, editors, reporters, and friendly congressional staffers. "I have talked to Stevens or Seaton eight or ten times this past week," Snedden wrote Bartlett at one point, "and they are really wheeling along in high gear."[14]

Appointed to the Alaska Statehood Committee by Mike Stepovich, Snedden had to miss his first meeting in Juneau in early March because he thought it a higher priority that he remain in Washington, and Bartlett agreed. "He is doing yeoman work here," Bartlett explained to committee secretary Mildred Hermann, who had complained that Snedden was going to be absent, "of a degree of importance even superior to being at his first Statehood Committee meeting, in my judgment." Because Bartlett's relations with the Tennessee Planners were so strained—he resented Gruening, had little respect for Ralph Rivers, and only truly felt comfortable with Bill Egan—in spite of his partisan differences with the Fairbanks publisher, the delegate often relied upon Snedden and confided in him more than he did his fellow Democrats. In his extensive correspondence files with Alaskans, Bartlett repeatedly singled out Snedden for his prodigious efforts as the territory's number-one citizen lobbyist:

"Bill Snedden is here, working like a Trojan . . ."

"Bill Snedden is here and . . . working actively. He is rather a unique character. One of the most persistent men I have ever met and for that reason and others, mighty effective."

"We owe, no matter what happens, a very considerable debt to Bill Snedden . . ."

"Mr. Snedden, publisher of the *Fairbanks Daily News-Miner*, has been here for over a month and has done some very effective work. He is a Republican and a close friend of Secretary Seaton."

"Bill Snedden is in the outer office. An extraordinary chap by whatever standard of definition one wants to use. He has kept himself very busy here, and usefully so. It is amazing the way he gets around and the contacts he makes."[15]

Thanks to Secretary Seaton, Snedden said he had ready access to "all the key individuals . . . on the Republican side from Vice-President Nixon on down the ladder," most of "whom I could never have reached" otherwise. "In many cases they gave us support because it was well known that Fred Seaton was 100% behind us."[16] As *Time* reported, "working hand in glove with Fred Seaton" Snedden stalked the corridors of the capital in 1958 with his stack of index cards and his little black book. "His influence was everywhere."[17]

Like all effective political operations, both the Republican and Democratic statehood lobbies compiled index cards and research files on all the members of Congress and their staffs, especially on those who were opposed or undecided, in order to formulate the best strategy to approach a particular legislator. For instance, a few of the surviving cards from those compiled by Ernest Bartley for Bartlett and the Tennessee Planners read in part:

Albert, Carl, 3rd Dist.—Oklahoma
Democrat—Attorney. Phi Beta Kappa—Veteran. Albert is definitely for us.

Alexander, Hugh Q., 9th Dist.—North Carolina
Democrat.
Sympathetic, but will probably vote against us because of his southern bias.

Andresen, August H., 1st Dist.—Minnesota.
Republican—Legal education.
Shows some interest in Administration's endorsement. Maybe [urgency] from White House spokesmen would swing him.

Ashmore, Robert T., 4th Dist.—South Carolina
Democrat—Lawyer.
Gave him all the arguments. Friendly to the extent that he won't actively oppose us, but probably won't vote for us.

Auchincloss, James C., 3rd Dist.—New Jersey
Republican businessman—military service. Veteran. Mayor. Very abrupt—very negative—rude.[18]

Snedden recalled that with Seaton's help he created a "list of all staff assistants for members of Congress who were former newspapermen" and could be counted upon as confidential sources. "This proved to be one of our most helpful assets. For all practical purposes, you could say that we had 'spies' planted at virtually all the key strategic spots in our opposition. This worked out so well that I remember Fred Seaton remarked in May 1958 that he believed I had the most efficient 'grapevine operation' Washington had ever seen."

According to Snedden there was also an element of what he bluntly described to George Lehleitner as "practical politics" sometimes bordering on blackmail that was hardly "all nice," but seemed to be essential. "We thoroughly combed the backgrounds of key known opponents, and where indicated did excavating in their own back yard (using for the most part people in the news business whom I employed through the advice of columnists or wire service executives in cases where I did not have a friend upon whom I knew we could rely)."

> When we struck "pay dirt," one of our top news men in Washington would have a casual conversation with the individual involved, mentioning lightly what we had stumbled across, and inquiring what their opinion was of the merits of Alaska statehood. This was a very delicate operation . . . and to be honest about it, a great many times I was greatly concerned over the distinct possibility we would fumble the ball and the whole project would blow up in our face, with possibly some very embarrassing results. However, it worked out nicely, and I am convinced that it undoubtedly was the only way we could have accomplished the job.

When Snedden learned that Nick Bez and Winton Arnold, the top two lobbyists of the salmon packing industry, had come to Washington, he said he "hired a total of four men to keep track of the activities of these two gentlemen and, of course received reports upon whom they called, how long they stayed, and in a couple instances parts of conversations when they talked to people in public." Snedden got hold of two different letters Arnold had sent to key senators on opposite sides of the aisle; the letter to Democratic senators argued that most new states typically elected Republicans, while the letter for Republicans made the case that Alaska was sure to elect nothing but Democrats.

"Fred Seaton, Ted Stevens and myself sat around until very late that evening discussing the incident," Snedden recalled. "We finally decided something had to be done, so Fred Seaton drafted a little covering note, we duplicated the letters and made another mailing—reversing the process" so that the Democrats could see what Arnold was telling the Republicans, and vice versa. This had the desired effect of neutralizing Arnold's message, and he left Washington the following day.[19]

Individually tailored letters were most effective. Snedden drafted a letter for Stepovich that was sent out with the governor's signature to every member of Congress, only needing the appropriate blanks to be filled. The master copy addressed "Dear Congressman" read in part: "Americans now living in Alaska include residents of every state in the Union, including your own state of [congressman's home state]. They miss the privileges formerly enjoyed as full-fledged citizens of [congressman's home state]. Your vote now means much to the future state of Alaska."[20]

Snedden masterminded an effort to have Wally Hickel and Alex Miller, the Republican and Democratic National Committeemen for Alaska, write "partisan" letters to their own party members in Congress telling them what they wanted to hear about which party Alaska would favor. "Wally said he would do so," Snedden told Bartlett, but Alex Miller was more difficult. "Unfortunately, Alex does not have any stationery as the Democratic National Committeeman (he has only had the job about four years!) but he does have some stationery as chairman of the Democratic Central Committee. He said he would use that if the Democratic women would volunteer to type the letters. George [Sundborg] will draft the letter and I hope they will get on the ball within a day or so."[21]

Beyond directly lobbying members of Congress, Snedden's primary campaign was drumming up support among newspaper publishers, wire services, editors, columnists, and reporters. Mobilizing the American press corps, from the biggest metropolitans dailies to the smallest rural weeklies, was the area in which he made his greatest impact on the statehood fight. Though public opinion polls continued to show overwhelming popular support for statehood—especially for Alaska—this mild and superficial interest was broad but not deep and failed to translate into a political movement or a cause célèbre; statehood never came close to rising to the level of a major national issue. The noncontiguous territories remained mentally noncontiguous to Americans, distant places far offshore, out of sight and out of mind, except in the realm of the Deep South, where obsession with keeping the forces of racial integration at bay made the two potential new states a loathsome threat. Elsewhere in the 1950s the status of the two territories evoked scant enthusiasm or controversy, and as a result Alaska and Hawaii seldom broke into the headlines or the national news, except for the annual struggle in Congress over admitting them into the Union. The one time that statehood was prominently featured on television in 1958 proved just how much of a non-story it was.

When CBS newsman Edward R. Murrow dedicated a one-hour special episode of his weekly news program *See It Now* to the statehood question in the spring of 1958, he did so because he claimed there had been "no great public debate" about the statehood issue on the national scene, and that Congress was showing "no sense of urgency" in resolving the matter. "We have presented this report in the hope of starting a small argument about it."

Tackling controversial issues that no one else on television dared to bring up, Murrow's *See It Now* had become "the most widely discussed, most electric, most admired and most rabidly condemned program on television."[22] But the hour-long Alaska-Hawaii statehood show gener- ated neither praise or condemnation; mostly it was just a time filler, and Murrow figured it to be one of his least important programs of the year. "It was what was known in the business as a soft show," according to author and journalist David Halberstam, a "minor, noncontroversial show" nota- ble only "by how ordinary it really was."[23] The few truly memorable parts of the program were the typically irrational conspiracy theories against statehood from men such as Nevada Sen. George "Molly" Malone. While Murrow tried to keep a straight face, the senator explained why opening the door to noncontiguous areas such as Alaska and Hawaii was a step towards totalitarianism. "That's the ultimate objective, Ed. You ought to think this thing through. What are you going to do with Canada in be- tween?. . . . If we took Canada we can take Alaska. . . . If we had the popu- lation of Europe . . . we'd take Mexico in the morning—before breakfast."

In the course of his ranting about Alaska, Senator Malone took pains to add that Washington, D.C., and New York City were hotbeds of "in- ternationalist" treason, and that he felt sorry that Murrow had to work in New York, because "if there's any city in the United States more dangerous to the United States of America than Washington, D.C., it's New York," where the buildings were so high "they can see the nations of Europe and Asia easier than they can those little States west of the Hudson River."

"Well, speaking of New York and what you had to say about New Yorkers," Murrow responded, "would you advocate throwing New York out of the Union?"

"It's been proposed," Malone stated ominously, "but I don't propose it. I just say don't let 'em run the United States."[24]

Struck by the bizarre nature of Malone's comments on the Murrow program, the *Washington Post* reprinted a verbatim transcript of his "choice, noncontiguous words" as an editorial entitled "Malone's Moonshine," noting that Mexicans, Canadians, Europeans, and Asians would be even more confounded by the senator's nonsense than Americans. According to the *Post*, the only doubt about statehood that Malone's remarks had confirmed was the wisdom of granting statehood—to Nevada.[25]

Since the statehood issue as a whole seemed to Murrow to be so lacking in real controversy, except for the complaints of obvious right-wing extremists, he was furious when CBS executives allowed Congressman John Pillion a fifteen-minute "rebuttal." Pillion had protested that "by the trick of association" and his choice of guests Murrow had "willfully created" the impression "that only 'old fuddy-duddies' oppose statehood." Frankly, since it was next to impossible to find young, thoughtful, and articulate opponents of statehood and civil rights, most observers believed Murrow had gone out of his way to showcase the "smokescreen and baloney" of George Malone and those who agreed with him. "If anything," Murrow's biographer wrote, "*See It Now* had bent over backward in presenting the viewpoint of a small minority, mostly old-line diehards in the House and Senate opposing statehood on grounds of race and supposed ideology."[26] In Murrow's view the network's simple-minded decision to open the airwaves to Rep. Pillion under the pretense of balanced reporting was a betrayal of journalistic ethics; if television executives adopted such a spineless posture in response to a man like Pillion, they clearly had no respect whatsoever for the program's editorial integrity. According to Halberstam, Murrow found "the decision to put on a dissent as silly as this on a show as mild as the Hawaii-Alaska one for reasons of self-serving cowardice . . . shattering," and it essentially marked the beginning of the end of Murrow's relationship with CBS.[27]

In his fifteen minutes of televised fame Congressman Pillion's accusations made George Malone sound like James Madison. As he had done for years, Pillion made his standard prediction: granting statehood to Alaska and Hawaii would be an open invitation for "four Soviet agents to take seats in our Congress." After statehood, he said, it would take only one hundred communist organizers to stage a bloodless coup in Alaska. "It will be apple pie to take over its politics. The chain of command, the line of discipline, will be completed from Moscow to . . . Honolulu and Juneau, Alaska, then into our Congress."[28]

The press and the public ignored Malone and Pillion as inconsequential crackpots, in spite of the fact that they were both members of Congress. That these two men—the type likely to argue that water wasn't wet—were the congressional face of the opposition to Alaska statehood highlighted one reason why the issue was not a naturally compelling story for the national press; among the vast majority of reasonable Americans, there was no genuine controversy or fear about Alaska's suitability to join the Union, but neither was there a groundswell of interest demanding it to happen. Out of the estimated fourteen million viewers of *See It Now*, the program generated only a handful of calls and letters in response.[29] With the myriad problems facing the people of the United States in the 1950s, adding a forty-ninth and fiftieth state would never be a critical issue for those in the other forty-eight, even though the public overwhelmingly believed it a good idea. A public opinion poll found only 6 percent of Americans opposed Alaska statehood in 1958. As the leaders of the "six percenters," all that Malone and Pillion really proved, the *Wilmington News* in Delaware suggested, was that the constitution did not require an "intelligence test" to become a member of Congress.[30]

Hard-core Southern opponents—such as Rules Chairman Howard Smith—were more cunning and less gullible. Even if they publicly continued to parrot the party line of "noncontiguity" or the Red menace—and at the last moment the cry of "giveaway"—these were all diversions, hiding as always the unspoken goal of protecting the filibuster and stopping the spread of civil rights legislation. Since Congress was an institution of representative democracy, but not fully democratic itself, the minority could rule until faced with a supermajority, and the challenge was to reach that threshold through an atmosphere of general indifference.

To combat the apathy of the American public and help coerce Congress into action, Snedden pushed newspaper publishers and editors across the country to demand Alaska's admission as a top editorial priority. This was not a hard sell. For years American newspapers had been overwhelmingly in favor of statehood. "Literally, almost every newspaper in the United States has urged editorially that Alaska be made a state," the Alaska Statehood Committee had declared in the early 1950s. "Newspapers which differ widely on almost every other subject of national concern unite in recommending the wisdom and necessity of Alaska statehood." After a "diligent" search the committee reported that outside of Alaska it had discovered "only four newspapers in the entire United States which have expressed doubts about the advisability of Alaska statehood."[31]

The challenge therefore was not to change the minds of editors but simply to encourage them to demand that their local congressmen and senators act on the admission of Alaska with the sense of urgency that was clearly lacking. Following up on a suggestion from Seaton, Snedden contracted with two or three news services that specialized in providing canned news copy for small weekly newspapers across the country, and to turn up the heat on members of Congress he began channeling statehood stories or editorials he had written, edited, or compiled to papers across the 435 congressional districts in the forty-eight states. "It was amazing to me," Snedden recalled in 1968, "to see how much of an impression it made on Congressmen and Senators when I would call at their offices and show them clippings of editorials from newspapers in their home districts." [32] It was no accident, for instance, that in the coal mining country of western Kentucky the *Madisonville Messenger* had an editorial that sounded like it had been ripped out of the editorial page of the *News-Miner*: "It is alien to the spirit of our institutions," the Kentucky paper stated, "to keep a large group of Americans—well over 200,000 now and rapidly increasing—in the second-class citizenship of territorial status." [33]

Between Snedden and George Lehleitner, who was also a boilerplate factory of statehood propaganda, they hardly missed a single newspaper in the entire country. Over the course of his long statehood crusade, Lehleitner may have written more letters to the editor than anyone in history (and he also sent "individualized" letters pushing statehood to every one of the 10,396 Lions Clubs in the United States). In one four-day span he wrote letters promoting Alaska's admission to the *Standard-Times* (Massachusetts), *Daily Iberian* (Louisiana), *Oakland Tribune, Denver Post, Louisville Courier-Journal and Times, New York Herald Tribune, Chicago Tribune, Detroit Free Press, Hartford Courant, St. Petersburg Independent, Jacksonville Journal* (Florida), *Mansfield News-Journal* (Ohio), *McComb Enterprise* (Mississippi), and *Brattleboro Reformer* (Vermont). [34] "When statehood becomes a reality," Lehleitner wrote in one letter that he sent to every daily newspaper in the country, "a substantial part of the credit will properly belong to our American editors, 97% of whom have staunchly supported Alaska's aspirations over the years." [35] Snedden was always particularly grateful that the three competing newspapers in Washington, D.C., the *Star, News,* and *Post and Times-Herald,* all opened their doors to him and were united in favor of admitting Alaska, delivering statehood stories to senators, congressmen, and staff from the bulldog to the final edition three different ways. "We Alaskans think our cause is just," Snedden wrote. "But even the best of causes seldom attract . . . support in the full measure Alaska statehood has received from the nation's press." [36]

The list of newspapers that directly or indirectly got Snedden's message reads like a gazetteer of the United States; according to one source 679 American newspapers endorsed Alaska statehood. To name a random dozen: *Toledo Blade, Los Angeles Herald-Express, Tampa Tribune, Salt Lake City Desert News, Dayton Journal, Cincinnati Enquirer, Norfolk Virginian Pilot, St. Paul Dispatch, St. Louis Post-Dispatch, Milwaukee Journal, Winston-Salem Journal,* and *Seattle Post-Intelligencer.* A dozen of the newspapers that endorsed statehood in Texas alone ranged from the *Victoria Advocate* and the *Sherman Daily Democrat* to the *Dallas Times Herald,* with others in Amarillo, Austin, Beaumont, Corpus Christi, Corsicana, El Paso, Fort Worth, Houston, and San Antonio.[37]

Syndicated newspaper columnists—with the exception of Drew Pearson—were another favorite target of Snedden's, including such popular figures as Roscoe Drummond (208 daily newspapers), Thomas L. Stokes (more than one hundred newspapers), and George Dixon (hundreds of newspapers). Snedden called Dixon, author of the political humor column "Washington Scene," the Groucho Marx of the District of Columbia, who had been deflating stuffed shirts on the Potomac for more than two decades. After Snedden had lunch with Dixon one snowy day in March 1958, Dixon's column was a wry profile of the Fairbanks publisher, the local weather, and the statehood cause.

We were having another of our snowstorms the other day when Mr. C.W. (Bill) Snedden of Alaska, came in. He said he found our Washington weather a little rigorous for a man used to the more clement climate of Fairbanks, but that he was prepared to endure hardship for the good of the cause. The "cause" naturally is statehood for Alaska. Mr. Snedden is prepared not only to brave our winter, but our spring and summer, if necessary to keep crowding the legislative and executive branches of government for the procrastinated project. . . . I asked the man from Fairbanks how he dressed away up there. He fingers his middle-weight overcoat and said, "Just the way I'm dressed now. But I wish I had a heavier one for this Washington weather."

Dixon said that Snedden and other Alaskans were among "the most dedicated non-governmental men this community has seen in a long time," staying here for weeks at a time and "running up tremendous bills, which they can't charge off to anything or anybody else." Publisher Snedden had to run "his *Fairbanks News-Miner* by telephone—and Washington-to-Fairbanks is something more than a dime call."[38]

Dixon was not the only newsman accustomed to political hacks and self-promoters wanting their names in the paper who found the sincerity and sacrifice of the Alaskans refreshing. Snedden went to New York in early April 1958 to pitch the Alaska story to the nerve center of the communications industry, and in a few hectic days he called on nearly half a dozen of the most influential men in the publishing world; he reported back to Bartlett that the members of the Fourth Estate were unanimously supportive.

1. *Life Magazine:* Chief Editorial writer, Jack Jessup, stated after I spent an hour and a half with him "certainly glad you came in to let us know what the status of this matter is, and I am sorry we have procrastinated so long. We will do our best to give you a good assist in the near future."

2. *Time Magazine:* Managing Editor, Roy Alexander, said he would inject a long needle into Chairman Howard Smith in this week's issue, "and we will put the Alaska article we have in the warming oven [about Stepovich] in the fire when it looks like it will do you the most good. . . . We are all for Alaska around here—you know that!"

3. **William Randolph Hearst, Jr.:** Will immediately write a personal letter to Speaker Rayburn mentioning that the Hearst Newspapers are planning a hard-hitting editorial series pointing our that the Democratic party is not making good on its campaign pledges (and Speaker Rayburn's statement last August) in not moving the Alaska statehood bills in the Democratic controlled Congress. If a strong reply is not received by April 14, the Hearst papers will start hitting it editorially. The editorials are being prepared right now. . . .

4. *New York Herald Tribune:* William J. Miller, Chief Editorial Writer, stated he would start another series about April 10 or 12 plugging our cause.

5. *New York Times:* Charles Mertz, Editor of the Editorial Page, said "we will hit it a few licks again in the near future. It is time something was done."[39]

Snedden believed Hearst should have been "given a medal" for all of his help; not only did he throw the Hearst newspaper chain behind statehood, and personally contact both Sam Rayburn and Lyndon Johnson, but he was also invaluable in keeping pressure on Washington Sen. Henry M. "Scoop" Jackson, who would be the floor manager of the statehood bill in the Senate. Fearing that Jackson might backslide, when Snedden learned that the senator was going home to Seattle for a weekend speech, he did his best to put pressure where it would count by ensuring statehood would be on the front page that weekend of Seattle's Hearst paper, the *Post-Intelligencer.*

> I called Bill Hearst, who agreed to change his weekly Sunday front page "Letter from the Editor-in-Chief" editorial which ran in all the Hearst newspapers, so that week it would deal solely with the merits of statehood for Alaska. Then I called the publishers of every newspaper in Washington state and asked them as a personal favor to send a staff man to meet Scoop when he arrived in Seattle and question him as to whether he felt he would be successful in pushing through the Alaska statehood bill. Also made arrangement with the *Life-Time* bureau in Seattle to attend the press conference.

Finally Snedden arranged with the airline on which Senator Jackson was returning to Washington, D.C., to place a copy of the *P-I* with the Alaska story on his reserved seat. Jackson's legislative assistant told Snedden after the trip that Scoop had been impressed and shocked at "how much interest there was in Alaska statehood around home!"[40]

Another newspaper chain that went all out for Alaska statehood was Scripps-Howard, at the time the largest newspaper chain in America with about twenty newspapers and close to three million readers. Walker Stone, the Washington, D.C., editor-in-chief of Scripps-Howard, became a personal mentor for Snedden; he not only proved to be the most passionate advocate for statehood in the American press, but he would repeatedly lobby both Johnson and Rayburn to move the bill along.

Originally from Okemah, Oklahoma, Walker Stone was a long-time supporter of both Ike and LBJ. In May 1945 Stone had been one of the eighteen editors General Eisenhower took to Europe to see first-hand the horror of the liberated concentration camps; he would be one of the first newspapermen Johnson would personally call following the death of President Kennedy. Stone's brother, Ewel, was an Oklahoma-Texas oilman and family friend of the Johnsons, and the senator had often stayed at their Texas home.[41] Due to the Stone family's warm feeling for Johnson, the Scripps chain would push for LBJ's nomination on the Democratic ticket in 1960 and endorse him outright for the presidency in 1964, the first time Scripps-Howard had supported a Democrat for the White House in a quarter-century.[42]

Looking back over the events of 1958, Walker Stone would later claim that in his estimation the Alaska Statehood Act was "by far the most important legislation" of the year, a notable contention since the session would also approve the National Aeronautics and Space Act of 1958 to establish NASA. In July 1958 Stone wrote a "Dear Bob and Bill" letter to Bartlett and Snedden, responding to their letters of thanks to Scripps-Howard for the chain's effort on behalf of statehood. In Stone's opinion Bartlett and Snedden were two sides of the statehood coin. "I trust you will forgive me for responding in one letter. But since your notes are so much alike, since one is a Democrat and the other a Republican, since one is a public official and the other is a newspaper publisher, I think it may be appropriate that I send to you both the same reply."

Stone said he first learned the Senate had approved the statehood bill while traveling behind the Iron Curtain, sitting in the bar of the landmark Bristol Hotel in Warsaw, Poland. "I celebrated in the best sourdough fashion I could, using Polish vodka, which was all that was available." He wished he was thirty years younger. "I genuinely regret that I am not now 20 years old. If I were I would move to Alaska. I happen to have been born in Indian Territory. As a child I saw it develop into the new state of Oklahoma. The people who developed it were the people who came there out of hunger and hope and eagerness to get ahead and building something peculiarly their own."

Stone envisioned Alaska statehood as a giant economic bonanza to the entire United States, the chance to "continue the development of our country along its traditional lines" with a golden opportunity not seen "since the states of California and Texas were added to the Union." He saw the reincarnation of the Old West in the New North and claimed to believe that someday the forty-ninth state might rival New York with "at least" seventeen million people.[43]

Snedden adopted Stone's economic argument in April and May of 1958 in his newspaper educational campaign. Rather than simply pleading the moral case for Alaska's cause, he began to aggressively point out the financial benefit that statehood could mean for the rest of the country, mired as it was in the recession of 1957–1958. This enabled the Alaskans to go on the offense for a change.

"I did not quite buy it at first," Snedden told Bartlett about Stone's suggestion, "but after I chewed on it a while I figured it did make sense, and I have been plugging that angle for the past several weeks. Wish we had started in on it sooner." He thought "we should really bear down on this angle of economic advantage to the United States in our statehood pitch. Many places in the country are hurting, and there are doubtless a few Congressmen who will go along with us on this angle ... that Alaska statehood will do something beneficial for the economy."[44]

In "Take Alaska Off the Ice," the editorial that *Life* published due to Snedden's prodding, the illustrated magazine readily adopted the economic argument. "You may remember I mentioned to you Walker Stone was the father of this idea," Snedden wrote Stevens, "and [at first] I thought it was a little bit too grandiose to be sold. However I emphasized it in my talk to Jack Jessup of *Life*, and he in turn emphasized it pretty strongly in his editorial."[45] The *Life* editorial blasted Howard Smith as "a Virginia gentleman whose impeccable manners include little real respect for either free enterprise or Democracy."

Snedden also tried to have the Hearst Corporation adopt the Walker Stone formula. "Perhaps I am not phrasing it in a delicate manner," he wrote Hearst's top editor, "but it is my considered opinion the most sensitive portions of Mr. American Citizen's anatomy is his hip pocket. If we can convince the average citizen Alaska's development will put more money in his pocket, I believe he will pay a lot more attention than he will to our plea that Alaskans want full citizenship rights."[46]

The most memorable collaboration between Snedden and Stone was an article on April Fools' Day 1958 that took up the entire front page of Stone's home paper, Scripps-Howard's capital city tabloid, the *Washington Daily News*. How it came about was one of Snedden's favorite stories, and the man at the center of the piece was Rules Chairman Howard Smith.

Once the February battle between Knowland and Johnson had stopped any progress on the Senate side of the Capitol, the focus had shifted back again to the House and into the unfriendly hands of Howard Smith of Virginia. To simply call Judge Smith an opponent of Alaska statehood did not do justice to the intensity of his feelings on the subject. He was statehood's nemesis. Bartlett called the Judge "a foe now of statehood, a foe before now, and a foe as long as he will live, who will use every stratagem, every parliamentary device he can conjure up to delay, to impede. And he is as skillful in parliamentary maneuverings as any man in the House of Representatives."[47]

Judge Smith's power was a product of the unique rules of the House, rules of necessity that had evolved since the nineteenth century to bring order out of chaos, enabling hundreds of representatives (421 men and 14 women as of 1957) to deal efficiently with the thousands of bills introduced each session. Unlike Senate rules, those of the House were designed to keep the talking at a minimum. Woodrow Wilson, noted as a political scientist before he entered politics, had written in 1908 that the House of Representatives was fundamentally different in form and character from the Senate, because the House "does not debate. It has not the time. There would be too many debaters, and there are too many subjects to debate. It is a business body and it must get its business done."[48]

The real duty of the House was performed in its dozens of standing committees and subcommittees. "The House sits not for serious discussion," Wilson wrote, "but to sanction the conclusions of its committees . . . Congress in session is Congress on public exhibition, whilst Congress in its committee rooms is Congress at work." As the legendary Speaker Thomas R. Reed explained, the committee was "the eye, the ear, the hand and very often the brains of the assembly." As such the committee system had close to a veto power over proposed legislation. James Bryce put it most eloquently in 1893: "a bill comes before its committee, with no presumption in its favour, but rather as a shivering ghost stands before Minos in the nether world."[49] But even more sweeping was the authority of the Rules Committee, which determined when legislation from all the other committees could or would go forward to the House floor, and decided the terms and conditions under which it could be debated or amended. Though theoretically intended only to regulate the flow of legislative committee traffic to keep bills moving efficiently and ensure the House use its time wisely, the committee of all committees often did more dictating to Congress than directing its traffic, granting rapid approval to bills it preferred, and slowing down or stopping those it wished to kill.

"Favored measures can go forward," a reporter explained, "under restrictions which make meaningful debate and amendments virtually impossible. Unwanted proposals can be pigeonholed forever." Controlling how a bill could be treated was more important than what the bill said. "If you let me write procedure and I let you write substance," one congressman said bluntly, "I'll screw you every time." As Chairman Howard Smith liked to say, "My people did not send me here just to be a traffic cop."[50]

Since the 1930s a coalition of conservative Republicans and Southern Democrats had controlled the twelve-member Rules Committee; as the Chairman of the Rules Committee in the 1950s, and the "brains" behind the Southern Democratic caucus in the House, Howard Smith repeatedly frustrated moderates and liberals of both parties by his uncanny ability to sink their legislation. An unabashed apologist for segregation, and almost always outnumbered, he was never outgeneraled, and no Virginian since Robert E. Lee was more cunning in protecting and defending the traditions of the Old South against long odds. A twenty-seven-year veteran of Congress, he owed his chairmanship to long seniority, not to the Speaker of the House, and in the late 1950s he found himself increasingly at odds with the more moderate policies of Sam Rayburn, brazenly defying the Texas lawmaker supposedly in charge of the House of Representatives. "The House substitute for the Dixie filibuster," said a longtime congressional observer from the South, "is Howard Smith." For good reason, in the generation before the governmental reforms of the 1960s and 1970s curbed its power, the Rules Committee was sometimes called the "third House of Congress," and Smith was proud that he had personally "killed, watered down or postponed more progressive legislation than any other Congressman in modern times."[51]

Howard Smith never made any secret of his intense hatred of Alaska statehood, largely because he knew adding a forty-ninth state might make it impossible to stop the creep of federal civil rights legislation. When the topic of letting the statehood bill escape from his Rules Committee came up in early 1958, Bartlett said the Judge's demeanor was a sight to behold: his "gasket bulged and swelled and almost broke under the strain. He foresees the end of the Republic; the doom of civilization as we know it, if Alaska is ever let in!"[52]

Smith would openly admit in May 1958 that he had been staging a one-man filibuster on the statehood bill for almost a full year. He swore it was his "dead body" bill and vowed he would never give in. On the morning of March 31 Snedden boarded an elevator in which he bumped into Judge Smith, who was chatting with another congressman. As they rode together Snedden was furious to hear the Judge repeat his "my dead body" claim about the statehood bill, but realized he could not say a word. Shortly afterward he had lunch with Walker Stone and told him what he had overheard in the elevator. "When we left the restaurant Walker took along one of the cloth napkins upon which he had made a dummy of the next day's front page of the *Washington News*."[53]

The layout was a unique slice of newspaper history. In the upper right-hand corner was a tiny one-quarter-column mug shot of Howard Smith; underneath the little picture of Smith was a row of eleven half-column mug shots of the other members of the Rules Committee, and below this was one large group portrait of hundreds of members of the House of Representatives in session. In descending order the three headlines/captions and pictures grew larger:

"THIS LITTLE MAN"
STALLS A VOTE BY THESE 11 MEN . . .
AND DEFEATS THE WILL OF THIS ENTIRE BODY . . .

Across the bottom of the page was Stone's editorial decrying the many months that Smith had been stalling the statehood bill, defying the will of the House, the will of the Senate, and the will of the American people, simply because he knew it would win if it ever came to a fair vote. Even worse, Stone argued, Smith was depriving the country of a "lasting spur to the economy comparable to the opening of the West."

"Congress frantically hunts a plan to spend billions and coax back the boom," he wrote. "But it can't find the time for a ready-made plan which historically always has been a stimulant to prosperity, and which wouldn't cost the taxpayers anything.

"This is the bill to grant statehood to Alaska."[54]

Naturally the "Little Man" editorial—copies of which Snedden and Lehleitner sent to everyone in Congress and to newspapers throughout the country—infuriated Judge Smith, but he would never relent in his opposition to statehood, no matter how intense the pressure. Snedden believed—as did Lehleitner—that only one man in Washington had the clout to make Smith move, or to pry the bill out of the Rules Committee: Sam Rayburn. Therefore, the real target of their lobbying effort in the press was to force the Speaker of the House to keep his promise to support Alaska's entry. Unlike the lambasting of Howard Smith, the approach to Rayburn was always respectful, never criticizing him directly but simply mentioning his promise to Bartlett in 1957 and praising him as a man of his word.

Lehleitner called Bob Estabrook of the *Washington Post and Times Herald*, asking that he "editorialize along the lines of reminding his readers—and the Speaker—of the unequivocal pledge" to support statehood in August 1957, a pledge that "would undoubtedly be redeemed by Mr. Rayburn because of his reputation for integrity." Estabrook not only agreed to put Rayburn on the spot but also said he "would simultaneously make a pitch for subsequent action by Lyndon Johnson."

After Estabrook's column on the Speaker and the Majority Leader appeared, Lehleitner suggested that Snedden, Bartlett, and the Tennessee Planners mail copies "to every influential editor and commentator" they knew in the country, asking them to apply "similar pressure" to Rayburn and Johnson. "In so doing, however," he wrote privately to Snedden and Bartlett, "may I suggest that we not tell the others [the Tennessee Planners and the editors] how Bob Estabrook's editorial came about; I believe it would be much more effective for each of them . . . to labor under the impression that it was completely spontaneous."[55]

Along these lines the *Washington Post* targeted the two Texas lawmakers. First Rayburn: "Last summer Speaker Rayburn stated unequivocally that he would support statehood for Alaska. Mr. Rayburn is known as a man of his word; but time is awasting." And then Johnson: "It would be encouraging if Majority Leader Johnson, who has shown such competence and responsibility on other measures, would voice his intention to assist in redeeming this pledge of both parties."[56]

The goal was to make Alaska politically important enough so that if statehood failed again, Rayburn and Johnson would be personally and politically embarrassed. To appease the moderate and liberal wings of the Democratic Party, the Speaker would have to find a way to force the bill out of the Rules Committee. "'Mr. Sam' is known as a man of his word," Snedden wrote in the *News-Miner*, "and is all powerful in the Congress."[57] But despite the public perception that the Speaker of the

House could simply order Smith to do as he was told, that was hardly the truth. Over decades the committees of Congress under the rigid seniority system tended to evolve into personal fiefdoms, none more powerful or independent than the Rules Committee. The hallmark of Rayburn's long tenure as Speaker—his seventeen years in the chair remains the longest in history—was his conciliatory but persuasive style of give and take. If "The Buck Stops Here" was the essence of Truman, "To Get Along, Go Along" was pure Rayburn. "The old day of pounding on the desk and giving people hell is gone," he said in 1950. "A man's got to lead by persuasion and kindness."[58]

But Smith had no desire to get along and no intention to go along with Sam Rayburn about the Alaska bill. A way around Howard Smith would have to be found, because no matter what anyone said, he would not be moved.

17

The Last Resort

Unable after eleven months to muster the necessary seven votes to pass the Alaska statehood bill out of Howard Smith's House Rules Committee, only two unlikely options were left. A majority vote of the full House could pull a bill from a reluctant committee, but such "discharge petitions" were almost never successful; only twice in the twentieth century were bills advanced in this manner able to become law.[1] The other remote possibility was to bypass the Rules Committee entirely. This was a last resort and could only be done by treating the statehood bill as "privileged" legislation, a designation that enabled a handful of standing committees to send certain types of urgent legislation—including tax measures, appropriations, and "matters of special import to the House as an institution or to the federal government"—immediately to the House floor.[2]

"All bills are not created equal," one student of Congress has written, and bills with privilege automatically go to the head of the line.[3] Statehood admission bills from the Interior Committee were eligible for this special status; however, since this extraordinary step had not been taken since the debates over Arizona and New Mexico half a century before, no one was eager to pursue it. Furthermore this procedure would be "cumbersome," Bartlett explained, because as a "privileged bill" under House rules "theoretically every member of the House would have the right to speak one hour on the bill," and it could therefore "tie up the House for an entire Congressional session."[4]

"I am sure all three of us will agree," Lehleitner wrote Snedden and Bartlett, "that it would be much, much better to bring the bill to the floor through the orderly procedure of the Rules Committee" rather than to try to force it through as "privileged legislation," since this would be a "measure of last resort" and "almost surely cost us some badly needed House votes."[5] Approving the bill as privileged would clearly be done for only one purpose, to avoid the Rules Committee, and some House members were bound to oppose the tactic on the principle that a bill did not deserve to pass if it could not do so by normal procedures.

By late April the public pressure on Rayburn in the press seemed to be working. On April 23 Bartlett, Clair Engle, and Leo O'Brien meet with the Speaker in his office. The mood was somber. "We had a very frank talk with him," Bartlett told Snedden the following day, "with Clair and Leo saying everything that needed to be said." O'Brien argued that even if it were now too late for the statehood bill to make it all the way through Congress, he hoped for at least a vote on the House floor so "the mourners . . . have a chance to see the body." For his part the Speaker admitted that he "has less than a consuming enthusiasm for statehood but he had committed himself for statehood for Alaska and that he intended to go ahead."

Just how aggressively he would go ahead was not decided. "Some discussion was had on bringing the bill to the floor under privileged status but no firm decisions were reached on that. At least I don't think there were but on account of what transpired later, perhaps . . . I am wrong."

Upon leaving the Speaker's office they found the *News-Miner's* Washington correspondent, Bob Smith, "waiting for a story," and Representative Engle spoke for the record as chairman of the Interior Committee. Bartlett relayed the back story of the interview to Snedden, which was never made public. According to the delegate, what Engle told Smith about their closed-door session with the Speaker was not how he remembered it. But he much preferred Engle's version anyway.

Engle told the reporter he had warned Rayburn that unless the Rules Committee acted "fairly promptly" on the statehood bill "he would ask for recognition for the privileged status move and that the Speaker had told him the recognition would be granted. For the life of me, I can't remember hearing the Speaker say that. . . . Anyway, I am glad Clair said what he did."[6]

Even if Engle had invented the story about Rayburn's intent to approve a privileged motion, Bartlett told Snedden there was "much more powerful" evidence that perhaps the Speaker was finally living up to his promise about the bill. The delegate said a "friend of mine who properly demanded anonymity" had been eavesdropping on a private conversation between Rayburn and Howard Smith in the Speaker's lobby next to the House floor.

"According to the story told me, Rayburn was positive as could be in his demand that this 'filibustering' in the Rules Committee be ended. He demanded a rule. . . . He wanted action. Smith allowed that he might be compelled to tell the prospective witnesses they couldn't be heard because of the Speaker's insistence on action."

"'I don't care what you tell them,' Rayburn is reported to have said. 'What I want is an end to the stalling.'"[7]

"RAYBURN PRESSES STATEHOOD" was the *News-Miner* banner the following day with the prediction that Rules Chairman Smith would soon "capitulate to the speaker's demand." After a few more days of showy opposition to Rayburn's "steamroller tactics," it was generally expected that finally, like old Pharaoh, Judge Smith would let the statehood bill go.[8] In the culture of Congress, so dominated by precedent and tradition, ripping a bill from the grip of the Rules Committee and taking it up under "preferential status" was such a drastic alternative, a violation of a cardinal principle of House organization, that hardly anyone believed it would prove to be necessary. The threat alone should have sufficed as leverage against the Rules Committee.

But it proved to be a mistake to underestimate the obstinacy of Howard Smith. "I am not interested in making progress," he boasted. Refusing to buckle under to "threats" from the House leadership, he said he was "perfectly willing to hear this bill hour after hour and day after day . . . I am not going to hurry it any."[9] This continued stalling put Rayburn in an embarrassing double bind. Not only was he unable to bring the statehood bill to the House floor, but also the national spectacle of the dictatorship of the Rules Committee, holding up a supposed Democratic priority, highlighted the breach in the Democratic Party between the South and the rest of the country. If the South ruled the Democratic Party, the Democratic Party would never again have a chance of ruling the country, and Johnson's hopes for the White House would be dashed. Due to Chairman Smith's refusal to heed the wishes of the majority of House members, he was the perfect foil for moderates, liberals, and the statehood cause. While Rayburn had never intended to become a champion of Alaska's candidacy, Smith's intransigence had left him no alternative; the more resistance that came from the Judge, the more force was applied by the Speaker.

In a biting editorial about ending Smith's nearly yearlong stall on
the statehood bill, the *Washington Post* praised Speaker Rayburn's commitment to push it past the Rules Committee as privileged legislation, if
necessary, as a "beam of hope" to reasonable Americans wishing to see an
end to this legislative charade. "Representative Smith could save himself
humiliation by ending the tyranny of the Rules Committee before the
issue is forced. Lest Mr. Smith, whose behavior sometimes seems to emulate that of Napoleon, be under some confusion, when Napoleon said, 'I
am the state' he was not talking about Alaska."[10]

The crucial day of decision for Alaska turned out to be May 21, 1958,
one year—short of two days—since Leo O'Brien's subcommittee had
passed the statehood bill. In order to bypass the Rules Committee, the
full House, under the guidance of the leadership, reluctantly prepared to
resolve itself into the Committee of the Whole—a parliamentary maneuver by which all 435 members comprised a single committee—to consider the Alaska statehood bill as privileged legislation. Bypassing the Rules
Committee in this manner was not an option that anyone preferred; the
move was sure to rile conservatives, who might otherwise have been supportive. Seaton acknowledged that going the privileged route would cost
statehood supporters fifteen or twenty votes. "Whether we can regain
part or all of that lost voting power remains to be seen." O'Brien assured his colleagues of his respect for both the Rules Committee and the
traditions of the House. Bringing up the bill as a privileged matter "was
not an impertinent gesture on the part of those who favor statehood for
Alaska" but a desperate measure "of last resort." When a reporter asked
"if pro-statehood forces were not setting sail on some 'uncharted' parliamentary waters" by trying to pull the bill from the Rules Committee,
O'Brien admitted that it was a radical step, but necessary because the
only alternative was being "put to death" at the hands of the high execu-
tioner, Howard Smith.

The congressional leaders of both parties thought, even if the privileged maneuver succeeded, the bill was likely to fail anyway. In advance of
the debate, both Speaker Rayburn and Republican Minority Leader Joe
Martin of Massachusetts told the press that they were "doubtful" the bill
would pass. Rayburn's exquisite feel for the temper of the House membership made him an extraordinarily effective Speaker, and he said he

detected "less enthusiasm" for statehood than in previous years. Even if the House agreed to take up the bill as privileged and voted to debate it, the Speaker warned Clair Engle that a majority of House members would likely be ready to kill it off immediately by voting to recommit it to the Interior and Insular Affairs Committee. Those backing statehood were in the familiar but uncomfortable role of the underdog. As Bartlett told Bob Smith, "I'd rather be in the position of the overdog," but at least thanks to Rayburn's promise they would have a chance to fight it out on the House floor.[11]

A few minutes past noon on May 21, with Sam Rayburn sitting in the chair, Colorado Democrat Wayne Aspinall—filling in for the absent Interior Committee Chairman Clair Engle—announced that by "direction of the Committee on Interior and Insular Affairs and pursuant to rule XI, clause 20," he moved that the House resolve itself into the Committee of the Whole to consider HR 7999 providing for the admission of the state of Alaska into the Union. Missouri Democrat Clarence Cannon, the chairman of the Appropriations Committee, immediately objected on the grounds that the bill contained elements that could not be heard under privileged status and therefore must be returned to the Rules Committee for approval. This was the opening shot in the historic showdown between Chairman Smith and Speaker Rayburn, and before the 386 members present in the "hushed and packed chamber," the fate of Alaska statehood hung in the balance.

Howard Smith was often reckoned to be one of the leading parliamentary strategists in Washington, D.C., but his ally Rep. Clarence Cannon, who would be Rayburn's principal adversary in this procedural debate, knew the history of the rules of the House of Representatives as well as any man who ever lived. Before winning election to Congress in 1923, Cannon had held the position of clerk at the Speaker's Table (the post later known as the House Parliamentarian) and had authored *A Synopsis of the Procedure of the House* (1918), *Procedure in the House of Representatives* (1920), and *Cannon's Procedure* (1928); the five-volume set of House precedents he compiled is still known as *Cannon's Precedents*, a compilation of the major House precedents from 1908 to 1936.

Cannon called the Alaska statehood legislation "iniquitous" and "reprehensible" from a parliamentary standpoint, "loaded with unprivileged matter" on "page after page." As he reminded his colleagues, "One unprivileged matter in a privileged bill destroys the privilege of the entire bill."

"Therefore, it follows that being unprivileged—which no one will deny—and not being necessary to the act—which no one will affirm—they destroy the privilege of this bill."[12]

Cannon had made a strong case. Under normal conditions having a man of his stature and legendary expertise object to a bill on parliamentary grounds would be a fatal blow, but fortunately there was one individual on the House staff as equally well versed in the rules of the game, Rayburn's indispensable "big brain man," Lewis Deschler, the House Parliamentarian since 1927. As of 1958 the House of Representatives was ruled by 169 years of precedents—estimated to total more than twenty thousand official opinions—and the reasoning behind allowing the statehood bill to reach the floor as privileged legislation was a momentous twist of an old procedure made possible by Deschler's expert knowledge of House history. Once described in the *New York Times* as "the only man who really knows the thousands of rules and procedures that govern what 435 Representatives may or may not do, and how," the Speaker's right-hand man devoted "long hours of study and research" before May 21 to prepare the memorandum Rayburn read in the House to overrule Smith and Cannon and justify privilege.

The record was clear that other statehood acts—including those of Arizona, New Mexico, Oklahoma, and Wyoming—had been considered privileged, but the core of Deschler's opinion was that despite the contention of his distinguished predecessor Clarence Cannon, the incidental "unprivileged matter" in the Alaska bill was not fatal to privilege as would normally be the case: "where the major feature of the bill relates to the admission of a new state, lesser provisions incidental thereto do not destroy its privilege . . . and therefore, for these and other reasons, the Chair overrules the point of order."[13]

Deschler wrote many historic opinions during his forty-six years as House Parliamentarian; he was responsible for selecting the exact day that beer began to flow with the end of Prohibition—April 7, 1933—and he sketched the procedures that led to the declaration of war in 1941, but it was his memo on statehood privilege for Alaska that he cherished above all. When he died in 1976, it was singled out for recognition in his obituary, and back in 1959 he had decided to put a copy of it in the foundation of the U.S. Capitol itself. As Deschler explained to Bartlett in 1965, "I thought the opinion I prepared was of sufficient historical importance, not only to Alaska but to the Union, that . . . in the cornerstone of the extension of the east front of the Capitol, I inserted . . . an extract from the *House Journal* containing the Speaker's decision together with my own explanatory remarks regarding it." The cornerstone was laid on July 4, 1959, by law the first day the forty-nine-star flag could legally be flown over the Capitol; Deschler's note inside the cornerstone reads:

> This star came into the Union primarily through a decision of Mr. Speaker Sam Rayburn of Texas, when on May 21, 1958, he made a decision in the House of Representatives which permitted the House to consider H.R. 7999.... Under the political and parliamentary conditions that prevailed in the Eighty-fifth Congress, it would have been impossible to have considered the Alaskan Statehood Bill had he not so decided. And, if that decision has not been made by Speaker Rayburn ... the flag flying over the Capitol today would contain but forty-eight stars.[14]

Rayburn's historic decision on the Alaska bill—which earned a detailed discussion in Chapter 17 of *Deschler's Precedents*, the parliamentarian's massive compilation of the "most significant rulings of the chair" from 1936 to 1974—permitted the full House of Representatives to decide if it should consider the statehood bill or not. This would be the first of many crucial votes the bill would face in the next seven days. When the roll was called the House had agreed to debate the statehood question by the surprisingly wide margin of forty-five votes, 217–172.[15] It was a stunning victory, but the *News-Miner* warned that "a long and bitter fight is in prospect." As C. P. Trussell reported in the *New York Times*, "The opponents of the Alaska bill, beaten in the initial vote, appeared to have many tactical plans in reserve."

During the opening rounds of the floor debate that long afternoon, Smith and his supporters interrupted the proceedings four times with quorum calls, a standard dilatory tactic that could consume anywhere from twenty-five to thirty-five minutes or more per roll call. Refusing to consent to a time limit on the bill, they left open the theoretical threat of more than four hundred hours of talking yet to come.[16] The fight on the House floor was certain to be tough because the conservative coalition of Southern Democrats and eastern Republicans had once again materialized to try to stop statehood.[17] Seventy-two Democrats had opposed bringing up the bill; all but five of those—four from Massachusetts and one from New York—were from the South. Of the one hundred Republicans who had voted no, all but five—four from California and one from Idaho— were from the East.[18] Minority Leader Joe Martin of Massachusetts led the Republican opposition. Angered at the exclusion of Hawaii, Martin had announced in advance that the Republican leadership in the House would oppose the legislation, and this had so alarmed House Republicans backing Alaska, including Pennsylvania Congressman John Saylor, he appealed to Seaton for help from the White House.

Only hours before the May 21 parliamentary battle between Rayburn and Cannon, Fred Seaton and two senior administration aides had gone to the Oval Office to get help from the president. The meeting lasted just eleven minutes, but that was more than enough time to demonstrate yet again that Fred Seaton was the man at the helm of the Eisenhower administration's Alaska strategy, and it was his responsibility to keep the president on course. A White House "diary memo" written for the files immediately after the meeting revealed just how resistant Eisenhower privately continued to be on the subject of bringing Alaska into the Union, especially without Hawaii.

"The President is not enthusiastic about the legislation," Ike's administrative aide Jack Z. Anderson wrote in the confidential meeting summary. "He finds it hard to understand why the House should act first on Alaska rather than Hawaii which is preferable as far as he is concerned. I explained that we were confronted with a condition and not a theory as the Alaska Statehood Bill was ready for consideration, whereas, the Hawaii bill has not even been reported by the Committee on Interior and Insular Affairs." According to a press report that appeared ten days later in the *New York Times*, Ike had "listened sympathetically" to Representative Martin's reasons for opposing the bill, and had decided that he would support the Minority Leader's campaign to block Alaska on the grounds of justice for Hawaii. At this point Seaton rose to the challenge. In his "earnest appeal" he reminded the president of the GOP's commitment to back Alaska, and pleaded that the linkage should not be used as the grounds to delay either one or the other. Furthermore, as Seaton had said at an earlier conference with the president, "Republicans are in a better situation currently in Alaska than in Hawaii," due in no small part to Snedden's promotion of the party and Stepovich's popularity, so there were clearly practical political reasons to move ahead that Martin and his allies did not appreciate.

One of Eisenhower's traits as a leader in both military and civilian life was his reliance on his most trusted advisors, and his willingness to delegate and to listen, even when the advice ran against his grain. As he had many times before, he begrudgingly agreed to follow Seaton's lead, telling the interior secretary to announce that the president "stands squarely behind" the 1956 Republican Party platform supporting the admission of both territories. Putting the best gloss possible on this rather tepid promise, Seaton relayed Ike's stance to the press as an unqualified endorsement of Alaska, neglecting any mention of Hawaii as the quid pro quo Eisenhower truly wanted: "President Eisenhower has authorized Republican supporters of Alaska statehood to take the floor and tell the House he wants the statehood bill passed."[19]

As the debate proceeded over the following week Seaton would not personally be on hand to reassure House members of the administration's support; unfortunately, both the secretary and Snedden were in Fairbanks. Never imagining that the statehood bill would be heard so late in the session, months earlier Seaton had agreed to be the commencement speaker at the graduation ceremony for the University of Alaska in Fairbanks at the end of May, and therefore he had to leave Washington the day after the debate began in the House. This meant he and Snedden were forced to keep tabs on events in the House via long distance and left Ted Stevens, as Snedden phrased it, in charge of Seaton's "big sector of the battle line" between Congress and the administration.[20]

All the top Republicans in the House, including Martin and his two chief lieutenants, former Minority Leader Charley Halleck of Indiana and Republican Whip Les Arends of Illinois, were actively fighting the bill. According to the *Washington Post*, Arends "summoned Republicans committed to statehood into the cloakroom and threatened them with political excommunication if they did not join the House Republican leadership in opposing the measure." Thus it was up to John Saylor, ranking Republican on the Interior Committee, to coordinate the GOP effort with the White House staff. Saylor reassured his colleagues on the House floor that he had been authorized by Seaton to say Eisenhower supported the bill, even though the president remained publicly silent. Saylor forwarded a list of twenty-two congressmen he wanted the White House to lobby. "I feel certain if the President will make personal contact with the following Republican members, the bill will pass the House." Though the president made no calls himself, his staff contacted those Saylor had targeted, while representatives from the Interior Department lobbied an additional nineteen congressmen.[21]

The statehood forces appeared to be doing all that was possible, knowing that the final showdown was going to come within six or seven days. Bartlett said the weeklong marathon statehood trial in the Committee of the Whole was like nothing he had ever experienced, and historians would "have to go quite a way back to discover when a bill has been under consideration for such a prolonged period. From one Wednesday to the next probably sets some kind of record." By the end of the eighth day Bartlett and his staff were exhausted. "I told Vide every night on going home at the conclusion of a session on statehood, I simply couldn't understand why I was so tired when I had done nothing but sit there all afternoon. But there is, indeed, a very considerable emotional strain which translates itself into physical weariness."[22]

Under a unanimous-consent agreement general debate on the bill expired on Monday, May 26, at five p.m., with the following Tuesday reserved for discussion of amendments under the five-minute rule, and a final roll call expected to be held on Wednesday, May 28. During debate over amendments on Tuesday afternoon Howard Smith's charge of "giveaway" prompted fierce discussions about how many millions of acres the state should receive. As House Speaker during the Carter administration a generation later, Massachusetts Democrat Thomas P. "Tip" O'Neill would help orchestrate passage of the Alaska National Interest Lands Conservation Act of 1980, which placed more federal land in conservation units than any act in American history. During the statehood debate O'Neill blasted the "giveaway" of millions of acres of federal property in Alaska that rightfully "belongs to the people who live in my District and who live in your District. . . . I do not think we have any right to delegate to a handful of people in a legislature in Alaska the authority to give away property that belongs to the people of America." Equally hot about the statehood "giveaway" was Texas Democrat Walter E. Rogers. Arguing that the Alaska land grant should be no more than twenty-one million acres—instead of the 102 million figure then on the floor—he chided the attitude of colleagues that seemed to be "Well, we are destroying the Republic so we might as well do a good job of it and give away all the land—we do not need it anyway." To California Democrat Chester E. Holifield, hearing traditional "state's righters" hypocritically wanting to deny the future state an adequate land base was "an amazing demonstration of how you can ride both ends of a horse going in different directions at the same time."[23]

At this point, as the statehood supporters were debating among themselves how much land the state should be given, Rogers, working in tandem with Howard Smith, moved that the Committee of the Whole— or at least the 250 of the 435 members who were present—recommend striking the "enacting clause" of the statehood bill, a common method of killing a bill without having to vote it up or down, by simply eliminating the italicized words that prefaced every bill in Congress: "*Be it enacted by the Senate and the House of Representatives. . . .*" According to Rogers he had yet to hear "one sound reason why Alaska should be granted statehood," and he alleged those supporting statehood had fallen victim to communist propaganda.

> Much has been said as to what the Russians might think about it if we do not grant Alaska statehood. . . . I do not care what the Russians think. . . . We could not please the Russians short of giving them complete domination of the world, and everyone in the sound of my voice knows it. It is high time we stopped listening to the propaganda from the Kremlin and started assuming our own responsibilities and taking care of our own business.

The move to delete the enacting clause had caught statehood supporters off guard, and O'Brien made it clear what was at stake. "In a very few seconds," he said, the American people would learn if the House was truly representative or not. "We will either accept or reject the overwhelming demand of all the American people and the solemn pledges of our two great parties that we enrich and strengthen ourselves by admitting this great new state of Alaska into the Union. . . . Vocal opposition has come largely and obviously from a handful of Members, distinguished though they may be, most of whom would oppose statehood if everything to which they have objected would be deleted from the bill."

As O'Brien's five minutes ran out he ended with a sea-to-shining-sea recitation of east and west, north and south. "When the roll is called on this motion, let us hear again in this Chamber, as we have during recent days, strong voices of men and women from Maine to California, from Vermont to Oregon, from New Jersey to Louisiana, from New York to

Texas, from Washington to Ohio, and from New Hampshire to Florida. Our people want this bill and we are their representatives."[24]

In truth, no strong voices would be heard on the motion as it was a "teller vote," an archaic and secretive House procedure—subsequently abolished—originally developed in England to protect the voting records of members of parliament from the wrath of the king. In a teller vote representatives voted with their feet by walking down the center aisle to either side of the chamber past one of the two designated "tellers" or head counters, in this case Rogers and O'Brien, except no names were recorded. Since teller votes protected the identities of individual congressmen, they typically drew fewer members than recorded votes, but were likewise more reflective of genuine feelings; as the members slowly filed through the chamber going left or right, the numbers were a shocking defeat to the statehood camp. By this advisory vote of 144 to 106, the Committee of the Whole recommended the full House strike the enacting clause and kill the Alaska statehood bill. And as if to kill the bill a second time to ensure it stayed dead, Rep. Rogers—on the instructions of Howard Smith—introduced a preferential motion to recommit the bill to the Committee on Interior and Insular Affairs.

When a reporter asked Smith why attempt to recommit the bill, since deletion of the enacting clause would suffice to stop it, "[h]e answered only that it was 'less bloody,'" or perhaps would appear so to constituents who did not understand how Congress worked. Sending a bill back to committee for more work could be portrayed as a positive step, rather than the death sentence it truly was.[25] Smith might have said, as he had once lectured reporters about his anti–civil rights strategy in 1957: "I am inclined to follow the course most likely to result in no bill. Am I making myself clear?"[26] The only saving grace for those who favored statehood was that by prior agreement a recorded vote in the full House to decide the motion could not be held until the following day, because Tuesday was election day in Kentucky, requiring that delegation to be absent.[27]

The lead of Bob Smith's next *News-Miner* dispatch from Washington began: "Alaskan statehood hung precariously in the balance last night as the House of Representatives retired to sleep on a proposal to kill the bill off." Bartlett called it a "fateful and terribly disturbing day." His analysis was that they had been outmaneuvered by Howard Smith, whose more disciplined troops had been "concentrated on the floor waiting for a vote while the supporters were scattered." Publicly, Bartlett tried to remain confident: "It's going to be a close squeeze, but I still think we've got the votes."[28] Privately, he agreed with O'Brien and Ted Stevens that the situation was grim, and along with all the other statehood supporters—including Fred Seaton by long-distance telephone—they would spend much of the night trying to round up votes among the 185 members who had been absent. This was the night that Stevens told Snedden on the phone to go down to St. Mathew's Church in Fairbanks and pray, because they were "fighting to save ourselves now instead of to get the bill through."[29]

Even if the bill survived the first test vote in the Wednesday session, if Howard Smith could manage to delay final consideration until Thursday or later, he would again have the upper hand. Wednesday was typically the preferred day for consideration of most controversial legislation, because almost invariably midweek saw the highest rate of attendance. Many congressmen from the east were regularly no-shows on Mondays and Fridays—the so-called "Tuesday-to-Thursday Club"—but due to the upcoming Memorial Day weekend, absenteeism was expected to be higher than normal starting Thursday. Theoretically Smith could kill the statehood bill with as few as 109 votes—half of the House quorum of 218—and with the combination of conservative Republicans and Southern Democrats, he clearly had more than that number at his command. Smith could defeat the majority if enough of them neglected to show up to vote.[30]

Ninety minutes before the noontime session in the House was set to begin on Wednesday, President Eisenhower held a regularly scheduled news conference at the White House, where *New York Herald Tribune* columnist Roscoe Drummond—who had been a fruitful contact for Snedden—assumed he would have to write the obit on the statehood bill that afternoon. Drummond asked for Eisenhower's reaction to the pending move by the Democratic-Republican House coalition apparently poised to kill Alaska statehood once again: "Mr. President, if the Alaskan statehood bill is defeated today, as appears rather likely in light of the adverse vote yesterday, what do you feel the American people should think about the integrity of party platforms?"

Ike responded with his standard Hawaiian-Alaskan one-two punch: "with both platforms urging statehood for both" Hawaii and Alaska "we should carry out the pledges of our platforms." In regards to the GOP statehood commitment to Hawaii and Alaska Eisenhower said, "I feel a duty."[31]

While Ike had consistently maintained that Hawaii was a better candidate than Alaska, and that ideally the statehood question should have been resolved as a package deal including both territories, the president's willingness to again publicly go along with Seaton and not oppose Alaska by itself surely helped a few hours later when the House took up the pending motion to recommit—and therefore kill—the statehood bill. In the crowded chamber that afternoon, with attendance 50 percent more than the day of the teller defeat on Tuesday, the House turned back the recommit motion by 174–199. Following this display of pro-statehood strength, the House quickly disposed the pending recommendation to strike the enacting clause on a simple voice vote.

Two major amendments would be debated and passed that afternoon: a reduction of the state's public land grant from 182 to 102.5 million acres, and temporarily requiring continued federal control of fish and wildlife—to appease conservationists and Seattle fishing interests—until the secretary of the interior determined the new state was ready to take over. Seaton had assured Bartlett he would make that ruling expeditiously.[32]

By that stage it had long since become apparent to Smith and everyone in the chamber who could count that the statehood bill was going to pass the House. Shortly before the final vote, Smith offered a technical amendment to remove a phrase indicating all new states must join the Federal Reserve System, because it might imply there would be an additional new state—Hawaii—in the future.[33] O'Brien's sense of humor could not be contained any longer, when to Smith's surprise he accepted the amendment as friendly. As soon as the clerk read Smith's proposed amendment and the Virginia Democrat rose to defend it, the encounter played out as follows:

> MR. SMITH: Mr. Chairman—
>
> MR. O'BRIEN: Mr. Chairman, will the gentleman yield?
>
> MR. SMITH: I yield.
>
> MR. O'BRIEN: The committee will accept that amendment.
>
> MR. SMITH: I want to make a speech.
>
> MR. O'BRIEN: If the gentleman will yield, that is what I was afraid of.

Even Smith could see the humor. O'Brien, he said, "took all the wind out of me" and, admitting defeat, he sat down for the last time. All were ready for the final vote except dead-ender Rep. Pillion of New York, who made another recommit motion, hopeless as it may have been, which lost 172–202, an even larger margin than the crucial vote at the start of the debate.[34]

At that point all the talking was over and the question before the House was the passage of the Alaska statehood bill; Rep. Rogers of Texas asked for the yeas and nays. Having been shunted aside to legislative Siberia for so many years, it was fitting that Alaska could emerge only after a final roll call vote. Of all the symbols of how slow Congress could be in adapting to change, the manual roll call vote in the House of Representatives—largely unmodified since the inaugural session in 1789—was the most obvious. By the 1950s, having a clerk call out 435 names for every recorded vote, a practice that would have been familiar to Benjamin Franklin, was a costly anachronism. Electronic voting machines had been available since 1869, two years after the purchase of Alaska, when Thomas Edison received his first patent for an invention he called the "Electric Vote-Recorder," "an apparatus which records and registers in an instant, and with great accuracy, the votes of legislative bodies, thus avoiding the loss of valuable time consumed in counting and registering the votes and names," and the refusal to install an automated system meant that by the 1950s Congress was wasting an estimated twenty-five legislative days every session simply in the act of voting.[35]

If less efficient than Mr. Edison's system, however, the traditional House roll call vote by the clerk—abandoned only in 1973 when an electronic voting system became operational—lent an air of unfolding drama and suspense to the proceedings, accenting one by one the importance of each member's decision from A to Z in the same leisurely style as would have been done for the thirty-five new states that had come before:

Abbitt	(D-Virginia)	No
Abernethy	(D-Mississippi)	No
Adair	(R-Indiana)	No
Addonizio	(D-New Jersey)	Aye
Albert	(D-Oklahoma)	Aye

During the voting Bartlett was sitting on the House floor with Leo O'Brien; watching anxiously from the gallery above was Constitutional Convention delegate and Operation Statehood member Vic Fischer of Anchorage. Fischer had been visiting Bartlett's office when the bell had rung for the final vote that afternoon, and he had accompanied the delegate and his assistants, Mary Lee Council and Marge Smith, to the House chambers.

"I remember walking ... from the House Office Building through the underground corridor to the Capitol Building," he told historian Claus-M. Naske in 1970, "and I had Marge Smith on my arm, and Bartlett and Mary Lee were walking ahead. And Marge was just broken up, she was shaking, she said, 'I just can't take this anymore. I just can't take it. If we don't make it now, I just can't go through this again.'"[36]

Unable in the gallery to track how the votes were accumulating, Fischer said it was a "tremendously tense affair," and with representatives constantly milling about it appeared to his untrained eyes like "turmoil on the floor." In the midst of the chaos Bartlett and O'Brien were focused and intent on tallying the votes. By the time the clerk had reached the Ps and Q—Quie (R-Minnesota, Aye)—Bartlett would have known that the bill was so far ahead (170–114) the only question that remained was the size of the victory, and when he gave his friends in the gallery the thumbs-up sign, Fischer said they broke down with emotion. With 210 yeas and 166 nays, HR 7999, "To Provide for the admission of the State of Alaska into the Union," had passed the House.[37]

Fred Seaton never forgot exactly what he was doing the moment he heard of the House vote. It was late morning—Alaska was six hours behind Washington, D.C.—and he was shaving in an Anchorage hotel room when he got the call that the House of Representatives had passed the statehood bill. He said next to the Japanese surrender in World War II, the House vote was "about the best news I have ever heard in my life."[38] Daunting obstacles remained before HR 7999 could become law, but at least in retrospect it is clear that the House approval practically guaranteed Senate concurrence, because it would force the hand of Lyndon Johnson.

Before May 28 the Senate Majority Leader had been pleased to watch from the sidelines, waiting to see how his colleagues in the other body would dispose of the statehood question, but the unexpected outcome in the House changed the game completely. Statehood's triumph in the House had been a rare victory over the same coalition of Southern Democrats and conservative Republicans that had ruled Congress for decades and had most resisted Johnson's 1957 Civil Rights Act. As of May 29 LBJ was still no more enthusiastic about making Alaska a state than Rayburn, but now that the statehood bill had landed on his desk, he could not afford to have it fail. Failure would antagonize moderates and liberals who suspected him of being an unreconstructed Dixiecrat at heart, while allowing the bill to get through could be justified to his diehard Southern allies as a necessary evil, the same rationale he had used to engineer the 1957 civil rights package.[39]

Bartlett had received an inkling of what role Johnson would be willing to play behind the scenes as early as February 7, 1958, when the Majority Leader—predicting statehood was dead for the year anyway—promised that if circumstances permitted he would be willing to go so far as to "act as a midwife in getting the bill on the floor. Just a midwife, he said, not a doctor. He was willing to do that Johnson told me."[40]

In refusing the role of "Doctor Johnson," LBJ apparently meant that he planned to let the legislation follow its natural course, without undertaking any extreme measures on its behalf. Snedden was aware of this after a private meeting on March 13 between LBJ and Walker and Ewel Stone. At Snedden's request the Stone brothers spent two intense hours with LBJ that evening trying to convince the senator from Texas of the benefits of Alaska statehood. Walker Stone relayed an account of the meeting to Snedden, who in turn forwarded to Fred Seaton a summary of Johnson's "hands off" approach: "Johnson, while not personally in favor and will not promise his affirmative vote, privately stated he will see the bill gets action. Stated further that action should come first in the House if there is to be reasonable chance of enactment [but that] House action 'is not my problem.'"[41]

Once the House vote made it his "problem," however, LBJ gave every indication that he was going to do all he could to bring the state of Alaska into the world in a timely fashion. "Lyndon Johnson is out of town," Bartlett wrote Snedden on the afternoon of May 29. "But from sources so close to him as to be absolutely authoritative ... he is planning to bring the bill up within ten days or two weeks. This assuredly means that he is not trying to give us the run around because just as well as not he could dally for another two weeks, which would bring us up on the Senate stage at a critically late date."[42]

Since the Senate had no formal system comparable to that of the Rules Committee to schedule bills, the procedure to get the bill to the

floor was far simpler than in the House. Whether the Senate would hear
the bill or not lay completely under the discretion of the Majority Leader.
"The fate of statehood in this session now rests . . . in the hands of Senator
Johnson," the *News-Miner* explained. "If he wants it, we are in. If he is
against us, we have no hope."[43]

After Johnson indicated to Democratic Senate leaders that he
was going to do what was needed to get the bill passed, Republican
Minority Leader Knowland agreed that the GOP would not stand in the
way. The gravest political threat appeared to be that Senate opponents
might attempt to graft Hawaii onto the Alaska bill—creating a Siamese
Frankenstein, according to Lehleitner. Though still anxious to see a commitment on Hawaii, Knowland consented to let the Alaska bill proceed
without a formal agreement to admit the fiftieth state.

In truth, however, even adding a single comma to the House version of the bill would be a killer amendment. The only viable strategy
was for the Senate to pass HR 7999 exactly as approved by the House.
Altering even one word or point of punctuation would force the bill back
to the House and certain defeat at the hands of the Rules Committee.
This was because Senate modifications would require the bill to be heard
by a House Conference Committee, a procedure that required either
unanimous consent of the House or a vote of the Rules Committee, both
of which were impossible. As Mary Lee Council later summarized the
situation, getting unanimous consent in the House was a laugh, getting a
two-thirds majority in order to bring the bill up under the suspension of
the rules "was an additional laugh," and getting anything out of the Rules
Committee was the biggest laugh of all. "If the other procedures provoked
laughter," Council wrote, "this produced hysteria."[44] The desperation was
a recognition that it was now or never. Bartlett told Snedden in early June
that "if Alaska goes down this year" by Senate amendment it would also
be the death knell for Hawaii, and then "goodness knows when either territory may hope to come in."[45]

Initially no one dared to believe the Senate would concur 100 per-
cent with the House version. With legislation as controversial as the
Alaska statehood bill, this would be at the very best "improbable." On
June 2 Bartlett thought the possibility that the Senate would adopt the
House version as is "is probably too much to hope for." The delegate wrote
Lehleitner—with a courtesy copy to Snedden—of his confidential analy-
sis. "The only copy of this being sent out is to our colleague in Fairbanks
[Snedden] and I shall add the injunction passed on to me that we must
not release a word in the papers on our account for fear that any applecart

might thereby be upset." The word was that Senator Johnson would be in Washington by Wednesday and the Democratic Policy Committee would meet on Thursday to schedule the bill. "You will be highly pleased to learn that the prospects as of June 2 are that Dick Russell is not disposed to make any all-out fight against Alaska statehood."[46]

The following day at a meeting with Washington Sen. Henry M. "Scoop" Jackson, who would mange the bill in the Senate as O'Brien had done in the House, Jackson confirmed that due to the impossible parliamentary thicket in the House of Representatives, the Senate leadership had agreed to drop S 49, the Senate version of the statehood bill, in favor of the House-approved bill, HR 7999, and make every effort to pass it unamended. Bartlett told Lehleitner and Snedden that Scoop acknowledged "he didn't know whether all amendments which might be offered could be denied but he certainly was firm in his conclusion that the old college try must be made in this direction."[47]

Meanwhile, Ted Stevens warned Snedden that they needed to "perform a miracle" to pass the House bill without any changes, because anything less "will kill the bill." Stevens asked if Mike Stepovich would return to Washington to help with the Senate battle, because he wanted to make sure the governor would be adequately briefed. "Frankly, Bill, he did a good job with the House members who knew very little about the bill, but I think the Senators are a little more astute. Mike pulled figures and facts out of the air in some of our conversations with the House members that would have gotten him into a great deal of trouble had he made the statement before Senators."[48]

As the days passed the tension mounted, because the early scheduling of the bill Johnson had promised was slow in materializing. Obviously there were enough votes in the Senate to pass the bill—the best guess was between fifty-two and sixty votes in support—but the parliamentary situation was growing increasingly precarious. "In this congressional world, nothing is absolutely definite," Bartlett informed the members of Operation Statehood on June 18. "But it seems fairly sure that debate on the Alaska statehood bill will start next Monday, June 23, in the Senate." The most positive news was that the Southern caucus, swayed by Lyndon Johnson, Richard Russell, and Russell Long, recognized they lacked the votes to prevent cloture and thus ruled out any concerted effort for an "organized" filibuster.[49] "Every Southerner is on his own. No doubt some of them will talk, and at length. We already hear that two of these gentlemen are prepared for long-winded speeches."[50] The first warning shot came when Strom Thurmond of South Carolina, the longest-winded man in Senate history during the 1957 struggle against civil rights, denounced the Alaska bill as an unconstitutional infringement of state's rights he was not about to resist without a lengthy fight—"SOUTH OPENS FIRE ON STATEHOOD" was the *News-Miner* banner headline on page one— and meanwhile rumors circulated that George Malone—a Southerner in spirit even if he hailed from Nevada—was preparing to talk for twelve hours all by himself.[51]

But if the danger of a coordinated filibuster was gone, the insertion of an extra "whereas" or a killer-comma amendment now seemed inevitable. Bartlett's spirits sank on the eve of the Senate debate when Scoop Jackson had concluded it would be "impossible to prevent amendments being added to the bill." This was the ultimate nightmare, the "fantastic and horrible possibility that a statehood bill might be passed by both houses . . . in this 85th congress and still not become law." Bartlett thought the scenario too awful to imagine: "Wouldn't that be horrible and devastating and almost incomprehensible?" A Senate amendment of HR 7999 would be the final revenge of the Rules Committee, leaving Howard Smith and his cronies to have the last laugh, even if it resulted in a "storm of national indignation."[52]

The cause of this impending catastrophe was a previously overlooked clause in the House bill that now appeared to be a self-destruct mechanism set to go off at midnight July 3, 1958. When Senator Jackson and his staff read line by line through the thirty-seven pages of the House-passed bill, they were shocked at what they found in the first sentence of Section 7, page fourteen: "Upon enactment of this Act, it shall be the duty of the President of the United States, not later than July 3, 1958, to certify such fact to the Governor of Alaska."

The House had passed a statehood bill with a July 3, 1958, expiration date that was seemingly impossible to meet. The date had been included in both House and Senate versions of the statehood legislation introduced eighteen months earlier on January 3, 1957, the first day of the 85th session, to serve as a symbolic reminder that statehood would be a confirmation of the beliefs of the founding fathers and to ensure Alaskans had a special reason to celebrate July 4, 1958. The idea was that following the notice from the president no later than July 3, the governor would have the privilege of calling for the first state elections on America's birthday. But after the bill was unexpectedly held up by the Rules Committee for nearly a year, no one remembered to change the July 3 deadline in Section 7 before the final vote in the House, and so what had been intended as a harmless firecracker now looked like a ticking time bomb.

On June 20 Jackson told the press the statehood bill would have to be amended—and therefore returned to the House—because he saw no way the bill could reach the president's desk before the Fourth of July holiday. Jackson said he hoped, however, that the bill would pass the Senate by "such an overwhelming majority that the powerful House Rules Committee will not dare to bottle it up when it goes back to the lower chamber."[53]

Bartlett informed Lehleitner and Snedden that with the help of LBJ and Fred Seaton, he still believed the July 3 deadline could be met, thereby averting the debacle of sending the bill back to the House.

> Now if Johnson is right in assuming that a vote can be had on [June] 27th or 28th and if the bill is not amended in any particular, very obviously the requirements of section 7 can be easily met. But even if that is too optimistic a forecast it still can be done. Let's say the bill doesn't pass until [June] 30th or July 1. The executive department knows about the bill's provisions and the mechanics of getting the bill to the President for signature can be speeded.

It was at this stage that Ted Stevens came to the rescue. Bartlett said Stevens's "offhand opinion" was that the date could be safely disregarded, and "that even if the President's signature is attached to the bill after July 3 that the error would not be fatal. He is going to do some more checking on this and then get in touch with me again."[54] Upon further investigation Stevens recommended to Seaton, with the concurrence of the Justice Department, that the administration advise the Senate that the July 3 deadline was immaterial and irrelevant. The purpose of the section was simply that the governor of Alaska needed to be officially notified after the passage of the bill. "The intent of the section," Stevens's argument ran, "would not be defeated if such notification is given after July 3." Seaton's message to Congress was that it would be a tragedy if Alaska's "hopes and dreams for political equality" were to be stymied by nothing but "an overabundance of patriotic zeal" for the Fourth of July, and he urged the Senate to adopt the bill without amendment.

Like Rayburn's ruling on privilege, the dismissal of the July 3 expiration date as an inconsequential technicality—which neutralized any threat of a mini-filibuster intended to push Senate deliberations past the due date—was the only possible way for statehood to proceed, even if the decision itself clearly stretched the letter of the law. Essentially, the Eisenhower administration was telling the Senate it could approve a law that did not mean what it said. As Stevens recalled about three decades later, the July 3 deadline was a near-fatal flaw in the statehood bill, and if the Senate had followed Jackson's reasoning that the date had to be amended, all would have been lost. In legal terms it "was a real problem," Stevens admitted in the 1980s, but luckily "I happened to be the one that was making the decision that [the date] was not a problem."[55]

When the Senate debate—more truthfully, a series of windy monologues in a nearly empty room—finally got under way in earnest on June 24, it was a "loud, lengthy show" in "the grand style of Dixie oratory" about the perils the country would face if Alaska became a state. A pair of Southern segregationists was first to perform, A. Willis Robertson of Virginia and "Big Jim" Eastland of Mississippi. News-Miner correspondent Bob Smith described the peculiar scene as the two Democrats, only two seats apart, "faced each other with clenched fists, waved their arms like erratic windmills and flung their verbal thunderbolts" that echoed in the mostly vacant Senate chamber. "Clearly it was a performance for the record—and for the southern newspaper correspondents in the press gallery who were dispatching their arguments to the home folks down south."[56]

The same day that the Senate began to talk, Fred Seaton sent a two-page memorandum to Eisenhower—apparently either drafted by or drawn from material compiled by Ted Stevens—anticipating the objections Senators would raise "concerning Alaska's population, income, per capital general revenue, and the costs of statehood." As he had done so many times before, Seaton reassured Ike that the bill under consideration needed their support, as it "represents a workable compromise on many conflicting issues difficult of reconciliation." "In my sincere opinion, these facts again demonstrate that Alaskans are ready for statehood."

As Seaton had come to expect, Ike's terse response was hardly enthusiastic. When the president paused to consider the statistics regarding Alaska's general revenue per capita, which at $161.60 was reported as higher than "39 of the existing states," Ike scribbled in the margin: "I don't believe it—unless we take into consideration Fed [federal] expenditures."[57]

Despite Eisenhower's personal skepticism, however, the president stoically agreed to go along with Seaton and keep his doubts to himself over the next six days, as an array of senators, mostly Southern Democrats but also a few northeastern Republicans, lectured hour after hour why bringing in Alaska would be a betrayal of American history and "a dangerous precedent" for the future, citing authorities ranging from the Bible and Shakespeare to the Articles of Confederation and the Constitution, and summoning up the ghosts of Washington, Jefferson, Madison, Daniel Webster, and Sam Houston. It was not so different from the orations heard against Arizona half a century before. "One marvels at the monotony of the debates," commented a historian of the Arizona fight, "filled with endless repetitions, burdened with useless details, and delivered to empty seats."[58]

Prescott Bush (R-Connecticut)—father of the first president Bush and the grandfather of the second—favored the no population and no economy argument, while Herman Talmadge (D-Georgia) reminded his colleagues that noncontiguity and the Polish Corridor had been Hitler's excuse for starting World War II, ominously warning that a thousand-mile-wide Canadian Corridor in the heart of the American continent was likely to provoke trouble; Olin D. Johnston (D-South Carolina) predicted outright that the state of Alaska might eventually force the United States and Canada into war.

Strom Thurmond envisioned a "deluge" of new states that would be forced upon the American people, and not just the usual suspects— Hawaii, Puerto Rico, Guam, American Samoa, the Marshall Islands, and Okinawa—but also "Cambodia, Laos, South Vietnam" and any "other politically threatened or economically demoralized nations in southeast Asia, the Caribbean, and Africa." Hours were spent criticizing the unconstitutionality of Section 10, the national defense withdrawal zone beyond the PYK line drafted by Stevens to meet Eisenhower's strategy concerns, with Thurmond damning the defense perimeter as a "glaring violation of the equal-footing doctrine," and charging that the Warren Court, which had done so much to tear down the constitution with the *Brown* decision, was likely to use the Alaska precedent as a ruse to "simply extend the principle of the withdrawal power to cover the present 48 States as well as Alaska" and make the whole country subject to military control. "I say that if the President of the United States can withdraw land from Alaska, he can withdraw land from Wisconsin, he can withdraw it from Idaho, he can withdraw it from Maine or Florida, or from any other State in the Nation." The Alaska statehood bill in general, and the Section 10 PYK line in particular, according to Thurmond, was a dagger in the heart of constitutional freedom and states' rights. "I do not hesitate, like Mark Antony, to attribute ambition to the ambitious. This Federal bureaucracy is ambitious, and worse, it is power hungry. It is a constant usurper of authority. It is a would-be tyrant."[59]

As the leader of the South in the Senate, Richard Russell took pains to explain that he and many of his staunchest allies were opposing Alaska statehood strictly on the merits of the issue, having nothing whatsoever to do with the "so-called civil-rights" problem. "Whenever a large segment of the press wishes to prejudice the country and the Senate against any position," Russell said, "it tries to argue, if it can find southern Senators in opposition, that there is some vague and nebulous connection between the opposition of some of us to the proposal and the misnamed civil-rights program." Sensitive to accusations of LBJ's horse-trading on civil rights—which were in fact true—Russell denied the "many fantastic charges ... that all kinds of trades and deals have been made in connection with various items of legislation relating to the so-called civil-rights issue." Downplaying the influence and denying the existence of the Southern bloc, Russell pointed out that "Senators from the so-called Southern States are seldom unanimous on any issue." Since a handful of Southern Democrats were supporting Alaska statehood— including Russell Long of Louisiana, Spessard Holland of Florida, and Lister Hill and John Sparkman of Alabama—that should have been sufficient to prove that their concerns were genuine and disprove the allegation that Southerners were primarily opposed because of their obsession with racial segregation and the survival of the filibuster. His personal opposition to Alaska was "not colored by my views with respect to any other legislation. I would be opposed to this bill, and to statehood for Alaska ... even if I had a guaranty in my pocket of 60 votes against any of the misnamed, mislabeled civil-right legislation. ... I do not believe that this Territory is prepared economically for statehood, or that it can support a State government."[60]

Richard Russell's patrician manner enabled him to sound logical and judicious even when he was neither, but not even the senior senator from Georgia could disguise the obvious, that the civil "so-called" rights question was the fault line of American politics in the U.S. Senate, and in the last week of June 1958 the admission of Alaska was caught in the center, as proved by the generally bizarre and outlandish Southern rhetoric against it. "The anti-statehood arguments used by the southerners have been specious in the extreme," stated a front-page *News-Miner* editorial. "Nobody really believes the United States would be risking war with Canada, or that we would be giving the world a demonstration of imperialist expansion . . . or that admission of Alaska practically guarantees that Guam, Samoa and other islands tidbits will be brought into the Union as states." These fatuous claims only underscored the fact that the Southerners were trying to "stall for time rather than to win adherents," and that the more they talked, the less likely it would be for anyone to believe them.[61]

The Senate majority leader was not there to hear any of it. Lyndon Johnson had quietly arranged to be out of town the entire week so his role as the "midwife" for the legislation remained invisible; staying out of sight he would not have to publicly betray the South or personally battle with any of the diehard segregationists. LBJ had committed himself to vote yes if he had been present, but since he was absent he never had to face the issue squarely. As Bartlett described the strategy, "Johnson made all the necessary arrangements to assure the vote's being taken, knowing that it would pass, and . . . then slipped out of town so that his southern colleagues could not hurl too many poison arrows at him."[62]

The most astute analyst of the Senate in the Washington press corps was Johnson's longtime friend and fellow Texan William S. White. The veteran reporter had known LBJ since their early days together in Washington in 1933, when Johnson had been secretary to a Texas congressman and White was the Associated Press regional correspondent for Texas affairs. By the time Johnson had become Senate Majority Leader two decades later, White was the chief capitol correspondent for the *New York Times*, winner of the Pulitzer Prize for his 1954 biography of Ohio Senator Robert Taft, and author of *Citadel: The Story of the U.S. Senate*, one of the most influential books ever written about the chamber.[63] As a member of Senator Johnson's inner circle, no reporter had a deeper appreciation for the Majority Leader's method of operation.

While White watched the Senate, despite the protests of a few diehards, move inexorably in the last days of June 1958 to add two new desks to the Senate floor for the first time since 1912—desks with Johnson's fingerprints all over them—he was struck by the significance of the proceedings in the grand sweep of American history. Physically, LBJ may have been absent, but politically, he was the trail boss running the entire show, convincing his Southern colleagues to do what did not come naturally. "The more traditional southerners . . . have gloomily concluded that they cannot threw in any all-out attack against what now seems to be the manifest destiny of the Alaskans to have a state capitol," White wrote. "All but a handful . . . were coaxed into this withdrawal from their old position of absolute and total opposition by some of their own people, chiefly Senator Lyndon B. Johnson of Texas." From White's perspective the acceptance of Alaska marked the surrender of the "old obstructionist South" to the Johnson-Rayburn moderate faction aligned with the West. This northward expansion of the Union—made possible by the fall of the South and the rise of the West—would herald a radical realignment of government power, stripping the Deep South of its chokehold on Congress and essentially forcing the Southern states into the mainstream of American politics, healing the lasting scars of the Civil War and providing "the opportunity to begin to bring the South, with all its backward-looking ideas but also with all its political grace and skill, back into the United States of America." The unspoken message was that the coalition of moderate Southerners and Westerners would be the foundation for Johnson's presidential ambitions. LBJ let the young Western senators such as Mike Mansfield and Henry Jackson handle the details of the Alaska bill because the Majority Leader didn't want to provoke his "still glumly resisting old southern colleagues any more than need be," reminding White of a quote from Winston Churchill that conveyed the essence of LBJ's courteous but forceful style. "When you are about to kill a man," the prime minister was reported saying, "it does no harm to be polite."[64]

The Senate deliberations were as polite as a funeral, because it was clear after the first preliminary votes on Friday, June 27, that any serious opposition to statehood had "crumbled," and the only genuine issue that remained was the size of the margin of victory. By surprisingly large majorities—"much bigger than we expected," according to Scoop Jackson—the Senate easily defeated an amendment that would have eliminated the PYK defense withdrawal zone (53–28) and another that would have substituted commonwealth for statehood (50–29). Since tax-free commonwealth status for Alaska remained a political and constitutional impossibility, the *News-Miner* noted that these twenty-nine senators were not actually voting "for" commonwealth or tax exemptions. "They were 29 votes for any change at all in the statehood bill," twenty-nine votes trying to "sidetrack the statehood express" by modifying the bill and sending it back to the House. Like the commonwealth proposal, each of the subsequent killer amendments was defeated by equally large or larger majorities—62–22, 55–31, 67–16—indicating that an "overwhelming" victory for the statehood bill was inevitable. Unwilling to prolong the agony, many opponents either cut short their remarks or chose not to speak at all, enabling the leadership to cancel a proposed Saturday floor session that would have been necessary in the event there had been more long-winded speeches.[65]

A nine-hour floor session beginning at eleven a.m. on Monday, June 30, was the last hurrah for the Southern holdouts, ending only after Strom Thurmond took several hours to explain the dire consequences of approving the "reckless, unwise and unnecessary step of admitting Alaska to . . . the Union." "I urge my fellow Senators," he pleaded, "to join with me in opposing this dangerous bill."[66]

But Thurmond might as well have saved his voice. There was no turning back and everyone in the chamber realized it. One senator after another rose to explain how honored and privileged they felt—like so many expectant fathers—as they were about to cast the historic vote to create the forty-ninth state. Barry Goldwater (R-Arizona) had been born in the Territory of Arizona on New Year's Day in 1909. "I knew that the Senate, in its wisdom, would smile kindly upon Alaska's appeal for statehood. This is a very pleasing moment for me. One of the first memories I have in my life, is that of my mother sewing two additional stars in the flag of the United States when the Territory of Arizona [and New Mexico] became a State. . . . I know something of the struggle . . . to become a State of the Union." Arthur V. Watkins (R-Utah) likewise recalled Utah's admission day in 1896. "I was a lad 9 years of age at the time. I can still remember the enthusiastic celebrations . . . when Utah, after 40 years delay, was finally admitted to the Union. The scenes of my childhood will no doubt be repeated tonight by the people of Alaska. I think I know how deeply they feel."[67]

It was all over but the voting when Scoop Jackson rose to give thanks to Delegate Bartlett, the Tennessee Planners, Fred Seaton and Mike Stepovich, and the bipartisan campaign that had made the day possible. "In any fair appraisal of the Alaska statehood bill," Jackson said, "one fact stands out very clear. Our work to date has not been the product of a single party. It has been the product of a bipartisan majority."

"This is not a Republican victory; it is not a Democratic victory; it is not simply a victory for Alaskans ... it is a victory for all Americans and for the Democratic process."

At that point, according to the *Congressional Record*, "several Senators" began to shout "Vote! Vote!" and at 7:53 p.m. the roll call began: Aiken, Allott, Anderson, Barrett, Bennett, Bible, and Bricker—all responded aye—followed by Bridges, Bush, Butler, and Byrd—all voting no. Exactly nine minutes later, at 8:02 p.m., the voting was closed and the final tally was a landslide: by 64–20 the U.S. Senate had approved the Alaska statehood bill. With seven of the twelve absent senators pledged as a yea vote if they had been present—including Majority Leader Lyndon Johnson—nearly 74 percent of the ninety-six members of the Senate had gone on record in favor of the forty-ninth state, close to the same percentage of the American public that had long favored Alaska statehood. Thirteen of the twenty opponents were Democrats, all Southerners except for Monroney of Oklahoma, who refused to budge on his commonwealth proposal.

When the total vote was announced, the galleries erupted with cheering and clapping, and even senators on the floor stood to applaud. As the concluding summary states in the *Congressional Record*: "So the bill (H.R. 7999) was passed. {Manifestations of applause in the galleries.}"[68]

So ended the congressional battle for Alaska statehood. It had been more than fifteen years—or, according to Mary Lee Council, "something like" 8,018,160 minutes—since the Senate's first Alaska statehood bill had been introduced back in April 1943. After those millions of minutes and countless "heartbreaks and setbacks," she called the long anticipated victory an "almost unbelievable ... numbing experience." Bartlett said personally "I imagine it will remain the most thrilling moment of my life." [69]

———

That night both Bob Atwood and Snedden were watching the historic proceedings from the crowded press gallery with a mixture of exhilaration, disbelief, gratitude, and a profound sense of accomplishment. The American press corps had played a vital role in breaking the grip of congressional inertia, and the publishers of the *Anchorage Daily Times* and the *Fairbanks Daily News-Miner* had been the catalysts that brought the statehood miracle of 1958 to life. Of the two men, Atwood was without question the statehood pioneer of the Fourth Estate, the man who made the first headlines. Beginning in the mid-1940s his *Anchorage Times*, closely allied with the ruling pro-statehood Democrats topped by Governor Gruening and Delegate Bartlett, had been the voice of the statehood movement. But ever since the Constitutional Convention in Fairbanks in 1955, and particularly since the appointment of Fred Seaton as secretary of the interior in 1956, Snedden—not Atwood—emerged as the most influential newspaperman in the statehood cause. It was not so much that Atwood became less passionate about statehood—he remained chairman of the Alaska Statehood Committee for its entire existence—only that Snedden became far more personally and professionally involved as the political landscape shifted between 1952 and 1958. Snedden's special relationship with Seaton was only one factor in the relative rise of his political influence.

Snedden's support for the constitution was a critical factor in the success of the convention, while initially Atwood had not been in favor of calling a constitutional convention at all, seeing it simply as another delaying tactic, and he never evinced enough interest to dispatch a full-time reporter to cover the day-to-day goings-on in Fairbanks, opting instead to rely on the *News-Miner* for regular coverage. Atwood had likewise been an early opponent of the Alaska-Tennessee Plan, and even though he ultimately agreed to accept the Republican nomination for one of the ATP Senate seats in 1956, his defeat in the general election at the hands of Democrat Bill Egan left him disillusioned. The election loss also revealed the electoral no-man's-land between the two parties in which Atwood found himself, a political estrangement that had crystallized after Eisenhower's election in 1952. Though Atwood was a lifelong Republican—his father-in-law, E. A. Rasmuson, was the Republican National Committeeman for Alaska until his death in 1949—he had been aligned for so long with Gruening and Bartlett that he was often perceived as more of a Democrat than a Republican, a donkey in elephant's clothing. When Gruening left office in 1953, Atwood infuriated the Republican establishment with an editorial praising his friend Ernest as "Alaska's Greatest Governor." For their parts Gruening and Bartlett both excused Atwood's affiliation with the GOP as a pardonable vice or a chronic ailment for which they hoped someday there would be a cure.

Atwood shared Gruening's contempt for Bill Strand, the conservative Republican and former *News-Miner*–editor–turned Interior Department official under Douglas McKay, thinking he was the root of the Eisenhower administration's anti-statehood stance. "When the Republicans took over in 1952, it seemed to many of us in Alaska that anti-statehood office seekers came out of the woodwork to take the key jobs." Atwood's memoir, *Alaska Titan: Bob Atwood and his Times,* co-written in the 1990s with journalist John Strohmeyer, dedicates almost half a chapter to a private meeting that Atwood had with Eisenhower in the Oval Office in the spring of 1954—shortly before the Operation Statehood delegation with John Butrovich had made Ike's face turn red with rage. Atwood had difficulty in getting to see the president, because, he said, "all my contacts were Democrats. They had no access." Furthermore Eisenhower had been "surrounded by anti-statehood bureaucrats"—Republicans such as Strand— "who wouldn't let me see him." In his rosy recollection of his conversation once he got through to the president in 1954, Atwood portrayed Ike as a true statehood believer being manipulated by shady advisors such as Strand, and said it "confirmed my suspicions that the salmon packers had surrounded Ike with anti-statehood administrators." Atwood's demonization of Strand and idealization of Eisenhower—according to Atwood, Ike's words were "music to my ears" and "I left the White House with spirits high"—revealed that he did not understand, or else failed to remember, the true divisions inside the administration or the GOP any better than the Democrats, and in particular the essential role Seaton would play in garnering and keeping Ike's support.[70]

Following in Atwood's footsteps, Snedden had likewise alienated conservative Alaska Republicans by supporting statehood and endorsing Bob Bartlett, and also refusing to back a straight Republican ticket when he judged the nominees undeserving; nevertheless, in comparison to Atwood, Snedden was a model Republican, untainted by suspicions of being a closet Democrat too close to Gruening. Snedden actually believed Strand was deep at heart a statehood supporter—a side of Strand invisible to everyone else—who had been vilified merely because he dared criticize Gruening. Trusting Strand, Snedden had been far more patient with the Eisenhower administration in its first two years, making his GOP credentials all the more sterling, and thus he was the natural choice to become the nucleus of the Republican revival in the territory.

Though Snedden's *News-Miner* had only about half the circulation of Atwood's *Times*—9,500 compared to 18,500—the Fairbanks publisher had a disproportionately larger impact on the national debate.[71] The alliance between Snedden and Seaton—which had resulted in the rising prominence of Mike Stepovich and Ted Stevens—was the seed of the resurgence of the Alaska GOP, making the *News-Miner* a powerful tool for "manufacturing Republicans," as Snedden phrased it. Combined with Snedden's tireless promotional activities, beginning with the annual Progress Editions that he distributed throughout the United States in the early 1950s and culminating in his 1958 public relations blitz with publishers and editors that landed Mike Stepovich on the cover of *Time*, the national GOP was encouraged to think the state of Alaska could become more fertile soil for Republicanism than the territory of Alaska ever had been.

Proof of the Republican faith in the future of Alaska and Snedden's effectiveness in getting the message across was the tally of the final Senate vote: astonishingly, more Republicans (thirty-three) than Democrats (thirty-one) voted for the admission of Alaska. As Scoop Jackson had said, the making of the forty-ninth state had certainly been a bipartisan victory, but the overwhelming and unexpected GOP support in the Senate for a new state that Democrats expected would be solidly Democratic was an unparalleled triumph for the Republican Party alone, thanks to Fred Seaton and the publisher of the *Fairbanks Daily News-Miner*.

The statehood struggle on Capitol Hill was over, but for Atwood and Snedden there remained one more race to be run: which newspaper would be the first to get the word back to Alaska. Correspondent Bob Smith was reporting for both the *Times* and the *News-Miner*, but the two publishers were nevertheless eager to scoop the other. Knowing a bit more about the facilities in the Senate offices, Snedden was better prepared. By prearrangement he had already secured one of the telephones in the press room adjacent to the gallery; about 6:30 p.m. in Washington (12:30 p.m. in Fairbanks) Snedden said he "phoned Fairbanks and told them to get the forms ready for the press" of the sixteen-page, four-color statehood supplement that had been prepared weeks earlier, and to hold the presses on stand by for the next two hours waiting to hear about the final vote.

When the Senate roll call began shortly before eight p.m. Snedden placed a long-distance call on the same phone to *News-Miner* editor George Sundborg in Fairbanks "to ensure an open wire." They chatted, killing time until 8:02, when Smith dashed back to the press room from the gallery to give the final tally to Snedden: "Here it is. You're in. The vote was 64–20." Snedden immediately relayed the news to Sundborg on the phone in Fairbanks, making the *News-Miner* managing editor the first person in Alaska to learn the bill had passed.[72]

Snedden had scooped everyone in Alaska with the story, but the *Anchorage Times* would run the best front page. The *News-Miner* chose a four-color rendering of Old Glory with forty-nine stars under a headline that was a prosaic statement of fact:

CONGRESS APPROVES
ALASKA STATEHOOD

But the triumphant banner in the *Times* better caught the spirit of the joyous occasion, even if it was not technically accurate; originally the Anchorage paper wanted to run "We're No. 49," but that wouldn't fit, so managing editor Bernie Kosinski composed a two-word headline of six letters in "end of the world" size wooden type to sum up the culmination of ninety-one years of American rule in Alaska, with the help of an apostrophe made from a sawed-off comma:

WE'RE IN!

When Sundborg had received the word from Snedden about the Senate action, he in turn relayed the news to Fairbanks civil defense officials; they were supposed to set off local sirens for five minutes of celebration, but as the *News-Miner* reported that evening, the "sounding of the sirens was delayed about ten minutes because those manning them had been relieved to eat lunch." Soon enough the sirens started blaring, accompanied, as *News-Miner* reporter Jack De Yonge wrote, by "every noisemaking device in the area" from whistles and car horns to pots and pans.[73]

While the sounds of victory resonated throughout Fairbanks, Snedden remained on the other end of the line with Sundborg trying to give him instructions, but neither could hear what the other was saying. "It cost me 20 minutes in long-distance time," Snedden said, "just waiting and fiddling with my hearing aid until things quieted down enough for me to give George the details for the special edition. It was probably the happiest money I've ever wasted in my life."[74]

The statehood issue rolled off the press about two hours late, and Sundborg immediately had about sixteen hundred copies trucked to Eielson Air Force Base twenty-six miles south of Fairbanks. Weeks earlier Snedden had laid the groundwork at the Pentagon for a classic newspaper stunt, arranging for the U.S. Air Force to fly copies of the statehood edition back to Andrews Air Force Base overnight on a Strategic Air Command B-47 Stratojet. "The idea was to have a graphic illustration in the Capitol," Snedden said, "of how close the newest state was to Washington in this day of jet transportation."

The timing of the bill's passage in the early evening provided an extra opportunity. Bulldog editions of the East Coast morning papers were already on the streets, and there would be little time for the later editions to "work up anything approaching comprehensive coverage," so Snedden planned for the *News-Miner* to scoop the Washington press corps with same-day coverage all the way from Fairbanks by personally hand delivering copies of the June 30 edition to 1600 Pennsylvania Avenue and to every senator and congressman in the Capitol by breakfast.

This best-laid plan to deliver the news from Fairbanks to Washington in less than half a day encountered some unforeseen obstacles; the B-47 loaded with a half ton of newspapers—including copies of the *Anchorage News* and the *Anchorage Times*, which had joined in on the stunt—did not take off from Eielson AFB until eleven p.m. Alaska time. According to the story, as Snedden liked to tell it, the bomber lifted off late because the crew wanted to finish watching *Gunsmoke*. Regardless, the plane touched down at Andrews AFB the following morning shortly before noon on the East Coast, where paperboys Bob Smith and Bill Snedden hand delivered the *News-Miner* to the White House, the Interior Department, and the House and the Senate, with the remainder sent to newsstands.[75]

The front page of the June 30 issue featured the story of the "Smashing 64–20 Vote Piled up in Senate," flanked by a Sunday-style editorial "Let Us Pause to Give Thanks," honoring at the top of the list Fred Seaton, the "No. 1 man on the administration team," and his entire staff, of whom the "most devoted and tireless was Theodore F. Stevens, former United States attorney in Fairbanks who is now legislative counsel for the Department of the Interior" and "Known as 'Mr. Alaska' in the Interior Department."

At the bottom of the page appeared a boldface notice, five columns wide, explaining why on Tuesday morning, July 1, 1958, the previous day's issue of "America's Farthest North Daily Newspaper" was being sold on the streets of Washington, D.C.:

THIS NEWSPAPER

*Was printed in Fairbanks, Alaska, after passage
of the Alaska Statehood Bill by the U.S. Senate the
afternoon of Monday, June 30, 1958*

A token shipment is being made to Washington, D.C., for delivery
to every member of Congress and for sale on the newsstands, as
a demonstration of the nearness, under modern transportation
conditions, of the nation's capital to the heart of Alaska, the 49th
State.

In this manner the small-town publisher and his newspaper that had
done so much to bring the forty-ninth state into the Union, and to push
the country closer to the ideals of American democracy, had proved once
again that distant Alaska was not so foreign or so far away after all. The
people of Alaska would be second-class citizens no more.

Epilogue

The Fourth of July came five days early for the people of Alaska on June 30, 1958, "Statehood Day." Senate passage of HR 7999 touched off a wave of "happy pandemonium," according to the *News-Miner*, that was a combination of Independence Day, St. Patrick's Day, and New Year's Eve; Bob Bartlett said it would forever be remembered as the "greatest day" in the history of Alaska. "JUBILANT ALASKANS WHOOP IT UP" read the *News-Miner* headline the following afternoon, and the people of the territory found forty-nine different ways to cheer. In Juneau they rang a replica of the Liberty Bell forty-nine times; in Ketchikan a carillon chimed forty-nine strokes; in Anchorage the National Guard fired a forty-nine-gun salute, and the community paraded down Fourth Avenue to pin a ceremonial forty-ninth star to a huge banner of the Stars and Stripes while a giant bonfire on the Park Strip blazed all night long. Back in Fairbanks Mayor Paul B. Haggland declared "S-Day" a local holiday for all citizens, 2,253 of whom signed a one-word telegram sent to every member of Congress that read "Thanks!" While children climbed on the city fire truck as it crawled down Cushman Street, above the crowd flags and firecrackers were flying everywhere. On top of the Federal Building the First National Bank carillon played "My Country 'Tis of Thee," "The Star-Spangled Banner," and "Auld Lang Syne," and the beer and hard liquor flowed free. "Bars threw open their doors here tonight," read a Fairbanks dispatch sent to the *New York Times*, "owners shouting, 'drinks on the house,' and within minutes . . . the streets were filled with backslapping, hugging celebrants, milling and dancing through stalled, horn-honking traffic."[1]

Two curious stunts chronicled by the *News-Miner*, both of which went slightly awry, highlighted the festivities in Fairbanks. Promoter Don Pearson had planned to make the Chena River run gold with thirty bags of orange dye that the air force used for rescues at sea; however, the orange coloring dumped in the river did not work so well on a freshwater stream laced with sewage. According to the *News-Miner* account the river turned bright "kelly green, not gold as expected," forcing locals to adopt the attitude that "Green gold is better than none." Meanwhile, at about four p.m., a team of volunteers on the roof of the Polaris Building, the tallest structure in Fairbanks, launched two helium weather balloons anchored with guy wires; suspended between the balloons was a golden silk star emblazoned with the number 49. For eight hours this forty-ninth star—fifty feet wide from point to point—floated about one thousand feet over Fairbanks until a few minutes before midnight, when the leaky balloons came crashing down in a gust of wind from the north. The *News-Miner* described what happened next: "The star dipped down, caught on a power line at 3rd and Lacey, and burned in half. . . . For 16 minutes power in some downtown areas was off until utilities systems crews . . . had cut-off switches turned on again."[2]

When the bars closed down and the cheering stopped, the real work of creating the forty-ninth state would begin, but not until President Eisenhower actually signed HR 7999 into law. So while June 30 might have been the highpoint of Alaska history as Bartlett claimed, in reality the law would remain a dead letter until Eisenhower saw fit to approve it. That he would readily sign the bill was taken for granted at the time, a mere formality, one last loose string of which Ike would quickly dispose. Thanks to Seaton, both the GOP and the Eisenhower administration could truthfully claim a major share of credit for the victory. While Democrats Rayburn and Johnson were at most reluctant converts to the statehood cause, Republican Seaton had been a true believer from the start. From drafting the bill, to lobbying, testifying, and counting votes on the Hill, and in the end convincing more Senate Republicans than Democrats to vote aye, Seaton and the Interior Department had done the impossible, taking the first step toward making a Republican state out of a Democratic territory. The signing of the statehood bill would set in motion the other formalities that needed to be dealt with in the coming months before the president could authorize an official statehood proclamation to formally bring the forty-ninth state into existence, including the calling of the statehood referendum, which everyone recognized would be passed by a landslide, followed by general elections for the first slate of state officials. "Unless Ike wants a revolution on his hands," one

Alaskan said in the first week of July, the president was sure to sign the bill, and publicly the most likely scenario appeared to be that the new state would be conceived on or before the Fourth of July, in honor of America's 182nd birthday.[3]

In truth, the president did not intend to wrap the GOP in the forty-nine-star flag on July 4 and had no wish to claim statehood as a partisan victory for the Republican Party for the same reason as always: though willing to back statehood for Hawaii, no matter how much "mental retching and vomiting" it took, as one GOP senator had said, Ike could not swallow statehood for Alaska.[4]

"If Dwight Eisenhower had ... followed his own inclinations instead of Interior Secretary Fred Seaton's, Alaska would never have become a state while Eisenhower occupied the White House." This was the judgment of a man who knew: William B. Ewald Jr., a veteran of both Ike's White House staff and an assistant to Fred Seaton, and author of one of the most insightful memoirs of Ike's presidency: *Eisenhower the President: Crucial Days, 1951–1960.* According to Ewald, Eisenhower never changed his mind about Alaska and never thought the forty-ninth state made economic sense. "Ike had thought statehood for such a territory ridiculous," and it was Seaton who stood up to Eisenhower. "Fred Seaton ... deserves all acclaim for his resistance to the President and the result. So does his assistant and legislative counsel ... Ted Stevens, who worked night and day on the hill, at one time provoking Republican minority leader Joe Martin, an old foe of statehood, to go straight to the White House to protest Interior's 'blitz.' On this cause Fred was a zealot, Ted a fanatic. Without them, Alaskan—and Hawaiian—statehood would not have happened."[5]

Even after he left the White House, Eisenhower's skepticism about Alaska's suitability to join the Union did not subside. When Ewald moved to Gettysburg to work with the former president as a research assistant and ghostwriter on his memoirs, the subject riled as much as ever. Ewald recalled that even "as late as 1963, as we worked on *Waging Peace*, he could still cuss about it: 'They were nuts to want to start paying their own way.'" Ewald also remembered how Seaton, ever the faithful Eisenhower man, made sure that Ike got the credit for Alaska statehood, even if he didn't want it. An early version of the presidential memoirs Ike dictated said that Alaska statehood had been a mistake. "When we mailed that draft out to Seaton in Nebraska for comment, Fred nearly had a heart attack, got on the phone at once to ask me what happened to my sense of historical perspective, and inundated me with additional information to turn the chapter around." Seaton reminded Ewald that there had been such strong opposition among Southern Democrats to admitting Alaska that Senate Majority Leader Lyndon Johnson had "predicted death for Ike's foreign aid bill in 1957 if I kept pushing Alaska statehood," and they were even more determined to keep out Hawaii. Seaton pleaded that Ewald not "make the President a reluctant dragon; give him full credit. I didn't disregard his counsel and insist on statehood for Alaska before Hawaii: we wanted to set a trap—get Alaska in, and thus make Hawaiian statehood inevitable." In the end Seaton thought it so important how Ike dealt with the subject in the book that he went to lobby his old boss in person at Gettysburg and once again managed to convince the president to reluctantly accept the laurels for the creation of the forty-ninth state. According to Ewald the incident illuminated a recurring theme in the Eisenhower presidency: Ike picked "strong lieu-tenants, gave them freedom to think and to innovate, backed them to the hilt despite his qualms," and in the end the admission of Alaska and Hawaii was a great "triumph of his administration" because he trusted Fred Seaton.

By downplaying his own role in the statehood battle—and indirectly that of Ted Stevens and Bill Snedden—Fred Seaton helped to muddy fur-ther the historical record, which was already jumbled enough by the seven days of limbo into which Ike had dropped the Alaska statehood bill after its passage. When Secretary Seaton and Governor Stepovich personally delivered the statehood bill to the White House on July 1, 1958, they re-ported that the president professed to be pleased that the Alaska bill had made it to his desk, even though Ike notably refused to say when it would be signed. Stepovich told the press that "indications were" Ike would affix his signature by July 2 or July 3 at the latest.

After leaving the White House Seaton held a press conference say-ing that the Senate action had been "not merely a victory for the 220,000 inhabitants of Alaska alone," but for "all who believe in government of the people, by the people, and for the people." Nevertheless he was quick to remind Democrats that "the statehood fight is not yet over," not until they were willing to take up the cause of Hawaii. "Every argument for Alaskan statehood buttressed the case for Hawaii. Now with the Senate action last night, that case is stronger than ever. The time for action on Hawaii is now."[6]

Frustrated with the Democratic stonewalling of Hawaii, Eisenhower pointedly refused to sign the Alaska bill by Thursday, July 3—the putative deadline written into the legislation even if Stevens had concluded the date was more of a suggestion than a requirement—and Bartlett began to fret. Knowing that a deal was not done until the ink was dry, he feared that Eisenhower was simply playing politics. But to what end? "What we can't figure out is why Eisenhower didn't sign the statehood bill on July 3." Seaton had issued an "opinion that signing after then would not constitute a fatal error. However, he is not the court of last resort. We know that the Interior Department and the Bureau of the Budget had made all preliminary clearances so that the President could have signed without trouble. But he didn't." Some Democrats suspected that perhaps Ike would sign the bill in private, in order to let Mike Stepovich "make the big announcement" by himself on July 4. But by the time the holiday was almost over, there was still no word from the White House.[7]

"This is being dictated into one of those Dictaphone machines on the 4th of July," Bartlett wrote Mike Walsh, an old friend from Nome.

> I mention this because you asked the question why the President did not sign the statehood bill Tuesday or Wednesday or Thursday. The question has even broader implications now. He did not sign it Wednesday, so far as we know. He did not sign it Thursday, so far as we know. This is all a great mystery. He left for Gettysburg by helicopter Thursday afternoon after signing a good many bills. The White House announced that statehood was not one of them. . . . We just can't figure it out. There is a lot of comment about this. Many reporters were on the phone to us Thursday afternoon; but of course we could give them no explanation whatsoever.

At the bottom of the letter Bartlett added a postscript written four days later, on July 8. "P.S. The time between dictation of the above and the actual typing process has been such that you will know long since that the President finally moved yesterday. Our word is that he moved alone—no audience was there whatsoever. We still can't figure all of this."[8] Lehleitner was equally mystified and disheartened—particularly for Bob Bartlett and Bill Snedden, whom he thought should have been invited even if no one else had been—that the president had ignored the "opportunity to accentuate a truly historical occasion" and had treated the signing as little more than a housekeeping measure.[9]

Eisenhower's puzzling decision to sign the bill in private after a week of suspense was his silent protest vigil for Hawaii, accentuated by the begrudging explanation that he offered on the official signing statement. Ostensibly welcoming Alaska into the Union, he devoted almost all his energy to complaining about the Democratic betrayal of Hawaii: "While I am pleased with the action of admitting Alaska, I am extremely disturbed over reports that no action is contemplated by the current Congress on pending legislation to admit Hawaii as a State."[10]

Ike's genuine concern about fair play for Hawaii in 1958 foundered on the rocks of political reality and further served to illustrate how delicate it had been to engineer the passage of the Alaska bill. To appease the Southern wing of their party, moderate and liberal Democrats had to settle with the hope that the entrance of Alaska would make that of Hawaii inevitable in the near future, perhaps in the 86th Congress, but not in the 85th under any circumstances. The *New York Times* and the *Washington Post* damned the Democratic refusal to take up Hawaii immediately as nothing but cynical partisanship, but Senate Majority Leader Lyndon Johnson was unfazed. Balancing Democrats on both ends of the political spectrum, LBJ had brokered the deal to admit Alaska with the promise that Hawaii was dead for at least the rest of the session, perhaps longer, and he had no intention of going back on his word to the Southern segregationists in the Senate. Neither Johnson nor Sam Rayburn would even publicly commit to consider Hawaii in the next Congress.

But all the sound and fury about the admission of Hawaii was soon to dissipate, as the ideological and partisan make-up of the U.S. Senate in 1959–1960 would be a world apart from that of 1957–1958. For one thing, the new U.S. senators from Alaska would champion the cause of Hawaii with a passion no senators had ever felt before. On the day Ike had signed the Alaska statehood bill, Bartlett had promised the editor of the *Honolulu Star-Bulletin*: "If the two United States Senators and the Representative from Alaska do not lead the fight for Hawaii statehood in the 86th Congress they should be kicked all over the lot. There will be no need to kick them all over the lot."[11] Four months later Bartlett and Gruening were elected as Alaska's first U.S. Senate delegation, and true to his word Bartlett demanded the Senate take immediate action on Hawaii. For the first time the former delegate had a vote to back it up: "Everything," he said, "that can be said . . . on the subject of Hawaii statehood, for or against, has been said."[12]

But the two new Democrats from Alaska were hardly alone. A Democratic landslide in the off-year elections in 1958 gave the liberal wing of the party a strength it had not known since the glory days of the New Deal. In addition to the two seats from Alaska, moderate and liberal Democrats picked up an additional thirteen new Senate seats in the 1958 elections, transforming the bare 49–47 Democratic majority in the 85th Congress to an insurmountable 64–34 supermajority in the 86th Congress. As a result of the Republican rout the power of the Southern caucus of the Democratic Party was severely diminished, and Southerners no longer had the automatic veto power to block progressive legislation, such as the admission of Hawaii. Quickly adapting to this new reality, LBJ and the other Democratic leaders would ramrod Hawaiian statehood through Congress like a shotgun wedding in the spring of 1959 "with almost embarrassing haste." Johnson and Rayburn arranged for both the House and the Senate to take up Hawaii on March 11, 1959. After sixty years of indecision and delay, according to a reporter for the *New York Times*, this "surprise move" "caused gasps among members of both houses." After a few hours of desultory debate, the Senate voted 76–15 to admit Hawaii, with the House concurring the following day 323–89. In retrospect, according to the *Times*, "The entrance of Alaska had made Hawaii's victory a certainty."[13]

The entrance of both Alaska and Hawaii reflected the erosion of the power of the Old South in the U.S. Congress and further accelerated that decline, even though the addition of four new senators did not produce the automatic four votes against filibusters as expected; in fact, the first votes that Bartlett and Gruening cast as senators from Alaska were in support of Majority Leader Lyndon Johnson's battle against resurgent liberals trying to change Senate rules to eliminate the filibuster. LBJ's successful strategy "to retain the filibuster as an instrument of government," the *New York Times* noted rather glumly, was yet another example of the Texas senator's dominance on Capitol Hill, a mastery of "parliamentary strategy, political pressure and personal sarcasm" that enabled him to handily beat back the liberals by rounding up votes not only from "the expected goats but also some of the sheep," and "even roped in the two brand new Senators from Alaska, whose records indicated they would go with the liberals on most questions."[14] Though Bartlett always thought of himself as a moderate, he was pegged in 1963 as one of the ten most liberal members of the Senate; yet he would repeatedly vote against cloture with a rationale that could have been scripted by any of the Southerners who had fought for so long to keep Alaska out of the Union. He championed the filibuster, he said in 1963, because "the right of unlimited debate is protective of the states with small populations which otherwise might and probably would be ridden over roughshod.... The minority has a right, too."[15]

But Bartlett's support for the right to filibuster did not come at any cost, and the difference that the addition of the four senators from Alaska and Hawaii made became most clear in the great showdown vote on President Lyndon Johnson's landmark Civil Rights Act of 1964. Before 1964 the South had never been defeated when it staged a filibuster against civil rights legislation. On eleven previous occasions Southerners had successfully talked civil rights bills to death, but after seventy-five days and an estimated six million words in 1964, the longest filibuster in Senate history, on June 10 the Senate approved cloture on the act that would redefine race relations in America by a vote of 71–29.[16] The margin of victory turned out to be four voters more than necessary, the four votes that came from Alaska and Hawaii.

After all the hoopla of the Senate passage of the Alaska statehood bill on June 30, Eisenhower's secretive and delayed signing on July 7 drained much of the excitement from the achievement, and is perhaps one reason why "Statehood Day" on June 30 did not come to be recognized in later years as Alaska's Independence Day, as many in 1958 supposed it would. The secret signing also helped perpetuate a myth—the actual Senate vote to the contrary—that the GOP deserved none of the credit for the passage of the legislation. As historian Claus-M. Naske notes, this was best summarized in a letter complaining about the secret signing that Gruening received from a Democratic senator, who alleged that Ike's unceremonial signing was strictly for partisan reasons:

> Rather than to have had pictures taken in the presence of yourself and all those other fine Democrats who played such instrumental roles

in bringing about the admission of the 49th state
into the Union, he chose to handle this momentous matter as though he were merely signing a
private bill for the relief of Mr. 'X.' Lord knows
where he's going to find two Republicans who
were sufficiently important to bring about statehood for Alaska to whom to present the two pens
he used in the signing.[17]

Thanks to Ernest Gruening and Drew Pearson, the question of
who should receive the most credit for the achievement of statehood
had already become a bitterly personal and partisan issue even before
Eisenhower signed the statehood bill into law. In his column on Sunday,
July 5, Pearson published the first draft of the history of the Alaska statehood movement with a blistering attack on Mike Stepovich and the
GOP, slamming the governor of Alaska as nothing more than a statehood
scalawag and opportunist, and claiming that the real father of the forty-
ninth state was former Governor Gruening.

"A lot of Johnny-come-latelies such as Gov. Mike Stepovich are now
claiming credit for making Alaska the 49th state in the Union," Pearson
wrote. "But the man who unobtrusively, but consistently, badgered senators, button-holed congressmen, maneuvered in the smoke-filled rooms
to bring statehood . . . is an ex-newspaperman named Ernest Gruening.
He more than anyone else is the father of the 49th state." Pearson inti-
mated that as a result of a family tragedy, Governor Gruening was more
than merely the metaphorical father of the new state; after Gruening's son
had committed suicide in 1955, Pearson wrote, the "grief-stricken father
more than ever threw all his heart and soul into the battle for Alaskan
statehood. In effect he made Alaska his child."[18]

Pearson's brief history of the statehood movement certainly stretched
the truth in several directions; for starters, no honest depiction of Ernest
Gruening could have ever described his style as "unobtrusive." "If you see
anybody being unobtrusive," the *News-Miner* responded, "you won't have
to ask his name to be sure it is not Ernest Gruening."[19] Pearson's most
serious distortion, however, was that of omission. To make no mention
whatsoever of Bob Bartlett—and likewise ignore Fred Seaton, Lyndon
Johnson, and Sam Rayburn—was inexcusable. While Snedden's press
campaign on behalf of Stepovich had pushed the young Republican governor into the national spotlight and showered him with excess praise,

Pearson's response of simplifying statehood into a one-man crusade by Gruening was equally misleading.

Pearson's attack on Stepovich initiated a long-running historical and political debate over who should receive the most credit for achieving statehood, and it would cause far more serious repercussions than the usual scholarly feud. The controversy Pearson ignited featured prominently in the irreparable final breach between Gruening and Bartlett, who after 1958 barely spoke to each other until Bartlett's death ten years later, and threatened Snedden with financial ruin and the loss of the *Daily News-Miner*.

Ever since Gruening had arrived in Washington, D.C., as the Tennessee Plan senator, Bartlett had chafed at the intrusion of his elder colleague onto the congressional turf he considered his own. When they were both sworn into the U.S. Senate in January 1959, Bartlett thought he should receive the designation as the "Senior Senator" because he had represented Alaska in Washington since 1944. Though Gruening—who repeatedly said he thought of Bartlett as his son—would later claim he was willing to let Bartlett take the honor, that was not how Bartlett angrily recalled the encounter two years later: "To this day I can vividly remember Ernest leaning back in his chair, putting his hands across his belly, assuming the small half smile so familiar, and informing me that we had better give further consideration to this." Gruening wanted to flip a coin to decide who would be senior and who would be junior, and ultimately Bartlett agreed to settle the matter by heads or tails, only to keep him out of Gruening's debt, vowing he "would not take one damn thing from him because to do so would be only to place myself in the position where I could be constantly reminded of the great sacrifice he had made . . . for me." Gruening lost the coin flip, and as a result ever after both Bartlett and Snedden privately called Gruening "Junior."

The feud between Gruening and Bartlett erupted into open warfare in the spring of 1961, when they publicly clashed on the merits of a fishing bill. Shortly afterward, on April 14, Gruening caught up with Bartlett at the end of a luncheon honoring West German Chancellor Konrad Adenauer. According to Bartlett, Gruening accosted him as follows:

> "I have been expecting you to come to see me," he said. My reply was that I had had no intention of coming to see him and if any calling were done it would have to be the other way around.
>
> "You don't like me any more, do you?" he queried. "You hate me, don't you?"

I told him I hated no human being.

"But you don't like me very well any more, do you?" he insisted.

I said I did not.

EG offered the thought that there isn't very much difference between dislike and hate.

Bartlett asked rhetorically: "How can you approach logically a man who distorts facts, always, to suit his own fancy and his own needs and desires? It is impossible."[20]

Over the years both Bartlett and Snedden were continually incensed at what they thought were "Junior's" misstatements of fact and omissions about the winning of statehood and his inclination to seemingly insert himself into the picture at every critical moment. In 1963 Bartlett wrote privately that the history of statehood had been "sadly distorted" by Gruening, who had spread so much misinformation in the public record "the history books will never record the exact truth." Bartlett's version of events had been recorded in the many thousands of letters he had written to Alaskans of all walks of life in the 1940s and 1950s; Bartlett was an articulate, witty, and insightful correspondent, and the personal letter was his favored literary art form. Following Bartlett's death a distraught friend found a cache of about twenty of his letters she had saved for the archives. Knowing she would never again receive one of his treasured missives, she said, is what "leaves me so bereft."

As gifted as he may have been as a personal correspondent, however, Bartlett never had the confidence nor took the time to write a book. In May 1967 he told Snedden, who repeatedly was begging him to write a memoir, that he hoped "the time may come when I shall have the leisure and the inclination to write of my recollections of the statehood movement. Since others [i.e., Junior] are doing their writing now, I must stick to business and to Alaska's continuing needs."[21] Knowing that he could never match Gruening's skill as a scholar or author, Bartlett gloomily predicted that future historians would "understandably give Ernest a place as the foremost leader of the statehood movement he simply does not deserve. They do so because he, farsighted, has written his own history of what went on and this is the published work to which historians of the present and the future have to refer. No one else has put down the true and contrary story. That is my fault."[22]

As part of the 1967 Alaska Centennial the newly established University of Alaska Press wanted to publish a collection of short reminiscences of the principal actors in the statehood movement, but Snedden was incensed to learn in late 1966 that the book—eventually published as *The Battle for Alaska Statehood*—had been written entirely by Ernest Gruening. As Snedden explained to Bartlett, "because Junior is known as a scholar, writer and historian, he was contacted asking to submit a monograph on statehood not to exceed 20,000 words. This of course let the camel get his nose into the tent. . . . Characteristic of Junior's usual modus operandi, the 20,000 words have now grown to something like 70 or 80,000, and the result of course will be a nice fat book."[23]

Bartlett responded in early 1967 that even if he had possessed the skill, he had no intention of going on the public record in his fight with Gruening over their conflicting historical interpretations of statehood:

> Bill, you cause me utmost agony in reporting that Junior had written a little old paper amounting to 70,000 or 80,000 words on statehood. I declined to write anything at all. . . . I don't want to be recorded under my name in any such undertaking. If I tell the truth about this it will cause a commotion greater in Alaska than any recent event. The truth should be told and eventually will insofar as I am concerned but after some of the actors have departed this vale to another. In saying this I am torn to beat the band because I realize that historians of the future turn to printed records written by participants and Junior has written more than any other person on this subject and will continue to write more than any other and his publications will form the principal source for what those who write later will have to draw upon.[24]

Though he refused to put pen to paper, Bartlett was exasperated when he continued to hear about how the Alaska-Tennessee Plan, and by implication Ernest Gruening, had been the winning weapon in the statehood campaign. The latest was from Tom Stewart, secretary of the Alaska Constitutional Convention, who appeared to Bartlett to be hopelessly under Gruening's spell. He confided in Snedden, as they both believed the Tennessee Plan had largely been a failure, and largely because of Gruening himself:

Tom Stewart was in Washington the other day and was out to the house for dinner in company with others. We got to talking about George Lehleitner. From there Tom proceeded to speak in a manner that indicated he thought that statehood came about by reason of the operation of the Tennessee plan. This was more than I could take so I told him that, although my regard for George was and is high and I, too, endorsed the Tennessee plan, the plain, brutal truth of the matter is that it had little or nothing to do with the accomplishment of statehood. You and I know how it broke down and why almost from the moment the delegation arrived in Washington.[25]

As much as Snedden disliked Gruening's statehood book, however, he believed the senator's worst historical transgression had been published by Drew Pearson beginning on July 5, 1958, with the "Johnny-come-lately" attack on Mike Stepovich. Snedden was still in Washington when he read Pearson's column that Sunday, and he furiously wired George Sundborg in Fairbanks telling him he was "permanently dropping" Pearson. Sundborg argued against the decision, replying that in essence Pearson's criticism of Stepovich was on target:

Feel it my duty as friend and loyal employee to communicate my judgment which is that reason for dropping Pearson will be all too obvious to loyal opposition which will make big thing out of it hurtful to News-Miner, Mike and Republicans generally. Sad truth is that Mike never did a thing for statehood till year ago and our dropping column saying so will only put frosting on Democratic campaign cake. Running column won't hurt Mike here but dropping it will.

Snedden followed Sundborg's advice and ran the Pearson column slamming Stepovich on July 7, but the *News-Miner* followed with its historic "Garbage Man of the 4th Estate" editorial on July 8 written by George Sundborg.

"Drew Pearson irritates us often. On days like yesterday he infuriates us." The editorial denied that Governor Stepovich was, as Pearson alleged, "'claiming credit for making Alaska the 49th state.'" "To the best of our knowledge Mike Stepovich hasn't been claiming a thing." After defending Stepovich, the editorial first took dead aim on Ernest Gruening. Not only had the former governor not been of much help in the capital, it charged he had actually been one of the greatest roadblocks to statehood, quoting an unnamed Washington insider: "It's a good thing the people of Alaska sent down two other Tennessee Plan representatives, and had Bob Bartlett on the job, because it has taken practically the full time efforts of three men for the past two years patching up the damage Gruening did."

And then the editorial dealt with Pearson, citing again an unnamed source—who was in fact Ted Stevens—who reported that Pearson had been called "'the garbage man of the fourth estate.' . . . This would seem to raise the point . . . of why we should give space in our newspaper to the printing of garbage. . . . For the time being we'll get a clothespin for our editorial nose while we decide what to do about this free-wheeling garbage man of the fourth estate."[26]

Snedden permanently dropped Drew Pearson at the end of July 1958, about the same time that he told editor George Sundborg that his services would no longer be needed. For a variety of reasons, both personal and political, Snedden had concluded that it was time to part ways with Sundborg and to find a new editor who could enthusiastically back the GOP. Additionally, he would come to believe that Sundborg, working behind his back, intentionally ensnared the *News-Miner* in the legal nightmare that grew out of the "garbage man" controversy.

While other newspapermen might have laughed off the criticism of a small daily newspaper four thousand miles from Washington, that was not Drew Pearson's style. His first response was to ask Gruening to instigate a letter-writing campaign to Snedden demanding the reinstatement of the "Washington Merry-Go-Round" in the *News-Miner*, saying that by doing so they could "almost guarantee that the dictatorial suppressor of news who runs this sheet will repent."[27] Pearson also pledged to help Gruening in his upcoming U.S. Senate campaign against Snedden's candidate, Mike "Johnny Come Lately" Stepovich, which gave Pearson the idea of suing Snedden for libel. Pearson explained to Gruening the plan behind the lawsuit, which he characterized as "a gold mine of opportunity," in late August 1958: "Libel suits are something I don't like to get mixed up in. But in this particular case I thought it might be interesting and might even be helpful regarding the coming campaign. If for instance, we could bring out in court in Alaska the biased position of Mr. Snedden and the truth of the fact that Stepovich was a Johnny-come-lately regarding statehood, it would be most helpful in bring a good senator to Washington."

By early September 1958 Pearson had decided he would wage an all-out campaign against the *News-Miner*, hiring Warren Taylor as his Fairbanks attorney. "I have concluded that it would be smart strategy for me to sue Snedden and the *News-Miner* for libel," Pearson wrote Taylor. "I have consulted with my old friend Ernest Gruening, who thinks that the juries in Alaska would be favorable to me and not too favorable to Snedden." Pearson said he was "not only endeavoring to collect a substantial amount of damages from Snedden" but was also planning to put "Stepovich on the witness stand" and force him to admit under oath "when he really came out for statehood."

Pearson's libel suit against the *News-Miner* for $176,000 plus court costs, formally filed in Fairbanks on October 13, 1958, may have contributed slightly to voters' doubts about the level of Stepovich's commitment to statehood, as Gruening's narrow victory the following month was the biggest upset of the election that turned out to be a Democratic sweep. In the words of the *New York Times* the morning after the first state election, "Alaska lay buried today under a white blanket of Democratic ballots."[28] But politics and justice move at different speeds, and just because the 1958 election came and went, Pearson was not about to drop his vendetta against Snedden. Senator Gruening, who quickly hired his old protégé, former *News-Miner* editor George Sundborg, to be his administrative assistant, would actually be reelected a second time in 1962—this time defeating Ted Stevens—before the libel lawsuit finally came to trial six years after it was filed in September 1964.

During the eight-day proceedings, it was not simply the *News-Miner* that was on trial but the history of statehood itself. Much of the testimony centered on the question of how sincere and how long Mike Stepovich had been in the statehood camp, and conversely how important Ernest Gruening's contributions had been. The Democrats took the lawsuit as the trial of Ernest Gruening. As Snedden later quipped to Bartlett: "For a time it appeared that the issue being resolved was: 'Is it not a fact that Ernest Gruening is actually the George Washington of Alaska'"?[29]

Snedden was gratified that Bartlett, whom he called the "star witness for the defense," flew to Fairbanks to testify on behalf of the *News-Miner* as to the general reputation of Drew Pearson on Capitol Hill, and ever after believed that "the principal reason our side emerged on top from this unique legal-political carnival was the fact that Alaska's distinguished senior senator was a witness for us!" For his part Bartlett and his staff were furious to hear Gruening honored in the libel suit as the principal architect of statehood by those who testified for the Pearson/Gruening side. The praise heaped on Gruening was intended to show the contrast between him and Stepovich, and therefore prove the substance of Pearson's "Johnny-come-lately" charge, but Bartlett felt the elevation of Gruening in the adversarial process and the total disregard of his own role was a travesty. The worst was the sworn testimony of Stan McCutcheon, a longtime Democratic legislator and Gruening ally, who came across in news accounts as if he had deliberately denigrated Bartlett vis-à-vis Gruening. When Mary Lee Council read that under cross-examination McCutcheon had admitted that James Wickersham, Tony Dimond, and Bob Bartlett had all played a role in statehood, but that "Senator Gruening was more responsible for statehood than any man"—she was dumbfounded. "I read it, and I couldn't believe it," she wrote McCutcheon. "And so I read it again. . . . I called it to Bob's attention with the suggestion that he might want to write you. He said he wouldn't bother. Perhaps he felt it impossible to alter the unalterable. However, I am so bothered that I decided to write you myself." Council said that if she "didn't write this letter, Stan, I should feel that history was being defaulted," because "Ernest Gruening wasn't even a midwife at the birth of the modern statehood movement." She went through Bartlett's record point by point:

> Who was it, Stan, who year in and year out made members of the Congress conscious that Alaska ever existed?
>
> Who was it, Stan, who during his 15 years in representing Alaska . . . led all members, both in the House and Senate, in the number of bills enacted into law?
>
> Who was it, Stan, because of this process of appearing before just about every Senate and House standing committee time after time was in position to tell Alaska's story repeatedly, thus performing a real Alaska "brainwashing"?

> Who was it, Stan, through sheer hard work, warmth, persuasion and creation of good will— and without a vote—advanced Alaska's cause?
>
> Who was the main force, Stan, through those long years in slowly but surely turning the strong tides of indifference and opposition to interest, enthusiasm, victory?[30]

Bartlett and Snedden's shared passion for the statehood cause and their equal indignation with Ernest Gruening, which had been highlighted during the Drew Pearson libel suit, forged a bond between the two men that other politicians could never comprehend. Two months before Bartlett's death in 1968 a friend reported that she had been asked by a Fairbanks Democrat how she could "stand" Snedden: "Such an inquiry would never be directed to you by me," Bartlett responded. "I understand the man although back in the days when he first came to Fairbanks it took some doing on my part." He said he not only admired Snedden for having the strength of character to reverse the *News-Miner*'s position on statehood, but also over the years had learned that in spite of Snedden's strong partisan orientation his "dedication, as I see it, to the public good in the long run outweighs all other considerations. . . . As we know so well and so gratefully . . . few there are in the statehood movement who did more to reach that goal. He is quite a man."[31]

Knowing that a Pearson victory in the libel suit would only further burnish the legend of Ernest Gruening, Bartlett was nearly as delighted as Snedden when Judge Everett W. Hepp ruled in November 1964 that following the reasoning of the recent U.S. Supreme Court landmark case *New York Times v. Sullivan*, since Pearson was an internationally known public figure, the *News-Miner*'s "garbage man" description lacking "actual malice" was privileged speech. Two years later the Alaska State Supreme Court upheld the decision.[32]

Washington syndicated columnist Robert S. Allen said Snedden's "epic victory" over a bully such as Pearson deserved "universal public acclaim," though he feared that few in the journalism profession would be brave enough to say it. "Unhappily, your fellow publishers and other newspaper people doubtless won't give you the resounding kudos you deserve, but that doesn't detract from the fact that you merit them one bit. If there were such a thing as a Medal of Honor in newspaperdom, you deserve it outstandingly. You had the guts and fortitude to take on this jerk bluntly and baldly, and you nailed him to the mast."[33]

In the final analysis the Pearson libel suit against the *Fairbanks Daily News-Miner* proved the extent to which the most powerful newspaper columnist in America would go to settle an old score. Ironically, the legal ruling protected Pearson probably more than anyone, as the case greatly expanded the latitude of the press in freely commenting on public figures. But Snedden found the victory particularly satisfying; he hung a framed clipping from *Time* about the case on his office wall, reminding him that he could now legally call Drew Pearson a garbage man anytime he wished.

Conclusion of the long legal battle with Pearson in 1966 resolved the unfinished business of the *News-Miner*'s statehood campaign, but in the eight years since the case had been filed both the newspaper and the state it had helped to create were vastly changed from 1958. Most of the certainties about what Alaska statehood would mean had turned out to be wrong. Admitting Alaska and in turn Hawaii did not open the floodgates for other new offshore states, and the most likely candidate, Puerto Rico, continues to prefer Commonwealth status. The conventional wisdom that Hawaii would go Republican and Alaska Democratic was turned on its head. While Hawaii became a Democratic stronghold, the state of Alaska proved to be far more amenable to the GOP almost from the start, shockingly even going for Nixon over Kennedy in 1960. JFK's defeat in Alaska—balanced by his surprising victory in Hawaii—was the start of a pattern that would continue: though Alaskans voted for LBJ in the 1964 landslide, that would be the only time they have ever voted Democratic in a presidential election. Conversely the Hawaiians have only gone Republican twice: during the Nixon and Reagan landslides in 1972 and 1984. As of 1966 Alaska had a Republican governor (Wally Hickel), a Republican congressman (Howard Pollock), and a Republican State House and Republican State Senate, and even though Gruening and Bartlett still held the U.S. Senate seats, an analyst concluded that the Republicans "have become the majority party, no longer subject to the taunts of being a mere faction or splinter group."[34]

Especially considering the newfound strength in Alaska of the GOP, that Gruening would still be one of the state's two U.S. senators as of 1966 was for Snedden almost unimaginable. Dismayed that Gruening defeated Stepovich in the first state election, Snedden thought Ted Stevens would be the top candidate to defeat Junior in 1962. (Gruening's first term was only four years, and Bartlett's two years, so as to ensure future staggered elections.) To promote Stevens's career and help prepare him to knock out Gruening, Snedden began lobbying hard after the 1958 campaign to have Stevens appointed as the sole federal judge for the new state, writing Vice President Richard Nixon in December:

> As you may know the Federal Judge will be required to travel almost constantly throughout Alaska, holding court in all principal cities. Admittedly my judgment is not infallible (I honestly thought we could elect Mike Stepovich to the Senate), but I believe if Stevens can receive the Judgeship appointment that within four or six years he will be an extremely strong candidate who could resign and successfully campaign for a Republican seat in the United States senate.[35]

Snedden gave a similar rationale to Fred Seaton, because as a judge Stevens "would be traveling over the whole state pretty constantly. I can't think of a better man than Ted to do some good for the Republicans, and at the same time get established so he would be in a good position in about four years to resign and take on our 72-year-old Democratic Senator in a real lively campaign."[36]

As of December 1959 the judgeship had still not been filled, and Snedden was dismayed when the Associated Press reported that state court Judge Walter H. Hodge—a nonpartisan Republican who eventually received the nod—was being touted for the federal post. He called Hodge's candidacy a Democratic "mousetrap maneuver" designed to block Stevens, ostensibly because Stevens could not win confirmation by the U.S. Senate or the Alaska Bar Association, but in reality, he felt, due to Stevens's stronger GOP credentials and political prospects. As a last-ditch effort Snedden appealed directly in December 1959 to Kentucky Senator Thurston B. Morton, the chairman of the Republican National Committee, to help win the appointment:

> I want very much to see Theodore Stevens appointed as Alaska Federal Judge. I know him very well and am fully convinced he is eminently qualified for the position. Also, perhaps equally important, I believe that, if appointed, Mr. Stevens during the coming two years will establish an adequate

foundation so that he will be in a position to resign
the position on the bench and successfully take on
Democratic Senator Ernest Gruening in the 1962
election. Stevens is the only strong possibility I can
see to accomplish this chore, which I consider of
high priority.[37]

Having failed to get the Alaska judgeship, Stevens would remain in
Washington until the end of the Eisenhower administration, rising to become the top lawyer under Fred Seaton in the Interior Department. After
President Kennedy's election, Stevens returned to Alaska in 1961, moving
to Anchorage to resume private law practice, but in Stevens's much-an-
ticipated run against Gruening for the Senate in 1962, the "cantankerous
old man," as thirty-eight-year-old Stevens called Gruening, handily won
reelection. Stevens was elected to the Alaska State House in 1964 and
in 1966, but in trying for a second shot at Gruening in 1968, he was
defeated in the Republican primary. Stevens's loss seemingly ended any
realistic chance of his rising to the U.S. Senate, as Gruening himself had
been knocked out in the 1968 Democratic primary by upstart challenger
Mike Gravel. But the fates would deal a different hand. On December 11,
1968, Bob Bartlett died unexpectedly in a Cleveland hospital from complications following heart surgery. He was sixty-four. Twelve days later
Governor Wally Hickel appointed Stevens to Bartlett's seat, one he would
hold for the next forty years, the longest tenure of any GOP senator in
U.S. history.[38]

Alaska was changing in the 1960s and so was the *News-Miner*. Always
ahead of the curve of technological innovations in the printing industry,
Snedden realized by the early 1960s that a revolution in newspaper production was in the offing, one that would render obsolete almost all of
the costly equipment in the *News-Miner* printing plant he had purchased
less than ten years before, including the Linotype machines and "Alice,"
the high-speed Goss rotary printing press. As a result of advances in elec-
tronics, transistors, chemical processing, inks, and photography, a new era
of practical printing technology was unfolding, which would cause the
most dramatic change in the printing of newspapers since the invention
of the Linotype machine in the 1880s and the most radical innovation
for printing of all kinds since Guttenberg: the end of typesetting with

movable type and the introduction of photocomposition and offset print-ing. Eventually most newspapers in America would make the shift from composing with "hot type" of molten lead slugs molded on a Linotype machine to "cold type" printed on photographic paper in a phototype-setter in the late 1970s, but despite the enormous costs involved, once Snedden realized the changes were inevitable, he was not content to wait. Starting in about 1962 he and his top technical staff, including Chuck Gray and Mark Campbell, traveled all across the country learning the latest developments in photocomposition, and at the same time began preparing employees for the transition.

In June 1964 Snedden announced his plans to equip the *News-Miner* with the most advanced newspaper production facilities in Alaska: "Our plans for a new building and the latest in newspaper equipment will give our readers and advertisers the most modern and readable newspa-per printed in Alaska."[39] The *News-Miner* tried to explain to readers the difference between the late-nineteenth-century Linotype and the mid-twentieth-century "Fotosetter": slugs of hot lead individually cast out of boiling alloys in the metal pot of the Linotype would be replaced by im-ages of letters produced by the "magic of a beam of light" with solenoid, transistor, and diode "no bigger than a match head." It was the dawning of the "electronic machine age."[40] In the fall of 1965 the *News-Miner* fired up the first rotary offset press in the state, a Goss Urbanite, Snedden called "Lulu," located in the new $1 million Aurora Building, a twenty-thousand-square-foot plant on the north side of the Chena River, imme-diately south of the recently completed passenger terminal of the Alaska Railroad, where the giant rolls of newsprint could be readily offloaded directly from freight cars to the printing press.

In the decades that followed, Snedden's *News-Miner* would continue to play a major role in covering and promoting the growth of Fairbanks and the development of Alaska. Though the 1960s campaign to build the massive Rampart Dam on the Yukon River—a project in which he fer-vently believed—failed, the arctic oil and gas development that he had also promoted since 1954 would prove to be the financial foundation for the state of Alaska. Establishment of the Arctic Wildlife Range in 1960 allowed Fred Seaton to lift PLO 82, the public land order that had closed the Arctic to private oil development since the 1940s, and ultimately led to the opening of the Prudhoe Bay oil fields. The discovery of oil would in turn set off a chain of events, including the settlement of the Alaska Native Claims Settlement Act, the construction of the Trans-Alaska Pipeline, the creation of the Alaska Permanent Fund, and the enactment of the Alaska National Interest Lands Conservation Act of 1980 that would determine the destiny of the state in the 1970s and 1980s.

Until his death in August 1989 after a decade-long struggle with cancer, Snedden's view through it all was that his newspaper's mission was to remind friend and foe alike of the need to keep the promises of statehood alive, in much the same manner and style in which he had promoted statehood in the first place. As Ted Stevens, echoing Fred Seaton, had told Snedden in 1958: "the only reason we really did anything this year . . . is that we would really have caught hell from you if we hadn't." Stevens thought Snedden's brimstone threat was a part of history that they needed to put down on paper. "When we get old, Willis, maybe we should write a story about this 85th Congress and its machinations re statehood."[41]

Snedden never published his story of the getting of statehood, or the keeping of it, except in nearly forty years' worth of newsprint in the pages of the *Fairbanks Daily News-Miner* from August 1, 1950, to August 7, 1989.

Notes

CHAPTER 1

1. Unless otherwise noted, Snedden's reminiscences are from a series of unpublished interviews in the 1980s, hereafter cited as Snedden Interview.

2. The main source for the general history of the newspaper's early years is an unpublished manuscript by Paul Solka Jr., who went to work as an apprentice printer at the *News-Miner* in 1922, rising to journeyman in 1929. In 1975 Solka completed a massive work titled "Adventures in Fairbanks Journalism, 1903–1975." The unwieldy tome was edited and abridged by Art Bremer and published by the *News-Miner* in 1980 in a much slimmer version called *Adventures in Alaska Journalism Since 1903.* See also the telling profile of W. F. Thompson by Mary Lee Davis in *We Are Alaskans* (Boston: W. A. Wilde Co., 1931).

3. *Fairbanks Daily News-Miner* (hereafter *FDNM*), 24 Jan. 1920; Davis, *We Are Alaskans*, p. 134; Solka, "Adventures in Fairbanks Journalism."

4. *FDNM* 13 Nov. 1963.

5. Davis, *We Are Alaskans*, p. 135; *FDNM* 5 Jan. 1926.

6. *FDNM* 15 July 1922.

7. Davis, *We Are Alaskans*, p. 138.

8. Solka, "Adventures in Fairbanks Journalism"; Robert F. Karolevitz, *Newspapering in the Old West: A Pictorial History of Journalism and Printing on the Frontier* (Seattle: Superior Publishing Co., 1966), p. 19.

9. Ibid., p. 23; see also George Corban Goble, "The Obituary of a Machine: The Rise and Fall of Ottmar Mergenthaler's Linotype at U.S. Newspapers" (Ph.D. dissertation, Indiana University, 1984).

10. *Dawson Daily News*, 13 Oct. 1903; 20 Nov. 1903; 3 Sept. 1904; 5 Jan. 1905; *Inland Printer*, June 1901; *Seattle Times*, 13 April 1901.

11. *Fairbanks News*, 19 Sept. 1903.

12. Terrence Cole, *Crooked Past: The Story of a Frontier Mining Camp* (Fairbanks: University of Alaska Press, 1991), p. 122.

13. Ibid., p. 27; *Tanana Weekly Miner*, 18 Oct. 1906; Porter A. Stratton, *The Territorial Press of New Mexico, 1834–1912* (Albuquerque: University of New Mexico Press, 1969), pp. 38–39.

14. W. F. Thompson, *The Low Down Truth About Alaska* (1923), p. 17.

15. Michael Carberry, *Patterns of the Past* (Anchorage: Historical Landmarks Preservation Commission, 1979), p. 133.

16. Joseph Driscoll, *War Discovers Alaska* (New York: J.B. Lippincott, 1943), p. 216.

17. Carberry, *Patterns of the Past*, p. 51; Jean Potter, *Alaska Under Arms* (New York: Macmillan, 1943), p. 111.
18. Elizabeth A. Tower, *Mining, Media, Movies; Cap Lathrop's Keys for Alaska Riches* (Anchorage: Roundtree Publishing, 1991).
19. Philip S. Smith, *Mineral Industry of Alaska in 1940* (U.S. Geological Survey, 1942), p. 83; *Jessen's Weekly*, 6 March 1952.
20. John C. Boswell, *History of Alaskan Operations of the United States Smelting, Refining and Mining Company* (Fairbanks: Mineral Industry Research Laboratory, 1979); Clark C. Spence, *The Northern Gold Fleet: Twentieth Century Gold Dredging in Alaska* (Urbana: University of Illinois Press, 1996).
21. *FDNM* 26 July 1950.
22. *FDNM* 8 Nov. 1929.
23. *FDNM* 26 July 1950.
24. *FDNM* 11 Sept. 1988.
25. Solka, "Adventures in Fairbanks Journalism."
26. Ibid.
27. *FDNM* "Goldfields Edition," 1937.
28. Maury Smith, "KFAR is on the Air," *Alaska Journal*, Autumn 1985, pp. 8–15.
29. Potter, *Alaska Under Arms*, pp. 116–117.
30. Driscoll, *War Discovers Alaska,* p. 223.
31. R. S. and H. M. Lynd, *Middletown: A Study in Contemporary American Culture* (New York: Harcourt, Brace, 1929), p. 269.
32. Solka, "Adventures in Fairbanks Journalism."
33. Ibid.
34. Ibid.
35. *FDNM* 26 July 1950.

CHAPTER 2

1. Richard A. Cooley, *Fairbanks, Alaska: A Survey of Progress* (Juneau: Alaska Development Board, 1954), p. 7; *New York Times*, 21 Feb. 1949.

2. Cooley, *Fairbanks*, p. 12; Merle Colby, *A Guide to Alaska, Last American Frontier* (New York: Macmillan Co., 1939), p. 301.
3. *FDNM* 17 July 1923.
4. Snedden Memo on Duties of Managing Editor, Oct. 1982, Snedden Collection.
5. *Vancouver Evening Columbian*, 29 May 1930.
6. *Vancouver Evening Columbian*, 29 May 1930; 28 April 1930.
7. *FDNM* 8 Nov. 1950.
8. *FDNM* 13 Nov. 1952.
9. *FDNM* 8 Nov. 1950.
10. *Jessen's Weekly*, 5 Nov. 1953.
11. *FDNM* 13 Nov. 1952.
12. Ibid.
13. *FDNM* 29 Feb. 1952; 7 Sept. 1951.
14. *FDNM* 2 May 1952.
15. Snedden Interview.
16. John J. Ryan, *The Maggie Murphy* (New York: Norton, 1951).
17. *FDNM* 13 Nov. 1963.
18. *FDNM* 8 Sept. 1995.
19. Snedden Memo on Duties of Managing Editor, Oct. 1982, Snedden Collection.
20. *FDNM* 9 June 1952.
21. *Seattle Post-Intelligencer*, 6 Sept. 1995.
22. *FDNM* 11 June 1952.
23. *FDNM* 8 Sept. 1995.

CHAPTER 3

1. U.S. Senate, *Conditions in Alaska: Report of Subcommittee of Committee on Territories*, 1904.
2. *The Forty-Ninth Star*, 1915.
3. H. G. Wells, *The Outline of History* (Garden City, NY: Garden City Publishing, 1931), p. 1028.
4. U.S. House of Representatives, *Russian America*, 40th Congress, 2nd Session, 1868, Ex. Doc. No. 177, p. 189.
5. Melvin Crain, "Governance for Alaska: Some Aspects of Representation," Ph.D. dissertation, University of Southern California, 1957, p. 190.

6. Terrence Cole, "Creating Alaska Museum Exhibit"; Henry W. Clark, *Alaska: The Last Frontier* (New York: Grosset and Dunlap, 1939), p. 135; J.A. Hellenthal, *The Alaskan Melodrama* (New York: Liveright Publishing Co., 1936), p. 284.

7. Robert David Johnson, *Ernest Gruening and the American Dissenting Tradition* (Cambridge: Harvard University Press, 1998), p. 158.

8. Ickes hoped FDR would fire Gruening late 1939 so that Charles Bunnell, the president of the University of Alaska, could take over as governor. See Claus-M. Naske, *Ernest Gruening: Alaska's Greatest Governor* (Fairbanks: University of Alaska Press, 2004), p. 27.

9. *Ketchikan Alaska Chronicle,* 15 Sept. 1949; Richard H. Bloedel, "The Alaska Statehood Movement," Ph.D. dissertation, University of Washington, 1974, pp. 212–213.

10. Claus-M. Naske, *Bob Bartlett of Alaska: A Life in Politics* (Fairbanks: University of Alaska Press, 1979), p. 204.

11. Bartlett to Tony Dimond, 4 May 1943, Personal Correspondence, Bartlett Collection.

12. Gruening to Paul Solka, 16 March 1948, General Correspondence, Gruening Collection.

13. Gruening Diary, 11 Aug. 1940, Gruening Collection.

14. Gruening to Bartlett, 17 March 1948, Bartlett Collection.

15. Gruening Diary, 11 Aug. 1940, Gruening Collection.

16. Ernest Gruening, *A Message to the People of Alaska,* 1941.

17. Gruening to James L. Fly, Chairman of FCC, 21 May 1941; Ernest Gruening, "Memorandum Concerning Radio Stations in Alaska," 15 April 1941. Thanks to Dermot Cole for copies of these documents.

18. *FDNM* Progress Edition, 13 Nov. 1963; Evangeline Atwood and Lew Williams Jr., *Bent Pins to Chains: Alaska and Its Newspapers* (Privately printed, 2006), pp. 393–394; Solka, "Adventures in Fairbanks Journalism."

19. *FDNM* 13 March 1948.

20. A. E. Lathrop to Charles D. Jones, 29 March 1948, Charles D. Jones Collection, Rasmuson Library.

21. Solka, "Adventures in Fairbanks Journalism."

22. Ernest Gruening, *Many Battles: The Autobiography of Ernest Gruening* (New York: Liveright, 1974), pp. 355–360.

23. *FDNM* 6 March 1950.

24. Atwood and Williams, *Bent Pins to Chains,* p. 354; for Gruening's account of his troubles with the *Empire* see *Many Battles,* pp. 372–376.

25. *FDNM* 10 Oct. 1950.

26. *FDNM* 26 July 1950.

27. *FDNM* 10 Oct. 1950.

28. Ibid.

29. Snedden Interview; Evangeline Atwood and R.N. DeArmond, *Who's Who in Alaskan Politics* (Anchorage: Alaska Historical Commission, 1977), p. 96.

30. Ibid.

31. C. W. Snedden, edited by J. S. Whitehead, "C.W. Snedden Recollects the Campaign for Statehood," *Alaska History* 20, no. 1 (Spring 2005).

32. Bloedel, "The Alaska Statehood Movement," pp. 157, 176. The most lopsided vote against statehood probably came from Fort Yukon, where all but two of fifty-four votes were opposed.

33. U.S. House, Alaska Hearings Pursuant to H. Res. 93, 80th Congress, 1st Session, p. 176; Bloedel, "The Alaska Statehood Movement," p. 158.

34. *New York Times,* 2 Sept. 1952, p. 23.

35. *FDNM* 3 Oct. 1951.

36. "Snedden Recollects."

37. U.S. House, *Statehood for Alaska: Hearing Before the Subcommittee on Territorial and Insular Affairs,* 85th Congress, 1st Session, March 1957, p. 154.
38. Ibid.
39. Naske, *Bob Bartlett*, p. 15.
40. *FDNM* Progress Edition, 13 Nov. 1963.
41. Ibid.
42. Naske, *Bob Bartlett*, pp. 21–22.
43. *New York Times*, 16 Oct. 1932, p. E6.
44. Naske, *Bob Bartlett*, p. 29.
45. *Anchorage Daily Times*, 12 Dec. 1968.
46. *New York Times*, 12 Dec. 1968, p. 43.
47. Naske, *Bob Bartlett*, pp. 230–231.
48. Ibid., p. 91.
49. Margaret Truman, ed., *Where the Buck Stops: The Personal and Private Writings of Harry S. Truman* (New York: Warner Books, 1989), p. 12.
50. "Snedden Recollects."
51. Ibid.
52. *FDNM* 27 Feb. 1954.
53. Snedden Interview.
54. "Snedden Recollects."
55. Snedden Interview.
56. Ibid.
57. "Snedden Recollects."
58. Ibid.
59. Mary Lee Council, "Three Steps Forward, Two Steps Back: Bob Bartlett and Alaska Statehood," unpublished manuscript, pp. 358–359.

CHAPTER 4
1. Peter Coates, *The Trans-Alaska Pipeline Controversy* (Fairbanks: University of Alaska Press, 1993), p. 82.
2. *FDNM* 23 March 1953; 25 Feb. 1955; 26 Feb. 1955; 28 Feb. 1955; 3 March 1955.
3. *FDNM* 28 May 1954; 4 June 1955.
4. *FDNM* 28 May 1954.
5. Ibid.
6. *FDNM* 20 Feb. 1953.
7. An excellent treatment of both Chariot and Rampart is Coates, *The Trans-Alaska Pipeline Controversy*.

For the Chariot fight in particular see Dan O'Neill, *The Firecracker Boys* (New York: St. Martin's Press, 1995).
8. *FDNM* "A Newcomer Gives Varied Impressions of Fairbanks," Progress Edition, 1953.
9. *Alaska Journal*, Autumn 1983.
10. Dermot Cole, *Historic Fairbanks: An Illustrated History* (San Antonio: Historical Publishing Network, 2002), p. 36.
11. *FDNM* 23 March 1953.
12. *FDNM* 8 Aug. 1957.
13. *FDNM* 23 Aug. 1957.
14. *FDNM* 7 Aug. 1957.
15. *FDNM* 3 Dec. 1958.
16. *FDNM* 10 April 1957.
17. *FDNM* 9 Dec. 1959; 14 Aug. 1959.
18. *FDNM* 4 Sept. 1953.
19. *FDNM* 13 Nov. 1952.
20. *FDNM* 15 Feb. 1957; 19 Feb. 1957; 27 Feb. 1957.
21. *FDNM* 30 Nov. 1954.
22. *FDNM* 17 July 1953.
23. *FDNM* 10 Aug. 1953.
24. Ibid.
25. *FDNM* 14 Aug. 1953.
26. *FDNM* 21 Aug. 1953.
27. *FDNM* 28 Dec. 1953.
28. *FDNM* 13 Nov. 1953.
29. *FDNM* 9 Dec. 1953.
30. *FDNM* 4 Feb. 1954.
31. *FDNM* 11 Feb. 1954.
32. *FDNM* 16 Feb. 1954.
33. *FDNM* 2 March 1954.
34. *FDNM* 9 Sept. 1954.
35. Hickel, *Who Owns America?* (Englewood Cliffs, NJ: Prentice-Hall, 1971), p. 68.
36. Ibid.
37. *FDNM* 30 Nov. 1954.
38. *FDNM* 3 Dec. 1954.
39. *FDNM* 1 Dec. 1954.
40. *FDNM* 21 Jan. 1955.
41. *FDNM* 16 Dec. 1955; 19 Dec. 1955.
42. *FDNM* 22 Jan. 1955.
43. *FDNM* 19 Dec. 1955.
44. Ibid.

45. *FDNM* 16 Dec. 1955.
46. *FDNM* 31 Dec. 1954.
47. *FDNM* 11 Jan. 1957.
48. *FDNM* 7 Dec. 1954; 8 Dec. 1954; 13 Dec. 1955.
49. *FDNM* 12 Aug. 1954.
50. *FDNM* 6 Dec. 1954.
51. *FDNM* 10 Jan. 1955.
52. *FDNM* 6 May 1953.
53. *FDNM* 14 Feb. 1957.
54. *FDNM* 4 March 1955.
55. *FDNM* 8 Dec. 1955.
56. *FDNM* 4 June 1955.
57. *FDNM* 15 June 1955.
58. *FDNM* 11 June 1955.
59. *FDNM* 8 April 1957.
60. *FDNM* 8 April 1957.
61. *FDNM* 10 May 1957.
62. *FDNM* 26 March 1957.
63. *FDNM* 2 Feb. 1951.
64. *FDNM* 1 Dec. 1953.
65. *FDNM* 28 April 1953.
66. *FDNM* 8 Sept. 1955.
67. *FDNM* 12 April 1957.
68. *FDNM* 3 May 1957.
69. *FDNM* 7 May 1957.
70. *FDNM* 27 Aug. 1957.
71. *FDNM* 9 Feb. 1957.
72. *FDNM* 23 Dec. 1954.
73. *FDNM* 3 May 1956.
74. *FDNM* 30 July 1957.
75. *FDNM* 18 July 1953; 24 Sept. 1953.
76. *FDNM* 16 March 1955.
77. *FDNM* 12 April 1955.
78. *FDNM* 8 May 1954.
79. *FDNM* 29 Aug. 1957.

CHAPTER 5

1. *Juneau Independent,* 22 July 1954.
2. State of Alaska, Legislative Affairs Agency, *Alaska Legislature: Roster of Members 1913–1982* (Juneau, 1982).
3. Peter Wood, "The Sorry State of Alaska," *Interlake Times,* Constitutional Convention, Anti-Statehood Materials, Egan Collection.
4. *FDNM* 15 June 1956; 1 July 1957.
5. *Congressional Record,* 23 March 2000.

6. The best and most detailed biographical portrait yet published about Ted Stevens is a series by reporter David Whitney in the *Anchorage Daily News* from Aug. 7 to 15, 1994. Whitney also wrote "Mr. Stevens Goes to Washington," a profile that appeared in the winter 2000 issue of *UCLA Magazine.* See also Donald Craig Mitchell, *Take My Land, Take My Life* (Fairbanks: University of Alaska Press, 2001), pp. 220–221; Mike Doogan, "Uncle Ted," *Alaska Magazine,* Nov. 2005; *FDNM* "U.S. Senator Ted Stevens," Special Edition, 29 Dec. 1993.
7. U.S. District Courts, Alaska, 4th Division, Fairbanks, Oaths and Orders, "Theodore F. Stevens, 1954" (hereafter Stevens oath), Pacific Alaska Region, National Archives and Records Administration (PAR, NARA).
8. Theodore F. Stevens, "Erie R.R. v. Tompkins and the Uniform General Maritime Law," *Harvard Law Review* 64, no. 2 (Dec. 1950): 246–270.
9. William Tetley, *Glossary of Maritime Law Terms.* For "Pole Star" see "From Swift to Erie: An Historical Perspective," Review by Gene R. Shreve, *Michigan Law Review* 82, no. 4 (1984): 869.
10. Stevens, "Erie R.R. v. Tompkins and the Uniform General Maritime Law," p. 270.
11. E. A. Kral, "700 Famous Nebraskans: Nationally Distinguished Nebraskans: A Brief Bio-Bibliography of 700 Individuals," http://www.nebpress.com/700/famousnebs.pdf; *New York Times,* 6 May 1980.
12. *FDNM* 4 Aug. 1962.
13. *Jessen's Weekly,* 19 Feb. 1953, p. 32. Mitchell says Stevens took Petro's job, *Take My Land, Take My Life,* p. 222.
14. David Whitney, "The Road North," *Anchorage Daily News,* 9 Aug. 1994;

Jessen's Weekly, 16 April 1953, p. 30; *Jessen's Weekly,* 28 Jan. 1954.

15. *Jessen's Weekly,* 16 April 1953.
16. *Jessen's Weekly,* 15 Jan. 1953; *FDNM* 17 Jan. 1953.
17. Michael Crowley, "The Jerk": In Praise of Ted Stevens, the Senate's Angriest Man," the *New Republic,* 10 Sept. 2007.
18. Alan Ehrenhalt and Michael Glennon, eds., *Politics in America: Members of Congress in Washington and at Home* (Washington, DC: Congressional Quarterly, Inc., 1983), pp. 39–40.
19. *Congressional Record,* 23 March 2000.
20. David Whitney, "The Road North," *Anchorage Daily News,* 9 Aug. 1994.
21. Stevens oath, PAR, NARA; *FDNM,* 31 Aug. 1953.
22. *FDNM* 16 Feb. 1953; 17 Feb. 1953; 18 Feb. 1953; 24 April 1953; *Jessen's Weekly,* 5 Feb. 1953; 19 Feb. 1953.
23. *FDNM* 3 March 1953.
24. *FDNM* 5 Feb. 1953.
25. *FDNM* 16 Feb. 1953.
26. *FDNM* 17 Feb. 1953.
27. *FDNM* 18 Feb. 1953.
28. *FDNM* 21 Feb. 1953.
29. Minutes of the Fairbanks City Council, 2 March 1953; *Jessen's Weekly,* 5 March 1953; *FDNM* 3 March 1953.
30. *FDNM* 24 April 1953.
31. *FDNM* 25 April 1953.
32. *FDNM* 28 March 1953; 11 May 1953.
33. *FDNM* 23 April 1954.
34. Floyd Oles to Charles F. Willis, 1 Oct. 1953; 8 Oct. 1953, General Files, 17-E-1, #313, 17-M, Alaska, 1952–59, Eisenhower Library.
35. *FDNM* 24 Jan. 1953.
36. *FDNM* 22 Jan. 1953.
37. *FDNM* 24 Jan. 1953; 24 Feb. 1953.
38. *FDNM* 2 Feb. 1953.
39. *FDNM* 30 Dec. 1953; 15 Jan. 1954.
40. R.N. DeArmond to Myrth B. Sarvela, 24 Aug. 1953. Thanks to Dermot Cole for a copy of this correspondence.
41. Ibid.
42. *Jessen's Weekly,* 22 Jan. 1953; 29 Jan. 1953; *FDNM* 2 Feb. 1953; *FDNM* 14 Aug. 1953.
43. *Jessen's Weekly,* 29 Jan. 1953; 26 Feb. 1953; *FDNM* 14 Aug. 1953.
44. *FDNM* 14 Aug. 1953.
45. Snedden to Stevens, 2 May 1986, Snedden Collection.

CHAPTER 6

1. William R. Hunt, *Distant Justice: Policing the Alaska Frontier* (Norman: University of Oklahoma, 1987), p. 9.
2. *FDNM* 11 Sept. 1953.
3. *FDNM* 28 Sept. 1953.
4. Richard Oestermann, "A Danish Journalist Views Alaska," *Alaska Life,* Aug. 1948, p. 22.
5. *FDNM* 23 Aug. 1957.
6. *New York Times,* 3 Feb. 1949, p. 16.
7. Dr. Charles Walter Clarke, ASHA Executive Director, to Gov. Gruening, 21 Feb. 1952.
8. *FDNM* 6 March 1952.
9. *FDNM* 11 March 1952.
10. *FDNM* 20 May 1952; 3 Sept. 1952.
11. Warren A. Taylor to Bartlett, 16 June 1958, Justice Files, Bartlett Collection.
12. David Whitney, "The Road North," *Anchorage Daily News,* 9 Aug. 1994.
13. *FDNM* 11 Sept. 1953.
14. Snedden to Heintzleman, 3 Nov. 1953, U.S. Department of Justice, Office of Legal Policy, Office of Information and Privacy, FOIA (Freedom of Information Act) Request.
15. *FDNM* 29 Oct. 1953.
16. Al Dorsch to "Bill" (Strand), 14 Jan. 1954, FOIA Request.
17. Ibid.
18. Snedden to Heintzleman, 3 Nov. 1953, FOIA Request.
19. Tanana Valley Bar Association to Honorable Herbert Brownell,

Attorney General of the United States, 19 Nov. 1953, FOIA Request.

20. *FDNM* 23 Nov. 1953; 27 Nov. 1953; Tanana Valley Bar Association to Honorable Herbert Brownell, Attorney General of the United States, 19 Nov. 1953, FOIA Request.
21. Ralph Rivers to Bartlett, 22 Jan. 1954, General Correspondence, Bartlett Collection.
22. Ibid.
23. Bartlett to Ralph Rivers, 27 Jan. 1954, General Correspondence, Bartlett Collection.
24. Al Dorsch to "Bill" (Strand), 14 Jan. 1954, FOIA Request.
25. Snedden to Heintzleman, 3 Nov. 1953, FOIA Request.
26. Snedden to Honorable Herbert Brownell Jr., 25 Nov. 1953, FOIA Request.
27. Judge George Folta to Attorney General James P. McGranery, 5 Aug. 1952, Alaska General Correspondence, Judiciary, Box 3, Gruening Collection.
28. *FDNM* 27 Nov. 1953.
29. G. T. Charlton, Fairbanks Ministerial Association, to U.S. Attorney General, 23 Nov. 1953, FOIA Request.
30. *FDNM* 3 Nov. 1953.
31. (Blacked out) to Herbert Brownell, 21 Nov. 1953, FOIA Request.
32. *FDNM* 10 Jan. 1955.
33. *FDNM* 12 June 1956.
34. *FDNM* 24 Oct. 1953; 14 May 1954; 15 May 1954; 24 May 1954; 26 May 1954; 29 May 1954; 23 July 1954; 10 June 1955; *Jessen's Weekly*, 20 May 1954; Michael Carey, "Con men and women," *Anchorage Daily News*, 17 June 2006, is an insightful reflection on the white slavery case.
35. *FDNM* 22 Feb. 1955.
36. Stanley McCutcheon to Gruening, 2 May 1955, Gruening Collection.
37. J. L. McCarrey to Legislators, 1 Feb. 1955, included in statement by Warren A. Taylor, "In the Matter of the

Disbarment of Warren A. Taylor," 24 April 1955, U.S. Attorneys and Marshals, Fairbanks, Alaska, Significant Civil and Criminal Case Files, 1955–1973, "In the Matter of Contempt of Court by Warren A. Taylor," (hereafter Taylor disbarment file), PAR, NARA.
38. Taylor disbarment file, PAR, NARA.
39. *FDNM* 9 Feb. 1955; 22 March 1955.
40. *FDNM* 9 Feb. 1955.
41. *FDNM* 11 Feb. 1955
42. *FDNM* 22 March 1955.
43. U.S. Attorney Ted Stevens to Special Agent in Charge, 23 Feb. 1955; Special Agent John A. Holtzman to Theodore Stevens, U.S. Attorney, 2 March 1955, Taylor disbarment file, PAR, NARA.
44. *FDNM* 23 March 1955.
45. Stanley McCutcheon to Gruening, 2 May 1955, Gruening Collection.
46. *FDNM* 5 April 1955.
47. Judge George W. Folta to Theodore Stevens, U. S. Attorney, 4 April 1955, Taylor disbarment file, PAR, NARA.
48. Warren A. Taylor to Bartlett, 16 June 1958, Justice files, Box 5, Bartlett Collection.
49. U. S. Court of Appeals Ninth Circuit, *Bergen v. USA*, No. 14158, 2 June 1955, 222 F.2d 949, 15 Alaska 548; *FDNM* 9 June 1955.
50. Stevens oath, PAR, NARA.
51. *FDNM* 13 Jan. 1955.
52. *FDNM* 4 Jan. 1955.
53. *FDNM* 13 March 1953.
54. *FDNM* 2 Oct. 1953.
55. *FDNM* 25 Sept. 1953.
56. *FDNM* 25 Sept. 1953.
57. *FDNM* 29 Sept. 1953.
58. *FDNM* 16 Jan. 1954.
59. *FDNM* 21 Dec. 1953; 28 Dec. 1953.
60. *FDNM* 29 Dec. 1953.
61. *FDNM* 17 Dec. 1953.
62. *FDNM* 15 Dec. 1953.
63. *FDNM* 29 Dec. 1953.
64. *FDNM* 5 Jan. 1954.
65. *FDNM* 5 Jan. 1954.

66. A. P. Brandt to Stevens, *FDNM* 21 Jan. 1955.
67. *FDNM* 10 Feb. 1955.
68. *FDNM* 1 Feb. 1955.
69. *FDNM* 10 Feb. 1955.
70. Ibid.
71. *FDNM* 21 Jan. 1955.
72. *FDNM* 10 Feb. 1955.
73. *FDNM* 24 Feb. 1955.
74. *FDNM* 1 Feb. 1955.
75. *FDNM* 17 Feb. 1955.
76. *FDNM* 3 March 1955.
77. *FDNM* 23 Sept. 1953; 1 Oct. 1953; *Jessen's Weekly*, 22 Oct. 1953.
78. Richard T. Fulton, "Death and the Midas Touch," *Front Page Detective*, Feb. 1954, p. 23.
79. *FDNM* 7 March 1953; 7 April 1953.
80. *FDNM* 23 Sept. 1953; 1 Oct. 1953;
81. *FDNM* 17 Oct. 1953; 9 March 1954; U.S. Attorneys and Marshals, Fairbanks, Alaska, Significant Civil and Criminal Case Files, 1955–1973, "Colombany, William," Fourth Judicial Division, Grand Jury, July 1954 Term, Typescript of Testimony taken 21 Jan. 1955 from Reuben J. Tarte (hereafter Colombany file), p. 20, PAR, NARA.
82. *Jessen's Weekly*, 29 Oct. 1953; 22 Oct. 1953.
83. *FDNM* 17 Oct. 1953; 19 Oct. 1953.
84. *FDNM* 7 Oct. 1953.
85. *FDNM* 21 Oct. 1953.
86. *FDNM* 19 Oct. 1953.
87. *FDNM* 20 Nov. 1953.
88. *FDNM* 23 Nov. 1953.
89. Ibid.
90. *FDNM* 24 Nov. 1953.
91. *FDNM* 30 Nov. 1953.
92. *FDNM* 2 Oct. 1953; 30 Oct. 1953; 31 Oct. 1953; 3 Nov. 1953; 4 Nov. 1953.
93. *Life*, "The Case of the Beat-Up Blonde," 30 Nov. 1953, pp. 52–54; *Newsweek*, "Drummer and Blonde," 16 Nov. 1953, pp. 38–39; *New York Times*, 18 Oct. 1953, p. 88; *FDNM*,

7 Nov. 1953; *Ebony*, "The Alaska Murder Case," Oct. 1954, pp. 99–102.
94. *FDNM* 17 Sept. 1954.
95. *FDNM* 4 Nov. 1953.
96. *FDNM* 6 Nov. 1953.
97. *FDNM* 7 Nov. 1953.
98. *FDNM* 24 Nov. 1953; 27 Nov. 1953.
99. *Newsweek*, "Drummer and Blonde," pp. 38–39.
100. *FDNM* 27 Nov. 1953.
101. Ibid.
102. *FDNM* 6 Feb. 1954.
103. *FDNM* 9 March 1954.
104. "Long Distance Telephone conversation [transcript] between Sgt. Boswell of the Los Angeles Police Department, and Mr. Stevens, U.S. Attorney, Fairbanks, Alaska, March 15, 1955," Colombany file, PAR, NARA.
105. *FDNM* 28 March 1955; 29 March 1955; 18 June 1955.
106. *FDNM* 22 May 1956; 1 June 1956; 8 June 1956.

Chapter 7

1. Bartlett to John J. Ryan, 5 March 1954, Bartlett Collection.
2. Bartlett to Snedden, 13 March 1954, Bartlett Collection.
3. *FDNM* 11 Oct. 1954.
4. Snedden to Bartlett, 18 March 1954; 22 March 1954, Bartlett Collection.
5. Bartlett to Snedden, 13 March 1954, Bartlett Collection.
6. Bartlett to Karl Armstrong, 24 July 1953, Bartlett Collection.
7. Bloedel, "The Alaska Statehood Movement," pp. 281, 617.
8. Bob Atwood to Kit Crittenden, 17 Feb. 1954, Bartlett Collection.
9. Snedden to Bartlett, 22 March 1954, Bartlett Collection.
10. Ibid.
11. Bartlett to Snedden, 26 March 1954, Bartlett Collection.
12. See also *FDNM* 24 March 1954.
13. Bartlett to John J. Ryan, 13 April 1954, Bartlett Collection.

14. Snedden to Bartlett, 22 March 1954, Bartlett Collection.
15. *New York Times*, 8 Feb. 1953, p. 58.
16. Ibid., 27 June 1954, p. E2.
17. "Membership Changes of 83rd Congress (1953–1955)," http://www.senate.gov/artandhistory/history.
18. Robert A. Caro, *The Years of Lyndon Johnson: Master of the Senate* (New York: Alfred A. Knopf, 2002), p. 94.
19. Bartlett to Victor C. Rivers, 22 March 1954, Bartlett Collection.
20. Bartlett to Karl Armstrong, 24 July 1953, Bartlett Collection.
21. Bartlett to Steve McCutcheon, 23 Jan. 1954, Bartlett Collection.
22. *New York Times*, 22 Jan. 1971, p. 38.
23. Ibid., 22 Jan. 1972, p. 43.
24. Gruening to William S. Carlson, 5 Feb. 1952, Bartlett Collection.
25. Bartlett to Lehleitner, 13 April 1956, Gruening Collection.
26. *Times-Picayune* (New Orleans), 3 Jan. 1993.
27. Clarence K. Streit, *Union Now: The Proposal for Inter-Democracy Federal Union* (shorter version) (New York: Harper Brothers, 1940), p. 246.
28. Streit, *Union Now*, p. 25.
29. Ibid., p. 83.
30. Clarence K. Streit, *Union Now with Britain* (New York: Harper and Brothers, 1941), pp. 209–210.
31. Lehleitner to Clarence K. Streit, 17 Jan. 1986, "How *Union Now* Inspired the Campaign to Bring Alaska and Hawaii Into the Union," website of the Streit Council for a Union of Democracies.
32. Lehleitner to James C. Wright, 12 Sept. 1963, Bartlett Collection.
33. Lehleitner to Sen. Russell B. Long, 14 Jan. 1955, Bartlett Collection.
34. Lehleitner to Clarence K. Streit, 17 Jan. 1986.
35. Rep. James B. Utt to Lehleitner, 12 Jan. 1956, Gruening Collection; Lehleitner to Members of Alaska State Constitutional Convention, 16 Jan. 1956, Egan Collection.
36. Lehleitner to Members of Alaska State Constitutional Convention, 16 Jan. 1956, Egan Collection.
37. Lehleitner to Mildred R. Hermann, 7 May 1956, Gruening Collection.
38. Lehleitner to Gruening, 16 May 1954, Gruening Collection.
39. Bartlett to Snedden, author's files.
40. *FDNM* 2 Dec. 1950.
41. Bloedel, "The Alaska Statehood Movement," p. 333.
42. Ibid., pp. 337–338.
43. *Juneau Independent*, 29 April 1954.
44. Ibid., 25 Feb. 1954; a slightly different version appears in Gruening to Barrie White Jr., Operation Statehood, n.d., Gruening Collection.
45. Lehleitner to James C. Wright, 12 Sept. 1963, Bartlett Collection.

Chapter 8

1. *FDNM* 8 Sept. 1955.
2. *FDNM* 27 Nov. 1953.
3. *Anchorage Daily Times*, 4 June 1954, p. 6.
4. *FDNM* 3 June 1955.
5. *FDNM* 8 Feb. 1955.
6. Minutes of the Alaska Constitutional Convention (hereafter Minutes ACC), Day 1, http://www.law.state.ak.us/doclibrary/cc_minutes.html.
7. "Snedden Recollects."
8. *FDNM* 1 Sept. 1954; 3 Sept. 1954.
9. Minutes ACC, Day 3.
10. Ibid.
11. Ibid.
12. Ibid.
13. Ibid.
14. *FDNM* 11 Nov. 1955; Gerald E. Bowkett, *Reaching for a Star: The Final Campaign for Alaska Statehood* (Fairbanks: Epicenter Press, 1989), p. 27.
15. Victor Fischer, *Alaska's Constitutional Convention* (Fairbanks: University of Alaska Press, 1975), p. 26.

16. Bowkett, *Reaching for a Star*, p. 27.
17. Fischer, *Alaska's Constitutional Convention*, p. 34.
18. Ibid., pp. 34–35.
19. *FDNM* 15 Nov. 1955.
20. Bloedel, "The Alaska Statehood Movement," p. 492.
21. Fischer, *Alaska's Constitutional Convention*, p. 168.
22. Minutes ACC, Day 76.
23. Ibid., Day 73.
24. Roger Bell, *Last Among Equals: Hawaiian Statehood and American Politics* (Honolulu: University of Hawaii Press, 1984), p. 180; George Lehleitner, "The Tennessee Plan— Admission of the Bold," Egan Collection.
25. Robert T. Mann, *Legacy to Power: Senator Russell Long of Louisiana* (New York: Paragon House, 1992), p. 185.
26. *FDNM* 4 Oct. 1954.
27. *Time*, 14 July 1958, p. 70.
28. Bartlett to H. H. Hilscher, 27 Nov. 1956, Bartlett Collection.
29. *FDNM* 30 June 1983.
30. Lehleitner to Hon. F. Edward Hebert, 31 Dec. 1957, Bartlett Collection.
31. Lehleitner to Hon. Sam Rayburn, 25 Jan. 1958; Bartlett to Lehleitner, 28 Jan. 1958, Bartlett Collection.
32. Lehleitner to Snedden, 24 March 1958, attached speech written by Lehleitner, Bartlett Collection.
33. Lehleitner to Delegates of Alaska State Constitutional Convention, 25 Jan. 1956, Constitutional Convention, Egan Collection.
34. *Anchorage Daily Times*, 14 Dec. 1955.
35. Ibid., 13 Dec. 1955.
36. Ibid., 10 Dec. 1955.
37. *FDNM* 12 Dec. 1955.
38. *FDNM* 13 Dec. 1955.
39. Ibid.
40. Snedden to Lehleitner, 3 Dec. 1955, Mattson Chronology.
41. Bartlett to Egan, 13 Dec. 1955, Constitutional Convention, Egan Collection.
42. Robert H. Estabrook to Lehleitner, 16 Nov. 1955, Constitutional Convention, Egan Collection.
43. Bartlett to Egan, 13 Dec. 1955, Constitutional Convention, Egan Collection.
44. *FDNM* 20 Jan. 1956; Minutes ACC, Day 59.
45. *FDNM* 24 Jan. 1956; Minutes ACC, Day 62.
46. George Lehleitner, "The Tennessee Plan—Admission of the Bold," Egan Collection.
47. *FDNM* 24 Jan. 1956.
48. Ibid.
49. Minutes ACC, Day 68.
50. *FDNM* 1 Feb. 1956.
51. Fischer, *Alaska's Constitutional Convention*, pp. 153–154; Bowkett, *Reaching for a Star*, pp. 78–79; Minutes ACC, Day 71.
52. Minutes ACC, Day 68.
53. Ibid., Day 72.
54. Ibid.
55. Ibid.
56. Ibid.
57. Ibid, Day 73.
58. Snedden to Bartlett, 13 Feb. 1956, Bartlett Collection.
59. Snedden to Rep. Edith Green, 27 Jan. 1957, Constitutional Convention, Bartlett Collection.
60. Bartlett to Egan, 15 March 1956, Constitutional Convention, Egan Collection.
61. *FDNM* 6 Feb. 1956.
62. Snedden to Bartlett, 13 Feb. 1956, Bartlett Collection.
63. Bartlett to Snedden, 13 Feb. 1956, Constitutional Convention, Bartlett Collection.
64. Bartlett to Snedden, 16 Feb. 1956, Bartlett Collection.
65. *Anchorage Daily Times*, 14 April 1956; *FDNM* 18 Feb. 1956.

66. *FDNM* 18 Feb. 1956.
67. *FDNM* 3 Feb. 1956.
68. Lehleitner to Egan, 23 Dec. 1955, Constitutional Convention, Egan Collection.
69. *Ketchikan Daily News*, 5 April 1956.
70. *Anchorage News*, 19 April 1956.
71. Lehleitner to Snedden, 9 April 1956, Constitutional Convention, Egan Collection.
72. Lehleitner to Mildred Hermann, 12 April 1956, Constitutional Convention, Egan Collection.
73. Snedden to Bartlett, 21 April 1956, Egan Collection.
74. *FDNM* 26 April 1956.
75. *FDNM* 29 May 1956; Bloedel, "The Alaska Statehood Movement," pp. 520–521.
76. Bartlett to Lehleitner, 13 April 1956, Gruening Collection.
77. Bartlett to Egan, 23 March 1956, Tennessee Plan, Egan Collection.
78. Bartlett to Earl E. Cook, 29 May 1956, Bartlett Collection.
79. Bartlett to Lehleitner, 13 April 1956, Gruening Collection.
80. Snedden to Bartlett, 21 April 1956, Egan Collection.
81. Lehleitner to Mildred R. Hermann, 7 May 1956, Gruening Collection.
82. Snedden to Bartlett, 21 April 1956, Egan Collection.
83. Ibid.
84. Ibid.
85. Ibid.
86. *FDNM* 29 May 1956.
87. *FDNM* 4 June 1956.
88. Ibid; Bloedel, "The Alaska Statehood Movement," pp. 521–522.
89. Bartlett to Egan, 1 May 1956, Constitutional Convention, Egan Collection.
90. Snedden to Egan, 22 May 1956 (dictated May 19), Tennessee Plan, Egan Collection.
91. Gruening to Mildred Hermann, 26 April 1954, Constitutional Convention, Gruening Collection.
92. Bloedel, "The Alaska Statehood Movement," p. 524.
93. Bartlett to Katherine Nordale, 3 July 1956, Bartlett Collection.
94. Bartlett to Egan, 1 June 1956, Constitutional Convention, Egan Collection.
95. Bloedel, "The Alaska Statehood Movement," p. 523.
96. Lehleitner to James C. Wright, 12 Sept. 1963, Bartlett Collection.
97. Lehleitner to Mildred R. Hermann, 7 May 1956, Gruening Collection.

CHAPTER 9

1. Bartlett to Paul Solka Jr., 2 March 1954, Bartlett Collection.
2. Fred I. Greenstein, "Eisenhower as an Activist President: A Look at New Evidence," *Political Science Quarterly* 94, no. 4 (Winter 1979–1980): 588.
3. John T. Woolley and Gerhard Peters, *The American Presidency Project* [online]. Santa Barbara, CA: University of California (hosted), Gerhard Peters (database). Annual Message to Congress on the State of the Union, Jan. 6, 1955. Available at http://www.presidency.ucsb.edu/ws/?pid=10416.
4. Michael Carey, "Fred Seaton of Nebraska and His Friend in Alaska," p. 3.
5. Elmo Richardson, "The Interior Secretary as Conservation Villain: The Notorious Case of Douglas 'Giveaway' McKay," *Pacific Historical Review* 41, no. 3 (Aug. 1972): 343; "The Old Car Peddler," *Time*, 23 Aug. 1954.
6. Tyler Abell, ed., *Drew Pearson: Diaries, 1949–1959* (New York: Holt, Rinehart and Winston, 1974), p. 234.
7. Thomas Soapes, "Transcript of Oral History Interview with Orme Lewis," p. 10, OH-361, 19 July 1976, Eisenhower Library.
8. Maclyn Burg, "Transcript of Oral History Interview with Elmer

Bennett," pp. 189, 149–151, OH-401, 23 Aug. 1976, Eisenhower Library.

9. Bernard DeVoto, "Conservation: Down and on the Way Out," *Harper's Magazine*, Aug. 1954.

10. Richardson, "The Interior Secretary as Conservation Villain," p. 336.

11. "The Old Car Peddler," *Time*, 23 Aug. 1954.

12. *FDNM* 14 July 1954.

13. *FDNM* 5 June 1954.

14. *FDNM* 16 April 1953.

15. *FDNM* 22 July 1954.

16. "Public Land Order No. 82," *Federal Register*, 4 Feb. 1943, Vol. 8, No. 24, p. 1599.

17. U.S. Department of Interior, Bureau of Land Management, *Table of Public Land Orders, 1942–2007*, www.blm.gov/wo/st/en/prog/more/lands/public_land_orders.html. PLO 82 was amended seven times before Seaton finally revoked it with PLO 2215 on 6 Dec. 1960, at the same time that he created the Arctic Wildlife Range with PLO 2214.

18. John C. Reed, *Exploration of Naval Petroleum Reserve No. 4 and Adjacent Areas Northern Alaska, 1944–1953, Part 1, History of the Exploration*, U.S. Geological Survey Professional Paper 301 (Washington, D.C.: U.S. Government Printing Office, 1958), pp. v, 169–173; Dalton, *Possibility of Commercial Development of Gubik Gas Field*, p. 8.

19. *FDNM* 27 Dec. 1954.

20. Robert W. King, "Without Hope of Immediate Profit: Oil Exploration in Alaska, 1898–1953," *Alaska History* 9, no. 1 (Spring 1994): 19.

21. Ibid., p. 27; David E. Jessup, "The Rise and Fall of Katalla: 'The Coming Metropolis of Alaska,'" *Alaska History* 20, no. 1 (Spring 2005): 24–41.

22. Hugh A. Johnson and Harold T. Jorgenson, *The Land Resources of Alaska: A Conservation Foundation*

Study (University Publishers, 1963), p. 242; Phil R. Holdsworth, "Oil and Gas May Transcend Gold and War Booms in Alaska's Economy," in *Lou Jacobin's Guide to Alaska and the Yukon* (Juneau: Guide to Alaska Co, 1954), pp. 47–53.

23. Holdsworth, "Oil and Gas May Transcend Gold and War Booms," p. 47; Reed, *Exploration of NPR No. 4*, pp. 134–138, 147–152, 161.

24. Reed, *Exploration of NPR No. 4*, p. 150; *FDNM* 31 Jan. 1953; *Jessen's Weekly*, 12 March 1953.

25. *FDNM* 9 March 1953; 14 March 1953.

26. *FDNM* 3 Sept. 1954.

27. For a biographical summary of Dalton see Joe E. LaRocca, *Alaska Agonistes: The Age of Petroleum* (North East, PA: Rare Books, Ink, 2003), pp. 333–348; *Jessen's Weekly*, 25 Aug. 1950; *FDNM* 8 Jan. 1955.

28. *FDNM* 12 Jan. 1954.

29. *FDNM* 12 Jan. 1954; 23 July 1954.

30. *FDNM* 12 Jan. 1954.

31. *FDNM* 13 Jan. 1954.

32. Dalton, *Possibility of Commercial Development of Gubik Gas Field*, p. 2; *FDNM* 27 Aug. 1954; 8 Jan. 1955.

33. *FDNM* 9 May 1977.

34. Dalton, *Possibility of Commercial Development of Gubik Gas Field*, pp. 4–5.

35. Ibid., pp. 33–35.

36. Ibid., pp. 2, 5.

37. *FDNM* 8 Aug. 1968; 9 May 1977; 11 May 1977.

38. *FDNM* 8 Aug. 1968; LaRocca, *Alaska Agonistes*, pp. 347–348.

39. *FDNM* 22 July 1954.

40. *New York Times*, 12 Oct. 1944, p. 28.

41. Donald A. Ritchie, *Reporting from Washington: The History of the Washington Press Corps* (New York: Oxford University Press, 2005), p. 135; Douglas A. Anderson, *A 'Washington-Merry-Go-Round' of Libel Actions* (Chicago: Nelson Hall, 1980), p. 10.

42. Steve Weinberg, "Avenging Angel or Deceitful Devil?: The Evolution of Drew Pearson, a New Kind of Investigative Journalist," *American Journalism* 14, no. 3–4 (Summer-Fall 1997): 299.
43. "Battle of the Billygoats," *Time*, 25 Dec. 1950, p. 11.
44. *Congressional Record*, 1944, pp. 3683–3688; Anderson, *A 'Washington-Merry-Go-Round' of Libel Actions*, p. 3.
45. "Core of the Corps," *Time*, 9 July 1951, p. 55.
46. Anderson, *A 'Washington-Merry-Go-Round' of Libel Actions*, p. 248; Douglas A. Anderson, "Drew Pearson: A Name Synonymous With Libel Actions," *Journalism Quarterly* 56, no. 2 (Summer 1979): 235–242.
47. Anderson, "Drew Pearson: A Name Synonymous With Libel Actions," p. 239.
48. *FDNM* 8 July 1954; 15 Aug. 1958.
49. "Querulous Quaker," *Time*, 13 Dec. 1948, p. 71.
50. Anderson, *A 'Washington-Merry-Go-Round' of Libel Actions*, pp. 1–2.
51. Ibid., p. 235.
52. Drew Pearson and Jack Anderson, *The Case Against Congress: A Compelling Indictment of Corruption on Capitol Hill* (New York: Simon and Schuster, 1968), p. 433.
53. Tyler Abell, ed., *Drew Pearson: Diaries, 1949–1959* (New York: Holt, Rinehart and Winston, 1974), p. 256.
54. Drew Pearson, "Washington-Merry-Go-Round," 30 Sept. 1954; 1 Oct. 1954, Special Collections, American University Library, Washington, D.C.; "Querulous Quaker," *Time*, 13 Dec. 1948, p. 70.
55. *FDNM* 15 Feb. 1954; 23 Dec. 1954; 27 Dec. 1954.
56. *FDNM* 12 Oct. 1954.
57. *Juneau Independent*, 14 Oct. 1954.
58. Snedden to Lehleitner, 19 March 1956, Mattson Chronology.
59. Bartlett to Mildred Hermann, 23 Feb. 1954, Bartlett Collection.
60. *Anchorage Daily Times*, 24 Feb. 1954.

CHAPTER 10

1. *FDNM* 13 April 1953.
2. *New York Times*, 26 Jan. 1954, p. 16.
3. *New York Times*, 2 July 1954, p. 19; Bloedel, "The Alaska Statehood Movement," p. 319; Justus F. Paul, "The Political Career of Senator Hugh Butler, 1940–1954," Ph.D. dissertation, University of Nebraska, 1966, p. 27.
4. Bloedel, "The Alaska Statehood Movement," p. 361; *FDNM* 13 Aug. 1953.
5. Paul, "The Political Career of Senator Hugh Butler, 1940–1954," p. 292.
6. Ibid., p. 291.
7. Sen. Hugh Butler to Hon. William F. Knowland, 12 March 1954, File 17-M-4, White House Central Files, Eisenhower Library.
8. Ibid.
9. Soapes, "Transcript of Oral History Interview with Orme Lewis," p. 46.
10. James Hagerty Diaries, 1 March 1954, Box 1, Folder 1, Eisenhower Library.
11. *New York Times*, 14 Aug. 1947, p. 12.
12. David Holloway, *Stalin and the Bomb: The Soviet Union and Atomic Energy* (New Haven: Yale University Press, 1994), p. 242; *Chicago Daily Tribune*, 4 March 1951, p. 10.
13. *New York Times*, 2 April 1950, p. 1.
14. *New York Times*, 30 March 1950, p. 2.
15. Hanson W. Baldwin, "Alaska: Rampart We Must Watch," *New York Times Magazine*, 23 April 1950, p. 34.
16. Soapes, "Transcript of Oral History Interview with Orme Lewis," pp. 46–47; Bloedel, "The Alaska Statehood Movement," pp. 388–389.
17. Bartlett to Bruce Kendall, 10 May 1954, Bartlett Collection.
18. Sen. Hugh Butler to the president, 12 March 1954; Sen. Hugh Butler

to Hon. William F. Knowland, 12 March 1954, File 17-M-4, White House Central Files, Eisenhower Library.

19. Cornelius P. Cotter, "Eisenhower as Party Leader," *Political Science Quarterly* 98, no. 2 (Summer 1983): 255.

20. Woolley and Peters, *The American Presidency Project*. Eisenhower Press Conference, March 16, 1955. http://www.presidency.ucsb.edu/ws/?pid=10434.

21. Ibid., Eisenhower Press Conference, 14 July 1954.

22. Bartlett to Barrie White, 25 Feb. 1955, Bartlett Collection.

23. *Anchorage Daily Times*, 27 July 1954.

24. Bartlett to Donald H. Eyinck, 2 April 1954, Bartlett Collection.

25. Sen. A. Willis Robertson to Hon. Howard W. Smith, 3 April 1954, File 147-D-1, White House Central Files, Eisenhower Library.

26. Wilton B. Persons to A. Willis Robertson, 5 April 1954, File 147-D-1, White House Central Files, Eisenhower Library.

27. *FDNM* 4 April 1955.

28. Bartlett to James F. Doogan, 13 Feb. 1957, Bartlett Collection.

29. Bartlett to Donald H. Eyinck, 2 April 1954, Bartlett Collection.

30. *FDNM* 19 May 1954.

31. *FDNM* 5 April 1954.

32. Barrie White Jr. to Sen. Hugh Butler, 14 April 1954, Bartlett Collection.

33. Bartlett to Henry A. Benson, 14 April 1954, Personal File, Bartlett Collection.

34. Bartlett to Jim Downey, 13 April 1954, Bartlett Collection.

35. *The Juneau Independent*, 27 May 1954.

36. Alsa F. Gavin to Bob Bartlett, 8 April 1954, Bartlett Collection.

37. *Juneau Independent*, 8 April 1954.

38. *FDNM* 4 Feb. 1955.

39. *FDNM* 23 Feb. 1955.

40. *Juneau Independent*, 29 July 1954.

41. Bill Egan to Bartlett, 11 April 1954, Personal File, Bartlett Collection.

42. Sen. Hugh Butler to Bob Atwood, 21 April 1954, Bartlett Collection.

43. Memo of Bob Bartlett, 1 May 1954, Bartlett Collection.

44. John Joseph Ryan to President Eisenhower, 21 April 1954, File 17-M-4, White House Central Files, Eisenhower Library.

45. Bartlett to Louis R. Huber, 8 May 1954, Bartlett Collection.

46. *FDNM* 3 May 1954.

47. *FDNM* 15 May 1954.

48. *FDNM* 10 May 1954; 11 May 1954.

49. *FDNM* 15 May 1954.

50. Bartlett to Louis R. Huber, 8 May 1954, Bartlett Collection.

51. Orme Lewis to Thomas E. Stephens, Secretary to the President, 13 May 1954, File 147-D-1, White House Central Files, Eisenhower Library.

52. Bartlett to Mildred Hermann, 20 May 1954; Bartlett to Sundborg, 24 May 1954, Bartlett Collection.

53. *FDNM* Golden Days Edition, July 1969, p. B30; Naske, *Alaska Statehood: The Memory of the Battle*, p. 52.

54. Bartlett to Mildred Hermann, 20 May 1954; Bartlett to Sundborg, 24 May 1954, Bartlett Collection.

55. Ibid.

56. Naske, *Alaska Statehood: The Memory of the Battle*, p. 52.

57. *FDNM* 14 May 1954.

58. Barrie White to the president, 27 May 1954, File 147-D-1, White House Central Files, Eisenhower Library. There is no evidence to support the often repeated myth that in the course of his monologue Butrovich pounded on Ike's desk. Such unruly behavior would have landed Butrovich on his seat on the pavement of Pennsylvania Avenue!

59. Ibid.

60. *Juneau Independent*, 29 July 1954.

61. *Juneau Independent*, 24 Aug. 1954.

62. *Anchorage Daily Times*, 8 June 1954; 9 June 1954; Bartlett to Mildred Hermann, 20 May 1954, Bartlett Collection.
63. *Anchorage Daily Times*, 9 June 1954; 15 June 1954.
64. *Anchorage Daily Times*, 14 June 1954.
65. *FDNM* 9 June 1954.
66. *Anchorage Daily Times*, 10 June 1954.
67. Bloedel, "The Alaska Statehood Movement," p. 387.
68. *FDNM* 21 July 1954; *Anchorage Daily Times,* 20 July 1954.
69. *FDNM* 21 July 1954.
70. *Anchorage Daily Times*, 29 July 1954.
71. *Anchorage Daily Times*, 27 July 1954.
72. Ibid.
73. *Juneau Independent*, 5 Aug. 1954; *Anchorage Times*, 27 July 1954.
74. *Juneau Independent*, 5 Aug. 1954.
75. *FDNM* 5 Feb. 1955.

CHAPTER 11

1. *New York Times*, 27 April 1956. Eisenhower outpolled both his Democratic rivals; however, as the *Times* noted, "the normally Democratic territory ran true to form by casting a higher [combined] total vote for the two Democratic contenders."
2. Bartlett to Egan, 26 April 1956, Constitutional Convention, Egan Collection.
3. Wendell P. Kay to Bartlett, 2 March 1956, Bartlett Collection.
4. Bartlett to Bruce A. Kendall, 19 March 1954, Bartlett Collection.
5. *Washington Post*, 11 Dec. 1951, p. 2.
6. *New York Times*, 18 Jan. 1974, p. 36.
7. *Christian Science Monitor*, 23 Sept. 1958, p. 14; *New York Times*, 30 May 1956, p. 20; 6 June 1956, p. 32.
8. *New York Times*, 5 Dec. 1952, p. 28; Herbert S. Parmet, *Eisenhower and the American Crusades* (New York: Macmillan, 1972), p. 313.
9. Kansas State Historical Society, "Fred Seaton: A Kansas Portrait,"

http://www.kshs.org/portraits/seaton_fred.htm.
10. *New York Times*, 18 June 1940, p. 29.
11. *New York Times*, 19 June 1940, p. 22.
12. *Washington Post,* 19 Dec. 1951, p. 2.
13. *New York Times*, 29 May 1956, p. 14.
14. "The Cabinet Game," *Time*, 17 Nov. 1952; Louis Galambos, ed., *The Papers of Dwight David Eisenhower: NATO and the Campaign of 1952*, Vol. XIII (Baltimore: Johns Hopkins University Press, 1989), pp. 1468–1470.
15. *New York Times*, 29 May 1956, p. 14.
16. *FDNM* 16 May 1956; 17 May 1956; *Washington Post and Times Herald,* 3 June 1956, p. E1; *Christian Science Monitor*, 2 June 1956, p. 14.
17. *New York Times*, 7 June 1956, p. 21; *Chicago Daily Tribune*, 31 May 1956, p. 8; *Washington Post and Times Herald*, 29 May 1956, p. 12.
18. U.S. Senate, *Nomination of Frederick A. Seaton to be Secretary of the Interior, Hearing Before the Committee on Interior and Insular Affairs*, 5 June 1956 (Washington, DC: Government Printing Office, 1956), p. 19.
19. Robert Welch, *The Politician* (Belmont Publishing Co., n.d.), pp. 233–234.
20. *FDNM* 12 Nov. 1955.
21. *Washington Post and Times Herald*, 16 Dec. 1957, p. A13; Burg, "Oral History Interview with Elmer F. Bennett," 23 Aug. 1976, Interview No. 4, pp. 163–166; *FDNM,* 12 Nov. 1955.
22. Allen Drury, "Eisenhower's Four Years," *New York Times*, 27 July 1956, p. 1.
23. U.S. Senate, *Nomination of Frederick A. Seaton*, 5 June 1956, p. 21.
24. *FDNM* 5 June 1956.
25. U.S. Senate, *Nomination of Frederick A. Seaton*, p. 31.
26. *FDNM* 1 June 1956.
27. Victor Fischer to Bartlett, 7 June 1956, Bartlett Collection.
28. Bartlett to Victor Fischer, 16 June 1956, Bartlett Collection.

29. Author Michael Carey was the first to make this observation.
30. *New York Times*, 18 Jan. 1974, p. 36.
31. "The Voice of the Opposition," *Time*, 23, Feb. 1953.
32. *FDNM* 1 June 1956; Newell B. Terry, director of personnel, to chief of examining divisions, U.S. Civil Service Commission, 4 Dec. 1958, U.S. Department of Justice, National Archives.
33. Ted Stevens to Warren E. Burger, 6 Aug. 1954; Fred G. Aandahl, assistant secretary of the interior, to Ted Stevens, 27 Sept. 1954; RG 118, Box 15, Significant Civil and Criminal Case Files, File No. 85, PAR, NARA.
34. Claus-M. Naske, "Bob Bartlett and the Alaska Mental Health Act," *Pacific Northwest Quarterly*, Jan. 1980, p. 31.
35. Naske, *Bob Bartlett of Alaska*, pp. 99–114; Naske, "Bob Bartlett and the Alaska Mental Health Act," pp. 31–39.
36. U.S. Senate, Committee on Interior and Insular Affairs, *Alaska Mental Health: Hearings Before the Subcommittee on Territorial and Insular Affairs of the Committee on Interior and Insular Affairs United States Senate, 84th Congress, 2nd Session, on H.R. 6376, S. 2518, S. 2973* (Washington, DC: Government Printing Office, 1956), p. 42.
37. U.S. House, Committee on Interior and Insular Affairs, *Alaska, 1955: Hearings Before the Subcommittee on Territorial and Insular Affairs of the Committee on Interior and Insular Affairs, House of Representatives, 84th Congress, 1st Session, Pursuant to H. Res. 30*, Pt. 1 (Washington, DC: Govt. Printing Office, 1956), p. 4.
38. Ibid., p. 1.
39. Naske, *Alaska Statehood*, pp. 115–116.
40. Bartlett to William P. Rogers, 9 Sept. 1955, Department of Justice, NARA.
41. Joseph H. Lesh, "Memorandum for the Files, Re: Request of Delegate E.L. Bartlett...for authority for Theodore Stevens to testify-Mental Health Bill," Department of Justice, NARA.
42. Dale C. Cameron, "Comment: Alaska Mental Health Survey," *American Journal of Psychiatry* 107, no. 3 (Sept. 1950): 226–227.
43. *FDNM* 22 Feb. 1956.
44. Stevens to William P. Rogers, Deputy Attorney General, 29 Aug. 1955, Department of Justice, NARA; U.S. House, *Alaska, 1955*, p. 162.
45. U.S. House, *Alaska, 1955*, p. 159.
46. Ibid., pp. 159–160.
47. Ibid., pp. 161–162.
48. *FDNM* 21 Sept. 1955.
49. *FDNM* 21 Sept. 1955; 11 June 1956.
50. *FDNM* 19 Jan. 1956.
51. Priscilla L. Buckley, "'Siberia, U.S.A.,' The Rocky Road of H.R. 6376," *National Review*, 25 July 1956, p. 10.
52. Leigh F. Burkeland, "Siberia, U.S.A.," reprinted in U.S. Senate, *Alaska Mental Health*, pp. 141–142.
53. Michelle M. Nickerson, "The Lunatic Fringe Strikes Back: Conservative Opposition to the Alaska Mental Health Bill of 1956," in *The Politics of Healing: Histories of Alternative Medicine in Twentieth Century*, ed. Robert D. Johnson (New York: Routledge, 2003), p. 126.
54. U.S. Senate, *Alaska Mental Health*, p. 182.
55. *FDNM* 14 Feb. 1956; 3 Feb. 1956.
56. Naske, *Bob Bartlett of Alaska*, p. 113; *Alaska Mental Health Enabling Act*, July 28, 1956, Public Law 830, ch. 772, 70 Stat., pp. 709–714; *FDNM* 4 June 1956; 7 June 1956; 8 June 1956.
57. Mitchell, *Take My Land, Take My Life*, pp. 224–225.
58. William P. Rogers to Theodore F. Stevens, 1 March 1956; Theodore F. Stevens to William P. Rogers, 1 March 1956; Theodore F. Stevens

to Joseph H. Lesh, 1 March 1956; FOIA request.

59. "Ted Stevens Denies Rumor of 'Pressure,'" undated clipping from *FDNM* Snedden Collection.

60. Theodore F. Stevens to Joseph H. Lesh, 1 March 1956, FOIA request.

61. Ted Stevens to Herbert Brownell Jr., 14 May 1956, FOIA request.

62. *FDNM* 29 Sept. 1955; 15 Nov. 1955.

63. Maclyn Burg, "Transcript of Oral History Interview with Ted Stevens," OH-484, 6 Oct. 1977, Eisenhower Library, pp. 2–3.

64. Burg, "Oral History Interview with Elmer F. Bennett," 2 July 1975, Interview No. 3, pp. 82–83.

65. Ibid., pp. 80–81.

66. Burg, "Oral History Interview with Ted Stevens," pp. 9–10.

67. Newell B. Terry, director of personnel to chief of examining divisions, U.S. Civil Service Commission, 4 Dec. 1958, U.S. Department of Justice, National Archives.

68. Ibid.; Burg, "Oral History Interview with Elmer F. Bennett," p. 137; *FDNM* 20 Feb. 1961; *New York Times*, 9 June 1956, p. 11.

69. Burg, "Oral History Interview with Ted Stevens," pp. 7–8.

70. Snedden to Lehleitner, 29 Sept. 1956; "Oct. 1956 Lehleitner visit to D.C.," Mattson Chronology.

71. Snedden to Seaton, 12 Nov. 1956, Snedden File, Seaton Collection, Eisenhower Library.

72. Memo by LK, 26 Nov. 1956, Snedden File, Seaton Collection, Eisenhower Library.

73. Elmer F. Bennett to Seaton, 13 Dec. 1956, Snedden File, Seaton Collection, Eisenhower Library.

74. Snedden to Lehleitner, 3 Dec. 1956, Mattson Chronology.

75. Ernest Gruening, *The Battle for Alaska Statehood* (College: University of Alaska Press, 1967), p. 94.

76. Snedden to Lehleitner, 6 Feb. 1957, Mattson Chronology.

77. Snedden to Seaton, 29 Dec. 1956, Bennett Collection, Box 20, Per Book II (4), Eisenhower Library.

78. Ibid.

79. Ibid.

80. *FDNM* 29 Jan. 1957.

81. Gruening to Gradelle Taylor, 7 March 1957, Gruening Collection.

82. Legislative Counsel to General Wilton E. Persons, 6 March 1957, A 76-26, Box 3, Alaska Statehood, Seaton Collection, Eisenhower Library.

83. Ibid.

84. Ibid.

85. As early as May 1954 the *News-Miner* reported that Sen. Hugh Butler said, "The idea of a military reservation within state boundaries instead of a partition seems to have merit and may be a good compromise. Supposedly such a reservation would embrace vast non-populous areas of Northern and Western Alaska." See *FDNM* 12 May 1954.

86. Legislative Counsel to General Wilton E. Persons, 6 March 1957, Alaska Statehood, Seaton Collection, A 76-26, Box 3, Eisenhower Library.

87. U.S. House Committee on Interior and Insular Affairs, *Statehood for Alaska: Hearings Before the Subcommittee on Territorial and Insular Affairs of the Committee on Interior and Insular Affairs, House of Representatives, 85th Congress, 1st Session, on HR 50, HR 628, and HR 849, etc.* (Washington: Govt. Printing Office, 1957), p. 97.

88. Ibid., p. 95.

89. *FDNM* 12 March 1957.

90. *FDNM* 11 March 1957.

91. Gruening, *The Battle for Alaska Statehood*, p. 95.

Chapter 12

1. U.S. House, *Statehood for Alaska*, p. 146.

2. U.S. Senate, *Alaska Statehood, Hearings Before the Committee on Interior and Insular Affairs, U.S. Senate, 85th Congress, 1st Session, on S. 49 and S. 35* (Washington: Government Printing Office, 1957), p. 9.
3. *Anchorage Daily Times*, 19 March 1957.
4. Estes Kefauver to Sundborg, 26 July 1957; Memo from Snedden to Bartlett, 29 July 1957; Bartlett to Snedden, 1 Aug. 1957, Bartlett Collection; Memo from Snedden to Seaton, n.d., Snedden File, Seaton Collection, Eisenhower Library.
5. Council, "Three Steps Forward, Two Steps Back," p. 369.
6. Snedden to Gruening, 27 Nov. 1956; Snedden to John B. Adams, 27 Nov. 1956, Tennessee Plan File, Egan Collection.
7. *FDNM* 18 Jan. 1957; 19 Jan. 1957; 21 Jan. 1957.
8. Egan to Bill Pettit, 11 July 1957, Egan Collection.
9. Bartlett to Ernest Bartley, 16 April 1957, Bartlett Collection.
10. *FDNM* 12 Jan. 1957.
11. *FDNM* 7 May 1957.
12. Naske, *A History of Alaska Statehood*, p. 243.
13. Homer E. Gruenther to Gerald D. Morgan, 3 Jan. 1957, General File #315, 17-M-4, Eisenhower Library.
14. *New York Times*, 1 July 1958, p. 16.
15. *Anchorage Daily Times*, 15 March 1957; *New York Times*, 22 Feb. 1957, p. 12; 7 March 1957, p. 1; 19 March 1957, p. 74; 8 April 1957, p. 13; 20 April 1957, p. D6; 4 May 1957, p. 10.
16. U.S. Senate, *Alaska Statehood*, p. 10.
17. U.S. House, *Statehood for Alaska*, pp. 116, 133.
18. Ibid., p. 130.
19. Ibid.
20. U.S. Senate, *Alaska Statehood*, pp. 120–121.
21. Ibid., p. 10.
22. U.S. House, *Statehood for Alaska*, p. 150.
23. Ibid., p. 156.
24. Ibid., pp. 152–156.
25. Ibid., p. 160.
26. Ibid., pp. 161–162.
27. Ibid., pp. 165–166.
28. Ibid.
29. *New York Times*, 13 March 1957, p. 18; *Washington Post and Herald Times*, 13 March 1957, p. 2.
30. U.S. House, *Statehood for Alaska*, pp. 303–304.
31. Ibid., p. 310.
32. Ibid., pp. 315, 322.
33. Ibid., pp. 335–336.
34. Ibid., pp. 269–270.
35. *FDNM* 8 Feb. 1951.
36. Bartlett to Snedden, 31 Jan. 1957, Bartlett Collection.
37. U.S. House, *Statehood for Alaska*, p. 332.
38. *FDNM* 10 July 1957.
39. Alice Stuart, *The Alaska Calendar for Engagements* (Fairbanks, 1953). Stuart's calendar was a spinoff of the Hastings House Publishing Company, which published similar engagement calendars for New England, Virginia, California, etc.
40. Bartlett to Stewart French, 25 Jan. 1958, Bartlett Collection.
41. Snedden to Milton Tabor, 18 March 1958, Bartlett Collection.
42. U.S. House, *Statehood for Alaska*, p. 283.
43. U.S. Senate, *Alaska Statehood*, p. 40.
44. *FDNM* 25 Aug. 1953; 10 April 1954; 20 March 1954; 21 May 1954; 19 March 1957.
45. J. William Barba to Bernard M. Shanley, 17 May 1954, White House Office Files, 147-D-1, Eisenhower Library.
46. *FDNM* 27 May 1954.
47. U.S. House, *Statehood for Alaska*, p. 276.
48. Ibid., p. 279.
49. Ibid., pp. 282, 286.

50. U.S. Senate, *Alaska Statehood*, p. 90.
51. Ibid., p. 86.
52. *FDNM* 21 March 1957.
53. *Anchorage Daily Times*, 29 March 1957.
54. *FDNM* 2 April 1957.
55. *FDNM* 21 March 1957.
56. U.S. House, *Statehood for Alaska*, p. 350.
57. *FDNM* 11 April 1957.
58. *FDNM* 20 April 1957.
59. *FDNM* 30 April 1957; 2 May 1958; 8 Feb. 1958.
60. *FDNM* 30 April 1957.
61. Bartlett to Sundborg, 4 June 1955, Bartlett Collection.
62. Sundborg to Bartlett, 20 June 1955, Bartlett Collection.
63. Ibid.
64. "Conquest of Mexico," *Time*, 2 Nov. 1942.
65. *FDNM* 22 Feb. 1956; 23 Feb. 1956; *New York Times*, 22 Feb. 1956, p. 18.
66. "Protecting Sources," *Time*, 5 March 1956; *New York Times*, 23 Feb. 1956, p. 28; 20 Oct. 1965, p. 27; 8 April 1956, p. 30; 10 April 1956, p. 33; *FDNM* 18 May 1956.
67. *New York Times*, 9 April 1956, p. 33; "Publisher Urges Elimination of Taxes," undated clipping from *Anchorage Times*, May 1956, Bartlett Collection.
68. *Congressional Record*, 19 March 1958, p. 4196.
69. Ruben Berrios Martinez, "Independence for Puerto Rico: The Only Solution," *Foreign Affairs* 55, no. 3 (April 1977): 567.
70. A.S. "Mike" Monroney, "Let's Keep It 48," *Collier's*, 4 March 1955, p. 36. For a summary of the Alaska commonwealth movement see Claus-M. Naske, "Commonwealth: A Historical Footnote," *Alaska Journal*, Summer 1972, pp. 57–59.
71. *Anchorage Daily Times*, 15 March 1954.
72. Naske, *An Interpretative History of Alaskan Statehood*, pp. 201–202.

73. *Alaska Weekly*, 26 Nov. 1954; U.S. Senate, *Alaska-Hawaii Statehood, Elective Governor, and Commonwealth Status*, "Hearings Before the Committee on Interior and Insular Affairs" (Washington, DC: Government Printing Office, 1955), p. 149.
74. U.S. Senate, *Alaska-Hawaii Statehood*, p. 135.
75. "Publisher Urges Elimination of Taxes," undated clipping from *Anchorage Times*, May 1956, Bartlett Collection.
76. U.S. House, *Statehood for Alaska*, p. 454.
77. *FDNM* 11 June 1957.
78. Bartlett to Egan, 16 Aug. 1957, Egan Collection.
79. Jack Ryan to Bartlett, n.d., Bartlett Collection.
80. Bartlett to Jack Ryan, 9 April 1957, Gruening Collection.
81. *FDNM* 22 April 1957.
82. *FDNM* 12 April 1957; 17 May 1957.
83. Snedden to Bartlett, 18 April 1957, Bartlett Collection.
84. Snedden to Bartlett, 22 April 1957 (dictated 18 April 1957), Bartlett Collection.
85. *FDNM* 23 April 1957.
86. Telegram from W. P. Allen to Snedden and Jack Ryan, 21 April 1957, Bartlett Collection.
87. Ibid.
88. Snedden to Gruening, 22 April 1957, Gruening Collection.
89. *FDNM* 23 April 1957.
90. Telephone Conversation WPA and Snedden, 26 April 1957, Bartlett Collection.
91. Telegram Snedden to Bartlett, 26 April 1957, Bartlett Collection.
92. Bartlett to Snedden, 29 April 1957, Bartlett Collection.
93. Snedden to Bartlett, 30 April 1957 (dictated 27 April 1957), Bartlett Collection.
94. Bartlett to Snedden, 4 May 1957, Bartlett Collection.

95. Jay Hammond, *Tales of Alaska's Bush Rat Governor* (Seattle: Epicenter Press, 1994), p. 124.
96. Bartlett to W. P. Allen, 9 May 1957, Bartlett Collection.
97. *FDNM* 27 May 1957.
98. U.S. Senate, *Alaska Statehood*, pp. 153–154.
99. Bartlett to Sewell Faulkner, 22 March 1957, Bartlett Collection.
100. Bartlett to Atwood, 22 March 1957, Bartlett Collection.

CHAPTER 13

1. *Wall Street Journal*, 3 April 1958; *Time*, 9 June 1958.
2. Snedden to Seaton, 4 March 1957, Seaton Collection, Eisenhower Library.
3. Bloedel, "The Alaska Statehood Movement," p. 542.
4. Snedden to Seaton, 20 April 1957, Seaton Collection, Eisenhower Library.
5. Stevens to Snedden, 5 June 1957, Mattson Chronology.
6. *FDNM* 2 July 1957.
7. *FDNM* 29 July 1957.
8. Snedden to Stevens, 26 June 1957, Seaton Collection, Eisenhower Library.
9. *Wall Street Journal*, 3 April 1958.
10. Bartlett to Mrs. E.A. Fischer, 20 Jan. 1958, Bartlett Collection.
11. *FDNM* 25 June 1958.
12. *FDNM* 3 July 1958.
13. *FDNM* 7 June 1958.
14. Council, "Three Steps Forward, Two Steps Back," pp. 415–416.
15. *FDNM* 18 May 1957.
16. Bartlett to Sundborg, 13 May 1955; 1 May 1957, Bartlett Collection.
17. Snedden to Lehleitner, 9 May 1957, Mattson Chronology.
18. Sundborg to Bartlett, 23 July 1957, Bartlett Collection.
19. Sundborg to Bartlett, 21 June 1957, Bartlett Collection.
20. *FDNM* 26 Aug. 1957; Bartlett to Sundborg, 28 Aug. 1957, Bartlett Collection.
21. Sundborg to Bartlett, 3 Sept. 1957, Bartlett Collection.
22. Bartlett to Sundborg, 5 Sept. 1957, Bartlett Collection.
23. Sundborg to Bartlett, 11 July 1957, Bartlett Collection.
24. Sundborg to Bartlett, 12 June 1957, Bartlett Collection.
25. Sundborg to Bartlett, 23 July 1957, Bartlett Collection.
26. Sundborg to Bartlett, 3 Sept. 1957, Bartlett Collection.
27. Bartlett to Sundborg, 5 Sept. 1957, Bartlett Collection.
28. Snedden to Seaton, 20 April 1957, Seaton Collection, Eisenhower Library.
29. Bloedel, "The Alaska Statehood Movement," p. 559; "Snedden Recollects."
30. Snedden to Stevens, 2 May 1986, Snedden Collection.
31. *Washington Post and Times Herald*, 17 Oct. 1960, p. 8.
32. Bloedel, "The Alaska Statehood Movement," pp. 559, 623; Burg, "Oral History Interview with Ted Stevens," 6 Oct. 1977, p. 20; U.S. House, *Statehood for Alaska*, p. 330.
33. *New York Times*, 29 March 1957, p. 45; Bartlett to John E. Longworth, 2 June 1958, Bartlett Collection.
34. *FDNM* 16 April 1957.
35. Council, "Three Steps Forward, Two Steps Back," pp. 382–383.
36. *FDNM* 24 April 1958; 7 May 1958.
37. *FDNM* 21 May 1958.
38. *Congressional Record*, 26 May 1958, p. 9496.
39. Ibid., pp. 9498–9499.
40. Bartlett to Rep. John D. Dingell, 12 May 1958, Bartlett Collection.
41. U.S. House, *Statehood for Alaska*, p. 403; *FDNM* 23 May 1958.
42. *FDNM* 17 May 1958.

43. *FDNM* 16 May 1958.

44. Snedden to Seaton, 9 July 1957, Seaton Collection, Eisenhower Library.

45. Snedden to Stevens, 16 June 1957, Mattson Chronology.

46. Roger Kaye, *Last Great Wilderness: The Campaign to Establish the Arctic National Wildlife Refuge* (Fairbanks: University of Alaska Press, 2006), p. 41.

47. Snedden to Seaton, 9 July 1957, Seaton Collection, Eisenhower Library.

48. Seaton to Snedden, 9 Aug. 1957, Seaton Collection, Eisenhower Library.

49. Snedden to Seaton, 31 Oct. 1957, Seaton Collection, Eisenhower Library.

50. Snedden to Seaton, 20 Nov. 1957, Seaton Collection; Stevens to Snedden, 25 Nov. 1957, Mattson Chronology.

51. *FDNM* 20 Nov. 1957.

52. *FDNM* 13 March 1958; 14 March 1958; 17 March 1958.

53. Fred Seaton, "America's Largest Wildlife Area," Ewald Research Files, Seaton Collection; Kaye, *Last Great Wilderness*, pp. 138, 143; Daniel Nelson, *Northern Landscapes: The Struggle for Wilderness Alaska* (Washington, D.C.: Resources for the Future, 2004), p. 51.

54. Olaus J. Murie to Fred A. Seaton, 9 Dec. 1960, Personal Correspondence, Seaton Collection, Eisenhower Library.

55. Johnson and Jorgenson, *The Land Resources of Alaska*, p. 234; John Strohmeyer, *Extreme Conditions: Big Oil and the Transformation of Alaska* (Anchorage: Cascade Press, 1997), p. 37; Philip W. Morgan to Director, Office of Territories, 25 July 1957, Kenai National Moose Range, Seaton Collection; *FDNM* 23 April 1958.

56. *FDNM* 22 May 1958; 5 Aug. 1957.

57. *FDNM* 23 April 1958.

58. *Congressional Record*, 30 June 1958, p. 12647; Egan to Bartlett, 8 April 1961, Bartlett Collection.

59. *Time*, 16 Dec. 1957.

60. *New York Times*, 26 July 1958, p. 21.

61. David W. Miller, "Historical Development of the Oil and Gas Laws of the United States," *California Law Review* 51, no. 3 (Aug. 1963): 529.

62. *New York Times*, 14 Feb. 1956, p. 28; 11 Nov. 1956, p. 171; 28 Dec. 1955, p. 22; Jack Roderick, *Crude Dreams* (Seattle: Epicenter Press, 1997), pp. 73–77.

63. Coates, *The Trans-Alaska Pipeline Controversy*, p. 93.

64. *FDNM* 14 Nov. 1957.

65. *FDNM* 11 Dec. 1957; 23 Dec. 1957.

66. Nelson, *Northern Landscapes*, p. 51; *FDNM* 16 Dec. 1957.

67. Ernest Gruening to Francis E. Mullen, 20 Dec. 1957, Gruening Collection.

68. *FDNM* 23 Dec. 1957; 16 Dec. 1957.

69. Bartlett confidential office memo, 20 Dec. 1957, Bartlett Collection.

70. *FDNM* 11 Dec. 1957.

71. Bartlett confidential office memo, 12 Dec. 1957, Bartlett Collection.

72. Stevens to Seaton, 23 Dec. 1957, Kenai National Moose Range, Seaton Collection, Eisenhower Library.

73. Bartlett confidential office memo, 29 Jan. 1958, Bartlett Collection.

74. Bartlett to Snedden, 12 Dec. 1957, Matson Chronology, Snedden Collection.

75. *FDNM* 26 Dec. 1957.

76. Roderick, *Crude Dreams*, pp. 84–85.

77. *The Oklahoman*, 28 Oct. 2007; *New York Times*, 28 Feb. 1952, p. 1; 29 Feb. 1952, p. 1; 2 March 1952, p. 75.

78. Gruening, *Many Battles*, p. 391; Hubert A. Gilbert to Bartlett, 11 Feb. 1958, Statehood Legislative Bill File, Bartlett Collection.

CHAPTER 14

1. Egan to George McLaughlin, 29 July 1957, Egan Collection; Bartlett Memo, 25 July 1957, Bartlett Collection; Bartlett to Lehleitner, 1 Aug. 1957, Bartlett Collection.
2. James Bryce, *The American Commonwealth* (Indianapolis: The Liberty Fund, 1995), pp. 122, 143.
3. *FDNM* 3 May 1958; *New York Times*, 15 Feb. 1955, p. 14; 3 July 1961, p. 16; 4 July 1961, p. 4; Drew Pearson, "Washington Merry-Go-Round," 26 Sept. 1964; U.S. House, *Statehood for Alaska*, p. 403.
4. Bartlett to Snedden, 24 May 1957, Bartlett Collection.
5. Egan to Snedden, 21 May 1957, Egan Collection.
6. Naske, *An Interpretative History of Alaskan Statehood*, p. 161.
7. Snedden to Bartlett, 27 May 1957; Snedden to Lehleitner, 21 June 1957, Bartlett Collection.
8. Snedden to Bartlett, 24 June 1957; Snedden to Lehleitner, 21 June 1957, Bartlett Collection.
9. Bartlett to Robert Atwood, 1 Feb. 1954; Bartlett to E. P. Chester Jr., 22 Nov. 1954, Bartlett Collection.
10. Bartlett to Snedden, 4 June 1957, Bartlett Collection.
11. Bartlett memo, 25 July 1957, Bartlett Collection; Egan to George McLaughlin, 29 July 1957, Egan Collection.
12. Bartlett to Lehleitner, 2 June 1958, Bartlett Collection.
13. *FDNM* 26 July 1957.
14. *FDNM* 9 July 1957.
15. Egan to George, Ruth, Mike and Frances McLaughlin, 9 July 1957; Egan to Yule Kilcher and Family, 22 July 1957, Egan Collection.
16. Bartlett memo, 25 July 1957; "Memorandum Which Will Not Bear a Title," 26 July 1957, Bartlett Collection.
17. Bartlett memo, 25 July 1957, Bartlett Collection.
18. *FDNM* 27 July 1957.
19. Bartlett memo, 25 July 1957, Bartlett Collection.
20. *FDNM* 30 July 1957.
21. Bartlett to Earle C. Clements, 2 Aug. 1957, Bartlett Collection; Egan to Lee Johnson, 4 Aug. 1957, Egan Collection; Bartlett to Lehleitner, 1 Aug. 1957, Bartlett Collection; Council, "Three Steps Forward, Two Steps Back," p. 393.
22. *FDNM* 26 July 1957.
23. Lehleitner to Bartlett, 30 July 1957, Bartlett Collection.
24. Bartlett to Lehleitner, 1 Aug. 1957, Bartlett Collection.
25. Brent J. Aucoin, "The Southern Manifesto and Southern Opposition to Desegregation," *Arkansas Historical Quarterly* 55, no. 2 (Summer 1996): 190–191.
26. *FDNM* 28 June 1957.
27. Robert Dallek, *Lone Star Rising: Lyndon Johnson and His Times, 1908–1960* (New York: Oxford University Press, 1991), p. 554.
28. For instance, in *Completing the Union* Whitehead argues that because there was no "softening" on civil rights by Southerners in the 1950s, "statehood and civil rights were not necessarily linked in the passage of statehood legislation" (p. 356).
29. Roger Bell, *Last Among Equals: Hawaiian Statehood and American Politics* (Honolulu: University of Hawaii Press, 1984), p. 337.
30. Bartlett memo, 5 June 1957, Bartlett Collection.
31. Bartlett to Sundborg, 24 June 1957, Bartlett Collection.
32. Lehleitner to Snedden, 30 Sept. 1957, Bartlett Collection.
33. *FDNM* 28 June 1957.
34. *New York Times*, 17 Nov. 1961, p. 28.

35. Merle Miller, *Lyndon: An Oral Biography* (New York: G.P. Putnam's Sons, 1980), p. xvi.
36. *New York Times*, 1 April 1956, p. 160.
37. Caro, *Master of the Senate*, p. 853; Howard E. Shuman, "Senate Rules and the Civil Rights Bill: A Case Study," *American Political Science Review* 31, no. 4 (Dec. 1957): 975.
38. Nadine Cohodas, *Strom Thurmond and the Politics of Southern Change* (New York: Simon and Schuster, 1993), pp. 294–297; Shuman, "Senate Rules and the Civil Rights Bill," pp. 974–975; Caro, *Master of the Senate*, pp. 997–998; *New York Times*, 1 Sept. 1957, p. 105.
39. Caro, *Master of the Senate*, p. 1009.
40. *FDNM* 8 Aug. 1957.
41. *FDNM* 8 Aug. 1957.
42. Transcription of phone conversation between Snedden and Stevens, 27 May 1958, Mattson Chronology.
43. *FDNM* "Miracle Recalled in Capitol," 30 June 1983; John Whitehead, *Completing the Union* (Albuquerque: University of New Mexico Press, 2004), p. 386; Lehleitner to Ted Stevens, 15 July 1958, Bartlett Collection.
44. Bartlett to Snedden, 18 July 1957, Bartlett Collection.
45. Lehleitner to Bartlett, Egan, Gruening, and Rivers, 11 March 1958, Bartlett Collection.
46. Burg, "Oral History Interview with Ted Stevens," 6 Oct. 1977, p. 27.
47. Council, "Three Steps Forward, Two Steps Back," pp. 430–431; Bartlett to Wendell Kay, 17 May 1960, Bartlett Collection.

CHAPTER 15

1. *New York Times*, 8 Jan. 1958, pp. 1, 9.
2. Bartlett memo, 25 July 1957, Bartlett Collection.
3. Snedden to Bartlett, 6 Jan. 1958, Bartlett Collection.
4. Bartlett to Snedden, 15 Jan. 1958, Bartlett Collection.
5. Bartlett to Snedden, 28 Jan. 1958, Bartlett Collection.
6. Snedden to Bartlett, 4 Feb. 1958; Bartlett to Snedden, 4 Feb. 1958, Bartlett Collection.
7. Drew Pearson, "The Washington Merry-Go-Round," 26 Jan. 1958.
8. Bartlett, confidential office memo, 28 Jan. 1958, Bartlett Collection.
9. *New York Times*, 6 Feb. 1958, p. 18.
10. Snedden to Seaton, 5 Feb. 1958; Stevens to Seaton, 5 Feb. 1958, Seaton Collection, Eisenhower Library.
11. *New York Times*, 7 Feb. 1958, p. 12.
12. Transcript of Phone Conversation between Stevens and Snedden, 7 Feb. 1958, Bartlett Collection.
13. Sundborg to Bartlett, 14 Feb. 1958, Bartlett Collection.
14. Council, "Three Steps Forward, Two Steps Back," p. 399.
15. Bartlett to Snedden, 11 Feb. 1958, Bartlett Collection.
16. Helen Fischer to Bartlett, 17 Feb. 1958; Bartlett to Fischer, 19 Feb. 1958; Mildred Hermann to Mary Lee Council, 1 Aug. [1960], Bartlett Collection; *FDNM* 8 March 1958.
17. Bartlett to Snedden, 11 Feb. 1958; Bartlett, "Statehood Memo," 7 Feb. 1958; Bartlett to Helen Fischer, 19 Feb. 1958, Bartlett Collection.
18. L. A. Minnich Jr., Legislative Supplementary Notes, 4 March 1958, Ann Whitman File, Eisenhower Diary Series, Eisenhower Library.
19. *Congressional Record*, 21 May 1958, p. 9219.
20. Council, "Three Steps Forward, Two Steps Back," p. 399; E. L. Bartlett office memorandum, 6 Feb. 1958, Bartlett Collection.
21. Council, "Three Steps Forward, Two Steps Back," pp. 400–401; Bartlett, confidential memo, 7 Feb. 1958, Bartlett Collection.

22. *FDNM* 15 March 1958; 20 March 1958; 26 March 1958.
23. Bartlett to Mr. and Mrs. Barrie M. White Jr., 24 March 1958, Bartlett Collection; *FDNM* 14 March 1958.
24. Bartlett to Lehleitner, 5 May 1958, Bartlett Collection.
25. Bartlett to Mr. and Mrs. Barrie M. White, Jr., 24 March 1958; Bartlett to John Kagel, 1 April 1958, Bartlett Collection.

CHAPTER 16

1. Snedden to Atwood, 18 March 1958, Bartlett Collection.
2. Bartlett to Lehleitner, 14 March 1958, Bartlett Collection.
3. Sundborg to Bartlett, 3 April 1958; Bartlett to Sundborg, 7 April 1958, Bartlett Collection.
4. *FDNM* 11 March 1958; Snedden to Bartlett 7 April 1958, Bartlett Collection
5. *FDNM* 31 March 1958.
6. Bartlett to Atwood, 18 March 1958, Bartlett Collection.
7. *Time*, 14 July 1958, p. 69.
8. Lehleitner to Stevens, 15 July 1958; Lehleitner to Gruening, Egan, and Rivers, 29 May 1958; Lehleitner to W.O. "Bo" Smith, 3 July 1958, Bartlett Collection.
9. *FDNM* 11 Dec. 1957.
10. *FDNM* 25 Nov. 1957.
11. Ibid.
12. *FDNM* 9 Dec. 1957; 11 Dec. 1957; Snedden to Bartlett, 24 April 1958, Bartlett Collection.
13. *FDNM* 2 June 1958.
14. Snedden to Bartlett, 29 April 1958, Bartlett Collection.
15. Bartlett to Mildred R. Hermann, 27 Feb. 1958; Bartlett to Sundborg, 1 March 1958; Bartlett to Atwood, 14 June 1958; Bartlett to Sundborg, 20 March 1958; Bartlett to Atwood, 18 March 1958; Bartlett to Mr. and Mrs.

Barrie M. White Jr., 24 March 1958, Bartlett Collection.
16. Snedden to Atwood, 18 March 1958, Bartlett Collection; "Snedden Recollects."
17. *Time*, 14 July 1958, p. 69.
18. Ernest R. Bartley to Egan, 7 Jan. 1957, Egan Collection.
19. "Snedden Recollects."
20. Governor of Alaska to "Dear Congressman," n.d., Bartlett Collection.
21. Snedden to Bartlett, 29 April 1958, Bartlett Collection.
22. A. M. Sperber, *Murrow: His Life and Times* (New York: Freundlich Books, 1986), pp. 485–486.
23. David Halberstam, *The Powers That Be* (Urbana and Chicago: University of Illinois Press, 2000), pp. 149–150.
24. *Congressional Record*, 21 March 1958, pp. 5040–5041.
25. *Washington Post*, 13 March 1958; *FDNM* 5 April 1958.
26. Sperber, *Murrow*, p. 529.
27. Halberstam, *The Powers That Be*, pp. 149–150.
28. *FDNM* 24 April 1958.
29. *FDNM* 3 March 1958; Whitehead, *Completing the Union*, p. 4.
30. *FDNM* 5 April 1958; Bloedel, "The Alaska Statehood Movement," p. 617.
31. Alaska Statehood Committee Flyer on statehood endorsements, Bartlett Collection; *FDNM* 25 March 1958.
32. Carroll V. Glines Jr., "Alaska's Press and the Battle for Statehood," master's thesis, American University, 1969, pp. 102–103.
33. *FDNM* 25 Feb. 1958.
34. Snedden to Lehleitner, 21 June 1957, Bartlett Collection; Letters to editors in Tennessee Plan Files, 1956–1958, Egan Collection.
35. Lehleitner to C. P. Manship Jr., 18 June 1958, Bartlett Collection.
36. *FDNM* 25 March 1958.

37. *FDNM* 25 June 1958; Lehleitner to Bartlett, n.d., Sample letter to Texas editors, Bartlett to Dean Chenoweth, 14 June 1958, Bartlett Collection; *Congressional Record,* 27 June 1958, pp. 12448–12449; 21 May 1958, p. 9218.

38. *FDNM* 25 March 1958.

39. Snedden to Bartlett, 7 April 1958, Bartlett Collection.

40. "Snedden Recollects."

41. Snedden to Seaton, 14 March 1958, Alaska Statehood, Seaton Collection, Eisenhower Library.

42. Stephen L. Vaughn, *Encyclopedia of American Journalism* (New York: Routledge, 2008), p. 477; *New York Times,* 21 July 1958, p. 14; 26 Sept. 1964, p. 11; 2 June 1960, p. 16; 19 March 1973, p. 38.

43. Walker Stone to Bartlett and Snedden, 17 July 1958, Bartlett Collection.

44. Snedden to Bartlett, 5 May 1958, Bartlett Collection.

45. Snedden to Stevens, 5 May 1958, Mattson Chronology.

46. Snedden to William S. Lampe, 4 May 1958, Bartlett Collection; *FDNM* 2 May 1958; *Life,* 2 May 1958.

47. Council, "Three Steps Forward, Two Steps Back," pp. 401–402.

48. Neil MacNeil, *Forge of Democracy: The House of Representatives* (New York: David McKay Co., 1963), p. 42.

49. Dealva Stanwood Alexander, *History and Procedure of the House of Representatives* (New York: Houghton Mifflin, 1916), p. 291; Bryce, *The American Commonwealth,* Vol. 1, p. 159; George Goodwin Jr., *The Little Legislatures: Committees of Congress* (University of Massachusetts Press, 1970), p. ix.

50. U.S. Congress, *Final Report of the Joint Committee on the Organization of Congress* (Dec. 1993), http://www.rules.house.gov/Archives/

JointComm.htm; *New York Times,* 24 Dec. 1966, p. 18; *New York Times Magazine,* 12 Jan. 1964, p. 85.

51. *New York Times Magazine,* 12 Jan. 1964, p. 13; Burdett A. Loomis, *The Contemporary Congress* (Boston: Bedford/St. Martins, 2000), p. 172.

52. Bartlett to Snedden, 28 Jan. 1958, Bartlett Collection.

53. "Snedden Recollects"; in Sue Mattson's Chronology, 1 June 1987, Snedden recalled that the "Little Man" editorial ran two days after he heard Smith's dead body comment.

54. *Washington Daily News,* 1 April 1958, p. 1.

55. Lehleitner to Bartlett and Snedden, 12 March 1958, Bartlett Collection.

56. *FDNM* 19 March 1958.

57. *FDNM* 31 March 1958.

58. *Guide to Congress* (Washington, DC: Congressional Quarterly Press, 2008), p. 507.

Chapter 17

1. MacNeil, *Forge of Democracy,* p. 56; Richard S. Beth, *The Discharge Rule in the House: Recent Use in Historical Context* (Washington, DC: Congressional Research Service, The Library of Congress), p. i.

2. Edward Brooke Hasecke, "Balancing the Legislative Agenda: Scheduling in the United States House of Representatives," Ph.D. dissertation, Ohio State University, 2002, pp. 43–44.

3. Loomis, *The Contemporary Congress,* p. 172.

4. Bartlett to R. F. Sullivan, 6 May 1958; Bartlett to John Kagel, 1 April 1958, Bartlett Collection.

5. Lehleitner to Bartlett and Snedden, 12 March 1958, Bartlett Collection.

6. Bartlett to Snedden, 24 April 1958, Bartlett Collection.

7. Ibid; Mary Lee Council in "Three Steps Forward, Two Steps Back" identifies the informant as Bartlett's

old friend Marietta Drake. See pp. 405–406.

8.   *FDNM* 24 April 1958.
9.   Bartlett to R. F. Sullivan, 6 May 1958, Bartlett Collection; Council, "Three Steps Forward, Two Steps Back," pp. 406–407.
10.   *FDNM*, 9 May 1958.
11.   *New York Times*, 20 May 1958, p. 21; 21 May 1958, p. 30; *FDNM* 16 May 1958; 20 May 1958; 23 May 1958; *Congressional Record*, 21 May 1958, p. 9218.
12.   *Congressional Record*, 21 May 1958, p. 9213.
13.   Ibid., 21 May 1958, p. 9216.
14.   Council, "Three Steps Forward, Two Steps Back," pp. 409–410; *New York Times*, 27 Sept. 1973, p. 28; 13 July 1976, p. 35; Lewis Deschler to Bartlett, 18 June 1965, Bartlett Collection.
15.   Ilona B. Nickels and Thomas P. Carr, *Congressional Parliamentary Reference Sources* (Nova Science Publishers, 2004), p. 108.
16.   *New York Times*, 22 May 1958, p. 1; 23 May 1958, p. 12; 19 June 1951, p. 10; *Congressional Record*, 21 May 1958, pp. 9217–9227.
17.   *FDNM* 23 May 1958.
18.   Ibid.; *New York Times*, 22 May 1958, p. 16.
19.   Jack Z. Anderson, "Memorandum for Mrs. Whitman, 21 May 1958, Ann Whitman File, Eisenhower Diary Series, Eisenhower Library; Seaton to General Wilton B. Persons, 29 May 1958, White House Central Files, 147-D-1, Eisenhower Library; L. A. Minnich Jr., Legislative Supplementary Notes, 4 March 1958, Ann Whitman File, Eisenhower Diary Series, Eisenhower Library; *FDNM* 5 June 1958; 21 May 1958; *New York Times*, 23 May 1958, p. 12; 2 June 1958, p. 17.
20.   *FDNM* 29 May 1958.

21.   *Washington Post*, 2 June 1958; John P. Saylor to Wilton B. Persons, 23 May 1958; Memo on Statehood Lobbying, 27 May 1958; Jack Anderson to John Saylor, 26 May 1958, White House Office Files, 147-D-1, Eisenhower Library.
22.   Bartlett to M.J. Walsh, 30 May 1958, Bartlett Collection.
23.   *Congressional Record*, 27 May 1958, pp. 9610–9611.
24.   Ibid., p. 9611.
25.   *New York Times*, 28 May 1958, p. 21.
26.   Ibid., 15 Aug. 1957, p. 14.
27.   Ibid., 23 May 1958, p. 12.
28.   Bartlett to Edward V. Davis, 4 June 1958, Bartlett Collection; *FDNM* 28 May 1958.
29.   Transcript of phone conversation between Snedden and Stevens, 27 May 1958, Mattson Chronology.
30.   *FDNM* 28 May 1958.
31.   *New York Times*, 29 May 1958, p. 12.
32.   *Congressional Record*, 28 May 1958, pp. 9743–9745.
33.   Bloedel, "The Alaska Statehood Movement," p. 635.
34.   *Congressional Record*, 28 May 1958, p. 9755.
35.   *New York Times*, 30 June 1949, p. 22; 19 June 1951, p. 10; United States Patent Office, T.A. Edison, "Electric Vote-Recorder," Patent No. 90, 646, 1 June 1869.
36.   Naske, *A History of Alaska Statehood*, p. 267.
37.   *Congressional Record*, 28 May 1958, pp. 9743–9745.
38.   Bloedel, "The Alaska Statehood Movement," p. 638.
39.   Bartlett to M. J. Walsh, 30 May 1958, Bartlett Collection.
40.   Bartlett, confidential memo, 7 Feb. 1958, Bartlett Collection.
41.   Snedden to Seaton, 14 March 1958, Alaska Statehood, Seaton Collection, Eisenhower Library.
42.   Bartlett to Snedden, 29 May 1958, Bartlett Collection.

43. *FDNM* 3 June 1958.
44. Council, "Three Steps Forward, Two Steps Back," p. 418.
45. Bartlett to Snedden, 10 June 1958, Bartlett Collection.
46. Bartlett to Lehleitner, 2 June 1958, Bartlett Collection.
47. Bartlett to Lehleitner, 3 June 1958, Bartlett Collection.
48. *FDNM* 3 June 1958; Stevens to Snedden, 2 June 1958, Mattson Chronology.
49. *FDNM* 10 June 1958; 23 June 1958.
50. *FDNM* 24 June 1958.
51. *FDNM* 17 June 1958; 27 June 1958.
52. Bartlett to Oliver C. Riggs, 18 June 1958, Bartlett Collection.
53. *FDNM* 20 June 1958.
54. Bartlett to Lehleitner, 20 June 1958, Bartlett Collection.
55. Stevens to Snedden, 6 Dec. 1958, Mattson Chronology; *New York Times*, 26 June 1958, p. 55; *Washington Post and Times Herald*, 26 June 1958, p. 2; *FDNM* 20 June 1958; Snedden Interview; *Congressional Record*, 30 June 1958, pp. 12649–12650.
56. *FDNM* 24 June 1958.
57. Seaton to Eisenhower, 24 June 1958, Ann Whitman File, Box 33, June 1958 Staff Notes, Eisenhower Diary Series, Eisenhower Library; William B. Ewald Jr., *Eisenhower the President: Crucial Days, 1951–1960* (Englewood Cliffs, NJ: Prentice-Hall, 1981), p. 202.
58. H. A Hubbard, "Arizona's Struggle Against Joint Statehood," *Pacific Historical Review* 11, no. 4 (Dec. 1942): 422.
59. *Congressional Record*, 30 June 1958, pp.12598, 12642–12643; 26 June 1958, pp. 12339, 12294; *FDNM* 27 June 1958.
60. *Congressional Record*, 30 June 1958, p. 12612.
61. *FDNM* 28 June 1958.
62. Bloedel, "The Alaska Statehood Movement," p. 645.
63. Transcript, William S. White Oral History Interview I, 5 March 1969, by Dorothy Pierce McSweeny, Internet Copy, LBJ Library; U.S. Senate Website, "Citadel." www.senate.gov/artandhistory/history/minute/citadel.htm.
64. *Congressional Record*, 3 July 1958, pp. 11810–11811.
65. *FDNM* 28 June 1958; Bloedel, "The Alaska Statehood Movement," p. 648.
66. *Congressional Record*, 30 June 1958, p. 12645.
67. Ibid., pp. 12645–12646.
68. Ibid., p. 12650.
69. Naske, *A History of Alaska Statehood*, p. 270; Bartlett to Kenneth A. Clem, 3 July 1958, Bartlett Collection.
70. John Strohmeyer, *Alaska Titan: Bob Atwood and His Times* (eventually published, slightly abridged, as *Bob Atwood's Alaska* by Robert B. Atwood, privately printed, 2003).
71. Robert U. Brown, "Shop Talk at Thirty," *Editor and Publisher*, 12 July 1958, p. 60.
72. *FDNM* 30 June 1958.
73. Ibid.
74. *Time*, 14 July 1958.
75. "Snedden Recollects"; *FDNM* 30 June 1983, p. B-10; 1 July 1958; *Editor and Publisher*, 12 July 1958, p. 15. In his reminiscences in 1964, Snedden said the newspapers arrived in Washington about seven a.m., while the *News-Miner* on 1 July 1958 says the time was 11:25 a.m. EDT.

EPILOGUE
1. *New York Times*, 1 July 1958, p. 62.
2. *FDNM* 26 June 1958; 30 June 1958; 1 July 1958; *New York Times*, 1 July 1958, p. 62.
3. *New York Times*, 4 July 1958, p. 20.
4. Ewald, *Eisenhower the President*, p. 202.
5. Ibid., pp. 202–203.
6. Statement of the Secretary of the Interior on Alaskan Statehood at his

news conference, 1 July 1958, White House Office Files, 147-D-1, Eisenhower Library.

7. Bartlett to John C. Doyle, 5 July 1958, Bartlett Collection.

8. Bartlett to M. J. Walsh, 8 July 1958, Bartlett Collection.

9. Lehleitner to Bartlett, 15 July 1958, Bartlett Collection.

10. Statement of the President Signing H.R. 7999, 7 July 1958, White House Office Files, 147-D-1, Eisenhower Library.

11. Bartlett to Riley H. Allen, 7 July 1958, Bartlett Collection.

12. Bell, *Last Among Equals*, p. 271.

13. *New York Times*, 11 March 1959, p. 1; 12 March 1959, p. 1; Bell, *Last Among Equals*, pp. 272–274.

14. *New York Times*, 12 Jan. 1959, p. 1; p. 38.

15. Council, "Three Steps Forward, Two Steps Back," pp. 437–439.

16. *New York Times*, 14 June 1964, p. E1.

17. Naske, *A History of Alaska Statehood*, p. 271.

18. *Washington Post and Times Herald*, 5 July 1958, p. C15.

19. *FDNM* 8 July 1958.

20. Bartlett Memorandum, 15 April 1967, Bartlett Collection.

21. Bartlett to Snedden, 15 May 1967, Bartlett Collection.

22. Bartlett to Helenka Brice, 17 Dec. 1963, Bartlett Collection.

23. Snedden to Bartlett, 28/29 Nov. 1966, Bartlett Collection.

24. Bartlett to Snedden, 23 Jan. 1967, Bartlett Collection.

25. Ibid.

26. *FDNM* 8 July 1958.

27. This account of the Pearson-Snedden lawsuit is drawn from an unpublished paper on the case by Dermot Cole.

28. *New York Times*, 27 Nov. 1958, p. 1.

29. Snedden to Bartlett, 18 Sept. 1964, Bartlett Collection.

30. Mary Lee Council to Stanley McCutcheon, 2 Oct. 1964, Bartlett Collection.

31. Bartlett to Helenka Brice, 7 Oct. 1968, Bartlett Collection.

32. Anderson, *A 'Washington Merry-Go-Round' of Libel Actions*, p. 235.

33. Robert S. Allen to Snedden, 30 Nov. 1964, Bartlett Collection.

34. Herman Slotnick, "The 1966 Election in Alaska," *Western Science Political Quarterly* (June 1967): 528.

35. Snedden to Vice President Richard Nixon, 22 Dec. 1958, Seaton Collection, Eisenhower Library.

36. Snedden to Seaton, 30 Dec. 1958, Seaton Collection, Eisenhower Library.

37. Snedden to Thurston B. Morton, 8 Dec. 1959, Seaton Collection, Eisenhower Library.

38. *New York Times*, 24 Dec. 1968, p. 10.

39. *FDNM* 24 June 1964.

40. *FDNM* 20 July 1965.

41. Stevens to Snedden, 28 Aug. 1958, Mattson Chronology.

Bibliography

In addition to the back files of the *Fairbanks Daily News-Miner*, available on microfilm, the main sources for this book are in the archives of the Alaska and Polar Regions Collection at the Rasmuson Library, University of Alaska Fairbanks. Three collections at the Rasmuson Library are particularly rich in statehood materials: the private and official papers of Governor/Senator Ernest Gruening, Governor William A. Egan, and Delegate/Senator E.L. "Bob" Bartlett. By far the most valuable collection is that of Bartlett, whose vast correspondence files—with Snedden and many others—constitutes almost a day-by-day record of Alaska's political and social history from the mid-1940s to the early 1960s.

At the National Archives in College Park, Maryland, numerous collection were useful, including Record Group 48 (Office of the Secretary of Interior during Seaton's era) and RG 126 (Office of Territories). At the National Archives facility in Anchorage RG 21 (District Courts of the United States) and RG 118 (U.S. Attorneys) contain material pertinent to Ted Stevens's career as U.S. Attorney.

Fred A. Seaton's papers, including Snedden's correspondence with both Secretary Seaton and Ted Stevens, is located in the Dwight D. Eisenhower Presidential Library in Abilene, Kansas. In addition to the official records of the administration, the Eisenhower Library contains the papers and transcriptions of oral histories of many of the top figures in the Eisenhower administration.

Finally, Helen Snedden, the widow of C.W. Snedden, graciously provided the publisher's old files, including some correspondence and abstracts of his correspondence compiled by Sue Mattson in the 1980s.

Abell, Tyler, ed. *Drew Pearson: Diaries, 1949–1959*. New York: Holt, Rinehart and Winston, 1974.

Alaska Department of Law. Minutes of the Alaska Constitutional Convention, http://www.law.state.ak.us/doclibrary/cc_minutes.html.

Alaska Legislative Affairs Agency. *Alaska Legislature: Roster of Members 1913–1982*, Juneau, 1982.

Alexander, Dealva Stanwood. *History and Procedure of the House of Representatives*. New York: Houghton Mifflin, 1916.

Anderson, Douglas A. "Drew Pearson: A Name Synonymous With Libel Actions." *Journalism Quarterly* 56, no. 2 (Summer 1979).

———. *A 'Washington-Merry-Go-Round' of Libel Actions*. Chicago: Nelson Hall, 1980.

Atwood, Evangeline, and R. N. DeArmond. *Who's Who in Alaskan Politics*. Anchorage: Alaska Historical Commission, 1977.

Atwood, Evangeline, and Lew Williams Jr. *Bent Pins to Chains: Alaska and Its Newspapers*. Privately printed, 2006.

Aucoin, Brent J. "The Southern Manifesto and Southern Opposition to Desegregation." *Arkansas Historical Quarterly* 55, no. 2 (Summer 1996).

Bell, Roger. *Last Among Equals: Hawaiian Statehood and American Politics*. Honolulu: University of Hawaii, 1984.

Beth, Richard S. *The Discharge Rule in the House: Recent Use in Historical Context*. Washington, DC: Congressional Research Service, The Library of Congress, 2003.

Bloedel, Richard H. "The Alaska Statehood Movement." PhD diss., University of Washington, 1974.

Boorstin, Daniel. *The Americans: The National Experience*. New York: Random House, 1965.

Boswell, John C. *History of Alaskan Operations of the United States Smelting, Refining and Mining Company*. Fairbanks: Mineral Industry Research Laboratory, 1979.

Bowkett, Gerald E. *Reaching for a Star: The Final Campaign for Alaska Statehood*. Fairbanks: Epicenter Press, 1989.

Brown, Robert U. "Shop Talk at Thirty." *Editor and Publisher*, 12 July 1958.

Bryce, James. *The American Commonwealth*. Indianapolis: The Liberty Fund, 1995.

Buckley, Priscilla L. "'Siberia, U.S.A.,' The Rocky Road of H.R. 6376." *National Review*, 25 July 1956.

Burg, Maclyn. "Transcript of Oral History Interview with Elmer F. Bennett." OH-401, Eisenhower Library.

———. "Transcript of Oral History Interview with Ted Stevens." OH-484, Eisenhower Library.

Burkeland, Leigh F. "Siberia, U.S.A." (Reprinted in: U.S. Senate, *Alaska Mental Health*, 1956).

Cameron, Dale C. "Comment: Alaska Mental Health Survey." *American Journal of Psychiatry* 107, no. 3 (September 1950).

Carberry, Michael. *Patterns of the Past*. Anchorage: Historical Landmarks Preservation Commission, 1979.

Carey, Michael. "Con Men and Women." *Anchorage Daily News*, 17 June 2006.

———. "Fred Seaton of Nebraska and His Friend in Alaska." Unpublished manuscript.

Caro, Robert A. *The Years of Lyndon Johnson: Master of the Senate*. New York: Alfred A. Knopf, 2002.

Clark, Henry W. *Alaska: The Last Frontier*. New York: Grosset and Dunlap, 1939.

Coates, Peter. *The Trans-Alaska Pipeline Controversy.* Fairbanks: University of Alaska Press, 1993.

Cohodas, Nadine. *Strom Thurmond and the Politics of Southern Change.* New York: Simon and Schuster, 1993.

Colby, Merle. *A Guide to Alaska, Last American Frontier.* New York: Macmillan Co., 1939.

Cole, Dermot. *Historic Fairbanks: An Illustrated History.* San Antonio: Historical Publishing Network, 2002.

———. "Drew Pearson against the *News-Miner.*" Unpublished manuscript.

Cole, Terrence M. *Crooked Past: The Story of a Frontier Mining Camp.* Fairbanks: University of Alaska Press, 1991.

Cooley, Richard A. *Fairbanks, Alaska: A Survey of Progress.* Juneau: Alaska Development Board, 1954.

Cotter, Cornelius P. "Eisenhower as Party Leader," *Political Science Quarterly* 98, no. 2 (Summer 1983).

Council, Mary Lee. "Three Steps Forward, Two Steps Back: Bob Bartlett and Alaska Statehood." Unpublished manuscript.

Crain, Melvin. "Governance for Alaska: Some Aspects of Representation." PhD diss., University of Southern California, 1957.

Dallek, Robert. *Lone Star Rising: Lyndon Johnson and His Times, 1908–1960.* New York: Oxford University Press, 1991.

Davis, Mary Lee. *We Are Alaskans.* Boston: W.A. Wilde Co., 1931.

DeVoto, Bernard. "Conservation: Down and on the Way Out." *Harper's Magazine,* August 1954.

Dierenfield, Bruce J. "Conservative Outrage: The Defeat in 1966 of Representative Howard W. Smith of Virginia." *Virginia Magazine of History and Biography* 89, no. 2 (April 1981).

Doogan, Mike. "Uncle Ted." *Alaska Magazine,* November 2005.

Driscoll, Joseph. *War Discovers Alaska.* New York: J.B. Lippincott, 1943.

Ebony Magazine. "The Alaska Murder Case," October 1954.

Edison, T. A. "Electric Vote-Recorder." United States Patent Office, Patent No. 90, 646, 1 June 1869.

Ehrenhalt, Alan, and Michael Glennon, eds. *Politics in America: Members of Congress in Washington and at Home.* Washington, DC: Congressional Quarterly, Inc., 1983.

Ewald, William B., Jr. *Eisenhower the President: Crucial Days, 1951–1960.* Englewood Cliffs, NJ: Prentice Hall, 1981.

Fischer, Victor. *Alaska's Constitutional Convention.* Fairbanks: University of Alaska Press, 1975.

Fulton, Richard T. "Death and the Midas Touch." *Front Page Detective,* February 1954.

Galambos, Louis, ed.. *The Papers of Dwight David Eisenhower: NATO and the Campaign of 1952.* Baltimore: Johns Hopkins University Press, 1989.

Glines, Carroll V., Jr. "Alaska's Press and the Battle for Statehood." Master's thesis, American University, 1969.

Goble, George Corban. "The Obituary of a Machine: The Rise and Fall of Ottmar Mergenthaler's Linotype at U.S. Newspapers." PhD diss., Indiana University, 1984.

Goodwin, George, Jr. *The Little Legislatures: Committees of Congress.* University of Massachusetts Press, 1970.

Greenstein, Fred I. "Eisenhower as an Activist President: A Look at New Evidence." *Political Science Quarterly* 94, no. 4 (Winter 1979–1980).

————. *The Hidden-Hand Presidency: Eisenhower as Leader.* New York: Basic Books, 1982.
Gruening, Ernest. *The Battle for Alaska Statehood.* College: University of Alaska Press, 1967.
————. *Many Battles: The Autobiography of Ernest Gruening.* New York: Liveright, 1974.
Guide to Congress. Washington, DC: Congressional Quarterly Press, 2008.
Halberstam, David. *The Powers That Be.* Urbana and Chicago: University of Illinois Press, 2000.
Hammond, Jay. *Tales of Alaska's Bush Rat Governor.* Seattle: Epicenter Press, 1994.
Hasecke, Edward Brooke. "Balancing the Legislative Agenda: Scheduling in the United States House of Representatives." PhD diss., Ohio State University, 2002.
Hellenthal, J. A. *The Alaskan Melodrama.* New York: Liveright Publishing Co., 1936.
Holdsworth, Phil R. "Oil and Gas May Transcend Gold and War Booms in Alaska's Economy." In *Lou Jacobin's Guide to Alaska and the Yukon.* Juneau: Guide to Alaska Co, 1954.
Holloway, David. *Stalin and the Bomb: The Soviet Union and Atomic Energy.* New Haven: Yale University Press, 1994.
Hubbard, H. A. "Arizona's Struggle Against Joint Statehood." *Pacific Historical Review* 11, no. 4 (December 1942).
Hunt, William R. *Distant Justice: Policing the Alaska Frontier.* Norman: University of Oklahoma, 1987.
Jessup, David E. "The Rise and Fall of Katalla: 'The Coming Metropolis of Alaska.'" *Alaska History* 20, no. 1 (Spring 2005).
Johnson, Hugh A., and Harold T. Jorgenson. *The Land Resources of Alaska: A Conservation Foundation Study.* University Publishers, 1963.
Johnson, Robert David. *Ernest Gruening and the American Dissenting Tradition.* Cambridge: Harvard University Press, 1998.
Kansas State Historical Society. "Fred Seaton: A Kansas Portrait," http://www.kshs.org/portraits/seaton_fred.htm.
Karolevitz, Robert F. *Newspapering in the Old West: A Pictorial History of Journalism and Printing on the Frontier.* Seattle: Superior Publishing Co., 1966.
Kaye, Roger. *Last Great Wilderness: The Campaign to Establish the Arctic National Wildlife Refuge.* Fairbanks: University of Alaska Press, 2006.
King, Robert W. "Without Hope of Immediate Profit: Oil Exploration in Alaska, 1898–1953." *Alaska History* 9, no. 1 (Spring 1994).
Kral, E. A. "700 Famous Nebraskans: Nationally Distinguished Nebraskans: A Brief BioBibliography of 700 Individuals," http://www.nebpress.com/700/famousnebs.pdf.
LaRocca, Joe E. *Alaska Agonistes: The Age of Petroleum.* North East, PA: Rare Books, Ink, 2003.
Life. "The Case of the Beat-Up Blonde," 30 November 1953.
————. "Take Alaska Off the Ice," 5 May 1958.
Loomis, Burdett A. *The Contemporary Congress.* Boston: Bedford/St. Martins, 2000.
Lynd, R. S., and H. M. Lynd. *Middletown: A Study in Contemporary American Culture.* New York: Harcourt, Brace, 1929.
MacNeil, Neil. *Forge of Democracy: The House of Representatives.* New York: David McKay Co., 1963.
Mann, Robert T. *Legacy to Power: Senator Russell Long of Louisiana.* New York: Paragon House, 1992.
Martinez, Ruben Berrios. "Independence for Puerto Rico: The Only Solution." *Foreign Affairs* 55, no. 3 (April 1977).

McSweeny, Dorothy Pierce. Transcript, William S. White Oral History Interview I, 5 March 1969, Internet Copy, LBJ Library.

Miller, David W. "Historical Development of the Oil and Gas Laws of the United States," *California Law Review* 51, no. 3 (August 1963).

Miller, Merle. *Lyndon: An Oral Biography*. New York: G.P. Putnam's Sons, 1980.

Minutes of Alaska Constitutional Convention, http://www.law.state.ak.us/doclibrary/cc_minutes.html.

Mitchell, Donald Craig. *Take My Land, Take My Life*. Fairbanks: University of Alaska Press, 2001.

Monroney, A. S. "Mike." "Let's Keep It 48." *Collier's*, 4 March 1955.

Naske, Claus-M. "Bob Bartlett and the Alaska Mental Health Act." *Pacific Northwest Quarterly* 71, no.1 (January 1980).

———. *Bob Bartlett of Alaska: A Life in Politics*. Fairbanks: University of Alaska Press, 1979.

———. "Commonwealth: A Historical Footnote." *Alaska Journal* (Summer 1972).

———. *Ernest Gruening: Alaska's Greatest Governor*. Fairbanks: University of Alaska Press, 2004.

———. *A History of Alaska Statehood*, 2nd ed. Lanham, MD: University Press of America, 1985.

———. *An Interpretive History of Alaskan Statehood*. Anchorage: Alaska Northwest Publishing Co., 1973.

Naske, Claus-M., et al. *Alaska Statehood: The Memory of the Battle and the Evaluation of the Present by Those Who Lived It*. Anchorage: Alaska Statehood Commission, 1981.

Nelson, Daniel. *Northern Landscapes: The Struggle for Wilderness Alaska*. Washington, DC: Resources for the Future, 2004.

Newsweek. "Drummer and Blonde," 16 November 1953.

Nickels, Ilona B., and Thomas P. Carr. *Congressional Parliamentary Reference Sources*. Nova Science Publishers, 2004.

Nickerson, Michelle M. "The Lunatic Fringe Strikes Back: Conservative Opposition to the Alaska Mental Health Bill of 1956." In *The Politics of Healing: Histories of Alternative Medicine in the Twentieth Century,* ed. Robert D. Johnson. New York: Routledge, 2003.

Oestermann, Richard. "A Danish Journalist Views Alaska." *Alaska Life* (August 1948).

O'Neill, Dan. *The Firecracker Boys*. New York: St. Martin's Press, 1995.

Parmet, Herbert S. *Eisenhower and the American Crusades*. New York: Macmillan, 1972.

Paul, Justus F. "The Political Career of Senator Hugh Butler, 1940–1954." PhD diss., University of Nebraska, 1966.

Pearson, Drew, and Jack Anderson. *The Case Against Congress: A Compelling Indictment of Corruption on Capitol Hill*. New York: Simon and Schuster, 1968.

Potter, Jean. *Alaska Under Arms*. New York: Macmillan Co., 1942.

Reed, John C. *Exploration of Naval Petroleum Reserve No. 4 and Adjacent Areas Northern Alaska, 1944–1953, Part 1, History of the Exploration*, U.S. Geological Survey Professional Paper 301. Washington, DC: Government Printing Office, 1958.

Richardson, Elmo. "The Interior Secretary as Conservation Villain: The Notorious Case of Douglas 'Giveaway' McKay." *Pacific Historical Review* 41, no. 3 (August 1972).

Ritchie, Donald A. *Reporting from Washington: The History of the Washington Press Corps*. New York: Oxford University Press, 2005.

Roderick, Jack. *Crude Dreams: A Personal History of Oil and Politics in Alaska*. Seattle: Epicenter Press, 1997.

Ryan, John J. *The Maggie Murphy*. New York: Norton, 1951.

Shreve, Gene R. "From Swift to Erie: An Historical Perspective." *Michigan Law Review* 82, no. 4 (1984).

Shuman, Howard E. "Senate Rules and the Civil Rights Bill: A Case Study." *American Political Science Review* 31, no. 4 (December 1957).

Slotnick, Herman. "The 1966 Election in Alaska." *Western Science Political Quarterly* (June 1967).

Smith, Maury. "KFAR Is On the Air." *Alaska Journal* (Autumn 1985).

Smith, Philip S. *Mineral Industry of Alaska in 1940*. U.S. Geological Survey, 1942.

Snedden, C.W. (ed. J. S. Whitehead). "C.W. Snedden Recollects the Campaign for Statehood." *Alaska History* 20, no. 1 (Spring 2005).

Soapes, Thomas. "Transcript of Oral History Interview with Orme Lewis." OH-361, 19 July 1976, Eisenhower Library.

Solka, Paul, Jr.. "Adventures in Fairbanks Journalism, 1903–1975." Unpublished manuscript, Snedden Collection.

Solka, Paul, Jr. and Art Bremer. *Adventures in Alaska Journalism Since 1903*. Fairbanks: Commercial Printing Co., 1980.

Spence, Clark C. *The Northern Gold Fleet: Twentieth Century Gold Dredging in Alaska*. Urbana: University of Illinois Press, 1996.

Sperber, A. M. *Murrow: His Life and Times*. New York: Freundlich Books, 1986.

Stevens, Theodore F. "Erie R.R. v. Tompkins and the Uniform General Maritime Law." *Harvard Law Review* 64, no. 2 (December 1950).

Stratton, Porter A. *The Territorial Press of New Mexico, 1834–1912*. Albuquerque: University of New Mexico Press, 1969.

Streit, Clarence K. *Union Now: The Proposal for Inter-Democracy Federal Union*. New York: Harper Brothers, 1940.

———. *Union Now with Britain*. New York: Harper and Brothers, 1941.

Strohmeyer, John. *Bob Atwood and His Times*. (Eventually published, slightly abridged, as *Bob Atwood's Alaska* by Robert B. Atwood. Privately printed, 2003.)

———. *Extreme Conditions: Big Oil and the Transformation of Alaska*. Anchorage: Cascade Press, 1997.

Stuart, Alice. *The Alaska Calendar for Engagements*. Fairbanks, 1953.

Time. "Battle of the Billygoats," 25 December 1950.

———. "The Cabinet Game," 17 November 1952.

———. "Conquest of Mexico," 2 November 1942.

———. "Core of the Corps," 9 July 1951.

———. "Magnificent Obsession," 14 July 1958.

———. "The Old Car Peddler," 23 August 1954.

———. "Protecting Sources," 5 March 1956.

———. "Querulous Quaker," 13 December 1948.

———. "The Voice of the Opposition," 23 February 1953.

Thompson, W. F. *The Low Down Truth About Alaska*, 1923.

Tower, Elizabeth A. *Mining, Media, Movies; Cap Lathrop's Keys for Alaska Riches*. Anchorage: Roundtree Publishing, 1991.

Truman, Margaret, ed. *Where the Buck Stops: The Personal and Private Writings of Harry S. Truman*. New York: Warner Books, 1989.

U.S. Congress, *Final Report of the Joint Committee on the Organization of Congress* (December 1993), http://www.rules.house.gov/Archives/JointComm.htm.

U.S. Department of Interior, Bureau of Land Management. *Table of Public Land Orders, 1942–2007*, http://www.blm.gov/wo/st/en/prog/more/lands/public_land_orders. html.

U.S. House. *Russian America.* 40th Congress, 2nd Session, Ex. Doc. No. 177, 1868.

U.S. House, Committee on Interior and Insular Affairs. *Alaska, 1955: Hearings Before the Subcommittee on Territorial and Insular Affairs of the Committee on Interior and Insular Affairs, House of Representatives, 84th Congress, 1st Session, Pursuant to H. Res. 30.* Washington, DC: Government Printing Office, 1956.

———. *Statehood for Alaska: Hearings Before the Subcommittee on Territorial and Insular Affairs of the Committee on Interior and Insular Affairs, House of Representatives, 85th Congress, 1st Session, on H.R. 50, H.R. 628, and H.R. 849, etc.* March 1957. Washington, DC: Government Printing Office, 1957.

U.S. Senate. "Membership Changes of 83rd Congress (1953–1955)," http://www.senate. gov/artandhistory/history.

U.S. Senate, Committee on Interior and Insular Affairs. *Alaska Mental Health: Hearings Before the Subcommittee on Territorial and Insular Affairs of the Committee on Interior and Insular Affairs United States Senate, 84th Congress, 2nd Session, on H.R. 6376, S. 2518, S. 2973.* Washington, DC: Government Printing Office, 1956.

———. *Alaska-Hawaii Statehood, Elective Governor, and Commonwealth Status Hearings Before the Committee on Interior and Insular Affairs, United States Senate, 84th Congress, 1st Session, on S. 49, S. 399, S. 402. . . .* Washington, DC: Government Printing Office, 1955.

———. *Alaska Statehood, Hearings Before the Committee on Interior and Insular Affairs, U.S. Senate, 85th Congress, 1st Session, on S. 49 and S. 35,* March 1957. Washington, DC: Government Printing Office, 1957.

———. *Nomination of Frederick A. Seaton to be Secretary of the Interior, Hearing Before the Committee on Interior and Insular Affairs,* 5 June 1956. Washington, DC: Government Printing Office, 1956.

U.S. Senate, Committee on Territories. *Conditions in Alaska: Report of the Subcommittee of Committee on Territories,* 1904.

Vaughn, Stephen L. *Encyclopedia of American Journalism.* New York: Routledge, 2008.

Weinberg, Steve. "Avenging Angel or Deceitful Devil?: The Evolution of Drew Pearson, a New Kind of Investigative Journalist." *American Journalism* 14, no. 3–4 (Summer–Fall 1977).

Welch, Robert. *The Politician.* Belmont Publishing Co., n.d.

Wells, H. G. *The Outline of History.* Garden City, NY: Garden City Publishing, 1931.

White, William S. *Citadel.* New York: Harper and Brothers, 1957.

Whitehead, John. *Completing the Union.* Albuquerque: University of New Mexico Press, 2004.

Whitney, David. "Mr. Stevens Goes to Washington." *UCLA Magazine* 12 (Winter 2000).

———. "Senior Senator," a weeklong series on career of Ted Stevens, beginning August 7, 1994.

Woolley, John T., and Gerhard Peters, *The American Presidency Project* [online]. Santa Barbara, CA: University of California (hosted), Gerhard Peters (database), http:// www.presidency.ucsb.edu.

Wright, Jim. *You and Your Congressman.* New York: Coward, McCann & Geoghegan, 1972.

Index

Note: Italicized page numbers indicate photographs or figures and their captions.

Washington Hand Press, 6
Washington News, 394
Washington Post, 301, 383–84, 395, 400
"We Like Mike" (song), 299–300
Wells, Cecil, murder of, 125–27, *140*
Wells, Diana, 126–27, 129–32, *140–42*
White, Barrie, 210–11, 213, 215, 372
White, William S., 353, 421–22
Whitney, David, 96, 109
Wickersham, James, 40, 51–52, 446
Wien Alaska Airlines advertisement, *62*
Wilderness Society, 315–16

Wildlife Management Institute, 311
wildlife refuges, 320–22. *See also* Arctic
    Wildlife Refuge
William Bergen v. United States of America,
    119
Wilson, Woodrow, 392
World War II, and drive to statehood, 41
Wrangell Sentinel, 4, 160

Yeager, George, *135*